Women & Men in the Prehispanic Southwest

Publication of the Advanced Seminar Series
is made possible by generous support from
The Brown Foundation, Inc., of Houston, Texas.

School of American Research
Advanced Seminar Series

Douglas W. Schwartz
General Editor

Women & Men in the Prehispanic Southwest

Contributors

Patricia L. Crown
Department of Anthropology, University of New Mexico

Suzanne K. Fish
Arizona State Museum, University of Arizona

Kelley Hays-Gilpin
Department of Anthropology, Northern Arizona University

Michelle Hegmon
Department of Anthropology, Arizona State University

Louise Lamphere
Department of Anthropology, University of New Mexico

Debra L. Martin
School of Natural Science, Hampshire College

Barbara J. Mills
Department of Anthropology, University of Arizona

Jeannette L. Mobley-Tanaka
Department of Anthropology, Arizona State University

Jill E. Neitzel
Department of Anthropology, University of Delaware

Scott G. Ortman
Department of Anthropology, Arizona State University

Katherine A. Spielmann
Department of Anthropology, Arizona State University

Christine R. Szuter
University of Arizona Press, University of Arizona

Women & Men in the Prehispanic Southwest

Labor, Power, & Prestige

Edited by Patricia L. Crown

School of American Research Press
Santa Fe

School of American Research Press
Post Office Box 2188
Santa Fe, New Mexico 87504-2188
www.sarpress.org

Editor-in-Chief: Joan K. O'Donnell
Editor: Jane Kepp
Designer: Context, Inc.
Indexer: Andrew L. Christenson
Typographer: Cynthia Welch

Library of Congress Cataloging-in-Publication Data:
Women and men in the prehispanic Southwest : labor, power, and prestige / edited by Patricia L. Crown.
p. cm. — (School of American Research advanced seminar series)
Includes bibliographical references and index.
ISBN 0-933452-74-8 (cloth) — ISBN 0-933452-17-9 (paper)
i. Indian women—Southwest, New—Social conditions. 2. Indian women—Southwest, New—Economic conditions. 3. Indians of North America—Southwest, New—Social life and customs. 4. Excavations (Archaeology)—Southwest, New. 5. Human remains (Archaeology)—Southwest, New. 6. Sex role—Southwest, New—History. 7. Division of labor—Southwest, New—History. 8. Social status—Southwest, New—History. 9. Southwest, New—Antiquities. I. Crown, Patricia L. II. Series.

E78.S7 W65 2001
305.897079—DC21 00-059538
CIP

Library of Congress Catalog Card Number 00-059538.
International Standard Book Numbers 978-0-933452-74-9 (cloth) and 978-0-933452-17-6 (paper).

First edition 2000. Third paperback printing 2021.

Cover: Possible Marau women's society petroglyph (detail), middle Little Colorado River, ca. A.D. 1150–1400. Drawing by Patricia McCreery from a photograph taken by Ekkehart Malotki, who discovered the site in 1994.

Contents

Figures

Tables

Acknowledgments

The authors thank the School of American Research and the Wenner-Gren Foundation for Anthropological Research for their generous support of this seminar. The School provided wonderful surroundings, and special thanks go to Douglas W. Schwartz for affording the opportunity for scholars to meet and discuss anthropological issues in such an intensive and pleasant atmosphere. The seminar house staff saw to our needs for an unforgettable week, and Duane Anderson took the group on memorable tours of Arroyo Hondo Pueblo and the SAR facilities.

I want to express my gratitude to Joan O'Donnell, of the School of American Research Press, and Jane Kepp, a free-lance editor in Santa Fe, who together guided us through the publication process with patience and encouragement. Joan O'Donnell and two anonymous reviewers provided insightful comments on the original manuscript. Thanks also to University of New Mexico graduate student Ann Winegardner for compiling the bibliography from the individual contributions.

I especially thank the seminar participants. The seminar in Santa Fe was one of the most exhausting and exhilarating weeks of my professional career. We did not always agree with one another, but the days of serious debating and discussion were offset by evenings of laughter. I can't imagine better company, and I have valued the continued camaraderie of this group. They all responded to timetables for manuscripts and refined their arguments in response to the reviewers with grace.

Thanks also to my family for tolerating my absence during the seminar and for encouraging me during the preparation of the manuscript. Chip Wills provided constant support for my work and stimulating discussions about many of the ideas set forth in my contributions. Finally, this book is dedicated to my son, Andrew Keith Wills, who was born the day after I learned that the seminar would be funded (not that I'm implying any cause and effect here). He was two when the seminar was held and is now five and a half as the manuscript goes to press. I hope that by the time he is old enough to read this book, a new generation of scholars will be building on the issues and ideas we raise here.

—Patricia L. Crown

Women & Men in the Prehispanic Southwest

1

Gendered Tasks, Power, and Prestige in the Prehispanic American Southwest

Patricia L. Crown

This book is about men and women in the prehispanic American Southwest. Its chapters discuss the activities undertaken by men and women in prehistory and the differential access that men and women had to sources and symbols of power and prestige. The authors compare different Southwestern culture areas, examining the varied contexts in which gendered relations were enacted and how these relations changed through time.

The volume compiles papers originally prepared for an advanced seminar titled "Sex Roles and Gender Hierarchies in Middle-Range Societies: Engendering Southwestern Prehistory," held at the School of American Research in Santa Fe, New Mexico, in March 1997. When I organized the seminar in October 1994, my primary goal was to assess evidence for changes in the division of labor and in gender hierarchies in Southwestern cultures from the time of earliest occupation through the protohistoric period. I argued that the Southwest presented an ideal situation for investigating issues central to gendered research in anthropology because of the wealth of data available, the secure dating of sites in the region, and the presence of multiple "cultures" that survived into protohistoric times. Previous research had indicated that the division of labor and gender hierarchies in at least some parts of the Southwest had not remained stable throughout the prehispanic era. The seminar would afford us the opportunity to examine the important issues of why the division of labor and prestige structures changed along with increasing economic intensification or increasing sociopolitical complexity. Participants were asked to probe the time period during which Southwestern populations shifted from living as migratory gatherer-hunters to practicing sedentary agriculture and from living in small bands to settling in large aggregated communities.

The seminar was not meant to produce another synthesis of Southwestern prehistory. A number of excellent volumes already provide outlines of the past for this area (for example, Cordell 1984, 1997; Cordell and Gumerman 1989; Gumerman 1994; Plog 1997), and we relied on them rather than trying to duplicate their efforts. In contrast, there are, to date, no overviews that attempt specifically to consider gendered relations in the prehispanic Southwest, despite an increase during the 1990s in the number of articles discussing gender (Crown and Fish 1996; Crown and Wills 1995a, 1995b; Ezzo 1992; Hays-Gilpin 1993; Hegmon and Trevathan 1996; Howell 1995; Lowell 1991b; Martin 1997; Mills 1995b; Mills and Crown 1995; Mobley-Tanaka 1997a; Rautman 1997; Schlanger 1996a, 1996b; Simon and Ravesloot 1995; Spielmann 1995).

Of particular relevance, researchers exploring the broad anthropological issues of changes in the division of labor and the development of gender hierarchies had not incorporated prehispanic Southwestern data (although a recent article by Claassen [1997] attempted to do so). Yet scholars knowledgeable about the Southwest have the means to inform us about these issues using data from a huge sample of well-dated, multicultural contexts. Anthropologists have abundant evidence of dramatic shifts in the division of labor and in gender hierarchies from "simple" foraging or gathering societies to complex societies, and understanding these shifts requires close attention to middle-range societies, or "societies between the band and complex chiefdom levels" (Kosse 1996:87). The Southwest is an ideal arena for examining gender in middle-range societies because of the variety of pre-state societies that existed there in the past. The goal of the seminar was thus not to explain Southwestern prehistory—why people became sedentary, aggregated in large villages, intensified their agriculture, or abandoned places. Rather, the goal was to examine the effects such changes had on the lives of the women and men who inhabited the Southwest—on their tasks, health, prestige, and power within the community. We sought to understand how men and women worked out relationships regarding the division of labor, power, and prestige as their societies shifted from mobile hunting and gathering adaptations to life in sedentary, aggregated villages.

In selecting participants for the seminar, I relied on four criteria: a record of publication and research on gender issues; a record of publication and research on a specific topic for the seminar; research in varied portions of the American Southwest to ensure expertise covering all of the subregions; and doctorates from varied institutions to ensure varied viewpoints. Besides me, the participants were Suzanne Fish (Arizona State Museum), Kelley Hays-Gilpin (Northern Arizona University), Michelle Hegmon (Arizona State University), Louise Lamphere (University of New Mexico), Debra Martin (Hampshire College), Barbara Mills (University of Arizona), Jill Neitzel (University of Delaware), Katherine Spielmann (Arizona State University), and Christine Szuter (University of Arizona Press). The sex of the participant was not a criterion, but the majority of scholars currently engaged in gendered research in the Southwest are female.

Apart from the discussant—Louise Lamphere, a Southwestern ethnologist and feminist anthropologist—the seminar participants each addressed evidence for changes in the sexual division of labor and gender hierarchies on the basis of a single data set, incorporating information from throughout the Southwest for the entire prehispanic sequence wherever possible (fig. 1.1, table 1.1). In practice, participants tended to concentrate on the post-Archaic time periods and on three to four regions: the Mogollon (particularly the Mimbres Branch), Hohokam, Ancestral Pueblo (particularly Chaco, Mesa Verde, and Rio Grande areas), and, where possible, Casas Grandes. In addition to the broader issues discussed by all participants, a year in advance of the seminar each participant was given a set of questions to address in her paper. Topics assigned included the organization of space (Hegmon), ritual activities (Hays-Gilpin), mortuary goods and burial facilities (Neitzel), gathering and agricultural production (Fish),

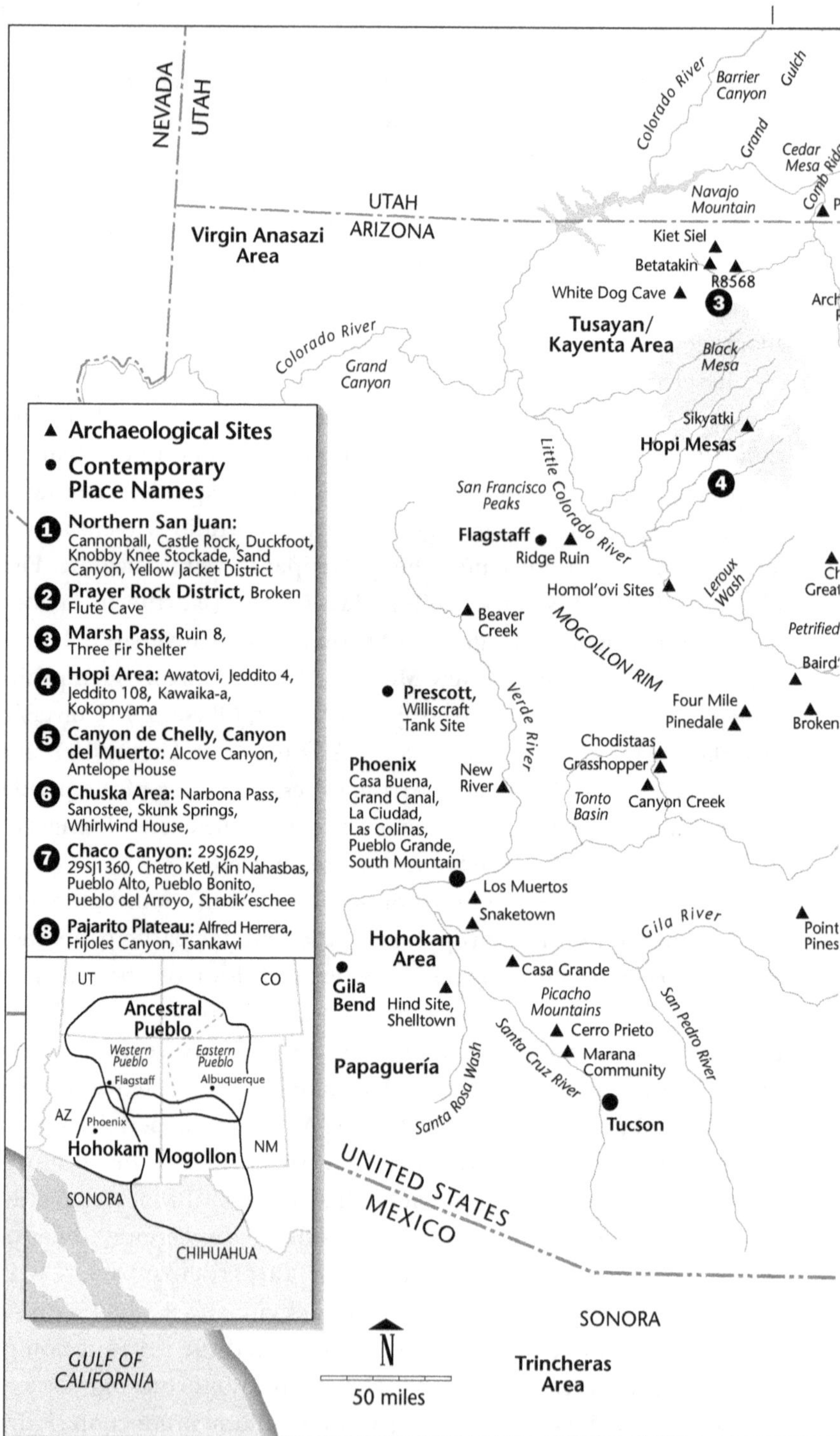

Figure 1.1

The greater American Southwest, showing sites, regions, and subregions discussed in this book.

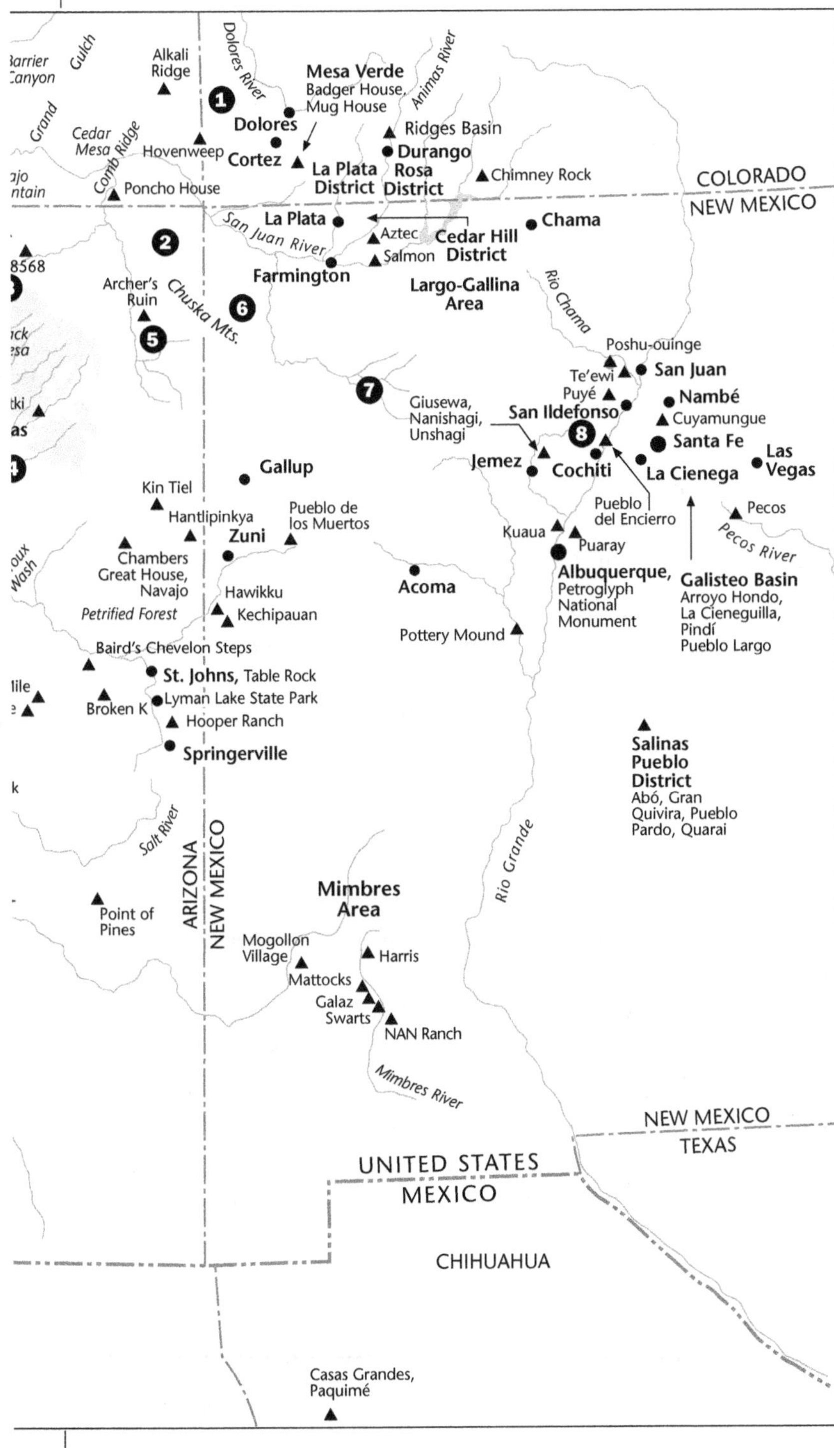

Alkali Ridge
Dolores River
Mesa Verde
Badger House, Mug House
Animas River
Gulch
Grand
Cedar Mesa
Comb Ridge
Hovenweep
Dolores
Cortez
La Plata District
Ridges Basin
Durango
Rosa District
Chimney Rock
Poncho House
COLORADO
NEW MEXICO
La Plata
San Juan River
Aztec
Salmon
Cedar Hill District
Chama
Farmington
Largo-Gallina Area
Rio Chama
Archer's Ruin
Chuska Mts.
Poshu-ouinge
Te'ewi
San Juan
Puyé
Nambé
Giusewa, Nanishagi, Unshagi
San Ildefonso
Cuyamungue
Santa Fe
Las Vegas
Jemez
Cochiti
La Cienega
Gallup
Kin Tiel
Pueblo del Encierro
Pecos
Hantlipinkya
Zuni
Pueblo de los Muertos
Kuaua
Puaray
Pecos River
Chambers Great House, Navajo
Acoma
Albuquerque,
Petroglyph National Monument
Galisteo Basin
Arroyo Hondo, La Cieneguilla, Pindí Pueblo Largo
Hawikku
Kechipauan
Petrified Forest
Pottery Mound
Baird's Chevelon Steps
St. Johns, Table Rock
Broken K
Lyman Lake State Park
Hooper Ranch
Springerville
Salinas Pueblo District
Abó, Gran Quivira, Pueblo Pardo, Quarai
Salt River
ARIZONA
NEW MEXICO
Rio Grande
Mimbres Area
Point of Pines
Mogollon Village
Harris
Mattocks
Galaz
Swarts
NAN Ranch
Mimbres River
NEW MEXICO
TEXAS
UNITED STATES
MEXICO
CHIHUAHUA
Casas Grandes, Paquimé

TABLE 1.1

Chronologies for three major regions of the Southwest: the Ancestral Pueblo region (including the Colorado Plateau and northern Rio Grande), the Mogollon Highlands, and the Hohokam region (southern Arizona)

Date	*Ancestral Pueblo*	*Mogollon Highlands*	*Hohokam*
A.D.1500			
1400			
1300	Pueblo IV		
1200			
1100	Pueblo III	Mogollon Pueblo	Classic period
1000			
900	Pueblo II		Sedentary period (950–1150)
800			Colonial period
700	Pueblo I		
600		Late Pithouse	
500	Basketmaker III		
400			
300			
200			
100			
100 B.C.	Basketmaker II	Early Pithouse	Pioneer period
Time gap			
1500 B.C.	Late Archaic	Late Archaic	Late Archaic
5000	Middle Archaic	Middle Archaic	Middle Archaic
7000	Early Archaic	Early Archaic	Early Archaic
12,000	Paleo-Indian	Paleo-Indian	Paleo-Indian

Note: These are the rough chronologies traditionally used in these areas, but they may not apply to the specific culture history of subregions (for instance, the Kayenta-area Ancestral Pueblo).

hunting and domesticated animals (Szuter), food processing and preparation (Crown), health, nutrition, disease, and violence (Martin), craft production (Mills), and exchange and interaction (Spielmann).

We spent the first two and one-half days of the seminar discussing the papers prepared by participants on these topic areas. On the fourth morning, Lamphere placed the conference issues and discussions in a broader context. She particularly reviewed the history of concepts of autonomy, hierarchy, and power in anthropology and how researchers have used these concepts in studying gender relations. The remainder of the seminar was spent discussing the broader issues and comparing each participant's conclusions. Shorter, revised versions of the papers were delivered during a symposium at the annual meeting of the Society for American Archaeology in April 1997. Questions raised at the symposium aided in completing final revisions to the papers, which form the chapters of this book.

In their contribution on the organization of space, Michelle Hegmon, Scott Ortman, and Jeannette Mobley-Tanaka draw together the massive record on architecture and the use of space in Southwestern prehistory. They particularly examine evidence for work places and task groups, as well as indicators of relative status, autonomy, and power. They conclude that gender differentiation increased through time and that there is some evidence for a negative correlation between women's prestige and autonomy. Thus, as women's prestige increased in the Hohokam area, their autonomy apparently decreased, and as women's prestige declined in the Puebloan area, their autonomy may have increased.

Kelley Hays-Gilpin examined the distribution of decorative styles on media produced by men and women, as well as the distribution of images of sexed figures in the Southwest, in order to evaluate the roles of men and women in ritual activities. In her chapter, she concludes that when ritual activity is most intensively visible in the record, gender symbolism is also most prominent. She suggests that gender roles were periodically renegotiated, particularly in times of aggregation and multiethnic mixing.

Jill Neitzel examined mortuary goods at a variety of sites in the Southwest and found that female adults were buried with "ordinary" goods more often than males, whereas male adults received ritual or ornamental goods more often than females. She discovered a strong correlation between the development of social differentiation and the development of gender hierarchies but also found that gender hierarchies did not always occur in societies with social hierarchies. In chapter 4 she argues that many mortuary populations suggest that a female-dominated gender hierarchy was present at many Southwestern villages.

In her study of farming and foraging in the Southwest, Suzanne Fish draws on a large body of ethnographic and archaeological data in order to examine the roles of men and women in plant gathering and production. She posits a number of significant changes in the roles of men and women in such activities through time in the Southwest and suggests possible differences among the various culture areas in terms of land tenure and individual involvement in the process of food procurement. She notes differences in the ritual use of plants, along with transfer of control over plant resources between acquisition and final disposition.

Christine Szuter, in chapter 6, argues that "hunting" includes activities taking place before, during, and after the "hunt" that made killing an animal possible. These activities thus potentially involved more personnel than simply the individual who killed the prey. Noting the importance of women in many facets of hunting and trapping, she reviews evidence for men's and women's involvement in the taking of small and large game animals in the Southwest, as well as the importance of large game animals and tended animals in ritual activities. She concludes that women were important in hunting in the Southwest but that resource depletion associated with aggregation might have pulled them out of hunting activities during later time periods. More distinct gender hierarchies in late time periods might have conferred greater status on the hunting of large game animals important for diet and ritual.

In my contribution on Southwestern cuisine, I argue that women were the primary personnel involved in food processing and preparation in the Southwest, on the basis of multiple lines of evidence. With increased sedentism, changes in cooking tools entailed efforts to reduce losses in time, nutrients, and wear on tools, all of which created greater energy expenditures for the cooks. Despite being pulled into more domestic work, women's crucial role in maintaining Southwestern societies led to the development of separate, complementary status hierarchies for women and men, with skill in food preparation a potential avenue to increased recognition in the community.

Debra Martin examined health differentials for and labor contributions by Southwestern men and women. Most of her conclusions in chapter 8 relate to Ancestral Pueblo groups, because data are unavailable or sample sizes are too small for other Southwestern populations. Among most Ancestral Pueblo groups documented she found declining health over time for women and indications of inadequate diet for both men and women, particularly after populations aggregated into villages. She also found evidence for violence against some women in the La Plata area, indicating a status hierarchy among women there.

In her examination of craft production, Barbara Mills found changes in the kinds of crafts produced by women and men through time and differences in societal response to increased demand for crafts. In Puebloan areas, increased demand for pottery was accompanied by increasingly gendered production of crafts within households. In contrast, in the Hohokam area, increased demand for shell ornaments led to household-wide involvement in their production. As a third alternative, gendered weaving of textiles (by men) was performed outside the household in the Puebloan area after A.D. 1000. Mills argues that items made specifically for ritual use as inalienable objects were likely made by men, which implies greater status for these producers. She also notes the importance of distinguishing between corporate and network leadership strategies and of recognizing the possible effects these different strategies had on the relative status of men and women in Southwestern societies.

In chapter 10, Katherine Spielmann provides an overview of gendered exchange relations in ethnographic contexts. She then turns to the archaeological record and considers three primary types of durable objects: ceramics, lithic raw material and projectile points, and ornaments. She argues that ceremonial contexts, particularly ceremonial feasts, might have presented women with opportunities in which their products, especially ceramics, brought them prestige. Interaction among women of different villages through exchange, ceremonies, and intermarriage provided mechanisms for circulation of material, design and technological styles, and ideas.

During the seminar, our discussions about individual contributions generally included overviews of the broad issues of changes in the sexual division of labor and the development of gender hierarchies.

Further comments encompassed concerns over methodology, additional relevant archaeological examples or ethnographic analogs, and questions about sampling. Every discussion raised issues that could not be addressed with available data and highlighted the need to address gaps in the record. The major difficulty, participants found, was the lack of complete reporting of data in published reports and monographs. Finally, an issue that arose repeatedly but that we were unable to address adequately because of a dearth of research on the topic was that of the socialization and labor of children in the precontact Southwest.

Nevertheless, participants agreed that there are general trends that appear to have characterized Southwestern prehistory in most subregions and that affected gendered relations. These trends included increasing ritual specialization, increased productive specialization, increasing exchange, increased time spent in food processing and preparation, intensified food production, increasing sociopolitical complexity, decreased birth spacing, and increased variability in health status within populations, but generally declining health. These trends accompanied increasing aggregation in large villages. It appears that work loads increased for both women and men, and evidence suggests that as work loads increased, unisex task groups may have taken on increasing importance. In other words, adult women spent more time with other adult women, and adult men more time with other adult men. This is particularly reflected in the spatial arrangements of activities—for instance, the appearance in many portions of the Southwest of special rooms for grinding corn, shared by the women of a number of different households.

We agreed as well that gendered relations became increasingly differentiated through time, so that similarities across space early in the sequence changed toward a greater variety of arrangements. No single generalization can be made concerning the sexual division of labor or gender hierarchies during the late prehistory of the Southwest. I argue later in this chapter that our inability to find a single overarching pattern in the archaeological record of the Southwest is due to the inherent ambiguity and "complexity" of gendered relations rather than to a failing in our reading of the record (see Kosse 1996:87 for a similar discussion concerning sociopolitical complexity in the Southwest).

Mortuary data provide some of the most direct evidence for status differentiation, although even here there are questions about the meaning of differences in quantities and kinds of grave goods, in burial locations, and in burial treatment. Jill Neitzel's study of burial data across the Southwest indicates that gender hierarchies were clearly present in mortuary contexts only when social hierarchies were clearly present as well. Particularly after A.D. 1300 there is evidence for declining relative status for many, but not all, women in the Southwest and evidence for parallel hierarchies for men and women in some areas. We agreed that in considering the relative status of men and women, we must also consider different realms (domestic, ceremonial, political) and different scales (household, task group, village, community, region) within society.

In contrast to perceiving general trends, participants also noted regional differences. For instance, Barbara Mills demonstrated the existence of two different trajectories in the intensification of craft production in the Southwest, one toward increasingly gendered production (especially prevalent in the northern Southwest) and one toward increasing engagement of the entire household in the production of crafts (particularly prevalent in the southern Southwest). Similarly, Kate Spielmann noted differences in the extent to which women were involved in exchange of the products of their own labor in different portions of the Southwest.

In her discussion of the papers, Louise Lamphere particularly highlighted the often contradictory interpretations of authors who used different lines of evidence. Rather than trying to reach a single conclusion about the relative status of men and women in Southwestern societies, she suggested that we consider Sherry Ortner's concept of hegemonic and counterhegemonic tendencies in reexamining our data. She pointed out that many of us were trying to make a theoretical leap from gender differences in the sexual division of labor to a notion of gender hierarchy, but that it was often difficult to evaluate whether separation of the sexes meant complementarity or actual differences in the control of resources, power, and social value.

DEFINING OUR TERMS

During our week in Santa Fe, we spent a great deal of time discussing definitions of terms used by archaeologists and anthropologists.

Louise Lamphere was particularly helpful in explaining current anthropological terminology. We focused especially on defining what we meant by sex and gender, division of labor, status, and the concepts of power, prestige, and hegemony.

Sex and Gender

In the simplest formulations, scholars often differentiate sex from gender by stating that sex refers to a biological fact and gender to cultural constructions of biological differences. Recently, some researchers have argued that these definitions are too simplistic and fail to take into account the constant interaction between sex and gender (Errington 1990; Sperling and Beyene 1997; see also Meskell 1998:182). Human genetic makeup provides certain basic parameters for our bodies, but cultural practices (including, minimally, diet and work load) ultimately shape our bodies in important ways: height, weight, posture, reproductive capacity, and hormone response in particular situations (Errington 1990:11–13; Sperling and Beyene 1997). This is aptly illustrated in table 1.2, which shows important differences between the reproductive life cycles of modern Western females and those of females in nonindustrialized societies. Despite their common sex, women in the two groups experience dramatic differences in their reproductive lives owing to differences in their diet, nutrition, work loads, and cultural practices. Some researchers even consider sex to be "a determination made through the application of socially agreed upon biological criteria for classifying persons as females or males" (West and Zimmerman 1987:127) and thus as much a social construct as gender. Following this line of thought, Shelly Errington (1990:28) argued that we should separate the concept of "sex," a feature of the human body, from "Sex," a culturally specific construction of human bodies.

Given these recent concerns with the simple separation of sex and gender, it is useful to review some aspects of the two concepts. In our own Western Euro-American culture, infants are classified at birth into one of two sexes based largely on genitalia. Yet the presence of specific genitalia takes on additional importance only many years later in a child's life, when reproductive capability is signaled through physiological changes. Human reproductive life-cycle events, including

Table 1.2

Comparison of reproductive life-cycle events for women in nonindustrialized societies and in Western industrialized societies

Culture	*Median Age at Menarche*	*Median Age at Marriage*	*Average Family Size*	*Years of Lactation per Child*	*Number of Menstrual Cycles*	*Age at Menopause (in years)*
Nonindustrialized societies	16–17	16–17	About 5 children	3–4 years	About 48	42–43
Contemporary Western societies	12.8	20.8	2.5 children	0 or limited	Up to 455[a]	51

Source: *Sperling and Beyene 1997:144–47.*

[a] *Calculated as 35 years times 13 cycles per year.*

menarche or onset of puberty, childbirth, and menopause, are often celebrated through cultural practices. "Sex" is thus not just about genitalia and biological difference; it is also about reproduction. Changes in reproductive capacity are significant in most cultures in affecting social constructs of gender and status (Meigs 1990). Such social constructs are determined to some extent, but not completely, by age. For instance, in many cultures, females are called by terms (glossed in English as "girls") that remain the same until they have children (when they become "women"), regardless of their age. Actual reproduction may thus be more important in determining a female's status than her potential for reproduction alone.

For the purposes of this book, we define gender as the cultural construction that Errington (1990:27) termed "Sex," which is a cultural construction of biological differences. Gender constructs are inextricably linked to age, reproductive capacity, class, and status. Gender is "about" socialization, labor, status, prestige, and power. It is a fundamental way of classifying humans in every society, but the specifics of how individuals are classified differ greatly from one society to another. In many societies, the specific treatment and behaviors of individuals change throughout their lifetimes depending on age *and* sex, so that it is impossible to tease out what is tied to gender and what is tied to age. Differences in rates of infanticide, in weaning ages, and in socialization practices for male and female children (Draper 1997; Morelli 1997; Schlegel and Barry 1991) indicate the importance of gender categories from birth. Although such distinctions may not appear in mortuary contexts (that is, children may be treated roughly equally at death regardless of their biological sex), this does not mean that gender is unimportant in child rearing (see, for example, an interesting discussion of changes in clothes for young children and their lack of impact on gender identities [Paoletti 1997], reviewed in greater detail below). As I noted earlier, reproductive capability is also important in gender constructs, so that males and females of reproductive age are usually treated differently from children. Young, unmarried women may enjoy relatively high status (Solway 1992:51). Married women often have less status, power, and prestige in a community during their reproductive years, and their productive output may decline (DeBoer and Lathrap 1979:124; see Lee 1992:37 for a contrasting view). Finally, postmenopausal or middle-aged women often enjoy freedom from restrictions on their behavior (including greater sexual freedom), the opportunity to exert authority over junior women, and higher status as well as eligibility for new roles, sometimes including roles otherwise held exclusively by men (Brown 1992; Lee 1992). Individuals' tasks, responsibilities, authority, power, and prestige are thus not static but may change throughout their lifetimes.

Societies always have two gender categories but may have more. And their means of placing individuals into these categories may vary, from strict placement based on genitalia to more fluid placement based on enactment of gender-specific actions, gestures, dressing, or language. A person with male genitals may thus be viewed as a "woman" (or an additional third gender category) if "he" behaves, dresses, and speaks like other persons in the "woman" category.

Division of Labor

Division of labor refers simply to the customary allocation of different tasks to different kinds of people. Universally, females versus males and children versus adults do different kinds of tasks. However, the specific tasks associated with each "category" of person differ from society to society. Although there are patterns in the types of tasks associated with each sex in societies worldwide (see, for instance, Brightman 1996; Brown 1970; Burton and White 1984; Draper 1975; Ember 1983; Estioko-Griffin and Griffin 1981; Kurz 1987; Murdock and Provost 1973; Peacock 1991; White, Burton, and Brudner 1977) and patterns in how the types of tasks performed change with increasing societal complexity (Ember 1983; Kurz 1987; Murdock and Provost 1973; White, Burton, and Brudner 1977), there are no universals in how labor is divided by sex. In the chapters in this volume, many of the authors argue that one sex or the other performed a particular task in a Southwestern society. In making such arguments, they are not suggesting that females in these societies performed *only* "female" tasks and males *only* "male" tasks, but rather that, statistically, the vast majority of people who engaged in particular tasks had genitals that corresponded to our traditional definitions of females and males. For instance, females cook most food in most societies. But males are generally fully capable of cooking and indeed often cook when away from home.

In all societies, the sexual division of labor is complemented by the age division of labor. The sexual division of labor is fundamentally important to how and by whom children are socialized (Draper 1997; Morelli 1997), which in turn is fundamentally important to the perpetuation of gender relations and gender ideologies. Robert Brightman (1996: 715–16) recently argued that a division of labor presupposes asymmetry in prestige and authority between the sexes. The way in which labor is divided between the sexes is thus not an adequate explanation of sexual inequality but rather reflects an existing gender ideology.

Status

If status is defined simply as "a position in the social structure" of a society (Kottak 1975:60), then explorations of the "status" of women or of men attempt to examine the general, and relative, position of each gender within a society. In recent years, anthropologists have noted a number of problems with trying to define the status of a gender.

First, status is highly context specific, so that an individual may have high status in one situation with one group of people and low status in another with a different group of people. As Errington pointed out (1990:7), "a woman acting in the capacity of sister is quite different for social purposes from a woman acting in the capacity of wife."

Second, status changes over the course of an individual's lifetime, so that even for a single woman or man there is no "set" status. For instance, a female child might have relatively low status until she reaches a marriageable age, after which she might enjoy a brief period of relatively high status until marriage. She might have relatively low status during her child-bearing years and then enjoy high status again after her reproductive years have ended. Conversely, she might enjoy high status throughout her child-bearing years and lower status afterward.

Third, Anna Meigs (1990:106–8; see also Hendon 1999) argued that men and women achieve statuses as individuals rather than as members of a group, yet we lump these individual statuses when we try to define the status of men or women for a society. A high-status woman might outrank a low-status man, making it difficult to determine which gender has higher relative status (Errington 1990:7).

Fourth, Meigs (1990:107) also argued that within societies, female or male status might be high in some respects (or for some activities) and low in others. "There is no formula by which to reduce all the complexity of variables to a single status 'score.'"

Fifth, males/men and females/women in many societies are viewed not so much relative to the opposite sex or gender in terms of status but rather relative to individuals of the same sex or gender. Often, genders appear to have complementary or parallel status hierarchies. Thus, there may be high- and low-status males and high- and low-status females, where status for each gender is based on different attributes of skill, power, or prestige.

Finally, there is no single attribute that measures status cross-culturally (Brightman 1996:717; Errington 1990:7). Status differences may be marked by clothing, hairstyles, or other traits, with subtle distinctions that might well go unnoticed by an outsider (Errington 1990:5). Archaeologists are even farther removed from observing the full suite of possible status markers for a society and undoubtedly miss many of the subtler clues that would be obvious to a member of the culture.

Power, Prestige, and Hegemony

The anthropological literature on power and prestige is vast. I discuss only a few salient points of this literature here; Louise Lamphere discusses these topics in chapter 11 as well. Power has been variously defined (Errington 1990; Schlegel 1977a; Wolf 1990). Most anthropologists consider power to be an abstract, secular relation between people (Errington 1990:41). In Western definitions, power is generally considered an attribute of an individual and is associated with force and the ability to exercise one's will (Robb 1999). Using such a definition as a foundation, Alice Schlegel (1977a:8–9) provided a useful discussion of three dimensions of power. By her definition, it is composed of "power," or the ability to exert control, "authority," or the socially recognized right to make decisions for others, and "autonomy," or freedom from control by others.

Alternatively, Foucault (1994) viewed power as a depersonalized quality of culture that constructs actors (Robb 1999), and he discussed the less coercive notion of "power to" rather than "power over" (Foucault 1980). Power is negotiated among individuals and is a process (French 1985; Wylie 1992:61).

In contrast, other cultures may conceive of power as something concrete. In Java, for instance, "power exists, independent of its possible users. It is not a theoretical postulate, but an existential reality. Power is that intangible, mysterious, and divine energy which animates the universe" (Anderson 1972:7). In societies with such a notion of power, political power involves the acquisition or demonstration of suprahuman powers (Errington 1990:41). Audiences and wealth are signs of access to such power. Thus, power is *revealed by* rather than based on the accumulation of wealth and followers. Errington (1990) suggested that we use the term "potency" to refer to this concrete type of power: "Yet a striking aspect of the demonstration of potency in these situations is that it is divorced from power as it is usually understood in the West, and (in most level societies) it is completely divorced from force. Those who aspire to demonstrate potency must persuade others to listen to them or be cured by them; the material gain may be negligible, the gain in influence in other contexts, uncertain. The prestige of having potency is its own reward" (Errington 1990:430). Benedict Anderson (1972) argued that such notions of power dominated world societies before the rise of secular nation-states.

Many anthropologists have pointed out that the concept of power as an abstract, secular relation generally involves a gendered bias (Robb 1999). For instance, using such an abstract concept of power, Michael Mann (1986) suggested that there are four sources of power: political, military, economic, and ideological. Although such sources certainly can provide the power, authority, and autonomy that Schlegel referred to, they almost universally bias perspectives of women's potential access to power (Duffy 1986:22; Rogers 1975; Wylie 1992:56). Possible alternative sources of power that would incorporate women in most societies include domestic, reproductive, and child-rearing activities. In running the household, in making decisions regarding reproduction, and in socializing children, women may have power, authority, and autonomy (see, for example, Browner and Perdue 1988; Rogers 1975; Schlegel 1977a; Strathern 1984). Indeed, Susan Rogers (1975:737) suggested that peasant women control virtually all aspects of community life *because* they are powerful in domestic contexts. Alternatively, researchers have suggested that women derive power by forming solidarity groups (Sanday 1981), by acquiring access to ritual knowledge (Paul and Paul 1978), by influencing powerful men, and by producing (or refusing to produce) the crafts, crops, or livestock that are the basis of men's power (Brumfiel 1991; Nash 1978; Sillitoe 1985:517; Strathern 1984:25; Weiner 1986:108; Wylie 1992).

Schlegel (1977a:9) suggested that we ask three questions about power and gender: "First, in what spheres and under what conditions are women or men in control of their own persons, activities, and products of their labor and the persons, activities, and products of labor of the other sex?.... Second, how do areas of female control compare with areas of male control—is one subsumed by the other, or do they exist in balance?.... Third, do areas controlled by women include institutions that are central to social organization?"

The concept of prestige is equally complex. Prestige is defined as social honor or social value (Ortner and Whitehead 1981:13). Sherry Ortner and Harriet Whitehead (1981:13) used this term, rather than status (Ortner 1996:231), as the basis for their concept of "prestige structures," which they defined as "the sets of prestige positions or levels that result from a particular line of social evaluation, the mechanisms by which individuals and groups arrive at given levels or positions, and the overall conditions of reproduction of the system of statuses." They examined such prestige structures largely separately from the practice of power (Ortner 1996:144).

Later, Ortner (1996:145) highlighted several problems with this initial formulation. For instance, it implies that each society has a single prestige structure, that this structure is unchanging, and that it is functionally beneficial to the people within the society. The concept has since been elaborated. Julia Hendon (1999:260) noted three issues crucial for the study of prestige structures: "first, that alternate or multiple prestige structures may exist; second, that these alternate avenues may be in competition even if restricted in who may participate; and third, that not all avenues of prestige will be equally obvious to outside observers or equally emphasized by all members of the society." Most importantly, gender is not the only social classificatory system of importance in achieving prestige. Lineage, age, birth order, affinal kin, and occupation are potentially more critical than gender in assigning social honor in a society. The concept of "prestige structure" thus suffers from the same problem as the concept of "status": there is no way to reduce the complexity of "prestige structure" to a single score for any one society (Ortner 1996:146).

Recognizing these problems, Ortner (1996) adopted the concept of "hegemony" as articulated by Raymond Williams (1977) in his adaptation of the Gramscian term. Hegemony combines culture and ideology. "What is decisive is not only the conscious system of ideas and beliefs, but the whole lived social process as practically organized by specific and dominant meanings as values" (Williams 1977:109). As Ortner suggested, the concept of hegemony is particularly useful because it highlights the notion of gender ideologies, practices, and institutions as historically mutable. She argued that "the most interesting thing about any given case is precisely the multiplicity of logics operating, of discourses being spoken, of practices of prestige and power in play. Some of these are dominant—'hegemonic.' Some are explicitly counterhegemonic—subversive, challenging. Others are simply 'there,' 'other,' 'different,' present because they are products of imagination that did not seem to threaten any particular set of arrangements" (Ortner 1996:146). The scholarly quest thus shifts from trying to add up the pieces for an equality "score" to evaluating the prevailing hegemony and whatever counterhegemonic tendencies may be present.

Other researchers have made similar arguments in suggesting that multiple gender ideologies were present in single societies and that they were under constant negotiation in social interaction (Bledsoe 1990; Lederman 1990b; Meigs 1990; Sanday 1990:6).

ARCHAEOLOGICAL APPROACHES TO GENDER ISSUES

Since the publication of Margaret Conkey and Janet Spector's 1984 article, "Archaeology and the Study of Gender," a steady stream of books, edited volumes, and articles has been devoted to the study of gender in the past (see, for example, Barber 1994; Bertelsen, Lillehammer, and Naess 1987; Claassen, ed., 1992, 1994; Claassen and Joyce 1997; DuCros and Smith 1992; Ehrenberg 1989; Gero and Conkey 1991; Marshall 1998; Miller, ed., 1993; Moore and Scott 1997; Nelson 1997; Walde and Willows 1991; Wall 1994; Wright, ed., 1996). Yet there exists no single notion of what we are attempting to elicit from this research or how we should go about it. Like the anthropologists just discussed, archaeologists have varied in their definitions, methods, and interpretations when attempting to study gender. This is not the appropriate place for a complete review of the many issues involved, so here I mention only a few basic aspects of gender studies in archaeology and add a few caveats.

In studying gender without historical records, archaeologists use five primary categories of data. First, they examine imagery of males and females. These images might be two-dimensional representations in rock art or on pottery, stone, bone, or shell, or they might be three-dimensional sculptures, effigies, or figurines. Second, they examine tools, using ethnographic, cross-cultural, or archaeological data to make inferences about who made, exchanged, used, and discarded them. Third, they examine skeletal material for evidence of differences in diet, nutrition, and disease between males and females or for evidence of musculoskeletal stresses that indicate differences in work loads and tasks. Fourth, they examine mortuary data, including burial practices and furniture. Finally, they examine space, including architecture, features, and task areas.

In order to formulate hypotheses about gendered relations in the past or to interpret those relations, archaeologists often rely on ethnographic analogy and cross-cultural generalizations. Although there have been many critiques of the use of analogy, it can be an important tool for understanding the past (Wylie 1985). Discussions of who made pottery in the prehispanic Southwest provide an excellent example of how analogy has been used in this area (Mills and Crown 1995:12). Ethnographic descriptions of ceramic production in the Southwest indicate that women were primarily responsible for the manufacture of pottery vessels (Bunzel 1972 [1929]; Fontana et al. 1966; Tschopik 1941). Worldwide cross-cultural comparisons indicate that pottery that is hand-built by nonspecialists or part-time specialists in the context of the household is almost always made by women (Arnold 1985; Murdock and Provost 1973). On the basis of such information, archaeologists have argued that women generally made pottery in the Southwest. This interpretation is borne out by burial data: burials that contain potters' tool kits (e.g., Ravesloot 1992; Shafer 1985) are those of adult females.

The ethnographic record for the Southwest is unusually rich, with an enormous variety of sources and cultures. Yet archaeologists working there often draw on ethnographic analogs from other parts of the world. They do this for several reasons. First, comparisons of ethnographic sources and the archaeological record demonstrate change through time, so that the cultures recorded by anthropologists in the nineteenth and twentieth centuries were not always the same as they would have been a millennium earlier. Second, there were forms of material culture and, apparently, arrangements of societies in the past that have no recognizable continuity into the present. For instance, the ball courts and platform mounds of southern Arizona and northern Mexico are not found among any historically or ethnographically known societies in the Southwest. Analogs from which to interpret these forms must be sought elsewhere, either in the ethnographic literature from other parts of the world or in our imaginations. Finally, scholars can often strengthen their arguments by finding generalized patterns in a wide variety of ethnographically known cultures rather than limiting themselves only to the cultures found in the historical Southwest. Although discussions of cultures in New Guinea, Europe, or South America may seem far removed from the Southwest, in fact consideration of the variety of potential social arrangements in the world provides a richer tapestry for interpreting the Southwestern past.

Archaeologists ask many questions about gender in the past, but most of them concern two major issues: the nature of the sexual division of labor and the presence of gender asymmetry or a gender hierarchy in a particular area or areas. As Robert Brightman (1996) argued, these issues are so intimately tied together that it is difficult to consider one without considering the other. Alternatively, some scholars concentrate on androcentric (or gynocentric) bias in the archaeological literature and in the profession. All of these issues require new ways of thinking about old data but depend largely on existing methods and materials.

In the chapters that follow, all of the authors employ data sets with which they have worked in the past, but they view them from a different perspective, highlighting considerations of gender. They rely on ethnographic examples to a greater or lesser extent, depending on the nature of the archaeological data they consider. For example, in interpreting evidence for violence against women in the past, Martin can interpret the skeletal data without using specific ethnographic analogies. In contrast, Fish and Spielmann each review a variety of ethnographic cases in order to interpret farming practices and exchange relationships, respectively. In these cases, the analogs furnish a wealth of potentialities, provide examples of cross-cultural regularities, and help bring largely inaccessible aspects of the past into focus (Wylie 1985).

REFRAMING OUR QUESTIONS

The SAR seminar discussions, particularly Louise Lamphere's comments and suggestions, led all of us to reconsider our interpretations. Recent theoretical statements from anthropologists were useful in reformulating our questions both during and after the seminar. I briefly review some of these ideas and how they might influence archaeological interpretations of the past.

First, there is the issue of gender relations as involving on-going social negotiation (Bledsoe 1990; Dobres 1995; Lederman 1990b; Meigs 1990; Sanday 1990:6). If social negotiation is of greater importance than strictly social identity (that is, if gender processes or relations are more important than gender identity), then we need to consider how and where such negotiation occurred in prehistory. Thus, a critical aspect of considering gender ideologies to involve social negotiation is that we must examine gender in social contexts: contexts in which men and women meet, interact, argue, exchange, and share their lives. Linda Donley-Reid (1990), for example, argued that decorated pottery was used in Swahili households only when women prepared food for and served men; the decoration acted to preserve the purity of the food from pollution by women.

A recent study of the history of baby clothes in America has some interesting and relevant information for such a perspective as well. In this study, Jo Paoletti (1997) found that children in the nineteenth century wore essentially the same clothes (usually dresses), regardless of their sex; they began wearing more gender-specific clothes beginning in the late 1890s. Children's clothing has gradually become more gender-specific in color and form since then. She attributed these changes to two processes. First, modern children lead more public lives than nineteenth-century children did and are exposed to many more people who do not know them or their parents. Gender-specific baby clothing is one way to signal the sex of the baby nonverbally and to ensure appropriate social responses from strangers. Second, there has been an important shift in the way we view the development of gender identity by children. In the nineteenth century, parents believed that "masculinity and femininity were innate qualities that would emerge naturally as the child grew" (Paoletti 1997:30). By the early twentieth century, parents, guided by child psychologists, believed that gender distinctions must be taught as early as possible.

For the archaeologist, there are several lessons in Paoletti's study. First, the absence of gender distinctions for small children did not mean that boys and girls were treated equally or believed to *be* a single gender. Second, the signaling of gender identity (and whatever other social negotiation accompanied public encounters) through material means became important only when the small child was exposed to a broader community that was unfamiliar with its sex. Finally, the change in material objects (clothing) occurred as a result of two processes: increased mobility in a larger community and a shift in gender ideology. We might expect, then, that expressing gender identity through material objects becomes more important as community size increases or as mobility increases, so that individuals meet strangers more often.

Next among the theoretical ideas that helped us reframe our questions were the concepts of power and prestige and how archaeologists might examine them from a gendered perspective. Here, the work of Shelly Errington (1990) provided some useful concepts. She argued that understanding a society's myths of gender requires examining first how people in that society view the "person." This, she suggested, entails comprehension of three issues: people's views of human bodies, people's views of personal behavior and the social attributes that signal identity (as she put it, "how a person goes about demonstrating convincingly that he or she is a proper person in that society" [Errington 1990:17]), and the access people with different categories of social identity have to power.

For the first issue, Errington (1990:35) suggested that societies viewing male and female bodies as profoundly different also tend to have more rigid separation of gender-related activities, language, dress, and ritual. In contrast, societies that view male and female bodies as similar, downplaying differences in anatomy, also tend to have more flexible gendered arrangements. From an archaeological standpoint, such distinctions are useful: where differences between males and females are emphasized materially or symbolically, we might infer that the society probably viewed males and females as fundamentally distinct in ways that informed other distinctions in the society. Where such differences are not emphasized materially or symbolically, we might infer that the society probably viewed males and females as basically similar. Such information might be available in imagery of males and females or in differences in mortuary furniture and treatment of the body.

The second issue, that of personal demeanor and social attributes, is the most difficult to grasp from the archaeological record. It may be possible to glean this information from imagery, however. Hendon (1999), for instance, argued that in prehispanic Mesoamerica, greater emphasis was placed on people's *actions* in determining their gender than on their temperament or appearance.

For the third issue, Errington (1990:58) convincingly argued that to understand the access different gender categories have to power and prestige, we must first understand local conceptions of power and prestige and then attempt to view how sex, age, and kinship map onto these power and prestige systems. The initial step for archaeologists thus involves understanding not simply gendered relations but power and prestige. Women and men may participate in the same or different power structures or prestige systems. And any single society may have multiple prestige systems. Different prestige systems may be complementary or competing (Hendon 1999).

The authors of the chapters in this volume could not address all of these important issues for Southwestern prehistory. Instead, we concentrated largely on the initial seminar goals of examining the sexual division of labor and gender hierarchies in the many middle-range societies that inhabited the southwestern United States during the period prior to A.D. 1540. We did bring in some additional issues as suggested by discussions during the seminar, and I mention these next, as I turn to the conclusions we reached. My goal in what follows is to draw together the individual authors' various interpretations to create an overview of the sexual division of labor and gendered power relations in the Southwest.

THE SEXUAL DIVISION OF LABOR

In examining the sexual division of labor in the prehispanic Southwest, we wanted to know, first, whether the division of labor was roughly equivalent among the different middle-range societies occupying the Southwestern landscape. Second, we assessed how the sexual division of labor changed in correspondence with changes in the settlement patterns and subsistence bases of those varied societies. Third, we questioned whether the division of labor in the Southwest was similar to arrangements found in other middle-range societies worldwide. We were also curious about whether the assumptions archaeologists often make about tasks undertaken by men and women had any empirical basis. Finally, we wanted to know whether the sexual division of labor in Southwestern societies roughly matched the domestic-public dichotomy (Rosaldo 1974) often used (and debated or disparaged) by cultural anthropologists—that is, a dichotomy between a public/community-oriented male sphere and a domestic/household-oriented female sphere. We were severely limited in our ability to examine these issues for Paleo-Indian and Archaic populations in the Southwest, primarily due to a lack of published data or a lack of the necessary studies carried out with the published data. Research over the next decade will probably change this situation. For the most part, however, my discussion concentrates on the sedentary farming groups that inhabited most of the Southwest after A.D. 500.

The archaeological record indicates that there were gross similarities in the sexual division of labor throughout the greater American Southwest. Moreover, the patterns seen in the Southwest roughly match patterns found worldwide and cross-culturally. Thus, men were generally associated with the hunting of large game with "male" weapons such as bows and arrows or spears (Szuter, this volume) and with long-distance exchange (Spielmann, this volume). Women were generally associated with the gathering of wild plants, with food processing and preparation (Crown, this volume; Fish, this volume), and with child care. Many of the chapters, however, emphasize the relative fluidity of such gendered task differences. For instance, Szuter discusses women's involvement in hunting throughout the prehispanic chronological sequence, and I note that men probably knew how to cook and would have done so on long hunting or trading expeditions.

Spielmann discusses women's probable involvement in exchange, particularly of pottery, in the Southwest. Mills and Spielmann discuss how both men and women became involved in the production of various crafts.

We conclude, then, that there *were* divisions of labor by sex for all Southwestern societies, but the specific arrangements permitted flexibility. As has been noted for the sexual division of labor in a modern Tewa pueblo (Jacobs 1995:204), it is likely that men and women were ready "to perform any task required to meet their individual and familial needs." Such flexibility is suggested as well by imagery on Mimbres vessels showing adults with genitals (thereby permitting sex identification) performing various tasks. This imagery indicates considerable overlap in the performance of tasks by the two sexes (Munson 2000). As I discuss later, however, for some portions of the Southwest, labor was associated with a particular gender more than with a particular sex. Thus, genitalia were apparently less important than the social presentation of self in determining which activities a particular individual undertook. For this reason, the term "gender division of labor" is more accurate than "sexual division of labor" (Munson 2000).

Changes in subsistence practices toward increasing reliance on domesticated crops were accompanied in all areas by changes in both the sexual division of labor and the time allocated to particular tasks. Evidence from bone morphology, stress markers, and pathologies on skeletal remains indicates increased time spent in food preparation, particularly grinding, for female adults, with increased reliance on cultigens. Females were also less mobile once they became sedentary, so that males and females became increasingly differentiated in lower body musculature (Ogilvie 1993, 1996; also see Crown, this volume; Martin, this volume). Women may have had fewer opportunities for involvement in hunting (Szuter, this volume) and perhaps assumed an increasing burden of child care as family size increased. Interestingly, Southwestern populations dealt with intensified craft production through two different strategies. In some areas, craft production was increasingly gendered, as one gender or the other took over production of particular objects. In other areas, intensified production involved the entire family and became less gendered (Mills, this volume). Thus, women, men, and children were probably involved in the production of Mimbres black-on-white vessels and some Hohokam shell jewelry (Mills, this volume).

Other types of changes in the sexual division of labor accompanied changes in settlement patterning. As settlement size increased and villages became more aggregated, there is evidence in many portions of the Southwest for increasingly gendered task groups. Corn grinding, for example, often moved from portable, individual grinding sets to facilities dedicated to grinding, with many (up to 12) metate-and-mano sets. In such facilities, girls and women interacted while grinding. Such a shift in the organization of work might have had important consequences for women in these villages. First, studies indicate that cooperation increases productivity. For example, nineteenth-century Plains Indian women who worked together processed twice as many bison hides as women who worked alone (Lewis 1942:39; see also Collier 1988:72). Second, cooperation also promotes solidarity and improves the "status" of women (Eggan 1950:131; Murphy and Murphy 1980:181). Indeed, Robert Murphy and Yolanda Murphy (1980:181) indicate that it is the organization of labor rather than the actual amount of labor that explains the relative status of women and men in different societies.

Yet the variable presence of such task-related facilities, along with the varied timing of the adoption of innovations both within and between Southwestern villages, indicates that there is no simple causative relationship between changes in settlement-subsistence arrangements and changes in the division of labor. Thus, some villages had separate grinding rooms, and others of equivalent age and size did not. Some households readily adopted new technologies that changed the amount of time allocated to particular tasks, and other households of equivalent age did not. Such patterning demonstrates the critical importance of individual decision making in the processes discussed. Southwestern men and women were not automatons; despite the clear availability and knowledge of innovations, many households chose to retain the old ways of doing things.

Although Michelle Rosaldo's (1974) original formulation of the domestic-public dichotomy has been the subject of critique for more than two decades now (for instance, Lamphere 1987; Reverby and Helly 1992; Rosaldo 1980; Strathern 1984), that formulation was sufficiently compelling that scholars continue to address both the dichotomies and the critiques. For the purposes of this chapter, I wish to emphasize only two points here.

First, for the Southwest, the validity of such a dichotomy for the sexual division of labor depends largely on how domestic and public are defined. If (following Lamphere [personal communication]), we define public as "where men are" or "what men do" and domestic as "where women and children are" or "what women do," then of course this dichotomy holds nicely. But if we define domestic and public on the basis of specific types of activities, then the situation becomes murkier. For instance, if domestic activities include cooking, eating, sleeping, and craft production, and if we can show that kivas were used for cooking, eating, sleeping, craft production, *and* ritual only by adult males and male initiates, then were they domestic spaces or public "integrative" spaces? If the latter, whom did they integrate?

The archaeological record confirms the complexity of the situation. There is abundant evidence that women were involved in activities both inside and outside of the village proper, including hunting (Szuter, this volume), exchange (Spielmann, this volume), gathering and farming (Fish, this volume), and carrying burdens (including water, wood, and dead animals [Munson 2000; Shaffer, Gardner, and Powell 1999]). Perhaps most significantly, women performed many "domestic" activities outside the household space proper. Much food preparation occurred in dedicated facilities such as grinding rooms, and cooking was often conducted outdoors. Indeed, the ethnographic record suggests that the domestic-public dichotomy does not fit the conceptions of Southwestern native peoples. Among Tewas at San Juan Pueblo, the pueblo and its immediately surrounding area are apparently considered to "belong" to women while the more distant hills "belong" to men (Alfonso Ortiz, personal communication, cited in Jacobs 1995:181). Socialization of children among Southwestern groups also confirms the flexibility of domestic-public arrangements. Historically, children were cared for by their mothers, often in cradleboards, until they were one or two years of age. After this time, older female children spent much of their days caring for young children, and they had freedom of movement throughout the village (and sometimes fields). In a sense, then, children spent the years from about one to twelve being raised in a public, community setting. At about ten to twelve, girls lost this freedom and were trained in cooking and craft production within the household proper. Taken together, all of these aspects of Southwestern life suggest that the "domestic sphere" there was encompassing, with women conducting quotidian activities throughout the entire village, often in "public" settings.

The second point is one that Fred Eggan (1950:131) emphasized for the Western Pueblos: many of men's productive activities involved solitary efforts, whereas women often worked together. Though Eggan was arguing that such cooperation maintained the integrity of the matrilocal extended family, his illustration also has implications for how we think of a domestic-public dichotomy. Men might have performed more tasks outside the village proper, but when such work was solitary it is difficult to conceive of any particular advantage that it afforded to men. In contrast, women working in cooperative task groups on different productive activities within the village might have had much more opportunity for interaction and influence.

A number of ethnographers have argued that Southwestern groups (and most other Native American groups [Klein and Ackerman 1995:14]) had clear sexual divisions of labor but that the two groups of tasks were seen as necessary, complementary, interdependent, and equally valued (Jacobs 1995; Schlegel 1977b; Young 1987). I turn now to the issues of power and prestige as they relate to gender, in order to explore whether such balanced ideologies obtained prehistorically among Southwestern groups,

GENDERED POWER

Shelly Errington (1990:58) argued that any understanding of gender must begin with an understanding of local ideas of power and prestige and then move to an understanding of how gender is mapped onto these local ideas. For historic Puebloan groups, ritual knowledge was the basis of power, but leaders did not accumulate wealth and did not use physical force in establishing their authority (Hays 1990). Ritual knowledge was also a critical aspect of power among the Pimas and Papagos historically (Bahr 1983). Indeed, Ruth Underhill's (1979b:92) description of power among the Papagos closely resembles Benedict Anderson's (1972) description of power as a concrete energy that must be derived from spirits. Most archaeologists would argue that power in prehispanic Southwestern societies also entailed ritual knowledge (Hays 1990; Wilcox 1991a), although in some times and place, leaders may have accumulated wealth and enforced their authority through physical means.

If ritual knowledge was the fundamental source of power in prehistory, then an understanding of power relations in the past must entail seeing how gender mapped onto ritual knowledge. This is no simple task. Even in ethnographic situations in the Southwest, scholars debate the amount and types of ritual involvement women had in various groups (Hays-Gilpin, this volume). For instance, Watson Smith (1990 [1952]:119) stated that Pueblo priests kept esoteric ritual knowledge from "lay fellow townsmen, and particularly from women." Elizabeth Brandt (1994:15) concurred: "Women are excluded from most knowledge of a ceremonial nature, though women's societies did and do exist in some communities." She suggested that women's participation in ritual had declined since Spanish contact. For San Juan Pueblo, Sue-Ellen Jacobs stated that although women did not play formal roles in religious or political leadership, they did participate in religious ceremonies, perform roles in sodalities, and influence male relatives who held leadership roles. For the Zunis, Ruth Bunzel (1932:543–44) noted both the limitations on women's participation in ritual and the fact that some women did enter the priesthoods, were initiated into the kachina society, and held ritual knowledge: "Some women who are well endowed mentally exert a good deal of influence indirectly upon religious affairs. Although their activities may be restricted, knowledge is not taboo to them. There are women who know prayers and rituals better than their men folks and some men customarily consult their wives, mothers or sisters on matters of sacerdotal procedure" (Bunzel 1932:544).

Jane Young (1987) indicated that women were central to the ideological basis of western Pueblo religion because the central metaphor of this religion was the reproductive power of women. Thus, although women did not play a central role or participate often in ritual performances, much of male ritual entailed imitation of the reproductive power of women. And women participated in significant ways by grinding sacred cornmeal for ritual, feeding ritual participants, feeding ceremonial masks, and painting pottery with sacred symbols that were then used in rituals (Young 1987:438). When asked by ethnographers about their relative status, women in historic Southwestern groups emphasized their critical role in reproduction—that is, their role as mothers (Schlegel 1977b:245; Underhill 1979b:92; Young 1987:437). Dennis Tedlock (1979) noted that boys were initiated into the kachina society at Zuni in order to "save them" or "make them valuable," but that, to a degree, girls were "valuable, protected" by their very nature and thus did not need such initiation. Female deities were among the most important as well (Young 1987:438).

Among the Piman-speaking groups, women could be curing shamans and herbalists but were usually not the "magicians" involved in weather control or war (Ezell 1961:81).

The ethnographic record thus indicates complicated relationships between women and ritual participation and ideology. The discussion of these issues for the prehispanic period by Kelley Hays-Gilpin (this volume) indicates no less complexity. She notes that both women and men were depicted in images of rituals, and both females and males were buried with ritual paraphernalia. Similarly, Jill Neitzel (this volume) found that when female burials contained higher-value grave goods than male burials, they also contained more ritual goods, and when male burials contained higher-value grave goods than female burials, they contained more ritual goods. She interprets this patterning as suggesting that ritual activities were important to a sex's dominant position in the society. At some times and places, particularly at Hawikku, in the Classic-period Hohokam region, and in the Mimbres area, women clearly participated in ritual and might have had access to ritual roles equivalent to those held by men, perhaps particularly after menopause (Crown and Fish 1996; Howell 1995; Munson 2000). However, Neitzel observes that the types of ritual items found in female burials tend to differ from the types of ritual items found in male burials, suggesting that the specific ritual activities of males and females might have differed.

Kate Spielmann's chapter (this volume) emphasizes the critical role of women in the production of items used in ritual and feasting. Among the Mimbres people, women usually acted as parrot or macaw handlers (Munson 2000; Shaffer, Gardner, and Powell 1999), thus performing an important role in raising birds whose feathers were probably used for ceremonial purposes. Generally, however, males are found buried with ritual items more often than females. More detailed research is clearly justified, for the presence of women in Southwestern ritual has been noted particularly when researchers made this issue a focus of their research and used large samples.

An equally important question is the obverse: is there evidence that women were powerless in Southwestern societies? Once again, the data are variable. Debra Martin (this volume) discusses burials of women in the La Plata area whose bones show evidence for repeated, nonlethal trauma. She suggests that they might represent either an "underclass" exposed to domestic violence, women accused of witchcraft, or slaves. Michelle Hegmon and co-authors (this volume) also discuss the relative autonomy of women in the Southwest and conclude that women had quite variable degrees of autonomy through time and across space. Whereas some women apparently had access to power in the prehispanic Southwest, females were potentially more likely to suffer from lack of power than males.

GENDERED PRESTIGE

Prestige is social honor or value; it may or may not equate with power in any single society (Ortner 1996). Archaeologists can examine prestige through different means. One is to examine ages at weaning for boys and girls as indicated by skeletal evidence. Unfortunately, this type of study is rare for Southwestern populations, but the available studies indicate that girls were generally weaned earlier than boys (Fink and Merbs 1991; Martin, this volume).

A second way to examine prestige is to assess access to valued foods by males and females. The results of such studies among Southwestern populations indicate a high degree of variability, even within individual sites examined at different periods of time. Females, however, appear to have suffered greater nutritional stress and disease loads than males in many portions of the Southwest at different times (Martin, this volume). Martin emphasizes that in some burial populations, some adult females *and* males show evidence of less dietary stress than other adult females and males, indicating the presence of prestige hierarchies within each sex.

Prestige can also be evaluated by examining the relative access each sex had to wealth and valued objects in the prehispanic Southwest. Jill Neitzel's chapter demonstrates that women often did have access to objects that we consider to have constituted wealth in the past. But she also emphasizes that females were buried with different types of ordinary goods, ornaments, and ritual goods. This finding echoes conclusions made for many individual burial populations throughout the Southwest (for example, Crown and Fish 1996; Mitchell 1991, 1994; Whittlesey 1984), which tend to show female adults buried most often with utilitarian objects and male adults buried more often with ritual items and ornaments. When females had ornaments and ritual items, they tended to be different from those found with men (Neitzel, this volume; Whittlesey 1984:283; although see Spielmann, this volume). Such findings suggest that females were honored in a different prestige structure from that of men; that is, there were distinct ways of honoring socially valued females and socially valued males.

There is some indication that women's prestige had the potential to improve with age; women over the age of 40 were honored with richer burial goods and graves in more valued locations (such as platform mounds) more often than their younger counterparts (Crotty 1983; Crown and Fish 1996). The specific reasons women were socially honored in these societies are not clear, although the strong association of women with utilitarian objects suggests that skills in craft production, food preparation, and housekeeping might have provided women with avenues to greater social honor. In contrast, men might have been honored more often for success in hunting and warfare. In the Hohokam area, preliminary findings suggest that the prestige of older males was generally less than that of younger males (Crown and Fish 1996; Mitchell 1994), providing a contrast with the opportunities afforded older women to improve their status. That males and females tend to be found with different types of valued objects suggests that women were competing more with other women for prestige, and men with other men. These prestige hierarchies appear to have arisen with other forms of social hierarchies in Southwestern societies (Lepowsky 1990; Neitzel, this volume). Parallel prestige hierarchies are relatively common cross-culturally and would fit well with ethnographic arguments for Southwestern societies that men and women were equally valued, but for different reasons. Women clearly did not occupy a single, simple status relative to men in prehispanic Southwestern societies.

CONCEPTIONS OF THE BODY AND GENDER SYMBOLISM

Many questions can be asked about the meaning of gender in Southwestern societies. Were males and females viewed as fundamentally similar or as critically different in their bodies, appearance, or actions? Were there more than two genders? How was gender symbolized in the past? Though I cannot provide detailed answers to all of these questions, I offer here a few glimpses into the issue of gender ideologies for the prehispanic Southwest.

To get at the issue of how bodies were viewed in the past, it is necessary to rely on imagery and sculptures of males and females. As indicated in the chapter by Kelley Hays-Gilpin, there is some variability in how bodies appear among different Southwestern societies. She notes that images of sexed figures are relatively uncommon but occur in association with aggregation in particular areas (particularly Ancestral Pueblo areas). In most areas and time periods, genitalia are not particularly emphasized, nor are male and female bodies depicted as greatly distinct. For all Hohokam crafts, Emil Haury (1976:261) noted that "when sexual characteristics were shown, they were both natural and incidental to the subject matter." Sizes of bodies and shapes of bodies of males and females are depicted roughly similarly in the Hohokam area. Likewise, two surveys of Mimbres Classic pottery (Munson 2000; Shaffer, Gardner and Powell 1999) indicate that few depictions of human figures display their sex, and when sex is indicated, it is seldom emphasized or exaggerated (although there are exceptions, such as those depicted in Anyon and LeBlanc 1984:573C). For most areas and times in Southwestern prehistory, then, archaeological evidence suggests that Southwestern societies downplayed the visual sexual differences between males and females.

In contrast, social attributes seem to have been important in indicating the gendered identity of individuals. Where imagery is available in the Southwest, studies indicate that certain items of material culture (particularly clothing, jewelry, and tools) and bodily "ornamentation" (particularly hairstyles and face painting) are associated in a statistically significant way with each sex (Hays-Gilpin, this volume; Munson 2000; Thomas and King 1985, although the last presents no statistical data). For instance, for sexed figures on Mimbres pottery, Marit Munson (2000) found that string aprons, striped lower legs (possibly indicating leggings), lines on the cheeks, necklaces, and burden baskets were associated with female figures. A solid band at the ankle, paint extending from the eye to the top of the head, and weapons (bows and arrows and spears) were associated with males. Similarly, Hays-Gilpin (this volume) has found a long history of female figures with hair whorls, possibly indicating their unmarried status, in the Ancestral Pueblo area. For Hohokam-area figurines, Charles Thomas and Jeffrey King (1985) found that males sometimes wore turbans and had more jewelry, including necklaces, cheek plugs, bracelets, ear plugs, and earrings, whereas females had red ochre on their abdomens and never wore necklaces.

How people presented themselves appears to have been more important than genitalia in their social enactment of gender. Interestingly, Munson (2000) found a number of figures on Mimbres vessels that display social attributes in conflict with their biological sex. One individual, for example, has male genitalia but the cheek paint associated with women. Such images might indicate that the ties between physical sex and gender identity were fairly loose, and that taking on a different gender identity was possible through a change in outward appearance (and probably demeanor, voice, and other intangibles). The possibility of changing gender identity in this way was certainly present during the historic period among the western Pueblos. Will Roscoe (1991:24–25) discussed evidence for prehispanic berdaches in archaeological contexts in Ancestral Pueblo burials and imagery, primarily items of material culture that "contradicted" the sexual identification of the individual. Alternatively, figures that combine different attributes of male and female might indicate something broader about how genders were conceptualized in the past. For instance, Roscoe (1989) suggested that at Zuni, women, as a category, incorporated both male and female qualities, whereas men emerged as differentiated from women. In contrast, Alfonso Ortiz (1969:36) argued for the Tewa that "qualities of both sexes are believed present in men, while women are only women."

That some of the material markers of gender were different for various Southwestern societies in the past raises interesting questions about social interaction between these groups. For instance, if Mimbres women alone wore necklaces and Hohokam men alone wore necklaces, what did such contradictions mean during encounters between these two groups?

Action might also have been important in defining categories of men and women, as it was in prehispanic Mesoamerica (Hendon 1999) and among the western Pueblos historically (Roscoe 1991:22). As discussed earlier, there was some overlap in the tasks undertaken by males and females (and by men and women as defined by their appearance, for instance, on Mimbres pottery), but there were also tasks particularly associated with one gender or the other. It is probable, then, that depicting a person with hunting weapons (bow and arrow or spear) or weapons of war (bow and arrow, shield, club) was a means of clearly indicating a man, whereas depicting a person grinding corn, giving birth, or carrying a burden basket was to clearly indicate a woman in most Southwestern societies.

In her interesting discussion of gendered imagery, Hays-Gilpin (this volume) suggests that the times when sexed figures were particularly emphasized in the Southwest were also the times associated with aggregation into larger villages. She suggests that societies undergoing such shifts in settlement size experienced a number of stresses, some of which might have led to greater contestation of gender roles. For instance, the demographic changes associated with this period, particularly the apparent aggregation of different ethnic groups in individual areas or sites, must have led to negotiation of gender roles and symbolism. Increases in mobility or population density might also have necessitated intensified gender symbolism, because individuals potentially encountered more people who did not already know them or their gender.

CONCLUSION

The American Southwest presents a varied picture of gendered relations in the past. As seminar participants, we ultimately concluded that we could make few worthwhile generalizations about sex roles or gender hierarchies in the middle-range societies of this area. Indeed, we were often struck by the contradictions in the evidence from individual areas: some data sets suggested complementarity and relatively egalitarian gendered relations, whereas other sets suggested male domination and female powerlessness or exclusion from roles of power. It is possible that such contradictions and ambiguity are the fault of the researchers and our inability to read the record correctly. However, I believe that such ambiguity is instead an accurate reading of the record and an indicator of the tensions and contradictions that characterized these middle-range societies. Krisztina Kosse (1996:87) made this point regarding sociopolitical organization in the prehispanic Southwest, and it applies equally well, I would argue, to gendered relations in the past.

Various factors undoubtedly contributed to the lack of evidence for clear-cut, intensive male domination in Southwestern societies. First, for most of Southwestern prehistory, population density was relatively low throughout the region. Most daily interaction involved face-to-face negotiation among individuals who knew one another well (Lepowsky 1990). Even in the centuries immediately preceding European contact, population levels in the largest individual communities were probably below 2,500 persons (Kosse 1996), and most (but not all) areas lacked regional integration of political authority. Most areas lacked clear social hierarchies throughout most of the sequence, a situation that tends to accompany a lack of gender hierarchies as well (Lepowsky 1990). Second, it seems likely that many (if not most) Southwestern societies were matrilocal or bilocal rather than strongly patrilocal, if the ethnographic and historical situation has time depth. Women generally enjoy higher "status" in such situations. Third, women were crucial to the maintenance of society, and men were dependent on them for productive activities, situations that tend to keep power in balance (Sillitoe 1985:518). Fourth, various factors, including a benign climate, subsistence practices, and settlement patterns, encouraged people to conduct many activities outdoors or in dedicated communal facilities, where women could interact with other women for much of the day. Finally, what little we can glean of gender symbolism suggests that few Southwestern societies emphasized differences in male and female bodies (or genitalia); instead, demeanor, dress, ornamentation, and action were apparently primary indicators of gender. Although men's and women's activities differed, so that there was a gendered division of labor, current evidence (from burials and imagery) suggests that specific genitalia were not requisite to fulfillment of those tasks. Such flexibility—the option for individual autonomy in selecting gender—combined with the apparent view in many areas of the complementarity of the genders, would also have promoted balance in gendered relations (Errington 1990:34–35).

I do not mean to imply that all women in Southwestern prehistory had wonderful, fulfilling lives. On the contrary, the record suggests that most women were burdened with work, family responsibilities, poor health, and marginal nutrition. Some women were powerless and mistreated; others held positions of prestige. What the record emphasizes is the variety of gender arrangements present in Southwestern societies.

Much work remains in understanding gendered relations in Southwestern prehistory. The lack of published data for many sites severely restricted our ability to maintain a broad perspective. It is important that researchers not only publish their data but also consider the relevance of gender to existing interpretations of the past in the Southwest. We must strive to bring the vast archaeological record to bear on these important and exciting issues.

2

Women, Men, and the Organization of Space

Michelle Hegmon, Scott G. Ortman, and

Jeannette L. Mobley-Tanaka

Our assigned task in this effort to engender Southwestern archaeology was to examine gender relations from the perspective of architecture and the use of space. Both feminist theorists and scholars concerned with the social dimensions of architecture have struggled to understand the relationship between what people actually do and the larger forces (societal or architectural) that structure their lives.[1] And scholars in both fields have found some solutions to these problems in practice theory—that is, in understanding social relations as part of the flow of history and in emphasizing the duality of human practice and the structure that is both created by and creative of those practices (Connell 1987; Ferguson 1995; Moore 1986; Ortner 1996). Practice theory, however, is not a panacea for all the interpretive difficulties involved in studying gender. Indeed, in many ways practice theory is not really a theory at all, in that it lacks an underlying narrative and an underlying norm of the social order (Ortner 1996:2). Rather, it is a perspective that directs our archaeological and analytical attention to various realms and their interaction.

First, practice theory reminds us that people are not automatons, mindlessly filling their assigned roles (see Connell 1987:chapter 3). Instead, people often do things for specific reasons, and their actions have intended as well as unintended consequences. The archaeological record is formed as a result of what people did in the past (Shennan 1993), and archaeologists have well-developed methods for making sense of this record (Schiffer 1987). At the same time, even when we are able to reconstruct past behavior and determine what women and men actually did, the implications for gender relations and the lives of women and men are far from straightforward (Conkey and Gero 1991). Such implications require insights from social and feminist theory, including concern with structure, its reproduction, and its transformation.

"Agency" refers to the capability people have for doing things (Giddens 1984:9), and agency is a process by which people affect (reproduce, reinforce, change) structure. Thus change is not always caused by outside forces; the impetus for change often comes from within. This is a bit trickier to discern archaeologically, but we do often have good data on change, such as the remodeling of a room indicated by the presence of a filled-in doorway or an abutting interior wall. The key is to focus on variability in the archaeological record; were some people doing things differently from "the norm," and what might the effects of those differences have been?

Structure is not an immutable entity, but it is also something more than a sum of people's day-to-day activities. Archaeologically, we can get at structure by focusing on how people represented and organized their lives—for example, through mortuary practices (see Neitzel, this volume), material symbolism (Hays-Gilpin, this volume), and the arrangement and construction of architecture (this chapter).

Architecture is itself a structure: it physically structures social interactions (Hillier and Hanson 1984) and metaphorically reinforces social relationships (Goffman 1976). Architecture is also created by people, and in the prehispanic Southwest it was mostly created by the people who lived in and used it, or by their immediate ancestors (Hegmon 1989; Swentzell 1990). Analytically, this perspective directs our attention to the boundaries and passages created by architecture as well as to the actual use of architecturally defined spaces, the symbolism of architecture,[2] and the processes and scale of construction. We focus on the use of space primarily at an intrasite level; later chapters by Fish and Spielmann discuss issues regarding land use and regional interaction.

CONCEPTUAL ISSUES AND ANALYTICAL APPROACHES

Much discussion during the SAR seminar dealt with the issue of women's status: what do we mean by status, how can we explain variability in women's status, and what does status mean for women's lives? For example, some Classic-period Hohokam women apparently received high-status burial treatment and lived in high-status walled compounds on platform mounds. How did this status affect their lives? Did they perhaps have less autonomy than "commoner" women living in other kinds of residences? Did elite or commoner Hohokam women have "better" lives (by our standards or theirs)?

These kinds of questions regarding women's status have become increasingly complex in recent literature (see Mukhopadhyay and Higgins 1988; Quinn 1977). Following the welcome suggestion of Louise Lamphere, we rely on a recent formulation by Sherry Ortner (1996:chapter 6). Ortner distinguished three often separable dimensions of gender status: (1) culturally affirmed relative prestige or value—this is what is commonly considered to be status; (2) women's autonomy, or (the obverse) the extent of men's control over women's behavior; and (3) women's power "to control some spheres of their own and others' existences" (1996:140). In most societies there exists a pervasive relationship such as male dominance or gender equality that is reproduced in cultural practices and appears "natural" to members of that society; this is what Ortner called gender hegemony (following Williams 1977). But there are also usually some aspects of gender relations that are contrary to the hegemony, and sometimes these contrary aspects are subversive and challenging and thus may be the key to change. Therefore, we should consider multiple lines of evidence and expect that not all of them will point to a unitary or consistent conclusion.

We focus on three components of architecture that have implications for gender as well as for other social relationships. These are (1) the locations of gendered workplaces and evidence for task groups; (2) residential architecture and the delineation of households; and (3) the accessibility or restrictedness of architectural spaces. In general, our data give us few direct insights into gender prestige; we have more to say about autonomy and power. Of the three components, the first (the locations of gendered workplaces) is most directly implicated in determining what women and men did in the past and where they did it. The other two inform us more about general social relations, including gender relations, than they do about particular activities.

Households

The rapidly expanding field of household archaeology has a great deal to offer to the study of gender. Although gender relations and women's roles were ignored in some of the earlier studies of households, a spate of recent work (e.g., Brumfiel 1991; Hastorf 1991; see summary in Hendon 1996) is beginning to correct the imbalance. We hope this chapter and our analyses of residential architecture can make an important contribution to household archaeology. At the same time, we use the term "household" somewhat sparingly, because of the difficulty of defining exactly what a household is or does (see Bender 1967; Hendon 1996; Verdon 1980; Wilk 1989, 1991; Wilk and Netting 1984; Yanagisako 1979). That is, households may be units of residence, production, consumption, and reproduction, but to extremely variable degrees. Specifically, although households (variously defined) are often important units of analysis, we should be careful not to conflate our analytical unit (often a room with a hearth and other adjacent rooms [e.g., Ciolek-Torrello 1989; Lowell 1991a]) with a social unit. Various lines of evidence are important in this regard (see Lightfoot 1994), including access between rooms and/or boundaries between households, evidence for various activities within households, the scale of construction and abandonment, redundancy or variability in household units, and possible symbolic references to the significance of household units.

The complexity of the household concept is made clear in a consideration of ethnographically known Pueblo Indians. Households are socially recognized and important units in the pueblos, but the extent to which an individual is a member of one particular household varies depending on gender and residence rules. Classic ethnographies disagree over the definition of a Hopi household (Eggan 1950; Titiev 1944),[3] but generally in matrilocal western Pueblo societies, men variously participate in their wives', sisters' and mothers' households. Thus, the grandmother's house may be a symbolic locus for a key conceptual unit (the matrilineage), but not all individuals who are part of that unit consistently reside in, eat in, or produce for that household. A more extreme example is found in the international development literature, where the term "hearthholds" is used to describe groups of people who share a residence and hearth at any one time but have few enduring ties (e.g., Ekejiuba 1995).

A consideration of households is relevant to gender relations in several respects. When households are basic social, economic, and decision-making units, they provide an important context for women's participation and thus may contribute to women's power in at least some realms (Rogers 1975). Household organization can also affect women and gender relations negatively, in at least three ways. First, households are often arenas of contestation between women and men (Wolf 1991). Second, households sometimes subsume women (and possibly also men) as individuals such that, in some contexts, women may lose their individual autonomy. Furthermore, although Marilyn Strathern (1984) argued that domesticity does not "denigrate" or limit the autonomy of Mount Hagen women (in the New Guinea Highlands), she also found that women's labor, in the domestic realm, is less valued than are the prestige exchanges pursued by men. Third, households may be contexts of abuse, particularly when women are isolated (Ward 1999:236–37).

One possible key to making sense of the link between household organization and gender is the domestic-public distinction. Michelle Rosaldo (1974) defined the domestic realm as the "minimal institutions and modes of activity that are organized immediately around one or more mothers and their children" (p. 23) and the public realm as activities and institutions that transcend, organize, or subsume these basic units. Using these definitions, she suggested that women's status is lower when the domestic-public distinction is clear and the association of women with the domestic realm is strong. In later work Rosaldo (1980) and others (Lamphere 1993) problematized this formulation for several reasons, including a lack of clear distinction between domestic and public realms and bias introduced by the importance of public activities in our own Western history. However, even more recent work has revived the distinction to a limited extent. Micaela di Leonardo (1991:16) suggested that the distinction is useful analytically, although not as a sweeping explanatory framework, and Ortner (1996:chapter 5) found the public participation of some Sherpa women and men to be a useful aspect of analysis (see also Mukhopadhyay and Higgins 1988:481). These more recent considerations assume fairly general definitions that link the domestic realm with the "household level" (rather than simply with child care and mothering) and the public realm with the extrahousehold level. In this chapter, we consider this general domestic (household)–public distinction to some extent; specifically, we attempt to discern what kinds of activities took place in various contexts and at various scales and involved various categories of people.

We consider household-scale architectural units but do not assume that households were always well-defined, symbolically important social units. Our analysis rests on the following interpretive principles: (1) Residential mobility contributes to social flexibility and thus to individual and household autonomy, as is the case in many forager societies. (2) Well-defined, redundant, relatively invariant household architecture is indicative of the importance of the household as a social unit. In such cases, households can have considerable autonomy, but individuals may be subsumed by the households. (3) Extrahousehold facilities indicate a public realm of activity. If women are excluded from public activities, their power and prestige will decline.

Gendered Workplaces

Over the course of time in the prehispanic Southwest, women and men had to work increasingly hard as agriculture was intensified and resources were depleted (Crown, this volume; Fish, this volume). We use information on the locations of archaeological features—including mealing bins, hearths, and loom holes—and of movable but not easily transportable metates in order to investigate the location and organization of this labor. Following arguments made by Crown (this volume) and Mills (this volume), we assume that the hearths and grinding equipment were used primarily by women, and looms were used primarily by men. The result is a bias toward women's activities, because hearths and grinding equipment were used throughout much of prehistory but loom holes are identified only in later (primarily Pueblo IV) sites.

We assume that there was a gendered division of labor, and the locations and organization of this labor provide insights into gender relations. Our analysis rests upon the following interpretive principles: (1) The spatial separation of gendered labor serves to reinforce and even naturalize gender differences. (2) The locations of features convey symbolic information regarding gender status. For example, the positioning of cooking areas (used by women) at the margins of a Berber house is linked to the relatively low position of women in that society (Bourdieu 1973). (3) Variability or uniformity in the distribution of features is indicative of flexibility or rigidity in the organization of labor and thus provides information on autonomy. (4) The positioning of features is relevant to both autonomy and power because it determines the degree to which a laboring person can be part of ongoing activities and the degree to which that person's labor can be monitored. For example, the activities of someone working in a ramada or plaza area are open to public scrutiny, but that person can also watch and participate in the general flow of social life. Labor in a special-purpose and enclosed space is less subject to public scrutiny, although it could certainly be monitored. Finally, labor within an enclosed residential or household context may be isolating and subject to monitoring (Brumfiel 1996b). (5) Task groups, particularly if they are culturally recognized with architecturally defined spaces, may be an important source of power.[4] At the same time, some women within task groups may be subject to the supervision of other women (Lamphere 1974); thus, although task groups may be sources of power, they may also impose limits on individuals' autonomy.

Access

Differences in status/prestige and power are often created or reinforced when some people are denied access to certain resources (including space or information). Ethnographically in the Southwest, differences in ritual participation are often key to differences between the genders as well as differences between elites and others (Brandt 1977). Unfortunately for archaeologists, differences in ritual participation are seldom manifested materially. However, we can gain insights into differential ritual participation by considering architectural accessibility. Space syntax analysis (Hillier and Hanson 1984) provides an important, although complex, methodology for describing and quantifying architectural boundaries and openings. We do not attempt our own space syntax analysis but rather draw on others' conclusions (e.g., Bustard 1996; Potter 1998).

In considering access, we focus on the locations and distribution of public or ritual spaces, the extent to which activities in them would have been hidden from view, and evidence (based on the distribution of features) for which gender(s) used those spaces. Our analysis of access is based on the following interpretive principles: (1) The secretive aspects of hidden public or ritual spaces impart a special degree of power and prestige to activities that take place in such spaces. Such activities are a special case of the public activities discussed earlier (principle 3 under households). (2) Restricted access is indicative of asymmetries in power and prestige. (3) Such asymmetries are relevant to gender relations even if we cannot determine precisely who (or which gender) participated in hidden activities.

THE MOGOLLON CULTURE AREA

Within the larger Mogollon culture area, we focus on the Mimbres region of southwestern New Mexico from the Late Pithouse through the Postclassic periods. Late Pithouse (A.D. 550–1000) data are drawn primarily from Anyon and LeBlanc's (1984) summary and from Mogollon Village and the Harris Site (Haury 1936). Mimbres Classic (A.D. 1000–1130/50) data are primarily from the Galaz (Anyon and LeBlanc 1984), Swarts (LeBlanc 1983), and NAN Ranch (Shafer 1982, 1991) ruins. Data on Classic field houses and the Mimbres Postclassic (A.D. 1150–1200) are from the eastern Mimbres area (Hegmon, Nelson, and Ruth 1998; M. C. Nelson 1993, 1999; Nelson and Hegmon 1995). Large-scale construction projects or obviously preplanned layouts are rare throughout the sequence, and there is no evidence of architectural restrictions on access. Thus we emphasize the location of work and the organization of residential architecture. Because of several parallels in Late Pithouse and Postclassic patterns, we first describe the archaeological evidence and then discuss the interpretations for gender for all three periods.

Late Pithouse period architectural sites are typically clusters of pithouses (ca. 14–16 m^2 [Anyon and LeBlanc 1984:94]) located on watercourse terraces. Few pithouses were occupied year-round, although residential mobility decreased and dependence on food production increased over time (Brady 1996b; Diehl 1996; Gilman 1987). Although many sites have 50 or more pithouses, it is unlikely that many more than 10 houses on a site were occupied simultaneously.[5] Almost all sites have large ceremonial structures (Anyon and LeBlanc 1980).

Pithouses vary in size and form, but they generally became deeper and more elaborate over time. Almost all pithouses have hearths located between the entrance and center. Early hearths are often just ash lenses; later ones are more formalized, although variable. No formal grinding features are known from any Mogollon pithouse site, although most pithouses have one (sometimes two) metates and one or a few manos in floor and roof assemblages. Grinding tools were also recovered in front of houses, set up so that grinders would face the entrance (Haury 1936). Thus cooking and grinding appear to have been organized at the level of the pithouse unit. In contrast, storage in external cysts (Anyon and LeBlanc 1984:87–89) was organized at a larger scale and may indicate more communal production.[6]

Classic-period pueblos often overlie pithouse sites and show evidence of more occupational permanence. In the Mimbres Valley about 15 large sites (50–100+ rooms) are located along a 55-kilometer stretch of river. Subsistence included agriculture with some water control (Herrington 1982), and environmental degradation combined with climate change contributed to subsistence stress (Minnis 1985). Field houses were established near small patches of land along smaller drainages (Nelson 1999). Most Classic sites have irregular central plaza areas, although usually the only built ritual structures are small kivas that seem to be associated with particular clusters of rooms. By the mid-twelfth century many large Classic villages were depopulated (although see Creel 1999).

The basic Classic residential unit is difficult to define. In some cases (e.g., NAN Ranch and possibly Swarts), there are clear-cut suites of interconnected rooms that were built at the same time. These suites comprise one (sometimes two) habitation rooms, each with a formal hearth and a roof entry, and one or more smaller storage rooms (Shafer 1982). In other cases (e.g., Galaz), no regular organization is apparent (the contrast between these two layouts is illustrated in figs. 2.1 and 2.2). In general, Classic habitation rooms are 8–26 m^2 (Anyon and LeBlanc 1984:98).

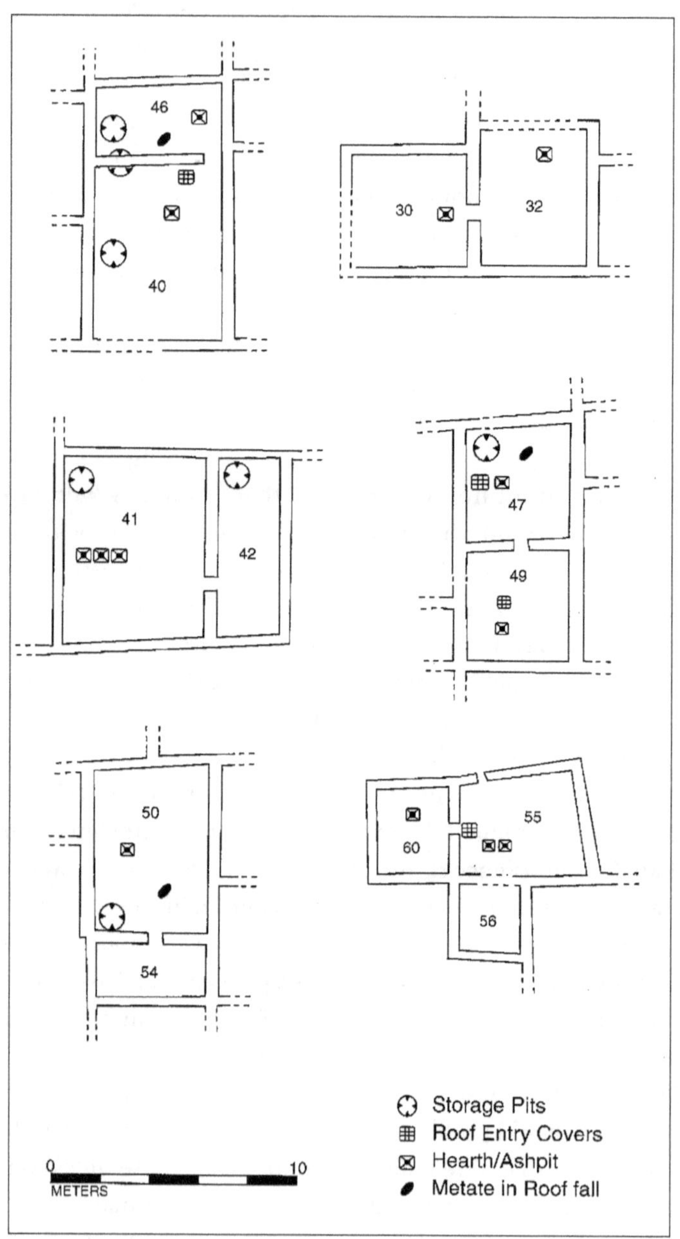

FIGURE 2.1.

Classic Mimbres residential organization at NAN Ranch Ruin, southwestern New Mexico. Habitation rooms (which are generally larger and have hearths) are organized in pairs or are connected to smaller storage rooms, which usually lack features. (After Shafer 1982: fig. 3.)

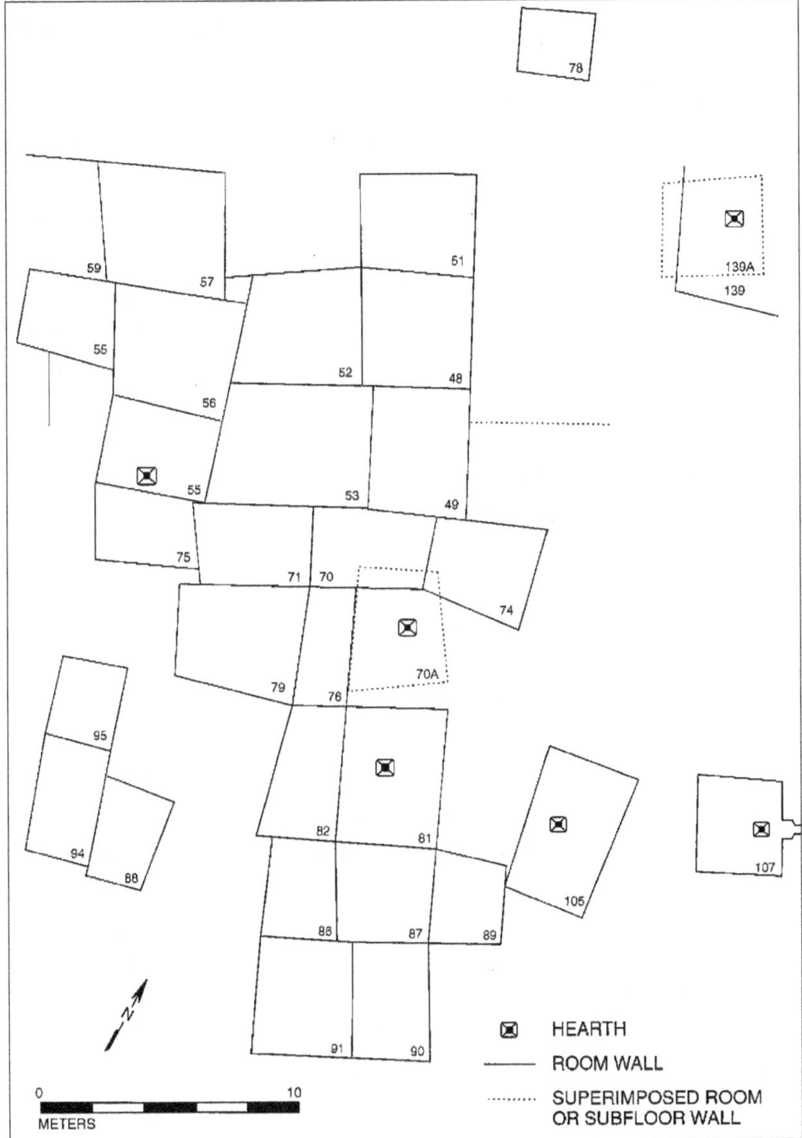

FIGURE 2.2.

Classic Mimbres residential organization at the south room cluster of Galaz Ruin, southwestern New Mexico. No suitelike organization is apparent, in contrast to NAN Ranch Ruin. Room 107 is a kiva. (After Anyon and LeBlanc 1984:fig. 6.1.)

Classic room clusters (groups of adjacent but not necessarily contiguous rooms) grew by accretion, and in some cases (e.g., NAN Ranch and the Mattocks site [Patricia Gilman, personal communication]), founding core rooms are identifiable. These core rooms began as regular habitation rooms and were extensively repaired and maintained throughout the life of a cluster; some (e.g., NAN Ranch room 29) have many burials under the floor. It may be that some core rooms were residences, perhaps of the founders, and some were later converted into ceremonial or mortuary areas. As agriculture became more intensive and more labor was needed, established residents may have attempted to entice people to join their group (a scenario proposed for the Hohokam [McGuire 1992]; see also Wilk's discussion of the Kekchi Maya [1984]). New construction at the sites is associated with relatively dry periods (Shafer 1996), suggesting that the relatively lush Mimbres Valley was particularly enticing at these times.

No mealing features are present in the Classic rooms; corn grinding was done primarily on single trough metates set on floors or roofs. In many cases (e.g., NAN Ranch and possibly Swarts), food preparation, consumption, and storage appear to have been organized at the scale of the room suite, although considerable variability is present (e.g., Galaz). Shafer (1995) has argued that the form of the hearths (rectangular and slab lined) symbolizes links with the underworld and with earlier architecture (i.e., rectangular pithouses), and the regular placement of hearths (just off center) provides some support for this interpretation. Although Classic architectural organization is quite variable, architectural details such as feature form and location and the arrangement of roof support posts are quite homogeneous (as is the pottery). This homogeneity, in the context of aggregated settlement and fairly intensive food production, is interpreted as indicating a high degree of social conformity (Hegmon, Nelson, and Ruth 1998).

Although some people may have left the Mimbres region just prior to A.D. 1150, others stayed and established new residences at the large sites (Creel 1999) or moved to other drainages (Nelson and Anyon 1996). Particularly in the eastern Mimbres area, many people established small (ca. 5–15 room) dispersed residential Postclassic hamlets along the smaller drainages (Nelson 1999). Many of these hamlets were built by adding to the field houses (M. C. Nelson 1993). The residents of these hamlets continued to rely heavily on plant cultivation, and they were residentially mobile (Nelson 1999). No public or ceremonial architecture is known.

Postclasssic hamlets in the eastern Mimbres area consist of an amalgam of habitation rooms (generally the size of larger Classic rooms) in one or two roomblocks. Almost all of the known excavated rooms (19 of 22) have hearths, about half have built-in mealing features, and items were stored in the rooms in large pits or hung from roof beams. Some of the mealing features (5 of 11) included places for two or three metates, and two rooms had two different and apparently contemporaneous mealing features. Thus food preparation, consumption, and storage were organized at the scale of the room, although it is possible that the residents of several rooms shared grinding features. Hearths are still consistently located just off center, and mealing features tend to be in corners or off to one side, positioned so that the grinder would face toward the room. Entry was usually through the roof, but entry locations are mostly unknown. Some slab-lined rectangular hearths are present, in conjunction with a variety of other forms. In general, feature form is extremely variable across and between sites, the variability cannot be explained in terms of differences in function, and there is no evidence for sitewide organization, suggesting that residents of each room were relatively independent of one another

The existence of a basic unit of residence, consumption, and to some degree storage in the Late Pithouse and then Postclassic periods probably facilitated household-level decision making and participation by all individuals. The Postclassic strategy of intensive cultivation linked with residential mobility has been compared (Hegmon, Nelson, and Ruth 1998; Nelson 1999) to that of the Tarahumara in northern Mexico (Graham 1994). Tarahumara residential units change during the course of a year as individuals or small groups move between residences.[7] This analogy suggests that Late Pithouse and Postclassic residential mobility might have contributed to individual (including women's) autonomy in that it would have allowed some choice of residence. Though some aspects of ritual and storage were apparently organized at the suprahousehold level in the Late Pithouse period, there is no evidence that these activities were exclusionary or that they were the source of gender-based differences in power or prestige.

The spatial context of labor also suggests a relatively large degree of social participation and autonomy for women in the Late Pithouse and Postclassic periods. There is no evidence for women's task groups (with the exception of a few small multiple grinding bins in the Postclassic) or for an intrasite spatial division of labor. Instead, women working at hearths or mealing features would have been in the middle of things, able to monitor and participate in various household activities. Late Pithouse women would have had considerable flexibility in deciding where they placed their metates, whereas Postclassic women would have had considerable flexibility in deciding how to construct a grinding feature. In general, tasks could have been organized to fit particular needs and situations. Overall, there is no evidence to suggest that the spatial organization of labor contributed to gender differentiation.

Throughout the course of the Late Pithouse period there seems to have been a growing emphasis on community at a larger scale, culminating with the Classic period. In comparison with redundant pithouses and Postclassic residential rooms, the basic organizational units are less regular in Classic pueblos. In some cases room suites appear to have constituted the basic unit; in other cases the basic unit may have been the larger room cluster, and small ritual structures were often associated with particular room clusters. To the extent that decisions were made at a scale larger than that of the room suite, participation by most or all adults was probably not possible, and some people must have been excluded. We lack evidence regarding who was excluded; it is possible that exclusion was gender based, but it might also have been based on other criteria such as length of residence and ancestral ties.

The central locations of hearths and movable metates in Classic Mimbres sites suggest a relatively large degree of social participation and autonomy for women, as in the preceding and subsequent periods. However, several other lines of evidence suggest that Mimbres Classic gender relations differed from those of other times. Classic material culture, including architecture, is quite homogeneous, in contrast to that of the Pithouse period and, especially, the Postclassic. Women apparently had little choice with regard to the form of the hearths they could build (rectangular and slab lined) or their mealing features (movable trough metates). However, if the hearths were symbolically significant, as Shafer (1995) suggested, then their use might have contributed to women's prestige and power. In general, life in Classic Mimbres times probably involved increasing amounts of hard work, such as irrigation and corn grinding, and increasing pressure for social control and conformity. Although the new labor demands might have fallen more heavily on women than men, we see no evidence for a marked increase in gender differentiation, spatially or otherwise. If ancestral ties were an important component of Classic Mimbres society, then women's role in reproduction might have been especially valued; such value might have translated into a certain kind of prestige but not necessarily into power or autonomy.

THE HOHOKAM AND SALADO CULTURE AREAS

Hohokam remains, in welcome contrast to Mimbres, evidence a multitude of spatial patterns, some with fairly specific implications for gender relations. Crown and Fish (1996) recently discussed the gender implications of the Hohokam pre-Classic to Classic transition, and here we draw on some of their conclusions, focusing specifically on issues regarding architecture and the use of space. We consider overall Pioneer-Sedentary (A.D. 300–1150) developments, drawing primarily on general summaries and of course on Snaketown (Haury 1976; Wilcox, McGuire, and Sternberg 1981). We then consider the Sedentary period (A.D. 975–1150) and the transition to the Classic period in more detail, focusing on the Phoenix Basin, particularly the detailed data from La Ciudad (Rice 1987; Henderson 1987b). Finally, we expand our spatial coverage and consider the Classic (A.D. 1150–1450) both in the Phoenix Basin (Pueblo Grande [Mitchell, ed., 1994a], and Los Muertos [Brunson 1989]) and at Marana near Tucson (Fish, Fish, and Madsen 1992). We also compare the Hohokam Classic with the Tonto Basin Salado sites (Elson, Stark, and Gregory 1995; Rice 1998). Much of our analysis focuses on the better known large sites, although we recognize that many people probably lived in small dispersed rancherías (P. Fish and S. Fish 1991). Also, we recognize that much living in southern Arizona was probably done out-of-doors and may have involved little permanent architecture; certainly many important Pima–Tohono O'odham social practices have few material correlates. For example, local groups had great longevity as social units, but the only material symbols of these groups were baskets of relics kept in the desert (Bahr 1983).

Pre-Classic Periods

The pre-Classic sequence is a time of Hohokam expansion and intensification, including the construction of more elaborate canal systems, which are equated with irrigation communities (Gregory 1991). Many sites, particularly the larger ones, were used throughout much of the sequence. Although there are major differences between sites, such as in the number and presence of ball courts and mounds, these differences are not reflected in the residential architecture, and there is little indication of marked social differentiation within or between sites. The biggest sites with the most public architecture appear to have had an instrumental role in community organization, indicated by their positions at important nodes on canal systems (Nicholas and Neitzel 1984).

Pre-Classic houses are typically shallow pit structures or houses in pits (hereafter called pithouses). Sedentary-period houses are typically elliptical, about 14–15 m^2 (but larger at Snaketown) (Crown 1991a:149; Mitchell, ed., 1994a:35; Wilcox, McGuire, and Sternberg 1981), with entrances on one long side. At any one time, there is little variation in house form or size; the sizes of subrectangular houses at La Ciudad exhibit a roughly normal distribution (Henderson 1987b:21). One of the key developments in Hohokam archaeology was the recognition by Wilcox, McGuire, and Sternberg (1981) that apparently scattered pre-Classic houses actually were arranged in courtyard groups, with the entrances of several (usually three to four) similar pithouses facing an open courtyard. Some courtyard groups (particularly in nonriverine areas) had their own cemeteries, but more often several courtyard groups (called suprahousehold groups or village clusters) shared a cemetery, midden, horno (oven), and occasionally other features (Wilcox 1991b:257, but see Sires 1984:138–39). The cemeteries are interpreted as symbolizing corporate groups (P. Fish and S. Fish 1991). Although there are some houses and groupings that do not fit this basic pattern (P. Fish and S. Fish 1991), in general the groupings and the cemeteries became more formalized over time.

Many researchers have suggested that courtyard groups strove to retain people and recruit new members (particularly young adults) because of the heavy labor demands associated with irrigation agriculture (Doelle, Huntington, and Wallace 1987; Henderson 1987a; McGuire 1992). At least two lines of evidence support this interpretation. First, the general expansion of pre-Classic (particularly Colonial-period) settlement suggests that people had the option of establishing new residences. Second, where detailed data are available, it appears that courtyard groups often began as a single house (often the largest house) and grew by accretion (fig. 2.3; Henderson 1987a), although such growth patterns might also have resulted from simple domestic cycling (J. Howard 1985).

Assuming that labor recruitment was an important aspect of pre-Classic courtyard group longevity, the composition of groups would have been fairly flexible, and at least some people would have had a choice of residence. This interpretation is supported by several lines of ethnographic evidence. Short-term movements (although not permanent changes in residence) are common among the Pima (Bahr 1983:182), and the Tohono O'odham had considerable flexibility in postmarital residence (see Bahr's [1983:182] summary of Underhill's [1939] data). Randall McGuire's (1992) interpretation of the Sedentary occupation at La Ciudad (which was based primarily on analogies with the Yuma but is not incompatible with Pima and Tohono O'odham practices) suggested that young people of all genders were recruited as household members and had considerable choice of residence. Although it is likely that residents of a courtyard group were linked by kinship, kin ties would not have determined residence. Rather, kinship is better interpreted as one of the resources people used to work out their strategies; for example, a mature leader could recruit his (or possibly her) offspring, and a young person could chose to live with parents or with other relatives. This situation might have benefited women in various ways. Some degree of residential choice would contribute to women's autonomy, and the recruitment of young women for household membership might contribute to their prestige and power. Furthermore, it is likely that women gained some prestige for contributing to the success of a household.

Most pre-Classic pithouses have one hearth (rarely two), positioned between the center of the house and the entrance, and small roasting pits are often adjacent to the houses (Henderson 1987b:34). Thus, some cooking appears to have been done by the residents of each house. In addition, large hornos, often on the periphery of a residential area and/or associated with multiple courtyard groups, indicate that

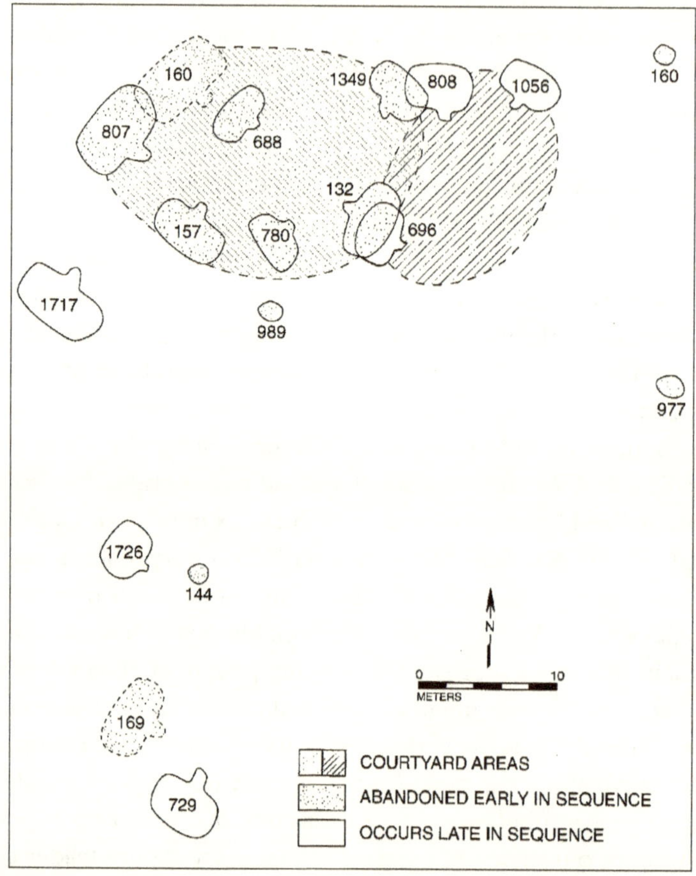

FIGURE 2.3.

The development of Sedentary-period Hohokam courtyard groups in the Moreland locus, La Ciudad, in Phoenix, Arizona. The upper left courtyard group was occupied between A.D. *950 and 1040; it began with the construction of pithouses 132 and 688, followed by 807 and then 157, 780, and 1349. Late in the sequence this courtyard was reoriented and a second group was constructed; it included pithouses 696, 808, and 1056 and was occupied from* A.D. *1005 to 1060. Pithouse 1717 was also built at this time and may represent the founding of a new cluster. (After Henderson 1987a:112–15, figs. 5 and 6.)*

some cooking was done on a more communal scale. Little information is available about the location of corn grinding (only seven whole metates were recovered at Snaketown [Haury 1976:280]), but it is likely that many food-processing and craft activities were conducted outside of the houses (Crown and Fish 1996:806; Kisselburg 1987). Information on food storage is also elusive. Many trash-filled pits are scattered across Hohokam sites, including inside houses, but the locations of areas specifically used to store food are unknown.

The distribution of pre-Classic architecture and features suggests considerable flexibility in the organization of labor. Residences were organized at the level of the pithouse dwelling, the courtyard group, and multiple courtyard groups. Cooking was done in pithouses, in extramural areas, and in communal hornos; storage may have been organized at similarly variable scales, and many activities were probably undertaken in the plazas and courtyards. Thus chores could have been done individually or at various communal levels. This kind of flexibility would have contributed to women's autonomy, would have facilitated the establishment of women's networks—a source of power—and might have eased women's labor burden because work could have been shared (e.g., child care) or at least done with company (e.g., grinding).

Although most pre-Classic structures were residences, there are also some special purpose structures including meeting houses (with schist risers), crematoria, and small huts with hearths but few other features that are interpreted as possible menstrual huts (Crown 1985a; Haury 1976:62, 68; Henderson 1987b:28). A late Sedentary–Early Classic possible menstrual hut was also identified at Pueblo Grande (Mitchell, ed., 1994a:79). These nonresidential structures usually are associated with multiple courtyard groups. Menstrual huts are known among the Tohono O'odham (Underhill 1939). Although the organization of households and labor suggests that pre-Classic women had fairly high status—including prestige, power, and autonomy—the presence of possible menstrual huts suggests that women's status was lower than men's in at least some respects. Menstrual huts are generally associated with beliefs in female pollution, and such beliefs are particularly prevalent in societies in which male prestige is dependent on female productive labor (Crown and Fish 1996:804 and references therein).

The Classic Period

Evidence for a social hierarchy is well established for the Hohokam Classic period and for the Salado phenomenon. Hierarchical relations are evidenced in residential architecture (discussed later) as well as in mortuary remains and other aspects of material culture (Neitzel, this volume; Wilcox 1991b). Many of the areas occupied during the pre-Classic continued to be occupied, but the integration or filling in of the canal systems (Nicholas and Feinman 1989), as well as the spacing of mounds (Crown 1987), suggests closure and intensification. Furthermore, primary sites (large sites with platform mounds) are commonly located near the ends of canal systems (e.g., Marana [Fish, Fish, and Madsen 1992], Casa Grande [Crown 1987], Las Colinas [Gregory 1991]), suggesting that their importance was based more on power than on instrumental position.

Variability in residential architecture increased markedly in the Classic period. Residence in single shallow pithouses continued in the early Classic, but a greater variety of house forms was built and used (six different types were identified at Pueblo Grande [Mitchell, ed., 1994a]). Some people continued to reside in these kinds of houses throughout the Classic, although by the later part of the period the most common residence was the compound, an above-ground adobe pueblo with associated open spaces. Most compounds included suites of habitation and storage rooms as well as other special-purpose rooms possibly used for craft production and ceremonies.[8] The spacing of houses within compounds was roughly the same as the spacing within a courtyard cluster (Sires 1987). Thus the basic organization indicated by courtyard groups seems to have continued into the Classic; the difference is that compounds were typically surrounded by substantial adobe walls. In addition, distances between compounds (100–300 m) were much greater than distances between courtyard groups (50 m) (Gregory 1991:181). Some compounds included only a few rooms, others had more than 50 (Brunson 1989:286), and groups of houses sometimes had separate walled plazas within the larger compound (Sires 1987).

The organization of activities established in the pre-Classic continued in the compounds. That is, most residences (single dwellings or suites of rooms) had hearths and small roasting pits (Mitchell, ed., 1994a:90–92), but there was often only one horno per compound (although one compound at Los Muertos had four hornos [Brunson 1989:286]). Basic food storage (in contrast to storage of prestige goods in or on the mounds [Jacobs 1992]) was done in small rooms attached to habitation rooms and in centrally located granaries (Brunson 1989:180); thus storage was organized at both the individual dwelling and the compound levels. Many productive and craft activities were carried out in the courtyards, as during the pre-Classic, the difference being that many courtyards were enclosed behind walls during the Classic period. A few pieces of ground stone were also found set up for use in the rooms (Jacobs 1994:158–59; Mitchell, ed., 1994a), indicating that some grinding was done indoors.

The flexible organization of labor noted for the pre-Classic, and its positive effects on women's lives, probably continued in the Classic, and compound organization might have promoted intragroup cooperation and eased burdens such as child care. For several reasons, however, we see an overall decrease in status for women in the Classic.

The increased interhousehold distance and of course the compound walls indicate a formalization of residential arrangements. That is, in contrast to pre-Classic courtyard groups, compound leaders might not have needed to worry about recruiting or maintaining members, and there would have been less flexibility in residential arrangements. Violence, for which there is growing evidence of during the Classic period (Rice 1998), would also have limited residential flexibility. Thus, whereas we interpreted pre-Classic household and residential organization as contributing to women's autonomy (and possibly also power and prestige), the formalization of that organization would have had the opposite effect.

Classic-period compound walls are an important example of restricted access. In addition, compound architecture represents a fairly dramatic increase in architectural differentiation, both within and between residences, which can be interpreted as an indication of increased social differentiation (Kent 1990b). Walls would have restricted access into the compounds and might also have limited the degree to which residents of the compounds could have interacted with others outside. "Women living in compounds could no longer see or communicate with the entire village community while working, effectively limiting their daily interactions" (Crown and Fish 1996:806). We have no evidence to suggest that Classic-period women never left their compounds or that they were subject to anything equivalent to purdah. However, it is likely that the walls limited both women's prestige—relative to men—and their autonomy.

The organization of Classic Hohokam architecture provides other evidence of vertical social differentiation and restricted access. David Wilcox (1991b:262) identified a four-tier intersite hierarchy topped by large sites with platform mounds and other ceremonial architecture. At an intrasite or intracommunity scale, differentiation and wealth differences are indicated by the forms and locations of residences. In general, the elites lived in compounds on or immediately surrounding platform mounds, and access to these areas was restricted by the mounds themselves and by surrounding walls. Higher-status people lived in walled compounds (those closer to the mounds may have been relatively higher), and lower-status people in pithouses.

Though there may be a general association between social hierarchies and gender hierarchies (Ortner 1981), it is likely that these forms of social differentiation crosscut gender differences. That is, women who lived on mounds apparently had more prestige than both women and men in other residences, and elite women might have had power over nonelites (Crown and Fish 1996). However, elite women might also have been in a worse position relative to elite men. That is, assuming the compound walls restricted their movements and interactions to some extent, elite women would have had limited autonomy and would have been cut off from the kind of power that derives from being part of a wide-ranging network and part of the ebb and flow of village life (a situation well portrayed by French [1977] for modern America). The complex dimensions of status (involving elites and commoners as well as men and women) bring to the fore the complexity of interpreting the meaning of social hierarchy and autonomy in women's lives. Who is better off, an elite woman who may have considerable social prestige but who spends most of her time behind compound walls, or a commoner woman who has personal autonomy and wide-ranging social interactions but must struggle for survival?

PUEBLO BEGINNINGS: BASKETMAKER III AND PUEBLO I

Turning to the Ancestral Pueblo culture area, we emphasize the northern San Juan region, particularly southwestern Colorado and northernmost New Mexico, including data from the Navajo Reservoir district (Eddy 1966), the Durango area (Carlson 1965), the Dolores River valley (Breternitz, Robinson, and Gross 1986; Kane and Robinson 1988; Schlanger 1988; Wilshusen 1991), the Yellow Jacket area (Mobley-Tanaka 1997b; Wheat 1984), the Duckfoot site (Lightfoot 1994), Badger House on Mesa Verde (Hayes and Lancaster 1975), and the La Plata district (Morris 1939; Toll 1992). We also draw information from Alkali Ridge in southeastern Utah (Brew 1946), from northeastern Arizona (Morris 1980; Nichols and Smiley 1985) and from Shabik'eschee Village in Chaco Canyon (Roberts 1929; Wills and Windes 1989).

Basketmaker III (A.D. 500–700) residences are typically pithouses with an antechamber to the south or southeast, a central hearth, and four roof support posts. Most pithouses are associated with external pits, cists, and shallow pit structures that were probably used for food storage. At large sites it is unclear whether these features are associated with particular pithouses, but at some smaller sites the arrangement of storage units to the north of the pithouse is clear (Carlson 1965; Mobley-Tanaka 1997b). Cooking was done in the central hearths and in exterior hearths, ovens, and roasting pits not obviously associated with any particular structure. Formal grinding features are rare, but metates (usually one, sometimes two or three) are common and—as in Mogollon pithouses—are typically located between the hearth and the entryway.

Most Basketmaker III sites comprise one or two pithouses and are widely dispersed across the landscape. A few sites with 14–20 pithouses are known (Eddy 1966; Morris 1980; Wills and Windes 1989), but these larger sites were probably not large permanent residences; they are better interpreted as important places and the loci of periodic aggregations (Wills and Windes 1989). Great kivas, usually located on the peripheries of larger sites, occur in the Basketmaker III and early Pueblo I periods and would have served as central places for dispersed communities.

Basketmaker III organization was probably fairly similar to that in the Mogollon Late Pithouse period. Some degree of residential mobility combined with the existence of a basic unit of residence, consumption, and to some degree storage would have facilitated household-level decision making and participation by many individuals, including women. The great kivas were probably used for suprahousehold activities, but there is no evidence that these were exclusionary. Women working at hearths or mealing features in or in front of pithouses would have been able to observe and participate in ongoing activities. Furthermore, the presence of communal as well as household-level storage and food preparation facilities indicates a flexible labor organization, and there is no evidence of gendered task groups. Thus Basketmaker III women probably had considerable power and autonomy, and there is no architectural evidence of a gender-based difference in prestige. However, Basketmaker III autonomy—for individuals as well as households—may have been limited as a result of the violence or threat of violence that characterized this period (LeBlanc 1999).

The unit pueblo (Lipe 1989; Prudden 1903) was the basic unit of residence, food preparation, construction, and trash disposal across much of the northern Southwest prior to A.D. 1300. Unit pueblo construction appeared in many areas by late Basketmaker III times (occasionally earlier [Dohm 1994]) and was ubiquitous by the Pueblo I period (A.D. 700–900). Its defining characteristics include a small (ca. 16 m^2) pit structure,[9] surface structures to the north or west of the pit structure and midden area to the south or east, and evidence (in the form of wall abutments) of accretional growth (B. Bradley 1993; Brew 1946; Leh 1942; Lightfoot 1994; Morley 1914; Rohn 1971). Pueblo I pit structures are generally deeper and more rectangular than their Basketmaker III predecessors; they lack antechambers but instead have vent-tunnel complexes and wing walls delineating separate areas. Pit structures have centrally located hearths, and many also have identifiable ritual features known as sipapus (Wilshusen 1986). At most Pueblo I sites in the northern San Juan region, pit structures and sets of surface rooms are clearly associated, although the arrangement is less consistent in other regions (see Hegmon 1994). The roomblocks often include two rows of rooms. The front multipurpose habitation rooms are larger, contain hearths, and usually provided access to one or more smaller, featureless storage rooms behind (Lightfoot 1994). Ramada and small plaza areas in front of the surface rooms often contain hearths. Formal mealing features are rare, but metates are found in various locations, including in pit structures, surface rooms, and ramada-plaza areas.

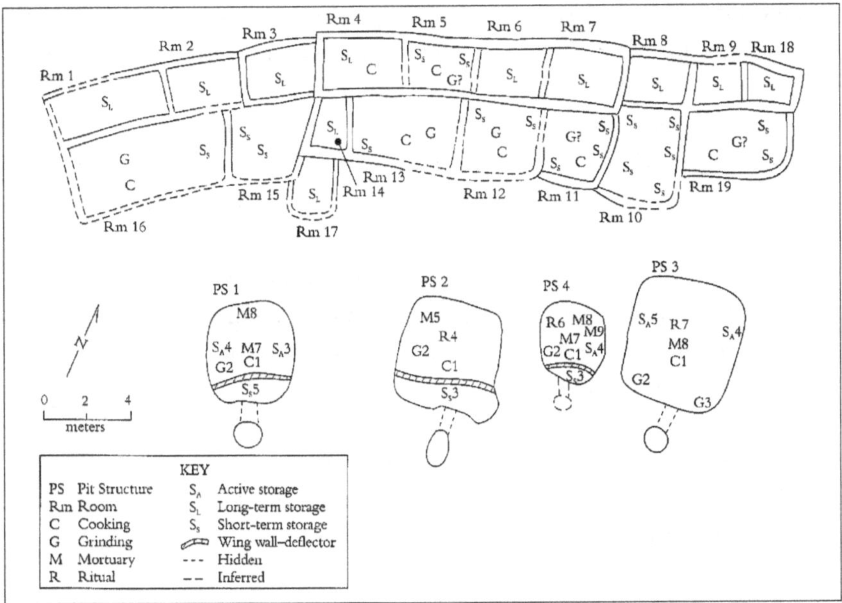

FIGURE 2.4.

The distribution of activity areas across and within households at the Pueblo I Duckfoot site in southwestern Colorado. The three household units are (1) rooms 1, 2, 3, 15, and 16 and pit structure 1; (2) rooms 4–7 and 11–14 and pit structure 2, possibly replaced by pit structure 4; (3) rooms 8–10, 18, and 19 and pit structure 3. (Reproduced from Lightfoot 1994: fig. 5.1, with permission of Crow Canyon Archaeological Center.)

Pueblo I household organization is fairly well understood, thanks to Ricky Lightfoot's (1994) detailed analysis of construction sequences, access, and artifacts at the Duckfoot site (fig. 2.4). Based on his finding that most domestic activities are redundant only at the scale of the entire unit pueblo, Lightfoot argued that the social correlate of the unit pueblo is a single large household and that various activities were organized at different social scales within the household. Storage was organized at the level of the household segment, which occupied an individual habitation room linked to the storage rooms (also see Gilman 1987; Hegmon 1996). In contrast, grinding and cooking were done in both the surface habitation rooms and pit structures, indicating organization at both the segment and entire household levels. Pit structure-based ritual would also have been organized at the level of the entire household. The well-established and redundant unit pueblo construction probably represents an increasingly formalized expression household organization, possibly symbolized by a shared ritual space.

The development of more restricted or private storage and a more robust expression of structured household organization in most Pueblo I contexts suggests a reduction in organizational flexibility—and concomitantly in individual (including women's) autonomy—in comparison with Basketmaker III patterns. At the same time, the presence of multiple cooking, storage, and grinding facilities within Pueblo I unit pueblos suggests an uncentralized and flexible domestic economy in which household segments could store and prepare their food separately or communally. Individuals and households would still have maintained considerable autonomy, and women probably had considerable power in the household-based organization. There is no evidence that either gender was restricted from access to ritual or other activities in the unit pueblo pit structures.

Large aggregated sites, possibly the earliest sedentary villages in the northern Southwest (Wilshusen 1991), developed by the A.D. 800s. Many of these villages were short-lived (ca. 40 years in the Dolores River valley) and appear to represent large-scale movements of preexisting communities (Schlanger 1988; Schlanger and Wilshusen 1993). Mid-800s villages typically consist of clusters of small roomblocks with unit pueblo architecture along with one or two large, U-shaped roomblocks. Some pit structures in these U-shaped roomblocks are oversized (ca. 66 m^2), contain elaborate ritual features, and are associated with relatively high frequencies of serving bowls and fauna used in rituals and feasting (Blinman 1989; Potter 1997). These oversized pit structure complexes appear to have replaced the much larger (180–400 m^2) great kivas—associated with earlier dispersed Pueblo I communities— as settings for large-scale ceremonialism (Wilshusen 1986). Similarities between these U-shaped roomblocks and the earliest (late A.D. 800s) construction at Pueblo Bonito (Windes and Ford 1992, 1996) suggest that these Pueblo I structures may represent early great houses (Schachner 1999).

The large Pueblo I villages represent one of the earliest examples of architecturally restricted access in the Ancestral Pueblo area (Schachner 1999). The oversized pit structures—in contrast to earlier great kivas—could have held only a fraction of the population of a village, and some U-shaped roomblocks also had walls restricting access into the plazas, indicating that some people were excluded from important activities. Furthermore, although surface rooms in these roomblocks are fairly typical, they are not consistently associated with individual pit structures in a unit pueblo arrangement (Brew 1946; Kane and Robinson 1988; Morris 1939:75–85; Wilshusen and Blinman 1992), suggesting that Duckfoot-style household organization was not ubiquitous. As was the case in our interpretation of the Hohokam Classic, we do not know whose access was restricted and whether restrictions were based on gender. Assuming that the oversized pit structures were used for feasting, women were probably involved in the preparation and serving of this food;[10] thus the gender-based division of ritual labor seen in the ethnographically known pueblos may have been established by this period. In general, though Pueblo I women probably maintained considerable power as important members of relatively autonomous households, that power may not have extended into all realms of society.

In the late 800s, large areas of southwestern Colorado were depopulated, and more dispersed communities with great kivas and early great houses developed in northern New Mexico, including the Cedar Hill area (Wilshusen 1995), Chaco Canyon (Windes 1993:337–339), and the eastern Chuska slope (Marshall et al. 1979). Wilshusen and Wilson (1995) argued that these settlement shifts represent a large-scale migration from the northern San Juan region, and the return to great kivas and dispersed settlement signals the reestablishment of more egalitarian, horizontally linked groups and household autonomy. These developments would have meant a return to earlier, more egalitarian gender relations as well.

THE CHACOAN ERA

Beginning by A.D. 900 and continuing into the 1100s, much of the northern Southwest was linked (ritually, economically, and/or stylistically) to developments in Chaco Canyon. On the north side of Chaco Canyon, nine elaborate great houses were constructed; most are multistoried, and the largest has more than 650 rooms. Less than a kilometer away, on the south side of Chaco Wash, are contemporary, apparently ordinary residences known as the Chaco small sites. Beyond Chaco

Canyon, extending across an area of more than 67,000 km^2, are a series of approximately 70 Chacoan outliers, that is, larger sites with great kivas that share some of the characteristics of the Chaco Canyon great houses. In some cases smaller residential sites are clearly clustered around the outliers; in other cases small sites are widely dispersed but are thought to be part of outlier communities (Kantner and Mahoney 2000).

There are enormous quantities of architectural data for this period. We focus primarily on residential architecture in relation to household organization, drawing data from the Chacoan small sites (Truell 1992; Windes 1993) and from several syntheses of the northern San Juan region (Lipe 1989; Mobley-Tanaka 1997a; Varien 1999; Varien, ed., 1999). We consider only a fraction of the great house and outlier data, specifically aspects of the architecture relevant to restrictions on access and the organization of labor, drawing primarily on the detailed Pueblo Alto report (Windes 1987) and Stephen Lekson's (1986) study of great house architecture.

Mortuary and biological data (Akins 1986; Martin, this volume; Neitzel, this volume), as well as the enormous differences in architectural elaboration, are indicative of some form of social inequality in Chaco Canyon, and it is likely that some women, as well as some men, enjoyed a privileged status. Many components of great house architecture would have placed severe restrictions on access. For example, plaza areas in most great houses are completely enclosed, series of storage rooms are hidden deep in Pueblo Bonito, and suites of rooms at Pueblo Alto are accessible only from the road (Lekson 1986:61–64; Windes 1987:fig. 10.3). However, the nature of Chacoan organization is not well understood. Several lines of evidence (including the distribution of hearths [Windes 1984] and the organization of room suites [Bernardini 1999]) indicate that there may have been only a small resident population in the great houses, and James Judge (1989) has suggested that Chaco Canyon was the locus of periodic pilgrimages. Thus the inequality evidenced in Chaco Canyon may not have been a pervasive aspect of most people's everyday lives across the northern Southwest (in contrast to the inequality signaled by Hohokam and Salado platform mounds). Researchers have only just begun to investigate the organization of outlier communities (Kantner and Mahoney

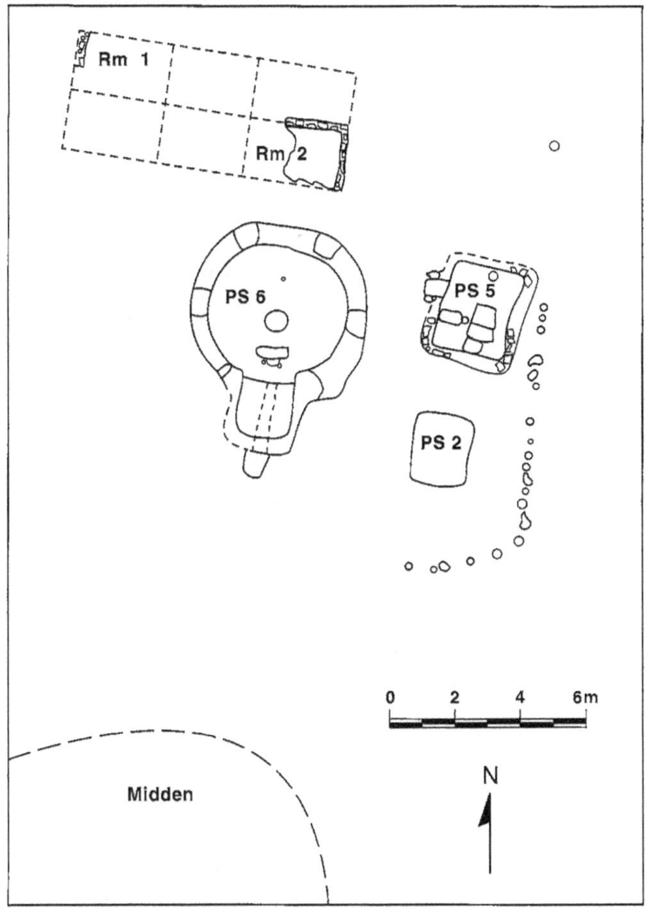

FIGURE 2.5.
Unit pueblo at Knobby Knee Stockade (ca. A.D. 1200) in southwestern Colorado (Morris 1991), showing surface roomblock (rooms 1 and 2), keyhole-shaped kiva (PS 6), and subterranean mealing room (PS 5).

2000; though see Breternitz, Doyel, and Marshall 1982).

Residential sites on the south side of Chaco Canyon and across the northern Southwest are characterized by unit pueblo construction: suites of surface rooms associated with well-constructed kivas and midden areas (fig. 2.5). Kiva form is standardized, although there are regional differences (e.g., Chacoan kivas are circular and have benches, in contrast to keyhole-shaped kivas with pilasters in the northern San Juan region). Kivas were sometimes accessed via tunnels that opened into surface rooms (Wheat 1984).

Substantial cooking hearths are present in kivas as well as in front surface rooms, indicating that the flexible organization of labor seen in earlier times continued to some extent. Other domestic activities became more centrally and formally organized, however. The most salient example of this centralization is the grouping of metates in clusters of fixed mealing bins (Mobley-Tanaka 1997a; Schlanger 1994, 1995).

The distribution of mealing bins is best understood in the non-Chacoan residential unit pueblos. At these sites, grinding complexes most often contained between two and six bins set in various locations including on kiva roofs, in subterranean mealing rooms adjacent to kivas (see fig. 2.5), in surface mealing rooms, and sometimes—when only one or two bins were needed—in kivas (Ortman 1998). Despite the variability, the common denominator is a single grinding complex that could be accessed directly from the kiva; thus mealing units were clearly isomorphic with kiva units.

The organization of grinding in the Chacoan small sites is more difficult to discern, since several specialized mealing rooms were constructed and dismantled during the course of each lengthy occupation. Space syntax analysis indicates that these mealing rooms were highly integrated spaces accessible from a number of adjacent surface rooms, pit structures, and extramural areas; thus Bustard (1996) argued that the mealing group was the fundamental social unit of Chacoan small sites. Because of the extensive remodeling, it is difficult to assess the relationship between mealing rooms and kivas, but we suspect they were linked.

Similar grinding complexes are present in the residential areas of Chacoan great houses such as Pueblo Alto (Lekson 1986:49; Windes 1987:386–91). In addition, Pueblo Bonito as well as some outlier great house sites (e.g., Aztec and Salmon [James 1994:258; Shelley and Irwin-Williams 1980] and Chimney Rock [Mobley-Tanaka 1990)]) have much larger communal grinding rooms, with 10 to 12 mealing bins, suggesting that at least some food preparation was done on a supra-household scale.

Unit pueblo architecture indicates that household organization—

already well established by Basketmaker III–Pueblo I times—continued to be important throughout the Chacoan era. Furthermore, the redundant unit pueblo organization and the elaborate and formalized nature of kivas suggest important symbolic associations that may signal the cultural importance of the resident household unit. These developments could have had various, and somewhat contradictory, effects on gender relations and the lives of women. Households probably maintained considerable autonomy (varying with mobility, as we discuss later), yet the pervasiveness of the organization may have limited individuals' autonomy to choose a style of residence.

The specialized mealing bins and grinding rooms are best interpreted from the perspective of these contradictory trends. On one hand, women would have had no choice regarding the location of their work, would sometimes have been separated from ongoing activities, and would have been subject to monitoring and supervision, often from other women. Thus these new features would have reduced women's autonomy and might be associated with an increase in women's labor burden. On the other hand, the construction of special facilities for women's work—facilities that were sometimes attached to kivas and were also found in great houses—suggests the importance of corn grinding and the power of women over this increasingly separate realm. Furthermore, the communal nature of grinding might have contributed to women's prestige. Ortman (1998) argued that the redundant and often elaborate unit pueblo form symbolized the cultural ideal of large, multigenerational extended family households and that the clustering of mealing bins in a single location expressed the ideal of economic solidarity among women from various segments of the household.

Although grinding facilities are sometimes found in Chaco-era kivas, they were much more common in earlier Pueblo I pit structures. This shift led William Gillespie (1976) to argue that the development of kivas represented the development of ritual spaces used primarily by men (although see Cater and Chenault 1988). We think a more reasonable interpretation has to do with variability in extended family households; that is, smaller families sometimes built their grinding facility in the kiva itself, whereas most larger families set aside a separate room in order to allow all of the grinders in the household to work together. The diverse features indicate that the kivas were used for various purposes, probably by all genders. We see no evidence that either gender was denied access to unit pueblo kivas.

In the northern San Juan region, and probably across much of the northern Southwest, household residential mobility was fairly high during the Chacoan era; many unit pueblo sites were occupied for only a generation (Varien 1999), although community centers show considerable longevity. In contrast, most Chaco Canyon small sites were occupied for more than a century and remodeled multiple times. Given this lack of mobility, as well as the small sites' proximity to the great houses, we expect that the households resident in the Chaco Canyon small sites enjoyed less autonomy than their contemporaries elsewhere. Thus it is interesting that our spatial data (i.e., unit pueblo construction, organization of grinding) indicate no differences in gender relations associated with these differences in household autonomy. A similar comparison is developed later.

Finally, although the great houses are much larger and more elaborate than the contemporary unit pueblo residences, the two types display a number of parallels in spatial organization that have important implications. The communal grinding facilities in great houses suggest mass preparation of food for rituals and appear to duplicate on the community level the more humble mealing bin complexes found in most unit pueblos. A second example is the existence in some great houses of what Thomas Windes (1987) calls "big room suites," which lack domestic features but otherwise appear to be large versions of unit pueblo room suites. In addition, kivas found in great houses parallel the small pit structures and kivas of contemporaneous small houses. Ortman (1998) suggested that the unit pueblo household concept was used metaphorically to structure community organization. If this was the case, and if our foregoing interpretations regarding women's power and prestige in unit pueblo households are correct, then women may have had considerable power and prestige in the large communities as well.

PUEBLO III, A.D. 1150–1300

Following the dissolution of the Chaco regional system, various areas of the northern Southwest evidence increasingly different patterns, culminating with the depopulation of much of the Colorado

Plateau. We focus here on the thirteenth century and develop comparisons between the northern San Juan region and the Kayenta region in northeastern Arizona, drawing on syntheses presented by Adler (ed., 1996), Lipe (1989, 1995), Ortman (1998), Rohn (1989), and Varien (1999; ed., 1999) and on detailed descriptions of sites such as Sand Canyon Pueblo (Lipe 1992; B. Bradley 1993), Mug House (Rohn 1971), Cannonball (Morley 1914), the Hovenweep Group (Winter 1977), and Betatakin and Kiet Siel (Dean 1969).

The Northern San Juan

Unit pueblo organization became increasingly formalized after A.D. 1200. Kivas were made with carefully shaped stone masonry (in contrast to the cruder masonry used in surface rooms). Kiva murals, niches with special pottery vessels, and carved kiva floors are found at some sites (B. Bradley 1992, 1993; Morris 1991), and tunnels between kivas and other rooms are fairly common (e.g., B. Bradley 1993:fig. 7; Luebben 1985). The construction of mealing bins and specialized mealing rooms also continued. And whereas cooking hearths were found in various locations in earlier periods, extramural cooking features were much less common in Pueblo III times; in most sites the only substantial cooking hearths are located in kivas.

Unit pueblo occupation length increased over time, and some later Pueblo III unit pueblos were used for more than a century (Varien 1999). Regional settlement data also show an increasingly crowded landscape over time, with indications of formalized land tenure (Adler 1996; Varien 1999) and violence (Lightfoot and Kuckelman 1994). As this social landscape developed, isolated unit pueblos began to cluster into multiple units and then into villages with as many as 100 households. Unit pueblo architecture remained strongly expressed in these large villages, and wall abutment data routinely reveal patterns of accretional growth (B. Bradley 1993; Leh 1942; Morley 1914; Rohn 1971).

The continuity and increased elaboration of unit pueblo organization in the context of village formation and decreases in mobility provide more data on the association of household mobility/autonomy and gender relations. The comparison already developed between more and less mobile Chaco-era unit pueblo households revealed no obvious differences in intrahousehold gender relations. Similarly, the decrease in unit pueblo household mobility seen in Pueblo III times might have reduced household autonomy but had little apparent effect on gender relations, at least as expressed in the architectural data. The only exception is that cooking hearth locations indicate less flexibility in the organization of labor associated with the later, less mobile period.

Thirteenth-century villages were typically built around the heads of canyons or in alcoves, often enclosed a natural spring, and were almost always bisected by a drainage or wall (Rohn 1971; Varien et al. 1996). Many had impressive rimrock architectural complexes, including ceremonial, residential, and storage architecture (B. Bradley 1996:246–47; Fewkes 1919), along with low masonry walls that defined village spaces (Kenzle 1993), great kivas, multistoried towers (Winter 1977), and in some cases suprahousehold storage structures (Bloomer 1989; Cattanach 1980; Lipe 1992). Much of this architecture seems to have restricted the access of outsiders, an important consideration during increasingly violent times, but there is little evidence of intrasite restrictions on access. It is possible that household-level social differentiation and competition was advertised in this impressive and creative architecture. Although some women might have gained prestige as members of important families, we expect that overall such competition would have increased women's labor burden and negatively affected most women's lives.

The Kayenta Region

Prior to the thirteenth century, the basic architectural unit in the Kayenta region was a local version of the unit pueblo, complete with kiva, midden, surface roomblock, and grinding room (Beals, Brainerd, and Smith 1945:15, 44; Dean 1996:34, 1970:149; Powell 1983:24). As villages began to form during the Tsegi phase (A.D. 1250–1300), the basic architectural unit changed into what Jeffrey Dean (1969:34) called the room cluster. This was essentially a unit pueblo that lacked a kiva and contained one or two habitation rooms with entry box-hearth complexes, several storage rooms or granaries, and in some cases a specialized mealing room. Central courtyards linked several of these room clusters into courtyard complexes. Differences between Betatakin and Kiet Siel also indicate that settlement and mobility were sometimes organized at the household level and sometimes at a more inclusive scale (Dean 1970). Tsegi Phase villages were short-lived, lasting only a few decades.

The effect of village formation on households and gender organization was quite different in the Kayenta and northern San Juan regions. In contrast to the persistent unit pueblo organization to the northeast, Kayenta household architecture became smaller, more variable, and less formally delineated (Dean 1969:36–37). Furthermore, the disappearance of unit pueblo kivas in favor of kivas shared by several room clusters suggests a decline in the importance of the household as a basic social unit.

These differences have several important implications for gender relations. On one hand, the variable organization and lack of residential permanence suggest that individuals, including women, might have had a relatively high degree of autonomy. On the other, the decline in the importance of unit pueblo organization signals a decrease in household autonomy. Women at different stages of life might have been differently affected by these changes in household and individual autonomy. Most women, however, would have been negatively affected by the decline or absence of well-defined grinding task groups and the minimal symbolic importance of households, trends that we interpret as indicating a decline in women's power and prestige.

The distribution of features in relation to kivas also indicates a decline in the power and prestige of women. Specifically, kivas lack mealing bins and occasionally have loom holes (Dean 1969:29–33; Smith 1952a), suggesting that they were increasingly becoming the purview of men, and possibly that the access of women to kivas was restricted, culturally if not materially. This possible change in kiva use, as well as the plaza orientation of some Tsegi phase villages, suggests that some of the important transformations in Ancestral Pueblo built environments that spread throughout the Pueblo world in the fourteenth century were already under way in the Kayenta region.

PUEBLO IV, A.D. 1300–1540

Several important changes occurred in the organization of Pueblo built environments coincident with the large-scale migrations of Ancestral Pueblo populations in the A.D. 1280s. The changes were so basic and widespread that it is possible to consider most of the Pueblo area (including the Mogollon Rim) in a single discussion. The first and perhaps most important change was the development of integrated villages that housed entire communities and enclosed central plazas with terraced, multistoried residential architecture. Some of the earliest fourteenth-century villages, including Pueblo de los Muertos (Watson, LeBlanc, and Redman 1980), Arroyo Hondo (Creamer 1993), and Homol'ovi II (Adams and Hays 1991) were highly formalized and carefully planned (fig. 2.6). Bonding and abutment data illustrate that, unlike their predecessors, early Pueblo IV villages were built in massive construction episodes that raised apartment-like houses for large segments of the community at the same time that central public spaces were created (Brown 1990; Creamer 1993; Hayes, Young, and Warren 1981; Watson, LeBlanc, and Redman 1980). Later, fifteenth-century villages tended to be less formally arranged, thus enabling more organic, long-term accretional growth (Potter 1998), but the plaza orientation has been maintained until the present.

The second change was the disappearance of unit pueblo kivas. Pueblo IV kivas have larger floor areas and occur much less frequently than their unit pueblo predecessors (Lipe 1989), never contain grinding features (Ortman 1998), often contain sets of loom holes (looms were used exclusively by male weavers in historic pueblos), and were usually located in the central plazas (Creamer 1993; Kidder 1958; Smith 1972). Judging from similarities with historic and modern pueblos, it seems likely that the social units using Pueblo IV kivas were not households but rather moieties, religious societies, clans, and/or sodalities. This shift away from household-based ritual represents a profound change in Pueblo organization and culture. Although access to some ritual areas (e.g., Pueblo I oversized pit structures) had been restricted in the past, in the Pueblo IV period it appears that access to all kivas was, or could be, routinely restricted.

The third change was the increased size and permanence of Pueblo IV villages. Most earlier villages were used for only a generation or so, but many villages first built in the fourteenth and fifteenth centuries were still occupied at the time of the European invasion (e.g., Hawikku [Smith, Woodbury, and Woodbury 1966], Awatovi [Brew 1979], Gran Quivira [Hayes, Young, and Warren 1981], Nambe [Ellis

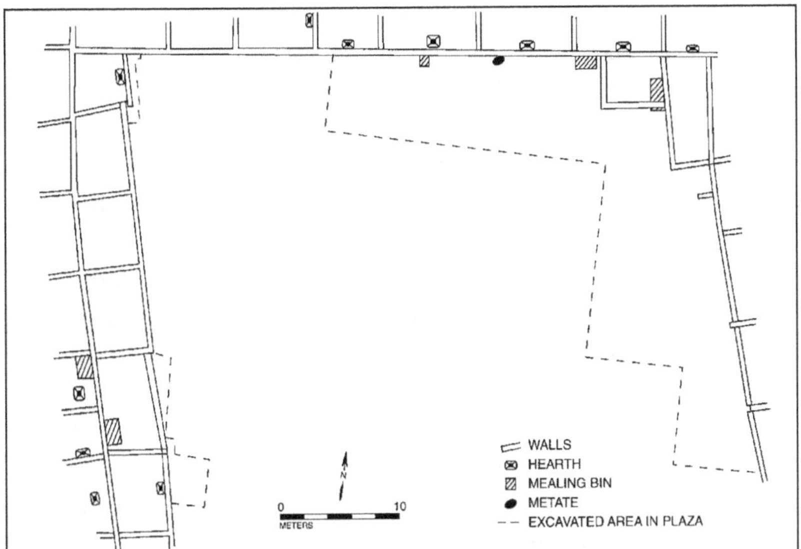

FIGURE 2.6.

Plaza C at the Pueblo IV site of Arroyo Hondo, northern New Mexico. The plaza is defined by regular rows of rooms. Grinding areas (mealing bins and metates) are found in rooms and in the plaza. (After Creamer 1993:79, fig. 4.16.)

1964], and Pecos [Kidder 1958]). Likewise, early Pueblo IV villages were often two, three, or even four times as large as the largest Pueblo III villages (Adler and Johnson 1996; Kintigh 1985).

The fourth important difference between Pueblo III and Pueblo IV communities has to do with the composition and cultural salience of households. Basic architectural units that probably represent households can sometimes be identified in formal, highly planned fourteenth-century villages. They usually consist of a front living room that opens onto a plaza, and one to five additional living and storage rooms. These basic units often encompass more than one story and are accessed through a combination of doorways and roof hatches (Ciolek-Torrello 1985:61; Creamer 1993:130–33; Kidder 1958:122–24). Grinding complexes in these residences, or at least ground-story facilities in the eastern Pueblo area, almost always contain a single mealing bin, suggesting that households were generally smaller and their composition less variable than was the case in unit pueblo households. Unfortunately, very few data on grinding facilities are available from fourteenth-century western Pueblo sites. An additional notable aspect of Pueblo IV "apartments" is their uniform nondescriptness, in contrast to earlier unit pueblos with their elaborate kivas. This is probably due in part to the large scale of construction episodes in fourteenth-century villages, but it also suggests that individual households were not considered to be as important as the overall community in which they were embedded.

The final change that is important for our purposes is a dramatic increase in the amount of food preparation that occurred outdoors, under open ramadas, in plazas, and on rooftops. Pueblo III outdoor grinding facilities are uncommon, but they are present in many Pueblo IV sites. Excavations at Pindi (Stubbs and Stallings 1953) and Arroyo Hondo (Creamer 1993; see fig. 2.6) have revealed that the central plazas of Pueblo IV villages contained roasting pits and turkey pens in addition to mealing bins. Outdoor bread ovens seem to continue this tradition of outdoor food preparation in most modern pueblos.

Two central points emerge from this summary. First, many basic organizational patterns of modern Pueblo communities date to the early fourteenth century. Second, Pueblo IV communities are organized quite differently from their predecessors. The disappearance of unit pueblo architecture in favor of integrated community architecture, the dissociation of kivas from households and their extension to larger organizations, the reduced social scale of households, and the increased visibility of food preparation all suggest that the household was a less important organizing principle in Pueblo IV society than it was in earlier times. In Pueblo mythology, it is the clan or moiety—not the household—that is the unit of emergence through the sipapu or earth navel of Pueblo cosmology. The long-term stability of Pueblo IV villages may have been enabled by the communal emphasis of this emergent ideology. In addition, there is a great deal of practical interdependence, particularly in the realm of agricultural production, among Pueblo households.

The significance of these changes for gender relations is not straightforward. We could argue that women's autonomy and prestige were reduced with the formation of plaza-oriented villages. In contrast to earlier times, in which large households were autonomous and culturally valued, Pueblo IV households were more seamlessly incorporated into a community in which important decisions were made by men in structures to which women did not have access on a daily basis. The disappearance of unit pueblos and their mealing rooms probably indicates a decrease in household–extended kin solidarity and thus in women's political influence. Finally, even if women entered and used the kivas on some occasions, it is likely that their access to kivas was, or could be, restricted at other times.

On the other hand, we do not suggest that the quality of women's lives deteriorated in all respects. The increasingly public and variable nature of food preparation, combined with the central role of prepared food redistributions in modern Pueblo ceremonialism (Ford 1972a), would have given Pueblo IV women prominent roles in community life and possibly new sources of ritual power. In addition, Pueblo III women spent much of their time in small kivas or mealing rooms, with no one to talk to other than their mothers, sisters, and in-laws. Although Pueblo IV households might have experienced an overall decrease in autonomy, some individual women might have gained some autonomy with regard to the organization and location of their labor, and at least they were able to observe and comment on village activities while doing their daily chores.

CONCLUSION

We began by emphasizing the importance of understanding (1) the practice of gender relations, that is, the structure as well as the agency of both women and men, and (2) the multidimensionality of women's status—as individuals and in relation to men—conceived in terms of prestige, power, and autonomy. In our analysis of the Mogollon, Hohokam, and Pueblo sequences, we focused on three components of architecture and the use of space: the location of gendered labor, household organization, and restrictions on access. These components are relevant to the various dimensions of women's status and to gender relations in general. Now, in order to bring some closure to the myriad information, we focus specifically on evidence of women's status in the three areas, relying on summary tables 2.1–2.3.

In the Mogollon-Mimbres sequence we see relatively little evidence for gender differentiation. There are suggestions of some social differentiation in the Classic period, but such differentiation

TABLE 2.1

Dimensions of Women's Status in the Mogollon-Mimbres Sequence

Period	*Prestige*	*Autonomy*	*Power*
Early Late Pithouse, A.D. 500–750	Little evidence; probably not much difference between women and men.	Residential mobility contributed to individual and household autonomy. Flexible labor organization.	Both genders contributed to household decision making and contributed economically.
Later Late Pithouse, 750–1000	Little evidence; probably not much difference between women and men.	Residential mobility contributed to individual and household autonomy, possibly less by end of period. Flexible labor organization.	Both genders contributed to household decision making and contributed economically.
Classic, 1000–1150	Little clear evidence; probably were differences, though not necessarily gender based. Importance of founders and ancestors suggests value placed on reproduction. Use of symbolically important hearths.	Less household and individual autonomy; emphasis on conformity.	Absence of household organization in some cases suggests less inclusive decision making. Probably not everyone had access to kivas; difference may not have been gender based.
Postclassic, 1150–1250	Little evidence; probably not much difference between women and men.	Residential mobility contributed to individual and household autonomy. Variable features suggest much freedom of choice.	Both genders contributed to household decision making and contributed economically.

apparently concerned ancestral ties and land tenure; it distinguished families and households, not genders. Both men and women may have worked to establish, symbolize, and perpetuate the important social and kin ties through mortuary practices and maintenance of core rooms. The homogeneous material culture suggests that Classic society was highly structured ideologically, although this structure is not evident in the architectural organization and probably did not involve highly redundant social units. The depopulation of villages at the end of the Classic period may represent an escape from this structure, and the diversity of the Postclassic, a resultant expression of individual autonomy.

The household organization suggested by Ancestral Pueblo unit pueblos and Hohokam courtyard groups would have facilitated important economic and decision-making roles for women and men; women probably had considerable power in both settings. The variable arrangements of courtyard groups and the possibility that group members were recruited suggest that individuals—again women as well as men—would have had considerable autonomy to choose where and how they wanted to live. The menstrual huts, however, suggest that Hohokam women were believed to be polluting and thus had less prestige than men. The dramatic increase in social differentiation in the Hohokam Classic seems to have crossed gender lines. Architectural variability and frequent rebuilding, as well as hoarding of valuables, suggest that the Hohokam power structure was never entrenched or routinely reproduced. The elites—possibly both women and men—had constantly to assert and maintain their power, and the trappings of power (mounds, compound walls, massive stores) were physical and possibly coercive as well as symbolic. This kind of power structure had repercussions at the household level, particularly in elite households in compounds. The organization of compound households was not much different from that in contemporary and earlier courtyard groups, with the exception of the surrounding walls. The walls may have served as markers of elite status, but they would also have limited the autonomy and power of women and others behind the walls.

Ancestral Pueblo peoples created an increasingly redundant and structured environment for themselves until the migrations of the late thirteenth century. The basic architectural form, the unit pueblo,

Table 2.2

Dimensions of Women's Status in the Hohokam Sequence

Period	*Prestige*	*Autonomy*	*Power*
Early Pre-Classic, A.D. 300–975	Little evidence; probably not much difference between women and men, though menstrual huts suggest belief in female pollution.	Courtyard group variability and need for recruitment suggest flexibility and residential choice. Flexible labor organization with work outside.	Both genders contributed to household decision making and contributed economically. Possibly both were recruited as courtyard group members. No restrictions on access.
Sedentary, 975–1150	Little evidence; probably not much difference between women and men, though menstrual huts suggest belief in female pollution.	Some decrease resulting from increased settlement packing, intensive irrigation, and violence. Flexible labor organization with work outside.	Both genders contributed to household decision making and contributed economically. Possibly both were recruited as courtyard group members.
Classic, 1150–1450	Social hierarchy cross-cuts gender lines. Architectural differentiation suggests multiple dimensions of social differentiation, though there is little direct evidence for gender-based differences in prestige.	Walled compounds restricted autonomy of those inside (women?), though organization within compounds was probably flexible. Non-elite women probably had more autonomy.	Lots of differentiation, restricted access to mounds and elite residences. Differences seem to cross gender lines. Elite women may have had power over non-elite but lacked other kinds of power because of their isolation.

delineated the basic social unit, the household. The unit pueblo also represented an important structuring principle in a larger social sense; people would have had little choice in residential organization. In contrast to the Hohokam courtyard groups, the redundancy and apparent symbolic importance of unit pueblo organization limited individual—although not necessarily household—autonomy. For the most part, we see little evidence of variable agency in the redundant architecture, although the evidence for competition and architectural ostentation that has been perceived in the aggregated Pueblo III sites and is obvious in Chaco Canyon probably represents a different kind of social strategy. Overall, the unit pueblo—as architectural unit, metaphor, and structuring principle—may be a good example of what Raymond Williams (1977) and Sherry Ortner (1996) meant by cultural hegemony. In this case, however, it is not a gender hegemony but rather a hegemony of organizational form that limited individual autonomy. At the same time, parallels between the organization of women's labor in mealing rooms and the unit pueblo kivas suggest that women had considerable prestige. This organizational hegemony broke down by the beginning of the Pueblo IV period, and the larger-scale community organization seems to have been linked to a decrease in women's prestige and power, although women may have had autonomy in some realms.

We realize that we have made a number of interpretive steps—perhaps leaps—in moving between architecture and gender relations. Assuming for the moment that these tentative steps are correct, we can assess relationships among the three dimensions of women's status. In the earlier periods, for which there are few indications of social differentiation, we see little evidence for gender differentiation. This conclusion is not surprising; many researchers have found links between social and gender hierarchies (e.g., Ortner 1981). Second, in the prehispanic Southwest, we see no case in which women had low prestige, little power, and little autonomy. Men probably had greater status in some times and places, but there is little evidence of a male-dominated gender hegemony. Third, two of the most dramatic transformations in the prehispanic Southwest—the beginnings of the Pueblo IV and Hohokam Classic periods—had major but different effects on gender relations. The Pueblo III–IV transition involved an end of unit pueblo

TABLE 2.3

Dimensions of Women's Status in the Pueblo Sequence

Time Period	*Prestige*
Basketmaker III, A.D. 500–700	Little evidence; probably not much difference between women and men.
Pueblo I, 700–900	Little evidence; probably not much difference between women and men.
Chaco era small sites, 900–1150	Symbolic importance of unit pueblo and association of kivas and grinding rooms indicate cultural recognition of women's value.
Chacoan great houses and outliers, 900–1150	Enlarged unit pueblo as concept in great houses probably indicates some at least symbolic recognition of women's value.
Late Pueblo III, northern San Juan region, 1200–1300	Symbolic importance of unit pueblo and link of kivas and grinding rooms probably indicate cultural recognition of women's value.
Tsegi phase, 1250–1300	Fewer indications of the recognition/ symbolism of women's value.
Pueblo IV, 1300–1540	Declines with end of elaborated household organization and unit pueblo kivas.

Autonomy	*Power*
Residential mobility contributed to individual and household autonomy. Threat of violence decreased autonomy.	Both genders contributed to household decision making and contributed economically.
Reduced mobility reduced individual autonomy, though flexible labor organization suggests autonomy in that realm. Unit pueblos → household autonomy.	Both genders contributed to household decision making and contributed economically. Some people may have been excluded from oversized pit structures.
Highly redundant unit pueblos limit individual autonomy, contribute to household autonomy. Grinding rooms → highly organized → less individual autonomy.	Both genders contributed to household decision making and contributed economically. Grinding work groups → source of women's power.
Residents of great houses probably had freedom linked to power, but within the context of a highly structured system.	Varies with status, not necessarily with gender. Some people (residents of great houses?) had much more power than others.
Highly redundant unit pueblos limit individual autonomy. Aggregation and violence reduce household autonomy. Highly organized labor → less individual autonomy.	Both genders contributed to household decision making and contributed economically. Grinding work groups → women's power. Some households may have become especially powerful.
Probably more individual autonomy though less household autonomy than in northern San Juan. Different in different communities.	Women's power probably less well defined than in northern San Juan as result of deemphasis of household and grinding room and possible exclusion from kivas.
Reduced household autonomy, more integrated communities. Variable and exterior grinding possibly indicates more individual autonomy for women at a certain (intracommunity) level.	Women lost power as a result of decline of household symbolism, exclusion from kiva, end of special grinding rooms; retained power as contributors of ritual food.

organization and women's important (prestigious and powerful) role in that organization, although individual women may have gained some autonomy. In contrast, there is little apparent change in household organization at the beginning of the Hohokam Classic, although the construction of compound walls around households and groups of households would have decreased the autonomy of the women who lived in those structures. Fourth, there seems to be something of a negative correlation between women's prestige and autonomy, both within a given society (e.g., the elite Hohokam) and over time (e.g., the Pueblo III to IV transition).

Several issues, both empirical and theoretical, should be pursued in future research. More detailed analyses of access and restrictions on access, possibly involving space syntax methods, would be useful. Such analyses could elucidate variation in the organization of Hohokam and Salado compounds in various contexts (on and off the mounds, walled and unwalled). Similarly, although architectural information is ubiquitous, detailed data on the distribution of rooms and features are often difficult to assemble. Many of the patterns we suggest could be examined in greater detail with more data from more sites, particularly in the Hohokam and Mogollon regions.

In considering the three components of our research—gendered workplaces, household organization, and restricted access—we are least satisfied with our interpretations regarding the third. That is, we were often able to identify what we thought to be architectural restrictions, but we were able to say little about whose access was restricted and what effects such restrictions had on women or gender relations. These issues could be considered theoretically and cross-culturally and by correlating the restrictions we identify in this chapter with trends identified elsewhere in this volume.

Finally, we came to realize (thanks to comments by Elizabeth Brumfiel) that our interpretive principles set up expectations that created negative correlations between autonomy, on the one hand, and power and prestige, on the other. For example, we interpreted unit pueblo household organization as contributing to women's power and prestige but limiting their autonomy. We need to reconsider this relationship and investigate (theoretically and empirically) cases in which women have autonomy as well as power and prestige.

Notes

A number of people contributed time, data, references, and ideas to this chapter. We are particularly grateful to Peggy Nelson in all respects, particularly with regard to households and the Mimbres material. Much of the eastern Mimbres data was collected by her and/or in collaborations with her, and the discussion of Mimbres features is based on her analysis. Elizabeth Brumfiel provided important and insightful comments. Jennifer Brady compiled much of the Mogollon data, Greg Schachner assisted with the Pueblo I data, and Ben Nelson, Bob Bolin, and Betsy Brandt contributed thoughts and references. We are also grateful for the comments of Patty Crown, Joan O'Donnell, and two anonymous reviewers. Linda Countryman drafted figures 2.1, 2.2, 2.3, and 2.6. Figure 2.4 is reproduced courtesy of Crow Canyon Archaeological Center, Cortez, Colorado.

1. For example, Connell (1987:chapter 3) concluded that neither sex role nor categorical theory provides a satisfactory account of gender asymmetry. See also Kent (1990a) regarding the extent to which culture "determines" architecture or vice versa.

2. The symbolic and conceptual importance of space in gender relations has been well documented in a number of ethnographic analyses—for example, the idea that women and men have different perceptual maps (Ardener 1981:27; see also Moore 1986; Spain 1992). Unfortunately, except in a general sense of providing ideas, the archaeological applicability of this work is limited.

3. According to Eggan (1950) the household is a matrilineal residential unit (including the husbands) that occupied a set of adjoining rooms. Titiev (1944), in contrast, considered a household to be a co-residential group of consanguineal kin (not including in-married men) that occupied a single room.

4. A number of influential early studies in feminist anthropology concluded that women universally have lower status than men (e.g., Ortner 1974; Rosaldo 1974), and many of the subsequent objections to these universalist conclusions emphasized the economic power of women working together and controlling important resources (e.g., Sacks 1979; Sanday 1981; Weiner 1976).

5. The large Galaz Ruin has approximately 135 pithouses and a maximum of about 38 per 100 years during the latest part of the Late Pithouse period (the Three Circle Phase [Anyon and LeBlanc 1984:91–92]). Assuming a pithouse use life of 21–28 years (which may be generous; see Cameron 1990), only about 10 would have been occupied at any one time.

6. A different pattern is evident farther to the north in the Pine Lawn Valley, where, in the early part of the Late Pithouse period, storage pits appear

to have been common inside pit houses and the pit houses tend to be larger than those in other areas and in later periods (Wills 1991).

7. Among the Tarahumara, individual houses are owned (or at least built and occupied) by fairly large extended family groups, but the units of residential mobility that move between those houses are generally nuclear families or sometimes individuals (Graham 1994).

8. These various room types are quite clear at some Phoenix Basin sites (e.g., Los Muertos [Brunson 1989]) and on Salado sites (Rice 1998). At Pueblo Grande, however, most structures, including the adobe-walled Classic rooms, appear to be simple dwellings [Mitchell, ed., 1994a:77]). We are not certain whether this apparent difference is chronological (i.e., Pueblo Grande is earlier), is due to different sampling or excavation strategies, or represents real differences in organization.

9. We use the term "pit structure" to refer to any semisubterranean structure in which the walls of the pit (lined or not) are the walls of the structure. Where it is clear that a pit structure was a residence, we use the term pithouse. Where pit structures may have had various uses (i.e., as a residence and/or as an early kiva), we retain the more general term "pit structure."

10. Data on food preparation in the oversized pit structures are scanty. Of the two excavated at McPhee Village (Kane and Robinson 1988), one had a broken mano fragment possibly associated with the floor, and the other had a broken trough metate probably associated with the roof fall.

3

Gender Ideology and Ritual Activities

Kelley Hays-Gilpin

Trying to understand ancient ideologies is endlessly fascinating and endlessly difficult. Ideology is an ideal representation of the world that attempts to "explain" the way things are. Ideologies often obscure, hide, or contradict the changes, ambiguities, and tensions inherent in social, political, and even economic processes. In trying to understand what Binford called "ideo-technic" behavior and its material correlates, we contend with evidence that is ambiguous by its very nature. For example, depictions of humans going about what may look to us like daily life rarely reflect "real" activities. Art (defined broadly here) may reflect prevailing ideas about how things should be, not they way they actually are. Art may resist or attempt to subvert dominant ideals. Individuals created visual representations, artifact decoration, and dress (like other important forms of art that are inaccessible to archaeologists, such as songs and prayers) in the context of physical and social environments. Art becomes part of environment, where it in turn influences behavior and ideas.

In middle-range societies, ideology is not necessarily an authoritative version of the world imposed by elites on commoners. Therefore, ideology becomes a more nebulous concept, impossible to reconstruct because no dominant, bounded, "official" version ever existed. Although it is difficult, perhaps impossible, to identify which themes seen in ancient visual arts represent a dominant ideology and which represent divergent or subversive statements, it is important to examine this material because art and ritual were not epiphenomenal activities in the lives of ancient peoples any more than they are today. Ritual behavior is and was very much part of the social and political fabric of society. Ritual not only reinforces existing roles and statuses, including (sometimes especially) gender roles, but also provides a context for the active negotiation of change. In the Southwest, archaeologists have unusual advantages, including detailed historic and ethnographic records, excellent preservation of architecture, ceramics, rock art, and perishables, and a higher degree of chronological precision than can be expected in most other regions.

Historic Pueblo ideology emphasizing gender complementarity contrasts with the gender hierarchies predominant in Old World and Euroamerican traditions. As described by Alice Schlegel (1977b) for the Hopi people, gender complementarity emphasizes the interdependence of male and female roles in cosmology and in crop and game animal fertility, as well as in human fertility and the need for daily cooperation between mortal men and women. Iconography, the association of decorative styles with items made and used by men and women, and evidence for gender roles in ritual activities can help trace the histories of gender ideologies in the past. Even in the patrilineal Tewa pueblo of San Juan, women and men have equal and complementary statuses and roles (Jacobs 1995). Evidence so far suggests that some form of gender complementarity has great time depth in the Pueblo and Mimbres areas, although the form and intensity of its material expression vary considerably in time and space, perhaps corresponding in some way to the degree of tension and renegotiation involved in maintaining varying degrees and forms of complementarity. Hohokam data suggest less emphasis on gender-based patterns in art and depiction of sexed figures, possibly suggesting that vertical social hierarchies or membership in corporate kin groups was more important than gender in the expression of social identities.

For this summary view of gender in prehispanic Southwestern art and ritual (table 3.1), I examined (1) the distribution of decorative styles on media that the other contributors to this volume concluded were likely to have been produced by men, women, or both, and the distribution of sexed figures in different media, localities, and time periods, as well as (2) depictions of figures that might represent deities or other immortal personages, life-cycle symbolism such as depictions of menstruation and childbirth, and links between such images and Puebloan oral traditions. Next, to find out about the roles of men and women in ritual activities, I examined rock art and pottery showing men and women engaged in what appear to be ritual activities, ethnography describing women's ritual roles, and sexed burials with associated ritual objects.

DECORATION, DIVISION OF LABOR, AND DEPICTION OF SEXED FIGURES

Men and women in some cultures use different decorative styles for their tools, clothing, houses, and other items. For example, Plains Indian women decorated buffalo hides with intricate, radial, geometric patterns, and men decorated hides with figures representing humans and animals. (I refer here to men and women as gender categories, not sex categories. I include male-sexed individuals who chose feminine dress and work roles in the category of "women," and vice versa.) Cross-cultural studies of the gendered partitioning of decorative styles suggest that where angular geometric and "free" naturalistic styles co-exist, women almost always produce the geometric style, whereas men depict life forms (Anderson 1989:86; Linton 1941:44). In addition, women often work with "soft" materials such as clay, leather, and fiber, whereas men work with "hard" materials such as wood, stone, bone, shell, and metal (Anderson 1989:86). "Hard" and "soft" are gendered as masculine and feminine in many cultures, including Euroamerican culture (e.g., the "hard" sciences and the "soft" [social] sciences).

Our own comfort level with such generalizations can promote unconscious assumptions about divisions of labor in other societies. In the absence of actual evidence, and contrary to ethnographic evidence, archaeologists usually think of the making of rock art and flaked stone as "hard" or masculine activities and the making of "soft" items such as textiles and pottery as women's work. These generalizations do not

TABLE 3.1

Changes in Gendered Imagery in Major Areas of the American Southwest

Time or Stage	*Basketmaker/Pueblo*	*Mogollon*	*Hokokam*
Archaic	Humans and animals depicted in rock art and figurines—no sex or gender indicated.	Humans and animals in Pecos River Style rock art, not sexed.	No data
Early agriculture	Basketmaker II—sex sometimes indicated in rock art, more males than females; females probably appear late in rock art. Textile menstrual aprons appear.	No data	No data
Early ceramic period	Basketmaker III—humans with hair whorls in rock art; female figurines (clay). Pottery, textile, and basket designs differ from rock art.	No data	Pre-Classic—male and female figurines; sexed rock art figures rare. Pottery, rock art, and textile designs often overlap. Possible menstrual huts. Ritual items most frequent in male burials.
Sedentary villages	Pueblo I—humans with hair whorls on pottery	No data	
Variety of settlement systems	Pueblo II—few human depictions in rock art. Male burials with ritual items. Sexed stone figurines in Puerco River of the West (both male and female). Male effigy vessels at Chaco.	Classic Mimbres—many sexed figures on pottery. Two pottery styles, life forms and geometric.	
Period of population movements	Pueblo III—many sexed figures in rock art. Textile/pottery designs also appear in rock art.	Post-Classic Mimbres—few depictions of humans?	Classic—a few female (post-menopausal) burials with ritual items, but most ritual items with males.
Aggregation into large communities	Pueblo IV—many sexed figures in rock art,including hair whorls, birthing, and menstruation; some sexed figures on pottery. Female and unsexed stone figurines in Rio Grande. Ritual items mostly buried with males, but some with females.	Western Pueblo—female stone figurines in upper Little Colorado. Male and female graves at Grasshopper have ritual items.	

hold for the Southwest, where both men and women worked with stone to make their own tools and where Pueblo men wove on looms while women made off-loom or belt-loom textiles. Style partitioning may refer in some cases to domestic versus ritual contexts, to household versus community contexts, or to regional scales of social interaction. These contexts, however, may or may not be dichotomous or gendered as feminine and masculine in other societies the way they are in ours. They should be investigated and not merely assumed valid.

Little or no cross-cultural comparison has been undertaken to explain why material expression of gender differences is sometimes pronounced and sometimes not. Perhaps the gender partitioning of decorative styles, the depiction of identifiable males and females, or both, indicate that a gendered division of labor is highly valued, and perhaps lack of partitioning indicates flexibility, but the ethnographic situation is never so simple. Just as likely, style partitioning (or frequent depiction of sexed individuals) indicates that division of labor (or gender identities and statuses) is not only important but *contested*, or subject to negotiation and change. Lack of partitioning, or lack of indication of sex, may indicate a stable, taken-for-granted situation that needs no visual emphasis. In addition, whether a design system is partitive (different styles for different media) or pervasive (same style on different media) affects the rate of style change. Partitive systems can admit more rapid change; pervasive systems tend to remain more stable (DeBoer 1991). Therefore, any specific case considered at one point in time depends to a large degree on its specific historical antecedents, rendering results of synchronic cross-cultural studies unreliable.

Who made what prehispanic Southwestern art? Data presented here will show that the degree of partitioning of design styles by medium varied among culture areas. For example, for the years before about A.D. 1050, when larger villages began to appear outside the Chacoan realm, the Puebloan area shows more partitioning than the Hohokam area. The degree of partitioning changed as well: textiles and rock art differed prior to the appearance of large villages or communities, but by the late Puebloan period, many designs crosscut media. Such variations probably do not directly indicate specific kinds of gender roles and hierarchies, but together with frequency or intensity of depiction of sexed figures, they provide initial clues about the relative importance accorded to gender as a structuring principle for social organization, organization of production, and ideology. To address these issues and to provide a spatial and chronological framework for the rest of the study, I looked at the distribution of decorative styles on different media to see how many distinct styles there were in any given time and region. I then considered evidence that men, women, or both, were likely to have made and decorated the items in question. I gleaned this evidence by examining records of sexed burials containing tools, raw materials, or both, by surveying depictions of humans with tools, by making cross-cultural comparisons, and by employing (cautiously) the direct historical approach.

The simplest stylistic classifications we can make include identifying geometric versus representational content, curvilinear versus rectilinear line treatment, predominance of singular versus repeated figures, and prevalence of mirror versus rotational symmetry. Geometric styles in Southwestern art emphasize grids, zigzags, interlocking key and triangle sets, dots, and wavy lines. Representational styles include depictions of humans, animals, birds, plants, and artifacts such as bows and arrows, crooks, flutes, bags, and atl-atls.

Archaic Hunter-Gatherers

Rock art of Archaic-period hunter-gatherers in the Southwest, like that of the Great Basin, consists mainly of wavy and zigzag parallel line sets, grids, and dots. Exceptions occur in the canyon lands of southern Utah, the middle Little Colorado drainage, and west Texas, where game animals and front-facing, static humans with lines and dots decorating their bodies appear. Some southern Utah and northwestern Arizona Archaic sites include elaborate paintings, such as the famous panel in Barrier Canyon, Utah, with large polychrome depictions of humans and sometimes snakes and geometric figures. The west Texas Pecos River polychrome style has these icons as well as plants, geometrics, and occasional animals.

Archaic split twig figurines found in the Grand Canyon and southern Utah represent game animals and, less frequently, horned humans. The body patterning of rock art figures resembles the way twigs form parallel lines with wrappings that cross the figurines' bodies. Clay figurines of this era are rare but also resemble the tapering, limbless shapes of rock art figures (Coulam and Schroedl 1996). In the Archaic period, then, representational designs cross media, including rock art, twig figurines, and clay figurines. Representations of humans never, to my knowledge, depict sex characteristics such as genitals or breasts. Geometric designs appear alone or as embellishments of representational figures. Basketry, sandals, and other textile arts seem to lack decoration but provide parallels to geometric rock art styles in their very structure of crossing, interlacing, and wrapping linear elements.

No direct evidence of who made what Archaic art and artifacts yet exists. Patricia Bass (1994) argued against assuming that only men made the Pecos River paintings, and her argument can be applied nearly everywhere that researchers attribute rock art to individual shamanic activity. Bass's review of worldwide ethnographic literature shows that hunter-gatherer shamans were mostly men but that women were rarely excluded from this role, and many societies encouraged women or husband-wife couples to be shamans. Women's rock art is documented in at least several regions of the world, including southern California, Australia, and southern Africa. In summary, Archaic period artisans seem *not* to have marked sex and gender as important representational features in spite of a rich and varied artistic corpus, and the genders of artisans remain unestablished.

Basketmaker II Mobile Farmers

Mobile, pithouse-dwelling maize farmers of the Basketmaker II era made rock art emphasizing large, frontal, static, humanlike figures. Body decorations appear to represent jewelry, string aprons, bandoleers, and elaborate headgear, although simple geometric patterning still occurs in many examples, and many figures are plain. These large and usually highly visible human figures of the San Juan Representational style tend to appear on canyon walls overlooking arable land and less frequently in rock shelters with storage or habitation features (Hyder 1997; Robins 1998). Some habitation and storage rock shelter sites also contain numerous colored handprints. Three Fir Shelter on Black Mesa, Arizona, an early Basketmaker II habitation site, contains not only handprints on the back wall but also small, incised geometric patterns on boulders on the floor, associated with grinding slicks (Hays 1984). I suspect that other Basketmaker sites contain similar low-visibility features and that excavators have simply dismissed such scratchings as irrelevant or of Navajo origin (that they *are* Navajo has not been completely ruled out). Their association with grinding areas, however, might indicate that they were done by women, if women ground corn then as they do now.

Basketry decoration of this period consists of sparse repeated geometric units, especially zigzags, rendered in black. Bags are plain or have simple black or brown stripes, and sandals are rarely decorated. Basketmaker II mobile farmers, then, had at least two decorative styles, one highly visible, representational, and widely distributed in rock art, the other geometric, confined to some habitation sites, and of relatively low visibility but crosscutting the media of textiles, basketry, and perhaps rock art to some degree.

Again, we do not know whether men, women, or individuals with other gender identities made the rock art. Although the majority of Basketmaker II figures lack sexual features, both sexes are depicted sometimes, in single-sexed groups, mixed-sex groups, and as male-female couples. Michael Robins (1998) suggested that depictions of rows of female figures, such as those at Cottonwood Canyon in the Grand Gulch, Utah, area, date late in the Basketmaker II sequence, perhaps around A.D. 200 to 400 (see Robins and Hays-Gilpin n.d. for discussion). Although shamanism remains a possible explanation for many of the images (Cole 1989), many others probably marked territory and group identity (Hyder 1997; Robins 1998). Neither explanation is necessarily gender linked. Likewise, we do not know who made decorated baskets and textiles, but ethnographic analogy with other small-scale societies in the world, as well as the direct historical approach with historic Pueblos and Great Basin tribes, suggests that these activities were women's work.

Basketmaker III Farming Hamlets

The partitioning of design styles by media that probably do have gender associations appears most prominently in the Basketmaker III period. Comparing decorated media in seventh-century-A.D. occupations of Broken Flute Cave and nearby Prayer Rock district Basketmaker sites of northeastern Arizona reveals that the earliest painted pottery designs appear to be very simple versions of the often elaborate red and black designs woven into coiled basketry trays (Hays 1992; Hays-Gilpin 1993, 1994, 1996). Made up of small geometric units usually repeated by rotation, these pottery designs are also simple versions of designs used on sandals, tumplines, and the very small proportion of women's string aprons that bear decoration. Because menstrual blood stains the string aprons, this geometric style can be linked to women. Moreover, ethnographic analogy with historic tribes in the western United States links baskets and pots to women, and tumplines may be linked to them via the association of ceramic effigies of carrying baskets with female figurines.

Basketmaker III rock art, in contrast, emphasizes birds, humans, animals, and asymmetric geometric designs such as squiggly lines and mazes. Rock art, then, has a completely different style from that of portable containers and clothing, and it is more visible and fixed in space. Portable decorated items such as baskets and pots appear mainly in association with pithouses and not with the feature Earl Morris called a great kiva in Broken Flute Cave (Morris 1980; see also Marshall et al. 1979). Rock art, on the other hand, is concentrated near the great kiva. At least some of its imagery—masks, lobed circles, and processions—apparently relates to ritual activities. Procession panels often include phallic figures and often appear away from habitation areas (for example, the Comb Ridge, Utah, procession panel depicted by Manning [1992] is isolated from any known habitation sites). Thus, a domestic-ritual or household-community dichotomy may help explain these dichotomous patterns, in addition to gender.

Although spatial and chronological data are far less precise for other Basketmaker III sites, the overall distinction between a geometric style on pottery and textiles and a representational style in rock art holds over a very wide region. Exceptions do occur: life forms sometimes appear on pottery and baskets, but they are rendered in a rectilinear "textilelike" style rather than in the mostly curvilinear and somewhat looser rock art style. Basket technology mandates this treatment, but pottery painting does not. Although most human and animal figures in Basketmaker III art remain sexless, depictions of phallic figures are fairly frequent, and figures with butterfly hair whorls (discussed later) may have represented pubescent women then as they do in the pueblos today.

FIGURE 3.1.

Rosa-phase petroglyph, Navajo Reservoir area, New Mexico, circa A.D. 800s–900s (drawing by K. Hays-Gilpin).

Pueblo I Village Farmers

The most exceptional stylistic cross-over of the Pueblo I period takes place in the Rosa district of the upper San Juan River region, Colorado, where early Pueblo I Rosa Black-on-white pottery (i.e., the I. F. Flora collection obtained by Harold Gladwin, now at the Arizona State Museum) bears diverse and mostly free-wheeling curvilinear designs, including stars, rayed circles, stick figures, and occasional animals that overlap to some degree with rock art. The hand-holding humans (sometimes sexed, sometimes not) diagnostic of Rosa phase rock art rarely appear on pottery, however, and geometric basketlike designs appear on some pottery but apparently not in rock art. I propose as a hypothesis that imagery shared by the two media implies that gender roles were less contested or more flexible in the ninth-century Rosa district than they were in the seventh-century Prayer Rock district. Note that in the most famous Rosa-style rock art panel (fig. 3.1), one figure is pregnant and depicted in a "family tableau," but the artists included no other sex or gender features.

In all other areas, Pueblo I rock art is either scarce or so closely resembles earlier or later styles that it cannot be distinguished. I suspect the former: that making rock art was an infrequent Pueblo I activity. The few decorated baskets and textiles preserved in Pueblo I sites closely resemble painted pottery. The Kana-a pottery style is remarkably uniform over almost the entire Ancestral Pueblo region, and it lasts about 200 years. Pottery found in sites with evidence for ritual activity in the form of kivas has greater stylistic diversity than pottery from smaller sites without kivas (see Hegmon 1995 for a thorough discussion of style in Pueblo I). Overall, however, the relative stylistic uniformity and stability of Pueblo I pottery may indicate a comparatively high degree of social interaction and stability. A similarly stable and uniform pattern persisted well into the 1000s in most areas, but again, evidence of style in nonceramic media is sparse.

Pueblo II Village Farmers

Pottery and rock art associated with small masonry villages of the Late Pueblo II and Early Pueblo III periods provide some contrasts to earlier patterns and to Mogollon and Hohokam patterns. Later Puebloan rock art emphasizes curvilinear, geometric designs based on wavy or wandering lines and spirals. Human depictions are simple, and most resemble lizards as much as people. Handprints and footprints continue to appear; snakes are frequent. Some rock art of this period almost certainly marks astronomical events such as solstices.

Life forms are extremely rare in pottery of this period, one of several stylistic characteristics that differentiate rock art designs from pottery. Geometric pottery styles become more varied. The Dogoszhi-Gallup style, probably earliest in the Chaco area, becomes widespread but exists alongside other styles (Sosi-Escavada, Puerco) that seem more regionally specific.

Chaco Canyon and Chacoan Great House Communities

The human form appears with most elaboration in rare male effigy vessels from Chaco Canyon (Pepper 1906, 1920) and stone figurines from Chacoan sites along the Rio Puerco of the West (Eaton 1991:52; Fane 1991:69; Langford 1986:35). The stone objects represent women or female immortal personages together with occasional male figures, snakes, a sandal, and a spotted dog. They are several inches tall, and although brightly painted, they would not have been highly visible objects except in small-group contexts. Unlike rock art and most pottery, these objects could have been "secret" rather than public. Hopi elders who were consulted about a cache found in the early 1990s in a Chacoan small-house site near Navajo, Arizona, asked that they not be made public because these objects were not traditionally seen by noninitiates (therefore, none is illustrated here). In an earlier consultation, one elder said the figurine group from Chambers Great House (Eaton 1991:52) would have been used to help tell stories. One seems to represent the Hopi personage known as "Child Sticking Out Woman." Rock art in nearby Chaco Canyon includes many sexed figures, both male and female.

Painted wood artifacts from Chetro Ketl and other Chaco sites, dating to the late 1000s or so, bear life forms such as birds and flowers as well as geometric designs that resemble those on pottery (Vivian, Dodgen, and Hartmann 1978). These items of ritual regalia, although rare, are among the most stylistically complicated media of the period. A painted wooden board has a complicated two-dimensional Escavada-style pattern of rotated interlocking barbed lines (Pepper 1920:pl. 8) that also appears on Chacoan pottery. This design structure, which may derive from loom-woven textiles, also appears in the Kayenta, Arizona, area on some Sosi-style pottery and later on Flagstaff Black-on-white pottery.

Post-Chaco Pueblo Towns

By the mid to late 1100s, two-dimensional patterns of interlocking barbs and hooks dominate pottery of the Kayenta, Hopi Mesas, and Hopi Buttes area, on types called Walnut and Flagstaff Black-on-white. The design also appears in rock art, especially in the Sinagua and Little Colorado areas (Christensen 1994). Although elements used in this style are indigenous to the Ancestral Pueblo area (triangles and broad lines appear on Black Mesa Black-on-white, for example), the structure appears to be new. Hohokam Sacaton Red-on-buff pottery designs are similar (Lindauer and Zaslow 1994; Zaslow 1981; Zaslow and Dittert 1977), as are rock art designs in the Hohokam area and parts of Sonora (Ballereau 1987) and designs on textiles found in the Verde Valley of central Arizona and as far south as Chihuahua, Mexico (Kent 1983; Teague 1998). In the late 1100s and early 1200s, then, a style horizon crosscut almost all surviving media. It seems to have been primarily a textile-derived phenomenon originating in Hohokam or northern Mexican cultures, arriving in Chaco in the early 1100s and appearing with greatest frequency in northern Arizona throughout the 1100s and 1200s.

In the 1200s, life forms, especially birds, begin to appear on pottery again, especially in the White Mountains and Mesa Verde areas, and they continue to appear in rock art with great frequency. By the late 1200s, Ancestral Puebloans had returned to rock shelters to build cliff dwellings, whose dry conditions preserved textiles and baskets that can be compared with rock art and pottery. Diverse styles burgeon and crosscut media. Rock art still emphasizes life forms, which are still rare on pottery and seem not to occur in textiles and baskets, but abundant textile-, basket-, and pottery-like designs also appear in rock art.

A possible explanation for some of the elaborate geometric designs may be sought in the introduction of cotton and loom weaving to the Pueblo area in the late 1000s or in an influx of southern design structures carried on imported textiles. In historic times, Spanish journals described western Pueblo textile production as extensive and intensive. Historically, men wove cotton blankets, kilts, and sashes on vertically mounted looms in kivas. Women continued to use belt looms and probably made most off-loom and belt-loom textiles from at least Basketmaker times onward. It becomes important, then, to know whether men were responsible for the production of loom-woven cotton textiles at the outset or whether there was a period of experimentation with gender roles. Did women resist loom work due to scheduling conflicts, or were there struggles to control production? Did men adopt it because textiles symbolized long-distance ties and perhaps extra–kin group high status by means of their association with more explicitly ranked Hohokam societies? Was cloth production an attempt to accumulate wealth for status or to have items that could be exchanged for food in hard times?

By the late 1200s, kivas contain loom anchor holes. Intricate textile designs, complete with tassels and fringes that certainly differentiate them from pottery designs, appear incised in the sooted plaster walls of a kiva at Archer's Ruin, a cliff dwelling in Alcove Canyon, just north of Canyon de Chelly (Hays-Gilpin 1996, field notes). Early kiva murals such as those in the Mesa Verde region most often consist of geometric, rectilinear, repeated units (Smith 1952b; Michelle Hegmon, personal communication re: Knobby Knee Stockade site). Textile designs abound in the rock art located near masonry kivas at the base of a mesa near Crack-in-Rock Pueblo, Wupatki National Monument. These geometric designs are rare at the contemporaneous Inscription Point site, located well away from any structures, across the Little Colorado River. Textile images do seem to be spatially related to kivas, then, in at least some places. If kivas were already localities of men's activities (see Schlanger 1994), then it seems that by late Pueblo III, men made loom-woven textiles with elaborate geometric designs that were often painted rather than in-woven but that strongly resembled southern-derived styles.

At the same time, pottery and textile designs continued to overlap. Potters' tool kits appear in female burials (Crotty 1983) when they appear in burials at all, suggesting that Pueblo women made pottery then as they do now. If this was the case, then men and women used similar design styles on different media. Designs no longer marked gender roles but perhaps referred to some other social domain such as community or regional affiliation, social ranking, or participation in a particular complex of rituals.

Large, Aggregated Pueblo IV Towns

In the Pueblo IV period, styles continued to cross media, and elaboration of the iconographic realm persisted, surpassing even Mimbres pottery in intricacy. Pottery, rock art, and kiva murals all exhibit religious icons such as kachinas and other holy personages, macaws, cloud terraces, rainbows, and flowers. Pottery and textiles display primarily geometric designs, but even geometric pottery designs now seem to diverge from those of textiles. Rock art continues to include geometric pottery and textilelike designs, and human depictions often have sex characteristics indicated.

The very wide distribution of some pottery types, such as Jeddito Black-on-yellow, Gila Polychrome, and (to a lesser degree) Fourmile Polychrome, together with a great volume of nonlocal wares at many sites and large production facilities such as clay pits and firing areas at some A.D.-1300s pueblo towns, suggests some degree of ceramic craft specialization. Craft specialization raises the interesting question of men's participation in pottery making at this time, and one must ask whether men painted some or many of the religious subjects found especially on later Jeddito yellow wares. Many researchers have addressed this issue for the Mimbres figurative pottery style (Brody 1977:115–17; Hegmon and Trevathan 1996; Jett and Moyle 1986:716; Mills 1995). Possibly, however, nothing prevented women from painting religious subjects on pottery. In historic times, Hopi women painted kachinas on pottery. Bunzel (1972 [1929]) reported that at Zuni, certain pottery designs were said to be a woman's way of offering prayers, equivalent to men's prayer sticks.

Historic records indicate that Hopi men were producing large volumes of textiles for exchange at the time of Spanish contact. Most of these are described as undecorated, but kiva murals of the fifteenth century depict elaborately decorated textiles, and analysis of the few remaining fragments from this era show brocade, tie-dye, and embroidery techniques (Kent 1983). As in Pueblo III times, loom holes and weaving tools are found in Pueblo IV kivas. Todd Howell (1995) reported that weaving tools were found in several male graves and several female graves at Hawikku.

Mogollon

Mogollon Red–style rock art emphasizes simple life forms, sometimes including sexed figures or probable feminine figures with butterfly hair whorls. Mogollon Red-on-brown and early black-on-white pottery styles are geometric, reflecting the partitioning of a figurative, representational style from a rectilinear geometric design similar to that seen in Ancestral Pueblo material. A different situation develops in the Mimbres branch in the A.D. 1000s. Mimbres Black-on-white pottery bears both geometric and naturalistic styles, with elements of both styles often appearing together on the same vessel. Indeed, the Mimbres figurative style is among the most naturalistic found anywhere in North America. Likewise, associated rock art, and rock art of the nearby Jornada Mogollon, contain both geometric and figurative subjects, often combined (see Short 1999 for detailed support of the argument that Jornada rock art and Mimbres Classic Black-on-white pottery belong to the same stylistic tradition). Human figures on Mimbres pottery often have sex indicated (Shaffer, Gardner, and Powell 1996). Rock art seems to emphasize faces, masks, or both, and when bodies occur, they are rarely sexed, so pottery does seem to emphasize sex identification more than rock art.

Hohokam versus Puebloan Arts

Stylistic partitioning between rock art and pottery does not appear to hold in the Hohokam area. Some pottery designs closely resemble those in rock art. Both media include life forms, especially humans and birds, and geometric designs, especially the interlocking scrolls and barbs with a "Y-frame" layout characteristic of Sacaton Red-on-buff (Lindauer and Zaslow 1994). Unfortunately, rock art chronology remains poorly developed in southern Arizona, so particular pottery styles cannot be compared directly with contemporaneous rock art. Because depictions of humans in Hohokam rock art and pottery do not seem to include sexed figures as often as they do among the Ancestral Puebloans, it is tempting to argue that these media were not particularly gendered or were not especially exploited to comment on gender roles and relationships. Many Hohokam clay figurines of humans are sexed, however (Haury 1976), indicating that gender *was* of symbolic import in some contexts. Figurine style, described later, does not seem to overlap with that of pottery and rock art.

In contrast to the Puebloan area, textiles in the south, where the Pueblo III style of interlocking hooks and barbs probably originated, may have been associated with women. The Classic-period Hohokam and many Mesoamerican groups used modeled clay spindle whorls on vertically oriented spindles supported in bowls, whereas the Pueblos used larger, flat disk whorls, usually wood, on horizontally oriented spindles supported on the spinner's thigh (Neff 1996). Bowl-supported spinning is a strongly feminine-gendered technology in Mesoamerica (McCafferty and McCafferty 1991), and women there were responsible for spinning and weaving. In Mesoamerica, the spindle and bowl represent sexual intercourse, and the growing spool of thread represents pregnancy. Spindles and weaving battens are symbolic feminine equivalents of masculine weapons.

The Hohokam shared with Mesoamerica the vertical spindle technology, judging by the frequency of stone and modeled whorls. We may never know whether they shared the symbolic complex. To date, the gender of textile artists in the Hohokam area remains unclear. Paul Ezell summarized historic data on Pima activities, noting that women were observed spinning and that "women sometimes wove but usually the weaving was done by old men" (Ezell 1961:26–27, 71). Crown and Fish (1996:805) and Mitchell (ed., 1994b) noted the association of modeled ceramic and stone spindle whorls with females in Hohokam burials at Pueblo Grande. Of Casa Buena and Grand Canal, Douglas Mitchell wrote that "generally, spindle whorls...were associated with adult females" (Mitchell 1991:116). Some kinds of spindle whorls, however, were found in both male and female burials (Mitchell, ed., 1994b), and Mitchell argued that correlation of bone awls with male burials might indicate that men worked with textiles, but awls were as likely to be used in basketry or hide working.

The Pueblos had a different spinning technology, and there is no evidence that spinning had much symbolic significance in gendered terms. Rather, spinning was part of the larger process of transforming cotton into cloth, symbolically analogous to the transformation of clouds into rain. If anything, this process was gendered masculine; Pueblo people equated falling rain with fertilizing semen. Historically, Pueblo men were responsible for spinning and weaving. They probably concentrated on these tasks in the off-agricultural season, when they also spent a great deal of time in the kivas preparing for rituals. Spinning and weaving are compatible in practical as well as ritual terms with practicing songs, stories, and prayers. John Loftin (1991) argued that because Spider Grandmother taught Puebloan ancestors to spin and weave, practicing these arts transports a Pueblo man into the primordial realm of ancestors, Spider Grandmother, and other holy beings. The activity is, in a way, a form of prayer. Hopi people, moreover, see no contradiction between the masculinity of weavers and Spider Grandmother's femininity.

In summary, prior to the emergence of Puebloan towns and great house communities between the A.D. 1000s and 1100s, depending on locality, potters, basket makers, and weavers, who were probably women, had a strong tendency to use small geometric design units repeated by rotational symmetry to decorate clothing and containers. Men were probably responsible for hunting tools and weapons, which were rarely decorated. Men may also have made most of the rock art, which emphasizes life forms and sometimes depicts ritual activities and regalia. Sometime after the introduction of cotton and the loom, we see (women's?) pottery and (men's?) textiles bearing intricate geometric design styles that may have had their origins in Hohokam or other southern cultures. In the Ancestral Pueblo area, then, women and men apparently used different design styles until the emergence of communities that were larger or more economically integrated than autonomous villages. Craft producers of both genders then converged on a new geometric style that developed alongside representational rock art, and representational decoration crossed over to pottery more frequently. Due to chronological imprecision, especially in dating rock art, it is difficult to assess whether Hohokam styles were partitioned along gender lines in autonomous villages and then crossed media once integrated communities appeared along irrigation systems, or whether Hohokam styles never were clearly partitioned along gender lines.

Reasons for such a shift in the Ancestral Pueblo and Mogollon areas are also difficult to know but probably have something to do with the scale at which families negotiated a division of labor. In small autonomous villages, gender might have been the most important aspect of social identity governing work roles, whereas in larger communities, labor specialization among households probably increased. As medicine societies and other ritually specialized social groups emerged within the same growing community, decoration might have signaled identities other than gender. In addition, women might have spent more time with other women, and men with other men, reducing the need to use household items such as containers to negotiate gender roles within the household (see Braithwaite 1982 for an interesting ethnographic case study of container decoration and household gender roles).

FEMALE AND MALE IN ICONOGRAPHY

Depictions of male and female humans or immortal personages abound in rock art and appear regularly but less frequently in pottery and other media. Learning to distinguish humans from immortals would be a tremendous feat, and I make no claim to having done this. Instead, I simply discuss what rock art specialists call anthropomorphic figures, taking the ambiguity between humans and immortal beings into account. Similar ambiguity pervades oral traditions, in any case. Even Pueblo stories about historic events such as the factional split at Oraibi in 1906 and the destruction of Awatovi in about 1702 include references to personages such as Spider Grandmother and the War Twins, whom European Americans would label immortal beings (or, problematically, "supernaturals"). Depictions of male and female per-

FIGURE 3.2.

Basketmaker III lobed circles, probably A.D. *600s, southeastern Utah (Manning 1992, reprinted with permission).*

sonages and of objects and animals associated with them, as well as their media and locational contexts, can tell us something about male and female in ideology and symbolic systems: the *ideas* of masculine and feminine and of gender complementarity.

Depictions of sexed humans, immortal beings, or both begin in the late Basketmaker II period in the northern Southwest. One of the earliest possible gendered icons—that is, something that is not a human figure but an abstraction that might have had a gendered meaning—is the Basketmaker III lobed circle, which Steven Manning (1992; see also Patterson and Patterson 1993) has argued represents a uterus. Lobed circles appear in rock art on the chests of male figures and the abdomens of females, and in a variety of other rock art contexts (fig. 3.2). Earl Morris recovered turquoise mosaic wooden pendants in the form of lobed circles from Canyon del Muerto (E. H. Morris 1925), where they were placed on the chests of adult male burials, and from Broken Flute Cave (E. A. Morris 1980).

Lobed circle shapes echo later kiva forms—especially keyhole-shaped kivas and those with southern recesses. The kiva, too, represents a womb, complete with sipapu-entrance to earth underworld as birth canal. Anthropologists usually view kivas as masculine spaces because ethnographically men meet in kivas for rituals, craft production, and political discussions. Young unmarried men often spend more time there than in their mothers' homes. Hopi women say a man's place is outside the home, which takes in not only the fields and distant pilgrimages but also kivas. Women may enter to deliver food to men, and women and children enter to view some proceedings at Hopi and Zuni. At Hopi only, women's religious societies use kivas in virtually the same way men's societies do, but at different times of the year. Most of the Rio Grande pueblos exclude women and children from kivas.

The archaeological situation is far more complicated. We want to know when masculine activities and feminine activities became spatially separated, but as Watson Smith (1990 [1952]) put it, "When is a kiva?" No single set of features distinguishes early ritual and domestic structures. Sarah Schlanger (1994, 1995) investigated the spatial organization of grinding activities by tracing the placement of grinding implements through the pithouse to pueblo transition (Pueblo I–II). She noted that this activity became increasingly segregated from what eventually became mostly masculine space (if ritual and weaving are taken as indicators of masculine activities). Subterranean mealing rooms that paralleled kivas in many early Puebloan sites disappeared. Grinding moved to surface rooms, and the site's central space became dominated by kivas only.

Exactly when the kiva became masculine space is unclear, but the keyhole-shaped and southern-recess kiva forms may represent masculine appropriation of a symbol of female fertility (Hays-Gilpin 1995). Jane Young's (1987) ethnographic research on Pueblo metaphors of birth and conception suggested that men's activities in this symbolically feminine space might be seen as an attempt to co-opt or at least imitate female conception and birth.

David Wilcox (1996) and others (Grenard and Grenard 1992) have noted the vulvalike shape of Hohokam ball courts. The Hohokam ball game should be investigated as a possible parallel to Puebloan kiva ritual: men manipulating the earth surface–subsurface interface in order to construct ritual space modeled on female reproductive anatomy.

Many worldwide ethnographic examples exist of ritual and iconography in which men extend the metaphor of conception and birth to crop and animal fertility and general well-being. Through their expenditure of a great deal of effort in ritual activities, men gain that which women are said to possess "naturally." For example, medieval European metallurgists called the smelter "Mutterschoss," or mother's womb (Jung 1968; Weigel 1989). Terry Childs's analysis of Bantu iron smelting in Africa contains similar elements. The master smelter, always a man, builds a furnace shaped like a woman, with breasts, tattoos, and legs. The furnace is his symbolic wife, and he causes her to give birth to the iron bloom. Women are excluded from all aspects of the smelt, lest their own inherent fertility interfere with the symbolic fertility of men and their furnace-wives (Childs 1991; Childs and Killick 1993). Bantu culture, like European culture, is gender stratified, and the male creative act is more highly valued than the female procreative act.

Marta Weigle (1989) examined cultural attitudes about birth and compared the origin stories of several diverse cultures. European cultures separate creation and procreation, assigning creation to males and procreation to females. They devalue procreation and motherhood as an automatic, natural, physical, unconscious, "animal" process that contrasts with the active, cultural, mental, conscious, "human" acts of males. In contrast, historic Pueblo culture makes no distinction between procreation and creation. Creation of anything is like birthing a baby. Making a pot, growing corn plants, weaving a blanket, even killing an enemy—all are like giving birth. At Zuni, "all forms of making were homologized to the act of birth and the ability of women to create life" (Roscoe 1991:140) . Therefore, birthing a baby is a creative act, valued as much or more than any other creative act.

"Fertility" Figurines

Archaeologists and art historians habitually label female figurines "fertility figures" (see, for example, Renaud 1929), and their interpretation has been "decidedly androcentric" (Dobres 1992). Clearly, ceramic female figurines were abundant in some times and places, such as the seventh century in the Four Corners Basketmaker area, where

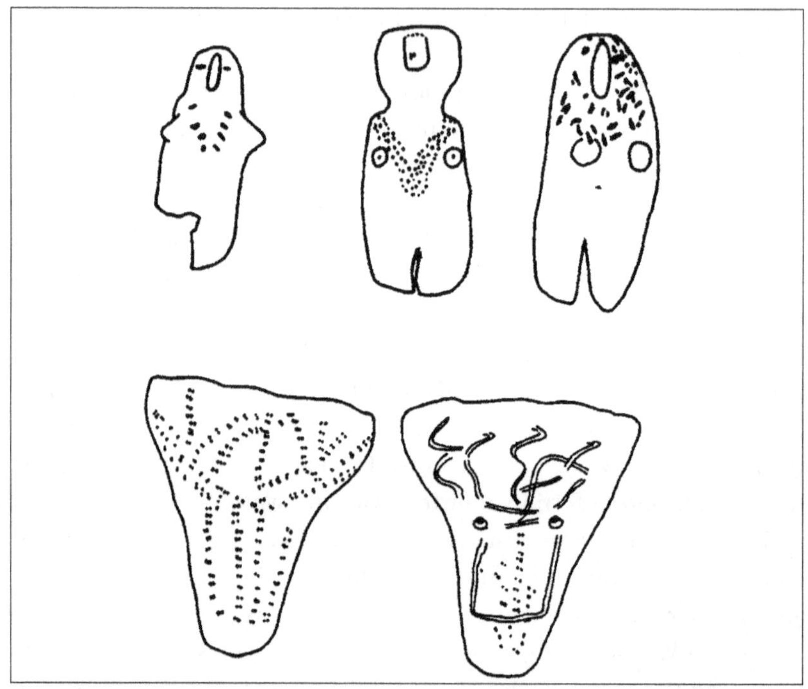

FIGURE 3.3.
Basketmaker III figurines (top row) *and carrying basket effigies* (bottom), *early* A.D. *600s, Prayer Rock district, northeastern Arizona (drawings by K. Hays-Gilpin).*

small figures with breasts and fiber aprons appear together with models of burden baskets (fig. 3.3). Earl Morris (1951) described them as signifiers of a "cult of female and plant fertility." I have argued for their possible use as toys designed to teach girls about future roles and activities that included bringing home food and firewood as much or more than becoming mothers or sex goddesses (Hays-Gilpin 1993, 1994). Female reproductive power was a key metaphor from this time period until historic times, but oddly, figurines may have had less to do with it than did birth and emergence symbols such as kivas, along with metaphors of corn maidens and mothers that I describe later.

In some, but not most, times and places in the Southwest, female figurines appear in large numbers, but they seem usually to be accompanied by figures of men and dogs rather than representations of tools, and very few are pregnant. The Pillings figurines from a cave in southern Utah are male-female pairs (as in some Basketmaker II rock art from southern Utah), but most Fremont figurines are female (Morss 1954). Numbers of male and female figurines were about even at Snaketown, and animals were also frequent there, but in many Hohokam sites females dramatically outnumber males (Haury 1976). In most Prescott culture assemblages of central Arizona, humans appear more frequently than animals, but the opposite is true for the Sinagua of north-central Arizona. Unsexed and female humans, including a few pregnant ones, appear in both areas (Batchelor 1996a, 1996b). In the Basketmaker III, Hohokam, Prescott (see Euler 1966:5), and Sinagua cases, figurines appear most frequently in midden deposits and architectural debris. In the last three cases, they often appear to have been deliberately burned and broken, but Basketmaker figurines rarely show this treatment. When they are burned, they usually appear to have burned in house fires.

Hohokam figurines often have detailed facial features, items of dress, and explicit genitals, both male and female. They most frequently occur in groups, often broken and burned, in cremation pits or trash deposits. Women are depicted working, holding babies, or standing. Sometimes they have a short vertical red stripe painted on their abdomens. Men are depicted standing, and they often sport jewelry and other ornaments (Thomas and King 1985). Little is known about who made figurines or how figurines were used in the Hohokam area or any other part of the Southwest. The Mohave people made pottery figurines for sale from the 1850s to the early 1900s. At least some of these appear to represent individuals, based on depiction of tattooing and body paint, rather than "rain gods," as some traders labeled them. Like the Hohokam, the Mohave practiced cremation, but whether some earlier version of these figurines was used in that ritual is unknown. A few of the dolls have human hair, however, and the Mohave did not cut their hair unless they were in mourning (Christy Strum, personal communication 1999). The Yuma also made pottery "dolls" dressed in typical traditional clothing and decorated with facial tattoo designs (Kaemlein 1955:2). Although these were made for sale to travelers, Eugene Trippel reported that "tiny clay dolls" were used in the Yuma mourning ceremony. "The women would walk among the mourners and touch them with dolls, thus reminding them that children would be born to fill the places of those departed" (Trippel 1889). The form and decoration of these "tiny" dolls was not recorded.

If precontact Hohokam and Patayan (ancestral Yuman) figurines were made for display at funeral rites, as is suggested by their breakage, burning, and association with cremations, they may have functioned in the renegotiation of intrafamily and intracommunity social relationships that inevitably takes place when an important individual dies. In this case, figurines might represent individual members of a community or, in a more general way, the roles and statuses of the deceased and their families.

Clearly, in the Southwest, as in the European Paleolithic, not all female clay figurines are "the same thing." In contrast to painted stone figures, described later, there is neither formal nor contextual evidence that any of the small pottery figurines represented deities. We can briefly examine the uneven distribution of female figurines in the Southwest in terms of Anna Roosevelt's (1988) comparative study of the context of these items in Central America and Mesoamerica and Ian Hodder's (1992) musings on the European Neolithic. Roosevelt argued that female figurines were most abundant and elaborate in garbage, house remains, burials, and caches (and not in temples or shrines) in sites that represented emerging chiefdoms or early states with economies undergoing a transition to intensive production of staple food crops. Women might have "gained in status due to their roles in reproduction and production" at times of economic and demographic growth, especially in societies that passed property and rank through the female line (Roosevelt 1988:1). Hodder argued that in Europe, "as domestication intensifies and settled villages are formed, so the elaboration of domestic symbolism, the numbers of female figurines and the subdivision and decoration of houses also increase" (1992:254). Not all of Roosevelt's and Hodder's conditions apply to the Southwest, but the idea that art can reflect changes in women's status linked to their role in production of crops and producing large families to increase labor supplies is certainly worth considering.

Conception, Birth, and Mother Earth

Female holy people in Puebloan oral traditions include the Clay Lady or Grandmother Clay, Spider Grandmother, Salt Old Lady, the

Mother of Game Animals, one or more mothers of hard substances such as shell and turquoise, Corn Maidens, Corn Mothers, and Thought Woman, the Acoma Creator. All or most of these personages represent the spiritual manifestations of substances, plants, or animals that reside in the earth or emerge from the earth. In contrast, sky phenomena such as sun, stars, lightning, and rain (sometimes viewed as the semen of the sun or clouds) are usually gendered masculine. A particularly detailed Mother Earth–Father Sky petroglyph dating from the Pueblo IV period appears in the Petrified Forest in Arizona (McCreery and Malotki 1994:fig. 4.12). This partitioning of the natural world is not absolute or truly binary, however. For example, the horned or feathered water serpent is both masculine and feminine and belongs both to the sky and the underworld beneath the waters. Loftin (1991) argued that for Hopi people, the notion of gender complementarity is both strong and flexible. Thus, the sky has both masculine and feminine aspects, the feminine aspect being symbolized by the serpent. The earth also has aspects of both genders. The masculine aspect is Muyingwa, the germination god, and Sand Altar Earth Woman personifies the feminine aspect. If this sort of flexibility has great time depth (and I expect it does), and if the specifics of gender ideology varied as much among pueblos in the past as they do now (and I expect they did), then interpretation of ancient imagery in these terms will always be tentative as well as useful.

Images of genitally explicit females, including menstruating and birthing women, and feminine-gendered images, indicated by butterfly hair whorls, abound in the rock art and pottery of the western Puebloan area and in the rock art but seldom the pottery of the Rio Grande—especially in rock art near large, aggregated Pueblo IV communities. Although most of these images could relate to earth or fertility in some way, there is no unitary explanation for them, and there is no single, pervasive Mother Earth figure. Rock art and pottery data support Patricia Crown's (1994) conclusion that ideology had become centered on earth and fertility cults by the late 1200s or so in the Salado and other areas, as well as Sam Gill's (1987) argument that a single Mother Earth figure is a recent phenomenon, growing out of more diverse prehispanic earth/fertility icons forged into one being via historic struggles over land and sovereignty.

FIGURE 3.4.

Hooper Ranch figurine, upper Little Colorado River, probably A.D. *1200s (drawing by K. Hays-Gilpin).*

The strongest possibility for an Earth Mother figure may be the Hooper Ranch figurine (fig. 3.4). Twenty-two centimeters tall, carved of igneous rock, and painted with a rainbow along her torso, she comes from a crypt inside a thirteenth-century rectangular great kiva at Hooper Ranch Pueblo on the Mogollon Rim (Martin 1961). Paul S. Martin described the crypt as a model of a great kiva embedded in an actual great kiva. A circular hole represents her birth canal. The eminent ethnographer Fred Eggan suggested to Martin that the figure might represent "an ancestral cult-deity" who "may have been regarded as the mother of all living things" (Martin 1961:5). This, then, might be an image of a female creator deity (see Weigle 1989) such as Acoma's Tsichtinako, or Thought Woman, who created Iatiku and her sister Nautsiti. She gave them baskets filled with all they needed to create plants, animals, and humans upon reaching the earth surface through

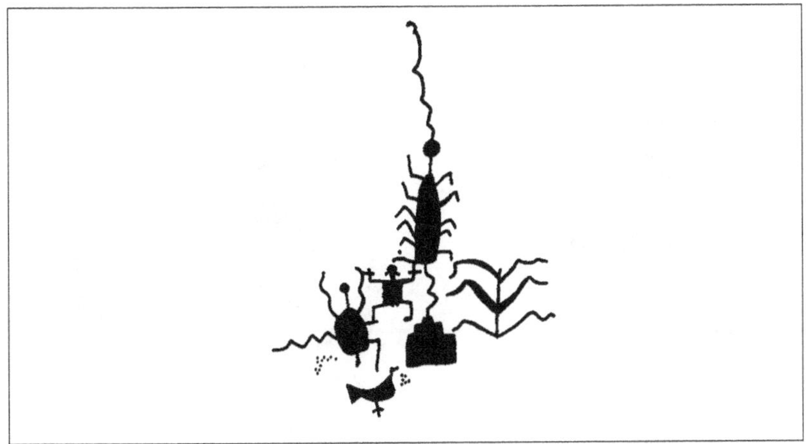

Figure 3.5.
The Iariko petroglyph panel at La Cienega, near Santa Fe, New Mexico, probably A.D. 1300s or 1400s (courtesy of Carol Patterson-Rudolph).

shipap (Gutierrez 1991; Stirling 1942). A Pueblo IV stone figure from Puye Pueblo on the Pajarito Plateau near Los Alamos, New Mexico, has breasts and a protruding abdomen, perhaps representing early pregnancy or an enlarged umbilical area (Hewett 1953:83). Most Rio Grande stone figures have no surviving indication of sex, however (collections of the Museum of New Mexico).

Graphic representation of an eastern Keresan version of the creator sisters story appears at the site of La Cienega, near Santa Fe (fig. 3.5). Carol Patterson-Rudolph (1990:61–91, 1997:7–10) carefully correlated Rio Grande–style petroglyph elements and their spatial relationships with the story of the sisters Uretsete and Naotsete and Spider Woman–Thought Woman. Depicted, too, is the corn mother fetish, or Iariko, that Uretsete created for the people she left behind when she returned to the underworld.

Several fourteenth-century images in the Little Colorado drainage may represent the Mother of the Hero Twins, a maiden who was impregnated by Sun and Water. She is analogous to the Navajos' Changing Woman, who is an earth mother of sorts, but not *the* Earth Mother. At least one image of a birthing woman in this area, at Baird's Chevelon Steps near Winslow, Arizona, might have functioned as a

FIGURE 3.6.

*Birthing scenes at (*left*) Baird's Chevelon Steps, middle Little Colorado River, and (*right*) Hantlipinkya, near St. Johns, Arizona, both probably* A.D. *1300s, Pueblo IV (drawings by K. Hays-Gilpin).*

fertility shrine (fig. 3.6). Hantlipinkya, near St. Johns, Arizona, the place where the Zuni Hero Twins were conceived, might also have served this function, by analogy with certain features of historic Zuni fertility shrines such as natural or pecked cupules (Stevenson 1887, 1904; see also Gough 1987; Hedges 1983; McGowan 1978; and Jeançon's 1923 mention of women pecking cupules at sites on the Rio Oso and similar cupules near Poshu on the Rio Chama). Both sites, however, probably commemorate a primordial birth, such as the birth of the Hero Twins, to a specific maiden or holy person. Individuals might have used the sites as fertility shrines owing to that association. Just as Spider Grandmother taught men to weave, and the act of weaving transports a man back to primordial times (Loftin 1991), so praying at the site of a holy conception or birth might bring supplicants into contact with powers that the ancients conferred on mortals long ago.

In contrast to the rock art images of birthing or otherwise fertile-looking Puebloan women wearing the hair whorls of maidens, two birth scenes on Hopi pottery (fig. 3.7) and several identified on Mimbres pottery (Hegmon and Trevathan 1996) may depict mortal, married women. These women lack the maiden hair whorls, and some

FIGURE 3.7.
Depictions on Pueblo IV pottery of women giving birth: (left) *Jeddito Black-on-yellow bowl (U.S. National Museum);* (right) *Jeddito Black-on-yellow bowl (Field Museum of Natural History, cat. no. 75698) (drawings by K. Hays-Gilpin).*

of the scenes have a more narrative quality. Attendants are present in the two Hopi examples, bearing the cleansing herbs a midwife uses today. A Hopi friend (Anonymous, personal communication 1995) suggested that these two bowls might be a visual form of prayer for a bride. Today, Hopi people pray that a bride will have at least two children and that one of them will be a girl. Pottery is often given as a gift at weddings, and Ruth Bunzel (1972 [1929]) noted that Zunis view some pottery designs as visual prayers that women make instead of prayer sticks.

Probable pregnancy and birth scenes also appear in southern Sinagua and Hohokam petroglyphs. One in the Beaver Creek drainage in the Verde Valley shows a spread-legged figure with a dot on her round stomach, next to a small figure with a squiggly line coming from it, possibly representing an umbilical cord (Hays-Gilpin, field notes). A birth scene in the Picacho Mountains between Phoenix and Tucson shows a round-bellied figure with spread legs above a small figure, a squiggly line, and a stipple-pecked oval that could represent a placenta (Henry Wallace, field photograph). Wallace also noted the figure of a pregnant deer near Gillespie Dam on the Gila River, suggesting that game animal fertility was also important to the Hohokam, whether literally or metaphorically.

Menstruation, Female Puberty, and Courtship

Menstruation is a potentially powerful gender symbol, often encoded with meanings about fertility, femininity, adulthood, holiness or pollution, weakness or power (Buckley and Gottlieb 1988; Paige and Paige 1981). Rock paintings in the Four Corners area sometimes display garments similar to the string aprons found on burials of adult females, on female figurines dating to the 600s, and on Mimbres pottery depictions of women. Discarded aprons from dry cave sites dating throughout the Basketmaker era bear blood stains and occasionally the tiny bones of miscarried fetuses. The presence of discarded menstrual aprons throughout deposits in dry sites suggests that Basketmaker people did not practice menstrual seclusion. In contrast, Crown (1985a) has suggested that some small Hohokam structures might have served as menstrual huts and that the Hohokam therefore *did* seclude menstruating women. Menstruation, then, seems to have had different meanings in the two areas.

Menstruation appears to be depicted in rock art in both the Pueblo and Hohokam regions, but again contexts differ. A painted and pecked Hohokam figure in the South Mountains near Phoenix, recorded by Todd Bostwick (1996), incorporates a natural hole and red iron stain into the depiction of an otherwise simple human figure with broad hips and with small breasts apparently indicated on the sides of her upper torso. She lacks the hair whorls of northern examples. Game animals, a snake, a bird, a probable dog, and other humans surround her. Pueblo IV examples at Leroux Wash and Lyman Lake in the Little Colorado area, at La Cieneguilla near Santa Fe, and in Catron County, New Mexico, wear the hair whorls of a pubescent Pueblo woman (fig. 3.8). On her first menstruation, a Hopi girl was secluded in her mother's home for four days, during which she ground corn (Stephen 1936). This "one-time" menstrual seclusion was not about "pollution" but, like other Hopi initiation rites, mimicked the four-day seclusion of an infant prior to naming and presentation to the sun. Afterward, the young woman's mother put up her hair in "butterfly" whorls, which she could wear from that day until her marriage. No further menstrual taboos or restrictions were observed. In contrast, no formal recognition was accorded a girl's first menstruation at Cochiti Pueblo (Lange 1959:408), but menstruation and hair whorls do appear in Rio Grande rock art.

FIGURE 3.8.
Depictions of menstruation: (left) *Catron County, New Mexico (courtesy of J. Louis Argend-Farlow), and* (right) *Lyman Lake (drawing by K. Hays-Gilpin), probably* A.D. *1200s or 1300s, Pueblo III or IV.*

Hopi-style butterfly hair whorls, which have a stem separating the "butterfly" from the sides of the head, appear on Pueblo I ceramics (for example, Lister and Lister 1978:11; Morris 1939:pl. 241) and in rock art of the Basketmaker III through Pueblo IV styles throughout the western Puebloan area. They also appear, albeit in fewer numbers, in Chaco Canyon (Jane Kolber, field notes), in some Verde Valley Sinagua sites such as Beaver Creek's V-Bar-V Ranch petroglyph site (Hays-Gilpin, field notes), in some Prescott culture sites (Williscraft Tank Site, Jane Kolber, field photograph), in some Rio Grande sites (they are fairly frequent at La Cieneguilla; see also Schaafsma 1992:fig. 167 for an example north of San Juan Pueblo, in the northern Tewa district; Hewett 1904:655 depicts one at Puye), and rarely in the Mimbres area (Snodgrass 1975:8, 126). Variants that may or may not have a similar meaning appear in the Big Bend area of Texas, where rounded but flattened hair "buns" are worn close to the head (Alloway 1994). Pueblo IV Rio Grande–style hair whorls include at least two styles that sit close to the head with no stems: round ones, as at La Cieneguilla (Renaud 1938:pl. 4) and Cochiti (Schaafsma 1975:84), and ones with two triangular points on each side, as at Petroglyph National Monument near

Albuquerque (Marcia-Anne Dobres, field photograph) and Cochiti (Schaafsma 1975:70). Patterson-Rudolph (personal communication 1997) has argued that many hair styles seen in Puebloan rock art seem to signal ethnicity rather than gender, and she cautions that neither the Hopi nor Rio Grande female hair whorl styles should be confused with "hair bobs" and other styles that hang closer to the neck.

Although elaborate headdresses appear on Basketmaker II figures, hair whorls are rare to nonexistent in that period and seem to occur earliest on one or two late Basketmaker II figures in Canyon de Chelly (John Campbell, personal communication 1997; Grant 1978:4.34; Robins and Hays-Gilpin n.d.). Hair whorls, then, may have symbolized female puberty specifically or a feminine identity more broadly from the seventh century to the present in the greater Puebloan area, but they appear rarely if at all in Hohokam art. A Hohokam petroglyph near Cerro Prieto, north of Tucson, appears to show two figures engaged in sexual intercourse (Henry Wallace, field photograph). One has possible hair whorls, but they are downward-drooping ovals with no stem. The other has one whorl with a stem, on only one side of the head. Neither closely resembles any of the Puebloan styles.

A flute player, historically an important symbol of courtship and fertility, serenades the Catron County "maiden." Similar tableaux appear on the San Juan River near Bluff, Utah (fig. 3.9), and in the Petrified Forest. Virtually all of the flute-player panels recorded so far place the male figure on the left and the female on the right (this gendered symmetry appears at least seven times in the Puebloan and Mimbres areas with one counterexample in the Mimbres, depicted in Snodgrass 1975:8). Were right and left gendered concepts in ancient Pueblo thought? Larger numbers of examples could answer this question and perhaps differentiate Mimbres from other Ancestral Pueblo cultures.

Flute players never appear with female genitalia or hair whorls. Many are male, and many are ithyphallic. Hopi has a Flute clan and flute ceremony, and the flute was the young man's instrument of courtship. Flutes appeared in male graves at protohistoric Hawikku (Howell 1995) and seventh-century Broken Flute Cave (Morris 1980). Pueblo oral traditions contain many references to flute players (Parsons 1939:41), such as the young masculine solar deity Paiyatamu

FIGURE 3.9.
Flute player and female figure near Bluff, Utah, circa A.D. *1000s to 1200s, Pueblo II or III (drawing by K. Hays-Gilpin).*

at Zuni, who courts young women with his flute playing. At Hopi, Locust plays his flute to bring warm weather and help crops grow. Flute players appear in pottery and rock art in the Hohokam region and in the eastern and western Puebloan areas, and in rock art in the Jornada Mogollon and Sinagua areas; the earliest dated examples are probably the seventh-century ones from the Four Corners area. Many Hopi elders note that although the famous Kokopelli is a prominent fertility figure, in their oral traditions and present-day kachina dances he does not routinely carry a flute but only occasionally "borrows" one from another kachina.

Gender and Hunting

The bow and arrow are, like the flutes, masculine tools of fertility in Puebloan thought, and men's hunting of large game is often viewed as analogous to a woman's giving birth. Yet the deity who bestows game animals on humans is often feminine—stories about mothers of game animals abound all over North America. A Hopi earth deity, Sand Altar Woman (also known as Child Sticking Out Woman), bestows human infants *and* guards game animals. Not entirely benevolent, she seduced and murdered young men, and when discovered, left Oraibi village to live alone along the Little Colorado River, according to one of several stories. Hunters who survived intercourse with her came away covered in blood but were thereafter lucky in the hunt (Parsons 1939:178, 964; Stephen 1936:261; Voth 1905:136–41).

The Mother of Game Animals herself appears in petroglyphs in the Little Colorado drainage, from the Petrified Forest to Crack-in-Rock Pueblo in Wupatki National Monument (McCreery and Malotki 1994:139–42; McCreery and McCreery 1986) (fig. 3.10). Birds and animals accompany her, some raising their tails in sexually receptive poses. Footprints with middle toes shaped like penises appear beside the female deity in the Petrified Forest petroglyph panel. Line and double-dot figures that appear between the footprints may represent penis prints or symbolic intercourse with the deity. Like a flute player and sets of bows and arrows, these symbols of masculinity are placed to the left of the female figure. They are probably an emphatic statement that men made offerings or prayers at this place.

Zuni, too, has a mother of game animals. Mathilda Coxe Stevenson (1904:34–39) recounted a story in which a female warrior deity is killed by a Zuni warrior, to whom the Sun reveals a secret: she carries her heart in her rattle. When the Zuni's arrow pierces the rattle, she falls dead, and the Zuni warriors "open the gates of the corral in which all game was kept by Cha'kwena (keeper of game).... Since that time game has roamed over the face of the earth." Elsie Clews Parsons (1939), however, noted that not all pueblos shared this deity. Iatiku, the female Acoma creator, for example, created a *father* of game animals.

Pueblo hunters do not rely on luck to find game. Large game such as deer and antelope must be treated with respect and accorded certain rituals so that if pleased, their spirits will go back to their "mother" and they can be born again and "give themselves" to the hunter. Human and animal sexuality and fertility are related. Hunters and their wives must abstain from sexual intercourse during the hunt (Parsons 1939:81). Alice Schlegel (1977b:259) wrote that at Hopi, "there is a subtle relationship between women and game animals, especially antelopes (the major type of hunted game), that crops up in various rituals and even in jokes about extramarital sexual adventures: men talk about hunting for 'two-legged deer.'"

An antelope maiden appears on a polychrome bowl from Sikyatki,

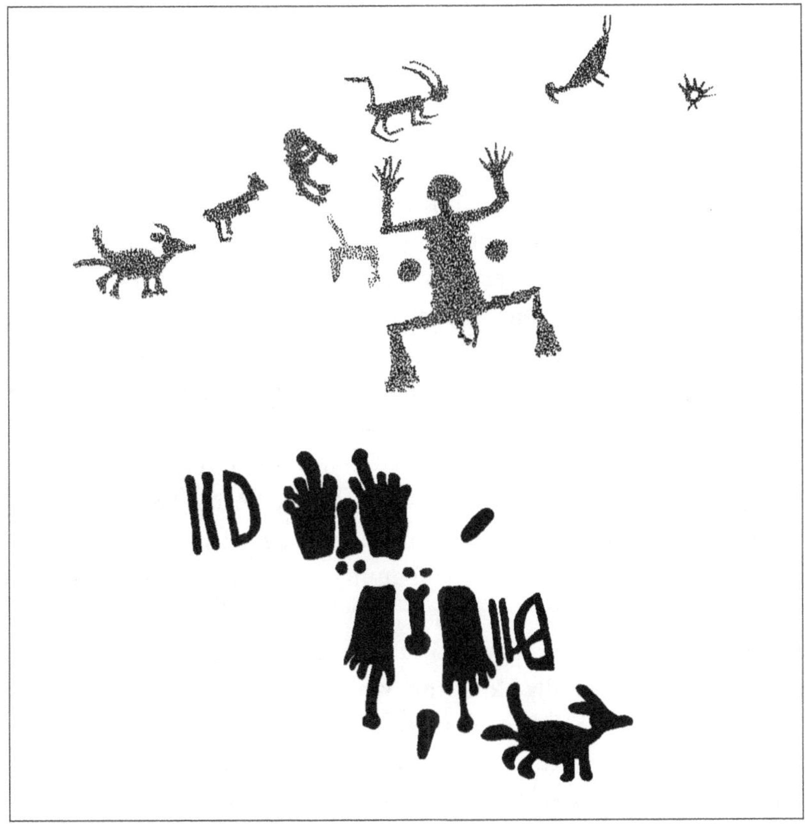

FIGURE 3.10.
Mother of Game Animals (top) *and phallic feet* (bottom), *middle Little Colorado River, probably* A.D. *1150–1400, Pueblo III or IV (drawing by K. Hays-Gilpin).*

a sixteenth-century Hopi village site (collections of the Field Museum of Natural History). At Inscription Point, an isolated rock art site across the Little Colorado River from the Pueblo III habitations at Crack-in-Rock Pueblo, copulating humans and copulating animals are depicted. Similar subjects appear in Chaco Canyon (W. H. Wills, personal communication, 1997) and the Petrified Forest's Cave of Life (McCreery and Malotki 1994:fig. 6.4).

Gender and Warfare

War is virtually always considered men's work, but in some cultures, some females have roles in warfare and occasionally even go to war. Oddly enough, Mohave *hwame*, women who took masculine gender identities, did not go to war, but "on occasion, women insisted on accompanying a beloved husband or brother on the raid" (Devereux 1937:518). Both Hopi and Zuni have female warrior kachinas. In the historic pueblos, women had important roles in warfare aside from fighting. Women at San Ildefonso and a few other Rio Grande pueblos performed "the war dance of the women" each night that the men of the pueblo were away at war (Hewett 1937:56). Pueblo IV petroglyphs in the Galisteo Basin depict tiny spear-bearing warriors in the wombs of women (Patricia Crown, field photograph). According to Ramón Gutierrez (1991:20), Pueblo women defused the dangers imposed by dead enemies by symbolically bringing the enemy into their homes and making them relatives through rituals mimicking intercourse with the scalps and then "feeding" them. Men had to be purified after bringing home a scalp, because "the scalp is dangerous: it and the warrior must be purified because it is like a woman having a baby" (Beaglehole and Beaglehole 1935:23–24).

Depictions of scalps appear in Basketmaker II rock art in the Utah canyon lands, especially along the San Juan River. Two scalps in one panel appear between flute players on the left and a possible female figure on the right. Not all of these figures date to the same period, but their arrangement nonetheless seems deliberate. Sally Cole (1989:71–76) noted that a Basketmaker-style scalp pictograph in Grand Gulch, Utah, corresponded closely to an actual painted human scalp interred with a young Basketmaker II woman and infant near Marsh Pass, northeastern Arizona (Kidder and Guernsey 1919:80–81, 190–91, pl. 87), suggesting that women's care of scalps has great time depth.

Corn Maidens and Corn Mothers

In addition to identifying the earth as a mother and the sun as a father, Pueblo people say, "Corn is life," and "Corn is our mother" (Ford 1994). At Hopi, the word *poshumi* refers both to corn seeds saved for planting and to the young clan women of child-bearing age (Black 1984). Corn plants are called maidens until they begin to produce ears. Then they are women, and the ears of corn are called their children. Some seeds are saved to become next year's maidens. The rest of the crop becomes "our mother," sustaining the Hopi people throughout the year literally as food and metaphorically in the form of perfect ears of corn given to infants and initiates (Black 1984; Ford 1994:515; Parsons 1939:319–23). There are seven corn maidens at Zuni, each with her own color and direction (including up, down, and center as well as the four cardinal directions) (Young 1987:440; see also Roscoe 1991:140–41). The life cycle of the corn plant is the same as the life cycle of humans. Corn is born with the consent of the earth mother and grows due to the prayers and nurturing of mortal men. Richard Ford (1994:513) argued that when Pueblo people say, "Corn is our mother," they mean "that corn creates culture, that it sustains life, and that it is the authority for social action." He suggested that corn likely has been a key metaphor in the Pueblo worldview for at least a thousand years, and he exhorted archaeologists to look more closely at the contexts of corn in the archaeological record, particularly the perfect ears called "corn mothers" or "corn guardians."

Corn maidens also appear in prehispanic art. Several pottery bowls from the Mogollon Rim area, circa A.D. 1300 to 1450, bear figures that may represent corn maidens, one with explicitly female genitalia (fig. 3.11). A nearly identical figure appears in a petroglyph near Springerville and dates to the same era (J. Louis Argend-Farlow, field photograph and personal communication, 1995). The Iariko panel at La Cienega, as noted earlier, includes a corn plant and is probably about the creation of the first Keresan corn mother fetish (Patterson-Rudolph 1990).

Masculine Tools of Fertility and Increase

Much rock art of the late Pueblo III and IV periods in the Little Colorado River area, and probably in other areas as well, is best interpreted in terms of ideas about gender complementarity and agricultural fertility and in terms of links between human sexuality and game animal fertility. For example, depictions of women giving birth, corn maidens, flute players, and perhaps snakes seem to refer to seasonal cycles of agricultural growth set down by certain deities, including the female earth and male deities who control fertilization and germination. Frequent accouterments of male and unsexed figures include flutes, staffs, crooks, bows, arrows, and possible digging sticks: the tools of farmers and hunters whose sexuality is intimately related to their

FIGURE 3.11.

*Corn maidens in pottery (*left, *drawing by K. Hays-Gilpin) and rock art (*right, *drawing by J. Louis Argend-Farlow, reprinted with permission), upper Little Colorado River area,* A.D. *1300s, Pueblo IV.*

success as providers. Note also the ithyphallic Mimbres male bearing a crook depicted by J. J. Brody (1977:fig. 150).

Loftin (1991) argued that Hopi religion can be viewed as having a female mode, emphasizing birth through women's internal space and blood, and a male mode "experienced through four implements relating to primordial hunting-gathering structures of meaning: bow and arrow, throwing stick, fire spindle, burden strap." The Sun and elder War Twin, Poqanghoya, gave humans the bow and arrow, Maasaw (a male fire and death deity) gave the fire spindle, and Kiisa, the sparrowhawk, gave the curved throwing stick, representing his wing. Bear gave the leather carrying strap (Loftin 1991:23). Loftin noted that "each implement is used in a direct engagement with the world to do something—fire making, gathering, and hunting." He argued that "Hopi men do not participate directly in the birth process as women do, but they can participate in other creative processes symbolically through the hunt. In the hunt, men shed blood external to themselves in external space in order to create new forms, that is, they give birth to meat, skins, furs, and other cultural artifacts (such as the carrying strap)" (Loftin 1991:25).

The inclusion of a burden strap cut from the hide of a bear (and not just a bear, but *the* Bear for which the Bear Clan was named) as a key male tool is interesting, because burden baskets in prehispanic iconography are, to my knowledge, almost always associated with women (as I discuss further later). Tumplines used to carry prehispanic burden baskets were textiles, not leather. Interestingly, one of Loftin's references to the carrying strap as a male tool pairs it with a "crate," not a basket. At some point, then, burden bearing may have shifted from being women's work to being men's work, perhaps sometime in Pueblo IV, or after Spanish and Navajo incursions made it dangerous for women to work in the fields.

RITUAL ROLES AND ACTIVITIES

The iconographic data, linked with oral traditions, suggest that the principles of female and male fertility and metaphors of conception and birth have been important in Pueblo ideology from prehistory to the present, and that feminine principles have been as important as, and at times more important than, masculine ones. As is demonstrated by the oft-depicted Virgin Mary in Mexico, however, veneration of female holy personages does not necessarily translate into access to ritual roles and knowledge for mortal women. Unfortunately, knowing what *anyone's* roles in ritual activities actually were in the past is difficult. First, most rock art depictions of humans are more iconic than narrative—that is, they depict one individual or a series in static poses. Second, most figures shown in ritual activities have no sex indicated. Perhaps sex was not of interest to the artist. Either sex was a certainty and therefore not worth depicting or it was irrelevant to the role and not depicted in order to include both sexes. Many members of processions and "staff bearers" are phallic, however, and depictions of recognizable females in such ritual poses are far rarer than those of males.

Burials with unequivocal ritual paraphernalia are rare in the Puebloan area but include a few males at several sites and a few females at at least one site, Hawikku. The Magician burial at Ridge Ruin near Flagstaff was an adult male. Hopi workmen argued that the only reason this individual was buried with recognizable ritual paraphernalia was because he had died without a successor. Todd Howell (1995) argued on the basis of mortuary data from Hawikku that Zuni women as well as men acted in leadership roles before Spanish contact. Howell used high diversity of offerings and grave elaborations to indicate access to multiple roles, including leadership. Three of the four prehispanic graves with the highest diversity indices held female bodies, and three other graves were identified as similar in terms of the kinds of goods present. Zuni workmen identified one of these as a "medicine priestess," partly on the basis of a shaped wood "rattlesnake bite shrine" in the grave (Howell 1995:143). She was also given a paint-grinding stone, a feather, and a gourd, all possible ritual items. This and the other two high-diversity female graves held human hair, possibly scalps. All six possible female "leaders" had prayer sticks. Most of the male graves identified as those of leaders had items related to warfare. Zuni workmen identified two graves as those of Bow Priests. Male offerings included scalps, pipes, and pouches containing pigments, probable ritual items that were apparently not found with females. Evidence from the historic graves suggests that after Spanish contact, women's access to leadership roles declined and all but disappeared, while the importance of masculine warrior roles apparently increased.

Jill Neitzel (this volume) notes that graves of females as well as males sometimes contain possible ritual items such as quartz crystals, pigment, miniature pottery vessels, and unusual minerals. At Las Colinas, near Phoenix, Arizona, females had more miniature vessels, quartz crystals, and asbestos than males. Pigments were about evenly distributed. At Grasshopper Pueblo in Arizona, both males and females were buried with arrays of exotic, possibly ritual, items. Females had more fossil shells, bird claws, stone disks, and body paint than males, whereas males had more projectile points, pigment mortars, pigment, bone wands, and animal scapulae. At Point of Pines, Arizona, females had more whistles, figurines, and palettes; males had more copper bells. Projectile points were about evenly distributed. At RB 568 near

Kayenta, females had more pigments, but other kinds of minerals were about evenly distributed, and evidence for any other likely ritual items was absent. All this indicates that some men and some women probably performed ritual activities, but not necessarily the same ritual activities, in the late prehispanic periods in the Hohokam, Mogollon, and Ancestral Pueblo areas. What those activities were probably varied a great deal among kin groups and communities, as much as or more than between genders.

Historically, Hopi women served as priests in the Marau, Lakon, and Oaqol ceremonies, using kivas and performing the same activities with the same paraphernalia as men in their kiva ceremonies (Fewkes and Stephen 1892; Voth 1912). Late Pueblo III or Pueblo IV rock art in the Little Colorado area depicts women undertaking ritual activities, including, perhaps, the Marau ceremony or something very like it. Patricia McCreery's drawings of a two-part petroglyph panel show Marau associations (fig. 3.12). Five human figures with butterfly hair whorls appear with fringed staffs, an elaborately decorated slab *paho*, concentric circles, spirals, and outlined crosses. Staffs with horsehair fringes are used in the Marau ceremony (Voth 1912), as well as in other ceremonies, and feathered staffs are also frequent in Pueblo ritual paraphernalia. Slab pahos are a hallmark of Marau. Dancers hold these painted wooden slabs with handles in their public dance, much the way Lakon dancers hold basketry plaques. Shapes and decoration of pahos and baskets are completely interchangeable in late Puebloan rock art, as well as in Mimbres pottery depictions, so the slab pahos may represent carrying baskets. If so, the slab paho is simply the Marau equivalent of the coiled or wicker basket tray carried by Lakon Society women in the Basket Dance. Carrying baskets appear to have a long history as a feminine icon in the Pueblo and Mimbres areas. Basketmaker III female figurines appear with models of conical burden baskets. Mimbres pottery shows women (and nonsexed figures) carrying wedge-shaped baskets that are nearly identical to the slab pahos carried by Marau women. Elaborate painted pottery figurines of carrying baskets appeared in Chaco Canyon (Judd 1954:pl. 88), but these were not associated with female figures.

In surveys of depictions of men and women engaged in activities of various kinds on Mimbres pottery, Brian Shaffer and colleagues

FIGURE 3.12.

Possible Marau women's society petroglyphs, middle Little Colorado River, probably A.D. 1150–1400, Pueblo III or IV (courtesy of Patricia McCreery).

(Shaffer, Gardner, and Powell 1996, 1997) discovered that most human figures had no sex indicated. Strictly on the basis of depictions with penises or breasts, they found that males were depicted farming, armed for warfare, hunting, fishing, and using snares. Females were shown making pottery, carrying burdens (water, game animals, firewood), caring for children, and giving birth. Both were shown tending crops, handling birds, engaged in sexual intercourse, and handling ritual items such as staffs, rattles, and "mobiles." Their study suggested that women were not excluded from ritual activities in Mimbres society, but this interpretation is not unproblematical. Virtually all of the depicted activities have at least some ritual associations in the ethnographic record; they should not necessarily be viewed as a simple, representational record of daily pursuits. Indeed, Barbara Moulard (1984) argued that the scenes represent the spirit world rather than this world. Although both men's and women's depicted activities are important, these depictions may tell us more about gender ideology than about actual sex roles.

Depictions of ritual activity, or at least what has been interpreted as people dancing, are frequent in Hohokam rock art and pottery decoration, but no indication of the sex of the participants is indicated. Perhaps further study of items of dress and hairstyles would be informative. Likewise, Hohokam evidence suggests that women were not barred from access to ritual activities. In the pre-Classic Hohokam, ritual items appeared more often with male burials: censers, bird effigy pots, plummets, turquoise, palettes, and turtle shell (also projectile points and many types of shell ornaments), but pre-Classic ball courts are open, accessible spaces. In contrast, Classic platform mounds are spatially and visibly restricted, so that ritual activities taking place there could not have been viewed publicly. Nonetheless, some platform mounds contain burials of female as well as male individuals, and most contain evidence for pottery making and food preparation, suggesting that elite women resided and worked there. Burials in the Classic-period sites reviewed by Crown and Fish (1996) suggest that women were not excluded from receiving ornamental or ritual items. Most of the women buried in platform mounds were over 40 or of indeterminate age, and the four females of known age with grave lots classed as wealthy were older. The only female burial likely to represent a ritual specialist was between 40 and 50 years old. She was buried on the top of a platform mound and had a leather pouch with a quartz crystal and asbestos. Her pelvis was covered with hematite. Crown and Fish (1996:811) concluded that "Hohokam women over the age of 40 may have been afforded costly burial in more prestigious locations because they were postmenopausal and had access to roles within the community that were closed to younger women."

CONCLUSION

Gender complementary as a key part of Pueblo worldview is fascinating because it provides an alternative to widespread ideologies of gender hierarchy in which masculine identities and activities are valued over feminine ones. Interpretations of the classes of data reviewed in this chapter suggest that gender hierarchies did develop in some places at some times in Southwestern prehistory. Indeed, ideology may reflect reality or may mask, challenge, or invert reality, and it is rarely static or homogeneous. Similarly, iconography may reflect ideology or serve to challenge it. Evidence for gendered iconography and ritual roles should next be examined for changes in context and intensity.

The depiction of males and females engaged in ritual roles and activities is unevenly distributed in space and time. Particularly intensive expressions of sexed figures, and of ritual activity generally, appear in larger Basketmaker III sites, in Chaco Canyon, in the Classic Mimbres Mogollon, and in the aggregated Pueblo IV villages. Gender symbolism is prominent in all of these cases but is especially frequent and graphically representational during Pueblo IV. These were times when community size grew dramatically in comparison with earlier times. Aggregation took place on a relatively small scale in Basketmaker, Mimbres, and Chacoan times and on a vast and unprecedented scale in Pueblo IV, when it seems likely that people from different regions who probably spoke different languages came together to form multiethnic communities. Craft specialization increased, and it seems likely that other roles, including ritual roles, also became specialized. Gender roles might have become more contested at this time, leading to a narrowing of sex roles in some cases or the overriding of sex roles by demands of increased productive specialization. Times when gender roles change are often times when ideas about gender are contested. For example, in the modern world, emotions run high as many women in Western nations demand equality and many men vigorously thump Bibles or Korans in response. It is possible that Puebloan gender complementarity should be viewed not as a set of ideas that keep the world in a state of harmonic peace but as a set of ideas for managing the tensions and conflicts that inevitably arise in small communities—ideas that must be periodically renegotiated through ritual performance and artistic discourse. For this reason, the attention accorded to sex and gender in iconography and other material culture patterning changes over time and varies among populations.

The Hohokam culture area presents a very different scenario, at least in the Phoenix Basin. Gender is most prominently represented in clay figurines of the pre-Classic period, when people lived in farming villages clustered along irrigation canals. Large, aggregated towns appeared in the Classic period, but figurines, rock art, and painted pottery from that time display few sexed figures. Even the gendered division of labor, such as pottery and textile manufacture, remains difficult to discern. Likewise, evidence for ritual roles for women appears sporadically. Were strong gender ideologies swamped by emphasis on other social identities, such as class or kin group? Or, in spite of competition between towns and among ethnic groups in these growing towns, were gender roles so stable and uncontested that they were no longer marked in material culture?

4

Gender Hierarchies

A Comparative Analysis of Mortuary Data

Jill E. Neitzel

An issue of primary concern to archaeologists is how prehistoric societies were organized. This question has dominated Southwestern archaeology since the late 1960s (e.g., Hill 1970; Longacre 1970), and it has been manifested over the past two decades in often heated debates about whether or not particular prehispanic Southwestern societies had nonegalitarian sociopolitical organizations (see Lightfoot and Upham 1989; McGuire and Saitta 1996). Throughout these debates, one critical component of societal organization has generally been ignored—gender relations. Only recently have a few Southwestern archaeologists (e.g., Crown and Fish 1996; Howell 1994, 1995; Simon and Ravesloot 1995) begun to investigate the relationship between gender and other organizational characteristics such as status differentiation and leadership roles.

In this chapter I focus on prehispanic Southwestern gender hierarchies, a topic in which questions about sociopolitical organization and gender relations intersect. The discussion is divided into four parts. First, I review the findings of cross-cultural, ethnographic research on gender hierarchies. Second, I consider issues related to the task of using mortuary data to study prehistoric gender hierarchies. Next, I use analyses of the values of grave goods interred with females and males from a series of burial populations in order to conclude that several kinds of gender hierarchies were present in the late prehispanic Southwest. Finally, I compare societies with these different kinds of gender hierarchies.

ETHNOGRAPHIC STUDIES OF GENDER HIERARCHIES

The concept of gender hierarchy comes from cross-cultural, ethnographic studies of gender relations. The term refers to a structural characteristic of societies in which members of one sex have disproportionately greater access to status, power, wealth, and/or resources (Gailey 1987a; Harris 1993; Miller 1993; Schlegel 1977a, 1977c). Although the term "gender hierarchy" is generally applied to this ranking of the sexes, the correct label in most applications would be "sex hierarchy," because the ranking applies to biological females and males and not to two or more socially defined genders. In order to conform to the common but terminologically inaccurate usage, I employ the label "gender hierarchy" throughout this chapter.

Although early gender researchers seldom used the term gender hierarchy, much of their work was concerned with the basic concept. One of their primary research questions was whether or not cross-culturally observed patterns of male dominance and female subordination were universal. Proponents of the universality view emphasized the effects of biological differences (e.g., Divale and Harris 1976; Ortner 1974; Rosaldo 1974; also see Quinn 1977 for an overview of this position). The subordination of females was attributed to their being weaker and constrained in various ways (e.g., time, movement) by pregnancy, nursing, and child care. The dominance of males was attributed to their being stronger and lacking the child-related constraints of women. As a result, males could be more involved in hunting and warfare, two activities that were assumed to be of greater importance for group survival. Some early gender researchers did reject the universality of male dominance and female subordination because of several biases in the supporting evidence: the research emphases of predominantly male ethnographers, expectations derived from the ethnographers' own state-level societies, and the impact of colonialism on indigenous sex roles (Gailey 1987a; Leacock 1978, 1981; Quinn 1977; Sacks 1976; Sanday 1974, 1981; Schlegel 1977a).

The focus of recent research has shifted as more ethnographic studies of gender relations have been completed. Although this work has verified that males tend to dominate the political realms of most societies, it has also demonstrated that the pattern is not universal (e.g., Awe 1977; Collier and Rosaldo 1981; Hoffer 1972; Leacock 1993; LeBeuf 1963; S. Nelson 1993; Ortner 1981; Quinn 1977; Sanday 1981; Schlegel 1977b, 1977c; Tiffany 1979b; Whyte 1978). There are societies in which females hold leadership roles, and in a few cases the political influence of females equals that of males.

Perhaps more significantly, recent ethnographic research has documented how difficult it can be to assess the relative ranking of females and males within gender hierarchies. It has become increasingly clear that concepts such as dominance and status are multidimensional, representing a composite of many factors (Kessler 1976; Meigs 1990; Quinn 1977; Sanday 1974, 1981; Schlegel 1977a, 1977b, 1977c; Spiro 1993; Tiffany 1979a, 1979b; Whyte 1978). Even if a researcher focuses solely on the political domain, the ranking of one sex versus the other can vary depending on whether comparisons are being made of power, authority, or prestige and whether they are being made for the public or the domestic realm. Complicating matters even further are the facts that politics is just one of a number of domains in which females and males can be ranked and that the relative position of members of either sex may change over their lifetimes.

The emerging consensus among ethnographers is that any effort to assess the relative positions of females and males within gender hierarchies must consider a number of measures (Cohen and Bennett 1993; S. Nelson 1993; Spiro 1993; Whyte 1978). Attempts to apply this approach have documented not only the diversity of variables that can be used in ranking but also how these variables can vary independently of one another. Thus, the position of females may, for example, be lower than that of males for one measure, higher for another, and relatively equal for still another (Meigs 1990; Quinn 1977; Sanday 1974; Spiro 1993; Tiffany 1979a, 1979b).

Table 4.1 lists some of the factors that have been found to affect the relative positions of females and males in gender hierarchies. Although some of these factors are clearly related, cross-cultural comparisons have demonstrated a remarkable degree of independence among others. Thus, multiple combinations of circumstances are possible, producing considerable variation in the positions of females and males within gender hierarchies. In addition, for societies in which members of the two sexes are ranked roughly the same overall, the causal factors may actually be quite different.

The cross-cultural, ethnographic findings on the relationship between female status and subsistence practices, sociopolitical organization, and descent and residence patterns summarized in Table 4.1 can be used to generate expectations concerning gender hierarchies in the late prehispanic Southwest. Subsistence practices there were based on agriculture, with the degree of intensification varying from case to case. Sociopolitical organization was similarly varied, spanning a range of complexity from tribes to complex chiefdoms. A variety of descent and residence patterns has been documented in the Southwest ethnographically and probably characterized the late prehispanic period as well.

These characteristics suggest that gender hierarchies were probably present in the late prehispanic Southwest and that the positions of females and males within these hierarchies probably varied depending on the combinations of circumstances found in different places at different times. More intensive forms of agriculture would have lowered the status of females. However, these negative effects might have been counterbalanced for at least some females in some cases by the presence of an ascribed sociopolitical hierarchy. In societies practicing matrilineal descent and matrilocal residence, female status might have been higher than male status.

STUDIES OF PREHISTORIC GENDER HIERARCHIES

The best data for investigating prehistoric gender hierarchies are mortuary data. The reason is that, unlike other kinds of archaeological information, mortuary data can clearly be associated with individuals whose sex is known (Cohen and Bennett 1993; Ehrenberg 1989; O'Shea 1984). Thus, given the generally accepted assumption that how individuals were treated at death reflects their treatment when alive

(Binford 1971; see Shanks and Tilley 1982 for an alternate view), mortuary data can be used to compare the roles and relative statuses of biological females and males. Three sets of studies provide guidance for performing such comparisons in the late prehispanic Southwest. They include cross-cultural, ethnographic comparisons of mortuary practices, archaeological investigations of gender relations using mortuary data from areas outside the Southwest, and previous Southwestern burial studies.

Ethnographic Studies of Mortuary Practices

Cross-cultural, ethnographic comparisons of mortuary practices demonstrate how multiple dimensions of an individual's identity may be signified in her or his mortuary treatment (e.g., Binford 1971; Carr 1994; Goldstein 1976, 1981; Tainter 1975; Vehik 1975). This is especially true for increasingly complex societies, because such societies encompass a greater range of social roles (Carr 1994; Wason 1994).

Christopher Carr (1994) compared the relative frequency with which five dimensions of social identity are signified in mortuary practices cross-culturally. Table 4.2 summarizes his results for the kinds of societies that characterized the late prehispanic Southwest. For each of these societal types, the same three dimensions are ranked highest, but in different orders. For horticultural tribes, the most frequently signified social dimension is age; for petty hierarchies, it is vertical social position; for paramount chiefdoms, horizontal and vertical position basically share primary importance. The two lowest-ranked dimensions exhibit the same order for all three kinds of societies, with personal identity being the least frequently signified and gender the next-to-least.

Carr (1994:53–54) offered two reasons why gender is consistently signified less frequently than age, vertical social position, and horizontal social position. First, gender does not require a special indicator because it is usually obvious from an individual's biological characteristics and dress. Second, compared with other dimensions of social identity, gender in many societies is usually less important in the final selection of leaders and thus does not need to be signified as much.

The task for an archaeologist studying a burial population is to disentangle which kinds of mortuary treatment reflect which dimensions of an individual's identity (see Binford 1971; Carr 1994; Goldstein

TABLE 4.1

Factors Affecting the Relative Status of Females

Circumstances in Which Female Status May Be Higher	*Circumstances in Which Female Status May Be Lower*
Subsistence	
Greater reliance on plants by hunter-gatherers	Greater reliance on animals by hunter-gatherers
Hunting-gatherering	Horticulture
Horticulture	Intensive agriculture
Hoe agriculture	Plow agriculture
Female and male contribution to diet roughly equal	Female contribution to diet either much lower or much higher than that of males
Economics	
Females are economically self-sufficient and males are dependent on female activities	Females are not economically self-sufficient and males are not dependent on female activities
Females own/control land and/or other key resources	Females do not own/control land and/or other key resources
Females control distribution of products of their own labor	Females do not control distribution of products of their own labor
Females engage in trading of goods and/or services outside household	Females do not engage in trading of goods and/or resources outside household
Kinship/descent	
Matrilineal descent/matrilocal residence	Patrilineal descent/patrilocal residence
Monogamous marriage	Polygynous marriage
Bridewealth given at marriage	Dowry given at marriage

Politics	
Female influence expressed in both the domestic and public domains	Female influence restricted to domestic domain
Egalitarian sociopolitical organization	Ranked/stratified sociopolitical organization
Ranked/stratified society with ascribed ranking of kin groups	Ranked society with ranking based solely on achievement
Warfare	
Males away at war for considerable periods	More warfare nearby
Ideology	
Magico-religious association between maternity, soil fertility, and social continuity/social good	Magico-religious association between hunting and/or warfare and social continuity/social good
Female life cycle	
Female is postmenopausal	Female is of reproductive age
Other	
Females able to form solidarity groups of some kind—e.g., matrilocal residence, co-wife coalitions, trade associations	Females unable to form solidarity groups

Sources: Aberle 1961; Berreman 1981; Brown 1979; Collier and Rosaldo 1981; Friedl 1975; Gailey 1987a; Goody 1973; Harris 1993; Kessler 1976; Leacock 1975, 1981, 1993; Lebeuf 1963; Lepowsky 1990; Martin and Voorhies 1975; Ortner 1981; Quinn 1977; Rogers 1975; Sanday 1973, 1974, 1981; Schlegel 1977a, 1977b; Spiro 1993; Whyte 1978.

TABLE 4.2

Rank Ordering of Frequency with Which Five Dimensions of Social Identity Are Signified in Mortuary Practices Cross-Culturally

Rank	*Horticultural Tribes*	*Petty Hierarchies*[a]	*Paramount Chiefdoms*
1	Age (34.9%)	Vertical social position (37.5%)	Horizontal social position (34.5%)
2	Vertical social position (24.9%)	Horizontal social position (22.1%)	Vertical social position (33.3%)
3	Horizontal social position (20.6%)	Age (18.1%)	Age (21.4%)
4	Gender (12.7%)	Gender (16.4%)	Gender (8.3%)
5	Personal identity (6.8%)	Personal identity (5.9%)	Personal identity (2.4%)

Source: Carr 1994:54.

Note: Numbers in parentheses indicate the percentage of observations of association between the dimension of social identity and mortuary practices within the societal type. Vertical social position refers to position in a hierarchy. Horizontal social position refers to family or corporate group membership, different kinds of leadership roles, or economic specialists.

[a] *Carr included big-man societies and simple chiefdoms in his category of petty hierarchies.*

1976, 1981; O'Shea 1981, 1984; Saxe 1970; Stickel 1968; Tainter 1975, 1978; Whittlesey 1978). Some correlations are relatively straightforward, such as that between an individual's age and quantity of grave goods (table 4.3). But material indicators that reflect more than one aspect of social identity are more difficult to interpret. For example, corroborating evidence is necessary to determine whether local grave location for a particular burial population reflects age, horizontal social position, or vertical social position (table 4.3).

Although questions about prehistoric gender roles can be investigated by comparing the kinds of utilitarian grave goods found in female and male burials (Binford 1971), the topic of prehistoric gender hierarchies is more difficult to study. The reason is that gender hierarchies conflate at least two dimensions of social identity: gender and vertical social position. Together, their material indicators include

TABLE 4.3

Types of Mortuary Treatment Associated with Different Dimensions of Social Identity Cross-Culturally [a]

Dimension	*Overall Energy Expenditure*[b]	*Kinds of Grave Goods*[c]	*Quantity of Grave Goods*[d]	*Local Grave Location*	*Formal Demarcation of Cemetery*
Vertical social position	1	2		3	
Horizontal social position[e]				X	X
Age			X	X	
Gender		X			
Personal identity		X			

Source: *Carr 1994.*

[a] *Numbers indicate frequency ranking found by Carr (1994); X indicates association found by Carr (1994) but no frequency ranking indicated.*

[b] *For Carr (1994), overall energy expenditure includes body treatment, grave construction, funeral duration, and material contributions to funeral.*

[c] *According to Binford (1971), the kinds of grave goods indicating vertical social position are usually nonutilitarian, and the kinds of grave goods indicating gender are usually utilitarian.*

[d] *Contrary to Binford (1971) and O'Shea (1981, 1984), Carr's (1994) analyses indicate that quantity of grave goods is not a frequent indicator of vertical social position cross-culturally.*

[e] *Contrary to O'Shea (1981, 1984), Carr's (1994) analyses indicate that body preparation/treatment is not a frequent indicator of horizontal social position cross-culturally.*

kinds of utilitarian and nonutilitarian grave goods, overall energy expenditure, and local grave location (table 4.3). If age and horizontal social position are also factors in ranking the two sexes, then the quantity of grave goods and formal demarcation of the cemetery may also convey information about the gender hierarchy. Thus, the initial task in trying to reconstruct a prehistoric gender hierarchy is to distinguish the most relevant burial practices (which may not be the same in every case) from those that reflect either other aspects of the society's social organization or its philosophical-religious beliefs.

Archaeological Studies

A number of archaeological studies of gender relations have been carried out using mortuary data from Bronze Age Europe (Ehrenberg 1989; Gibbs 1987; Gilman 1981; Kristiansen 1984; Levy 1982; O'Shea 1995; Randsborg 1974, 1986; Shennan 1975, 1982) and elsewhere (e.g., Ames 1995; O'Shea 1981, 1984; Schulting 1995; Wason 1994). All of this work has focused on comparing the treatment of biological females and males at death, rather than on identifying the genders defined by the society being studied (Claassen 1992). In most of these female-male comparisons, the emphasis has been on the kinds and overall value of grave goods (see Ehrenberg 1989).

Together, these previous mortuary analyses have produced two important sets of results, one substantive and the other methodological. Substantively, they have confirmed the ethnographically observed pattern in which females and males are buried with different kinds of objects (e.g., Binford 1971; Ehrenberg 1989; Kristiansen 1984; Levy 1982; O'Shea 1981, 1984, 1995; Shennan 1975, 1982), although these differential distributions are often not exclusive (Claassen 1992). They have also documented the presence of gender hierarchies prehistorically and the way in which the relative statuses of females and males within such hierarchies can vary considerably (e.g., Ames 1995; Shennan 1975, 1982; Wason 1994).

While generating these substantive results, previous mortuary analyses of prehistoric gender relations have also produced five important methodological lessons (see Ehrenberg 1989). First, in order to avoid tautological reasoning, individuals must be sexed independently of their mortuary treatment. Second, to avoid focusing on just the wealthy members of a society, sex identifications should be done for all individuals rather than just those with grave goods. Third, to avoid projecting contemporary notions about gender onto past societies, the same interpretive standards concerning how a grave good was made, obtained, and/or used and what its social significance may have been should be applied to both sexes (see also Conkey and Spector 1984). Fourth, while grave goods do provide a relative measure of an individual's social position, one should not automatically assume that all grave goods were owned and/or used by the deceased. Some objects might have belonged to the deceased's family or other mourners. Such offerings could inflate the deceased's status, especially if their purpose was to impress the broader community or to declare aspirations for the deceased in the afterlife.

The final methodological lesson, and one that is especially pertinent to the task of investigating prehistoric gender hierarchies, is that interpreting grave good distributions can be complicated by problems of equifinality (Ehrenberg 1989). For example, there are two possible explanations for the presence of "rich female burials." One is that the wealth was the women's and reflects their high status. Alternatively, the wealth and its associated high status might have belonged to the women's male relatives. Another example of the potential problem of equifinality is found in the two possible explanations for situations in which rich female burials outnumber rich male burials. These females could have been either wealthy, high-status women in a matrilineal society or the wives of wealthy, high-status men in a patrilineal, polygynous society.

Altogether, these lessons drawn from archaeological studies confirm the major conclusion of cross-cultural, ethnographic comparisons: that the relationship between gender and burial practices is complicated and subtle. Consequently, the investigation of prehistoric gender hierarchies can be difficult.

Previous Southwestern Burial Studies

Mortuary analyses have a long tradition in Southwestern archaeology, and some of this previous work reinforces expectations about the presence of different kinds of gender hierarchies in the late prehispanic Southwest. For example, two sets of evidence suggest the existence of male-dominated gender hierarchies. The first is descriptions of the Southwest's small number of well-known, truly rich burials (table 4.4). All of those with sex identifications are males.

The second is Patricia Crown and Suzanne Fish's (1996) gender-based analysis of Hohokam mortuary practices. According to Crown and Fish, the richest Classic-period Hohokam burials were always males interred on platform mounds. Crown and Fish interpreted this evidence as indicating that male status during the Classic period was higher than female status. In addition, these status differences were derived from different realms, as is indicated by males being buried

TABLE 4.4

The Prehispanic Southwest's Best-Known Rich Burials

Site	*Sex*	*Age*	*Reference*
Pueblo Bonito	Male	35+	Pepper 1909, 1920; Akins 1986:115–17
	Male	25+	Pepper 1909, 1920; Akins 1986: 115–17
Aztec Ruin	Unknown	Adult	Morris 1924:155–61
	Unknown (2)	Adult (2)	Morris 1924:163–67
Ridge Ruin	Male	35–40	McGregor 1943
Grasshopper	Male	40–45	Griffin 1967

with more exotic items, ornaments, and ritual paraphernalia and females with more tools and locally produced items. Crown and Fish attributed the occasional, not-quite-as-elaborate female mound burials to kin ties that these women had, through either blood or marriage, to elite families living on the mounds. If this interpretation is correct, it suggests that the Classic-period Hohokam were patrilineal.

In contrast, two other Southwestern mortuary analyses have produced conclusions about matrilineality. The first is Helen Crotty's (1983) study of the Late Pueblo III Ancestral Pueblo (Kayenta) site of RB 568. Her analysis revealed the presence of two extremely rich burials, one female (age 30–35) and the other male (age 20–25). Of the remaining burials, the richest were always those of senior women. In turn, the less rich burials of senior men were always richer than those of junior women. These patterns indicate that in addition to sex and age, other factors also affected the kinds and quantities of grave goods buried with an individual. Crotty's (1983) interpretation was that the social organization of RB 568 was characterized by ranking within and among matrilineal clans.

The other mortuary analysis to indicate matrilineality is Todd Howell's (1994, 1995) study of the protohistoric Zuni site of Hawikku. There, four disproportionately rich and diverse burials were recovered. The richest and most diverse was that of a female; among the remaining three, two were female and one was male. Howell also found both similarities and differences in female and male leadership roles. Prehistorically, both sexes served as ritual leaders, but females also served as matrilineage heads and males as war leaders.

Together, the mortuary analyses of the Classic-period Hohokam, of RB 568, and of Hawikku raise the question of whether there is an automatic correlation between descent rules and the form of a gender hierarchy. Among the Classic-period Hohokam, the preferential treatment of males can be interpreted as evidencing a male-dominated gender hierarchy and patrilineality. At RB 568 and Hawikku, conclusions about matrilineality suggest the presence of a female-dominated gender hierarchy. While these correlations may in fact be true, there is also suggestive evidence that prehispanic Southwestern gender hierarchies were more complicated. In a matrilineal system, high-status male burials could be attributed to family ties through blood or marriage with highly ranked matrilineages (cf. female burials on Classic-period platform mounds). Alternatively, the probability that Hawikku males served as war leaders might indicate that some of their high status was truly their own. Thus, as the results of previously discussed cross-cultural ethnographic comparisons have shown, the relative ranking of the two sexes in prehispanic Southwestern gender hierarchies may have varied in different realms of social life.

GENDER HIERARCHIES IN THE LATE PREHISPANIC SOUTHWEST

To investigate further the kinds of gender hierarchies present in the late prehispanic Southwest, I compared the values of grave goods interred with females and males from a series of burial populations. My approach was comparative; I not only compared females and males excavated at individual sites but also made intersite comparisons. In this section I describe the data and assumptions, then briefly discuss the calculations, and finally present the results of the female-male comparisons.

Data and Assumptions

The primary difficulty encountered during this research was in locating well-documented burial populations. Though literally thousands of human skeletons have been excavated throughout the

Southwest, only a small fraction have both sex identifications and grave good counts. Systematic documentation of human remains and their associated grave goods has been the exception rather than the rule in Southwestern archaeology. Even for sites for which there are some published data, the record is extremely uneven. Frequently, what is published consists only of summary totals and percentages, with none of the raw data from which these figures were derived. Where there are raw data, they are often incomplete; sex identifications are often lacking, or else only the presence (but not the numbers) of associated grave goods is recorded.

Well-documented Southwestern burial populations—that is, ones with sex identifications and grave good counts—are often characterized by other data problems such as low sample sizes and the effects of disturbance, poor preservation, excavation biases (e.g., an emphasis on roomblocks versus extramural areas), and inadequate or inconsistent data recording. Sample size is especially critical for investigating prehistoric gender hierarchies, because such studies require comparisons between females and males both within and among burial populations. Deciding how large a burial population should be in order to enable valid comparisons is problematical. In my review of Southwestern mortuary studies, I found that sex identifications were made, on average, for only one-third of the members of each analyzed burial population. Thus, to enable a comparison of 30 females with 30 males, a burial population would have to contain approximately 200 burials. Unfortunately, the number of prehispanic Southwestern sites with 200 well-documented burials (i.e., having both sex identification and grave good counts) is extremely small. Consequently, if the goal is to compare a number of populations, then sample size requirements must be reduced. The trade-off is that reducing sample size increases the probability that an infrequently occurring individual (e.g., one with many valuable grave goods) would be omitted from the analysis. If this did happen, then any conclusions about the kind of gender hierarchy represented by the burial population could be incorrect.

For the purposes of this chapter, burials from 16 cases were analyzed (table 4.5).[1] These cases included both sites and areas containing multiple sites. All cases dated to the late prehispanic period, and all of the Southwest's major culture areas were represented. Sample sizes

TABLE 4.5
Cases for Which Burial Samples Were Analyzed

Site	*No. Females*	*No. Males*	*Source*
Arroyo Hondo	31	18	Palkovich 1980
Casa Buena	22	12	Effland 1988; Pueblo Grande Museum
Casas Grandes[a]	51	41	Ravesloot 1988
Chaco Canyon[b]	64	52	Akins 1986
Convento Site	19	15	DiPeso, Rinaldo, and Fenner 1974b
Dolores[c]	15	13	Stodder 1987
Galaz[d]	27	37	Anyon and LeBlanc 1984
Grasshopper[e]	49	27	Clark 1967; Griffin 1967
Las Colinas[f]	22	16	Saul 1981, 1988
Point of Pines	63	48	Arizona State Museum
Pueblo Grande[d]	169	170	Mitchell, ed., 1994b, and personal communication
RB 568	19	6	Crotty 1983
Starkweather	14	18	Nesbitt 1938
Tijeras	14	23	Maxwell Museum of Anthropology
Turkey Creek	87	70	Arizona State Museum
Yellow Jacket[b]	21	14	Mobley-Tanaka, personal communication

[a] *Medio period only.*
[b] *All periods combined.*
[c] *McPhee phase only.*
[d] *Classic period only.*
[e] *Only burials excavated as of 1967.*
[f] *Inhumations and cremations combined.*

for many of the cases were low, so the analytical results should be treated as preliminary.

Grave Lot Values

The comparison of female and male burials relied on the calculation of "grave lot values" (GLVs), a measure that has been employed in several previous Southwestern mortuary analyses (e.g., Brunson 1989; Effland 1988; Hagopian 1995; McGuire 1992). A grave lot value is an estimate of the aggregate value of all grave goods buried with an individual. As such, it represents one measure of the energy invested in an individual's burial. Given that energy investment has been found ethnographically to be the most frequent indicator of vertical social position (see table 4.3), comparisons of female and male grave lot values should indicate whether or not a particular society was characterized by a gender hierarchy, and if so, the relative ranking of the two sexes.

To calculate an individual's grave lot value, each of her or his grave goods is assigned a rank based on its function, origin, and labor investment (see McGuire 1992). Then the rankings of all of the individual's grave goods are totaled to produce her or his GLV. This value is a heuristic device for making comparisons (see Effland 1988). It should not be treated as absolute or "correct," because the values are assigned by the archaeologist and not elicited from informants. Different investigators might assign different ranks to the same artifact depending on their research goals and knowledge about the object's source, labor requirements, and function at a particular place and time.

There are two inherent limitations in the grave lot value measure. One is that GLVs are derived solely from the kinds and quantities of grave goods and do not incorporate information about other potentially significant aspects of mortuary practices (e.g., tomb construction, burial location). The other limitation is that individuals with equal GLVs may in fact have been buried with very different kinds and/or quantities of grave goods, signifying very different roles and statuses.

Analytical Results

Two sets of comparisons were made of female and male grave lot values (table 4.6). First, the highest female and male GLVs for each case were compared to see which sex had the higher value. Second, the overall distributions of GLVs for each case were examined to determine whether the overall pattern for each sex was continuous or hierarchical.

At least five groups of cases were defined. One group consisted of McPhee-phase Dolores River sites and Tijeras Pueblo. For these cases, the maximum female and male grave lot values were approximately the same, and the distributions of both female and male values were

TABLE 4.6

Comparison of Female and Male Grave Lot Values (GLVs)

GLV Distribution	*Maximum Female GLV Greater than Maximum Male GLV*	*Maximum Male GLV Greater than Maximum Female GLV*	*Maximum Female GLV Approximately the Same as Maximum Male GLV*
Continuous distribution for females and males			Dolores Tijeras
Continuous distribution for females, hierarchical distribution for males		Arroyo Hondo Galaz Yellow Jacket	
Continuous distribution for males, hierarchical distribution for females	Convento Las Colinas		
Hierarchical distribution for females and males	Casa Buena (?) Grasshopper Point of Pines RB 568	Casas Grandes Chaco Pueblo Grande Starkweather Turkey Creek	Casa Buena (?)

continuous. These characteristics suggest the existence of relative gender equality.

Two groups of cases seem to be characterized by female-dominated gender hierarchies, as evidenced by the maximum female GLVs being notably greater than the maximum male value. The two groups of cases differed in the distributions of the two sexes' GLVs. At Las Colinas and the Convento site, the narrower range of male values exhibited a continuous distribution, whereas the wider range of female values exhibited a hierarchical distribution. In contrast, at RB 568, Grasshopper, Point of Pines, and perhaps Casa Buena, the GLVs for both sexes exhibited hierarchical distributions.

Two other groups of cases seem to be characterized by male-dominated gender hierarchies, as is evidenced by the maximum male GLV's being notably greater than the maximum female value. Again, the two groups of cases differed in the distributions of the two sexes' GLVs. At Yellow Jacket, Galaz, and Arroyo Hondo, the narrower range of female values exhibited a continuous distribution, whereas the wider range of male values exhibited a hierarchical distribution. In contrast, at Chaco Canyon, Turkey Creek, Starkweather, Pueblo Grande, and Casas Grandes, the GLVs for both sexes exhibited hierarchical distributions.

The case of Casa Buena raises the possibility that a sixth type of gender hierarchy might have been present in the late prehispanic Southwest: one with relative gender equality but hierarchical patterning for both females and males. Determining whether or not this is so requires specifying a standard for how close maximum grave lot values must be in order to be judged approximately the same. At Casa Buena, the maximum female and male GLVs were 3,317 and 2,031, respectively. Are these values roughly the same or different? Considering how few burials were excavated from Casa Buena (table 4.5), either alternative, along with the resulting conclusion that the site was characterized by either relative gender equality or a female-dominated gender hierarchy, could easily be disputed. As a result, I excluded this case from subsequent analyses.

FURTHER COMPARISONS

The preceding sections of this chapter indicate why variation should be expected in late prehispanic Southwestern gender hierarchies, and they present evidence that such variation did in fact exist. In the remainder of the chapter, I compare cases identified as representing different kinds of gender hierarchies in order to determine whether they can be distinguished in other ways as well. I make comparisons of overall sociopolitical complexity, cultural affiliation, time period, and sex role differentiation.

Organizational Comparisons

In the beginning of the chapter, I stated that prehispanic Southwestern gender hierarchies represent a topic in which questions about sociopolitical organization and gender relations intersect. That this is so should be apparent for the five kinds of gender hierarchies defined for the cases analyzed here. Relative gender equality was found in the two cases (Dolores, Tijeras) for which there was no hierarchical pattern in the distribution of grave lot values for either sex. This suggests that egalitarian societies in the late prehispanic Southwest lacked gender hierarchies, at least gender hierarchies that can be detected through analyses of GLVs.

In contrast, hierarchical patterning was evident in the distributions of GLVs obtained for the other four groups of cases. This hierarchical patterning occurred not just between females and males but also among the values for one or both sexes.

To further investigate the relationship between kind of gender hierarchy and degree of social differentiation, I made two sets of comparisons for the cases as a whole (females and males combined): one of grave lot value ranges and the other of Gini Indices. Ranges of GLVs can serve as a measure of overall differentiation because the greater the range, the richer the richest individual and presumably the greater the extent of social differentiation within the group. The Gini Index is a relative measure of the degree of inequality (and thus of social differentiation) within a group (McGuire 1992:128–32). It is calculated by first plotting the cumulative percentages of burials against the cumulative percentages of grave lot values. Then a diagonal line, representing absolute equality, is plotted. The Gini Index is the area between these two lines, with a larger area (and thus a larger Gini Index) indicating greater inequality.

Identical patterns were found when the GLV ranges and the Gini

Indices for the five groups of cases were compared (figs. 4.1–4.2). Not unexpectedly, the two cases evidencing no hierarchy for either sex exhibited the lowest ranges and the lowest Gini Indices. Cases with intermediate ranges and intermediate Gini Indices were those with female- and male-dominated gender hierarchies in which only the dominant sex exhibited a hierarchical distribution of GLVs. Cases with the highest ranges and highest Gini Indices were those with female- and male-dominated gender hierarchies in which both sexes exhibited hierarchical distributions of GLVs.

These patterns indicate that the relationship between kind of gender hierarchy and overall degree of social differentiation in the late prehispanic Southwest is fairly straightforward from one point of view and more complicated from another. The straightforward relationship is between the number of sexes with hierarchical distributions of grave lot values and how differentiated the group is overall. In the late prehispanic Southwest, it appears that if there was no hierarchy for either sex, then both sexes were also ranked approximately the same and the group as a whole was egalitarian. If only one sex evidenced a hierarchy, it is that sex that was ranked higher than the other, and there was an intermediate degree of differentiation. The maximum differentiation occurred when both sexes evidenced hierarchical distributions of GLVs.

What makes the relationship between type of gender hierarchy and overall degree of social differentiation complicated is that the straightforward relationship just described applies to both female- and male-dominated gender hierarchies. In other words, whether females or males are ranked highest seems to vary independently of organizational complexity.

Cultural Comparisons

There is no obvious relationship between kind of gender hierarchy and cultural affiliation (table 4.7). Two or more kinds of gender hierarchies were found in three of the four major culture areas considered here. Indeed, variation occurred at smaller scales even among roughly contemporaneous, neighboring sites. Examples include Hohokam cases located in the Lower Salt River valley (Las Colinas versus Pueblo Grande), Mogollon cases located in the Mimbres area (Galaz versus Starkweather), and other Mogollon cases in east-central

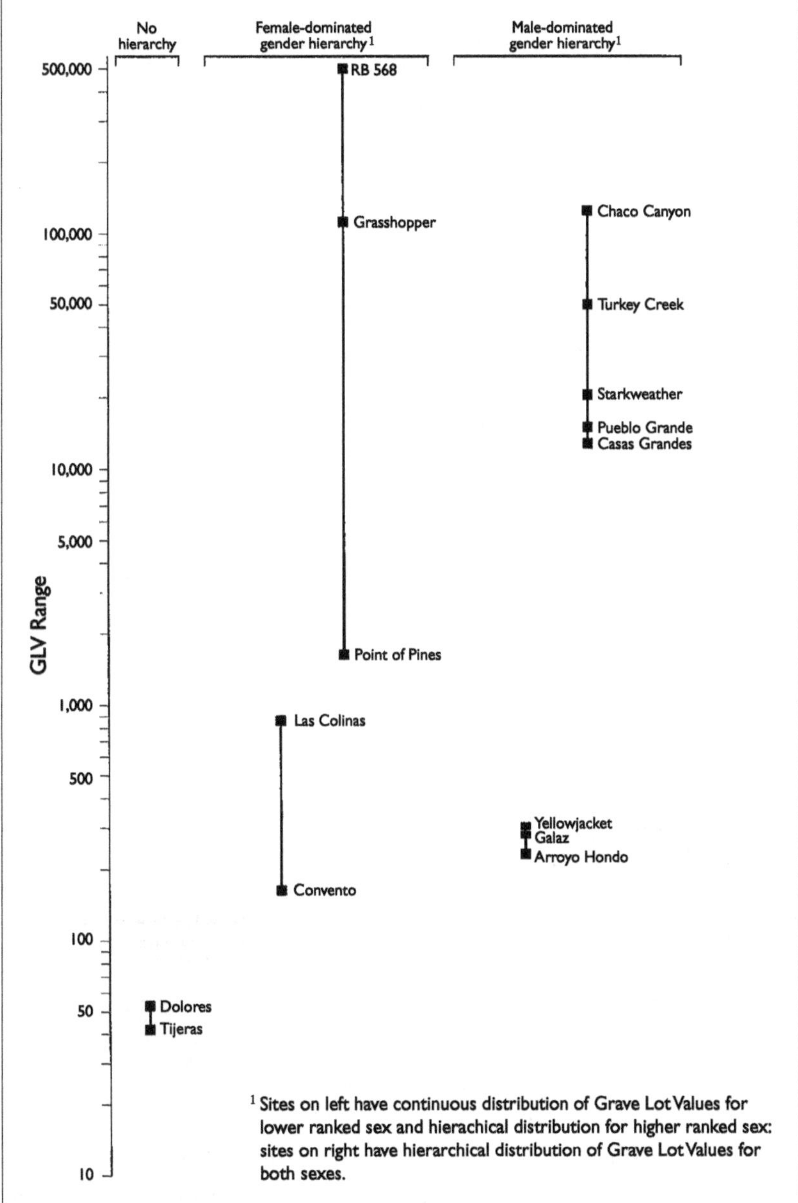

FIGURE 4.1.

Ranges of grave lot values (GLVs) for sites with different kinds of gender hierarchies.

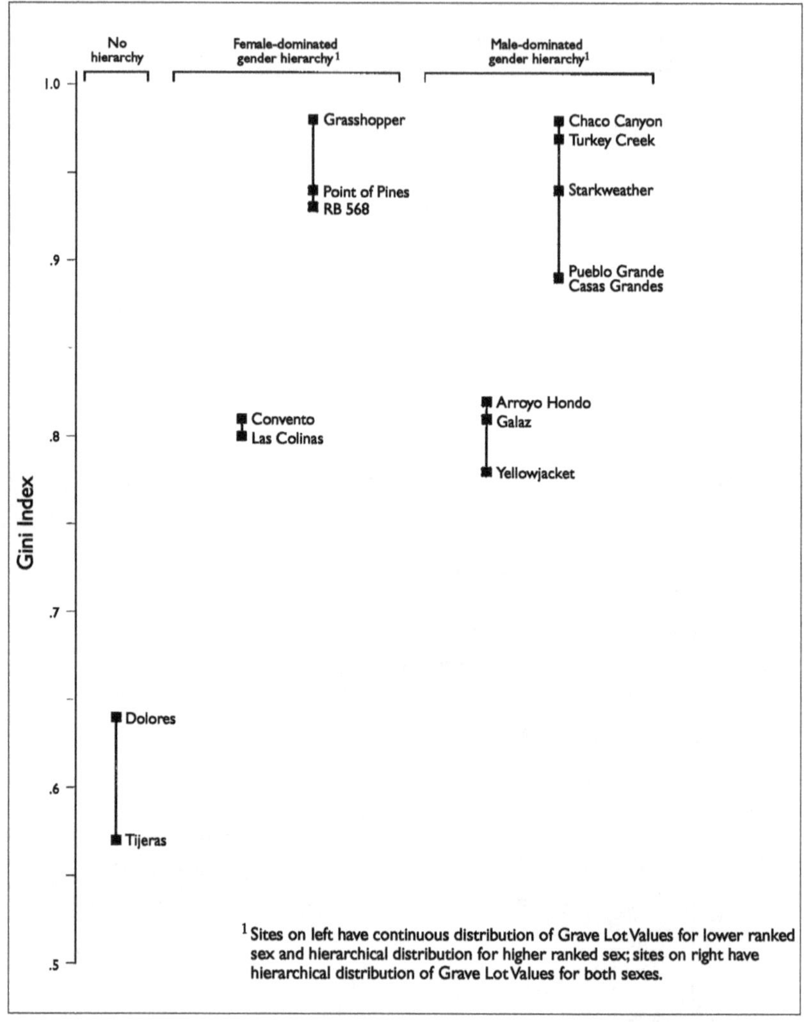

FIGURE 4.2.

Gini Indices for sites with different kinds of gender hierarchies.

Arizona (Grasshopper and Point of Pines versus Turkey Creek).

There are two possible interpretations of this diversity. One is that it is the product of data problems that have undoubtedly affected the analyses to some unknown extent. Cases in both the Mimbres and Hohokam areas (Starkweather and Las Colinas, respectively) are characterized by small sample sizes that could have produced false conclu-

TABLE 4.7

Relationships between Different Kinds of Gender Hierarchies and Major Southwestern Culture Areas

Kind of Gender Hierarchy	*Ancestral Pueblo*	*Hohokam*	*Mogollon*	*Salado*
No hierarchy	Dolores Tijeras			
Female dominated, type 1		Las Colinas	Convento[a]	
Female dominated, type 2	RB 568		Grasshopper Point of Pines	
Male dominated, type 1	Arroyo Hondo Yellow Jacket		Galaz	
Male dominated, type 2	Chaco	Pueblo Grande	Starkweather Turkey Creek	Casas Grandes[a]

Note: For type 1, dominant sex has hierarchical distribution of GLVs, and subordinate sex has continuous distribution of GLVs. For type 2, both sexes have hierarchical distribution of GLVs.
[a]*Convento and Casas Grandes are neighboring sites dating to different time periods; they are associated with different culture areas due to a shift in culture area boundaries.*

sions about the kinds of gender hierarchies present at those sites and, in turn, a false picture about spatial diversity.

An alternative interpretation is that variation in the kinds of gender hierarchies present within relatively small areas reflects a social reality of the late prehispanic Southwest. This alternative does not deny the existence of data problems; but eliminating problematical cases would not necessarily preclude the possibility that contemporaneous, neighboring sites could be characterized by different kinds of gender hierarchies.

Further examination of one area demonstrates that such small-scale variation could in fact occur. The analyses presented earlier for all sites in Chaco Canyon suggested that the area was characterized by a male-dominated gender hierarchy with the grave lot values of both females and males exhibiting a hierarchical distribution (table 4.6). However, when great house and small house burials are analyzed

Table 4.8

Summary of Chaco Canyon Grave Lot Values (GLVs)

Characteristic	*All Sites*	*Great Houses*	*Small Houses*
Sex with higher GLV	Male	Male	Female
Distribution of female GLVs	Hierarchical	Hierarchical	Hierarchical
Distribution of male GLVs	Hierarchical	Hierarchical	Continuous

separately, two different patterns emerge (table 4.8). Great houses exhibit the pattern seen previously for the canyon as a whole: a male-dominated gender hierarchy with GLVs of both females and males exhibiting a hierarchical distribution. In contrast, small houses are characterized by a female-dominated gender hierarchy with the GLVs of females evidencing a hierarchical distribution and those of males a continuous distribution. Thus, two different kinds of sites located close together within a single society exhibit different kinds of gender hierarchies. Possible reasons for this variation include the different historical trajectories characterizing the two site types and the different functions they might have served within Chacoan society. Given the results of the preceding organizational comparisons, the differential GLV distributions (e.g., hierarchical for one or both sexes) for the two kinds of Chacoan sites reinforce the widely held notion that the degree of differentiation was greater at Chacoan great houses than at neighboring small houses.

Diachronic Comparisons

Although the Chacoan data suffer problems of low sample sizes when they are subdivided by sex, site type, and time period, they nevertheless indicate that the forms of prehispanic Southwestern gender hierarchies could change through time (table 4.9). The available data indicate that, initially, Chacoan society as a whole (all sites) was characterized by a male-dominated gender hierarchy in which both male and female grave lot values exhibited a hierarchical distribution. This was followed by two periods with female-dominated gender hierarchies in which female GLVs exhibited a hierarchical distribution and male

TABLE 4.9

Gender Hierarchies in Chaco Canyon

Time Period	*All Sites*	*Great Houses*	*Small Houses*
Red Mesa (A.D. 900–1050)	Male dominated, type 2 (n = 11)	Male dominated, type 1 (n = 6)	Female dominated, type 1 (n = 5)
Gallup (A.D. 1030–1150)	Female dominated, type 1 (n = 39)	? (n = 7; no male burials)	Female dominated, type 1 (n = 32)
McElmo (A.D. 1100–1175)	Female dominated, type 1 (n = 24)	Female dominated, type 1 (n = 5)	Female dominated, type 1 (n = 19)
Mesa Verde (A.D. 1175–1300)	No hierarchy (n = 5)	? (n = 0)	No hierarchy (n = 5)

Note: For type 1, dominant sex has hierarchical distribution of GLVs and subordinate sex has continuous distribution of GLVs. For type 2, both sexes have hierarchical distribution of GLVs. Sample size (n) indicates numbers of individuals analyzed.

GLVs a continuous distribution. During the final period, Chacoan society seems to have been characterized by relative gender equality within an egalitarian sociopolitical system.

The temporal trends for great houses differ from those of the canyon as a whole in three ways. First, during the initial period, both great houses and the canyon as a whole were characterized by a male-dominated hierarchy, but the distribution of grave lot values at the great houses was hierarchical for males alone, whereas it was hierarchical for both sexes in the canyon as a whole. The second difference occurs in the second period, for which no male burials have been recovered from great houses. This absence of male burials may evidence a female-dominated gender hierarchy, as has been suggested for the canyon as a whole. The final difference occurs in the last period, for which there are no great house burials, female or male.

The temporal trends for small house burials are the same as those for the canyon as a whole except during the initial period. Unlike the great house and the canyonwide patterns, small house burials in the initial period evidence a female-dominated gender hierarchy with females displaying a hierarchical distribution and males a continuous one.

Among the other cases considered in this chapter, there is further suggestive evidence that prehispanic Southwestern gender hierarchies could change through time. For example, Medio-period Casas Grandes (A.D. 1200–1450 [see Ravesloot, Dean, and Foster 1995]) was characterized by a male-dominated gender hierarchy with both sexes evidencing a hierarchical distribution of GLVs. However, the nearby and earlier Viejo-period site of Convento (A.D. 700–1060 [Di Peso 1974]) was characterized by a female-dominated gender hierarchy with only females evidencing a hierarchical distribution of GLVs.

A shorter-term sequence of changing gender relations may be represented by the three neighboring Mogollon sites in east-central Arizona. The earliest site, Turkey Creek (A.D. 1225–1286 [Lowell 1991a]), had a male-dominated gender hierarchy with both sexes evidencing a hierarchical distribution of grave lot values. The two later sites of Point of Pines (A.D. 1275–1325 [Robinson 1959]) and Grasshopper (A.D. 1300–1375/1400 [J. Reid 1989]) had female-dominated gender hierarchies with both sexes evidencing a hierarchical distribution of GLVs. Further investigation is necessary to determine whether the variation in gender relations found among these three Mogollon sites is, in fact, spatial (as I suggested earlier), temporal (as I suggest here), or a product of data problems.

Sex Role Comparisons

Though grave lot values have proven to be quite useful in distinguishing different kinds of gender hierarchies in the late prehispanic Southwest, they may obscure important sex role differences. The reason is that individuals with equal GLVs might have been buried with completely different grave goods. Here, I briefly summarize the distributions of ordinary goods, ornaments, and ritual goods.

All Females versus All Males

To investigate possible sex role differences, I compared the distributions of ordinary goods, ornaments, and ritual goods found with one sex but not the other for all analyzed females and males. The results suggest that the greatest sex role differentiation occurred in the everyday realm. The two sexes were generally distinguished more frequently by sexually restricted ordinary goods than by sexually restricted ornaments and ritual goods. In addition, the fact that females were generally distinguished more frequently than males in the occurrence of sexually restricted ordinary goods suggests that female responsibilities lay more in the everyday realm than did those of males.

The analyzed females and males differed somewhat in the distributions of sexually restricted ornaments and ritual goods. Whereas females tended to have roughly equal proportions of ornaments and ritual goods, males tended to show an emphasis on one category of goods over the other. If ornaments and ritual goods served as status markers of some sort, then this patterning indicates that male status in the late prehispanic Southwest might have been derived from a more restricted set of activities or roles than female status.

Females and males may also have differed in the materials and forms of their ornaments. For example, females are in general distinguished more frequently by turquoise pendants, shell beads, shell rings, and stone beads. Males are in general distinguished more frequently by turquoise beads, shell pendants, shell tinklers, and stone rings. These various ornaments might have conveyed multiple messages (e.g., age, social rank, and/or gender), with the association of message(s) and ornament possibly varying from case to case.

Different kinds of ritual goods are also found with females and males. This suggests that although both sexes engaged in ritual activities, the specific activities associated with females and males may have differed. In addition, the lack of overlap in the kinds of ritual goods found for different cases suggests that the kinds of goods that symbolized ritual activities, as well as the activities themselves, might have varied from population to population.

Gender Hierarchy Comparisons

Another set of comparisons was made between cases with different kinds of gender hierarchies to see which sex had the higher percentage of sexually restricted ordinary goods, ornaments, and ritual goods. No obvious patterning was evident in who had the greatest frequency of sexually restricted ordinary goods. The same was true for ornaments except for cases with no hierarchy of any kind, social or gender; for these cases, ornaments distinguished males more frequently than females.

The strongest pattern was evidenced by ritual goods. Ritual goods generally distinguished females more frequently than males in cases with female-dominated gender hierarchies, and males more frequently than females in cases with male-dominated gender hierarchies. This patterning suggests that for cases in which one sex dominated the gender hierarchy, ritual activities were important to that sex's dominant position.

Highest-Ranking Female versus Highest-Ranking Male

A final comparison was made between the kinds of grave goods found with the highest-ranking female and male in cases with different kinds of gender hierarchies (table 4.10). Unlike the previous comparisons, which considered only those grave goods found with one sex but not the other, this comparison considered all grave goods buried with the highest-ranking female and male in each case. The same kinds of grave goods were buried with the highest-ranking females and males for three sets of cases: those with relative gender equality, those with a female-dominated gender hierarchy in which both sexes exhibited a hierarchical distribution of grave lot values, and those with a male-dominated gender hierarchy in which both sexes exhibited a hierarchical distribution of GLVs. For the cases with relative gender equality, the females and males with the highest GLVs were buried primarily with ordinary goods. Ritual items were present in lower quantities, and ornaments were completely absent. For the cases with female- and male-dominated gender hierarchies in which both sexes evidence a hierarchical distribution of GLVs, ornaments made up virtually all of the grave goods buried with the highest-ranking females and males.

Different kinds of grave goods were buried with the highest-ranking females and males for cases with female- and male-dominated gender hierarchies in which only the dominant sex evidenced a hierarchical distribution of grave lot values. For cases with female-dominated gender hierarchies in which female GLVs exhibit a hierarchical distribution and male GLVs exhibit a continuous distribution, the highest-ranking females were buried primarily with ornaments, and the highest-ranking males primarily with ordinary goods. For cases with male-dominated gender hierarchies in which male GLVs exhibit a hierarchical distribution and female GLVs exhibit a continuous distribution, the highest-ranking males were buried primarily with either

Table 4.10

Percentages of Different Categories of Grave Goods among All Grave Goods Found with the Highest-Ranked Female and Male at Each Site

	Ordinary Goods		*Ornaments*		*Ritual Goods*	
Kind of Hierarchy	*F*	*M*	*F*	*M*	*F*	*M*
Gender equality						
Dolores	71	67	0	0	29	33
Tijeras	50	100	0	0	50	0
Female dominated, type 1						
Convento	0	100	93	0	7	0
Las Colinas	1	85	99	15	0	0
Female dominated, type 2						
Grasshopper	<1	9	100	66	0	25
Point of Pines	6	3	94	91	0	6
RB568	<1	<1	100	100	0	0
Male dominated, type 1						
Arroyo Hondo	88	13	0	0	13	88
Galaz	86	4	14	0	0	94
Yellow Jacket	71	7	0	93	29	0
Male dominated, type 2						
Casas Grandes	<1	0	100	100	0	0
Chaco	2	<1	93	100	5	<1
Pueblo Grande	0	0	100	99	<1	<1
Starkweather	<1	<1	100	100	0	0
Turkey Creek	<1	1	100	96	<1	3

Note: For type 1, dominant sex has hierarchical distribution of GLVs, and subordinate sex has continuous distribution of GLVs. For type 2, both sexes have hierarchical distribution of GLVs. F indicates females, M indicates males.

ritual items or ornaments, and the highest-ranking females primarily with ordinary goods.

These results indicate that when the distribution of grave lot values is continuous, then the individuals the highest GLVs are buried primarily with ordinary goods. When the GLVs exhibit a hierarchical distribution, then the kinds of goods buried with the individuals with the highest GLVs consist primarily of ornaments. The only exception to this latter pattern is in cases with male-dominated gender hierarchies in which only the male GLVs exhibit a hierarchical distribution. For two of these cases, the grave goods found with the highest-ranking males are primarily ritual items, not ornaments.

CONCLUSION

The study of gender hierarchies has the potential to add much to our understanding of how prehispanic Southwestern societies were organized. The analyses reported in this chapter have demonstrated that such hierarchies were present in the late prehispanic Southwest and that their forms varied. Both female- and male-dominated gender hierarchies were identified, along with subtypes of each. Some but not all characteristics of gender hierarchy form were found to correlate with overall sociopolitical complexity. The results also suggested that gender hierarchy form could vary synchronically within relatively small areas as well as through time. Finally, a relationship was found between gender hierarchy form and the social realms from which female and male status were derived.

There is much left to be learned about gender hierarchies in the late prehispanic Southwest. Future research should expand the sample of cases considered in this chapter and seek to identify and eliminate cases that suffer from unresolvable data problems. Analyses of a larger sample of cases could verify and refine the conclusions presented here.

Apart from analyzing more data sets, the other major task for future research is to compare changes in gender hierarchy form to changes in those social variables that have been documented ethnographically as affecting the relative status of females and males. Such comparisons are necessary if Southwestern archaeologists are to understand why gender hierarchies at different times and in different places took the forms that they did.

NOTES

This chapter could not have been written without the help of many individuals. I am especially grateful to those who shared unpublished data with me: Jeanne Mobley-Tanaka (Yellow Jacket), Douglas Mitchell (Pueblo Grande), Geoffrey Clark (Grasshopper), Harry Shafer (NAN Ranch), Chuck Hilton and Bruce Huckell (Tijeras), and Raymond Thompson and Mike Jacobs (Point of Pines and Turkey Creek). Others shared advice gained from their own mortuary analyses: Nancy Akins, Kenneth Ames, Lane Anderson Beck, Judy Brunson, Helen Crotty, Richard Effland, John Hohmann, Jerry Howard, Todd Howell, Chris Loendorf, Ann Palkovich, John Ravesloot, Arlynn Simon, Ann Lucy Stoddard, and Stephanie Whittlesey. The Interlibrary Loan staff of the University of Delaware's Morris Library was ever resourceful in locating publications with Southwestern mortuary data for me. Leads on sources of unpublished data were provided by Roger Anyon, Larry Baker, Ethny Barnes, Marietta Davenport, Becka DuBey, Glen Fulfer, Pat Gilman, Keith Kintigh, Debra Martin, Charles Merbs, Lee Newsome, Judy Reed, Anibal Rodriguez, Leah Rosemeir, Brenda Shears, Ruth Trocolli, and Holly Young. Conversations with Joanna Grand, Jonathan Haas, and Tom Killion made me more aware of the sensitive issues involved in working with mortuary data in the era of NAGPRA. Willett Kempton wrote a computer program for calculating Gini Indices. Rob Schultz drafted the figures. Linda Clifton typed the tables. My greatest debt is to Patty Crown, who got me started and then was a paragon of support and patience throughout the long process of finishing. Finally, I dedicate this paper to my youngest son, Isaac Star Kempton, who was born during the course of this research.

1. The four criteria for including a burial population were that (1) sex identifications had been made, (2) both females and males were represented, (3) grave good counts were available, and (4) the data were accessible. Because of difficulties in obtaining data, no fixed sample size requirements were used.

Only grave good data from deliberate burials with sex identifications were analyzed. Consequently, accidental deaths and most children were not considered. Multiple burials were included if there was a clear association with a set of grave goods, in which case all grave goods were attributed to all burials. However, instances in which multiple burials and their grave goods were severely disturbed (e.g., room 33 at Pueblo Bonito) were excluded from the analysis.

A series of assumptions were made in the analyses. First, I assumed that the grave goods buried with an individual reflected her or his status when alive (even if the grave goods did not all belong to the deceased). Second, I ignored problems of preservation, disturbance, and poor data recording, assuming that these problems affected females and males equally. I also ignored the problem of excavation bias in favor of certain contexts over others (e.g., roomblocks versus trash mounds) and assumed that the sample of burials excavated from a site was representative of the site's population. Finally, I assumed that the sex identifications were correct.

5

Farming, Foraging, and Gender

Suzanne K. Fish

For more than three millennia, activities related to farming consumed the workaday lives of most women and men in the prehispanic Southwest. If the behavior toward plants that we term "agriculture" is viewed as a progressive intensification of the interventions practiced by foragers, then this generalization could be extended much farther back in time. It follows, then, that a majority of the gender relations of ancient Southwesterners found expression in a context of gathering or farming.

Societal frameworks for gender relations and their expression in social and economic interactions have not been focal issues for most Southwestern archaeologists. This thematic neglect is virtually absolute with regard to gender relations in the organization and primary contexts of foraging and farming. A review of paper titles and abstracts from the Society of American Archaeology meetings between 1990 and 1999 confirms that regional scholars are not unique in this omission. If broached at all, the subject of gender in subsistence production is approached indirectly. For example, in Katherine Spielmann's introduction to a pioneering journal issue on gender in Southwestern archaeology, topics under the heading "Agricultural Production" include the role of corn in the diet, the physical and social consequences of grinding technology and tasks, ceramics in farming economies, and the exchange of agricultural products, but not farming itself (Spielmann 1995:95–98). As Spielmann (1995:95) noted: "Corn production and distribution have yet to be engendered...in the archaeological record."

Why might this be? There are numerous examinations of gender in agriculture in the literature of ethnography, economic development, and women's studies, often focusing on women's roles and relations. Although such inquiries encompass the postproduction factors treated in other chapters in this volume, they also address the gender implications of land, labor, and produce in the primary context of production, the purview of the following discussion. The lack of attention to these themes in Southwestern archaeology is attributable in large part to relatively limited investigations of the settings of farming and foraging; archaeologists frequently pass over the more ephemeral remains of subsistence activities in favor of residential settlements. Another obstacle is the difficulty of discriminating gender in these situations, with their minimal artifacts and architecture. Moreover, the analyses that most unequivocally identify individual gender, such as those of skeletal morphology, burial accompaniments, and representational art in this volume, provide few clues concerning roles in subsistence production. The goal of this chapter, therefore, is an initial programmatic examination of variables relevant to gender in Southwestern foraging and farming, along with suggestions on how they might or might not be reflected in the archaeological record.

Cross-cultural studies of gender roles in subsistence systems identify factors that affect sexual divisions of labor in foraging and agriculture (e.g., Boserup 1970; Brown 1970; Burton and White 1984; Burton, White, and Dow 1982; Ember 1983; Guyer 1988; Hill et al. 1985; Hurtado et al. 1985; Murdock and Provost 1973; Schlegel and Barry 1986). Maxims include the suitability of males for tasks requiring maximum strength and maximum bursts of energy, the customary assignment of females to repetitive activities, the greater restriction of females with children to efforts near camps and habitations, the greater propensity of males to engage in distant travel, and the need for women with children to avoid dangerous locations and undertakings. In hunting and gathering activities, a widely noted corollary of these contrastive generalities is the more prominent role of men in the pursuit of large game and of women in the acquisition and processing of wild plants. In agriculture, commonly cited correlates are a foremost role for men in the tasks of initially clearing land and in situations involving draft animals for plowing or other purposes.

It is a leap from cross-cultural maxims, all of which have exceptions (Brightman 1996; Peacock 1991), to the archaeological elucidation of gender in the provisioning of past societies. Southwestern ethnography is an obvious starting point for framing questions to be asked of the archaeological record, although it offers multiple possibilities for any variable we choose to examine. Nevertheless, as the outcomes of the most relevant historical processes, practices of the postcontact era offer a counterbalance to universalistic and cross-cultural generalizations, and such analogs are referenced throughout this chapter.

PREAGRICULTURAL PATTERNS AND PROCESSES

Southwestern gender patterns pertaining to plant resources in Paleo-Indian through Middle Archaic economies are outside the scope of this chapter. Information is insufficient to enable a characterization of local or regional patterns. Reports of Paleo-Indian botanical remains and related equipment are generally lacking, in part because many excavated sites correspond to hunting localities and activities (Grayson 1988).

The central importance of vegetal foods appears to be of great antiquity in some parts of the Southwest, as is indicated by abundant grinding implements in sites of the post-Clovis Sulphur Springs stage of the Cochise tradition in southern Arizona (Sayles 1983). Among sites of similar age elsewhere, grinding tools typically are more occasional. The regular use of such implements by men in subsistence tasks is rare worldwide, and these tools are potential indicators of distinctive plant procurement and processing roles for women in economic orientations that are traditionally described as big game hunting. Ground stone increases through time and becomes more widely associated with Southwestern Middle Archaic assemblages after 4000 B.C. (Cordell 1997; Irwin-Williams 1973; Matson 1991a).

TRANSITION TO MEXICAN DOMESTICATES

Discoveries of Late Archaic occupations yielding corn (e.g., Mabry 1998; Matson 1991a; Wills and Huckell 1994) have progressed rapidly in recent years. The missing element for assessing the gender implications of the foraging to farming transition is the baseline of prior conditions. The emerging archaeological visibility of Late Archaic farmers contrasts with our inability to recognize and locate their immediate predecessors and thus to resolve competing assumptions about the economic configurations of the societies that first adopted the Mexican domesticates corn, beans, and squash.

At one end of a continuum of possible precursors to Late Archaic farmers are the routinely referenced bands of mobile hunters and gatherers, seasonally shifting locations in order to obtain sequentially available resources in an annual round (Binford 1980). At the other end are intensive gatherers and plant manipulators with extended residence and investments in land and resources (e.g., Arnold 1996; S. Fish and P. Fish 1991; Hayden 1981, 1990; Keeley 1995). Archaic societies resembling both extremes and many intermediate forms may have been present in the Southwest, but those already engaged in intensive manipulations could have incorporated domesticates most readily.

In the eastern United States, close examination of the precorn botanical record has established that this exotic cultigen was a late addition to a long tradition of cultivated indigenous species including marshelder, sunflower, chenopods, and native squash (Smith 1992). The few analyses of Southwestern botanical assemblages similarly predating corn have not as yet produced this sort of evidence for native plants, although indigenous cultigens such as agave and little barley are now widely reported for the subsequent ceramic period (Bohrer 1991; S. Fish and P. Fish 1994; Fish and Nabhan 1991; Gasser and Kwiatkowski 1991). Agave is an example of a prehispanic cultivated staple that had virtually disappeared from Southwestern farming by postcontact times (Fish, Fish, and Madsen, eds., 1992; Gasser and Kwiatkowski 1991). Corn may have replaced other, earlier indigenous Southwestern cultivars, much as it appears to have largely displaced native Eastern crops in some Mississippian and later farming societies.

Only a few Southwestern species may have been transformed into domesticates, but there are numerous ethnographic analogs for the intensive manipulation and cultivation of indigenous plants, particularly among foragers along the margins of the Southwest. A wide variety of practices designed to increase the productivity of plant resources can be cited, including irrigation and the collection and storage of seed (Bean and Saubel 1972; Castetter and Bell 1951; Downs 1966; Fowler 1986; Shipek 1989; Steward 1938). Such economies, which often also entail use rights and improvements to productive land, exhibit the attributes that would have best enabled a Late Archaic population to adopt new domesticates fully dependent on human intervention.

Gender Roles among Intensive Foragers

How were gender roles structured in the subsistence systems of Archaic foraging societies with immediate capabilities for incorporating the Mexican domesticates? Women's contributions to the acquisition and consumption of plant foods are usually central in the diets of ethnographically observed societies assumed to be similar to Archaic foragers. One archaeological measure of such centrality might be the prominence of grinding implements in overall assemblages. On the basis of detailed local distributions of prehispanic bedrock mortars in the western Sierra Nevada of California, T. L. Jackson (1991) suggested that women's food procurement and production activities were fundamental in structuring settlement systems and defining social and economic relations. He further interpreted the appearance of these pivotal features as a marker of innovation and change from preceding gathering patterns. Similarly detailed distributions of such facilities for Southwestern Archaic occupations prior to corn are unavailable. Nevertheless, informal manos and metates are conspicuous constituents and virtual diagnostics for Late Archaic sites.

The primacy of women in supplying plant foods and of men in actively pursuing at least the larger game is a regularly observed feature of hunting and gathering societies. The gathering and processing of plant foods, however, is only one aspect of gender roles with regard to vegetal resources. The rich ethnographic record of intensive manipulators and cultivators of indigenous plants at the fringes of the Southwest demonstrates more complicated economic behavior with respect to gender.

Whole families, rather than women alone, were often involved in initially obtaining critical resources, even though women may have been the primary processors. In Jackson's (1991:318–19) archaeological study of the bedrock mortars, he acknowledged two alternative analogs in opposite ethnographic patterns: the Northfork Mono practiced matrilocality (women used their mothers' mortars), and women claimed oaks and seed plots, whereas among the neighboring Miwok, a woman moved to her husband's group and used the bedrock facilities of that locale. Mono women may have claimed acorn granaries and their contents, but men apparently controlled the flow of products in extensive intergroup exchange (Jackson 1991:319–21).

Among the Cahuilla of southeastern California, ownership of oaks was associated with patrilineal groups, and the use of trees belonging to others was negotiated by men (Bean and Saubel 1972:131). Men climbed the trees to knock down acorns while women and children gathered them below. Men hunted in the vicinity of groves during the subsequent processing. In terms of closely associated material culture, men possessed long sticks for knocking down acorns and women owned portable or bedrock mortars, pestles, and related items for processing.

Mesquite beans stored in granaries permitted the Cahuilla a high degree of residential sedentism. The trees were pruned for improved yields and better access (Bean and Saubel 1972:107–17). Lineages controlled groves, and men defended the boundaries for gathering areas. Individual families within lineages owned particular trees. Because ownership was clear, women confidently left their prized mortars near the trees they harvested year after year. Archaeologically, the resulting distribution of mortars would map women's subsistence activities but would provide only a glimpse into the complicated relationships of both sexes to this important resource during the entire course of production and consumption.

Gender Roles in Crop Introduction and Development

Annual crops, and especially those that developed out of weedy progenitors, have been linked to a gendered origin. Patty Jo Watson and Mary C. Kennedy (1991) proposed women as the innovative agents in the domestication of weedy plants in the eastern United States because women would have been the principal creators of domestic soil disturbances and thereafter would have maintained the closest contact with the opportunistic species of residential environs. Gender-specific intensive manipulation stems from the assumption of a relatively limited radius of activity for women with children.

Ethnographic situations in western North America qualify this model. Among intensive plant manipulators historically, the economic activities of both sexes conformed spatially to locations of abundant fixed resources such as trees or to fixed requisites of cultivation such as water sources. In most locales, supplemental water was an additional mandatory ingredient for dense growth of weedy species. Among the Owens Valley Paiute, women tended plots of indigenous annual crops that men irrigated (Lawton et al. 1976; Steward 1938:53), whereas Yuman men along the Colorado River broadcast seed in panic grass plots that women later harvested (Castetter and Bell 1951; Gifford 1931). If similar joint plant tending were practiced by Late Archaic Southwesterners, either sex could have added exotic corn to the indigenous crop repertoire.

Given that either men or women might have been in a position to incorporate exotic crops into an existing system of plant management, the initial acquisition of seeds, cuttings, or other propagules represents a separate question. Men could be candidates in view of their roles as the foremost long-distance travelers and as influential participants in intergroup exchange. It seems equally plausible, however, that there was down-the-line transfer of seed from woman to woman, family to family, and village to village, necessitating only routine travel and trade.

Gendered interests might have spurred differential investment in newly available crops. Women might have valued corn, for example, for supplying an improved weaning food for babies (Braun 1987; Crown and Wills 1995a; Nerlove 1974). Guy Prentice (1986:104–6) attributed the appearance of gourds and gourdlike squash as the earliest domesticates in eastern North America to their use by male shamans as rattles. Tobacco might similarly be considered of male inception because of its ritual use and tending by men in various cultures of the western United States, although, like rattles, tobacco is not necessarily the exclusive province of men. These sorts of gender attributions for the introduction of new crops are not easily tested. It may not be possible to relate early crops to gender in the context of production, but sex-differentiated associations conceivably could be recognized in any period through botanical remains and artifactual correlates such as pipes in burials of known sex or in cave caches where possessions such as clothing or weapons might identify the user's gender.

In the Southeast, a largely ritual or social significance for early corn has been proposed because it appears to have constituted a minor element in botanical assemblages and in the diet for centuries after its appearance (e.g., Bender 1985; Hayden 1990; Prentice 1986). This kind of initial limited use is not apparent in the Late Archaic period of the Southwest. In most of the earliest archaeological contexts containing corn throughout the region, analyses that allow quantitative assessments show corn to be a major component of overall plant remains (e.g. Huckell 1998; Matson 1991b; Wills and Huckell 1994). Recovery patterns suggest that tropical cultigens soon became mainstays of widespread subsistence systems, and probably most often mainstays of those systems that involved relatively stable residence in conjunction with previous reliance on managed plants.

Historically, there are plausible regional analogs for Southwestern precorn economies with intensive plant manipulation, extended residence, and rights in productive land. Such models are consonant with current understandings of the processes leading to food production (e.g., Harris and Hillman 1989; Smith 1992) and, indeed, with cultivation as a precondition for domestication (e.g., Hillman and Davies 1990). According to Southwestern versions of appropriate analogs, men and women may control the same intensively managed plant resource in different stages of production and use, although worldwide women are the foremost processors (Kurz 1987; Murdock and Provost 1973). It is a minor transition from ditch irrigation of indigenous species, as was practiced in the postcontact Great Basin, to canal irrigation of corn, as is evidenced in the earliest farming in the Tucson Basin (Ezzo and Deaver 1996; Mabry 1998).

IMPLICATIONS OF EMERGING AGRICULTURAL DEPENDENCE

Jane Guyer (1988) employed the concept of the key task to analyze the organization of productive labor and the direction and impact of change. The key task is one that is unavoidable and obligatory and thus is the pivot around which other tasks revolve. The concept of the unavoidable and obligatory key task provides a perspective from which to view changes in gender roles following the adoption of Mexican cultivars. The tropical domesticates corn, beans, and squash are more dependent on human intervention than are the most heavily manipulated wild resources or indigenous cultivated plants. The prominence of domesticates in the plant remains of Late Archaic cultivators suggests that the repetitious and temporally prescribed tending of these crops had rapidly become a key task.

Reliance on corn strengthens the locational tie between primary resources and residences. Crop tending is time consuming and seasonally extended. The secure storage of agricultural seed for planting, in addition to the storage of harvests for sustenance, becomes critical. Many of the routine components of cultivation likely became key tasks for women, already responsible for the care of young children.

As crops became firmly established as the major share of diet, and particularly where that trend was coupled with larger family size, men's labor, too, would have been increasingly pulled into agricultural pursuits (Ember 1983). In the archaeological record, this process might be marked by decreasing proportions of large game among faunal remains as men's time for hunting forays diminished. However, agricultural labor adjustments would be concurrent with depletion of large game by sedentary and expanding populations and with the proliferation of small animals in culturally modified vegetation (see Szuter, this volume).

Changes in Gathered Resources

With commitment to agriculture, changes in women's gathering patterns might be reflected in a greater breadth of minor wild resources and successional species among archaeological plant remains. Mobile foragers tend to concentrate on momentarily abundant and easily processed resources. With greater sedentism, a fuller range of plants is often exploited, including those ignored in mobile seasonal rounds (e.g. Brown 1985; Hayden 1981; Johns 1990; Keeley 1995). New ecological niches created in agricultural landscapes further increase the potential diversity of gathered plants.

The languages of small-scale cultivators reflect the greater diversity of their interactions with plants compared with those of foragers. Small-scale cultivators consistently name wider arrays of plant species than do hunters and gatherers (Brown 1985). Women are typically the procurers of these more diverse resource plants in agrarian landscapes during the course of their more repetitive and homebound tasks (e.g. Messer 1978; Murdock and Provost 1973:212, 215; Rea 1997:200). In view of the early ubiquity of corn in currently well-studied assemblages (e.g., Huckell 1998; Matson 1991b; Wills 1988a), the transition to agriculturally modified settlement landscapes probably was well under way in Late Archaic times (see Crown's discussion of Southwestern dietary diversity and change, this volume).

Family and Household

The timing of the transition to corn-based farming, with its attendant gender implications, undoubtedly was quite variable across the Southwest. Complicating the picture, every household in the same settlement need not have followed the same economic strategy (for example, see Hard and Merrill 1992 for Tarahumara intravillage variability). In instances of mixed mobility and cropping within single settlements or settlement systems, however, households containing women with small children might often have been the ones that sustained residential and agricultural continuity. Once some households, settlements, or cultural groups became sufficiently committed to agriculture to maintain large and predictable seed supplies, their neighbors could have enjoyed greater flexibility so long as they could reinitiate cultivation by borrowing seed.

For a variety of reasons (summarized in Ember 1983), births of children tend to increase among small-scale agriculturalists relative to mobile foragers. In addition to biological reasons for higher birth rates, additional children offer significant economic advantages in agricultural labor. Several consequences might have affected women in such societies in the prehispanic Southwest. The familial and social value of elderly women might have increased in that they could be more effective child tenders under sedentary conditions, freeing younger women for farming tasks. At the same time, additional siblings undoubtedly added responsibilities to the childhood duties of older female children.

The efficiency of pooled child care with a closer spacing of births might have contributed to the frequency of coresident nuclear families in extended family groupings. The inclusion of upper- and lower-generation adult women or other "unattached" members offers additional advantages in child care duties. But the benefits to enlarged households in terms of female responsibilities were not necessarily the primary rationale for enlarged residential groups; extended households also provide labor for cooperative agricultural tasks.

PATTERNS IN AGRICULTURAL PRODUCTION

The spatial arrangements of gathering and farming have implications for sexual divisions of labor, although gender attribution is particularly difficult in such nonresidential archaeological settings. Differences between men's and women's productive activities at a distance from home may have been responsible for some spatial partitioning along gender lines. Gathering sites at increasing radii from residences might exhibit gender distinctions. Relatively numerous and diverse ground stone items and cooking pots might be markers for sites at which extractive activities regularly included women, assuming that unaccompanied men would tend to cook more simply. These same markers could also denote extended stays and regularized visits as opposed to brief stops; activities distant from home that included women with young children might necessarily entail overnight stays.

Some of the same distance considerations apply to fields nearer and farther from residences. Because they represent a greater investment in travel time, in addition to agricultural labor per se, distant fields are likely to coincide with the need to intensify production. Fields at increased distances also might reflect environmental diversification as a counter to localized risk or the need to utilize limited and dispersed sources of agricultural water. As in special activity sites, participation by men and women that covaried with field distance might be indicated by artifactual markers.

In addition to cultural norms, the spatial configuration of residential settlement is a potential factor in the participation of the sexes in gathering and farming. In aggregated settlements, labor pools would have been available for joint activities performed exclusively by men or women. These efforts might have been wide-ranging for male task groups but perhaps more restricted in radius for women with children—for example, local gathering or hoeing in nearby fields. For women, same-sex task groups would have been convenient for pooling child care as well as for working; alternatively, children might have remained with nonparticipating women in the village.

Dispersed settlement, on the other hand, would have tended to limit the immediate pool of male and female laborers and maternal helpers. Particularly in settlements with no more than a few households, the membership of day-to-day task groups would necessarily have been flexible. To the extent that same-sex task groups offered men and women support and networks outside the boundaries of household and kin, these benefits would have been fewer in small settlements or in seasonally dispersed occupations such as those at field houses.

Gender divisions of agricultural labor along single dimensions are apt to be misleading. Differential participation probably is inherent in a cycle of field use. For instance, men often play a primary role in the initial clearing of large vegetation, and there may be seasonal rhythms to subsequent gender-specific labor. The rarity of Southwestern representational art in most media inhibits one method of identifying prehispanic gender tendencies with respect to agriculture (but see Hays-Gilpin, this volume). Painted Mimbres bowls with naturalistic life scenes are a promising exception. However, in a study of the sexual division of labor encompassing 500 Mimbres human figures, the authors' single observation related to agriculture was the portrayal of several men with possible farming tools adjacent to a field (Shaffer, Gardner, and Powell 1999:115). Even if gender patterns could be derived from a more exhaustive inventory of farming scenes, any broad projection of Mimbres practices would be speculative, considering the diverse expressions documented in Southwestern ethnography.

The organization of the agricultural landscape might offer other clues to gender roles. Archaeological indicators include field boundary or ownership markers, field shrines, field extent and layout, fieldside processing or storage facilities, special activity loci, and field houses. Distributions of such features should pattern with organizational principles such as individualized or communal activities and tenure. Locations of repetitive activities should be particularly conducive to gender attribution by virtue of yielding sufficient numbers of artifacts to identify recurring categories clearly; permanent facilities such as roasting pits might provide analytical opportunities of this sort. The diversity of cooking assemblages and the amount of wear on ground stone in these contexts might be correlated with the degree or duration of female participation.

Field Houses

As indicators of more than passing occupations near fields, field houses concentrate gendered activities connected with cultivation. Patterns of land use, plot sizes and yields, and aspects of tenure may have correlates in the spacing and distribution of field houses (e.g., M. A. Adler, ed., 1996; P. Fish and S. Fish 1984; Kohler 1992a; Preucell 1988). Variation in the arrangement and content of such isolated structures is well documented (e.g., Ward 1978). Agricultural activity loci at field houses might be sufficiently distinct from those of ordinary domestic functions to reveal specialized and gender-specific agricultural tasks such as the initial processing of crops.

To the extent that storage features are associated with fields and field house locations, they may represent independent nuclear family or individual household control over stores, at least during the primary stages of production. Ethnographically, residence in field houses is frequently cited as a mechanism by which nuclear families escape the pressures and strictures of extended households and kin groups during the agricultural season. Relative isolation would have provided opportunities for both sexes to express individual motivations and preferences and to adjust socially prescribed gender roles. At the same time, unequal power relationships between males and females of a household might have been readily expressed in the absence of outside observation and intervention.

Field houses are more common in the Puebloan Southwest than among southern peoples in postcontact times. Maximum dispersal of such structures and physical segregation of their occupants could be expected in those restricted upland sectors where precipitation was adequate for rain-fed farming without supplemental water. Even in upland zones, however, prehispanic field houses often occur in the hinterlands of larger settlements. In many northern areas and in most of the southern Southwest, field houses are apt to be spatially clustered in conjunction with limited sources of agricultural water. Canals or other shared water delivery systems also linked groups of these structures. Proximity and systematic interaction in such cases might have permitted the formation of same-sex task groups similar to those of more aggregated settlements.

Women's Gardens

House gardens or kitchen gardens near habitation areas are facilities for agricultural production with recurrent ethnographic ties to women, including women's special rights to the produce. These gardens are small but often subject to intensive tending. In some ethnographic cases, such as Hopi and Zuni, gardens were irrigated (e.g., Page 1940) or involved hand watering from walk-in wells (Bohrer 1960; Stevenson 1904). The heavy investment of labor in these plots was commensurate with the appreciable time women spent in residential environs and with pauses between other domestic tasks.

Intensively cultivated gardens of postcontact times are commonly located within residential precincts or border roomblocks (Maxwell and Anschuetz 1992:41). Men may help to build and maintain the structural components of gardens, but women are the usual cultivators. Among groups of the southern Southwest, including adjacent Mexico, house gardens are located within immediate household space or in the most favorable locations nearby. Prehispanic gardens may be demarcated by rock borders or may occupy more elaborate structures such as terraces and grids that have greater archaeological visibility (Doolittle 1992). During excavations, which are typically focused on residential architecture in Southwestern archaeology, rock alignments or other constructions related to gardening are seldom encountered, but they could be sought through systematic extramural exploration.

Gardens do not provide the bulk supplies in household subsistence. They are apt to provide off-season or specialty items that demand individualized or repetitive care such as intensive weeding and watering. The diversity of plants grown in gardens is a source of dietary variety and nutrients underrepresented in starchy staples. Thus, a garden's nutritional and culinary contribution and its benefits to women tenders may overshadow its relatively modest yield.

In the prehispanic Southwest, kitchen gardens also might have been locations for innovation and experiments with novel cultivars and crop varieties. Female owners could have planted new crops and conveniently observed their progress. Indian gardeners of northwestern Mexico often transplant native species furnishing desirable products. Agave and cacti, for example, are regular constituents of such gardens (Pennington 1963, 1969, 1980), suggesting one mode of gendered origin for indigenous cultivars. Transplanting near residences offers a means to counteract the depletion of favored wild plants near long-term or heavily populated settlements. As probable women's domains, house gardens also hold potential for production and accumulation for personal negotiations and benefits, thus providing sources of independently enhanced standing for their cultivators.

Labor Exchange

Among Southwestern groups historically, the labor of men and women in the social unit that controlled an agricultural plot and its produce was often supplemented by the labor of external kin and neighbors (e.g. Underhill 1939; Pennington 1963). This supplemental and often season- or task-focused labor could be carried out by persons in variable combinations of age and sex, from a few hours for a few individuals to days or weeks for whole families in temporary residence, as in the case of the Tohono O'odham (Papago) who helped Pima irrigators (Russell 1975; Underhill 1939). Among the Tohono O'odham, inviting relatives to assist with the harvest and repaying them in kind was considered a favor. The wife's and the husband's relatives were invited in alternating years (Underhill 1939:104), giving both sexes an occasion for expressing generosity.

In Southwestern cases where payment was not made simply through reciprocal labor or with a part of the harvest, women of the host household often provided food for the duration of work. In addition to the immediate feeding of workers, reciprocal obligations could include gifts of agricultural stores or processed products. In each of these cases, an initial investment of time and effort by women was an integral part of obtaining extra labor. To the extent that their cooperation was critical and they contributed stores under their control, the position of women could be enhanced both within their own households and among the external participants.

Work parties could entail quite formalized patterns of hospitality and obligations, as they did among the Tarahumara. For them, labor exchange mandated the serving of *tesguino*, a fermented beverage, and thus a carefully scheduled advance effort by women to assemble supplies and prepare needed quantities (Kennedy 1963; Merrill 1978). Material correlates of Tarahumara agricultural work parties were the specialized vessels for preparing large amounts of tesguino. Similar obligations for obtaining external agricultural labor in the past might be archaeologically expressed in kinds and quantities of implements and utensils needed to feed numbers greater than the immediate household. Southwestern archaeologists usually look for distinctive distributions of items for processing, preparing, and serving only in the context of feasting as a ritual, integrative, or political activity. Evidence of disproportionate facilities, artifacts, and food residues might also be sought in association with field houses or small settlements adjacent to fields.

GENDER AND LAND TENURE AMONG SOUTHWESTERN AGRICULTURALISTS

Systems of tenure or use rights to farm land, residence after marriage, and patterns of inheritance are important variables in the gender relations of agricultural societies. In the postcontact Southwest, practices regarding these matters contrasted between the western Pueblos and the peoples of the south. The more formally articulated institutions and rules based in unilineal kinship were Puebloan, whereas groups to the south exhibited bilateral tendencies and more flexible, situational solutions. Eastern Pueblo customs included some instances of access to land through clan affiliation, as in the matrilineal system of Jemez (Sando 1979), but also followed a variety of alternative patterns.

Puebloan Land Tenure

Strongly matrilineal and matrilocal societies, exemplified by Hopi and Zuni, offer advantages to women because rights to clan land are bestowed on the basis of kinship through the female line (e.g. Kennard 1979; Ladd 1979a; Smith and Roberts 1954). In combination with matrilineal inheritance, fields were associated with particular households centered around women and their female offspring (Kennard

1979). In the case of divorce, women were not separated from their subsistence base, although they may have lost spousal labor. Continuity in claims to the means of production is a secure position from which to negotiate future marital partnerships. Clan ownership of the prime arable land was signaled by stone boundary markers and rock art with clan symbols (e.g., Cushing 1920). With the possible exception of late prehistoric or protohistoric markers on land recognized as ancestral by postcontact pueblos, however, archaeological boundary markers cannot be attributed with certainty to similar matrilineal systems.

Separate, if not economically equal, male rights to land could be established at both Hopi and Zuni (Cushing 1920; Kennard 1979:555). This was done by clearing and preparing new fields at a distance from the village, beyond the boundaries of clan holdings. Further, these plots could be inherited outside clan rules by heirs designated by the male owner, including his own sons. Archaeological fields isolated from contemporaneous habitation sites and identified by agricultural features, markers, or field houses might indicate agricultural land of this sort. Because villages were likely to have been initially settled near the best available land, more entrepreneurial male ownership might be anticipated in the development of marginal areas.

There is no comprehensive and well-recorded patrilineal system of kinship, tenure, and inheritance in the Southwestern ethnographic record comparable to the matrilineal systems of Hopi and Zuni, although there are rules prescribing inheritance by males alone. At San Juan Pueblo, for example, these rules passed land along male family lines for many generations. Patrilineal and patrilocal ideals were simply a tendency there, however, for women owned and inherited property almost as often as men (Ortiz 1979:290). Similar rules were expressed among some non-Puebloan peoples of the northern Southwest. The Havasupai allowed widows and daughters to retain use rights to land but not to inherit it unless there were no male relatives (Weber and Seaman 1985:125). In situations of solely male inheritance, the connection of women to productive fields could be severed by circumstances such as divorce. Patrilocal residence also meant that women entered households built around the kinship ties of their husbands, in which they were outsiders.

Some of the pueblos detached unilineal reckoning of kinship

from land tenure. Although there were matrilineal clans at Laguna, fields could be inherited through the mother or the father and transferred to other owners within the pueblo (Ellis 1979a:444). Kinship was essentially bilateral at Taos (Bodine 1979:261) and Isleta (Ellis 1979b:356). However, only males could inherit farmland at the latter. These examples demonstrate the variability among historic Puebloans in matters of gendered access to arable land. Accordingly, considerable caution is in order in projecting any given gender-linked system to archaeological cases.

Stringent unilineal rules of inheritance may reflect the circumscription of arable land through its inherent scarcity or high population demands. Population growth and in-migration are conditions under which such rules could provide a solution to the need to delineate ownership rigorously and to maintain workable plots of sufficient size over succeeding generations. Any archaeological evidence for the prominence of unilineal social structure heightens the likelihood that access to land was subsumed by associated rules. The distinction between matrilineal and patrilineal systems, with differing gender implications, is a further and more difficult inference.

Among Puebloans, another means of access to land and produce was formerly through the rights of high officeholders to fields and to communal labor for their cultivation. At Hopi, for example, fields were assigned to leaders of ceremonial societies (Kennard 1979:54). The eastern pueblos gave such rights to leaders of sodalities, who often had the added power to demand communal duties and to revoke the use rights of those who did not comply (Jorgensen 1983:696). Ostensibly, officeholders received the harvests of designated fields not as personal wealth but as resources to offset the time demands of their attention to institutional affairs, to supply needs for communal hospitality and welfare, or to fulfill obligations of the special events they directed. Nevertheless, the benefits of the ability to control and disburse communal resources accrued differentially to these men.

Land Tenure in the Southern Southwest

In the postcontact southern Southwest and adjacent portions of northern Mexico, unilineal kinship was less in evidence as a primary principle in social structure and access to land. With the exception of the Yumans, among whom males had exclusive rights to land (Castetter and Bell 1951), bilateral reckoning and inheritance by both sexes were the usual ideals among the various groups of Piman speakers and their neighbors to the south. Sons and daughters should share equally in land as well as in other possessions.

Tendencies toward patrilocal residence in groups such as the Tohono O'odham (Bahr 1983:181–82; Underhill 1939) and the Lower Pima (Dunnigan 1983:224) resulted in more frequent inheritance of land by the sons who were already farming it. Nevertheless, the rights of daughters had to be acknowledged through other forms of compensation. Among the Tarahumara and Tepehuan (Bennett and Zingg 1935:189–92), newly married couples worked land that might be claimed through any available tie, often piecing together plots in several locations. Throughout the southern Southwest, women as well as men had expectations, if not always fully equal ones, and recognized bases for negotiating use and future rights in productive land.

WARFARE AND AGRICULTURE

Warfare has broad implications for the gender structure of food production. Not only does it deflect male energies from agriculture, but also it may create special needs in war party provisioning and the concealment of subsistence supplies. It heightens the risk of geographically dispersed and distant activities, especially for women and children. Gathering of plant resources at any distance would be inhibited without accompaniment by male defenders. Male energies would be further siphoned away from agriculture by the need to maintain vigilance during day-to-day cultivation.

Where endemic conflict affected the spatial arrangement and extent of routine subsistence activities, it could have acted as a force toward agricultural intensification within a reduced but easily defended perimeter. Diminished evidence for residence and especially for the presence of women and children in detached fields might in fact be one indicator of endemic conflict. During the historic period, constant threats by mounted and highly mobile raiders such as Apaches undoubtedly heightened the prominence of males in ethnographic cultivation. An additional postcontact factor probably was the adoption of draft animals and plows by the time of many ethnographic accounts, practices cross-culturally associated with males. Observer bias in dealing primarily with male informants also may have been involved.

AGRICULTURAL INTENSIFICATION

Cross-cultural scholars have observed that male roles in agricultural production become more prominent with intensification (Boserup 1970; Martin and Voorhies 1975; Sanday 1973). To some extent, these correlations devolve on increased use of the plow and animals, issues irrelevant to the prehispanic Southwest. Carol Ember (1983) proposed that women's contributions do not decrease in an absolute sense as a result of intensification, but rather that men's roles increase disproportionately. She further suggested that limits are placed on increases in women's agricultural labor by simultaneously increased demands for domestic labor, particularly in more extended processing of foodstuffs (see Crown, this volume). These demands are typically coupled with a greater investment of time in child rearing as numbers of offspring rise.

Biological factors may promote greater fertility among intensive cultivators, but the creation of future household laborers for intensive practices is also perceived as advantageous in most situations (Ember 1983). In this sense, decisions for maximum participation by women in agriculture might satisfy short-term goals but hinder the long-term benefits of rearing additional children, a conflict in the demands of women's two key tasks. For the same reasons that larger families become desirable with intensification, extended households become increasingly useful for pooling child care and securing the participation of any unattached adolescents or adults. The benefits of additional laborers in the prehispanic Southwest would have been tempered, however, by the degree to which intensified production was able to absorb and support them without boosting population to levels that exacerbated environmental risk.

Cultivation of Marginal Land

Intensification took multiple forms in the ancient Southwest, and these arid-land versions do not necessarily conform to Boserup's (1965) classic definition of shortened fallow in an agricultural system. One strategy for increasing overall production was to bring marginal land into cultivation. Especially in the later centuries before contact in the Southwest, large tracts of land at varying distances from residential settlements were made productive by the construction of terraces, check dams, rock piles, mulches, grids, and other features (S. Fish and P. Fish 1984; Toll, ed., 1995; Woosley 1980). These sorts of fields utilized tertiary drainages or depended solely on direct rainfall or surface runoff. Usually more distant from habitations than better-watered fields, plantings on marginal land might have been somewhat less amenable to tending by women with small children. The presence of camps and field houses would identify extended stays at such fields.

In the case of Hohokam rock-pile fields, large pits for roasting agave mark one kind of associated activity locus that could be carefully examined for gendered evidence (Fish, Fish, and Madsen, eds., 1992). Specific roles for men and women are encountered among postcontact practices related to the acquisition and processing of gathered agave (e.g., Castetter, Bell, and Grove 1938). The regular spacing of huge communal roasting facilities in extensive Hohokam fields suggests that well-defined groups of cultivators cooperated in roasting harvests year after year. Evidence of this sort for the organization of agricultural labor and for fieldside processing of crops, residence, and domestic cooking might also be present in other agricultural situations.

Gender Roles in Irrigation

Irrigation is another version of intensive Southwestern cultivation. Among the Hohokam in particular, irrigation had become a dominant agricultural technique by the early part of the ceramic era. A simultaneous contraction and aggregation of settlements during the late prehispanic period throughout the region resulted in geographically concentrated settlement configurations encompassing the most favorable locales for gravity irrigation (S. Fish and P. Fish 1994:100–102).

In the largest irrigation systems, intervillage networks undoubtedly created an arena for male more than female leadership. Because the control of water and the coordination of communal labor had to be negotiated among multiple social units and settlements, men probably assumed the prominent public roles in allocation, construction, and maintenance. Among the Pima and Tohono O'odham, organizers of canal affairs were men, and men acquired the initial rights to irrigated land for their households as a result of their participation in canal construction (Castetter and Bell 1942; Russell 1975:88–89; Underhill 1939). Like all other communal efforts, irrigation involves a need for supporting labor and provisioning. Through their ties to male leaders or through their own organizational skills, women in prehispanic times might have had opportunities to play influential roles in these undertakings.

Robert Netting (1993) noted a strong worldwide tendency toward household control, as opposed to corporate or clan control, over agricultural land in which farmers have invested heavily in improvements. The investment criterion fits irrigated land, and this sort of tenure prevailed in the postcontact southern Southwest and among various eastern pueblos where irrigation was also practiced. In turn, independent rights in land may provide a basis for differential household accumulation and, ultimately, for unequal access to the means for agricultural production. Depending on rules of inheritance, individuals of both sexes in prehispanic irrigation societies might have had opportunities to negotiate economic advantages, with increased social standing as a possible result. If rights in land were vested primarily in males, then the women of successful households should have profited secondarily.

Agricultural Specialization

Yet another pathway to agricultural intensification is through productive specialization. Although attention is often directed toward craft manufacture as an economic alternative, specialization can also be achieved through distinctive emphases in farming and gathering. The previously discussed expansion of cropping on marginal land could be viewed in this way, as could investment in specialty produce in women's kitchen gardens through labor-intensive techniques such as pot irrigation. Larger-scale specialization in crops—for example, producing appreciable agave and less corn and other annual crops—maximizes productivity by focusing on the cultigens most suited to available land, labor, and demand rather than on generalized production for all household needs.

Specialization in agricultural labor itself is a further strategy that was exemplified in the last few centuries by the Tohono O'odham, who lacked access to perennial rivers and worked seasonally in the irrigated fields of the Pima (Castetter and Bell 1942; Russell 1975). Such arrangements are most probable where labor rather than land or water is the limiting factor in production, or at least where additional labor has the potential to increase yields. In the case of the Pima and Tohono O'odham, labor involved whole families rather than individual women or men.

The gendered structure of craft production may in turn foster specialization in the gathering or growing of raw materials. Men and women may take differential roles in acquiring plant resources for their manufactures. Working backward from probable male and female craft items, evidence of correspondingly differentiated acquisition or production could be sought. Some ethnographically gendered craft items such as baskets, however, are rare in the archaeological record. A further significant complication is the possibility that both men and women contributed raw materials or ancillary efforts to an item that was ultimately manufactured by persons of only one sex (see Mills, this volume).

The use of medicinal and ritual plants is structured by gender in many Southwestern societies. Ethnographically, practitioners include both sexes, although older women rather than younger ones tend to hold such roles. The association of spiked jimson weed effigy pots with Hohokam platform mounds (P. Fish et al. 1993) is an archaeological example of probable male roles in mound observances; ritual use of jimson weed is predominantly associated with men in the Southwestern ethnographic record.

THE PUBLIC SPHERE

Among Southwestern cultures, public events frequently involved amassing and distributing subsistence resources. The magnitude of food and other goods was often substantial (e.g., Ford 1972a). Recently, Southwestern archaeologists have begun to focus attention on ceramic distributions and other indications for large-scale food preparation and feasting, particularly in the context of centralized events.

Public events in the past would have affected farming and gathering if their staging involved alterations of normal subsistence production. The requisite stores might have been supplied in part by communal donations or from dedicated sources such as the communally worked fields of leaders in the eastern pueblos. It is likely that prominent leaders, largely men and heads of economically successful households (whether matrilineally or patrilineally organized), also would have been expected to contribute heavily. The production of both sexes in affiliated units would have been affected by these obligations. Disproportionate facilities and equipment for food storage, processing, and preparation in households at sites with public architecture might be related to the requirements of such events.

Women in the households of male leaders or the female kin of leaders in separate households might have had parallel roles in marshaling extra production, accumulating stores, organizing women's labor, and directing the logistical support for public events. Large households and even polygyny would have been advantageous for male leaders with socially ordained and repetitive public obligations. As a consequence of their critical logistical functions, perhaps codified in formal roles, attached women also might have gained recognition. Likewise, in their own right or as supporters of their prominent male kin, female heads of prominent matrilineal households might have had opportunities to invest agricultural resources toward social gains.

As institutions crosscutting other social divisions, prehispanic sodalities might have offered alternative opportunities for individuals or households to invest their productive efforts toward social goals. By contributing resources to the public activities of these organizations, members might have achieved standing at least partially outside the framework of kinship and other predetermined structures. Sodality participation is commonly prescribed along sex and age lines, and Southwestern examples include membership for both men and women. Sodalities may even be exclusively for women, as in a Tewa instance (Ortiz 1969). Currently there are few archaeological indications of sodality membership (but see Whittlesey 1978) and as yet no recognition of resources linked to such institutions.

GENDERED RESOURCES AND GENDER HIERARCHIES

It is difficult to approach gender hierarchies solely from the standpoint of subsistence production. The production of resources is less relevant to hierarchical relationships than is their consumption. From the ethnographic record of both Southwestern foragers and agriculturalists, control over resources may be transferred from one sex to the other more than once in a progression from acquisition to final disposition. The purview of this chapter is directed primarily toward the acquisition or production of plant resources, whereas hierarchical relationships are usually determined and most clearly expressed outside this topically delimited realm rather than within it.

In Southwestern ethnography, men are most often described as controlling agricultural land and crops growing in fields, with the exception of matrilineally acquired rights to land among the western Pueblos. Women are commonly described as controlling harvested and stored resources, and women often influence the distribution of prepared food, issues also addressed in other chapters. Despite these mid-level roles for women in the disposition of subsistence products, the higher-order structure of gender relationships is related to power over resource investment and ultimate distribution. Such power in postcontact times was usually reserved for heads of households, kin groups, villages, or more inclusive sociopolitical units, roles largely assigned to men, with the exception of domestic leadership in matrilineal societies.

Gender hierarchies in subsistence production, along with the hierarchical positions of men and women as a whole, cannot be decoupled from a society's pervasive social institutions. In any Southwestern society of the past, evidence for strong principles of unilineal kinship presages similarly vested rights in land and corporate strictures on autonomous subsistence-based accumulation by households and individuals. At the same time, hierarchical ranking of kin units might itself have provided the rationale and access to productive advantages.

Rights to land detached from comprehensive systems of unilineal affiliation most likely developed in prehispanic situations of intensive production and heavy investment in agricultural improvements. Such conditions represent sources of societal inequality and hierarchy that are not isomorphic with kinship. In societies where these conditions prevailed, situational advantages, including the inherent productivity of land or the ability to deploy agricultural labor, might have been manipulated to accrue social benefits and status for the heads of households or other socioeconomic units and their male and female members.

Although societal expectations regarding interpersonal behavior undoubtedly affected hierarchical gender relations in the precontact Southwest, direct archaeological investigation of this level of economic interaction is seldom possible. The organization and positioning of households or other basic economic units is a more archaeologically accessible determinant of the relationships of members with regard to subsistence pursuits. Gender relations reflecting higher-order control over resource production must be understood in the context of the principles and rationales underlying the hierarchical structure in a society as a whole.

RELEVANT VARIABLES AND ARCHAEOLOGICAL RELEVANCE

Bridging the gap between variables relevant to gender in foraging and farming and their archaeological manifestations is a daunting challenge. Gendered artifactual signatures represent an especially weak link in the research arsenal. Two examples from the thirteenth to fourteenth centuries in southern Arizona illustrate contrasting spatial organization of agriculture with differing gender implications. Both involve well-studied agricultural locales near relatively populous regional centers surrounded by outlying settlements.

The first instance is a compact irrigation system occupying 10.8 hectares of prime arable land in a triangle formed by the juncture of Beaver Creek and a secondary drainage in the Verde Valley (P. Fish and S. Fish 1984). The cultivators appear to have been the inhabitants of Sacred Mountain, a Sinagua center on a prominent hill 3 kilometers distant. Gridded fields supplied by runoff are situated at the base of this hill. In the Beaver Creek fields, the wall outlines of 25 rudimentary field houses are spaced along the main canal branches. Elaborate cobble grids and alignments were constructed to further conserve and control water in planting allotments delimited by upright elongated stones as boundary markers.

Labor-intensive cultivation at a distance from the home base and estimated corn yields per field house sufficient for five persons annually were inducements for fieldside residence at Beaver Creek during the growing season. The small size of field houses suggests that nuclear families camped and cultivated individually, probably storing their harvests separately before eventually transporting them back to Sacred Mountain. Women and men might have welcomed these circumstances liberated from sustained close contact with extended families in the roomblocks of the permanent village. Nevertheless, shared canals necessitated cooperation and coordination among field-house families; the proximity of structures also would have permitted pooled child care and same-sex task groups. Household involvement in irrigated labor and its produce at Beaver Creek might have contrasted with women's gardens in the gridded areas a short walk down the hill from the central settlement.

Farther south in the Tucson Basin, a series of large fields for the specialized cultivation of drought-adapted agave occupies almost 500 hectares of dry slopes at a maximum distance of 2 kilometers uphill from a Hohokam center containing a platform mound (Fish, Fish, and Madsen, eds., 1992). Corn was grown elsewhere in floodwater fields of limited magnitude in the immediate Marana Mound site environs. Women's gardens are not ethnographically associated with floodwater fields, and the gathering and roasting of agave in postcontact times usually involved both men and women. The agaves were planted on slopes in the moisture-enhanced microhabitats of cobble features that acted as mulches. Maturing over a decade, these desert succulents, which supply both food and fiber, require less maintenance than annual crops; the absence of field houses correlates with round trips during the day from the mound site to fields for nonintensive tending.

Rare instances of boundary stones bearing rock art suggest individual plots within extensive arrays, but it is the huge roasting pits for communal agave processing that reveal the overarching organization of fields and farmers. Relatively standardized ratios of field area per pit indicate a customary amount of land cultivated by the group using each roasting facility. Initial control of agave harvests by individual nuclear families would have been inhibited by immediate transport and storage in the mound site's compounds, which enclosed up to four or five multiroom households. These walled architectural units provided a secure situation for pooled child care, and such arrangements might have sometimes allowed women's task groups as well as mixed parties in the agave fields. It is also likely, however, that compound coresidence focused labor sharing among the conjoined households rather than toward external linkages (Crown and Fish 1996:812). Easily expanded investment in marginal land might have allowed leaders and ambitious households to better negotiate status through increased production of prized sweet foods or fermented beverages. Both sexes probably benefited from entrepreneurial opportunities in agave fiber crafts.

Given the difficulties of discerning the gender structure of foraging and farming solely from the archaeological record of primary contexts, the most compelling reconstructions are likely to emerge through inclusive syntheses of direct and indirect evidence. Innovative, fine-grained studies discriminating gender in productive behavior must be combined with more encompassing considerations of the layout of foraging and farming landscapes, the spatial relationships of production to habitation, and evidence for gender relations in other societal realms. The most insightful future reconstructions will also be firmly based in studies that transcend the technology of foraging and farming and approach these subsistence settings as the scenes of recurrent and socially structured interactions.

6

Gender and Animals

Hunting Technology, Ritual, and Subsistence

Christine R. Szuter

Archaeologists have implicitly if not explicitly discussed the roles of men, women, and children in prehistory. They have assigned some specific activities, such as hunting large game, and some particular classes of material, such as projectile points, to the male domain and others, such as ceramic containers or gathering small seeds, to the female domain. In addition, they have treated gender as involving two mutually exclusive categories, male and female, between which the lines are sharply drawn. The basis for making these assumptions often goes unstated, and criteria for evaluating the assumptions are not developed.

Margaret Conkey and Janet Spector (1984:21) have discussed gender as "a system of social rather than biological classification that varies cross-culturally and changes over time in response to a constellation of conditions and factors that are as yet poorly understood.... Most of the questions about culture process raised by contemporary archaeologists have a gender component or dimension: site functions, site use, subsistence systems that are, of course, based on task-differentiation; inter- and intrasite spatial phenomena; settlement systems; the power and role of material culture; mechanisms of integration and cultural solidarity; extradomestic trade and exchange systems, and above all, the course of culture change."

Gender theory, therefore, is about social relationships. It is about the relationship between women and men and the changing and dynamic roles of women and men in society. From an archaeological perspective it is about making a finer examination of prehistory that zeroes in on the impact of "changing adaptive systems," "changing subsistence systems," or "changing social stratification." Gender theory asks, What does the change mean in terms of relationships between men and women?

In this chapter I discuss the dynamic relationship between gender and animals throughout Southwestern prehistory by focusing on how animals were a part of everyday life and how the changing relationships between people and animals had a profound impact on gender hierarchies and the sexual division of labor. I examine changes in the hunting of wild animals and the tending of both wild and domestic ones through an examination of the archaeological and ethnographic record, with a focus on technology, ritual, and diet and nutrition.

THE MEANING OF HUNTING

Archaeologists have glossed endeavors such as hunting and gathering, along with items of material culture such as lithics and pottery, as male and female, respectively. I argue that if the archaeological record is to become "engendered," then archaeologists need to acknowledge that a gloss such as "hunting" or "gathering" hides a multitude of activities that cannot be simply labeled masculine or feminine. The contribution of both sexes to any activity can be better understood when we analyze all that is involved in hunting an animal or gathering a plant. The assignment of categories of artifacts to the female or male domain is equally damaging without a full consideration of the conditions under which women and men might have manufactured, used, and discarded those items.

The anthropological literature once featured abundant references to "man the hunter," a phrase that left women out completely. The complementary phrase "woman the gatherer" emphasized the primal importance that gathered foods played in the diet, along with an acknowledgment that women contributed the substantial portion of the food eaten. "Woman the gatherer" acknowledged the role of women in subsistence activities, but it did not provide a complete definition of women's roles in subsistence endeavors. Although hunting and gathering are often assumed to be synonymous with men's work and women's work, respectively, they are not sex-specific activities. Hunting, particularly of small animals, is often done by all members of a society, including women, men, and children. Although sex and age are key components in who hunts what animals in a society, older males have no exclusive rights over hunting activities. The manner in which females and children contribute animal products to the diet, to ceremonies, and to the manufacture of items such as bone tools or clothing is substantial.

When archaeologists, through implication or assumption, restrict the definition of "hunting" to the killing of large game alone, they immediately bias what is examined in the archaeological record and relegate hunting to the male domain. Hunting is not merely the pursuit and killing of large animals; it involves more than merely a group of men heading out to kill an animal; and it is not restricted to the use of a bow and arrow in active pursuit of a large animal. "Hunting" glosses all of the activities that take place before, during, and after the hunt that make the kill possible.

Depending on the size of the animal hunted, projectile points, spear shafts, and bows must be made, snares and traps built, nets woven, and pits dug. These tasks require quarrying lithics, gathering plants, tending birds (for arrow feathers), and looking for sign before the hunt begins. The actual hunt requires looking for sign, coordinating the hunters, driving the animals, killing, eviscerating, and skinning the animals, and carrying the game home. Once the hunters are home, the hide must be processed, the butchering completed (if it was not done in the field), the meat cooked or dried, the bones processed for marrow, grease, and tools, and the meat shared and eaten. Many of these activities can be accomplished while people are gathering plants, collecting firewood, visiting neighbors, or even playing.

If hunting is examined in its full complexity, then a wider range of activities that involve all members of a society can be examined. Such an examination can contribute to an understanding of the development of a sexual division of labor and gender hierarchies. Hunting is both active and passive, because a wide variety of techniques can be used to kill animals. Our focus should not be solely on the methods used, nor on the size of the animal captured, nor on who is doing the hunting. Rather, we need to focus on all of the activities carried out in the capture of wild animals and on how those animals are used in diverse contexts within a society: for food, clothing, tools, or ceremony.

TECHNOLOGY AND SMALL GAME HUNTING

Differences in hunting technology, as observed in the ethnographic record worldwide, are determined by the sizes of the animals hunted. There is a sharp distinction between the hunting of small animals (less than 40 kg) and the hunting of large animals (greater than 40 kg) (Ellis 1997; Szuter 1991a). Small animals of the Southwest that were hunted for food included birds, rodents, lagomorphs, reptiles, amphibians, and fish. The major large mammals hunted were artiodactyls such as deer, antelope, and bighorn sheep.

The hunting of small animals involved a simple, expedient technology that probably was not restricted to people with special knowledge or access. Information about the hunting technology used for small game would have been available to all members of a group, regardless of sex or age. Snares and traps, direct capture from burrows through flooding or probing, and the use of stones or bows and arrows were means used to kill small animals (Szuter 1991a:16, table 2.1). Although the manufacture of stone arrow points would have required more specialized knowledge, Christopher Ellis (1997) has argued that ethnographically, stone arrow points were not used to hunt small game. Instead, organic materials such as wood, reed, and bamboo were the materials of choice for tipping arrows used in killing small animals.

In addition to requiring only an expedient technology, small game hunting was known ethnographically to have been an unspecialized activity (Underhill 1936:49). Magic, ceremony, and ritual generally were not associated with small game hunting. Rather, it often accompanied other subsistence activities such as gathering wild plants, collecting firewood, or tending fields.

Hunting small game in prehispanic times, therefore, probably involved a simple technology, was embedded within other activities, and was unspecialized. There were no restrictions on who could hunt small animals; therefore, women and small children as well as older boys and men brought them home. As Southwestern groups came to depend more upon maize agriculture, and as large game near settlements became depleted, small game became a steady, constant source of meat in the diet, a contribution made by men, women, and children. The power and prestige associated with large game hunting might have become more concentrated in the hands of specialists, thus contributing to the development of hierarchies among and within genders.

Although jackrabbits (*Lepus* sp.) are small animals, they were likely pursued communally rather than through individual hunts. Communal hunting as it is known from the ethnographic record required a different technology from that of individual hunting, including the use of nets, rabbit sticks, clubs, and brush fences. Ceremony and ritual were often associated with communal hunting. Plants had to be gathered to make the nets and brush fences, rabbit sticks had to be shaped, and the hunt had to be planned and coordinated. Whereas an individual could hunt small game at will, communal hunting demanded greater cooperation between the two sexes and people of all ages. Among the Ituri of Africa (Bailey and Aunger 1989) women are known for their net hunting; in contrast, men hunt with a bow and arrow. Communal hunting among foragers worldwide is often a seasonal activity related to the maximum fat levels and the dense aggregation of animals (Driver 1990). Among agriculturalists, seasonality may be even more important in determining not only when people hunt but also who actually hunts. In addition—returning to the prehispanic Southwest—communal hunting of jackrabbits might have become more common as settlement size, and therefore population, increased (Anyon and LeBlanc 1984; Szuter 1991a). The inhabitants of village sites, as opposed to smaller hamlets, would have had a greater impact on the environment through land clearing, wood gathering, and house construction. The sort of cleared habitat preferred by jackrabbits because it enables them to escape their predators would have developed, thereby increasing their populations. The larger population of the villages, including women, men, and children, would have provided the necessary labor pool for communal jackrabbit hunts.

The technology associated with small game hunting, such as the use of nets, snares, and traps, is generally a perishable and ephemeral one, so other means of assessing the significance of small game hunting in the past must be devised. Joan Gero (1991) discussed the possibility that lithic tools and debitage were not necessarily confined to the male domain. She argued that women might have used an expedient technology that has been overwhelmingly ignored by archaeologists, who tend to focus on formal tool categories. An expedient technology in the form of flakes and debitage might have been extremely useful in skinning and eviscerating small game. Although formal stone tools, specifically projectile points, might not have been used to kill the animal, sharp flakes could have been used to butcher it.

Frank Bayham (1976) interpreted isolated lithic scatters in the Hohokam region as butchering sites for rabbits. The small quantities of lithic flakes, their isolated locations away from settlements, and the flake angles and use patterns suggested expedient small game processing. The manufacturing of such "tools" requires relatively little time and effort. They could have been made by females, males, and children at a moment's notice and left where last used.

Brian Shaffer and Karen Gardner's (1995) examination of Mimbres pottery designs focused on portrayals of human and animal interactions. Several pots show the hunting of small game, although care must be taken when interpreting painted images and other art. The drawings on Mimbres pottery are not necessarily recordings of daily activities (see Hays-Gilpin, this volume) but might provide some general insights into what types of activities, symbolism, and items were important to record.

One scene reproduced by Shaffer and Gardner (1995) depicts humans engaged in a communal jackrabbit drive using nets, rabbit sticks, and crooks. The humans are not identifiable as female or male on the basis of sexual characteristics. In two different scenes in which the human is identifiable as male, the hunter is carrying a turkey along with a bow and arrows in one, and in the other he is setting snares for birds. A painting of four humans (two identifiable as male on the basis of sexual characteristics) catching a large fish shows communal fishing.

The depiction of crooks in many Mimbres paintings warrants mention because both females and males hold them. Shaffer and Gardner (1995) discussed previous scholars' descriptions of these poles as hunting probes used to dislodge, poke, and pry animals from burrows. A male gathering firewood in one painting is carrying a probe, which may indicate the co-occurrence of hunting and foraging. The crook is carried by women when they are carrying game or tending macaws (I discuss these images later). The pole, however, might be a multipurpose tool used in agriculture or hunting or even for support and protection while walking. An analysis of the Mimbres crook and its use by females and males might provide greater insight into the hunting of small game.

Like the technology used to hunt small game, the processing and eating of it is relatively uncomplicated. With the exception of game taken by communal hunting and widely shared, meat was probably shared within a small group or was consumed individually. Small game might have been spitted over an open fire, but if it were stewed in a cooking pot, then smaller amounts of meat might have been distributed more equitably among a larger group of people (Crown and Wills 1995a). Yohe, Newman, and Schneider (1991) identified small-mammal blood protein residue on milling equipment recovered from two California sites. Milling equipment is known ethnographically in the Southwest to have been used to pulverize rats and mice. Because women are associated with grinding stone technologies archaeologically (Schlanger 1994; see Hegmon, Ortman, and Mobley-Tanaka, this volume), their role in food preparation probably involved more than grinding only corn. Yohe, Newman, and Schneider have offered an empirically supported perspective that milling equipment was used for grinding animal as well as plant material and that rodents were eaten. Their research expands our views on how women might have been involved in animal processing and provisioning meat to their families. This type of processing, along with the technology of cooking pots, would have extended the small package of meat to a wider group of people (see Crown, this volume; Crown and Wills 1995a).

TECHNOLOGY AND LARGE GAME HUNTING

The hunting of large game in the prehispanic Southwest and among ethnographically documented groups contrasts with the pursuit of small game because a wider variety of hunting technologies and ceremonies was used in it (Szuter 1991a:16, table 2.1). A hunter could passively kill a deer by setting up traps, snares, or pitfalls or by waiting for deer to pass by on a trail or come to a water hole. More active means of capture, often by hunters wearing headdresses made from artiodactyl skulls and skins, included chasing or stalking the animal, conducting deer drives, and using a bow and arrow.

Historically, hunting parties were generally small and restricted to older males, although young boys sometimes accompanied hunts as apprentices (McGee 1898:196; Spier 1928:109; Underhill 1939:77, 91, 1946:86, 87). Large game hunting, therefore, may have been a restricted activity in Southwestern agricultural societies in earlier times, excluding some males as part of a larger order of task differentiation.

Large game hunting is also known ethnographically to have been accompanied by elaborate ceremonies, rituals, and magic in the form of songs, dances, purification, and taboos before the hunt (Densmore 1929:210; Laski 1958:20; Spier 1928:290, 1933:69; Stevenson 1904:439; Whitman 1940:402). The ritual component of large game hunting will be discussed later, but it required a great deal of preparation. In actuality, few members of a prehispanic society might have participated in the kill of large game, and they would have been men. Yet many other participants might have been involved in making traps, snares, pitfalls, and nets or in looking for sign, carrying game, or preparing for the accompanying hunting ceremonies—all activities that needed to be accomplished for a successful hunt.

Although a broader definition and understanding of hunting allows for a fuller discussion of the role of women in procuring meat, it does not attribute to women the power and prestige associated with killing large prey, whether human or animal. Although women in some societies provide more food, do more work, expend more energy, and overall produce more than men, they do not regularly kill large game and they do not engage in warfare.

Barbara Miller (1993), however, has urged caution in claiming the exclusion of women from hunting and warfare. "While it is generally true that men hunt and women do not, and that men fight in wars and women do not, important counter cases exist" (Miller 1993:5; see Harris 1993). These counterexamples are valuable in understanding how changes in large game hunting affected the sexual division of labor and gender hierarchies.

The Agta of the Philippines (Estioko-Griffin and Griffin 1981; Goodman et al. 1985; Peterson 1978) are often singled out because Agta women hunt large game with bows and arrows. Hunting patterns vary among the different Agta groups, however. Among the Dipagsanghang and Dianggu-Malibu Agta, both men and women hunt. Close to Palanan and Casiguran, only males hunt. In Isabela, most Agta women do not hunt, but they do help male hunters by carrying game out of the forest and guiding dogs in game drives. When women do hunt, the techniques chosen are dependent upon their skills, not upon their sex. Some women prefer some techniques over others, but generally traps are used by the less able male and female hunters, and bows and arrows by the skilled ones. Women will make their own arrows but not do the actual blacksmithing.

Agta women hunt during their reproductive years, carrying their children during the hunt (Goodman et al. 1985). Older women claim to have learned hunting skills during their unmarried teen years, but they hunt only when food supplies diminish. Most hunts are day hunts and do not require long-distance travel, which might have been necessary in the Southwest as large game became depleted around settlements. Katherine Spielmann (this volume) argues, however, that women might have been involved in traveling greater distances than previously thought. In addition, hunting among the Agta decreased as the demands of cultivation increased, a situation that might have been paralleled among Southwestern groups for whom specialization increased through time. Finally, hunting by Agta women may have been a recent phenomenon resulting from colonialism.

Although there are such counterexamples, the question of why women rarely hunt large game remains unanswered. Robert Brightman (1996) considered this question through a review of previous explanations that focused on women's strength, menstruation, pregnancy, and role as primary child-care providers. He offered an alternative perspective by examining access to the technology used to hunt large game. Women overwhelmingly have limited access to large game hunting technology. When they do have access to it, it is a restricted technology, such as nets or dogs used for tracking.

The restriction may relate to the reasons men hunt large game. Provisioning one's family is often thought of as the primary reason, but sharing meat throughout the community may provide a stronger incentive because of the prestige and power it brings to the hunter. Kristen Hawkes (1991) discussed meat sharing as a way to show off in a community—but showing off is an undesirable trait among many groups. Sharing, however, may be extremely valuable as a means of cementing relationships and alliances within and among families.

In the Southwestern United States, stone projectile points and bows and arrows are the most direct archaeological evidence of large game hunting. On the basis of worldwide ethnographic data, Ellis (1997) argued that stone projectile points were used exclusively for hunting large game and killing humans in warfare. Their presence in the archaeological record indicates hunting, warfare, or associated ritual use. He examined 79 societies that used stone tips and found that in 96 percent of them, stone-tipped projectile points were used almost exclusively to kill large game such as deer, elk, caribou, moose, and bison, and not small game. Small game did not require the expenditure of energy that the manufacture of a stone point entailed. The small game could be more easily hunted with simpler equipment such as slings, traps, and throwing sticks or with points made from organic materials.

Ellis argued, however, that stone projectile points were more lethal than most organic-tipped ones and therefore were more effective in the hunting of large game. When arrows are used to hunt small game, the ethnographic record indicates that their tips are made of organic materials. These materials provide a wider blunt striking area that increases the striking surface, making it easier to stun and capture a small animal. Organic-tipped points do not tear or damage the skin, and they are less likely to penetrate the animal completely (allowing it to escape).

The implications of the association of stone projectile points with the hunting of large game (and with warfare) bear on questions relating to the sexual division of labor and the development of gender hierarchies associated with hunting. What is the patterning of stone projectile points at a site, and does that patterning change through time? What is the significance of the association of projectile points with human burials? Do we find that projectile points in burials decrease through time, indicating a decrease in the significance and importance of large game hunting? Do men lose power with a decrease in large game hunting, or does the power become concentrated in the hands of a few hunters? What replaces the loss of male power and prestige? Is there greater equality between men and women in agricultural societies where crop production is key? I do not have the answers to all of these questions but can offer a few insights from the Southwestern archaeological record that show the relationship between projectile points and male and female burials (also see Neitzel, this volume).

The image on a Mimbres pot of male large-game hunters with bows and arrows stalking a deer is a typical representation of "man the hunter" (Shaffer, Gardner, and Powell 1996). Complementing this image in the Southwest is the association of projectile points with male human burials and rarely with female ones (Crown and Fish 1996; McGuire 1992; Palkovich 1980:159–64). At Arroyo Hondo Pueblo in northern New Mexico (A.D. 1300–1425), 120 burials were excavated, and 27 females and 18 males were identified. Four arrow points and an obsidian point, respectively, accompanied two male burials; these were the only points found with any burials at the site (Palkovich 1980:159–64). Randall McGuire's analysis of Hohokam burials also found a strong association between male burials and projectile points. He suggested that distribution of projectile points with burials might have been part of the mourning ritual (Teague 1984:157) and that the points might have been made intentionally for burial use (Haury 1976:297).

There are some examples, however, of females being buried with projectile points, including burials at Las Colinas, Casas Grandes, San Xavier, and Chaco Canyon. At Las Colinas, a female and an infant were buried together, and a projectile point accompanied them. It was not possible to tell whether the point was associated with the female or the infant. All other projectile points recovered from burials at Las Colinas were found with male burials (Saul 1988). At Casas Grandes (Ravesloot 1988), one female mid-adult, 36–50 years old, was buried with a projectile point. At the San Xavier Bridge site, an adolescent female was reported buried with a projectile point that was anomalous when compared with those found in male burials (Ravesloot 1987). The point was made of basalt, was crudely manufactured, and was longer and wider than the projectile points found with male burials. The sexing of an adolescent is extremely problematical, however, and therefore this association is questionable.

Nancy Akins (1986) reported that at a Chaco Canyon site, 29J627, a female 22–29 years old was buried with 10 well-made projectile points. At Pueblo Bonito, projectile points were associated with graves that contained males, females, and children. At Talus Unit, a female 29 years or older had two projectile points buried with her. With these few exceptions, Southwestern burials with projectile points are all of males.

These exceptions, however, may prove key to understanding gender hierarchies and the sexual division of labor, because they contrast with the normative statement that projectile points are exclusively associated with males. Nevertheless, projectile points were rarely buried with females, suggesting a strong sexual division of labor in the realm of killing game or in the ritual expression of killing prey. Bows and arrow shafts have been recovered from several Ancestral Pueblo sites, including Pueblo Bonito (Judd 1954). They are assumed to have been male tools, although the sizes of a few (at Pueblo Bonito) indicate that they were children's bows. Neil Judd (1954:250–51) referred to them as boy's bows because of his ethnographic observation that boys were given bows and arrows at a very young age.

Although evidence for large game hunting by women in the American Southwest is weak, women's participation as "hidden producers" (Mills 1995b) in large game hunting might have been added to the demands placed on them by agriculture, food preparation, and pottery manufacture. Recognizing the fluidity of the multitude of tasks that compose any larger activity, such as making a pot or hunting an animal, acknowledges the broad spectrum of women and men who were involved in those tasks.

For example, although arrows might have been shot by males, the feathers on them might have come from birds tended by women. A Mimbres pot shows a woman, her belly distended, probably pregnant, with a crook in her hand, carrying an antelope after the kill (Shaffer, Gardner, and Powell 1996). Is this a depiction of a woman as a "hidden producer" carrying game for male hunters, or is she a woman hunter carrying game that she killed? If the former, then does "producing" in this manner (carrying game) confer the same power and prestige as actually killing the animal? Kelley Hays-Gilpin (this volume) argues that women and game animals are often depicted together in iconography and stories. The relationship between women and large animals, however, may be one of "mother of game animals" rather than "woman as hunter."

RITUAL AND LARGE GAME HUNTING

Animals in the Southwestern archaeological record are not only the result of hunting but are often also associated with ritual activity. George Gumerman IV (1996) has advocated research that extends beyond an interest in nutrition in order to "understand the dynamic social and symbolic nature of southwestern foodways."

David Whiteley's (1994) study of the Numic people, hunter-gatherers of the Great Basin, demonstrated the social and symbolic nature of animals and subsistence. He examined the social ramifications and changing gender relations in Numic society when the subsistence base changed from broad-based hunting and gathering to intense seed gathering. During the period of intense seed gathering, rock engravings depicting the hunting of big-horn sheep became plentiful. Whiteley sought to understand the "paradox [of] 'hunting art' produced by a seed gathering culture" (1994:361). Multiple lines of evidence from art (rock engravings), ethnographic literature, subsistence data, settlement patterns, and chronology led him to an elegant argument that engendered the archaeological record. His critical point was that if a society undergoes a major change in its subsistence base, then it also experiences a major change in social relations between men and women. This point is pertinent to the Southwest, where the change was from a broad-based and diverse pattern of hunting and gathering to a more focused agricultural system.

"Subsistence change is not simply a mechanical or even evolutionary alteration in diet.... A subsistence system is, after all, a conceptual entity, only indirectly expressed in the archaeological record, that is based on cultural perceptions of food preference, sexual divisions of labor, decisions about scheduling, selections between competing resources, social organization, and so on" (Whiteley 1994:370). Whiteley not only documented a major subsistence change from broad-based hunting and gathering to intense seed gathering but also asked what that change meant for social relations between men and women in Numic society.

An examination of the ethnographic and archaeological record of the Southwest indicates that large game animals were more than a meat source. Ritual was important not only during the hunt but also when the animals' bones were thrown out (Szuter 1991a). Most Southwestern hunters, including Mimbreños, Apaches, Zunis, Hopis, Yavapais, Havasupais, and Navajos, wore antelope, deer, or mountain sheep headdresses as disguises when they stalked large game (Spier 1928:120). Deer or antelope heads were brought to the village, where they were prepared by removing the skin, stuffing it with grass, drying it, and then fitting it to the hunter's head (Castetter and Underhill 1935:40–41). Antlers, or tree branches resembling them, were attached. In addition to wearing the headdress, the hunter would apply paint to his body or wear a skin so that he would resemble the animal he stalked.

Ceremony in the form of rituals, charms, and magic often accompanied the deer hunt. The Tohono O'odham smoked a mixture of flowers and tobacco and sang hunting songs in order to attract game (Densmore 1929:210). During the winter, young Tewa men and a special priest were responsible for arranging a deer dance (Laski 1958:20). Tewa hunters also washed and purified themselves four days before a hunt, besides remaining sexually abstinent and avoiding menstruating women (Whitman 1940:402). Zunis used owls' wings and Havasupais used the deer calculus (Spier 1928:290), a hard substance found in the stomach of a deer (Iliff 1954:196), as charms for hunting large game (Stevenson 1904:439). O'odham men were not allowed to hunt if they had an unborn child. If an O'odham hunter's own young children saw a dying deer or merely observed certain parts of deer meat, the hunter would begin to move like and imitate the sounds of a dying deer (Densmore 1929:210). These observations indicate the power of the kill and the ways in which women and children could affect and be affected by men hunting large game.

Like hunting itself, the disposal of artiodactyl bones had ritual significance, and they were not merely tossed onto a trash heap. The O'odham placed the horns of mountain sheep near waterholes (Castetter and Bell 1942:67) and put the bones out of the reach of dogs (Underhill 1946:86). Likewise, the Tewa people treated deer bones with care by returning them to the forest (Whitman 1940:401).

Seventeenth- and eighteenth-century Spanish explorers reported that along the Gila River they saw huge middens of deer antlers and mountain sheep horns that numbered over 100,000 (Castetter and Bell 1942:67; Castetter and Underhill 1935:41). The ritual, ceremony, and respect that accompanied the hunting of artiodactyls also accompanied the manner in which their remains were treated. The ethnographic documentation of the ritual aspects of artiodactyl hunting is mirrored in the archaeological record.

Artiodactyl remains have been recovered archaeologically throughout the Southwest. At Hohokam sites, however, they account for only 15 percent of the identified faunal remains, compared with 67 percent for lagomorphs (Szuter 1991a). Although three-quarters of Hohokam sites have some artiodactyl remains, the majority of them have very few. They include primarily cranial elements—antlers, horn cores, mandibles, skulls, and teeth—followed by lower limb elements—metapodials, tarsals, carpals, and phalanges that have been burned. High meat-bearing skeletal elements are not commonly recovered from archaeological deposits.

Whereas lower limb elements would have provided marrow as well as sources for bone tools, the skulls, antlers, and horns might have been used for headdresses worn to attract animals during a hunt. The brains might have been used to tan hides. The ethnographic record certainly indicates special treatment of cranial elements, and their abundance in archaeological sites may be associated with their use in headdresses (Di Peso 1956).

At Hohokam sites, burned artiodactyl cranial elements have been found on the floors of some large pithouses. Several common characteristics were observed in the pithouses and deposits that contained these remains. The artiodactyl remains were overwhelmingly antler racks or horn cores, skull fragments with attached antlers or horn cores, mandibles, or teeth. Only at Muchas Casas was this pattern different; there, an abundance of artiodactyl pelves was recovered (James 1987). These represented big horn sheep, mule deer, and pronghorn, all in the upper size range for these species. The artiodactyl remains were found in large pithouses with quite distinctive floor assemblages and indicated special treatment of these remains. Whole pots, *Glycymeris* shell bracelets, turquoise pendants, bone awls, manos, stone beads, and pestles have all been recovered from these contexts. The presence of artiodactyl cranial elements, often burned, on the floors of large houses that have either abundant or unusual artifacts indicates special treatment of these body parts.

In an earlier publication (Szuter 1991a), I discussed nearly a dozen Hohokam sites that exhibited these special contexts in which artiodactyl remains were concentrated in one feature, generally on a pithouse floor or in fill. Julian Hayden (1957:101) reported not only an abundance of pronghorn, bighorn sheep, and deer skulls and antler racks or horn cores but also cranial elements of elk in the fill of D4:Room 2 at University Indian Ruin in Tucson. The presence of elk, however, was a field observation unverified by further analysis, and only one other specimen comparable to elk has been identified in the Hohokam region (at Big Ditch by Johnson [n.d.]). The association of multiple species of artiodactyls within one pithouse is a common feature of these special contexts.

At Las Casitas (AZ U:15:27), John Sparling (1974) observed adult and fetal artiodactyl mandibles on the floor of room 7 that were associated with scraping tools. The mandibles had wear and striations that resulted from their having been used as tools, according to Sparling. The room in which they were found was large (7.3 x 6.3 m) (Doyel 1974:68, fig. 14) and had been destroyed during a catastrophic fire, so that the floor assemblage was left intact. Several reconstructible Casa Grande Red-on-buff vessels, a plain-ware scoop, and a Gila Red Ware jar were on the floor. The room was unique because of the presence of a wall niche near the southwest corner containing a Casa Grande Red-on-buff olla, a large cardium shell, and a small rectangular pumice stone (Doyel 1974:67). Although Sparling interpreted the "special-context" mandibles as tools, other "special-context" artiodactyl remains have not been interpreted that way. The notable floor assemblage and the large size of the structure at Las Casitas, however, are characteristics of these types of deposits observed elsewhere.

The Muchas Casas finds were recovered from a large pithouse with a stepped entryway (Hackbarth 1987:152–55); it was inferred to have functioned as a dwelling. The floor assemblage included a spindle whorl, three broken pots, and a stone bead. The artiodactyl remains represented an abundant minimum number of elements (MNE) of horn cores, antlers, and skulls as well as pelves (James 1987:186, table 8.7). The MNE was calculated as "the total number of right and left pelves which were refit" (James 1987:185). None of the other Hohokam sites appears to match the quantity of refitted elements, although quantification at the sites is variable. Nine bighorn and 36 deer pelves were recovered from pithouse 496 at Muchas Casas. At least one bighorn sheep skull lay between the two broken pots on the floor. In this same area, other large mammal bones were recovered from the fill.

At the Waterworld and Fastimes sites in Avra Valley, Arizona, William Gillespie (1988) reported large numbers of artiodactyl mandibles on the floors of several pithouses and in a pit in a cremation area. The bones from the pit were different from the pithouse remains in being highly fragmented (less than 4 cm in length) and burned white or gray. Gillespie (1988) also measured the antler racks and bighorn sheep horn cores and found them to be from very large adults. Their spans often exceeded those of the largest recorded archaeological and modern specimens in the area. As in the aforementioned sites, deer, pronghorn, and bighorn were represented.

Although a few of these structures with associated remains date to the Hohokam pre-Classic, the majority date to the Classic period. The presence of artiodactyl cranial elements, often burned, on the floors of large houses that have either abundant or unusual artifacts indicates special treatment of these body parts related to large game hunting. The increase in ritual activity associated with large game hunting during the Classic period might reflect a greater need to ensure a successful hunt. As large game resources were depleted through intensive local hunting, greater specialization in hunting might have occurred (Bayham 1982; Speth and Scott 1989; Szuter and Bayham 1989). Scheduling of an increased number of activities associated with hunting, gathering, and agricultural pursuits might have led to the specialized hunting of large game. Smaller, more specialized, and probably all-male hunting parties would have traveled farther afield in order to capture large animals. Although a greater differentiation of tasks among males and between males and females might have developed, the overall community might have been more involved in the ritual activities accompanying and associated with the hunt, such as the construction of the larger Hohokam pithouses that contained the artiodactyl remains and the production of accompanying artifacts such as pottery, shell bracelets, bone awls, and turquoise pendants. Males might have been critical in the use of these houses, judging from the association of artiodactyl cranial elements and the headdresses used by males in hunting large game. This association, nevertheless, does not preclude women, who might have prepared or orchestrated the ritual performed for large game hunting.

RITUAL AND THE TENDING OF ANIMALS

Other animals in the precontact Southwest, including macaws, turkeys, dogs, and snakes, were tended rather than hunted. Behavior with regard to them differed from that of hunting small and large game, because their primary purpose was rarely for food. Ethnographically, these animals have been more often used for companionship or assistance in hunting (dogs), for feathers used in prayer sticks, arrows, or rituals (macaws, turkeys, hawks, and other birds), or for ceremonies (snakes). All of these animals could have been eaten, but their low numbers, their lack of butchering marks, and their burial (except for snakes) argues that they did not contribute a large portion of meat to the diet.

The presence of dogs extends throughout the precontact record, whereas macaws were present during later times. Snakes and wild birds such as eagles and hawks are present throughout the archaeological sequence, but they may have been used only during select times. This discussion of ritual and animal tending examines who tended the animals, where the animals were buried, and where the bird pens and cages were located.

Because dogs are scavengers, it is unlikely that they needed as much care as macaws, which were taken from their natural habitat and placed in pens and cages. Formal burials of dogs, turkeys, and macaws occur throughout the Southwest, indicating that they were accorded a kind of attention not associated with other animals.

Direct evidence of animal tending is found on Mimbres pots (Shaffer, Gardner, and Powell 1996), where one scene shows a male and a female holding crooks and macaws. At the base of the painting are a bow and arrows and another bird. Shaffer, Gardner, and Powell (1996) stated that females more commonly handled parrots and macaws in paintings on Mimbres pots, even though this one example includes a male figure. Bird handling may be viewed as falling in the same realm as child care—that is, as an activity associated with the domestic sphere.

The Southwestern archaeological record displays numerous examples of females and males being buried with macaws and other birds. An elderly woman at Freeman Ranch was buried with a fledgling macaw, suggesting the association of women with macaw tending. Other macaw and human burials occur at Cameron Village, Pecos Pueblo, Jackson Homestead (a child burial), and Tuzigoot Pueblo, but the sex of the human burials is not given (Hargrave 1970). At Casas Grandes, a male (mid-adult, 36–50 years old) was buried with two military and five scarlet macaws. A young female adult (age 18–35) was buried with two common turkeys and two scarlet macaws. Other cases in which humans were buried with birds at Casas Grandes include those of a juvenile, age 7–8, with three lilac crowned parrots, and a male, age 36–50, buried with a turkey (Ravesloot 1988).

Macaws were associated with ceremony and ritual, and their feathers were plucked for different occasions. Although macaws were sometimes buried with human males and females, they were often buried separately in kivas, in rooms adjacent to kivas, or in rooms that contained a wide variety of ritual paraphernalia, as at Grasshopper, Galaz Ruin (3 burials in kiva 73), Pueblo Bonito, and Arroyo Hondo (Hargrave 1970; Lang and Harris 1984). Pueblo Bonito (Pepper 1920) had 13 macaw burials in room 38, a ceremonial room that might have been a Macaw clan room. The room also contained an inlaid bone scraper, a frog of jet inlaid with turquoise, a sandstone metate and 25 manos, stone pipes, and 4 piñon jay skeletons. Several ceremonial sticks were recovered that appear to have had feathers attached to them.

At Arroyo Hondo, two scarlet macaw burials were recovered from plaza G. One of them, dating from the late 1320s, had a chip of turquoise with it, and the other, dated to the early 1330s, was located east of the ventilator tunnel of kiva 12-14-6 (Lang and Harris 1984:115). Kivas have been discussed as male space, although women might have been allowed access to them during certain times. A division of labor in handling macaws might have been practiced, with women caring for the birds and men performing rituals with them.

At Arroyo Hondo, the remains of domestic turkeys (including dung and eggshells) and their pens were also found in plazas. The macaws from room 38 at Pueblo Bonito (Pepper 1920:194) might have been kept in cages or on perches, judging from the presence of bird droppings that extended the width of the room and measured 10 inches deep. Casas Grandes had puddled adobe nesting boxes, eggshells, and 234 macaws below plaza 3 (Ravesloot 1988). The tending of macaws and turkeys could have been done by the community rather than solely by females, males, or children.

The association of dogs with males, females, or children is not easily discerned. Dogs might have served as companions to all members of society, although the ethnographic record does not suggest that dogs were fed, cared for, and groomed as pets. They fed themselves by scavenging and thereby served to clean an area that otherwise would have needed care. Agta women who hunted often cared for and trained dogs for their hunting forays (Estioko-Griffin and Griffin 1981). Dogs might have accompanied Southwestern hunters, too, but their use in this way has not been clearly documented either archaeologically or ethnographically. A Mimbres pot (Shaffer and Gardner 1995) shows a male carrying wood with a dog trailing behind. A further examination of Mimbres pots might reveal additional scenes with dogs.

A large number of dogs at San Xavier were buried in the cremation burial area, but no association of dogs with specific burials could be made. Limited evidence that dogs were eaten comes from butchering marks on a dog limb from the Santa Rita mountains (Glass 1984). Overall, the involvement of females, males, and children in the care, feeding, and tending of dogs is unclear.

Shaffer, Nicholson, and Gardner (1995) described three depictions of snake handling and ceremonies on Mimbres pottery. The snakes are wrapped around the humans, one of whom is an identifiable male. Snake ceremony paraphernalia such as temporary storage facilities for the snakes would not have been preserved. These Mimbres vessels, therefore, provide a glimpse into snake ritual that would otherwise be unknown except for inference from the ethnographic record.

DIET AND NUTRITION AND ACCESS TO MEAT

Debra Martin (this volume) examines the health status of precontact Southwestern populations and shows that the quality of health—particularly women's health—decreased through time. Health status is a result of many factors, including nutrition, exercise, labor, and social relationships. Although meat consumption is often considered critical for adequate protein intake, meat is probably more important for its fat content, iron, and other minerals (Speth and Spielmann 1983). Humans do not need large quantities of protein, though they do need small quantities of it consistently. Meat, however, has value beyond its nutritional composition, and the selective sharing and distribution of meat throughout a community can reflect power and prestige relationships. Meat consumption, meat sharing, and changes in hunting patterns reflect gender and social hierarchies.

Joseph Ezzo's (1992) analysis of 230 adult burials from Grasshopper Pueblo shows a change through time in dietary differences between males and females. Although the techniques Ezzo used have been criticized, an examination of his results leads to some interesting questions regarding dietary differences between males and females. Males initially (A.D. 1275–1325) had greater access to meat and to cultigens, whereas females ate more wild plants. Later (A.D. 1325–1400), male and female diets looked the same; cultivated crops formed the core of the diet, and meat and wild plant foods decreased. Ezzo correlated the decrease in meat with a decrease in status differences between males and females. Anthropogenic modifications to the environment, such as wood clearing that reduced deer herds, along with a growing human population and depletion of deer through hunting, caused economic stress that led to a breakdown of status differences. Ezzo argued, in essence, that with greater economic uncertainty, there was greater equality and less status differentiation as determined by dietary differences and by the distribution of grave goods between females and males.

Patricia Crown and W. H. Wills (1995a:180) argued that the introduction of cooking pots in the Southwest might have ensured a more equitable distribution of meat and overall nutrition through the preparation of stews in clay pots. They also noted that John Speth (1990) had earlier indicated that meat sharing among foragers would be inequitable because men would control who received highly valued cuts of meat.

The archaeological record does show that resource depletion occurred through time in the prehispanic Southwest and at particular locales at any time (Anyon and LeBlanc 1984; Bayham 1982; Shaffer and Schick 1995; Szuter 1991a). Large game hunting decreased as settlements increased in size, agriculture became established, and anthropogenic changes decreased habitat. This change may have meant that more women and children engaged in small game hunting to make up for the loss of large game in the diet, thereby "equalizing" the diet for most, but not all, men and women.

The question, therefore, becomes, Was there a lessening of gender hierarchies and the sexual division of labor in the prehispanic Southwest with economic stress? Was that equality the result of shared misery? Was equality more likely with greater economic stress and a decrease in large game hunting? Although nutritional levels might have become more equitable through time, the reason might have been that females' consumption of meat remained constant while men's consumption of meat decreased. The decline in large game through time might have led to more equitable relationships between men and women but to less equitable relationships between males who hunted and those who did not.

John Speth and Susan Scott (1989:72), however, documented examples showing that inhabitants of Southwestern horticultural sites sometimes increased their reliance on large mammals as their communities became "larger, less mobile, and more heavily dependent on cultivated crops." Large game hunting at these sites, including Snaketown, some Salt-Gila Aqueduct sites, Point of Pines, Grasshopper, Arroyo Hondo, and Chaco Canyon, may have become more specialized in the hands of males who formed small hunting parties to travel farther afield in search of larger game. Coupled with this pattern is the selective distribution of large game at Hohokam platform mound sites, where larger quantities of artiodactyl remains are associated with the higher-status mound areas of the sites. Such differences might also have created greater status differentiation between males who hunted and those who did not, and between females associated with male hunters and those associated with males who were not hunters. Crown and Fish (1996) argued that some women occupying domestic spaces and buried on the tops of platform mounds had higher status than both men and women living in the compounds. This higher status for women might have given them access to the meat of large game that was denied to men and women living in the compounds.

CONCLUDING THOUGHTS

In the 1980s I did fieldwork on the social dimensions of the butchering of domestic animals in Cucurpe, a small ranching and farming pueblo in Sonora, Mexico. I observed that certain tasks were relegated to males and others to females. I asked both men and women, Who butchers the animals? They responded that men did so. But when I examined the butchering of animals, I found that not only men but also women and children were involved. Men did indeed kill the animal by sticking it, and they then removed its hide and quartered it, but women defleshed the bones, prepared the meat, cleaned out the stomach, cracked the bones, prepared the food, and ultimately served the meal. In terms of time and energy expenditure, women put in seven hours of work compared to one hour for the men.

In another circumstance, I observed women's knowledge of men's butchering activities after an all-night wedding celebration. The celebration included all the festivities and formality of the event. Swirling dresses, *norteño* dancing, a three-tiered wedding cake, a *barbacoa* (pit barbecue), and, for the men (and only the men, Cucurpe being a pueblo with a rigid sexual division of labor), plenty of beer and *lechuguilla* (moonshine mescal). The celebration went on throughout the next day. By noon, the men were still drinking. The women had gotten some rest during the night, but everyone was hungry. We traveled to a nearby ranch where someone had a goat that was soon to become our lunch. As the men awkwardly hung the goat up by its hind legs and pulled out their pen knives (the butchering tool of choice in Cucurpe) to stick its throat, the women began to make huge, paper-thin tortillas to accompany the meal. But the men were clumsy, and it quickly became apparent that they were unable to complete their butchering job. Without a word, a friend of mine, Angelita Montijo, walked up to the goat, pushed the men aside, and then reached into the pocket of her jeans and pulled out her own pen knife. She deftly skinned, eviscerated, and quartered the goat. Within a short time we were eating untainted, roasted goat meat. Angelita had the knowledge, the skill, and her own tools for butchering the animal, all hidden until circumstances demanded their display. Cucurpe women know how to kill domestic animals but are generally restricted from doing so unless the men are absent or unable to perform, in this case because of excessive consumption of alcohol.

These examples from a modern ethnographic context suggest that women may overwhelmingly do one task in a society and men another, but knowledge of those activities is fluid, as are the activities themselves. Access to knowledge may not be limited, but demonstration or exercise of that knowledge may be restricted. The behavior is fluid and dependent on circumstances (even in this case, where there was a strong division of labor between the sexes), and a multiplicity of tasks is glossed when terms such as "butchering" or "hunting" or "gathering" are used. These tasks are not single actions, and there are many ways to hunt an animal or gather a plant or sow a seed.

In the precontact Southwest, relationships between humans and animals changed through time. During the Archaic period, a wide variety of wild plants was gathered and animal resources hunted. Throughout the precontact sequence, small game such as cottontails, jackrabbits, and rodents provided small amounts of meat to the diet. Large game hunting became more specialized through time as a result of resource depletion near settlements and general segmentation and specialization of all activities. Ritual activity associated with large game hunting increased. With increased agricultural intensification, women may have been pulled from hunting even small game as food processing became more intensive (see Crown, this volume). With large game hunting more specialized, more distinct gender hierarchies might have formed in the precontact Southwest, and the association of women with male large game hunters might have increased their status in precontact societies.

7

Women's Role in Changing Cuisine

Patricia L. Crown

From earliest occupation to the arrival of Europeans, the diets and cuisines of people living in the American Southwest changed in ways that reveal expanded effort in preparing meals that increasingly revolved around the staple, maize. Evidence indicates that women were primarily responsible for meal preparation and that they took on this increasing work load. Patterned changes in the tools used to process and prepare food thus reflect changes in women's work loads and the division of labor—and these changes are in turn useful in evaluating the relative statuses of men and women in Southwestern prehistory.

In this chapter, I first review evidence for the primacy of women's involvement as cooks in the prehispanic Southwest. I then distinguish diet and cuisine. Although arguing for the conservatism of diet and cuisine, I present possible reasons for change in each. Finally, I review the precontact record of dietary and culinary change, concentrating particularly on changes in grinding tools, containers, and cooking hearths.

Evidence is largely lacking for a causal relationship between changes in diet and changes in cuisine. Prior to sedentary village life, mobility constrained tool design, and the archaeological record is dominated by small, portable tools suited for generalized use. With increasing sedentism, such constraints were lifted, and new tools appeared with increasingly specialized functions. Changes in tool design after this time reflect new concerns. Food processing and preparation entailed potential losses in four components of the cooking system: loss of time and energy for the cook, loss of nutrients in the storage or cooking process, loss of fuel, and wear on cooking tools. With sedentism, the major changes in cooking tools reduced losses to all of these components except the cook's energy. Instead, women gradually expended more effort in preparing meals using tools that saved time and fuel, optimized the nutritional value of the food prepared, and were more durable.

Although evidence is lacking for any change through time in the sexual division of labor associated with food preparation, women clearly took on increased work loads in preparing food throughout the sequence of Southwestern occupation. Yet despite their being pulled into more domestic work, I posit that women's contribution to food processing was so critical to the maintenance of Southwestern societies that their relative status did not decline over time. The increasingly marked spatial division of men's and women's work probably led to the development of separate, complementary status hierarchies, with skill in food preparation becoming a potential avenue to increased recognition in the community.

FOOD PROCESSING AND THE SEXUAL DIVISION OF LABOR

Cross-cultural regularities, Southwestern ethnographic data, and archaeological evidence from skeletons, tools found in burials, and imagery provide strong support for interpreting the sexual division of labor with regard to food processing in prehistory.

Cross-cultural data indicate a strong relationship between specific food preparation tasks and a worker's sex (Kurz 1987; Murdock and Provost 1973). George Murdock and Caterina Provost (1973) examined activities in 185 societies worldwide and derived an "index of average percentage of male participation" for each activity. Their indices ranged from 100 to 5.7 for 50 activities, with a higher number indicative of greater male participation. Activities associated with men included butchering (with a male "index of participation" of 92.3) and generation of fire (62.3, although for North American societies alone this index was 68.6). Women undertook most other food preparation activities, including preservation of meat and fish (32.9), fuel gathering (27.2), preparation of drinks (22.2), dairy production (14.3, not including milking), water fetching (8.6), cooking (8.3), and preparation of vegetal foods (5.7). With the exception of preservation of meat and fish, these activities were all considered "quasi-feminine activities." Although there are reasons to question the coding of variables in such studies and the reliability of the results (Bradley 1989), in this case the linkage between women and food preparation seems valid.

R. B. Kurz (1987) used a sample of 44 tribal societies to examine the importance of food processing to women's contribution to subsistence. He concluded that women made a heavy contribution to subsistence tasks, in the majority of societies performing more than 80 percent of the tasks associated with food processing, with a mean and median contribution of 77 percent. Interestingly, he found that women predominated in processing activities regardless of their contribution to productive activities (Kurz 1987:45). He also ranked four food processing activities in terms of women's contributions to each. The processing of plant products was most strongly associated with women's labor, followed by fetching water and fuel, cooking, and processing animal products. Despite the predominance of women in food preparation, cross-culturally men often roast meat (whereas women boil it), cook away from home, and cook for ritual occasions (Goody 1982:71).

Ethnographies for Pueblo and Piman-speaking groups confirm that women were primarily responsible for food preparation and serving (Castetter and Bell 1942; Cushing 1920; Dennis 1940; Ezell 1961; Longacre 1970:49; Lowell 1991; O'Kane 1950; Parsons 1919; Underhill 1979b). Women processed plants for consumption, each recipe involving a variety of steps. For instance, Michael Schiffer (1975:table 9) presented a behavioral chain analysis of maize preparation among the Hopis in A.D. 1900, documenting that women participated in 14 separate tasks from harvesting to serving, performing 7 of these tasks several mornings a week and 4 of the tasks twice daily. Ethnographic monographs also reveal the importance of childhood enculturation in food preparation skills. Among the Southwestern groups, girls began contributing to cooking tasks by about age 8, first learning to grind small amounts of cornmeal and tend the household fire. By age 10–12, when they were no longer permitted to play freely around the village, girls were expected to grind all of the meal and learn to cook as well. Among the Pueblos, girls of 15 had learned to cook the more difficult dishes, including *piki* bread at Hopi, and were prepared to run their own households (Dennis 1940:84–85; Parsons 1919:94; Underhill 1979b:37). Young Hopi women had to master *piki* preparation in order to marry (O'Kane 1950:82).

Despite the primacy of women in food preparation, Southwestern ethnographies confirm that men contributed to some tasks involved in cooking. First, men often gathered firewood at a distance from the village and brought it home (Parsons 1919; Underhill 1979b:14); however, this might have been a consequence of increased danger from raiding during the historic period or increased distance to firewood sources associated with aggregated sites. Regardless of who collected the wood, women were responsible for chopping it for use in a fire pit or hearth. Second, men helped with food preparation performed at a distance from the village or involving particularly heavy labor, including agave roasting (Castetter, Bell, and Grove 1938:48). Finally, men were capable of cooking and did so when away from home (Parsons 1919).

Archaeological data support this sexual division of labor in prehistory. In reconstructing particular activities, researchers have examined long-bone diaphyseal morphology (Ogilvie 1993, 1996), musculoskeletal stress markers (Hawkey 1988; Munson 1996; Nagy and Hawkey 1993), and activity-induced pathologies (Benson 1986; Merbs and Vestergaard 1985). After the introduction of corn, bone morphology, stress markers, and pathologies indicate that female adults spent considerable amounts of time grinding meal by kneeling and extending their arms across the metate (Benson 1986; Merbs and Vestergaard 1985:96; Munson 1996; Nagy and Hawkey 1993). The upper arms show symmetry, indicative of activity patterns that affect right and left sides equally, assumed to be corn grinding (Ogilvie 1993). This contrasts with male skeletons, which show preferential use of right upper limbs (Ogilvie 1993) and sometimes stress on the left elbow (Merbs and Vestergaard 1985:96), which has been interpreted as indicating the use of a bow and arrow. Data also indicate that males were more mobile than females (Ogilvie 1993, 1996).

Mortuary furniture, too, reveals differences in tasks associated with males and females that indicate an association of women with tools used in food preparation (Crown and Fish 1996:808; Howell 1995:142; Mitchell 1991:116; Whittlesey 1984:283).

Finally, figurines and imagery on pottery and in kiva murals support the role of women in food preparation. Hohokam figurines include women grinding on miniature manos and metates or carrying large mixing bowls (Thomas and King 1983:730). Mimbres pottery depictions show men trapping, hunting, fishing, foraging, and farming; they show women also foraging, carrying water, and carrying dead animals from the kill site (Shaffer, Gardner, and Powell 1999). A kiva mural at Pottery Mound reveals a woman cooking while a child watches (Hibben 1975).

Taken together, cross-cultural, ethnographic, and archaeological data strongly support the primacy of women's roles in food processing and preparation in the prehispanic American Southwest. Although I cannot assume that women prepared every dish or every meal throughout prehistory, I do assume that women were primarily responsible for meal preparation and food processing, and that changes in diet and processing technology affected their labor and work loads more than they did the lives of men or children.

DIET AND CUISINE

In distinguishing diet from cuisine, anthropologists define diet as the actual foods consumed, their proportions, and their nutritional values. In contrast, cuisines are cultural constructs that include rules for the appropriate manner of preparation of foods (recipes, tools, combinations of foods), the traditional flavorings of staples, the number of meals consumed per day, the manner of serving completed dishes, the use of food in ritual activities, and the importance of food taboos (Farb and Armelagos 1980:190; Weismantel 1988:87). Scholars note important distinctions between diet and cuisine. First, interhousehold differences in diet may be significant within a community, owing to differences in wealth, access to resources, or yearly variation in harvest, but all members of a community generally share a cuisine, unless social stratification or the presence of multiple ethnic groups provides some people with access to tools or cooking patterns that are unavailable to all (Weismantel 1988:87). Thus, people generally agree on what foods belong together and on how to process, cook, and serve them. Second, diet and cuisine affect men and women differentially. Although researchers document differences in *amounts* of particular foods consumed, men and women share common dietary components, particularly the staples, so that changes in diet affect adults equally. In contrast, because women hold the knowledge behind a cuisine and also execute the preparation of food more often than men, changes in cuisine affect women more than men, and they may not affect men at all.

Despite these differences, both diet and cuisine are conservative. Diet is conservative because people develop taste perceptions and preferences early in life. Every culture has categories of food considered acceptable, categories considered low-preference or "famine" foods, and categories considered inedible (Farb and Armelagos 1980; Minnis 1985:35–36). Studies document considerable resistance to change in diet. For instance, in 1946 an extension agent introduced a new hybrid corn to a northern New Mexico town. Although the corn produced yields more than double those of traditional varieties, virtually all of the farmers abandoned planting the hybrid within a few years because their wives did not like its texture, its taste in tortillas, or its color (Apodaca 1952). In this case, dietary conservatism took precedence over economic gain. Resistance to change is also met because people often view new foods as dangerous. In fact, several factors make adjusting to new foods difficult, particularly the presence of new pathogens in different foods and the physiological necessity of adjusting a body's enzyme-substrate system and bacterial flora to new foods (Wing and Brown 1979:4).

Food choices ultimately depend on several factors: expense, health, taste, and status (Crockett and Stuber 1992; Farb and Armelagos 1980). Expense relates to costs of obtaining and preparing the food, including energy expenditure. Health includes the anticipated nutritional value of the food. Taste includes texture, color, odor, and flavor (Farb and Armelagos 1980). Status is the perceived prestige value of food, particularly food that is scarce or consumed by high-status individuals. In complex societies, foods high in prestige are often associated with urban, affluent groups (Crockett and Stuber 1992), and foods may become symbols of cultural transformation and resistance (Weismantel 1988).

Cuisines are similarly conservative (Farb and Armelagos 1980:190; Goody 1982:150–53), in part because they incorporate the technological style of a group (Lechtman 1977:14; Mills 1999). Meals can be seen as "renderings of appropriate technological behavior communicated through performance" (Lechtman 1977:14). Cuisines are also conservative because, like other aspects of technological behavior, they entail knowledge and motor habits that are passed from generation to generation through teaching frameworks in domestic contexts (Goody 1982:151). Once ingrained, these are difficult to change, particularly because learning new motor skills takes time and effort that individuals often are unable or unwilling to devote to the task (Schiffer and Skibo 1987). Costs of obtaining new technology may be prohibitive.

Diet and cuisine are also conservative because food is crucial to the maintenance of any society and is a fundamental aspect of many interactions and transactions in middle-range societies, including the enactment of ritual (Appadurai 1981). As Mary Weismantel (1988:195) argued, "the etiquette of the meal reproduces household relations," while food exchange between households "creates the larger social structure" of the village. Furthermore, diet and cuisine are potent cultural markers. As Sidney Mintz (1985:3) observed, "people who eat strikingly different foods or similar foods in strikingly different ways are thought to be strikingly different, perhaps even less than human." People may thus be reluctant to innovate, even if innovation leads to greater efficiency, because change in either diet or cuisine may alter existing social dynamics (Bender 1978; Sassaman 1995:232).

Food preparation and presentation are more than diet or cuisine, however. In preparing food, women occupy a critical role between food production and consumption (Ninez 1984:9). They take a variety of items produced outside the household and transform them into meals for consumption within the household. The kitchen is one of the primary loci for the enculturation of children, particularly females, not only in the practices of food preparation but also in the social structure of the family and in ideological practice (Weismantel 1988:18). And the position of women in food preparation and serving is important in understanding their social status relative to men. Rosalind Coward (1985:12) suggested that "the preparation of food is considered an act of servitude, the demonstration of a subordinate and servicing social position.... The meal is the product of woman's domestic labor, demonstrating her willingness to serve the family." Yet to the extent that prestigious transactions or ceremonial activities rest on resources transformed into food (Strathern 1984), women hold a crucial position in relations outside the domestic sphere.

For example, rituals and festivals worldwide include the preparation and consumption of food. Generally, food associated with feasting takes time to prepare, is scarce, and is highly valued or costly to obtain (Farb and Armelagos 1980:147). Even within the domestic sphere, serving meals affords women the opportunity to use the culturally prescribed rules of food preferences and etiquette to communicate "messages about social position and relative power and even create opportunities to readjust the status quo" (Weismantel 1988:29). A meal then becomes an important arena for change, through the subtle insults, snubs, or favoritism associated with serving food to family members and outsiders (for a further discussion of gastropolitics, see Appadurai 1981). Examination of food preparation and presentation thus has the potential to inform us about household social organization, economic practice and the organization of production, and ideological practice and female political power (Weismantel 1988:34–36).

CHANGE IN DIET AND CUISINE

Given the conservatism of both diet and cuisine and the centrality of food in structuring social relations, a question of continuing importance becomes why diet and cuisine change at all. Migration or diffusion may bring populations into contact with new foods or new ways of preparing them, but that contact does not explain why some foods and techniques are adopted and others rejected. In this section, I review a variety of possible factors that researchers have posited as responsible for such change.

Scholars suggest that dietary change is related to the following:

1. Food shortages or overexploitation of natural resources, leading to the necessity of adopting new foods or utilizing low-preference

or famine foods (Minnis 1985:32; Ulijaszek and Strickland 1993)

2. Acceptance of new foods because they are considered high-value or prestige items due to their rarity, difficulty of preparation, or association with higher-status social groups (Ulijaszek and Strickland 1993; Wing and Brown 1979:12)

3. Adoption of particular crops that produce yields in difficult or otherwise unused environmental conditions (poor soils, poor drainage; Ulijaszek and Strickland 1993)

4. Development of food processing technology that makes otherwise inedible plants usable—for instance, removal of the cyanide-forming agent from bitter manioc (Wing and Brown 1979:4)

5. Exploitation of newly available species expanding into or colonizing an environment

Researchers note that people are most likely to adopt new foods if the food fits the existing cuisine, can be processed using existing tools, and substitutes easily for other foods in existing recipes or diets (Ezell 1961; Weismantel 1988; although see Mills 1999 for interesting examples of changes in cooking technology associated with the introduction of European domesticates at Zuni). Sweet, salty, or fatty foods are also more likely to be accepted (Farb and Armelagos 1980).

Scholars attribute changes in the technological aspects of cuisine to many factors as well:

1. Change in diet, leading to new techniques for food processing (Adams 1999:492; Crown and Wills 1995a; Doebley and Bohrer 1983; Minnis 1989:559; Snow 1990). Expectations here include the appearance of a new food or a new variety of an old food at the same time as or directly preceding the appearance of a new food processing technology.

2. Degree of population mobility, which is associated with the size and permanence of processing facilities (Morris 1990; Schlanger 1996a). Here the expectation is that greater mobility constrains the size and durability of cooking tools, so that they tend to be smaller, lighter, and nonbreakable. Cooking tools

become larger, heavier, and less portable as populations become more sedentary.

3. The necessity of conserving one or more components of the cooking system at the expense of others. The four components generally involved in cooking a recipe are the cook, the food, the fuel, and the cooking tools.

a. The cook. Cooking involves expenditures in time and energy for the cook. Time allocation and scheduling conflicts may lead to new techniques for processing food (Crown and Wills 1995a; Diehl 1996:106; Hard, Mauldin and Raymond 1996:257; Pierce 1996:8). Changes in cuisine associated with scheduling conflicts might include the development of weaning foods to reduce the conflict between subsistence activities and child care (Braun 1987; Buikstra et al. 1987:79; Crown and Wills 1995a; Nerlove 1974; Pierce 1996) and the development of techniques that increase the speed of food processing, even if they require more energy per unit of time (Crown and Wills 1995a:180; Diehl 1996:107; Torrence 1983:12). Alternatively, women might have saved time by making larger batches and fewer meals.

b. The food. Cooks can conserve nutrients in the foods they prepare by employing different culinary techniques (Crown and Wills 1995a:180–81; Diehl 1996; Katz, Hediger, and Valleroy 1974; Pierce 1996:8; Stahl 1989; Wing and Brown 1979; Snow 1990). One of the most common is increasing the surface area of food particles through finer processing, which makes food more digestible and speeds the absorption of nutrients (Stahl 1989:174). Lower cooking temperatures also retain more nutrients, whereas cooking in water tends to lose nutrients (Wing and Brown 1979:65). Alkali treatment improves the nutritional quality of corn; this can be achieved by soaking the corn in an alkaline solution, mixing ground maize with ashes, or even using particular lithic raw materials in grinding maize (Ivanhoe 1985; Katz, Hediger, and Valleroy 1974; Kuhnlein and Calloway 1979; Snow 1990; Stahl 1989; Walker 1985). More intensive extraction of portions of plants and animals higher in particular nutrients is a related phenomenon (see, for instance, Potter 1995), but it may not lead to changes in culinary technology.

c. The fuel. Shortages of fuel may lead to the adoption of cooking techniques that conserve fuel or cook more efficiently (Farb and Armelagos 1980:10, 192). When fuel is scarce, culinary changes include consumption of more raw foods, cutting or grinding food into smaller particles to decrease cooking time by exposing a maximum surface area to high heat, cooking more foods in a single container, using thinner-walled vessels to transmit heat to food without delay, and cooking foods at high heat for short periods rather than at low heat for prolonged periods. With increasing residential stability, fuel depletion became a problem in many areas of the Southwest (Kohler 1992b).

d. The cooking tools. Food preparation degrades cooking tools, so cooks want tools that are durable and efficient. Archaeologists assume that tool makers will experiment with materials and manufacturing techniques until they achieve a product that embodies minimally acceptable performance characteristics, including use life and maintenance (Bleed 1986; M. C. Nelson 1991; Schiffer and Skibo 1987). Changes in cuisine may be characterized by periods of experimentation to achieve the appropriate compromises.

4. Changes in the organization of food preparation that lead to changes in cooking technology. When the ratio of cooks to consumers decreases and cooks are preparing food for more than their own households, cooks may begin using different, or larger, tools to process and prepare larger batches. Such a change might also be reflected in a change in the ratio of cooking vessels to serving vessels (Welch and Scarry 1995). In small-scale societies, such changes may be intermittent and associated with communal feasts (Blinman 1989; Blitz 1993; Mills 1999; Toll 1985; Welch and Scarry 1995), whereas in more complex societies, full-time specialized cooks may prepare food in commercial settings for large groups of consumers on a daily basis. There is no evidence

for such full-time specialization in the precontact American Southwest.

In the remainder of this chapter, I explore the sequence of food preparation technology that characterizes Southwestern prehistory. My purpose is to examine broad trends through time and across the major environmental zones in order to evaluate why such patterning occurred. I am particularly interested in the relationship between changes in cuisine and associated changes in the sexual division of labor, the time allocated to tasks, and the development of gender hierarchies. Because many arguments for changes in cuisine hinge on a hypothesized change in diet, I turn first to evidence for dietary stability and change in the greater American Southwest.

CHANGE IN DIET IN THE GREATER AMERICAN SOUTHWEST

Tables 7.1–7.3 review the major dietary changes known for the greater American Southwest for each of the major environmental zones, based on secondary sources reporting evidence from pollen, macrobotanical data, paleofeces, and fauna. Fuller discussions are presented in the chapters of this volume by Fish and Szuter, respectively. At present, the data from northern Chihuahua are too scanty to enable completion of a fourth table, so the available data are discussed only in the text. The tables reveal a number of changes over time. The first major change in diet occurred in all three regions at the transition from the Paleo-Indian period to the Early Archaic, around 8500 B.C. Paleo-Indian sites are characterized by the presence of extinct megafauna and little else in the way of plant or animal remains. However, many researchers assume that the dietary picture afforded by Paleo-Indian sites is biased in favor of large game rather than revealing the complete composition of the diet. Paleo-Indian populations probably included gatherers as well as hunters, and they probably consumed plants and small game as well as large game.

Environmental change toward higher average temperatures and greater aridity initiated vegetation changes beginning around 10,000 B.C. Plant resources and small game animals are more evident in Archaic sites, dating after 8500 B.C. A variety of wild plants and animals

TABLE 7.1

Changes in Diet and Cuisine Technology in the Southern Arizona Desert

Date	*Diet*	*Grinding Tools*	*Container Technology*
Paleo-Indian, pre-8500 B.C.	Big game		
Early Archaic, 8500–5000 B.C.	Seeds, nuts, plants, small game	Unshaped ground handstones	Basketry?
Middle Archaic, 5000–1500 B.C.		Grinding slabs, one-hand manos, nutting stones	
Late Archaic, 1500 B.C.–	Maize (flint/pop)	Basin metates, one-hand manos	
500 B.C.			
200 B.C.			
100 B.C.			
A.D. 1			Ceramic containers
100			
200			
300		Trough metate, two-hand manos	
400	Cultivated little barley		
500	Domesticated beans		
600	Cotton		
700	Cultivated Mexican *crucillo*	Tabular knives	
800	Cultivated agave, tobacco		
900	Maize (flour)		Smudging
1000	Cultivated chenopodium and amaranth		
1100	Cultivated cholla (?)		
1200			
1300			*Comal*

Sources: Abbott 1984; Adams 1994; Bernard-Shaw 1984; Bohrer 1991; Breitburg 1993; Crown and Wills 1995a; Cutler and Blake 1976; Doyel 1991a; Gasser and Kwiatkowski 1991; Haury 1945; Huckell 1984; Lancaster 1986; Miksicek 1984; Wills 1988a.

TABLE 7.2

Changes in Diet and Cuisine Technology in the Mogollon Highlands

Date	*Diet*	*Grinding Tools*	*Container Technology*
Paleo-Indian, pre-8500 B.C.	Big game		
Early Archaic, 8500–5000 B.C.	Seeds, nuts, plants, small game	Unshaped ground handstones	Basketry?
Middle Archaic, 5000–1500 B.C.	Maize (flint/pop)	Grinding slabs, one-hand manos, nutting stones	
Late Archaic, 1500 B.C.–500 B.C.	Squash (C. *pepo*)	Basin metates, one-hand manos	
200 B.C.	Turkey		
100 B.C.	Beans		
A.D. 1			
100			
200			Ceramic containers
300			
400		Trough metate, two-hand mano	Smudging, neck banding, texturing
500	Tobacco (?)		
600		Metate sets—Pinelawn	
700	Maize (flour) (A.D. 500–700)		
800			
900			
1000		Metate sets—Mimbres	Overall corrugation
1100	Cotton		
1200			
1300			

Sources: Adams 1994; Breitburg 1993; Crown and Wills 1995a; Haury 1940:89–94; Lancaster 1986; Rinaldo and Bluhm 1956; Wheat 1955; Wills 1988a, 1996.

TABLE 7.3

Changes in Diet and Cuisine Technology on the Colorado Plateau

Date	*Diet*	*Grinding Tools*	*Container Technology*
Paleo-Indian, pre-8500 B.C.	Big game		
Early Archaic, 8500–5000 B.C.	Seeds, nuts, plants, small game	Unshaped ground handstones	Basketry?
Middle Archaic 5000–1500 B.C.	Maize (flint/pop)	Grinding slabs, one-hand manos, nutting stones	
Late Archaic, 1500 B.C.–	Squash (*C. pepo*)	Basin metates, one-hand manos	
500 B.C.			
200 B.C.			
100 B.C.	Maize (flour)		
A.D. 1			
100			
200	Turkey		Ceramic containers
300			
400	Beans		
500	Maize (flour)	Trough metates, two-hand manos	
600			
700			Smudging, neck banding
800			
900		Slab metates, faceted mano, mealing bins	Overall corrugation
1000	Maize (flour)	Metate sets	
1100	Cotton		
1200			
1300			*Comal*

Note: The variety of dates for the appearance of floury corn reflect different dates for different portions of this large area. The earliest dates are from the Albuquerque area, followed by Canyon de Chelly and then Mesa Verde.

Sources: Adams 1994; Blinman 1993; Breitburg 1993; Crown and Wills 1995a; Lancaster 1986; Schlanger 1996b; Snow 1990; Wills 1988a.

appear in sites of this time period, associated with a mobile lifestyle.

Domesticates first appear in the Southwest between about 2000 and 1500 B.C. The earliest domesticate in all areas was a flint or pop corn (Adams 1994). Current evidence indicates that corn was adopted slightly earlier in the northern and central Southwest than in the desert of southern Arizona (Wills 1992). Other traditional domesticates appeared in the Southwest at different times, including squash, tobacco, beans, and cotton (which provided both fiber and edible seeds). Ethnobotanists have identified at least 10 different *Zea* races, including pop, flint, dent, and flour corns (Adams 1994), but researchers generally caution against placing too much weight on corn race identifications, owing to transformations associated with drying shrinkage and heat or charring shrinkage, as well as variability within single cobs (Adams 1994; Doebley and Bohrer 1983).

Domesticated beans and squash generally do not preserve as well as corn, so the dates given for these species may be less reliable than those for corn. Nonetheless, a general sequence of appearance of corn followed by squash, beans, and, finally, cotton appears to hold for all environmental zones in the Southwest. In southern Arizona, the Hohokam domesticated, cultivated, or encouraged a variety of additional plants, including little barley, Mexican *crucillo*, agave, amaranth, and cholla (Bohrer 1991; Gasser and Kwiatakowski 1991). Farmers added flour varieties of maize at different times in the various environmental zones as well, although they never abandoned the flint and pop varieties they had grown for centuries. Evidence indicates that a floury corn was grown in the northern Rio Grande region as early as 138 B.C. (Adams 1994), although it was not grown in other portions of the Southwest until considerably later.

The record suggests that by A.D. 400, the general dietary components of precontact meals were present in the Southwest and in use in these broad environmental zones. Farmers apparently experimented with cultivation or domestication of additional plants, although there is every indication that these plants had already been used by cooks in their wild state. The general picture, then, is of a fairly static repertoire of plants available for use in cooking in the precontact Southwest after A.D. 400.

Studies of paleofeces provide the only available opportunity to view the actual importance of various plants in the meals eaten in the Southwest. Mark Stiger (1977) examined paleofeces from a number of Puebloan sites dating between A.D. 300 and 1250. He compared groups of paleofeces from three time periods, A.D. 300–600, 1100–1150, and 1250. He reported an increase in dependence on corn in the diet through these time periods, a decrease in the use of pinyon nuts and squash, and an increase in the use of cotton seeds, insects, and grass seeds for food (Stiger 1977:47–50). He noted a high incidence of wild plants in the diet but pointed out that most of the species used were disturbance plants or plants that grew in areas unfavorable for agriculture. He also argued for an increase in general dietary diversity, on the basis of an increase in the number of different components in the paleofeces from each time period (19 in 23 paleofeces from A.D. 300–600, 19 in 24 paleofeces from 1100–1150, and 47 in 139 paleofeces from 1250). He argued that this dietary change occurred due to environmental change associated with human disturbance and mounting population pressure.

Paul Minnis (1989) used these same data to examine dietary changes in the northern Southwest. He argued for general stability in the dietary regime from A.D. 500 to 1300. He also examined available data for the number of plant taxa per paleofeces and found a decrease in the number of taxa from A.D. 900–1100 to 1100–1300 (Minnis 1989:559), results that seem to contradict Stiger's. He concluded that this represented a change in one aspect of dietary diversity. Interestingly, the percentage of corn in the paleofeces did not change, averaging 40 percent in both time periods. While noting the general similarity in the core of plants consumed in all areas, Minnis found that plants were consumed in varying proportions in different parts of the northern Southwest.

Unfortunately, paleofeces are unavailable in sufficient numbers from other portions of the Southwest to provide comparable data. However, evidence from macrobotanical remains supports similar conclusions for the Hohokam area. Maize is identified in roughly 40–70 percent of all flotation samples from riverine sites and in comparable percentages of samples from many nonriverine sites (Gasser and Kwiatkowski 1991:424–25). The presence values of maize do not appear to have changed substantially from A.D. 300–1450 (Gasser and Kwiatkowski 1991:444). Studies do not reveal any substantial change in the diversity of taxa used or in dependence on nonagricultural resources (Gasser and Kwiatkowski 1991:444), despite the apparently increasing number of cultigens and encouraged species through time in the area.

The general conclusions of these studies support an interpretation of high dependence on corn in much of the prehispanic Southwest by at least A.D. 500, with estimates of dependence running from about 50 to 80 percent of the total diet (see Hard, Mauldin, and Raymond 1996 for a discussion of the variability in maize dependence in the Southwest). Results also suggest that farming groups depended on a greater variety of wild plants than did strictly foraging groups (as is common ethnographically [Johns 1990:245]), and the diversity of wild and encouraged plants gathered may have increased through time. As farmers became more dependent on cultigens, they may have supplemented their high corn diet with a greater variety of other plant foods.

Scholars indicate similar changes in the use of fauna through time (for example, see Szuter 1991b, and this volume). The only domesticated animal species used for food were the turkey (Breitburg 1993) and, possibly in some times and places, the dog (Mick-O'Hara 1994). Major animal species used throughout the Southwest included artiodactyls, jackrabbits, cottontails, and various rodent species. Additional species utilized in lesser amounts include birds, fish, and insects. The actual mix varied with environmental zone, degree of human environmental modification, and probably cultural preference (Szuter 1991b). Differences in species found at contemporaneous, closely spaced sites may relate to a community's ability to form task groups for long-distance hunting parties (Barbara Mills, personal communication, 1997). As with plant species, there is little indication of major change in the animal species utilized during prehistory after the Pleistocene, but the actual proportions of animals consumed and the portions of the carcass eaten varied greatly within and between sites.

Several aspects of Southwestern dietary change may have affected Southwestern cuisine. A major change in diet occurred at the end of the Pleistocene, with the extinction of several megafauna species and their replacement by smaller game, and with apparently increased use of wild plants in the diet. The major domesticates, corn, beans, and squash, were incorporated into the existing diet at different times in different parts of the Southwest. New varieties of corn appeared at different times as well. By around A.D. 300–500, the major components of the diet in all areas became largely stabilized, and the changes we see after this time are primarily changes in the relative importance of various taxa in the diet and changes in the amount of human intervention in their growth cycle. Where sufficient data exist to enable assessment of temporal and spatial variation, it is clear that populations in different areas used different proportions of these plants in their diets. To some extent this may have been due to differences in availability, but preference and cuisine probably were also important in shaping the nature of dietary differences in the Southwest.

CHANGES IN CUISINE IN THE GREATER AMERICAN SOUTHWEST

Food processing and preparation generally involve a series of steps, each of which may be characterized by distinctive tools. I present a brief overview of these steps for Southwestern cuisine prior to discussing changes in food processing technology in prehistory. Actual food preparation for Southwestern dishes involved many individual steps (Cushing 1920; Schiffer 1975:108). These can be grouped according to their purposes and the tools used, as follows.

The first step is preservation. Foods may be eaten fresh or may be preserved for later consumption. All plant and animal products undergo gradual deterioration through time, so that fresh foods have higher nutritional value than preserved foods (Wing and Brown 1979:61). Techniques available to Southwestern populations to preserve food for later use included moisture removal (drying, dehydration, concentration), heat treatment (blanching, sterilization), low-temperature treatment (cooling, freezing), acidity control (fermentation, acidic additives), and use of processing additives (salting, smoking) (Wing and Brown 1979:64). In the Southwest, there is some evidence to suggest use of most of these techniques. For instance, historically, corn was generally subjected to moisture removal through drying prior to storage, and corn found in prehispanic contexts at Mummy Cave appeared to have been parched prior to storage, a type of heat treatment (Adams 1994).

A second step in processing generally involves some trimming and discarding of plant or animal parts that are viewed as inedible (Wing and Brown 1979:65). This step involved such tools as knives and husking pins or pegs (Schiffer 1975:108; Wing and Brown 1979:105). Both trimming and washing contribute to nutrient loss. Fractionation or comminution reduces edible plants or animals into smaller parts through cutting or pulverizing. In the prehispanic Southwest, cooks employed knives, graters or abraders (Haury 1976:227), mortars and pestles, and manos and metates in this stage of food processing.

As a third step, cooks often mix particular plant and animal products together to create a dish. The combination may actually increase the nutrient value of the individual components by freeing otherwise unavailable nutrients. For instance, adding alkaline material such as ashes to corn increases the availability of amino acids and vitamins (Katz, Hediger, and Valleroy 1974). Cooks might use a variety of tools at this stage, particularly containers (bowls, jars, colanders) for mixing, soaking, or washing foods and utensils for stirring them.

A final step may involve heating. Heating of foods prior to consumption destroys toxins, bacteria, and parasites in food, makes food easier to digest, and may increase nutrient accessibility and caloric value (Farb and Armelagos 1980:53), but it also may cause additional nutrient loss, particularly if water or fat is used in cooking (Wing and Brown 1979:65). There are three types of heating (Farb and Armelagos 1980:53; K. Reid 1989:168–69). Dry heating includes direct application of heat, generally at high temperatures, such as roasting or broiling, as well as baking and parching. Baking and parching entail the use of containers such as pots or baskets for heating foods. Moist heating uses water or steam to cook food at lower temperatures than dry heating. It includes simmering, boiling, and steaming food. As K. Reid (1989:169) pointed out, simmering is best for stews or soups and for rendering oils from seeds and nuts or grease from bone fragments. Boiling is better for cooking starchy seeds. In the Southwest, cooks often steamed food in pits, but they used containers for simmering and boiling food. Finally, cooks could heat with fat by frying food, generally at a temperature intermediate between that of cooking in water and that of cooking in air.

Tables 7.1–7.3 list a number of significant changes in cooking technology for three major environmental areas of the greater American Southwest. Many tools used in cooking would have been perishable containers and utensils, so I cannot list the entire inventory. In the following discussion, I concentrate particularly on container technology and on tools for pulverizing food.

Tools for Pulverizing and Grinding Food

Ground handstones and simple grinding slabs represent the earliest nonperishable tools for processing food recovered in the American Southwest. Indeed, these tools are hallmarks of the Archaic period and are taken as important indicators of increasing reliance on wild seeds and nuts. Although plant materials were almost certainly consumed during the Paleo-Indian adaptation, no Paleo-Indian tools for processing plant foods remain.

The use of flat slab milling stones and nutting stones correlates well with the beginning of the Archaic and indeed is used to define this "stage" or adaptation in Southwestern prehistory. By the Middle Archaic, cooks began using shallow basin metates for processing food with simple one-hand manos as an addition to, rather than a replacement for, the earlier processing equipment. Many of the one-hand manos associated with these early milling stones were made of sandstone or quartzite (Morris 1990:186). Trough metates appeared throughout most of the Southwest between A.D. 300 and 500 and were used with two-hand manos (Doyel 1991a; Schlanger 1996a; Wills 1996). A change in raw material to increased use of basalt, particularly vesicular basalt (Lancaster 1986:183), for manos and metates usually accompanied this change in metate design. Finally, populations in some portions of the Southwest had adopted the use of sets of manos and flat or slab metates by about A.D. 900 (Schlanger 1996a). These metates were often set into mealing bins that were permanent, not portable, facilities (Adams 1993; Schlanger 1996a). In addition, sets of multiple metates are present in some portions of the Southwest. These consist of two to four metates of graded coarseness; most researchers argue that they were used in a multistage grinding technique to reduce corn into increasingly finer particles, from meal to flour (Lancaster 1986).

I can make several general observations about this sequence. First, populations often retained earlier forms despite the adoption of new forms of grinding tools (Wills 1996:349). Second, populations did not adopt new forms simultaneously, or even rapidly, between or within the different environmental zones or culture areas. Third, the complete sequence does not apply to all areas. Women and children grinding in the Hohokam, northern Chihuahua, and western Mimbres areas never used flat metates in mealing bins (Haury 1945:127; Lancaster 1986:187; mealing bins were adopted in the eastern Mimbres area after A.D. 1150 [Brady 1996a]), and mealing bins have a variable distribution among eastern Puebloan sites (Green 1996; Wetherington 1968). Fourth, the general sequence in virtually all areas made finer grinding possible. Finally, the general design of manos was toward larger grinding surfaces (Hard 1990; Hard, Mauldin, and Raymond 1996; Mauldin 1993; Morris 1990).

Earlier, in discussing possible reasons for changes in cuisine, I presented four major interpretations used by archaeologists. All four may apply to the sequence of changes in ground stone technology in the Southwest. The first was that change in diet leads to change in food preparation technology. Early attempts at understanding why this general ground-stone sequence characterizes most of the Southwest generally focused on the foods processed and argued that changes in diet led to changes in tool design. For instance, several researchers argued that basin metates and one-hand manos characterized seed-based diets, whereas trough metates and two-hand manos characterized the introduction of agriculture (Haury 1950; Martin and Rinaldo 1950). More recently, some scholars have suggested that trough metates were associated with a shift from pop and flint varieties of corn to flour and dent varieties (Adams 1999; Diehl 1996:105), because the latter varieties were used in recipes that required more dry-grinding into flour, and trough metates do this more efficiently. Yet a detailed study from the Four Corners area suggested the opposite pattern.

John Doebley and Vorsila Bohrer (1983) examined changes in corn varieties and changes in metate shapes at Salmon Ruin for two time periods, a Chacoan occupation between A.D. 1090 and 1130 and a Mesa Verdean occupation between A.D. 1250 and 1285. They found a shift from primary use of trough metates (75 percent) for processing corn in the Chacoan occupation to primary use of slab metates (77 percent) for that purpose in the Mesa Verdean occupation. Macrobotanical remains revealed a shift during the same time period from 72.7 percent pop or flint corn to 51–63 percent pop or flint (the range is due to sampling issues). Doebley and Bohrer interpreted the change in technology as resulting from an increase in the amount of flour corn used in later time periods. They particularly argued that trough metates were better suited for initially crushing the hard pop and flint kernels, which tend to bounce when first crushed by a mano. The high sides and concave trough of the metate would have concentrated the grains in the center of the metate while serving as an "anvil" for crushing. Flour varieties of corn are softer and easier to grind; hence the shift to slab metates with increased use of flour corn.

Comparison of the earliest dates for various cultigens and the earliest dates for new tool forms (tables 7.1–7.3) suggests a lack of correspondence between the adoption of new foods and the adoption of new ground-stone tools. In all portions of the Southwest, corn appears in the archaeological record in abundance long before trough metates are used. But trough metates appear in the desert of southern Arizona and in the Mogollon Highlands before there is evidence for floury varieties of corn (*harinoso de ocho/maiz de ocho* [K. Adams 1994; see also Ford 1981; Galinat 1988; Minnis 1985]), whereas flour corn appears along the northern Rio Grande before the appearance of trough metates. There is little evidence, then, that dietary change led to the development of new ground-stone technology, except possibly at the beginning of the Holocene when ground-stone tools were apparently first developed in conjunction with a shift to consumption of more seeds and nuts. It seems likely that the lack of relationship between technological change and dietary change is due to the conservatism discussed earlier. New foods are generally accepted into the existing diet when they do *not* necessitate a concomitant change in cuisine and when they substitute easily for ingredients in existing recipes. Following this line of reasoning, W. H. Wills (1988a:119) argued that the adoption of cultigens in the Southwest did not necessitate a change in the existing grinding technology.

Doebley and Bohrer's research is intriguing because it carefully documented changes in relative proportions of tools and foods rather than assigning causality in the appearance of one or the other. Their research does suggest that subtle shifts in the way cooks prepared existing varieties of corn were accompanied by shifts in the proportions of tools, rather than their presence or absence.

The second possible reason for changes in cuisine described earlier had to do with degree of population mobility, which was associated with the size, portability, and permanence of food processing tools. The general sequence of technological change in processing tools indicates a shift from versatile, generalized tools to tools designed to accomplish a narrower range of tasks or to process foods most effectively, and from portable, lightweight, and smaller tools to less portable, heavier, and larger tools. D. H. Morris (1990:187) argued that this sequence reflects increasing sedentism and associated changes in tool design as logistical limitations on tool size and design were "relaxed." Thus, the early small slab and basin metates and one-hand manos were relatively lightweight, portable tools associated with fairly mobile populations. With greater sedentism, larger tools became the norm. Although the trough metate and two-hand mano were less portable than earlier forms, they could still be moved easily within the settlement, from inside to outside of houses or from rooftops to plazas, depending on a host of factors, including weather conditions. Metates set in mealing bins are permanent facilities and indicate a further degree of commitment to long-term occupation of a site (Adams 1993:41–42; Schlanger 1996a).

The third reason was the necessity of conserving one or more components of the cooking system, beginning with conserving the cook's time and energy. Several researchers have argued recently that increases in mano size and changes in metate and mano shape were due to increasing time pressure and scheduling conflicts. Morris (1990:188) indicated that as dependence on corn grew, basin metates and one-hand manos became inadequate for grinding the amounts of corn needed to feed families, but that trough metates and two-hand manos were suitable for the task. He noted that "the combination of increases in surface area of the tools, sharing the work load between both hands, the use of vesicular basalt, and probably postural changes to reduce fatigue in the grinding process all served to make possible the grinding of large amounts of corn, amounts that were never required previously and which would have been impossible with the older grinding tools." Jenny Adams (1993:334) expanded on this argument, stating that with improved and larger tools, grinders could either grind the same amount of grain in less time or grind more grain in the same amount of time. However, grinding on a trough metate requires greater energy expenditure and produces greater fatigue, because women cannot shift the positions of their arms and bodies in order to reduce muscle stress as they can with a basin metate (Adams 1993:338–39). Grinding maize repeatedly to achieve smaller particle sizes would result in even greater energy expenditure. The trade-off for women would be decreasing the amount of time spent in grinding maize by increasing tool efficiency. Several researchers have noted that as consumption of maize increased through time, the time required to grind and cook it would have become prohibitive, creating scheduling conflicts. The solution was to develop tools that ground maize more rapidly, despite the increased energy expenditure (Bartlett 1933:28; Crown and Wills 1995a: 180; Diehl 1996:107; Hard, Mauldin, and Raymond 1996:257; Lancaster 1986:188). As Morris (1990:188) noted, the prehispanic record in the Southwest generally shows that grinding tools increased in size until new constraints appeared; these constraints were ones of weight, comfort, and ease of use (see also Lancaster 1986:188).

Changes in material type reinforce the importance of greater efficiency in grinding maize. During the Archaic, most ground-stone tools were made of nonvesicular basalt, quartzite, or sandstone, superior materials for grinding small seeds. With the adoption of the trough metate, tools shifted increasingly to vesicular basalt for grinding corn because it cuts easier, resharpens itself, and processes material more rapidly (Morris 1990:186).

A final aspect of increasing efficiency was a gradual shift from generalized tools suitable for grinding both seeds and maize to the development of more specialized tools designed to accomplish a narrower range of tasks or to process specific foods most effectively (Crown and Wills 1995a:181; Lancaster 1986:187). Individual households thus had a greater variety of tools for grinding and pulverizing food, each used for particular recipes or food types.

During the historic period, when grinding tools were certainly as time-efficient as their prehispanic counterparts, Hopi women ground corn three to five hours per day (Bartlett 1933; Dorsey 1899:741). The argument that time constraints and scheduling conflicts led to the development of tools for processing maize more efficiently appears to fit the data for all portions of the Southwest. However, fine-scale examination of the data from smaller areas of the Southwest reveals considerable variation in the timing of changes in ground-stone tool morphology and size (Hard, Mauldin, and Raymond 1996), indicating the importance of individual decisions and strategies in adopting new technology.

The need to conserve nutrients in food or to increase the nutritional value of foods might also have led to changes in processing techniques. Historically, cooks prepared maize in a variety of ways, only some of which required mealing. Although time pressure and decreasing mobility are compelling explanations for change in ground-stone technology, to some degree they beg the question of why cooks chose to prepare maize by the time-consuming technique of grinding. One plausible reason that cooks chose to use meal or flour, rather than preparing corn in simpler recipes, was to increase the nutritional value of the corn.

Changes in cooking tool design may reveal concerns with intensifying the nutritional yield per unit of food. For instance, increasing the surface area of food particles is one way of improving the nutritional value of food (Stahl 1989:174). Grinding seeds or corn into smaller particle sizes increases its surface area and makes the meal more digestible (Adams 1999; Crown and Wills 1995a:180–81; Hard, Mauldin and Raymond 1996:255; Stahl 1989), so the mere introduction of grinding technology would have increased the nutritional value of seeds and maize over most other preparations. The use of graded metate sets would have further reduced particle sizes. Finer grinding might also have been associated with the production of tortillas, made using *nixtamal,* a mixture of corn soaked in alkaline water (Snow 1990:293; Stahl 1989). Alkali treatment (Ivanhoe 1985; Katz, Hediger, and Valleroy 1974; Kuhnlein and Calloway 1979; Snow 1990; Stahl 1989; Walker 1985) increases the amino acid and calcium uptake of maize. Even grit from milling stones increases the iron and calcium content of the maize (Kuhnlein and Calloway 1979; Walker 1985).

In general, the sequence of milling stone use in the Southwest indicates that women were able to grind increasingly finer flour through time. However, many historic recipes for corn, such as roasting of green corn and stewing of posole, did not entail grinding. Furthermore, coarser types of milling stones were not abandoned as finer forms were adopted, indicating that a variety of grinding stones was used to produce a variety of types and textures of meal and flour. This suggests that improving the nutritional yield of maize might have been an important consideration but that variability in the preparation of this staple was a consideration as well.

Another conservation motive behind changing technology might be the need to conserve fuel. One way to decrease cooking time and conserve fuel is to grind food into smaller particles in order to expose the maximum surface area to heat. The use of metate sets to grind maize into finer particle sizes would have aided in reducing cooking time and saving fuel. *Piki* bread and tortillas cook quickly and thus require less fuel than recipes that require long-term simmering or boiling. However, data suggest that cooks employed a variety of recipes in the later precontact periods, suggesting that fuel conservation was perhaps only one of several concerns. To date, no one has examined the relationship between fuel depletion and ground-stone technology, and such an assessment would be worthwhile.

A last conservation need is that of conserving tools. Trough metates and two-hand manos required a much greater labor investment to produce and maintain than did basin metates and one-hand manos (Fratt and Biancaniello 1993:388; Phagan 1988:182), but they were often made of vesicular basalt and had longer use lives than earlier types (Morris 1990:186).

The fourth and final reason archaeologists have given for changes in grinding technology involves change in the organization of food preparation. Both Jenny Adams (1993:41–42) and Sarah Schlanger (1996a) have argued that the appearance of multiple mealing bins permanently affixed in special-purpose rooms represents a shift in the organization of food preparation. There is certainly reason to suggest that the presence of multiple mealing bins in rooms accessible to multiple households created a new social atmosphere for grinding meal and that it reflects a shift in the ratio of grinders to tools; it is less clear whether this was associated with a shift in the ratio of meal grinders to consumers. That particularly large mealing facilities, with up to 12 mealing stations, were associated with the Chacoan great houses suggests the possibility that women and older children were indeed grinding corn above the needs of the household for consumption in communal feasts, so that food preparation had indeed become a part-time specialized activity for some members of these communities.

Ground-stone morphology, size, and material types hold important clues to understanding why culinary technology changed in the pre-contact Southwest. At present, there is little evidence to support the argument that changes in diet led to changes in grinding technology, except possibly at the Paleo-Indian–Archaic interface, where chronological sensitivity is so poor that illuminating the primacy of one over the other may be impossible. Other major dietary changes appear to have occurred without major changes in ground stone, and major ground-stone changes appear to have occurred without concomitant changes in specific components of the diet. It is likely, however, that new ground-stone designs do partly reflect changes in the relative mix of dietary components or changes in the recipes used to prepare the staples. As populations became less mobile, ground-stone tools became larger, heavier, less portable, more permanent, and more durable. Once populations were largely sedentary, data suggest that changes in ground stone were aimed at increasing efficiency in grinding particular varieties of maize while retaining earlier, more versatile tool forms, indicating an expanding cuisine through time. Evidence indicates that cooks elaborated and intensified the ways of preparing corn through time, developing tools that processed maize in the most efficient manner possible. Time appears to have been an important consideration. The design of tools to grind maize into finer particles appears to have been of importance as well, suggesting that increasing the nutritional yield and conserving fuel were both important considerations of changing cuisine. Late in prehistory, changes in grinding tools and facilities suggest possible changes in the organization of food preparation.

The data also support increasing spatial differentiation in tool types. The fairly stable sequence of tool use in the Hohokam area contrasts with the greater variety of tools used in some portions of the Mogollon and Puebloan areas and the more rapid changes in tool use in those areas. Even within particular "culture areas," there is considerable variation in the timing of adoption of particular tools. Within sites, some rooms held mealing bins and flat metates while others retained the movable trough metates. Apparently, women made individual decisions for their households about the types of tools they employed and the range of recipes they prepared. Expansion of the range of food processing techniques might reflect their attempt to keep the narrow range of staples interesting (Farb and Armelagos 1980:11).

Containers for Preparing Food

Tables 7.1–7.3 also review the major changes in container technology for the prehispanic American Southwest. Prior to the production of pottery containers, women processed and prepared food in baskets, textile or hide bags, gourds, or pits. Unfortunately, most of these forms do not preserve well, so that examining change in forms, sizes, materials, or uses is not feasible. There are hundreds of roasting pits known from Archaic sites, so we know that dry heating through roasting or moist heating through steaming food were options for food preparation. Women probably used circular baskets or trays for parching seeds, another dry-heating method. Although there is no direct evidence to demonstrate the use of baskets for stone-boiling food in the Southwest, cooks may have employed this technique. The use of fat as a cooking medium might not have been feasible due to a lack of suitable containers for frying food.

Ceramic figurines appeared in southern Arizona around 800 B.C. (Huckell 1990:238–40), but women did not begin manufacturing containers out of clay until centuries later. Pottery vessels appeared first in the deserts of southern Arizona about A.D. 1, in the Puebloan area between A.D. 200 and 300, and in the Mogollon area between A.D. 200 and 400 (Blinman 1993; Blinman and Wilson 1993:72; Burton 1991; Doyel 1991a:236; Eddy 1966:384; Haury and Sayles 1947; LeBlanc 1982; Varien 1990:88–91; Wilson and Blinman 1991). The earliest ceramics throughout the Southwest have thin walls, rounded bases, simple profiles, and sand inclusions (Burton 1991:50–52; Haury and Sayles 1947:326–29; Skibo and Blinman 1999; Wilson and Blinman 1991). Forms particularly include bowls and "seed jars," neckless globular jars similar to the early *tecomates* found in Mesoamerica (Heidke, Miksa, and Wiley 1996; Skibo and Blinman 1999). The early jars were generalized forms that could be used for cooking, storage, or food processing. Use-alteration analysis demonstrates that some were used for cooking with water, whereas other vessels were used for cooking dry food, cooking a thick food such as gruel, or reheating food with little water in it (Skibo and Blinman 1999). Other vessels lacking evidence for use over a fire were apparently used for storage. Bowls may have been used for food processing, including mixing, soaking, and rinsing, as well as for serving.

In the following centuries, potters produced an increased array of vessel forms. In the Puebloan and Mogollon areas, techniques for manufacturing cooking jars changed. Women created the earliest vessels by coiling and then scraping the coil joints to create a smooth surface. Potters then polished the vessels. Through time, the variety of surface treatments increased. Potters began leaving coils around the neck unobliterated at about A.D. 400 in the Mogollon area (Wheat 1955:79) and in the late 700s in the Puebloan area (Blinman 1993). Plastic manipulation of surface texture shifted in both areas from neck banding to overall unobliterated coils and corrugated (usually finger-indented coils) vessel walls. Overall corrugation was present in the Mogollon area by A.D. 1000 and in the Puebloan area by A.D. 900 (Blinman 1993; Rinaldo and Bluhm 1956). Potters in northern Chihuahua also used an array of plastic decoration above the shoulders of cooking jars but virtually always left the lower portions smoothed (Di Peso, Rinaldo, and Fenner 1974a, vol. 6).

Other types of surface treatments were common in the Southwest as well. Vessel interiors were sometimes "smudged," or blackened, in a process that deposits carbon and tarry products of fuel combustion in the vessel wall. This practice began in the Mogollon area as early as A.D. 400 and was present on some Puebloan vessels around A.D. 700, on some Hohokam vessels after A.D. 900, and on some vessels in the Casas Grandes area after about A.D. 1300 (Abbott 1984:77; Di Peso, Rinaldo, and Fenner 1974a, vol. 6; Haury 1940:89; Wheat 1955:79). Finally, in most areas where researchers have provided adequate measurements, there is a general trend toward increasing cooking-vessel size through time (Di Peso, Rinaldo, and Fenner 1974a, vol. 6:4; Haury 1938:222; Mills 1999; Turner and Lofgren 1966; data from Black Mesa in north-central Arizona show an increase from A.D. 800 to 1150 and then a sharp decline [Smith 1988]).

In addition to ceramic containers, new "containers" for cooking included the flat stones sometimes referred to as *comales* for cooking *piki* bread, which appeared around A.D. 1250–1300 in the Puebloan and Casas Grandes areas (Adams 1991:81; Di Peso, Rinaldo, and Fenner 1974a, vol. 6; Snow 1990:293). After A.D. 1300, Hohokam cooks used circular ceramic *comales* (Haury 1945).

As with changes in ground-stone technology, archaeologists have interpreted the changes in containers in many different ways. I discuss these in terms of the same four possible reasons for changes in cuisine already described: changes in the foods produced, or the diet; changes in population mobility; the necessity of conserving any of four components of the cooking system; and changes in the organization of food preparation.

Might a change in diet have led to changes in Southwestern container technology or forms? As discussed, the earliest cultigens appeared in the Southwest at approximately 1500 B.C., but the earliest pottery containers did not appear until about A.D. 1. Although it is tempting to argue that women originally made pots in order to cook and store the new cultigens, this obviously could not be the case. Such a lack of contemporaneity is common throughout the world; ceramics precede the advent of farming in many societies and postdate farming in others (Arnold 1985; Birket-Smith 1965; J. A. Brown 1989:211; Crown and Wills 1995a). The situation in the Southwest is similar to that in other parts of the world where people adopted ceramic technology for manufacturing figurines long before pottery containers appeared (Klima 1953; Mellaart 1975; Vandiver et al. 1989).

Various scholars have suggested that potters began making containers in conjunction with other dietary changes. For instance, W. H. Wills and I (Crown and Wills 1995a:180) argued that pottery containers might have appeared to enable processing of new varieties of maize, particularly the floury *maiz de ocho* (or *harinoso de ocho*), which women could make into a gruel through boiling and grinding. Jenny Adams (1999; see also Crown and Wills 1995a:176) suggested that pottery might have been an important addition to containers for storing corn with the advent of floury varieties of corn; floury varieties lack a thick, hard endosperm, which makes them much more susceptible to pests than flint and pop varieties of corn. In contrast, James Skibo and Eric Blinman (1999) examined use alteration traces on early pottery and suggested that cooks might have adopted pottery for long-term boiling of beans. All three arguments suffer from a lack of correspondence between dates for the advent of pottery and dates for the advent of new foods, either beans or floury varieties of corn. In some areas, these new cultigens preceded the adoption of pottery, and in others they postdated that adoption. Interestingly, later changes in ceramic technology have not been attributed to changes in diet.

Southwestern pottery production began at a time of increasing residential stability, suggesting that pottery containers were produced in conjunction with decreasing mobility (Crown and Wills 1995a:174–75). Women might have started making pottery at this time because the increasing dependence on cultigens required more secure storage facilities (LeBlanc 1982; Morris and Burgh 1954; Smiley 1985) and containers with greater heat effectiveness and thermal conduction for preparing cultigens by boiling them (Arnold 1985:136). The properties characterizing the earliest Southwestern ceramics are suitable for storage and cooking: thin walls, rounded bases, simple profiles, and sand inclusions (Burton 1991:50–52; Crown and Wills 1995a:176; Haury and Sayles 1947:326–29; Skibo and Blinman 1999; Wilson and Blinman 1991). As noted, use alteration marks indicate that vessels were indeed used for both cooking and storage (Burton 1991:50–52; Skibo and Blinman 1999; although see Heidke, Miksa, and Wiley [1996], who argue that early vessels in the Hohokam area were used only for storage).

Like ground-stone tools, the earliest vessels appear to have been designed to serve multiple functions (Skibo and Blinman 1999). As populations became less mobile, the range of pottery forms increased. For cooking jars, potters employed a greater range of materials, shapes, and sizes to elicit specific performance characteristics for specific cooking tasks. The sequence matches that of ground stone, from generalized small, portable cooking tools to larger, more cumbersome tools better suited to specific tasks and processing larger batches.

Did the necessity of conserving one or more components of the cooking system lead to changes in container technology? First, in terms of conserving the cook's time and energy, researchers have attributed several changes in ceramic technology to time allocation and scheduling conflicts. Wills and I (Crown and Wills 1995a) argued that women maintained a heavy work load in the late Archaic and that scheduling conflicts might have *deterred* them from adding pottery manufacture to that work load until increased sedentism and greater dependence of cultigens required more frequent use of existing containers (baskets, bags, pits, and gourds) for storage and food processing. One possible reason for adding pottery production to their overburdened work schedule was that pottery was particularly suited for long-term boiling of food and preparation of corn as gruel. Following the work of S. B. Nerlove (1974), we noted that women often accommodate incompatible subsistence and child care activities through early weaning. Gruel prepared from corn would have been an ideal weaning food. Use of weaning foods is associated with increased fertility and decreased birth spacing. This argument follows that of Jane Buikstra and colleagues (1987; see also Braun 1987), who made a similar argument for the advent of pottery in the midwestern United States. Skibo and Blinman (1999) indicated that the use alteration traces found on early ceramics in the northern Southwest supported an argument for preparation of gruel in the early vessels.

In contrast, Heidke, Miksa, and Wiley (1996) estimated numbers of vessels produced yearly in an early site in the Tucson area and argued that the number of vessels manufactured was so low that women would not have been overburdened in producing pottery. Although it may be correct that the manufacture of vessels alone was not a particularly difficult addition to women's tasks, these researchers did not consider the broader contextual implications of the adoption of this technology discussed by Wills and me (Crown and Wills 1995a:179), which included more intensive food preparation techniques, new skills, a variety of new tools, new types of materials collection, and new burdens in gathering fuel and water, not to mention the conservative nature of technological styles in general.

Several later changes in pottery technology may reflect continuing concern with time allocation. Based on replication of prehispanic cooking jars using appropriate materials and methods, Blinman (1993:18) recently argued that it takes about one-third less time to manufacture a corrugated vessel than to obliterate the coil joints on both surfaces (Blinman 1993:18). It is possible, then, that the gradual transition from completely smoothed vessels to vessels with unsmoothed neck coils and then to corrugated pottery reflects increased concern over the time demands of pottery production. However, in a second replicative study, Chris Pierce (1996) challenged Blinman's results and argued that corrugated pots take three times longer to manufacture than plain vessels.

Research does demonstrate significant advantages in manipulating the surface treatment of vessels through smoothing, polishing, smudging, or adding other substances to the surface. All of these treatments reduce permeability and improve heating effectiveness (Rogers 1980; Schiffer 1990; Shepard 1938). By reducing the flow of water through the vessel wall, such surface treatments act to reduce the time needed to heat the vessel contents. Adding time in ceramic manufacturing tasks thus pays off significantly in reducing cooking time, as well as in preventing too much loss of vessel contents in the cooking process.

Changes in cooking vessel sizes over time might also relate to changing time allocation strategies. Scholars have documented increases in the sizes of cooking jars for several portions of the Southwest. In the Hohokam area, Haury (1938) noted a gradual increase in the sizes of cooking jars from the Pioneer through the Sedentary periods (approximately A.D. 500–1150). For Paquime, Di Peso, Rinaldo, and Fenner (1974a, vol. 6) noted increases in the volumes of cooking jars and bowls from about A.D. 1050 to 1500 (using the revised sequence dates). Barbara Mills (1999) demonstrated increases in cooking jar sizes for the Tusayan and Kayenta portions of the Puebloan area between A.D. 1000 and 1300 (see also Turner and Lofgren 1966). Marion Smith (1988) also demonstrated increases in cooking vessel sizes for sites in the Puebloan Black Mesa area from A.D. 800 to 1150, followed by a decline in size. H. Wolcott Toll and Peter McKenna (1987) documented increasing plain-ware jar sizes in Chaco Canyon. Various scholars have interpreted these changes as associated with changes in household size (Mills 1999; Nelson 1986:125; Smith 1988; Turner and Lofgren 1966) or with changes in the number or size of feasts (Mills 1999; Toll and McKenna 1987; see also Crown 1994; Graves and Eckert 1998; Nelson 1986; Spielmann 1998), interpretations that are discussed further below.

Changes in cooking vessel size might relate instead to scheduling conflicts. In an ethnographic study, Ben Nelson (1986:124) found that Maya women prepare all of the corn for the entire day in the morning in a single large jar. They also use smaller jars for cooking additional foods for individual meals. Although it is generally assumed that Southwestern women prepared food on a meal-by-meal basis, the trend toward larger cooking vessels might reflect a shift toward preparation of larger batches of food for multiple meals in response to increased time pressure. Such an interpretation would parallel that suggested for many of the changes in ground-stone technology; both developments were toward processing larger batches of corn more efficiently to save time, despite the greater initial effort involved. This interpretation also fits with contemporaneous evidence for a lack of comparable change in the size of consumption vessels in some areas (Smith 1988:921; although see Mills 1999). Historically in southern Arizona, women prepared enough gruel in the morning to last the entire day (Underhill 1979b:37).

Next there is the possibility that changes in containers were designed to conserve nutrients in food or or to increase the nutritional value of foods. In comparison with cooking in baskets or pits, pottery was a superior product that greatly expanded the range of cooking techniques for the same foods and was generally used in conjunction with techniques that derived greater nutritional value from those foods. The moist heating method associated with cooking cultigens in pottery containers, particularly long-term boiling, promotes greater absorption of nutrients, produces a more readily digested product than dry heat, and sterilizes food (Arnold 1985:136; Skibo and Blinman 1999; Stahl 1989:179–81). Rendering grease from bone is considerably more efficient and easier in pottery containers as well (Crown and Wills 1995a:176). In addition, pottery would have provided containers for fermentation, which also improves digestibility (Arnold 1985:136; Stahl 1989:179–80). Use of pottery probably resulted in greater equality in the nutritional values of foods consumed by different members of a single commensal unit, particularly through the preparation of stews (Crown and Wills 1995a:180). Meat sharing among foragers may be inequitable, with women receiving less-desirable portions (Speth 1990); cooking stews might have helped alleviate such inequities in protein consumption.

Later changes in pottery improved the nutritional quality of foods as well. Smudged vessels retard the growth of bacteria and fungi, preserving the largest possible yield from stored foods. They would have been particularly useful for producing and storing alcoholic beverages (Rogers 1980). The shift to overall corrugation of cooking pots in the

Mogollon and Pueblo areas might have been associated with increased cooking times to increase the digestibility of corn and beans (Pierce 1996:8). David Snow (1990) argued that several new types of cooking technologies appeared in the late thirteenth century in association with pretreatment of maize by soaking it in a warm lime-alkali solution. The new tools included *comales*, fire dogs (adobe or stone knobs constructed surrounding a fire pit and used to hold cooking containers above a fire), and rectangular fire pits, all used to prepare tortillas or wafer bread. In the northern Rio Grande, these changes were accompanied by a return to smoothed cooking jars, possibly because the making of tortillas largely replaced long-term boiling of corn (Pierce 1996:8). Ben Nelson (1991:169) discussed how different ways of processing corn result in different assemblages of vessels: processing involving soaking in lime, boiling, wet grinding, and then boiling again requires a much larger inventory of vessels than dry-grinding and then boiling, yet both processes are used to create the same dishes in different cultures. Evidence from sites in the Salinas area suggests increased breakage of animal bones to extract marrow and grease in the late prehispanic period (Potter 1995). The use of larger cooking jars would have facilitated more intensive rendering of grease from bones through simmering or boiling as well.

Cooks attempting to conserve fuel might have cooked meals in a single vessel on a daily rather than a meal-by-meal basis. They might also have used techniques employing high heat for shorter periods rather than long-term simmering and used thinner-walled vessels to transmit heat more quickly and effectively from the fire to the food (see Braun 1983; although Tani [1994:64] argued that larger cooking vessels generally have thicker walls).

The trend discussed previously toward larger cooking vessels through time might reflect a shift toward cooking more foods, such as stews, in a single pot. High-heat techniques that employ containers include parching, boiling, and frying. It is not known whether the incidence of parching and boiling increased through time in the Southwest, but the appearance of *comales* in the late thirteenth to early fourteenth centuries indicates the use of frying to prepare tortillas and *piki* bread. Fine grinding of meal or flour prior to preparation, thin batter, and use of oil for frying ensure that this is a fast (albeit labor intensive) cooking technique. The appearance of this technique and associated tools at this time might reflect increased concern over fuel. It is possible also that cooks cut down on fuel use in winter by simmering foods for a long time on the same fire used to heat the dwelling. Unfortunately, data for monitoring such a proposition are lacking. Longitudinal studies of cooking vessel wall thickness are rare for the Southwest, so it is not possible to track this relationship.

In terms of conserving tools, changes in cooking vessel design might reflect concern with improving their durability and prolonging their use life. Exterior texturing of cooking vessels through corrugation and other plastic techniques in the Mogollon and Puebloan areas did not improve the rate of diffusion of heat over the vessel or the rate of cooling after heating (Schiffer 1990; Young and Stone 1990:202), but it did improve the durability of vessels subjected to repeated thermal shock (Pierce 1996). Cooks or potters could alleviate problems with heat loss in textured vessels by treating the interior either before or after firing to reduce permeability (Schiffer 1990). Smudging has additional advantages, because the combustion products implanted in the vessel wall in smudging have bactericidal and fungicidal properties that would have allowed women to cook, serve, or store food in the same vessel for a longer period of time before bacterial or fungal growth became problematic (Rogers 1980).

Finally, I consider whether changes in the organization of food preparation might have led to changes in container technology. A change in the ratio of food preparers to consumers should produce predictable patterns in the archaeological record, including the presence of larger cooking vessels and a change in the ratio of cooking vessels to serving vessels. Such changes might be associated with increased feasting and the preparation of food above the needs of the household by a few women particularly skilled at cooking the special foods generally associated with feasts. A trend toward larger cooking vessels did occur in the Southwest but could have been a response to several possible factors. Blinman (1989) documented differences in the ratios of cooking to serving vessels and the sizes of cooking jars between assemblages from roomblocks with different ceremonial rankings in southwestern Colorado. Roomblocks with the higest ranking had fewer cooking jars per serving bowl, and the cooking jars were smaller than those from roomblocks with lower rankings. Blinman argued that such patterning reflects potluck-style feasting associated with the highest-ranked ceremonial structures. It might also reflect some degree of specialized food preparation for large-group gatherings. Additional data for assessing shifts in the organization of food preparation are currently lacking.

As in the case of ground stone, I conclude that there is little evidence to suggest that major changes in diet led to changes in Southwestern cooking containers. The initial appearance of pottery was probably tied in part to decreasing mobility, and the early forms suggest generalized shapes designed to fulfill a variety of functions while remaining lightweight and portable. With increasing sedentism, the range of pottery produced increased, and potters achieved different combinations of forms, surface finishes, and materials that best fulfilled specific food preparation and cooking tasks. Once Southwestern populations were largely sedentary (after about A.D. 500), changes in the forms, surface finishing, and materials of cooking containers indicate a general concern with saving time in cooking, increasing the nutritional yield from cooked foods, increasing the efficiency and durability of the containers, and decreasing fuel consumption associated with cooking. There is a possibility that increased feasting led to shifts in the organization of food preparation and to the use of larger cooking vessels to prepare larger batches.

Change in Facilities for Cooking in the Prehispanic Southwest

Features for cooking food included roasting pits, ovens, fire pits within houses, and fire pits in outdoor areas. A recent attempt at comparing such features in the Mimbres area suggests that indoor fire pits burned hardwood and might have been used for slow cooking, whereas outdoor fire pits used softwood and might have been used for faster, hotter cooking (Sobolik, Zimmerman, and Guilfoyl 1997). Unfortunately, there have been relatively few attempts to document change through time in the morphology and size of cooking facilities. Comparison of fire features at the Chodistaas site and Grasshopper Spring Pueblo (both dating to the late 1200s) indicates the presence of four types of features, three of them used for cooking. The four are circular, clay-lined hearths interpreted as all-purpose domestic features used for heating, cooking, and light; rectangular slab-lined hearths used for cooking (these occur in association with grinding activities, suggesting use for particular types of cooked foods); unlined circular hearths used primarily for heat and light; and roasting pits found in outdoor areas used for food preparation (Lowell 1995). A study of change in room and hearth size through time at Grasshopper Pueblo (A.D. 1300–1425) revealed no significant change in habitation room size but a steady decline in hearth size over time. Richard Ciolek-Torrello and J. Jefferson Reid (1974:44) interpreted this change as one associated with a decrease in household size, but they noted that Richard Woodbury suggested it might be due to decreasing fuel supplies. The latter interpretation seems to fit the evidence better, given the lack of a concomitant change in habitation room size. Grasshopper Pueblo postdates the Chodistaas and Grasshopper Spring sites and is a much larger site. In addition to the fire features noted at the earlier ruins in the area, Grasshopper has a number of outdoor ovens. The presence of such ovens suggests a changing cuisine, a change in the ratio of cooks to heating features, or a change in the organization of food preparation with a concomitant shift in the ratio of preparers to consumers.

In the eastern Puebloan area, cooks began using *comales* in the late 1200s in conjunction with new, rectangular slab-lined hearths featuring fire dogs (Snow 1990).

Such studies suggest that features used for cooking food increased in variety and form through time. This finding parallels the increasingly specialized forms of grinding tools and pottery containers through time. The evidence also suggests an increasing concern with fuel efficiency as easily available fuel surrounding villages was depleted.

UNDERSTANDING CHANGES IN CUISINE IN THE AMERICAN SOUTHWEST

I conclude, then, that various factors were responsible for changes in cuisine in Southwestern prehistory. Comparison of dates of adoption of new foods with dates of changes in cooking technology do suggest that populations were most likely to adopt new foods that fit the existing cuisine. However, later shifts toward increasing reliance on cultigens, along with changes in the relative mix of existing foods in the diet, might have encouraged women to utilize novel techniques for processing and preparing their meals. Changes in cooking technology in all areas of the Southwest between about A.D. 1 and 500 were probably largely responses to decreasing mobility, increasing reliance on cultigens, increasing work loads, and scheduling conflicts. Once Southwestern populations were largely sedentary, changes in cooking technology seem to represent attempts to minimize loss to the four components of the cooking system, although each change also reflects trade-offs in balancing one type of loss against another. Cooks saved time by using larger ground-stone tools, but they expended greater physical energy in doing so. They created new recipes that increased nutritional yields from a given quantity of food, but they expended greater time and energy in preparing those recipes. Cooking tools were made more durable and permanent but in some cases took more time to create (Fratt and Biancaniello 1993). Techniques that used less fuel typically entailed significantly greater initial processing time in order to reduce cooking time. In virtually every case, cooks were willing to expend more energy or time to minimize expenditures of nutrients, fuel, or wear on their tools.

The significant variation in the timing of adoption of most techniques for processing food after A.D. 500 suggests that women adopted new tools when the benefits of conserving one or more of the components outweighed the costs of depleting their own time and energy supplies. Of course, one way to minimize this loss was to increase kitchen help, especially through having more children and socializing them in food preparation earlier (Schlegel and Barry 1986:143). The available record limits our ability to pursue this line of reasoning, but the evidence does suggest that human time and energy were less critical than nutrients, fuel, and even tool use-life in creating the changes researchers have documented.

ALTERNATIVE EXPLANATIONS

Two alternative explanations for the increased tool sizes recorded through time are worth noting (see Mills 1999 for an excellent review of these models). One common explanation is that commensal unit size increased, creating a need for larger tools that processed bigger batches more efficiently. For instance, increases in the size of milling stones would have allowed women to intensify grinding and create more meal in the same amount of time that smaller tools ground smaller amounts

(Adams 1993). Likewise, increased cooking vessel size might reflect increases in the sizes of domestic units (Mills 1999; Turner and Lofgren 1966). In situations where concomitant changes in serving vessel sizes or in habitation unit sizes are documented, this explanation may be correct. The changes in tools do not signal a change in cuisine but merely a change in the size of the group consuming food in the household. In at least some instances, however, where change in the sizes of cooking containers or fire features was attributed to change in the sizes of the domestic units, habitation unit sizes or serving vessel sizes remained stable (Ciolek-Torrello and Reid 1974; Smith 1988).

Another alternative is that changes in tool size are related to increased feasting activity. This explanation is similar to the first in suggesting that increased tool size relates to increases in the size of the group consuming food, but in this instance it is not the domestic unit that grows but rather the scale or incidence of communal eating occasions. Several researchers have suggested that larger cooking and serving vessels reflect their use in communal feasts (Blinman 1989; Crown 1994; Graves and Eckert 1996; Mills 1989, 1993, 1995a, 1999; Nelson 1986; Snow 1982; Spielmann 1996; Toll and McKenna 1987; Turner and Lofgren 1966). Because all societies have feasts of one sort or another, it is certain that populations in the Southwest did as well. It is also plausible that larger containers were useful for feasting. The largest cooking vessels in all time periods are arguably most suited for cooking food for feasts. However, this does not explain the general trend toward larger cooking vessels through time. Feasts might have necessitated a large pot or two per household, but they would not have necessitated change in the mean or modal cooking vessel size. Feasting can be used as an explanation for the gradual, continuing change in cooking vessel size documented in many portions of the Southwest only if the argument is made that feasts simultaneously and gradually increased in size as well. Furthermore, it is doubtful that special grinding tools were created to process food for feasts alone. Instead, women probably expended additional energy and time processing food for feasts on their regular grinding tools, just as they did historically in the Southwest (Adams 1993). Ethnographically, Pueblo women used large vessels to prepare food for feasts and for any other occasions involving large groups of people (Wyckoff 1985).

I conclude that some shifts toward larger tool sizes may relate to increases in the size of the commensal unit or to increased feasting behavior, but other shifts that are not accompanied by clear evidence for changes in the size of the domestic unit or in the scale of feasting were probably due to changes in Southwestern cuisine associated with the number of meals prepared per day.

THE SEXUAL DIVISION OF LABOR AND CHANGES IN CUISINE

The purpose of the School of American Research seminar was to document and evaluate changes in the sexual division of labor (J. K. Brown 1970) and gender hierarchies in the middle-range societies occupying the precontact Southwest. Several cross-cultural studies indicate that women make the primary contribution to food processing and preparation regardless of their contribution to food production (Burton and White 1984; Ember 1983; Kurz 1987; Murdock and Provost 1973; White, Burton, and Brudner 1977). The actual amount of work associated with processing domesticated crops is generally greater than the amount of work associated with wild plants, particularly those found in the American Southwest. In many historical societies, this increasing burden in food processing was not offset by less time in food production (Ember 1983).

While it is thus probable that the sexual division of labor relating to food processing and preparation remained stable throughout the precontact sequence, with women always undertaking the burden of work associated with these tasks, there is strong evidence that the specific tasks and work load associated with food processing changed over time. Data suggest that the first major shift in food processing occurred at the Paleo-Indian–Archaic interface, for which there is increased evidence of plant processing and hunting of small game. Increased reliance on small seeds and nuts required changes in tools. This shift in tools to increased seed grinding may reflect an initial increase in the cook's work load (Wright 1994).

A second shift occurred with increasing reliance on cultigens and increasing residential stability in the Late Archaic. A recent study compared prehispanic skeletal material from Late Archaic sites in Texas (where cultigens were never incorporated into the economy) with remains from preceramic, early agricultural (Late Archaic) sites in southeastern Arizona and from the late prehispanic site of Pottery Mound in New Mexico (where intensive agriculture was practiced). Examination of cortical bone on femurs from the three groups revealed declining mobility, from foraging to early agriculture to intensive agriculture (Ogilvie 1996). Thus, the female skeletons reveal that women undertook fewer tasks involving mobility, including gathering wild plants, and were more involved in sedentary activities, particularly food preparation within the village.

A third shift occurred between A.D. 1 and 400 with the appearance of pottery containers, which are associated with increased sedentism. These containers allowed more intensive processing of cultigens and secure long-term storage of cultigens. More intensive processing and long-term storage placed additional burdens on women's time, in part because dried foods require longer processing times than fresh foods. The appearance of trough metates within 200 to 300 years of the appearance of pottery suggests a final stage in the move toward sedentism. Trough metates are not designed for long-distance movement, nor are they generalized tools for processing a variety of plants; instead, trough metates are designed to process maize efficiently and yet be moved from house to outdoor area. Women expended more energy grinding on trough metates with two-hand manos but were able to grind more corn more time-efficiently, and the tools had great durability. Tool forms increased in size and weight until limitations in utility were reached. Once again, studies of skeletal material reveal the effects of this increased work load and the use of two-hand manos. At the site of Pottery Mound alone, women showed greater upper-body robusticity than adult men, as well as greater symmetry in upper-body bone density, undoubtedly due to their work loads, which likely included grinding meal, gathering fuel and water, child care, and burden carrying (Ogilvie 1993).

From this point onward, cooking tools in the Hohokam area remained unchanged until the addition of the *comal*, whereas tool designs in the Mogollon and Puebloan areas postdating A.D. 500 display parallel trends toward increasing effort in processing food through time. In these areas, women developed a variety of new tool forms that saved time, fuel, nutrients, and tool wear while they expended increasing effort in preparing meals. There is the possibility that women dealt with losses of time and fuel by cooking fewer meals and cooking more food at once. The final major change in food processing occurred throughout the inhabited Southwest around A.D. 1300 with the appearance of tools for making tortillas or *piki* bread, highly labor-intensive foods.

Dramatic differences in the timing of adoption of various cooking tools indicate that the decision to make pottery or grind corn using a new form of metate was made on a family by family basis (Skibo and Blinman 1999). Southwestern families largely shared the same dietary components (particularly the staples) after A.D. 1, yet the variety of cuilinary tools used in different areas at different times suggests significant differences in the cuisines in the Southwest. However, the general trend toward development of an array of tools for processing maize suggests shared concerns with variety in meals and with conserving losses of time, nutrients, fuel, and tool wear and tear. The solutions to these concerns differed slightly from area to area, but they all reveal the importance of food preparation in these societies. The possibility that the organization of food preparation changed late in prehistory should be explored further in the future.

GENDER HIERARCHIES AND CHANGES IN CUISINE

Intensification of food processing was an important response to food stress, nutritional deficiencies, and fuel depletion. But this solution came at the expense of women's work load. An important issue then becomes how this increasing burden in food processing affected women's status relative to other women and to men in these societies.

Anthropologists document associations between women's contributions to subsistence and their status. For instance, Peggy Sanday (1974) argued that women's status is low in societies where the two sexes do not make equal contributions to subsistence, so that women are subordinate both in societies where they make a low contribution to subsistence and in those where they make a high contribution. Several researchers have documented declining status for women with increasing intensification of agriculture (Ember 1983; Whyte 1978:138). Other researchers suggest that women are more highly regarded when they make a high contribution to subsistence (Schlegel and Barry 1986). Patricia Draper (1975) found declining influence with decreased mobility.

Unfortunately for my purposes, these studies generally considered production of food rather than processing of food. Several studies that have discussed a relationship between food processing and status suggest that the more time women spend in activities within the home, including food processing, the lower their status (Ember 1983; Martin and Voorhies 1975). Such domestic work for women creates inequalities in access to knowledge, community activities, and gossip. The decreased birth spacing associated with sedentism and dependence on cultigens created additional burdens in child care that may have reduced women's influence outside the domestic sphere (Ember 1983:300–301).

On the basis of these discussions, I might conclude that women's status declined throughout the prehispanic sequence in the American Southwest as their work load increased. I question this simple answer, however. First, researchers who study particular societies in detail, rather than analyzing cross-cultural codes, generally argue that the apparent status of women in the eyes of outsiders may be quite different from their actual status and power. To some extent this is because of Western bias about what constitutes status and power, which is generally assumed to be political power. It is also because women in these cultures often perceive their own roles and status quite differently from those suggested in reports by their male counterparts or in the cultural ideology. Whenever men are dependent on women's productive activities, particularly for acquiring their own prestige, women often wield considerable influence (Brumfiel 1991; Nash 1978; Sillitoe 1985; Strathern 1984:25; Weiner 1986; Wylie 1992). The importance of food in many transactions and interactions in Southwestern society suggests that women's status might not have declined through time, even if they were less involved than men in political activity (Crown and Fish 1996). Instead, it is likely that parallel, complementary status hierarchies existed for women. Such separate prestige hierarchies have been posited for the Classic-period Hohokam on the basis of the presence of high-value items in adult females' burials that are different from the high-value items in male graves and that include the tools of productive activities (Crown and Fish 1996).

Second, if the incidence and scale of feasting or the use of food in ceremonial activities increased throughout the prehispanic sequence (Blinman 1989; Graves and Eckert 1996; Mills 1999; Spielmann 1995; Toll and McKenna 1987), then women held a crucial role in social interactions outside the domestic sphere. As noted previously, food associated with feasting and ritual generally takes time to prepare, is scarce, and is highly valued or costly to obtain (Farb and Armelagos 1980:147). Recipes for foods used in feasts and ceremonies may be particularly enduring, as is the recipe for *piki* bread, which has not changed during the historic period and which cooks must still prepare in the traditional way. Obtaining the skill to prepare such foods is an important part of socialization for Pueblo girls and may have been required before marriage (O'Kane 1950). If this were the case in prehistory, then mastering the recipes and technology of Southwestern cuisine was obviously a critical step in becoming an adult woman. And acquiring the skill to prepare certain dishes might have been one avenue to increased status within the community. Much of cuisine involves knowledge rather than hardware (McGaw 1996), and an adult woman who had the knowledge to prepare difficult and socially important dishes possessed a valuable skill that could be passed on only through teaching or demonstration to the next generation.

Third, coordination and cooperation within work groups are important aspects of food processing in many societies as well (Murphy and Murphy 1980:189–90) and may be associated with improved status for women. The appearance of special rooms with multiple mealing bins set in the floor and used by several women at once suggests the presence of task groups in at least some Southwestern villages after about A.D. 1000 (Hegmon, Ortner, and Mobley-Tanaka, this volume; Schlanger 1996a). The appearance of architecturally distinct loci for food processing at a time when food processing was requiring more time and effort from women suggests that the formation of such task groups might have been an important means of offsetting the isolation of women for long portions of their day.

Finally, as I discussed at the beginning of this chapter, cooks may influence and manipulate opinion in subtle ways, insulting or charming family or guests through the foods they serve and the manner in which they serve them. Through socialization, women in the domestic sphere create the future adults whose power and prestige may ultimately influence their own. I conclude, then, that because kitchen life and gastropolitics played crucial roles in the maintenance of society, Southwestern women must have continued to wield influence in the face of ever-increasing work loads.

8

Bodies and Lives

Biological Indicators of Health Differentials and Division of Labor by Sex

Debra L. Martin

The health status and labor contributions of men and women underpin every facet of community life. Poor health and occupational stress are empirical, nonrandom in distribution, and almost always related to ideology, social relations, politics, and economics (Doyal 1995). Health data on the effects of gender inequality presented at the 1995 World Conference on Women in Beijing, China, revealed that on a global scale women experience more chronic illness and disability over a lifetime than do men, and up to 50 percent of women are affected by trauma and/or physical abuse in their lifetimes (Hartman 1996). Along with men, women play a significant role in the labor force, especially in agrarian economies, but their contributions are often poorly understood and not well documented.

Recent scholarly work on women's health and labor in broadly cross-cultural contexts demonstrates that gender-based differences in access to resources, knowledge, and political power figure prominently in shaping patterns of ill health (e.g., Doyal 1995; Finkler 1994; McElmurry, Norr, and Parker 1993). There is a relationship connecting women's multiple roles and lower socioeconomic status with poorer health in many societies today (United Nations 1995), and recent bioarchaeological studies suggest that the trajectory of gender asymmetries, inequality, occupational hazards, and increased health risks for subgroups extends into the past as well (Goodman, Martin, and Armelagos 1995).

In exploring patterns of health and labor by gender for groups such as the Ancestral Pueblos, Mogollon, and Hohokam in the precontact Southwest, there is a large but highly variable literature on analyses utilizing human remains. Bioarchaeology, the study of human biological remains in archaeological contexts, made tremendous advances during the 1990s. Taking leads from studies in human adaptation and processual archaeology, it developed from being a descriptive science that delineated disease in time and space to being an explanatory science focused upon the processes by which people in antiquity became susceptible to illness and early death. Bioarchaeology has been limited, however, both materially (in terms of access to large, well-preserved collections) and theoretically. Theoretically it has been held back by the ecological biases inherent in the parent disciplines of archaeology and human adaptation, which emphasize environmental determinants. This has restricted the study of the relationship between health and social relations. A political-economic perspective, when applied to bioarchaeology (the focus of a 1992 Wenner-Gren Foundation conference), provides a framework for analysis of the biological consequences of social relations, differential access to resources and power, and regional influences (Goodman and Leatherman 1995). Although "ideology" and "power" do not leave unambiguous biological signatures, bioarchaeology is poised to enter a new era of research that integrates biology into analyses of cultural systems (Martin 1998).

In this chapter I use biological data to demonstrate the value of framing bioarchaeological research questions that utilize bodies as texts for "reading" the biological consequences of gender relations and differences in habitual activity and labor on health and longevity. I make no attempt to provide an exhaustive summary of all the biological studies to date that focus on health, labor, or gender. Instead, I focus on studies informed by a biocultural perspective that use biological data synthetically to assess the collective and accumulative forces of *physiological stress* (resulting in morbidity and mortality from differential risk factors) and *biomechanical changes* (resulting in modifications in skeletal size, shape, and form from occupational hazards and activity-induced strains and injuries). These types of integrative studies provide a way of evaluating the effects of gender hierarchies and sexual division of labor, the twin themes explored in this volume.

MONITORING AND INTEGRATING RISK FACTORS FOR MEN AND WOMEN IN THE PRECONTACT SOUTHWEST

It is clear that many of the health problems facing people worldwide today were endemic and vexing difficulties for groups living in the precontact Southwest. For example, iron deficiency anemia was ubiquitous among children and adults throughout the occupation of the Southwest (Walker 1985). Children experienced disruptions in their growth (Martin et al. 1991). Helminthic parasites such as pinworms and hookworms have been revealed in desiccated feces (Reinhard 1988, 1990). Treponemal infections and tuberculosis have likewise been documented (Baker and Armelagos 1988; Palkovich 1984; Stodder 1990). This list of potentially life-threatening illnesses does not address reverberations at the household or community level, because many osteological studies in the Southwest have been narrowly designed to isolate disease in time and space, and this has limited the investigation of health in larger synthetic studies (Martin et al. 1991).

Understanding the impact of biological disruption (dietary, nutritional, pathogenic, biomechanical, and traumatic) requires a systematic analysis that links biological data from individuals to the environmental and cultural world in which they lived. Disease states compromise individuals but can also affect activities at the household and community levels.

For an analysis of gender-related health risks, the interpretation of patterns of skeletal pathologies requires a systematic evaluation of a wide range of ecological and biocultural factors that can increase the risk of and susceptibility to morbidity and early mortality for women and/or men (fig. 8.1). This task is analytically challenging, but it is crucial that skeletal data be integrated with other archaeological data. This model highlights those factors most likely to be significant in the interpretation of health and longevity, particularly for adult men and women.

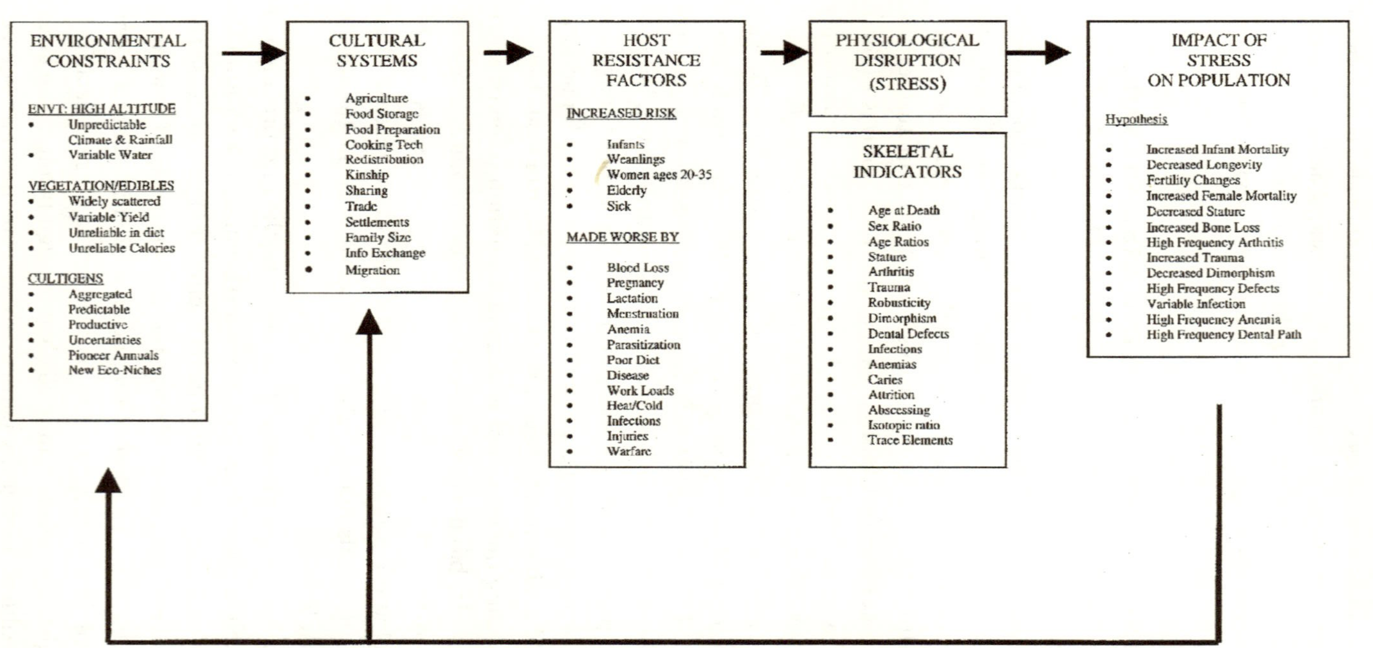

FIGURE 8.1.

Model for the analysis of biological indicators of health and habitual activities for adult women in precontact agricultural communities. The factors outlined in the boxes include environmental variables, cultural behaviors, subgroups most at risk due to compromised physiologies, and the possible outcomes that can be measured on the human skeleton. Hypotheses listed in the box at far right cover ways in which women can become at risk for ill health and early mortality.

Environmental Constraints and Diet

Cultigens (primarily maize, squash, and beans in the Colorado Plateau area and maize and agave in southern Arizona) are aggregated, nonrandom in distribution, and predictable in location, yield, and caloric content. But given the climatic vicissitudes of the southwestern United States, annual productivity of the crops was likely uncertain at times, and farming was a labor-intensive activity (Powell 1983; Schlanger 1988). Given the storage facilities found at some sites, it is conceivable that several years' worth of maize was grown during good years and stored for use during seasons when crops failed (Minnis 1989).

Naturally occurring edible wild plants are low in density in the Southwest, widely scattered, unreliable as dietary staples, and unpredictable in caloric contribution, particularly in areas such as the Colorado Plateau. Land cleared for agricultural use can attract a variety of "pioneer annuals" that are edible and might have contributed to the dietary base (Ford 1984). These plants, which include *Chenopodium*, *Portulaca*, and *Amaranthus*, are particularly attracted to newly cleared and planted plots of land. Older, abandoned fields attract Indian ricegrass and cacti, both of which are edible. These plants would have been found in localized dense patches and could have provided a predictable addition to the diet (Minnis 1989).

Animal protein was fundamental in the Southwestern diet, although faunal studies suggest variability and decreases over time in the larger game animals (e.g., Ezzo 1992; Stiger 1979). Michelle Semé (1984) demonstrated that gardening creates new niches that attract animals into an area in greater numbers (primarily rodents and rabbits). Although these animals might not ordinarily have been hunted as food sources (especially rodents), their high numbers in human-made fields might have contributed a predictable and localized protein source to the diet.

From a health perspective, it is important to remember that adults need very little animal protein to meet the the U.S. Department of Agriculture's Recommended Dietary Allowance (RDA). It is growing children and pregnant women who need high-quality protein daily. The most recent USDA dietary guidelines suggest that for optimal health, most calories should come from plants. The 1992 U.S. government

Food Guide Pyramid argues graphically that 85 percent of calories should come from plant foods and the rest from a combination of animal products.

For example, an adult female needs approximately 2,000 calories and 45 grams of protein per day (FoodPro 1996). RDAs are exceeded with a daily diet of six cups of maize, two tortillas, two cups each of beans and squash, one cup of amaranth, one ounce of turkey meat, and one-half ounce of pine nuts. If turkey and pine nuts are removed, the RDA for protein is still met but calories dip below the RDA. Pregnant women need 15 percent more calories and 65 percent more protein than nonpregnant women, which suggests that one to two ounces of meat need to be in the daily diet in order to reach the RDAs. Wilma Wetterstrom (1986) modeled diet for the fourteenth-century Arroyo Hondo community in good versus lean years and demonstrated that lean years were hardest on children and pregnant women. Several studies have documented the existence of "food stress" and its impact on communities such as Arroyo Hondo (Palkovich 1980) and the Mimbres pueblos (Minnis 1985). The exact effects on any member of the community would have been determined by a wide range of factors as outlined in figure 8.1.

One common finding in studies of Southwestern skeletal series is the presence of nutritional anemias. Mahmoud El-Najjar and colleagues (1976) compared numerous Southwestern skeletal populations in terms of their dependence on maize, which is a poor source of iron, protein, and other nutrients (Cravioto et al. 1945). Their sample was drawn primarily from Colorado Plateau sites, and they concluded that maize dependence in marginal areas such as those found in the Southwest predisposes people, particularly women and children, to nutritional anemias.

Phillip Walker (1985) expanded these findings with an exhaustive review and synthesis of the published literature on nutritional anemias from major Southwestern sites. Using a broadly ecological and biocultural perspective for his analysis, Walker concluded that the prevalence of bone lesions indicative of anemia resulted from the interaction of a complex set of factors relating to both nutrition and infectious disease. "Lack of iron in the diet, prolonged breast feeding, diarrheal and helminth infections, and living conditions conducive to the spread of disease all appear to have contributed to the prevalence of anemia" (1985:153).

Women need approximately 18 milligrams of iron daily, and for pregnant or lactating women, the RDA doubles. Children and adult males need 15 milligrams daily. With one ounce of meat and one-half ounce of pine nuts added to daily cultigens, the iron in the diet falls short by 10 percent. If there is no meat or nuts in the diet, the iron falls short by 40 percent. It is easy to see how an indigenous diet based largely on cultigens with sporadic additions of meat could produce a endemic problem with iron depletion.

Ann Palkovich (1985) summarized health in general terms for a number of Southwestern sites. She suggested that endemic nutritional stress prevailed throughout the Colorado Plateau region during all phases of occupation (Basketmaker II through Pueblo III). She speculated that this was a different pattern from that found in recent times in other parts of the world, where nutritional stress is episodic, not endemic. Her regional and temporal analysis suggests that inadequate diet and poor health were continual problems.

There are many other ways in which knowledge about the environmental, climatic, ethnobotanical, palynological, faunal, and floral conditions in the Southwest could be used to fine-tune interpretations of the effects of diet on health, as I discuss later.

Cultural Systems

In bioarchaeological studies, the environment is only one of several important variables that must be carefully evaluated. Changes in health should be measured not as a direct function of environmental constraints but rather as the result of a combination of forces filtered through a cultural system that can either link women and men to poor health or buffer them and enhance good health and a long life. Integration of health data with knowledge and ideas about cultural systems necessarily involves collaboration with archaeologists whose work includes the analysis of factors such as the gendered use of space, ritual activities and objects, differences in mortuary treatment, the sexual division of labor in craft and pottery production, agricultural activities, gathering, hunting, and food processing and preparation, and other political, ideological, and economic areas of gendered activities. The chapters in this volume all contribute in important ways to the bioarchaeological investigation of gender differentiation and can be used as models for considering where linkages across data categories are most useful.

Taken together, environmental constraints in the Southwest suggest a marginal and unstable ecosystem that may have produced food shortages and crop failures in prehispanic times. Cultural mechanisms, however, can effectively buffer such events. Precontact groups employed a diversity of food procurement strategies that included agriculture, harvesting wild plants, and hunting (Gumerman 1988). Structures for storing food increased in kind and number over time across the Southwest (Wills 1988b, 1991). The preparation of food became more efficient with a shift to new techniques. Basin metates and one-hand manos were replaced with trough metates and two hand-manos, suggesting that corn was ground into finer particles prior to cooking. This might have had beneficial nutritional effects.

A variety of other cultural and behavioral responses were probably operating in the Southwest. Stephen Plog and Shirley Powell (1984) suggested that mating networks of given communities were probably quite large and widespread during periods of low population density. As communities became more sedentary and densely populated, social and mating networks out of necessity would have become more proximally located. This might have led to an intensification of cooperation and social integration within villages. At the same time, local exchange between villages might have become more important as an aid in buffering productive variation. Thus, as the more marginal upland areas became the sites of sedentary communities, groups might have been forced to organize themselves in such a way as to maintain cohesive social networks within which food and other resources could be shared (Plog and Powell 1984:213). Recent work by Carla Van West and Timothy Kohler (Kohler 1996) in southwestern Colorado explored potential maize production and demonstrated that sharing was particularly evident during high-yield years, whereas hoarding occurred during unfavorable years.

Although many such cultural and behavioral responses might have effectively buffered inhabitants during some environmental perturbations, it could be argued that the Southwest was marginal enough to have produced stressors of a magnitude that could not be effectively buffered. For example, if people relied increasingly on cultigens through time, they would have had difficulty meeting dietary requirements if they experienced crop failures several years in a row. This problem would have been compounded if group size was growing and if groups had invested in a rigid set of adaptive strategies. On the other hand, increased sharing, storage capacity, trading, and redistribution of limited resources, along with flexibility in resource type and procurement, could have offset the stress produced by unsteady crop production.

Cultural innovations can be both good and bad. For example, when Hohokam people built canals to bring water from the source to their villages, they created the potential for contaminating their water supply (Fish, Fish, and Madsen 1990). Humans and animals many miles from the village could have contaminated the water with parasites, bacteria, amoebae, and other infectious agents, thereby spreading disease quite efficiently among widely dispersed groups. Issues of sanitation and aggregation are crucial to consider for large and dense sites. Grasshopper Pueblo, for example, is located next to an artificial reservoir, and use of that water for domestic purposes could have put many people at risk if there were contaminants in the reservoir. As another example, it was a mixed blessing to live in the cliff dwellings at Mesa Verde. Andrew Christenson (1991) demonstrated that the microenvironments of cliff dwellings provided warmer winter temperatures, protection from moisture, and ease of defense, but they were also highly conducive to the spread of transmissible diseases such as respiratory illness and diarrheal diseases (Stodder 1990).

Host Resistance Factors

There are important immunological and physiological factors that can place individuals at risk because of their reduced capacity to ward off disease and other physiological disruptions. For example, groups such as infants, weanlings, reproductive-aged women, and women (or men) who are elderly, frail, or sick are more vulnerable because of reduced immune responses. Persons in these categories are automatically at increased risk to any further problems in the social arena that might affect them, such as inadequate diet and nutrition, exposure to the elements, and accidents or trauma. Any potentially negative condition in the social or ecological realm can further reduce the capacity of women, infants, and the elderly to survive. These conditions include blood loss, pregnancy, lactation, menstruation, anemia, parasitization, inadequate diet, multiple simultaneous diseases, heavy work loads, exposure to heat, cold, or dampness, chronic infections, acute injuries, and violence.

Physiological Disruption

The adult human skeletal system is relatively immune to mild and short-term nutritional stress. However, the skeletal system is in constant communication and cooperation with other systems. The primary functions of the skeleton are support and locomotion, storage and regulation of minerals (especially calcium and phosphorus), protection of the brain, spinal cord, and other organs, and production of red blood cells (Raisz 1982). This diverse set of functions in one system indicates the degree to which the entire body is dependent on the skeleton. Thus, a careful reading of a variety of subtle morphological changes reveals physiological disruptions.

Although the adult skeleton may not show the effects of mild stressors, the growing bones and teeth of children are often altered in measurable ways (Adams 1969; Goodman et al. 1988). Specifically, chronic or episodic physiological stress can disrupt growth, and these disruptions often leave permanent markers on bone and teeth that persist into adulthood (Buikstra and Cook 1980; Goodman et al. 1993; Larsen 1987). These retrospective markers of previous physiological insults are among the most useful indicators of diet and disease for prehistoric skeletal remains.

Many diseases leave their "signatures" on bone. Tuberculosis, syphilis, and leprosy cause skeletal changes that are specific to each pathogen. Many other pathogens, however, leave only generalized changes in the skeleton. One frequently observes a reaction on the bone periosteum (outer layer) reflecting a pathogenic change of unknown origin. These periosteal reactions—inflammations that leave a roughened appearance on the outer layer of bone—occur when the fibrous outer layer is stretched and subperiosteal hemorrhages occur (Steinbock 1976). Microorganisms such as staphylococcus and streptococcus can cause these changes in bone. These are precisely the common transmissible diseases that account for a great majority of sickness and death in populations worldwide even today (Ortner and Putschar 1981).

Agriculturalists experience a distinctly different disease ecology from that of nomadic gatherer-hunters, and for the prehistoric Southwest, agriculture has been documented to have been an important part of the subsistence base since at least 1000 B.C. (Wills 1988b). Corresponding increases in sedentism and in population size and density, along with the domestication of animals, would all have increased the disease load. It is estimated, however, that a population of about 300,000 (such as that in Mexico at Teotihuacan) is required in order for a disease such as measles to become endemic (Storey 1988). The lower population sizes and densities estimated for the American Southwest indicate that this level was likely never reached (Nelson et al. 1994).

In the Southwest, the turkey (domesticated by at least A.D. 200 during the Basketmaker II period at Canyon de Chelly) might have been a source of ornithoses, shigella, and salmonella (Kunitz and Euler 1972). Ectoparasites such as head lice (*Humanus pediculus*), endoparasites such as ascarids (nematode worms), and bacteria such as staphylococcus would also have been present. The sedentism associated with agriculture brings people into close contact with their wastes. Often, disposal of excrement in or near the source of potable water increases the potential for contamination.

Karl Reinhard (1988) provided a detailed regional study of parasitism based on an analysis of prehistoric human fecal remains from Southwestern sites. This important study documented the presence of a variety of helminth infestations in specimens from the Colorado Plateau. Reinhard also compared agriculturalist specimens with Archaic hunter-gatherer specimens and reported a marked increased in the numbers and types of parasites for the agriculturalists. Interestingly, *Chenopodium* has anthelmintic properties and could have been widely used as a treatment for intestinal parasites (Kliks 1985).

Contagious and transmissible diseases that likely were present in the Southwest include tick-borne fevers, Q fever, rabies, tularemia, giardia, and sylvatic plague, all carried by dogs, rabbits, and coyotes (Woodbury 1965). L. M. Van Blerkom (1985) has provided an inclusive list of viruses thought to have been present; it includes staphylococcal and streptococcal viruses, some forms of herpes and hepatitis, poliomyelitis, pertussis, and rhinoviruses.

Impact on Community

Understanding physiological disruption and the effects of stress on a population feeds directly back into an understanding of cultural buffering and environmental constraints. It is extremely important to understand how disease and death have important functional and adaptive consequences for the community. Poor health can reduce the work capacity of adults without necessarily causing death (Leatherman et al. 1986). Decreased reproductive capacity might occur if maternal morbidity and mortality are high in the youngest adult females (Population Reports 1988). Individuals experiencing debilitating or chronic health problems might disrupt the patterning of social interactions and social unity and might strain the system of social support.

TEMPORAL AND SPATIAL PATTERNING IN BIOLOGICAL INDICATORS

Summarizing patterns in health and labor by gender for the Southwest is difficult because researchers often do not collect or present data in ways that permit their direct use in other studies. Osteologists and bioarchaeologists have been interested in different questions and therefore have structured their analyses differently. In light of this, I present selected data here that provide information useful in thinking about the development of adult health and longevity, gender hierarchies, and sexual division of labor. The objective is to provide examples of how data can be integrated across biology and culture. It is hoped that others will then collect or reanalyze data from their areas of expertise and continue to build on the understanding of the gendered patterns of health and labor presented here. Although this presentation focuses primarily on Ancestral Pueblo data from the Colorado Plateau and Rio Grande areas, data do exist from the Mogollon, Mimbres, and Hohokam regions, and it is hoped that others will take those studies and integrate them with the method, theory, and data presented in this volume.

A.D. 200–850

For the Ancestral Pueblos living in the Four Corners region, Basketmaker III–Pueblo I human remains from Black Mesa, Canyon de Chelly, and the Prayer Rock district present to varying degrees pathologies suggesting that mild dietary inadequacies, infections, and childhood illnesses were problems that affected both sexes equally (El-Najjar et al. 1976; Martin et al. 1991; Morris 1980). The reported cases of infection and anemia are less severe than those of later groups, and the data suggest that low-level disease affected community members equally. Although agricultural productivity was moderate, wild plants and animals were fairly abundant throughout the region at this time (Duke 1965).

Human remains from the Ridges Basin region near Durango, Colorado, provide additional evidence that the disease burden was equally shared (Martin and Goodman 1995). In the adult population (n = 67), nutritional anemia was an almost equal liability for males (36.6 percent) and females (25.0 percent), suggesting that it was a function of shared dietary resources. Rates of transmissible infectious disease for males (11.1 percent) and females (15.3 percent) likewise suggest shared morbidity loads. Four males (25 percent) and five females (30 percent) had traumatic injuries that included a wide range of cranial and postcranial manifestations.

A.D. 850–1150

Black Mesa in northeastern Arizona is a marginal and isolated environment that was abandoned during the height of Puebloan development in other areas (circa A.D. 1150). Although agriculture was practiced there, people exploited many other local resources in order to exist year-round. There is evidence that maize was supplemented by a wide variety of nondomesticated plants and small game such as rodents and rabbits (Ford 1984; Semé 1984). Black Mesa was never a major population center or a "focal point for trade or Anasazi culture innovation" (Gumerman 1984:6). There is virtually no evidence of exotic trade items there, nor an abundance of nonutilitarian goods (Gumerman 1994; Powell 1983). Black Mesa was populated largely by farmers living in dispersed small groups.

Analysis of Black Mesa vital statistics (Martin et al. 1991) shows that young adult females (n = 38) had a slightly higher mortality rate than did age-matched males (n = 22). The mean age at death for all females was 21.6, and for all males, 24.4. Fewer males than females died in the age categories from 20 to 35 (20.6 percent and 44 percent, respectively).

Young adult females also showed more severe cases of infection than did age-matched males (16.7 percent versus 0 percent), but virtually all females and males showed some cranial lesions associated with iron deficiency anemia (83.5 percent). The overall picture is one of shared morbidity across all ages and sexes. A close examination of children reveals no differences in growth disruptions between boys and girls (judging from dental hypoplasia data).

Many studies of precontact North American populations report higher mortality for reproductive-aged women, suggesting that pregnancy and birth placed them at risk for high morbidity and early mortality (e.g., Blakely 1977; Lallo, Armelagos, and Rose 1978; Lovejoy et al. 1977). Worldwide literature on pregnancy-related deaths in agrarian societies demonstrates that prolonged and obstructed labor, combined with hemorrhage and infection, accounts for the deaths of at least 600,000 women yearly (Crossette 1996). A report on maternal deaths in Third World nations concluded that "for the most part, these are the deaths not of the ill, or the very old, or the very young, but of healthy women in the prime of their lives" (The Progress of Nations 1996:136).

A detailed examination of birth trauma was conducted utilizing obstetrical measurements obtained from the pelves of adult males and females from Black Mesa (Martin 1990, 1992; Martin and Seefeldt 1991). The design of the research involved calculating how constricted the birth inlet, midplane, and outlet were for women from Black Mesa who had died between the ages of 20 and 30 (n = 15), compared with women who had survived the reproductive years (n = 14) and with men (n = 10). Obstetric measurements for young females revealed a predominantly transverse oval (or platypelloid) shape with a brim index of 78.4. Females over the age of 30 had a generally circular (gynecoid) shape with a brim index of 81.1. These data demonstrate that women who died young most likely did so because of prolonged and obstructed labor due to flattened birth canals. Anatomical and clinical studies indicate that nutrition plays a critical role in the development of the pelvis (Angel 1978; Gebbie 1981; Thoms 1947). Lawrence Angel (1978:378) stated that "suboptimally nourished women have flatter pelvic inlets with shorter sagittal diameters than upper class and well nourished subjects."

An additional piece of data on fetal and infant health from Black

Mesa is that 23 percent of newborns dying before the age of one had dental defects from physiological stress while in utero. Furthermore, 83.3 percent of the one-year-olds had infections at the time of death. Normally, infants are protected from infections by immune factors in their mother's milk until weaning (Russo and Cramoy 1984; Worthington, Vermeersch, and Williams 1990). These data strongly suggest that ill or malnourished mothers gave birth to compromised infants (Martin et al. 1991:210).

This picture of maternal health is at odds with the classic notion of early precontraceptive populations, in which all women were assumed to be biologically prepared to bear children easily and at full fecundity levels. In reality, the effects of childbearing on morbidity and mortality were most likely devastating for females in antiquity, just as they are for women in rural farming communities today (Population Reports 1988). To view pregnancy and lactation as natural functions to which women are well adapted is misleading. Multiple pregnancies, long lactation periods, and inadequate nutrition can place even healthy women at risk.

In terms of the skeletal effects of work, carrying heavy loads on the back causes strain on the sacroiliac joint, which responds by buttressing the point of biomechanical stress. The habitual carrying of heavy loads causes accessory sacroiliac articulations that can be found on the sacrum and pelvis. As evidence of a gendered division of labor, Black Mesa women had more cases and showed greater severity in expression of the sacral and pelvic accessory sacroiliac articulations, with 80 percent of adult females and only 37 percent of adult males demonstrating involvement (Wesson and Martin 1995). This suggests that women habitually carried heavy loads on their backs.

In contrast, habitually sitting in either cross-legged or straight-legged fashion causes changes in the pelvic region around the ischial tuberosities. Osteophytes and raised ridges, or what is referred to in the literature as "weaver's bottom," are related to sitting. Among Black Mesa males, 75 percent had distinctive and pronounced morphological changes of this sort, whereas 25 percent of the females exhibited such changes. Thus, male work patterns involved activities that were done while sitting, whereas female's occupational stressors related more to active movement.

Studies were also conducted on bone size and width in order to calculate overall robusticity and strength (see Molleson 1994 for an excellent review). Many recent studies have shown strong correlations between behavior and skeletal morphology (Bridges 1989, 1990; Kennedy 1983, 1989; Merbs 1983). Utilizing the methods of Bass (1971), Genoves (1967), and Lovejoy and Trinkaus (1980), we took an exhaustive battery of measurements on all of the major muscle-bearing bones in the Black Mesa burial population (Bayendor and Martin 1989).

Results showed that Black Mesa male and female adults were significantly dimorphic (different) only in stature; they were indistinguishable in all measures of robusticity, strength, and muscularity (Martin et al. 1991: 214). These measurements control for length, so that what is revealed is comparative strength. The Black Mesa overall results were slightly higher than those for precontact Mississippian groups (Lovejoy and Trinkaus 1980). Further studies were conducted to assess bone mineral content to see whether male and female bones were equally well mineralized (Chan 1989). Cortical area was determined by placing a transparent grid of known area over a thin section and counting intersects following the methods of Sedlin, Frost, and Villanueva (1963). The percentage of bone relative to the size of the bone cavity was calculated. Cortical area is a direct function of both cortical thickness and bone diameter and therefore is a good indicator of bone development and maintenance (Garn 1970). No significant differences were found between cortical thickness measurements in males and females (male and female mean cortical thicknesses equaled 54.5 mm and 55.9 mm, respectively). Likewise, the figures for percentage of cortical area were very similar (male and female means equaled 72.3 percent and 71.7 percent, respectively).

These data suggest that both adult males and females had cortical thickness and percentage of cortical area measurements that fell well within the normal values for healthy individuals (Martin, Magennis, and Rose 1987:258–59). The relatively well-maintained bones of the Black Mesa adult population signify two concomitant processes that directly affect bone density: constant and habitual biomechanical use and consumption of an adequate diet, particularly in terms of calcium (Raisz and Kream 1983).

Because Black Mesa females were as robust and muscular as the males, it is likely that these women had lifestyles that were physically demanding. One interpretation is that both males and females participated in tasks, and although the tasks might have been different, they required strength in both upper and lower body. In a cross-cultural review of the sexual division of labor in traditional societies, Judith K. Brown (1970) suggested that the degree to which women participate in subsistence activities depends on the child-care situation in the community. On the basis of her research, she described four situations in which womanpower could be drawn on to maximize the efficiency of women in the labor force. These included work that is close to home, work that is monotonous and requires little concentration, work that is not dangerous for women and attendant children, and work that can be performed with many interruptions. In these circumstances, women can sustain both economic activities and child care simultaneously.

At prehispanic Black Mesa, a life of hard work and arduous tasks began to take its toll on both males and females at around age 30. Assessing the relationship of lower back (lumbar) osteoarthritis to age showed that 25 percent of adults experienced degeneration by the age of 25. By age 30, the figure increased to 33 percent, and by age 40, to 60 percent. Among the elderly, 86 percent had lumbar degeneration (Martin et al. 1991:220). Overall, females showed more involvement in vertebral degeneration than did males (63 percent to 47 percent, respectively).

Why were strong women dying young in childbearing at Black Mesa? Marvin Harris and E. B. Ross (1987:49) suggested that with agricultural intensification comes a concomitant pressure on women to increase their economic productivity simultaneously with an increase in their reproductivity. This places an enormous burden on women to partition their time, energy, and activities among different and competing tasks. Harris and Ross (1987:50) cited summary data on the number of hours that women work daily (seven days a week) in agriculturally based villages. The figures ranged from 6.7 to 10.8 hours a day.

Historically, anthropologists have looked at reproduction and mothering as universal categories (Rosaldo 1980). Women's economic roles were thought to be determined primarily by their reproductive function. Empirical data from Black Mesa support a prominent role for women in the economic arena that disrupts these older stereotypes.

Black Mesa inhabitants, although suffering from health problems, shared equal responsibilities all across the community in order to make a living on relatively sparse resources. In my mind, Black Mesa represents ordinary farmers living in small, remote, hamlet-type villages. They were connected in a variety of economic, trade-related, and ideological ways to the larger, centralized communities east and south of Black Mesa. The empirical data on health suggest no status differences between males and females except in the arena of reproductive risk. The biomechanical data strongly suggest a balanced work force, again except in the added area of childbearing and child rearing.

Women may have generally enjoyed status and power relatively equal to men's in these villages. Traumatic injury and signs of violence are virtually absent at Black Mesa (Martin 1998). Interestingly, women survived into old age at a higher rate than men (there were twice as many females aged 50 and older than males). This suggests two alternative hypotheses. One is that women who survived the risky reproductive years had better health care and nutrition and were in some manner buffered or aided differentially over other women. The other hypothesis calls into question the normative role of women as reproducers, suggesting that perhaps not all women bore children. This notion gains some support from a recent comparative study of fertility rates in the Southwest in which Ben Nelson and colleagues (1994) demonstrated that Black Mesa had the *lowest* fertility rate in a comparison with Mesa Verde, Arroyo Hondo, Chaco Canyon, and Casas Grandes.

Ancestral Pueblo people in southwestern Colorado in the Dolores River valley and at the Duckfoot site appear to have experienced a similar pattern of health. Health summaries provided for Duckfoot (A.D. 850–875; Hoffman 1993) and Dolores (Stodder 1987) suggest that there were no discernable differences by gender. Nutritional anemias, low-level infectious diseases, and minimal traumatic injuries are reported for both populations. Unfortunately, no detailed studies were conducted beyond those of basic observable pathologies. However, these preliminary and incomplete data do parallel the trends observed at Black Mesa and for that reason are intriguing, but more detailed studies clearly must be conducted.

A.D. 1150 to 1300

For prehispanic people living at Mesa Verde, data from the analysis of more than 500 individuals from early (pre–A.D. 975) to late periods (A.D. 975–1275) reveal that health declined significantly with age (Stodder 1984, 1987). Subadults exhibited a gradual increase in the probability of dying, in the prevalence of nutritional anemias, and in the frequency of developmental defects from birth to age five. Late adult females had more indicators of stress than younger females. A closer look at the raw data for the Pueblo II population reveals that in comparison with females, males were protected from illness during the young adult years (30 percent of the females reaching reproductive aged died by age 20, and an additional 30 percent died by age 25, compared with fewer than 10 percent in each category for males). Furthermore, females had higher frequencies and more severe manifestations of nutritional anemias in every age category than males (for example, in the age group 21–30, 28 percent of males and 42 percent of females demonstrated lesions).

During the early period, peaks in childhood morbidity at ages two to three suggest weaning stress at that time. In contrast, for the Pueblo II–III sample, the peak occurrence is later, at ages four to five, suggesting delayed weaning. Nutritional anemia and developmental defects are more prevalent in the Pueblo II–III children as well.

Why would women breastfeed their children longer? Data from Third World agrarian-based groups demonstrate that once weaning begins, a second peak in both morbidity and mortality of children is frequently seen (Gordon, Chitkara, and Wyon 1963; Gordon, Wyon, and Ascoli 1967). Young children become dependent on their own natural defenses at a time when those defenses are just beginning to develop. If nutrition is inadequate and transmissible infectious diseases rampant, as is frequently the case for children of this age in marginal communities, then these defenses will be further hindered. Thus, it is not unusual for mothers to attempt to forestall this stress on their children by breastfeeding them for longer periods, particularly during hard times (McNeish 1986).

However, even if Mesa Verde mothers were weaning their children later, they were still operating at full reproductive capacity. Nelson and colleagues (1994) suggested that the rate of fertility during the late period was extremely high—higher than that of Black Mesa, Chaco Canyon, or Casas Grandes.

It is impossible to assign sex to subadult skeletons, but dental defects recorded in adult teeth can be used to retrodict childhood stress. Judging from Ann Stodder's dental defect data, girls at age three at Mesa Verde had more defects than boys, suggesting that girls were more physiologically compromised, owing either to earlier weaning or to poorer nutrition and/or increased disease load.

Together, these data suggest that boys and adult males were buffered during what is interpreted as having been a stressful time at Mesa Verde. Why would boys and adult males demonstrate vitality in the face of population growth, strain on resources, increased exposure to communicable diseases, and a narrowing food base at Mesa Verde? If there was a bias toward protecting boys that systematically placed girls at increased risk, then the repeated insults might have had a lasting adaptive cost even to those girls and women who survived in terms of growth, reproduction, activity patterns, cognition, behavior, and social performance (Allen 1984; Haas and Harrison 1977). The literature on child preference for boys and benign neglect of girls relates these cultural practices to political-economic systems that subjugate women (Doyal 1995).

These data are intriguing for what they imply about life in more densely settled, politically centralized areas. However, the data are also sorely lacking in completeness, and few linkages between the biological data and the archaeological reconstruction can be made on the basis of Stodder's research.

Contemporaneous with Mesa Verde, Chaco Canyon probably supported thousands of people, though only several hundred burials have been excavated. Nancy Akins (1986), in an analysis of 132 Pueblo II–III remains, divided her sample into those from the largest Chaco Canyon site (Pueblo Bonito) and those from smaller sites throughout the canyon. Akins was interested in delineating differences in health for high-status (Pueblo Bonito) and low-status (small-site) individuals. She provided detailed analyses of a variety of indicators of growth and development, degenerative diseases, and mortality profiles.

According to Akins, "authority-holding elites" had greater access to nutritional resources and enjoyed better health (1986:137–40). The overall rate of nutritional anemia for all Chaco sites was 25 percent, significantly lower than rates at contemporaneous sites elsewhere (Walker 1985). The overall infectious disease rate was low, too, at 17 percent. Akins also discovered that Pueblo Bonito males and females were taller (by 4.6 cm) than males and females from the outlying pueblos (1986:136). Achieved adult stature is influenced by genetics and by nutritional and other developmental factors, and it is quite possible that the greater stature of the Pueblo Bonito adults was attained through better access to dietary resources and less exposure to disease (Nelson et al. 1994:89). Demographic analyses comparing life expectancy and fertility at Pueblo Bonito and the small sites demonstrate that life expectancy was greater and fertility lower at Pueblo Bonito (Nelson et al. 1994:100).

Although there are no available published data with which to do a more detailed analysis of status, gender, and health at Chaco Canyon, it is provocative that both males and females at Pueblo Bonito demonstrate better overall health and taller stature. Strong status differentiation usually implies the existence of an elite or privileged group. The relationship of health and nutritional status to ranked social organization is an important factor in understanding gender hierarchies and power relations. On the basis of contemporary traditional cultures, status differentiation is thought to be marked by the delivery of more and better food to high-status individuals (Rosenberg 1980).

Tracking status and health in antiquity is often difficult because we must rely on settlement patterns in order to distinguish central from peripheral groups and on mortuary behavior to distinguish high- from low-status individuals. M. L. Powell (1988), for example, presented a detailed analysis of status and health for prehistoric Mississippian cultures at Moundville in Alabama. Moundville was highly stratified, and these divisions within the cultural system were assumed to have had effects on health for different segments of the population. Although elite males were found to be taller than nonelite males, no stature differences were found for females. Furthermore, there were no statistically significant differences in the rates of infections or nutritional pathologies among the different groups. Analysis of strontium indicated that elite males had a diet richer in meat. Powell contrasted these findings with those for neighboring chiefdoms. At Chucalissa, elite males were found to have more fractures than any other subgroup (Powell 1988:194). Powell's detailed analysis of status and health for the prehistoric Mississippian chiefdoms provides a cautionary note that relationships among variables may be complex and not easily identified.

Marvin Allison (1984), on the other hand, showed that for precolonial groups living in Chile and Peru, high-status shamans had a lower prevalence of fractures, arthritis, and infections than did commoner males and females. The differences between commoner males and females were also noteworthy, with commoner males having fewer nutritional and infectious pathologies than females.

These studies suggest that causal relationships between health and status may be difficult to ascertain without a careful and systematic analysis of several kinds of information. Differential rates of mortality and morbidity should be apparent if the status differentiation among subgroups sufficiently buffered the high-status individuals from the vagaries of food resources in the Southwest while linking lower-status individuals to increased risk for infections, nutritional inadequacies, and decreased longevity.

Other kinds of skeletal data may be useful in analyzing the effects of political centralization and hierarchy on health. Occupationally related stressors such as degenerative joint disease (osteoarthritis), trauma, and bone degeneration from wear and tear might not be present in high-status burials if elites did not participate in the daily labors of food production (Kennedy 1989). Differences in these indicators of the degree of involvement with work and labor should also to be analyzed with respect to age and sex within a given population. Division of labor within a community might fall along gender or age lines, and in some cases occupational stress might not be related to status differences. Careful analyses of these indicators within groups and between groups is necessary in order to tease out the causal relationship between work and status.

Contemporaneously with Mesa Verde and Chaco Canyon, the La Plata River valley in New Mexico is considered to have been a relatively advantageous place to live from about A.D. 950 to 1100. It was a permanently watered, productive agricultural area in which more than 900 sites have been reported (H. W. Toll 1993). Archaeological reconstruction suggests that communities along the La Plata had access to food resources, were aggregated, had an abundance of trade goods, and were centrally located with respect to important communities in regions to the north and south. This area was lush by local and regional standards, and the density of available resources was high. Agricultural potential was likewise very good, and there is ample evidence of hunted and domesticated game in the diet (M. Toll 1993). This area lay in the middle of a large and interactive political sphere of influence, with Mesa Verde to the north and Chaco Canyon to the south (Spray 1996).

Evidence for trauma in the La Plata burial series includes healed fractures or traumatic injuries that are in the remodeling (healing) phase (therefore, injuries that were nonlethal) (Martin et al. n.d.). Cranial wounds found on individuals from La Plata fit the description of depression fractures caused by blows to the head that occurred sometime during an individual's lifetime (Merbs 1989; Walker 1989). Frequencies of healed trauma for adults at La Plata reveal that females had a frequency of cranial trauma three times greater than that of males (42.8 percent versus 14.2 percent), and twice the frequency of postcranial trauma (35.7 percent versus 18.7 percent). Adult frequencies greatly outnumbered those for subadults, who had an overall rate of 4.7 percent for cranial trauma and virtually no cases of postcranial trauma.

La Plata male and female adults with cranial and/or postcranial trauma clearly demonstrate different patterns. For males (n = 18), there are three cases of cranial trauma. Among females (n = 14), six demonstrate healed cranial traumas (largely in the form of depression fractures); the ages of these women range from 20 to 40. However, the inventory of healed nonlethal cranial wounds among females is longer and more extensive, with three of the six cases involving multiple head wounds. For example, the youngest female (in her early twenties) had a healed broken nose. Another young female (in her early twenties) with a cranial trauma demonstrates two depression fractures, one on the forehead and one on the back of the head. A 25-year-old has multiple depression fractures about the front and side of her head. A women in her early thirties has a large, nonreunited but healed series of fractures at the top of her head. Of the two women in their late thirties, one has a healed fracture above her right eye, and the other, a depression fracture at the back of the head.

In addition to this, five females demonstrate postcranial trauma, and two features of their lower-body trauma are distinctly different from the male pattern: (1) in four out of six cases, cranial and postcranial fractures co-occur, and (2) the postcranial fractures in females occur in younger age categories, from 20 to 40. For example, the youngest female (age 20) has fractures in the atlas and axis vertebrae of her neck (she also had a broken nose). A 25-year-old has several fractures (right shoulder, left upper arm, neck) along with multiple depression fractures about the head. This female also had a severe case of osteomyelitis that affected numerous bones. There appears also to be localized, trauma-induced osteophytes (painful bone growths) on the third through fifth cervical vertebrae. It is possible that this woman was struck with an object hard enough to have caused not only cranial fracturing but also lacerated wounds on the shoulders and chest area.

Reviewing other factors associated with health for adult males and females at La Plata, females have more cases of infection (30.7 percent) than males (6.2 percent), and some of these may have been sequelae to the injuries that produced the fractures. Females demonstrate higher frequencies of childhood growth disruption (for four out of six teeth, females had more hypoplastic lines). Other characteristics of the females with cranial trauma are that their skeletal elements as a group generally display more frequent involvement of anemia and systemic infection. Several of them exhibit more left-right asymmetry (from 2 to 6 mm) in long-bone proportions than do other females and more pronounced cases of postcranial ossified ligaments, osteophytes at joint surfaces (unrelated to general osteoarthritis or degenerative joint disease), and localized periosteal reactions (enthesiopathies). Whether these conditions were the result of occupational stress (Kennedy 1989) or the sequelae of injuries that caused unusual and differential biomechanical problems is unclear. Regardless of their etiology, these markers suggest increased physiological trauma in some subgroup of women.

An association emerges when the mortuary contexts of the individuals with cranial trauma are examined. The majority of burials in La Plata sites were flexed or semiflexed and were placed in abandoned structures or in storage pits. Often burials contained associated objects, usually ceramic vessels or ground stone. Every female at La Plata with cranial trauma had a mortuary context that diverged from this pattern. All were found in positions that were loosely flexed, prostrate, or sprawled. Unlike their age-matched counterparts without signs of trauma, they were generally placed haphazardly in abandoned pit structures, without associated grave goods.

Violence and fear of injury may have played a significant role in repressing some members of the La Plata community. Trauma is absent in children and generally benign in adult males (particularly postcranial trauma, all of which was minor and occurred in elderly males). Females carried the unequal burden of traumatic injuries and poor health in this group. The locations and sizes of the cranial injuries show that by overall dimensions and size in area, female injuries covered a larger area, involved more bony elements, often occurred in multiples, and in some cases caused internal (endocranial) damage. Furthermore, the comorbidity factors of cranial and postcranial trauma, infections, and decreased life expectancy (very few females were represented in the older age categories) suggest truly suboptimal conditions for some adult females. Females with these health problems were more likely to have been found in mortuary contexts described as haphazard, with no associated grave offerings. As a group, they were younger when they died than were females who had traditionally prepared graves.

An examination of other attributes suggests that women with evidence of trauma at La Plata were part of the larger Pueblo culture to the extent that most of them show occipital or lambdoidal skull flattening consistent with the use of cradleboards during infancy. The one physical characteristic that distinguishes at least several of these women is a pattern of nonpathological lesions and abnormalities associated with occupational stress or habitual use of select muscle groups. Particularly, the humerus, radius, and ulna are most affected. Trinkaus, Churchill, and Ruff (1994) examined modern, extant, and extinct groups and found that humeral bilateral asymmetry related most often to activity-related functional changes, such as those that might occur with an increase in the number of hours spent grinding corn.

Another attribute of some of these women is the presence of isolated osteophytes in places that correspond to muscle insertions, suggesting biomechanical stress. Because as a group these women were generally too young to have experienced the osteoarthritic changes associated with aging, these morphological changes might have been related to habitual use of certain muscles, which can lead to the buildup of bone and changes at the site of the greatest biomechanical stress. Patricia Bridges (1990) examined the osteological correlates of weapon use in two precontact groups from Alabama and showed that the shift from hunting and gathering to agriculture could be correlated with non-pathological changes in morphology relating to different uses of tools and weapons. Bridges noted that there were changes in porosity and osteophytic lipping at the shoulder joints and the elbow in particular. She also found bilateral asymmetry between the groups in the diameters of the radius and ulna. Although the observation is somewhat subjective (osteophytes are difficult to measure and occur in many forms), many of the La Plata females in the subgroup with trauma do demonstrate osteophytes and asymmetries, and therefore the most distinguishing element of their physical makeup is one that is developmental and relates to occupation or habitual performance of certain activities.

Although the subgroup sample sizes limit a detailed quantitative analysis of occupational stress markers, it is possible to speculate about a division of labor by sex and possibly by "class" as well. Spencer and Jennings (1965), Titiev (1972), and Dozier (1970) summarized the sexual division of labor for Pueblo people, suggesting that traditionally, women ground corn, prepared food, gathered wood, built and mended houses, made pottery and clothing, gathered wild foods, and made baskets. Men were responsible for farming, occasional hunting, and religious and ceremonial activities. The difficult task of grinding a season's crop of corn into meal to be stored for the year belonged to the women, who might spend as many as eight to nine hours a day at the grindstone for several weeks.

There are several alternative hypotheses that could explain these La Plata data. One is that as the population of the La Plata Valley increased (through a combination of immigration and increased fertility), conditions arose that enabled one subgroup to exploit another. It is possible that as more people moved into the valley, the more local or "native" population maintained access to and control of resources. That is, natal groups retained preferred access to food and other resources over nonrelated newcomers, even as the need to increase production of food to feed greater numbers of people demanded an increased labor pool. This might have effectively established an underclass of people who were exploited in any number of ways. Reproductive-aged females might have been the most advantageous group to exploit because they could aid in domestic tasks and food production as well as in child rearing. This does not rule out the exploitation of males as well, but there is no physical evidence that this occurred.

Other explanations for the observed pattern could involve violence directed at women thought to be involved in witchcraft (Darling 1993) and the hypothesis that these women and their children were enslaved persons acquired from other groups through raiding and abduction. Yet another hypothesis is that these women were injured through spouse abuse or domestic violence.

Violence against women in an area where resources were abundant makes sense only in the context of a regional model of shifting political and economic strategies. Although the Ancestral Pueblo world was becoming increasingly connected, it may not have been unified. Social change at La Plata might have taken place in an arena of increasing domination and resistance. Health at La Plata, with its abundant agricultural and wild resources, cannot be understood without looking at the local and regional dynamics involving control of those resources.

This more complex set of explanations for the empirical evidence disrupts the standard narrative about life in the precontact Southwest in several ways. The environment, while playing a crucial role in constraining the productivity and use of the landscape, ends up being a poor predictor of group cohesion or of individuals most at risk. Population growth is not, in and of itself, the major factor underlying illness and eventual population decline. Violence might have contributed as much to the maintenance and growth of population as it did to its decline.

Violence has been documented by a number of researchers for other areas of the Southwest as well. Recent research in the areas of Castle Rock and Sand Canyon in southwestern Colorado suggests that evidence for violence increases dramatically in the mid-1200s (Haas and Creamer 1993; Wilcox and Haas 1994).

Sand Canyon was a large settlement built around a spring and enclosed by a sandstone masonry wall (Lightfoot and Kuckelman 1995). Major occupation took place during the 1200s. Archaeological signatures of both the threat and the reality of warfare and violence include walls and towers, limited entryways, burning of some structures, and disarticulated and randomly scattered human remains (Katzenberg and Walker 1992). Human remains recovered from this site represented 31 individuals, 9 of whom (mostly subadults) were formally buried. The rest were disarticulated and heavily weathered. Analysis revealed skull fractures, bones broken at the time of death (spiral fractures), and chipped and broken teeth. Although difficult to age and sex, the assemblage appears to consist mostly of women and teenagers. These preliminary analyses suggest violent death, though not necessarily all at the same time. Ricky Lightfoot and Kristen Kuckelman (1995) provided convincing evidence that there was long-term, low-intensity fighting at the site and a gradual abandonment of the village, with evidence of closing-down rituals.

Castle Rock Pueblo, on the other hand, was a smaller village built very defensively. Its structures were crowded onto a large rock outcrop that juts out of the ground. All of the skeletal remains retrieved were disarticulated, and many showed signs of spiral fractures, burning, cut marks, and postmortem weathering and neglect. The assemblage represents at least 40 individuals, and these came from a number of pit structures on the site. The demographic profile of this assemblage, although preliminary, appears to include six females, two males, and eight children; the rest are adults of unknown sex.

Lightfoot and Kuckelman (1995) suggested that violence occurred on at least two levels of intensity in this region. The evidence from Sand Canyon suggests long-term, small-scale conflict of the hit-and-run raiding variety, whereas the mass assemblage at Castle Rock indicates a large-scale conflict and catastrophic fighting that led to the abandonment of the pueblo. Although the research is in its preliminary stages, there appears to be an abundance of women and children in both of these assemblages.

Other places have yielded evidence of strife. For the Transwestern Pipeline series, from a region encompassing the San Juan Basin (circa A.D. 1200), Nicholas Hermann (1993) noted that several adult females had postcranial fractures in the fibula, sacrum, radius, and tibia. Several women had multiple healed fractures on their lower bodies. One female had three depression fractures on her frontal bone (she also had postcranial healed fractures), and one female had a perimortem fracture on her jaw.

At Carter Ranch Pueblo in Arizona (A.D. 1200), Danforth, Cook, and Knick (1994) summarized trauma for 24 nonsexed adults. One-quarter had healed fractures: two nasal fractures (one accompanying a broken jaw and the other a broken humerus), two radius fractures, a clavicular fracture, and a femur fracture. The fractures were interpreted to have resulted from blows to the body (Danforth, Cook, and Knick 1994:96).

Allen, Merbs, and Birkby (1985) analyzed 10 cases of scalping at Navakwewtaqa (A.D. 1200–1300) and Grasshopper Ruin (A.D. 1300). Some of the individuals who had been scalped showed depression fractures as well. For example, at Navakwewtaqa, there were four males ranging in age from 25 to 40 who were scalped, and three females ranging in age from 25 to 35. One female had a depression fracture on the left frontal, and one had an ovoid-shaped hole in the left parietal suggesting penetration by a weapon as the probable cause of death. At Grasshopper, two males were scalped, and one young female (age 15) exhibited a depression fracture. Most of these individuals had been buried with many grave goods, such as bowls, beads, awls, and crystals. The authors suggested that this "indicates that it was members of these two communities themselves who were the victims of the practice [scalping]" (1985:30). However, the authors go on to suggest that the 10 individuals described might have been victims of isolated raids of the hit-and-run variety.

A review of the literature on violence presents a complex view of the past. No strong patterns are emerging yet for the full range of injurious actions that sometimes occurred in the Southwest. Mass slayings, individual dismemberments, burning, scalping, intentional injury, and hand-to-hand combat are all attested to in the archaeological record, and they span the years from A.D. 800 to 1300. The extent to which such incidents occurred and their relationships to other political, economic, and ideological developments must be examined. These cases of violence may be relatively isolated examples, or they may be indicative of large-scale and integrated systems of power dynamics, show of force, oppression, coercion, or conflict resolution. It is possible that in order to maintain unanimity across economically, linguistically, and ideologically diverse communities, some show of force might have been necessary, but the extent to which it was practiced on women versus men is an area of research that would prove productive and useful in understanding its extent and impact.

A.D. 1300–1450

Analyses of human remains from the Hohokam Classic period (A.D. 1000–1450) are not abundant but represent an important data base for the southern Arizona region. Reinhard (1988) analyzed the paleofecal remains and found no helminthic infections. Michael Fink and Charles Merbs (1991) demonstrated that children from this region had dental defects that peaked between the ages of 2.5 and 4 years. Nutritional anemias were present in 50 percent of the individuals, with two cases of childhood rickets. This presents an interesting counterpoint to the ethnobotanical evidence, which shows a diverse and varied diet. The skeletal remains indicate that not everyone had access to those resources.

C. Kuzawa (1996) examined patterns of age-related bone loss from Pueblo Grande and showed that females lost bone more rapidly than males. Similarly, K. E. McCafferty and D. M. Mittler (1996) demonstrated that Pueblo Grande women exhibited higher frequencies and rates of development of vertebral osteoarthritis than men. This indicates that there may have been some sexual division of labor that placed women at higher risk for backaches and osteoarthritis.

For the Rio Grande Pueblos, Palkovich (1980) analyzed 120 burials from Arroyo Hondo in north-central New Mexico. This large site was occupied during two separate periods referred to as Component I (A.D. 1300–1330) and Component II (A.D. 1370–1420). Each occupation saw growth, prosperity, and sudden decline. Palkovich focused her analysis on nutrition- and disease-related pathologies and did not report trauma and degenerative conditions. Although few trends in health status differentiated Component I from Component II, the Arroyo Hondo populations in general experienced severe nutritional problems; children in particular suffered from a variety of ailments.

Palkovich painted a harsh picture for the Arroyo Hondo community. Most individuals were inflicted with some pathology, and infant mortality was high. She further documented a very high rate of active infections and anemia in infants under the age of one (Palkovich 1987). Normally, breastfed infants receive automatic protection from these problems from the mother, if she herself is healthy. Palkovich speculated that Arroyo Hondo infants had immediately acquired infections from their mothers, implying that maternal health was greatly compromised during pregnancy. Palkovich's study of the skeletal remains, together with Wetterstrom's (1986) ethnobotanical reconstruction of Arroyo Hondo food and diet, suggest strongly that there was endemic malnutrition.

SUMMARY AND CONCLUSIONS

This investigation demonstrates that there was great variability in overall health for women and men both within and among groups in the prehispanic Southwest. A wide range of factors intersected in some places and diverged in others, protecting individuals in some cases and putting them at risk in others. In general, the least gender differentiation in health is found in the earlier and smaller settlements (Black Mesa, Dolores, Duckfoot), with the more densely aggregated settlements of the twelfth and thirteenth centuries showing distinctly different patterns of morbidity and mortality (Mesa Verde, Chaco Canyon) and increasing evidence of violence (La Plata, Castle Rock, Sand Canyon) (fig. 8.2). Females in some of these settlements died earlier and with a burden of morbidity and trauma not seen in males. These trends suggest shifting ideological and political-economic processes that placed some, but not all, women at risk at some sites.

There are clear trends of declining health over time for many Ancestral Pueblo groups, but they cannot be linked directly with ideas about declining social status for women. When there is a differential burden of morbidity for women, as at Mesa Verde, the underlying reasons may include differential access to food resources or differential exposure to disease agents. In terms of food resources, however, the data reveal that males were *never* immune to nutritional anemias related to inadequate diet in the Southwest. Iron deficiency anemia was an equal opportunity disease. Thus, there is little evidence to suggest that females, by virtue of being subordinate, received less food to eat.

In general, age-matched males do appear to have been protected from some maladies such as infectious disease, but this may relate to

DIFFERENTIATION AND HIERARCHY: BIOLOGICAL INDICATORS

High		**Pueblo Bonito** Some males and females doing better than other males and females	**Mesa Verde – Late** Males doing better than females **La Plata Valley** Some males and females doing better than a subgroup of women	
Moderate		**Chaco Small Sites** Males moderately better off than females		**Arroyo Hondo** **San Cristobal** **Hawikku** Males moderately better off than females
Low	**Black Mesa** **Duckfoot** **Dolores** Males and females equal	**Mesa Verde** Males equal to or doing slightly better than females		

FIGURE 8.2.

Positions of various precontact groups along a continuum of low to high social differentiation and hierarchy by time period, from Pueblo I to Pueblo IV. Ranking is based on differences and similarities between male and female morbidity, mortality, and occupational stress markers.

patterns of activity that kept them from coming into contact with infectious agents (e.g., infant diarrhea, sick children, household garbage). Women tended to become exposed to infectious disease from reproductive factors such as prolonged and obstructed labor, as well as from proximity to infants and children, who transmit diseases such as staph and strep to whomever they contact (Gordon, Wyon, and Ascoli 1967). Thus, the increased morbidity load on women at some sites does not necessarily imply that they had lower status, but it may confirm their more active role in child rearing.

For the La Plata Valley, there are better empirical data to suggest status differentiation for some subgroup of women who frequently suffered blunt-force trauma. La Plata women with healed injuries on their heads tended to have a wide range of healed and unhealed injuries on their lower bodies as well. These women, as a subgroup, show right-left asymmetries and bone degeneration consistent with injuries related to trauma such as arduous muscle straining and with injuries to the musculoskeletal system that failed to heal properly. Upon death, these women singularly failed to receive formal burial treatment. It is difficult to imagine that these women were not part of an emergent underclass, possibly exploited by both men and women. There is little evidence for violence directed against men in these and other communities.

In biological data on biomechanical stress and bone development related to habitual activities there is evidence to suggest that women's work loads were heavy throughout the inhabitation of the prehispanic Southwest, and they may have increased in places where intensification of agricultural activities increased (e.g., Mesa Verde and La Plata). The sexual division of labor may be too difficult to track through skeletal evidence, because even with rigid categories of labor activities, variations in daily patterns may obscure direct correlates on the body (e.g., carrying babies and carrying wood will strain the same muscle groups). Furthermore, the indicators of stress reveal only in general ways which muscle groups were strenuously used, not the specific activities in which they were used. For example, corn grinding builds up certain parts of the arm, but a wide range of other activities involving arm muscles, such as lifting and carrying heavy loads in the arms, pulling on objects, and performing sustained upper body motions, would have left similar signs (Bridges 1990; Kennedy 1989).

At Black Mesa, there is virtually no sexual dimorphism in any of the measures that track muscularity and robusticity. It is common to assume that males tend to be larger and more muscular than females, but Black Mesa females were robust, full-bodied women with clear evidence of strength matching that of males. Is this because men and women performed identical tasks or because they performed different tasks but worked equally hard at them? There may be ways to tease apart these alternative hypotheses by looking closely at food processing techniques and other facets of work, as well as continuing to develop more finely tuned ways of measuring muscle use.

Archaeological evidence of patterning in the tools used for food processing (manos and metates) demonstrates that each family or extended family household on Black Mesa produced its own food (Powell 1983). Women there must have worked largely in solitary fashion grinding corn for daily meals. This evidence contrasts with that from rooms with multiple grinding stones found at Mesa Verde and La Plata, where women presumably worked together and, in doing so, were able to spend time together and share information. How this relates to division of labor and gender hierarchy is clearly complex and suggests no immediate causal relationship.

At La Plata, there does appear to have been a division of labor *among* females, and this disrupts the notion of simple dual gender divisions. The subgroup of women with skeletal trauma seems also to have been engaged in distinctive activities that might have been more punishing to the body. In order to continue to fine-tune analyses of labor and biobehavior, future studies must consider tracking variability within the sexes to be as important as tracking variability between the sexes.

Biological data have the potential to reveal much about the gendered influences that shape health, occupation, and lifestyle. The documentation of stressors written on the body can be channeled back into the discussion of gender, division of labor, hierarchies, ideology, and power. This presentation of biological data demonstrates the ways in which a reformulated research agenda can open new interpretations regarding men and women in the past. Understanding the conditions that create and maintain gendered divisions is challenging, but it is possible to reveal the important underlying cultural and historical processes and to show how these reverberated within the social system.

9

Gender, Craft Production, and Inequality

Barbara J. Mills

Most archaeological models of gender and craft production have been based on studies of complex societies, especially states (e.g., Brumfiel 1991; Costin 1993, 1996; Wright 1991, 1996), whereas ethnographic studies of gendered relations of production have been situated in societies that were part of colonial or world market settings (e.g., Etienne 1980; Nash 1993; Tice 1995). The variable contexts of archaeologically documented societies of the American Southwest provide an opportunity to study gendered production of craft items in precapitalist, middle-range societies. Within the prehispanic Southwest are examples of varied ecological settings, subsistence economies, settlement patterns, and social and political inequality. Each of these contexts has implications for the way in which labor was organized in the production of material culture. My goals in this chapter are to explore how the gendered organization of craft production can be investigated archaeologically, the evidence that exists for gendered divisions of labor in the prehispanic Southwest, and how these organizational patterns can be used to interpret differences in status and leadership.

My research on gender and craft production operates from several basic premises. First, gender is a fundamental principle of labor organization (Brightman 1996; Brumfiel 1992; Burton, Brudner, and White 1977; Burton and White 1984; Murdock and Provost 1973; White, Burton, and Brudner 1977). Second, gendered production is about both men's *and* women's roles. This is especially important in the study of small-scale societies where the household is one of the most important units of production (Hendon 1996). And third, gender attribution is only a reconstructive first step toward understanding how gendered relations of production varied through time or between archaeologically documented societies.

To investigate the dynamics of gender and craft production in the prehispanic Southwest, I begin with a general discussion of models based on ethnographic as well as archaeological evidence. These models point to a number of factors that contribute to the structuring of male and female labor for craft production. I then focus on archaeological evidence for changes in gendered craft production in the Southwest. Lines of evidence include ethnographic, mortuary, iconographic, and spatial data. These data indicate more variation than is often realized in the gendered production of specific goods and in how the gender of the producer varies with the process of craft specialization. Finally, I discuss how gender, craft production, and status intersected within the varying sociopolitical contexts of the prehispanic Southwest.

INTERPRETING GENDER IN THE ARCHAEOLOGICAL RECORD: METHODOLOGICAL CONSIDERATIONS

Specific attribution of crafts to female or male producers is highly variable in the ethnographic record, making interpretations difficult for archaeologists. For example, it is clear that men were not the sole producers of all stone tools (Conkey and Spector 1984; Gero 1991; Sassaman 1992a, 1992b). Even among nonhuman primates such as chimpanzees, females who are more intensively involved than males in some subsistence activities "precisely select raw materials, manufacture tools, and transport them for use in different areas" (McBrearty and Moniz 1991:76).

Gender attribution has been one of the major goals of cross-cultural studies of gender and the division of labor in craft production. These studies provide a basis for building models about how the gendered organization of production might be expected to vary under certain boundary conditions. Ethnographic cases do not document all the possible ways in which craft production and gender might covary, but they do point to major trends that can then be tested with independent data.

George Murdock and Caterina Provost's (1973) cross-cultural study found that although some activities in nonindustrial societies were almost exclusively male (e.g., hunting large aquatic fauna and metalworking) or female (e.g., cooking and other domestic chores), a significant number of activities were not exclusively male or female. Even within regions such as North America, considerable variation was found in what they termed "swing" tasks, or those that could be performed by either men or women (see also Jorgensen 1980). Many of these dual-gendered tasks were tasks of craft production, such as weaving, basket making, mat making, and manufacture of leather products; in general, males and females made the crafts that they would use. Pottery production was mostly (but not always) carried out by women, ranking 43 out of the 50 activities showing highest female participation (Murdock and Provost 1973; Skibo and Schiffer 1995:87). Only cooking, water fetching, clothes washing, and other domestic chores showed greater participation by women, and all of these were activities that frequently required pottery vessels.

The degree of variation found in the Murdock and Provost study makes it impossible to label all crafts in the archaeological record according to the gender of their producers. Murdock and Provost's explanation of this variation was that other variables such as physical strength, women's involvement in child care, degree of sedentism, processing of animal products, intensity of agricultural production, and occupational specialization must be taken into account, factors that are themselves intercorrelated (Byrne 1994).

Some of the variation in the gendered division of labor in technological activities can be accounted for by looking at the sequence of tasks involved, from tending or procuring raw materials to completing the finished product. As Burton, Brudner, and White (1977) noted, if women are engaged in one activity of the sequence of production, such as procurement of raw materials, then they are more likely to complete later tasks in the sequence. By knowing the gendered division of labor in the previous step, these authors were able to predict the sexual division of labor in specific tasks about 70 per cent of the time. They found that craft production, however, was less likely than other tasks to be correctly predicted, and a significant number of craft items were made by both sexes across the sample. However, men and women participated differentially in production steps for some crafts. Spinning was almost always a female task, but loom weaving was conducted by both women and men (Burton, Brudner, and White 1977). In this study, men's involvement in loom weaving was attributed to the fact that loom weaving was often done outside the household in workshops, which points to specialization as a key process for interpreting gender in the archaeological record. Physical strength was rejected as a factor, but women's involvement in child care was considered to be an essential variable that tethered women's activities to the household (see also Brown 1970; Ember 1983). Burton and his colleagues also concluded that dangerous or high-risk activities were more likely to be conducted by men outside the home.

Carol Ember (1983:297) reached similar conclusions in her cross-cultural study of women's participation in agricultural activities. She wrote that "men in agricultural societies are more likely to be 'pulled' out of work with food crops into other activities...particularly hunting, warfare, and trade." Hunting is an unusually time-consuming task that contributes important protein resources but takes men away from their residences for extended periods of time, leaving women to tend agricultural crops and make the utilitarian items for food collection, storage, processing, and consumption. In terms of craft production, Ember's observation suggests that men might make weapons used in warfare and hunting and might participate more frequently in high-risk, long-distance journeys to procure raw materials.

Although we tend to think about division of labor in terms of adult men and women, children also contribute labor to the household. Indeed, one way of increasing household production is by expanding household size through increasing the birth rate (Netting 1993). Children do not perform all tasks, nor do all children perform tasks equally. In one study comparing children's labor with adult labor, Candice Bradley (1993) found that children's labor helped to decrease women's work loads more than men's. Craft production was not included in her study, but one implication is that children might be more likely to share tasks in the production of women's crafts than in men's, because all children tend to participate in women's activities but usually only male children participate in men's activities. Even if they do not engage in the actual production of an item, children might share in activities such as procuring materials. A second implication is that larger households would enable women to concentrate on craft production more than smaller households, especially once children have reached the age of 10. By this age children in nonindustrial societies are full participants in child care and subsistence activities themselves, a trend that begins at ages 6 to 10. Thus, inequalities between households in both subsistence and nonsubsistence production might be fostered by differences in household size.

GENDER AND THE PROCESS OF CRAFT SPECIALIZATION

The process of craft specialization is closely related to changes in the gendered division of labor. For example, pottery making is considered to be a female task in nonindustrial contexts, and men's involvement to be a correlate of increasing specialization (Arnold 1985; Balfet 1965; Murdock and Provost 1973; Rice 1991; Skibo and Schiffer 1995). The shift from female to male production has been tied to the presence of larger consumer markets and declining agricultural production (Arnold 1985; Byrne 1994; Mills 1995b; Mohr Chavez 1992; Nash 1961; Netting 1990). Bryan Byrne made an explicit connection between decreased access to agricultural production and the production of ceramics as commodities. However, William Longacre's (1996) work in a relatively urban population with a market economy in the Philippines suggests that it is when pottery making becomes a more lucrative occupation that men take over its production and distribution. An archaeological test of the association of craft specialization with decreased access to subsistence resources in the Tucson Basin concluded that intensive production was independent of differences in access to faunal and floral resources (Harry 1997). These ethnoarchaeological and archaeological studies demonstrate that the reasons for intensification of craft production are complex and that differences in distribution and consumption should also be taken into account.

What these studies do not always address is that female potters are not entirely replaced by male potters with increasing intensity of production. Instead, the labor of the entire household is aggregated in the production process (Hendon 1996). Individual tasks may be partitioned to different members of the household, as hinted at in the Burton, Brudner, and White study (1977), and the labor of specific individuals may be "hidden" when the products reach consumers (Kramer 1985; Mills 1995b; Wright 1991). The probability that more members of the household participated in the production activity can be scaled according to increasing intensity of production. In this way, time spent in labor on craft production is assessed, and reliance on specific attributions of gender of producer to a particular craft is avoided.

Ethnoarchaeological findings about the intensification of production at the scale of the household parallel recent research results on the scale and intensity of production in prehispanic Mesoamerica. Both Patricia McAnany (1992) and Gary Feinman (1999) found that high-intensity household production characterized complex societies in the lowland Maya and Oaxaca areas of Mexico, respectively. Feinman argued that workshops unassociated with household compounds were absent from Mesoamerican sites in which intensive production had been identified. Instead, *households* rather than workshops were the maximal scale at which specialization in production took place in this region. Because the degree of specialization that can be accomplished at the scale of the household is quite high, very complex economic systems can be associated with household-based craft production, illustrating the great versatility of this production unit (Hendon 1996; Moore 1992). In addition, a variety of goods from utilitarian to wealth items (Brumfiel and Earle 1987) can be produced within the domestic unit.

PATHWAYS TO SPECIALIZATION IN THE AMERICAN SOUTHWEST

The Southwest is often thought of as an area in which craft production was unspecialized. However, recent studies of ceramics (Mills and Crown, eds., 1995), shell (Howard 1993), textiles (Webster 1997), and other materials offer evidence to the contrary. Craft production in the Southwest frequently took place at a level that exceeded consumption by the unit of production—the most basic definition of specialization. In talking about craft specialization, I use Cathy Costin's (1991) dimensions of craft production: production scale (individual, household, or suprahousehold), context (degree of control over alienation of goods), intensity (how much produced), and concentration (the spatial clustering of producers). I argue that there were three pathways toward craft specialization in the Southwest, depending on the product, other demands for labor, and the social and political contexts of consumption. Each of these pathways was affected by and affected gendered divisions of labor in the manufacture of nonsubsistence goods.

The first pathway to specialization was a change from gendered to nongendered division of labor at the scale of the household. As intensity of production increased, what was formerly produced by one member or segment of the household was supplemented by additional labor from other members of the household. As discussed later, examples of change along this pathway are the production of shell ornaments and some ceramics in the Hohokam area and of textiles during the late Pueblo III period in Canyon de Chelly. The intensification of production by entire households would have contributed to asymmetries in subsistence production between those households and their consumers as labor was reallocated to nonsubsistence production.

Another pathway toward specialization was an intensification of gendered production in which male and female roles became more differentiated. Role specificity in these cases was likely caused by the process of aggregation and the need for task groups to be involved in subsistence activities. Nonsubsistence production was structured along similarly gendered lines. Intensified production of ceramics throughout much of the Southwest was probably structured in this way.

The third pathway was one in which intensification of production resulted in a shift in the scale of production from the household to extrahousehold production, again along gendered lines. In contrast to the previous pathway, this one enhanced gendered divisions of labor by moving production out of the household and into other social contexts. An example is the intensification of cotton textile production in the Puebloan area during the Pueblo IV period. There, cotton textile weaving took place in structures that were used for nondomestic, ritual purposes. These contexts tended to segregate craft producers, probably men, from domestic contexts of production. Instead of creating asymmetrical relations between households, this pathway had implications for economic relations within households, the organization of suprahousehold corporate groups, and the transmission of ritual information.

The implications of each of these pathways toward specialization for the status of producers involve a number of factors, including the value of the goods produced. Different forms of value, from utilitarian and exchange value to social and ritual value, might be attached to different goods. In some situations, differences in productive power can be a means of creating social identities and maintaining social power (Brumfiel 1991, 1996a; Costin 1993, 1996; Joyce 1992; Weiner 1994; Wright 1996). Ethnologists have also stressed the political dimension of women's productive status in order to understand how households work beyond neoclassic economic models of decision making and maximizing (Hart 1992; Moore 1992). These theoretical frameworks hold much potential for interpreting gendered production in the prehispanic Southwest, but in practice they must be "rescaled." Political leadership there was not at the same scale of complexity as it is in many ethnographically known societies; indeed, many ethnographic studies have been based on explicitly capitalist economies (e.g., Young, Wolkowitz, and McCullagh 1981). Nonetheless, they point to the importance of incorporating political concerns into approaches toward gendered organization of production, the value of different kinds of goods, and the ways in which labor is scheduled and allocated at the household and community levels.

For the prehispanic Southwest, it is becoming increasingly evident that a major locus of power was ritual (see Mills, ed., 2000). We may infer from ethnographic accounts that objects used in these contexts were highly valued. I distinguish between objects used in ritual activities that could be exchanged and those that could be made and handled only by members of the group responsible for their care and that were not subject to mundane exchange transactions. Ceramic bowls used in ritual feasting are examples of the former. These bowls may not have been used exclusively in ritual, but red wares and especially polychromes in the Southwest were used in a number of contexts that included communal feasting (Blinman 1989; Graves 1996; Mills 1999; Spielmann 1998). That these bowls were also widely exchanged is clear from compositional data (see Mills and Crown, eds., 1995).

In contrast, the second class of items fits well with what Annette Weiner (1994) called "inalienable possessions," or goods that are made to be kept. The knowledge of how to make inalienable ritual artifacts and the roles these objects played in constructing and maintaining social and ritual power are key to understanding additional differences in producer status in the prehispanic Southwest. Perusal of ethnographic sources on the Southwest suggests that this class of objects was more likely to be made by men (e.g., Bunzel 1932; Parsons 1939), except for those that were used specifically by women's societies (see also Hays-Gilpin, this volume). Analyses of protohistoric mortuary data suggest that some women were given special treatment at death (Howell 1995), possibly because of their role(s) in women's ritual societies. Production of both alienable and inalienable ritual items probably conferred status on producers by virtue of their social contexts of use.

What follows is a summary of examples of direct and indirect evidence for changes in the allocation of labor for craft production in several of the major archaeological areas of the Southwest. I concentrate on evidence for division of labor in craft production as well as for changes in labor intensification through time in several areas. Division of labor can be looked at from direct evidence of the tools of production found in mortuary contexts, depicted in iconographic evidence, and inferred from spatial concentrations of tools, debris, and finished products in spaces used in gendered ways. Mortuary data are often considered one of the most clear-cut data sets for this purpose, but I consider them highly ambiguous in terms of the actual use or production of goods. Items found as mortuary accompaniments might have been used by the deceased but also might have been offered by friends and family. In the case of tools, they are more likely to have been used by the deceased, but tools of production in burials are uncommon, some well-documented cases notwithstanding. This is not only true of the Southwest but is also a common pattern in most middle-range societies (Crabtree 1991:386). The other problem with mortuary data is that they indicate the sex of the deceased but not gender in its cultural context. Less direct but equally important is evidence for labor intensification that affects the division of labor, especially as inferred from concentrations of tools, debris, and finished products.

THE ARCHAIC PERIOD

The southern Southwest saw earlier and more sedentary occupations than the northern Southwest during the Middle and Late Archaic periods because more reliable, storable resources (such as mesquite) were available in concentrated areas (Fish, Fish, and Madsen 1990). These resources would have encouraged more sedentary communities even before the adoption of cultigens. Middle Archaic pit structures and storage pits in southeastern New Mexico are evidence for the tethering of activities to fixed locations for at least part of the year (O'Laughlin 1980). Unfortunately, direct evidence for craft production is rare for this period. Models must be based on cross-cultural evidence for the division of labor in craft production congruent with the processes of increased storage, sedentism, and variation in the use of seasonally differentiated sites.

It is not uncommon in situations of increased sedentism among hunter-foragers to see increased differentiation in men's and women's spheres of production (Kornfeld and Francis 1991; Sassaman 1992b). In general, women's production was likely to be more tethered than men's, because of women's responsibilities in food processing (see Crown, this volume). Chipped-stone production was probably shared, with increasing differentiation by gender in the production of items for hunting versus activities situated around residential sites (Sassaman 1992a, 1992b). However, women's participation in some hunting activities cannot be ruled out. Judging from studies of western North American foragers (Jorgensen 1980:150–52), we would expect women to have been associated more frequently with weaving of nets, basketry, and mats, whereas men were more likely to have made weapons and dressed hides.

The northern Southwest was characterized by more pronounced seasonality and more spatially dispersed resources, which encouraged higher mobility than in the southern Southwest (Wills 1995:219–23). The implication of these contrasts is that the amount of labor devoted to producing different kinds of tools should show marked spatial and temporal differences between the southern and northern Southwest (with the probable exception of the Mogollon Highlands). Decreases in mobility generally indicate increased differentiation in men's and women's activities (Kelly 1991). Thus, during the Middle Archaic, gendered divisions of labor in production were probably more pronounced in the southern Southwest than in the north.

There is little direct evidence to enable gender attribution of craft production during the Late Archaic. On the basis of cross-cultural data, however, we would expect the adoption and intensification of domesticated crop production to have increased the production of associated implements along gender lines. To the degree that intensification of agricultural production was associated with sedentism, changes in the organization of men's and women's labor probably occurred with a reduction in mobility, increases in the number of children, decreases in birth spacing, and decreases in women's foraging areas (Bar-Yosef and Meadow 1995:93). In the southern Southwest, these changes may have been less dramatic from the Middle to the Late Archaic because of the use of analogous food resources in both periods.

Patricia Crown and W. H. Wills (1995a, 1995b) have tied the first production of ceramic containers in the Southwest during the Late Archaic to changes in women's time allocation. With the increased importance of agriculture, more demands were placed on women's labor, and their tasks became more tethered to residential sites. Because pottery manufacture is less easily interrupted than that of baskets, the benefits of using ceramics for cooking must have outweighed their more concentrated demands on women's labor (see also Hunter-Anderson 1986:121). The production of other classes of material culture, such as ground-stone and chipped-stone tools and textiles and other perishables, would also have been affected by the gendered divisions of labor present in hunting, foraging, and processing activities.

During the terminal Archaic (Basketmaker II in the northern Southwest), women's use and probable production of some textiles can be inferred directly from clothing such as menstrual aprons (Guernsey 1931:76; Lindsay et al. 1968:90; Morris and Burgh 1954:66; see also Hays-Gilpin 1996 and this volume, and Morris 1980, for similar interpretations of Basketmaker III clothing). The increased use of pits to store goods indicates a change in mobility patterns to one in which households became tethered to locations on the landscape. The contents of these pits indicate a concern with labor scheduling. Goods that were cached were those with a high degree of labor investment, including baskets, belts, nets, and other textiles, such as the artifacts found in cists and pits at White Dog Cave (Kidder and Guernsey 1919).

The Late Archaic caches indicate that labor allocation and scheduling for craft production were of increasing concern. Caches by their nature hide their contents and allow control over retrieval and use by those who construct them. The frequency and locations of these storage pits suggest that they were constructed and used by individual households. The contents of the caches were labor-intensive but commonly used items, a high proportion of which were probably made by women. The cached items would have allowed household activities to be resumed more easily upon site reoccupation. Because the items were usually relatively light and easy to carry, concerns other than weight seem to have been more important. Caches were a means by which women's and men's labor could be better managed over the long term. Producers made surpluses when time permitted and then had important household items available upon return to the site.

THE HOHOKAM AREA

The Hohokam area provides an excellent test case for examining the intensification of craft production and how it intersected with gendered division of labor and producer status. Intensive production of ceramics, shell ornaments, ground stone, and textiles is now well documented for many parts of the Hohokam area (Abbott 1996; Abbott and Walsh-Anduze 1995; Haury 1976; Hoffman, Doyel, and Elson 1985; Howard 1985; Huntington 1986; Kisselburg 1987; McGuire and Howard 1987; Seymour 1988; Van Keuren, Stinson, and Abbott 1997). Few of these studies address gendered production, however, and views differ on other aspects of craft production, including the extent of specialization, whether goods were made within systems of independent or attached production, and the role of craft specialization in establishing and maintaining a prestige goods economy. Here I look at the spatial organization of production activities and the intensity and scale of production in order to assess how Hohokam craft production was structured and what the implications might be for gendered divisions of labor.

The spatial organization of Hohokam communities can be viewed at a number of nested scales, from the house to the household cluster (or courtyard group) (Wilcox, McGuire, and Sternberg 1981) and from the site to the multisite community (Fish, Fish, and Madsen 1992). Communities were tied together by ball courts and plazas during pre-Classic times and by platform mounds in the Classic period. A shift in the organization of houses and household clusters also occurred across these periods, with a transition to above-ground adobe architecture and house clusters surrounded by compound walls. Irrigation agriculture tied communities together in the Salt and Gila basins, but away from those areas, communities were linked by complementary uses of ecological zones from floodplains to *bajadas.* The subsistence resources used and the relative concentration on different resources varied widely across the Hohokam area, creating local specializations in subsistence production (Fish, Fish, and Madsen 1992). These contrasts and specializations in subsistence production were paralleled by those in nonsubsistence production throughout the area.

If there is one hallmark of Hohokam craft production it is shell working. For the pre-Classic period there is evidence of substantial shell production at many sites in the Hohokam area. Both the quantity and the spatial concentration of shell-working debris at Snaketown during the Sacaton phase (A.D. 950–1100+ [Dean 1991]) demonstrate that some houses were associated with much more shell working than others, and these houses were clustered in several areas of the site (Seymour 1988). In addition, much of the debris was discarded in trash mounds, including some concentrations of waste disposed of on mounds and in pits. A similar concentration of shell production in only a few houses at the site of La Ciudad suggests that this pattern of differential production within sites was not limited to Snaketown (Kisselburg 1987). In both cases, production for more than the immediate household is suggested by the quantities of debris and raw materials.

Procuring shell from the Gulf of California has often been suggested to have been a male activity, on the basis of ethnographic accounts of men's participation in long-distance procurement trips. The idea that men's collecting parties periodically left the Phoenix and Tucson Basins to procure shell was based on incomplete knowledge of the nature of settlement in the Papaguería. Although some procurement might have been conducted by residents of the Phoenix and Tucson Basins, and it might have been conducted by men, archaeological work in the Papaguería indicates the presence of domestic sites associated with reliable water sources and trails that might have been used in procuring shell from source areas in the Gulf of California (e.g., Masse 1980).

Sites located along the Santa Rosa Wash in the Papaguería due west of Snaketown and southwest of the Salt River irrigation communities show clear evidence for a high intensity of shell production. Two pre-Classic sites, Shelltown and the Hind Site, are remarkable for the amount of shell working present; even more intensive production is suggested for these sites than for Snaketown. Quantities of *Glycymeris* shell bracelets were produced in a high proportion of structures at these two sites (Howard 1993), and shell dust on house floors was so thick that the archaeologists had to use chemical tests to distinguish it from caliche. Besides shell dust, these sites had concentrations of debris, broken ornaments, and even caches of whole-shell raw materials. A variety of shell types besides *Glycymeris* were present, as were unworked crab legs and other items picked up from coastal beaches.

At Shelltown and the Hind Site, shell dust and flakes were distributed around pit-structure hearths in "aprons" that clearly delineated activity areas (Howard 1993; fig. 9.1). The quantity and spatial distribution of debris seems too great to have been produced by one or two members of each of these households. Rather than a gendered system of production, it seems more likely that most members of each household in a cluster participated in different tasks leading to the completion of shell items. Shell working is a labor-intensive process that combines flaking, cutting, and abrading of the raw material. Reamers and a variety of ground-stone abraders were found in nearly every structure. Although shell working might have been a men's activity in situations of less intensive production, women and children's labor was probably used at these sites to increase output.

The spatial concentration of Classic-period shell production shows marked contrasts with pre-Classic patterns. The products themselves show less labor investment, but more items were actually produced and consumed (Neitzel 1991). Instead of a concentration of production in Papaguería villages and an uneven distribution of producer households in sites in the Phoenix Basin, production became more widespread (Howard 1985; Neitzel 1991). A recent analysis of evidence from the multisite Marana community in the Tucson Basin, however,

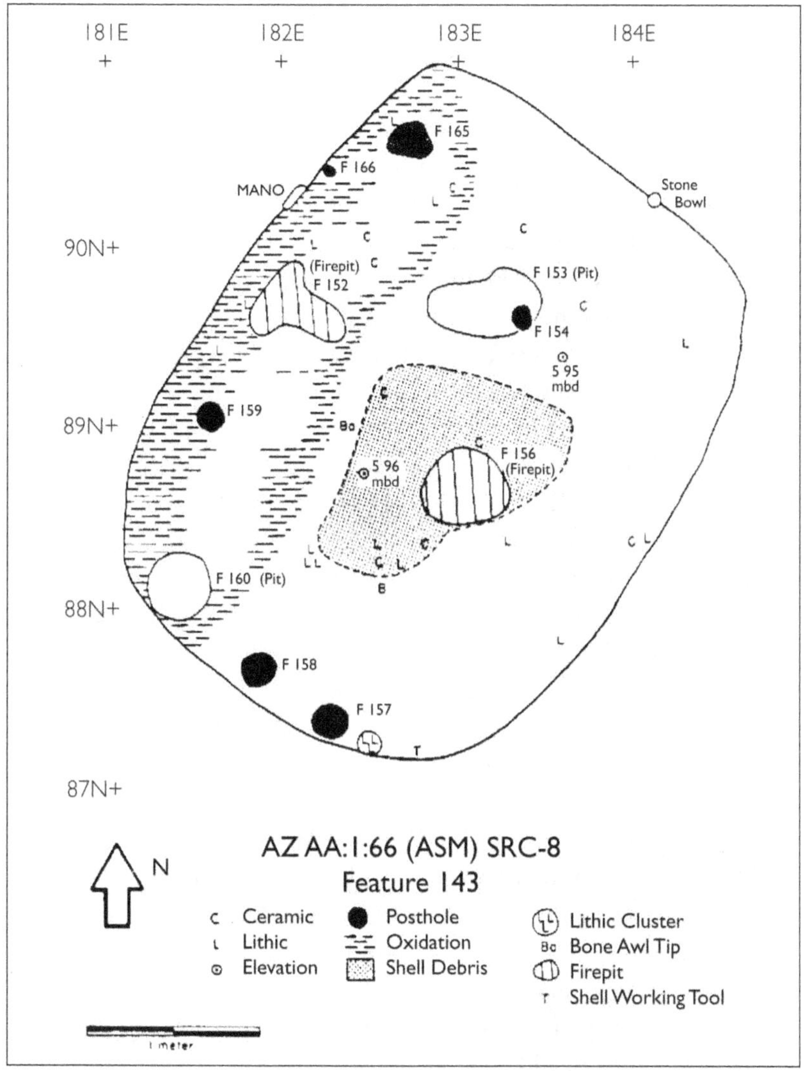

FIGURE 9.1.

Plan of pit structure (feature 143) at Shelltown (AZ AA:1:166 ASM), showing shell debris concentrations around central hearth (from Marmaduke and Martynec 1993:fig. E.15).

shows that not all households within compounds were similarly productive. Households in compounds associated with platform mounds seem to have made and used a greater proportion of shell items than did households farther away from the platform mounds (Bayman

1996). The same pattern is found at Pueblo Grande in the Phoenix Basin, where at least one household showed a greater variety of modified and unmodified shell than did other, contemporaneous early Classic sites (Gross and Stone 1994:193–94). This variation demonstrates differences between compounds in the production and consumption of ornamental goods that might have enhanced the status of households. I interpret these shell-working households as examples of "embedded specialists" as defined by Kenneth Ames (1995), in counterpoint to the idea that elite households controlled the production of crafts by other producers (i.e., "attached specialists"). Instead, elite households were themselves directly involved in the production of craft items, often producing intensely for consumers outside the household.

Few investigators of Hohokam shell artifacts have addressed the gendered division of labor in shell ornament production. Given that the intensity of production in any of the Classic-period contexts excavated was less than that at Shelltown or the Hind Site, it seems likely that Classic-period shell production was more exclusively a gendered activity. The gender of producers is not well indicated by the archaeological data, however. The value of these shell items in trade and as ornaments for status differentiation would have conferred status on producers. Judging from their unusual recovery contexts, some shell items were clearly different from others and were probably in the class of objects not exchanged or subject to only limited exchange. Such inalienable possessions would have conferred status upon an entire household. Judging from the presence of production areas in households on or adjacent to platform mounds, I think that individuals of high status were probably producing items of value. On the basis of ethnographic descriptions of inalienable possessions in the Southwest, it is likely that men produced shell items meant to be used as symbols of authority or in ritual, but this interpretation needs further testing.

Ceramic production shows some parallels with shell production across the pre-Classic to Classic span. As in the case of shell production, some pre-Classic sites show uneven concentrations of production locations. Ceramic production was concentrated in certain household clusters within the site of Snaketown (Seymour and Schiffer 1987). Clay mixing basins that hint at how labor was organized were found during Emil Haury's excavations. Several of these basins were excavated within an open area or courtyard surrounded by a cluster of pit structures. The number of basins and their locations near houses suggested to Haury (1976:194–97) that the residents of each house were involved in ceramic production. Kilns were also located close to the houses. The quantity of debris from pottery firing, the sizes of the mixing basins, and the concentration of production facilities in only parts of the site suggest that the producers might have been manufacturing pottery in excess of household needs. Production does not appear to have been at a scale that would have required the participation of more than the women of the household (and perhaps their children).

Outside the Phoenix Basin, a number of sites have been identified as production locations for pottery. One site in particular has been identified as showing evidence of community-level specialization, the West Branch Site in the western Tucson Basin (Huntington 1986). Several houses at this site were found with large numbers of anvils, polishing stones, grinding stones (some with pigment staining), pigments, temper sources, and samples of caliche. As at most Hohokam pre-Classic sites, houses were arranged in clusters. At least one house in each cluster contained high densities of ceramic tools and raw materials, suggesting that although production might have been intense, each household participated.

As yet, no other site in the Tucson Basin shows as much evidence for ceramic production as the West Branch Site. Karen Harry (1997) compared floral and faunal resource consumption at this site with that at other sites in the Tucson Basin to assess whether the nutrition of West Branch Site residents was distinctive. Her results suggested that potters at the West Branch Site had no differential access to resources that could be used to explain the site's higher production intensity relative to that of other sites in the basin, counter to the expectations set forth by Dean Arnold (1985). Although the spatial distribution of production debris at the West Branch Site shows that most households participated in ceramic manufacture, the intensity of production is not great enough to suggest production by more than the women of the community. Nonetheless, the distinctive composition of pottery made at the West Branch Site indicates that the products were traded throughout the Tucson Basin.

David Abbott's compositional analyses of Salt-Gila Basin ceramics also demonstrate widespread production for exchange. Although many pots were made and circulated within the boundaries of each community during the early Classic period, red-ware vessels were made more exclusively in Gila River communities and traded to Salt River–area communities (Abbott 1996; Abbott and Walsh-Anduze 1995). The amount of Gila Red Ware that was produced suggests that many households must have been involved in the manufacture of these vessels. If women were exclusively the potters, then demands on their labor would have been exceptionally high. Both the quantities exchanged and the association of Gila Red Ware with mortuary contexts indicates that these vessels were highly valued, possibly conferring status on their producers. Van Keuren, Stinson, and Abbott's (1997) more recent work suggests that other wares were also made in large quantities in the Phoenix Basin during the late pre-Classic, especially large plain-ware jars. In this case, the quantities made in one or a few locations were great enough to suggest a parallel to shell working in the Papaguería: that is, the entire household was probably involved in pottery production.

Spinning and weaving were also important economic activities in Hohokam society. Along with other wild plants, agaves were used for fibers as early as the Archaic period. Cotton cultivation became common in central Arizona by A.D. 500 (Teague 1998:13–14), and cotton fiber was the predominant fiber for textile production by A.D. 900 in the southern deserts (Teague 1998:23). Eighteenth- and nineteenth-century descriptions of Piman textile production indicate that women did most of the spinning, and men most of the weaving (Ezell 1961:70–72).

During the late pre-Classic period, spindle whorl technology changed to allow spinning of finer threads (Kent 1957). On the basis of ethnobotanical analyses and the number of whorls, several researchers have suggested that textile production intensified during the Classic period (Gasser and Miksicek 1985; Neitzel 1991; Wilcox 1987). That spinning was women's work in Hohokam society can also be inferred from the presence of more whorls in female Classic-period mortuary assemblages than in male assemblages (Crown and Fish 1996; Mitchell 1991, 1994). At Pueblo Grande, however, men, too, were commonly buried with spindle whorls, with some differentiation of whorl types by gender. Pueblo Grande women were more likely to have been buried with stone whorls, which are slightly lighter, and men with modeled clay whorls (Stone and Foster 1994:218). The differences in weight probably represent differences in the sizes of the fibers being spun (Teague 1998), evidence of further task differentiation by men and women and an additional burden on women's labor.

Ground stone was another craft item that was intensively produced in the Hohokam area. Basalt sources are concentrated around the irrigation communities of the Salt-Gila Basin but seldom lie immediately adjacent to sites. One of these sources is in the New River area, on the northern edge of the Phoenix Basin (Hoffman, Doyel, and Elson 1985). Domestic structures near the quarry indicate that people lived and manufactured tools close to the procurement area, perhaps seasonally. Stone working is, by ethnographic analogy with other groups in the western United States, a male activity (Jorgensen 1980; Schneider 1996), but given the proximity of the outcrops to the reduction and finishing areas at New River, some participation by other members of the household may also be posited. The basalt products from this and other quarries were widely distributed throughout the Phoenix Basin and are found at sites as far as 50 kilometers away (Bostwick and Burton 1993). Although some of the producers might have returned seasonally to residential sites in the central Phoenix Basin, bringing with them manufactured ground-stone tools, the quantity produced and circulated seems to have been in excess of the consumption needs of the producer households alone.

The combined evidence for craft production in the Hohokam area shows that there was more than one pathway to craft specialization there. Shell working, textiles, ceramics, and ground-stone items were intensively produced in the Hohokam region, in greater amounts than were needed for household consumption, but the gendered organization of production was different for each class of artifact. One of these pathways involved intensification of production by the entire household—that is, a change from a gendered system of production to a nongendered system. An example of this trajectory lies in the pre-Classic sites of Shelltown and the Hind Site in the Papaguería, where the intensity of production implies participation by most household members. Within the entire production sequence, individual tasks might have become gendered, but the final product was the result of multiple hands. Textile production also fits this trajectory. Spinning (by women) and weaving (by men) became gendered tasks, but each was a necessary step in the production of a single item. Along this pathway, the labor of an entire household was scheduled, allocated, and coordinated toward the completion of a single class of product. This is evidence that dichotomized divisions of labor do not always describe craft production or trajectories of specialization in small-scale societies. Nonetheless, who was credited as having been the producer might have been more gendered, on the basis of who was involved in the final steps of production.

A second trajectory toward specialized production entailed a more gendered division of labor. Ceramic production might have remained a female task, despite intensified production in many areas. Shell production in the Classic period might also have become a more gendered activity within the household. Some highly traded goods might have lent status to the producers through the products of their labor. Certainly, items that were made to be used by the household as status indicators must have conferred greater status on their makers.

As Patricia Crown and Suzanne Fish (1996:808) have discussed, there was a greater tendency for Classic-period Hohokam women to be buried with utilitarian objects, including spindle whorls, pestles, manos, and relatively large numbers of ceramic vessels, whereas Classic-period men were more likely to have been buried with ornamental or ritual items, axes, abraders, and smaller numbers of ceramic vessels. Crown and Fish suggested that this distinction could be interpreted as an extension of the division of labor that took place in life, and that it was more pronounced in the Classic period than in the pre-Classic.

The implication of increasing intensification of production is that for many households, women's work loads increased (Crown and Fish 1996). Demands on men's labor must have paralleled demands on women's labor. The weaving of cotton increased during the Classic period, providing strong evidence for demands on men's labor. Men might even have been involved in some of the spinning of certain fibers, judging from the presence of spindle whorls in men's burials during the Classic period. Ethnographic data suggest that textile production was a seasonal activity (Russell 1975:150), conducted outside the agricultural season. Alternatively, some men might have substituted nonsubsistence production for subsistence production. For example, older men might not have worked in the fields as much as younger men, diverting their labor to fiber processing and weaving, as Paul Ezell (1961) suggested for the Gila River Pimas. Like shell ornaments, cotton textiles were probably socially necessary items that conferred and maintained differences in household status in Hohokam society.

THE MIMBRES AREA

Evidence for a gendered division of labor in craft production is less well documented for the Mimbres area. Ceramics were clearly made by women during the Late Pithouse period, however. A women buried in a pit structure from the Late Pithouse component at NAN Ranch Ruin was associated with several ceramic production tools, raw materials, and even three unfired Boldface Black-on-white jars, probably dating to the late A.D. 800s or early 900s. Fragments of basketry in the grave suggest that the tools might have been kept inside a basket, and red pigment was found inside a black-on-white bowl as it might have been kept during the woman's life (Shafer 1985).

Classic-period Mimbres burials rarely contain tools of production or have been so disturbed by looting that many of the skeletons have not been sexed. One exception to the scarcity of production tools is a group of bead-working blanks and finished products found along with raw materials with a male buried beneath room 98 at Swarts Ruin (Cosgrove and Cosgrove 1932:62, pl. 69). The only tool from an identified individual burial at Galaz Ruin is an arrow-shaft smoother from a male interment (Anyon and LeBlanc 1984:399).

The many examples of representational art on Mimbres pottery can also be used to support interpretations of gendered production of ceramics. Male and female figures are clearly represented in a variety of activities, from hunting to wood collecting. On the basis of the variety and quantity of vessels and the quality of the painting, Steven LeBlanc (1983:138–39) suggested that it could not be assumed that Classic Mimbres women were always the potters. Stephen Jett and Peter Moyle (1986) argued that certain fish depicted on Classic Mimbres pottery dating between A.D. 1000 to 1150 represent species that can be found only in saltwater. If it can be assumed that only Mimbres men traveled to the distant seacoasts, then the painters presumably were male. I have used this interpretation, along with the fact that the end of the Mimbres Classic period was characterized by marked depletion of many resources, to suggest that if men participated in ceramic manufacture, this might have been a response to changes in subsistence labor (Mills 1995b). However, the assumption that only men could travel long distances to procure raw materials or completed objects through exchange may not be valid (Spielmann, this volume).

Other tantalizing iconographic evidence includes, first, a Mimbres bowl depicting a human figure behind a Classic-period geometric vessel; the figure has been identified as male by one observer (Scott 1983:65, pl. 18) and as female by others (Jett and Moyle 1986:716). Second, there are birth scenes on Classic-period Mimbres pots that seem not to represent accurately the way in which a female would paint the birthing process (Hegmon and Trevathan 1996). In the first case, however, it is unclear, aside from the gender ambiguity, whether the figure is making or using the vessel. In the second case, it should be noted that realism is not always a factor in artistic representation, and Mimbres art included a use of perspective that could produce distortions of realistic depictions (Espenshade 1997; LeBlanc 1997).

Besides evidence for gender ascription, there is compositional evidence to suggest that some Mimbres sites were producing ceramics more intensively than necessary for their own consumption. Undecorated ceramics were made from temper types restricted in their distribution within the Mimbres Valley, suggesting intensive production by potters at villages closest to the sources (Minnis 1985:179–80). Chemical analyses of black-on-white ceramics show that they were made in multiple villages within and outside of the Mimbres Valley (Gilman, Canouts, and Bishop 1994). In addition, the quality of the painting suggests that some people were producing vessels more intensively than others (LeBlanc 1983:138).

The extent to which this production affected household labor for other activities was probably not great. Similarly, turquoise and obsidian artifact production increased from the Late Pithouse period to the Classic period but was never very intensive (Minnis 1985:182–83). Indeed, it is surprising not to see more evidence for craft production and intensification in the Mimbres area, given dramatic increases in population size, irrigation agriculture, and use of nonriverine sites for resource procurement. It may be that the resolution of compositional analyses is inadequate to pick out uneven production. In addition, the overall population size was never so great that nonsubsistence production could substantially supplement subsistence production.

CHACO CANYON

The Pueblo II period in the northern Southwest was a time of contrasts in site size, access to resources and ritual, and, in all likelihood, gendered roles in craft production. Families living in dispersed communities outside the San Juan Basin inhabited a social and political frontier. Those living in Chacoan outlier communities participated in a system of labor organization that was replicated many times over. Differences between great houses and their surrounding communities, at least in Chaco Canyon itself, were marked by differences in the way household labor was structured and in access to resources. Direct evidence for gendered craft production during the Pueblo II period is slim, however, and only a few great-house communities have been systematically investigated.

For Chaco Canyon, burials and burial accompaniments have been inventoried by Nancy Akins (1986:table B-1). Only a small number of burials contained utilitarian items that might indicate production roles. Two burials unequivocally contained polishing stones. Both were of adult females, but in one of these burials, two females were interred with two infants (whose contemporaneity is unknown). These two associations were out of at least 200 sexed burials from Chaco Canyon. There was also a remarkable lack of prepared clay and pigments that might have been used in pottery manufacture.

The paucity of evidence for ceramic production tools in Chaco Canyon burials and site assemblages in general is correlated with the large number of ceramics that were imported into central canyon sites. As Anna O. Shepard (1939) pointed out long ago, judging from distinctive temper sources, potters in the Chuska area made many of the vessels found at Chaco Canyon sites. Between A.D. 1040 and 1200, about 30 percent of all ceramics at Chaco were made in the Chuska area (Toll 1991:94). The sources of at least some of the tempers in them have been traced to a limited area of the Chuska Mountains, especially near Narbona (Washington) Pass (Mills, Carpenter, and Grimm 1997).

Because so little excavation has been done at sites along the Chuska slope, little is known about the social contexts of this production. H. Wolcott Toll (1991) suggested that one of the reasons Chaco potters made no more pottery than they did was the paucity of wood for firing. I suspect that because sources of wood, temper, and clay are clustered away from the main residential sites of the Chuska slope, such as Whirlwind House, Skunk Springs, and Sanostee, some tasks in ceramic production, such as the procurement of raw materials and wood for firing, were shared within the household. In addition, temper sources lie adjacent to the well-known Washington Pass chert source. Even if women formed, decorated, and fired the vessels with wood and materials supplied by men, the quantity of ceramics made in the Chuska area argues for some impact on women's overall labor scheduling there. Indeed, if Chuska residents were responsible for bringing vessels to Chaco Canyon during "pilgrimages" or feasts, then their time would have been doubly affected. Nonetheless, the vast quantities of this pottery and its use in probable ritual contexts of consumption (Stoltman 1999; Toll 1985) suggest that the products and women's labor were highly valued.

Turquoise ornament production is another facet of Chacoan craft production that is often cited as instrumental in regional production and exchange. At least 11 ornament production areas were excavated in Chaco Canyon sites dating between A.D. 920 and 1220 (Mathien 1984). Two of these areas were in kivas, suggesting that men were the ornament producers. Debris, completed ornaments, partially completed ornaments, and manufacturing tools were found on a kiva bench at site 29SJ1360. In addition to one active abrader found on the bench, four passive abraders were found on the kiva floor. Although a diversity of materials was present, the total quantity suggests a relatively low intensity of production, possibly by one or two persons. A second Chacoan kiva suggested to have been the location of ornament production is the great kiva at Kin Nahasbas, where turquoise fragments, stone and shell beads, a clay ring, and possibly ground stone associated with ornament manufacturing were found.

In addition to the two kiva contexts, production tools, turquoise debris, and finished products were found on a pit-structure floor at 29SJ629. Hundreds if not thousands of pieces of worked and unworked turquoise and other materials were recovered from floor 1 of pithouse

2 (Mathien 1984:178), indicating intensive ornament production.

Given that many resources consumed at Chaco were unavailable in the central San Juan Basin, men's absences from the household were probably frequent. Labor for procurement of turquoise, timbers for Chacoan houses, and game to supplement what must have been a depleted faunal population had to be balanced with agricultural labor. Men's absences would have increased the burden of women's work in Chaco Canyon households, as well as in households at many of the Chacoan outlier communities in the central San Juan Basin.

The high intensity of ceramic production in the Chuska area is often considered an enigma in terms of general models of craft specialization, because these models often predict that specialization should occur in areas of poor subsistence resources. What the models seldom consider is a situation in which resources for ceramic firing are so poor, as they probably were in Chaco, that intensifying ceramic production would be unfeasible. Nor do they consider how a gendered division of labor might have operated to deplete the labor pool.

THE PUEBLO III AND IV PERIODS

Interpretations of the gendered division of craft production for the Pueblo III through Pueblo IV periods in the northern Southwest are based on the fact that these periods show marked changes in population aggregation (see Adler, ed., 1996). Although subsistence intensification is often considered a correlate of aggregation, intensification of crop production in the northern Southwest from the thirteenth through the sixteenth century was not due to increased reliance on maize (Mills 1999). Maize consumption was relatively stable throughout the Pueblo area by the Pueblo III period (Hard, Mauldin, and Raymond 1996). Instead, the organization of food processing and consumption hints at important changes in labor allocation and scheduling, especially toward increasing time-efficiency (see Crown, this volume).

One of the consequences of aggregation is that men's hunting becomes restructured as populations deplete faunal resources around aggregated sites (Speth and Scott 1989; Szuter and Bayham 1989; Zack-Horner 1996). The new hunting pattern requires more use of logistical sites by men at greater distances from residential sites, resulting in more time absent from the residential unit (see also Bar-Yosef and Meadow 1995; Szuter, this volume). Related to this change in site use is Eric Kaldahl's (1997) suggestion that there was a "bifurcated" chipped-stone technology at this time in which men produced bifaces for hunting and for ceremonial use and women produced more expedient tools at residential sites for a variety of domestic activities. Archaeological evidence for this gendered division of labor in chipped-stone production is present in the form of spatial clustering of debitage from biface reduction versus expedient tool reduction in different parts of sites during late the Pueblo III and Pueblo IV periods. Although these different deposits are discard assemblages, they probably resulted from gendered activities in different areas (Kaldahl 1999).

At the Pueblo IV site of Grasshopper, two manufacturing rooms contained extensive chipped-stone debitage and tools for producing weapons (Whittaker 1987:474–75). One room had 14 arrow-shaft smoothers in association with evidence for the production of other craft goods. Because the shaft smoothers had different shapes and decorations, John Whittaker inferred that they had been made and used by different men. He believed that production of arrow points was not exclusive to a small number of men at the site and that the points in the richest burial could have been made by as many as 16 individuals.

Polishing stones and other tools of ceramic production were found clustered together on several room floors at Grasshopper (Triadan 1989). Polishing stones, grinding slabs, and prepared (sherd-tempered) clays were found at the nearby and contemporaneous Bailey Ruin, just above the Mogollon Rim (Mills, Herr, and Van Keuren 1999). The clustering of tools in some room spaces does not directly implicate gender but does suggest a separation of work spaces commensurate with the idea of task specificity and more intensive production by members of some households than of others.

Utilitarian objects in the Grasshopper mortuary assemblage demonstrate a highly gendered division of labor. Polishing stones, pecking stones, and rubbing stones were associated exclusively with female burials. Male burials were associated with "inferred" ritual tool kits, flint-knapping tools, and projectile points that were probably placed in the grave originally as part of a quiver of arrows. The last might have been not utilitarian but symbolic of membership in a hunting sodality (Whittlesey and Reid 1997). The presence of burials with many arrows and the concentration of arrow production debris in at least two rooms suggest that hunting was an important activity for men at the site.

Ceramic manufacturing tools in Grasshopper mortuary contexts included polishing stones, but apparently none of the burials had the extensive ceramic tool kits found in the Kayenta area. During the late Pueblo III period, the Kayenta area shows clear-cut evidence of gender differences in tools of production in mortuary contexts (Beals, Brainerd, and Smith 1945; Crotty 1983). Ground stone, ceramic manufacturing tools and materials, awls, hammerstones, and jewelry were all found with adult women at Site RB 568, excavated by the Rainbow Bridge–Monument Valley Expedition. A total of seven graves contained pottery tools, and all but one of them held the remains of women (the seventh burial being unidentified). With one of these women was a large number of items in what Helen Crotty called a "potter's kit," in which *pukis* (turning plates), perforated plates used as *pukis*, polishing stones, and scrapers were interred with an adult female (Crotty 1983:30). The large number of pottery-making tools in the Kayenta area suggests that some women's roles as potters might have been more time-consuming than those of others. Like other activities, ceramic manufacture might have been practiced more intensively by some individuals than others as part of a process of task specialization.

Compositional studies also attest to the intensification of ceramic production during the Pueblo III and Pueblo IV periods. Ceramics were extensively made for more than the producing households in the Mesa Verde (Wilson and Blinman 1995), Rio Grande (Habicht-Mauche 1995), and Mogollon Rim (Stinson 1996; Triadan 1997; Zedeño 1994) areas. In most cases, increases in productive output could probably have been accommodated through the sharing of domestic activities at the household level. Larger household sizes would have encouraged such extra production by making more labor available for corn grinding, child care, and subsistence production.

Spinning and weaving, too, were gender specific. Cotton took on increased importance in the Pueblo area after A.D. 1000 (Kent 1983). It was cultivated in Canyon de Chelly, the middle Little Colorado River, the lower Rio Chama, and around the Hopi Mesas (Adams 1996;

Magers 1986; Teague 1998). As in the Hohokam area, cotton textile production placed additional labor demands on Pueblo spinners and weavers. Unlike in the Hohokam area (so far as we know), weaving became a cooperative activity by men in the context of ritual structures. This pattern is not uniform, however, and historic production hints at greater complexity, as does some of the archaeological evidence.

Spinning and weaving tools have been found in many sites throughout the Pueblo world. Because so many of the tools of textile production are perishable, estimating increases in labor intensification from them is difficult, but patterns of gendered production can be inferred. Spinning was clearly a women's task in the western Pueblo area. An entire spindle-full of cotton was found with a female at Canyon Creek Ruin in east-central Arizona (Haury 1934). At the Zuni sites of Hawikku and Kechipawan, the only spindle whorls from identified burials were found with women (Webster 1997). Weaving tools have been found at Mug House in the Mesa Verde area with a male interment (Rohn 1971) but at Hawikku with both men and women (Howell 1995; Webster 1997). One of the men at Hawikku was even buried with a loom.

Cotton textiles were increasingly made by men in segregated ritual settings in many of the eastern and western pueblos after A.D. 1100 (Kent 1983). Specialized ritual structures with loom anchor holes in their floors have been found at a number of sites in the northern Southwest (table 9.1), especially after 1325 (Peckham 1979). Much of this was for cotton weaving, although cotton was not grown in all of these pueblos. Raw cotton (as well as finished cotton products) was widely traded in the historic period, providing raw materials for production over a wide area.

In the western Pueblo area, loom anchors are often associated with kivas identified on the basis of other features such as benches and flagstone floors (Smith 1990 [1952]; fig. 9.2). These structures have been found at a variety of sites in the Tusayan, Mogollon Rim, and upper Little Colorado areas (table 9.1). Antelope House in Canyon de Chelly shows evidence for such intensive spinning and weaving that these activities must have begun to affect the time people spent in other tasks. Several kivas at the site have loom holes, and rooms within the pueblo had raw cotton and spinning and weaving tools, which suggest

TABLE 9.1

Pueblo Sites with Floor Loom Holes

Site	*Reference*	*Site*	*Reference*
Eastern Pueblo Area		Western Pueblo area	
Alfred Herrera Site (LA 6455)	Webster 1997	Antelope House	Magers 1986
		Awatovi	Smith 1972
Arroyo Hondo	Creamer 1993	Betatakin	Smith 1952b
Bandelier's Puaray (LA 326)	Webster 1997	Broken K Pueblo	Martin, Longacre, and Hill 1967
Cuyamungue (LA 38)	Webster 1997	Four Mile Ruin	Fewkes 1904
		Hawikku	Hodge 1939
Frijoles Canyon cavates	Toll 1995	Homol'ovi II	Walker 1996
		Homol'ovi III	Hays-Gilpin, pers. com., 1997
Frijoles Canyon Rainbow House	Webster 1997	Jeddito 4	Smith 1972
Giusewa (LA 679)	Webster 1997	Jeddito 108	Smith 1972
Gran Quivera (LA 120)	Webster 1997	Kawaika-a	Smith 1972
		Kiet Siel	Guernsey 1931; Smith 1990 [1952]
Kuaua (LA 187)	Webster 1997		
Largo-Gallina area (LA 12063, 12072)	Webster 1997	Kin Tiel	Haury and Hargrave 1931
Nanishagi (LA 541)	Webster 1997	Kokopnyama	Haury and Hargrave 1931; Smith 1972
North Bank Site	Webster 1997		
Pecos	Kidder 1958		
Poshu-ouinge	Webster 1997	Marsh Pass Ruin 8	Kidder and Guernsey 1919; Smith 1990 [1952]
Pottery Mound	Crotty 1994		
Pueblo del Encierro (LA 70)	Webster 1997		
Pueblo Pardo (LA 83)	Webster 1997	Pinedale Ruin	Haury and Hargrave 1931
Puye	Webster 1997	Poncho House	Guernsey 1931; Smith 1990 [1952]
Te'ewi (LA 252)	Webster 1997		
Tsankawi cavates	Toll 1995		
Unshagi	Webster 1997	Table Rock	Martin and Rinaldo 1960
		Waterfall Ruin	Kidder and Guernsey 1919; Smith 1990 [1952]

that many members of the household participated in some aspect of cotton textile production. Cotton seed was extensively consumed at the site, probably as a backup or starvation food during the mid- to late 1200s (Magers 1986).

Intensive textile production by men in separate ritual structures or kivas is well described in ethnographic accounts (e.g., Stephen 1936). Men were so productive in historic Hopi kivas that one Mormon missionary described the kivas as "workshops" (Brooks 1944:85). Spinning, weaving, and moccasin repairs were all carried out by men in the kivas. Weaving fit with the agricultural cycle, provided an activity during religious retreats, and produced an item for exchange outside the household. Textiles were highly valued goods in historic Pueblo society. The value of men's labor during the Pueblo III and IV periods was probably as high as it was in the historic period, when textiles were more highly commodified.

Although the spatial segregation of women and men is often interpreted as decreasing women's status (Spain 1992), weaving by men in kivas may not have limited women's access to ritual knowledge across the Pueblo world during the Pueblo IV period. Some women buried at the Zuni site of Hawikku, which was occupied from the fourteenth through the seventeenth centuries, were clearly associated with a large diversity of mortuary goods that imply participation in a variety of ritual settings (Howell 1995). Judging from ethnographic accounts, eastern Pueblo women had more restricted access to kivas, but at Hopi, women had their own ritual societies and their own ritual structures, and they owned the land, its products, and the products of men's work (Parsons 1939). There was a complementarity of roles within the corporate group (Schlegel 1977b) that transcended the spatial unit of the household. The idea of role complementarity was an essential part of the corporate nature of the group, and there was a balance between ritual and economic roles, much as Rosemary Joyce (1996:180–81) described for Classic Maya women. In the Pueblo world, men and women take part in different activities, but their roles are highly complementary. As Elsie Clews Parsons (1939:40) wrote of the historic Pueblos, "in most economic activities, men and women are engaged in one part or another of the same general process." This complementarity might have extended to the division of labor in tasks for the completion of single

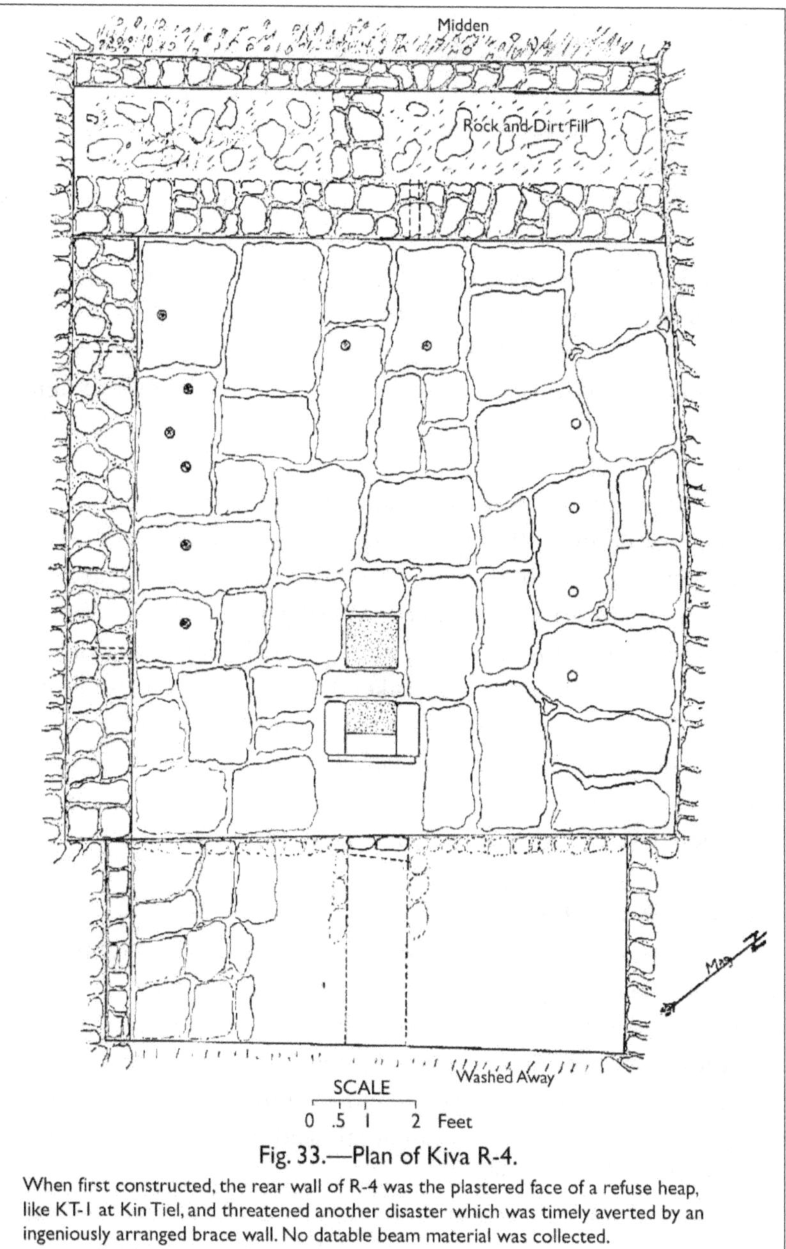

Fig. 33.—Plan of Kiva R-4.

When first constructed, the rear wall of R-4 was the plastered face of a refuse heap, like KT-1 at Kin Tiel, and threatened another disaster which was timely averted by an ingeniously arranged brace wall. No datable beam material was collected.

FIGURE 9.2.

Plan of kiva R-4 at Kokopnyama in the Tusayan area (from Haury and Hargrave 1931:fig. 33). Small circles on floor denote loom anchors.

items, especially if women were spinning and men were weaving.

In sum, textiles, pottery, and other craft items were produced within a highly gendered system of production during the Pueblo III and IV periods. Aggregation provided a means by which labor could be allocated for different tasks within the community, and that allocation was made largely along gendered lines. Intensity of production increased in several areas, a process enabled by increasing efficiency in other tasks such as cooperative hunting and corn grinding. The different forms of specialization evident in the late Pueblo periods were not the same, however, and all three pathways toward specialization of production are evident. Ceramics made in a highly gendered system of production were, for the most part, made within the household by women. One exception might have been the manufacture of whiteware ceramics in the Mesa Verde area, where trench kilns were used (Wilson and Blinman 1995). Judging from the quantities of ceramics fired at one time, firing might have been conducted by groups of women above the level of the household (Bernardini 1997). Weaving is an example of intensive production above the level of the household, most likely carried out by men linked by their membership in ritual societies. One exception to this pattern is seen at Antelope House, where entire households were involved in some task of cloth production to the extent of sitewide specialization. This case is analogous to the production of shell ornaments in the Papaguería.

CASAS GRANDES

The Casas Grandes region presents an intriguing case study for the investigation of craft production because of the quantity of raw and finished materials recovered from the site of Paquimé. In addition to ceramics, chipped stone, textiles, and bone, Charles Di Peso (1974b:483) estimated that 97 percent of craft production was in luxury goods, including shell and mineral beads and pendants, mosaics, and pseudo-cloisonné work.

A total of 4 million pieces of shell, totaling 1.5 tons, was recovered from Medio-phase contexts (ca. A.D. 1250 to 1450) at Paquimé. Of this total, 96.2 percent came from two adjacent rooms in unit 8, rooms 15 and 18 (Di Peso 1974b; Minnis 1988:185). Unit 14, room 26, also contained a large quantity of shell and nonshell artifacts and raw materials associated with subfloor caches. Di Peso suggested that two of these rooms were where slaves worked, because of the cramped space produced by 1-meter-high walls in the lower story. It is more likely, however, that these "walls" were in fact platforms or shelves (see Di Peso 1974b:fig. 69-2), which better fits with R. J. Bradley's (1996) interpretation that these rooms warehoused hoards of prestige goods that were maintained by elite members of the community. Few production tools were present in them, suggesting that actual production activities took place elsewhere (Minnis 1988:186–87).

The distributions of tools and raw materials associated with the production of ceramics, textiles, bone beads, and shell and mineral ornaments throughout the excavated portions of Paquimé do not suggest that production was limited to certain house clusters. Even when the contents of storage rooms are subtracted from the totals, I suspect that there were still more modified and unmodified shell items at Casas Grandes than at any other Southwestern site, and certainly more than at any other contemporaneous site in the greater Southwest. This great degree of regional concentration supports the interpretation of a high intensity of production that may have exceeded what one individual in each household could produce. Rather, the involvement of multiple members of each household in the production and distribution of both utilitarian and highly valued items seems more likely. Whether men and women worked together on the same items or whether this production was gender specific is difficult to determine on the basis of available contextual data.

Di Peso (1974b) often mentioned the gender of producers in his interpretations of Casas Grandes craft production at Paquimé, but he did so almost exclusively in terms of direct analogy with Sahagun's accounts of Aztec society. Burial assemblage data compiled by John Ravesloot (1988:79–89) show that both men and women at Paquimé were interred with production tools and materials. Mined deposits, pigments, and awls were found with both men and women. There was a greater tendency for women to be buried with clays and polishing stones, suggesting their involvement in pottery production. More exclusive to men were hammerstones, unfinished stone and shell ornaments, rubbing stones, and stone debitage, suggesting their greater involvement in chipped-stone tool and stone and shell ornament production.

The current evidence for craft production at Paquimé suggests the presence of large quantities of nonutilitarian goods, clear-cut hoarding of raw materials in a few rooms at the site, and widespread distribution of production tools and debris. Combined with the identification of clear differences in social status based on mortuary remains (Ravesloot 1988), these data suggest that many households practiced nonutilitarian craft production to enhance their status, as has been suggested for Classic-period Hohokam society. Contextual data from the site of Paquimé should be analyzed more closely, but this site may contain the best examples yet found in the Southwest of Ames's (1995) "embedded specialization," in which elite households are full participants in the production, distribution, and use of craft items.

CRAFT PRODUCTION, GENDER, AND STATUS

From foragers to committed agriculturalists, Southwestern societies have often been characterized as epitomizing egalitarianism. In anthropology as a whole, however, the interpretation of what constitutes egalitarianism has changed as differences in social equality within all nonstate societies have been recognized (Flanagan 1989). Age, gender, and kinship mark differences in status that may or may not be institutionalized. Moreover, it is becoming increasingly clear that models of political organization have been constrained by the assumption that hierarchy, status, and centralization should change in lockstep. New models that emphasize alternative forms of leadership suggest that political organization was highly varied across the Southwest (Mills, ed., 2000) Here, I consider the interplay of craft production, labor organization, and women's status in prehispanic Southwestern societies.

On the basis of studies of hunter-forager groups throughout the world, several implications can be outlined for women's status with increasing dependence on seed crops and on the production of craft items used in processing and cooking. These implications are for decreased mobility, increased alliance building, increased processing time, and decreased women's status (Jones 1996; Kelly 1991:146). On the basis of Brian Hayden and colleagues' (1986) comparisons of hunter-forager groups, we might expect that in situations of increased resource stress, especially in times of lower than average rainfall and/or increases in conflict, the status of women would be especially low.

Similarly, one of the often-cited effects of the transition to agriculture and increasing technological complexity is that women's status declines (Flanagan 1989:259; Sanday 1981). Many of the studies citing this effect, however, have been based on changes coincident with the transition from precolonial to colonial societies and may not accurately reflect changes in the prehispanic Southwest. Agricultural intensification is generally accompanied by an increase in task-specific activities such as long-distance faunal acquisition, food processing, and craft production. These activities may enhance rather than lower the status of women, particularly if women maintain control over the storage and distribution of food for daily consumption and ritual feasting activities. Moreover, even if few nonsubsistence goods were produced by women in the prehispanic Southwest, they might have been stored in the household, again enhancing women's status. These goods might have ranged from bridewealth to ritual objects maintained within matrilineages, both of which are documented for historic Pueblo societies. Indeed, prehispanic Southwestern society probably provided many contexts in which women's status was relatively high and others in which it was relatively low, highlighting the need to assess particular cases with as many lines of evidence as possible.

Craft production can influence and be influenced by social status. Many objects undoubtedly had ritual or symbolic significance within communities. In some cases, the users were also the producers, as in the production of masks, fetishes, and specific ritual paraphernalia. Other objects, such as shell bracelets, cotton clothing, and decorated serving bowls, might have been produced by a few but used by many in the construction of social identities. Production of goods made in a gendered organization of production might have enhanced the status of producers, whether men or women, by converting subsistence goods into tangible wealth. Whether production was at the scale of the entire household or at the suprahousehold scale, inequalities within the community might have been created and/or maintained through the process of craft manufacture.

Larger families can have higher status by virtue of having greater labor pools for engaging in communal activities and the ability to assign labor to specific tasks at other times. As noted earlier, children in agricultural societies can make significant contributions to household labor, potentially freeing some women's labor for other tasks. In multi-household communities where tasks such as child care and food processing could be pooled and where older children were full helpers in household and agricultural tasks, labor for craft production would have been more easily released. This was likely to have been the case in the late prehispanic pueblos, where we see changes in ground-stone technology toward greater efficiency without increases in consumption per person (Mills 1999). Fewer women would have been needed to grind the same amount of corn per person, allowing other women's labor to be diverted to more intensive craft production.

An example of how women's status might have declined in the Southwest is a situation in which household size was increased not just through the birth rate but through polygyny. Polygyny is one strategy for increasing household production and can be found when the fruits of women's labor become commodities, as hides were for historic-period Blackfoot families (Brumfiel 1992:555). Larger households created in this way do not provide equal status for women as they do for men, nor are all women in the household equal to each other. Structural inequalities between households are reinforced in societies that practice polygyny because families in them tend to be larger. A cross-cultural study of pre-state sedentary communities in the Americas conducted by Gary Feinman and Jill Neitzel (1984) found that the households of about one-third of all leaders practiced polygyny.

Hide processing was more often a man's task than a woman's in western North America, unless a high degree of hide processing for clothing was involved (Jorgensen 1980). As is indicated by the Blackfoot example just cited, hides were important trade items in the historic period. Judith Habicht-Mauche (1998) recently suggested that Rio Grande Pueblo women might have married into Plains Indian households in order to provide labor for processing hides that were subsequently traded to Pueblo families for subsistence items. She based her interpretation on the fact that late prehispanic Pueblo-style ceramics were not only present in Plains households but were also made there. Polygyny could have been practiced in these Plains households, as it could have been in some Pueblo households located at the interface of Pueblo-Plains territories and even in the Hohokam and Casas Grandes areas, where large households seem to have been present. We might expect to find such a strategy for incorporating women's labor into these households, and if we do, it will probably indicate the lower status of at least some women in that society.

GENDER AND THE PRODUCTION OF INALIENABLE POSSESSIONS

One of the most interesting recent contributions to the literature on anthropological economics is Weiner's (1994) model of "inalienable possessions." Although she based her model in exchange theory, she looked not only at what items were exchanged but also at those not exchanged—that is, items that were not alienated from their producers. The focus on inalienable possessions is thus more about production and how production enhances the status of the producer and her or his household.

Inalienable possessions may be goods, land use rights, or even ritual knowledge. Goods that do not circulate or that circulate only under special circumstances form the core of Weiner's examples: "inalienable possessions are symbolic repositories of genealogies and historical events; their unique subjective identity gives them absolute value placing them above the exchangeability of one thing for another" (1994:33). Inalienable material possessions are rarely food and almost always crafts. "Of all objects...food is the most ineffectual inalienable possession because its biological function is to release energy rather than store it" (Weiner 1994:38).

Mirrors, palettes, censers, trumpets, turquoise mosaic work, masks, fetishes, and dance costumes are among the possible prehispanic Southwestern examples of inalienable possessions. These items were produced in small quantities, were passed on through lineages and religious societies, and enhanced the status of their producers because of their great value. They were not commodities, which are usually "easy to give" (Weiner 1994:6). In general, these objects had to be ritually discarded rather than being desecrated by profane use. Many of the objects in burials and caches throughout the Southwest fall into this category and could be identified as inalienable possessions on the basis of context.

Weiner's model challenged traditional notions of reciprocity because she saw exchange as being as much about what is held back as about what is given. Objects that are held back are symbols of authority, connoting and legitimating distinctions between individuals and the roles those individuals play within society. The ability to keep while giving is therefore a position of power. Inalienable possessions, such as cloth, can be and often are made by women. Gender, production, and the construction and maintenance of social status are all therefore interrelated.

Judging from the kinds of objects considered to be inalienable possessions in ethnographic contexts in the Southwest, such as altars, prayer sticks, fetishes, and dance costumes, it is more likely that these objects were made by men than by women (e.g., Parsons 1939:279). Women did produce some inalienable possessions ethnographically, such as the ritual ceramics used to hold corn pollen that are still occasionally commissioned at Zuni. More often, however, men made the objects and women helped care for them by virtue of their relationships with men who held positions in the ritual hierarchy. Senior men were trustees or guardians of these ceremonial items, which were considered to be group property (Beaglehole 1937:12).

Ceramic serving vessels used in both daily meals and communal feasting probably conferred status on their makers as well, but these objects were alienable and often widely traded, perhaps even becoming commodities in some situations (Triadan 1997). Most important were the social contexts of their use, which might have increased in importance with village-wide ritual feasting (Mills 1999). Similarly, the high labor input in textiles made by men in the northern Southwest probably conferred status on their makers, but because these objects were sometimes alienable they had economic as well as social or ritual value.

GENDER, CRAFT PRODUCTION, AND POLITICAL INEQUALITY

The different political contexts in which material culture was produced and used across the Southwest also affected the gendered organization of production. Recent "revisionist" ethnological interpretations of historical and contemporary pueblos suggest greater political complexity than had been previously acknowledged (Brandt 1980; Levy 1993; Plog 1995). These interpretations hint at a form of political power in Pueblo society that was very different from that of

Classic-period Hohokam or Casas Grandes society (see Mills, ed. 2000). The way in which authority is organized in Pueblo society cannot be regarded as a stepping-stone toward more complex organization, however; it is better viewed as a fundamental characteristic of the way in which power is used and expressed in middle-range societies.

The pathways to power outlined by Richard Blanton and colleagues (1996) and by Feinman (1995) provide a particularly useful way of considering how prehispanic Southwestern societies might have been organized and how women's status might have been expressed in each context. Their model centers on leadership strategies characterized as corporate based and network based. These two strategies are not mutually exclusive in any particular society, but one mode tends to dominate. A corporate strategy is one in which power derives from a local group and individual prestige is de-emphasized. By contrast, the network strategy derives power from the development of exchange networks or alliances. Architecturally, one finds more evidence for labor investment in communal architecture with corporate strategies, whereas network strategies result in highly differentiated dwellings that emphasize personal power and differences between households. Economically, household production is the source of labor and power under corporate strategies, and manipulation of access to long-distance prestige goods characterizes network-based modes. The latter mode is more likely to be characterized by polygyny and gender hierarchies (Blanton et al. 1996:5).

Although these strategies are idealizations of a reality that probably falls along a continuum, the description of the collective and individualizing power that underlies the two strategies seems particularly applicable to the prehispanic Southwest. The late prehispanic western Pueblos, Chacoan society, and the pre-Classic Hohokam might represent examples of corporate-based or collective power. The Classic-period Hohokam and especially Casas Grandes better fit a model of power relations that is more network based or individualizing (Mills 2000).

These distinctions help us to understand different pathways toward specialization, especially the corporate-based production of textiles by men in suprahousehold contexts on the Colorado Plateau. A Pueblo IV kiva mural from Pottery Mound depicting richly decorated walls on which hang labor-intensive strands of beads and textiles illustrates how corporate production and use might have enhanced the status of a group in ritual settings (Vivian 1994:pl. 6). The sizes of groups and the responsibilities of their members are displayed through the massing of material belonging to the household of each member. Randall McGuire (1986) argued that the material depicted in the Pottery Mound mural indicates that the items were no longer being made and used but reflected their former significance in ritual. Instead, I suggest that the production and display of ornaments and other intensively produced items continued in ritual settings, much as they do to the present day. In contemporary and historic Zuni society, ornaments and textiles are displayed as "house jewelry," and their use is tied to a high degree of status for women because of the nature of corporate ownership at Zuni.

In Classic-period Hohokam society, platform mounds composed the public architecture, but these mounds were related to more individualized leadership within descent groups (Elson and Abbott 2000). Compounds effectively limited public access not only to the enclosed household but perhaps also to certain ritual activities. Some households clearly produced more than others and produced more goods with higher prestige value. The spatial concentration of these higher-status goods at some sites and in some households within sites closer to platform mounds reflects this more individualizing power. Casas Grandes production was probably similarly structured, and craft objects were made to enhance the prestige of individual households.

Women's status must also have varied in these contexts, with greater potential for complementarity in Pueblo and pre-Classic Hohokam societies and greater asymmetries of power along gender lines in Classic-period Hohokam and Casas Grandes societies. The historic western Pueblo pattern provides one example of how corporate-based power enhanced women's status. Western Pueblo women had autonomy in selecting marriage partners, who generally joined the wife's household upon marriage. The matrilineal household owned fields and the products of men's work in the fields. Storerooms maintained by the matrilineal household contained not only subsistence resources but also inalienable items that were related to the roles of individuals within the household and were passed down through the lineage by virtue of the lineage's position within the clan. Although they did not hold positions of ritual authority, women helped to maintain many of the objects used in rituals that were part of their household's ritual obligations. Although land tenure and residence patterns varied widely in the ethnographically documented Southwest (see Fish, this volume), corporate-based ritual was widely practiced, and households participated differentially in the care of ritual objects.

The status of women in Hohokam society was more dependent on individual household productivity, especially during the Classic period. During that time there were greater asymmetries of economic and political power between households than was the case earlier. Craft production of utilitarian items for consumption outside the household probably enhanced the statuses of producers, whether men or women, only marginally. The greatest status-enhancing productive activity would have been to make goods that did not circulate or that circulated only among a limited subset of the population as symbols of ideology or wealth.

CONCLUSION

Craft production played an important part in the gendered division of labor in prehispanic Southwestern societies. Changes in the kinds of crafts produced by men and women indicate changes in the organization of subsistence labor and time allocation for different tasks. Demands on labor for craft production probably affected the organization of labor for subsistence production, and vice versa. These demands also affected the relative statuses of men and women within their respective societies. Arrayed on a relative scale, the case studies discussed in this chapter show that demands on labor were differentially constructed. Plateau Late Archaic groups probably experienced fewer demands on their labor, and Classic-period Hohokam and Medio-phase Casas Grandes society probably experienced the greatest. I have suggested that changes in demands on labor for craft production were closely correlated with the process of aggregation, although how labor was organized and the meaning of that organization for differences in women's and men's status may have varied widely among the groups discussed.

Intensification of production for more than the household unit was part of the reorganization of labor for craft production. Three different pathways toward specialization of craft production have been identified for the Southwest, all of which have implications for gendered division of labor and for the statuses of men and women within their respective households and communities. One trajectory was toward increasingly gendered production within households, as was the case with most ceramic production in the Pueblo area. Another trajectory was toward intensive household-wide production of specific goods as part of a regional complementarity in production and exchange; this entailed a change from highly gendered to nongendered production. The intensive production of shell ornaments and ceramics in some pre-Classic Hohokam sites and of cotton textiles in Canyon de Chelly offers examples of this trajectory. A third trajectory was the highly gendered production of goods outside the household, of which men's weaving of textiles in the Puebloan area after A.D. 1000 is the best example.

In addition to these alternative trajectories of items made for use or exchange, special items used for ritual were made by a more limited set of producers. These items had embedded status distinctions, because the knowledge needed to make many of them was not or could not be shared with everyone. These goods conform to what have been called "inalienable possessions." In general, these items were probably made by men in most of the Southwest, providing men with the means of acquiring greater status, but they used that status in different forms of leadership across the Southwest. Even if women produced few of the ritual items, their status was probably higher in societies organized around corporate-based leadership strategies, illustrating the important linkages between craft production, social context of use, and status in the prehispanic Southwest.

ACKNOWLEDGMENTS

I would like to thank all the participants in the School of American Research advanced seminar for their stimulating and constructive comments. I especially thank Patty Crown for inviting me to participate and for all of her efforts in bringing this seminar to publication. Doug Schwartz, Duane Anderson, Joan O'Donnell, and the staff of the School of American Research are to be thanked for making the seminar such an enjoyable experience. William Longacre, Lynne Teague, Laurie Webster, and Stephanie Whittlesey provided critical bibliographic references and unpublished manuscripts. I also thank T. J. Ferguson and Carol Kramer for their advice and comments on various aspects of the research.

10

Gender and Exchange

Katherine A. Spielmann

Southwestern archaeologists have long been interested in the exchange of commodities and dissemination of styles, but rarely have they made gender the focal point of their analyses. In part, this lack of a gendered understanding of exchange stems from the inherent difficulty of using material remains to identify the individuals who interacted with one another. Ethnographic data provide us with potential scenarios about men, women, and exchange, but evaluation of these scenarios with archaeological data is often difficult.

In this chapter I begin with a discussion of anthropological research on gender and exchange in middle-range societies and identify the kinds of data we need from such studies to help us infer gender from the material remains of precontact exchange relations. I then review data on Southwestern exchange for the Archaic period in general, followed by data for the Hohokam, Ancestral Pueblos, and Mogollon. I conclude with a discussion of what I infer the intensity and extent of men's and women's exchange to have been in the precontact Southwest. I also consider the degree to which each gender participated in exchange for wealth, because such exchange relates to the issue of gender hierarchies.

THE ANTHROPOLOGICAL RECORD

Because the gender of the participants in exchange relations is not self-evident in the archaeological record, it is useful to examine ethnographically known systems of exchange that are similar in complexity to those that have been documented archaeologically for the Southwest. Two areas of the world are particularly relevant for comparison with the Southwest because of similarities in the extent and organization of their production and exchange systems.

The !Kung of southern Africa, whose generalized exchange system, called *hxaro*, has been documented in detail by Polly Wiessner (1977), provide an excellent analogy for the kind of exchange system that appears to have developed among the highly mobile foragers who inhabited the arid landscape of the Archaic Southwest. !Kung long-distance exchange relations were important in maintaining social ties as well as provisioning trade partners with material goods. According to Wiessner (1977), both women and men had multiple trade partners, and 75 percent of the material goods a !Kung household contained was acquired through long-distance exchange. A gender hierarchy is not apparent in this generalized long-distance exchange system.

Similarly, the production and exchange systems well documented for Melanesia and the Philippines provide insights into exchange relations among agricultural village dwellers in the Southwest. These areas are particularly relevant because their production and exchange systems tend to be characterized by community specialization in the absence of market systems and by the large-scale movement of products over long distances. Two hallmarks of production and exchange in the later precontact Southwest are the development of community specialization and long-distance exchange. In community specialization, households in villages specialize in the production of a single item, which they then exchange with other villages for their specialized products. What is remarkable about the Southwestern cases is the quantity of material that was transported long distances in the absence of the boat transportation typical of some Melanesian long-distance exchange.

Recent analyses of Melanesian exchange systems are also the only cases for middle-range societies in which gender is an explicit focus of analysis. This literature is thus important for developing an understanding of gender and exchange in the precontact Southwest.

Although I focus on these areas of the world for the following discussion, data from other middle-range societies are mentioned where relevant in order to amplify certain points. These ethnographic data allow us to analyze women's and men's participation in both local and long-distance exchange and to identify the relationships and contexts that are central to our understanding of gender and exchange in middle-range societies.

At the local level, in village-level societies women control the products of their labor when those products are subsistence items. In Melanesia, for example, Sio women trade pots for bananas (Harding 1967), and fish is traded for sago on the Sepik River in New Guinea (Gewertz 1983; Healey 1990). Elsewhere in the world, similar patterns have been documented: in the early 1800s, Plains women traded food for clothing (Blakeslee 1975; Griswold 1970); in the early 1900s, Southwestern Hopi women traded food with one another and with Navajo traders (Udall 1969); and in the 1950s, Tongan women of Zimbabwe traded baskets for food (Scudder 1962).

The situation changes when products are exchanged over long distances or when they constitute wealth. In Melanesia, men and women engage in exchange outside their communities to varying degrees. Among men, the variation appears to relate to differences in ability to amass surpluses to exchange and in ability to develop exchange partnerships (Feil 1984; Lilley 1985; Lederman 1990a). Among women, factors not directly related to exchange may reduce their ability to engage in long-distance exchange.

Central among these factors is women's control over the products of their labor, an issue discussed in the wider literature on gender and exchange (e.g., Friedl 1975:62; Josephides 1985). Although women's products often circulate through exchange systems, in some cases women exchange the products themselves, whereas in others men appropriate the products. Women's participation in external exchange is affected by other variables, including (1) the degree to which men control women's movement (Mintz 1971); (2) child-rearing obligations (which can also apply to men) (Lepowsky 1993; Mintz 1971; Quinn 1977; Tsing 1993:128; Wiessner 1977); (3) the intensity of warfare (Barlow 1985; Macintyre 1983; Sanday 1974; Stark 1992); and (4) women's access to public contexts of prestige building. In several

Melanesian societies, women may be active in personal exchange networks but have no access to the public ceremonial exchanges in which political relations are negotiated (Feil 1978; Josephides 1985; Lederman 1986; see also Quinn 1977). Women's products may circulate in both spheres, but in the public sphere, women no longer have control over their distribution.

Of particular interest is whether women and men have access to the same contexts for personal prestige building and whether socially valued goods (wealth) are the same for men and women, because these goods often circulate through long-distance exchange. In some societies, women and men operate in the same ceremonial sphere and with the same wealth items. Among the Vanatinai of Melanesia, for example (Lepowsky 1993), both women and men are active in the production and exchange of wealth, which they both use for prestige building in the same ceremonial context, mortuary feasts. Women and men both lead exchange expeditions to acquire wealth.

Kathleen Barlow (1985) described a somewhat similar system among the Murik of Papua New Guinea, although men there appear to have been more active in the ceremonial sphere. In this case, women produced many of the traded goods (e.g., baskets, fish) and had long-distance trading partners. They were more likely, however, to give male relatives items to trade in their name than they were to mount or accompany trading expeditions. In addition, Murik women could hold ritual feasts to advance their own name, and thus they traded for feasting food (garden produce and pigs) (Barlow 1985).

In some Melanesian societies, women and men are prominent in different ceremonial contexts and use different wealth items. Among the Kiriwina of the Trobriand Islands, for example, women's wealth is composed of banana leaf bundles, which women distribute by the thousands during mourning ceremonies. Men's wealth (yams, pigs) is also mobilized in the context of these ceremonies because men contribute to the accumulation by exchanging their wealth for bundles. Annette Weiner (1976) equated women's prestige building in the mourning ceremonies with men's prestige building in yam displays and the kula.

Aside from cases in which women have explicit ceremonial contexts in which to engage in prestige building, most examples of wealth exchange among men and women in Melanesia involve ceremonial contexts that privilege men. Thus, although women may be active in exchange relationships and may even decide who gets what in the ceremonial distributions, it is men who make these distributions and build a public name for themselves (Feil 1978; Lederman 1986).

Finally, there are a number of Melanesian cases in which women are involved marginally or not at all in exchange for wealth. Still, in many of these cases, women's products are critical for men to use if they are to participate in long-distance exchange networks designed partly to circulate wealth (Harding 1967; Healey 1990; Hughes 1977; Weiner 1976).

Several anthropologists have analyzed not only the physical exchange of items but also women's role as nodes in Melanesian exchange networks. Interpretations vary; some writers exalt the role of women in linking affines (Feil 1978; Weiner 1992), and others emphasize the marginality of women's participation when their only role is in linking their husband's group with their natal group (di Leonardo 1991; Josephides 1985; Strathern 1972). The Strathern-Weiner debate on the value of women's products and women's exchange relations in New Guinea illustrates the great variability of women's status as it relates to exchange.

In summary, ethnographic data document the diversity in men's and women's participation in exchange of subsistence and wealth items. Such diversity cautions us that the nature of women's and men's exchange relations is an empirical question that requires knowledge about a society's food production, social relations, and contexts of prestige building. The data also suggest the kinds of contexts to monitor in the archaeological record.

With regard to subsistence items, women are involved in exchanging the fruits of their labor within the village or with nearby villages. In a number of cases, from Melanesia (e.g., Barlow 1985; Gewertz 1983; Macintyre 1983) to the Puebloan Southwest (e.g., Hill 1982), women gain local prestige by being especially good at producing subsistence items such as pots and baskets for exchange. Long-distance exchange of women's subsistence items, however, is generally undertaken by male kin who act on the women's behalf or on their own behalf.

Turning to socially valued, or wealth, items, the degree to which women are active in prestige-building activities affects the degree to which they are active in long-distance exchange, and especially the degree to which they accumulate (as opposed to simply exchange) wealth. In many cases women do not build prestige for themselves, but their products (pigs, baskets, pots, shell ornaments) are used in exchange for valuables. In such cases, the intensity of women's production and exchange is affected by the tempo of men's ceremonial activities.

ARCHAEOLOGICAL CORRELATES

The anthropological record on gender and exchange in middle-range societies documents a great deal of variability in women's and men's participation in exchange but indicates that women tend to be much less active in long-distance exchange than men, even though women's products commonly circulate through long-distance exchange systems. Evaluating whether this was the case in precontact long-distance exchange requires that we be able to reconstruct behavior from material remains. So far, unfortunately, the necessary data are unavailable.

There are two lines of inquiry using ethnographic data that would be particularly helpful in inferring gender from archaeological exchange data. The first concerns technological style, which refers to how an item is made (Zedeño 1994). Similarities in technological styles imply direct contact, because these styles require instruction in order to be replicated. It would be helpful to know how technological styles pattern when men are engaged in the long-distance exchange of men's and women's products as opposed to when women participate in the long-distance exchange of their own products.

Patterning in design style is the second kind of information that would be useful to have from the ethnographic record. Similarities in design style do not necessitate direct contact, for designs can be copied. Ethnographically, however, design styles can be "owned" by certain production groups, and copying is actively discouraged. Again, analyses of the patterning of design styles in systems in which men are the traders and ones in which women also trade might help identify which gender or genders were involved in long-distance exchange.

In the absence of clear material referents linking gender and exchange, in the following review of Southwestern exchange data I postulate possible gendered exchange scenarios that should be considered hypotheses for future research.

THE SOUTHWESTERN ARCHAEOLOGICAL DATA

In the Southwest, archaeologists have amassed an enormous quantity of data on the loci and scales of durable-goods production and the areas over which these commodities were distributed. This analysis focuses on three kinds of durable items: ceramics, projectile points and lithic raw material, and ornaments. Although the literature on Southwestern ceramics is voluminous, the same cannot be said for lithics, with the exception of obsidian. Thus, my discussion is weighted heavily toward ceramics. I assume that women made and decorated most of the pots (Crown and Wills 1995a), that men made most of the projectile points (Gero 1991; Peterson 1994), and that producers had control over the local distribution of their products. I consider ornaments to have been socially valued goods, and I infer the gendered nature of wealth exchange from the association of ornaments with women and/or men in mortuary assemblages or paintings (on pots or in kivas).

As in other chapters in this volume, my data are presented by area and time period, beginning with a general discussion of the Archaic period and proceeding to the Hohokam, Ancestral Pueblo, and Mogollon areas.

ARCHAIC PERIOD (8000 B.C. TO A.D. 200)

Owing to inadequate data on basketry and other fiber products, the record of interaction in the Archaic period depends on lithic artifacts and thus is probably largely a male record. Stylistic diversity in the Early Archaic (8000 to 5000 B.C.) was limited, suggesting to both W. H. Wills (1988a) and Steven Shackley (1990) that Early Archaic populations were highly mobile and that social boundaries (for men) were lacking across a large portion of the Southwest.

During the Middle Archaic period (5000 to 1500 B.C.), point styles involving both the blade and hafting elements proliferated (Wills 1988a; Shackley 1990), as did the use of many different sources of obsidian. Shackley, following Wiessner's (1977) model for !Kung point styles, suggested that this reflected the closing of social boundaries at a scale larger than that of a hunter-gatherer band. Male interaction, then, remained at a fairly broad scale but was nonetheless more bounded than it had been in Early Archaic times.

Because the vast majority of obsidian on Middle Archaic sites is from sources in the general area of a hunter-gatherer band's seasonal round, Shackley argued that exchange of obsidian was minimal (1990:406). Todd Bostwick (1988), however, suggested that multiple point styles on individual sites in the Harquahalla area might signal exchange among different bands.

Settlement data suggest increasing sedentism during the Late Archaic period (1500 B.C. to A.D. 200) (Wills and Huckell 1994), which is reflected in the lithic record. Points were less reworked, and obsidian sources were less variable on individual sites. Barbara Roth and Bruce Huckell (1992) documented the development of point styles unique to southern Arizona and southwestern New Mexico. Shackley (1996) noted the presence of distinctive point styles in western Arizona sites, which he suggested might indicate ethnic differences. Other point styles were more widespread, however, and Wills (1995) argued that social boundaries remained fluid.

Several distributional patterns suggest relatively sustained interaction among Southwestern populations during the Late Archaic period. Like some point styles, Southwestern pithouse morphology was strikingly uniform. Moreover, corn and the knowledge necessary to cultivate it were rapidly adopted (Ford 1984; Wills and Huckell 1994). Whether women, men, or both were responsible for corn production during this period is unknown.

Relatively few ornaments have been found in Late Archaic sites. Those recovered in the vicinity of Chaco Canyon were made of local materials—seeds and bone (Mathien 1984).

In sum, although women's products (e.g., baskets, potentially), are not obvious in the Archaic record, the patterning in projectile point styles and the rapid dissemination of corn agriculture suggests that exchange connections were diffuse and widespread, much as in the !Kung system of generalized exchange. I expect that women and men participated equally in such a system.

THE HOHOKAM AREA

Pre-Classic Period (A.D. 300 to 1150)

Both women's and men's items and ornaments are well represented in the Hohokam pre-Classic record. One hallmark of the

Hohokam pre-Classic, buff ware, was made during the Snaketown phase of the Pioneer period (Fish 1989). Although buff ware is technologically homogeneous, geographical variation in design style suggests that the ware was produced throughout the Phoenix Basin rather than mass produced in a few locales (Crown 1984a). On the basis of these data, I suggest that the most intense interaction among women took place within individual drainages, within which design styles were fairly uniform. Nonetheless, commonalities in design-element repertoires and buff-ware technology suggest sustained interaction among women throughout the basin.

Plain ware was locally produced in many portions of the Phoenix Basin (Abbott 1984), but there was also a substantial quantity of phyllite-tempered plain ware that was traded across the basin (Crown 1984b). Plain ware composed the majority of ceramics exported from the Hohokam area (Crown 1985b). Because the vast majority of the exported vessels were jars, Patricia Crown suggested that they were traded for what they contained, perhaps a liquid like saguaro syrup.

People in the Phoenix Basin imported a large quantity of finished shell ornaments, principally *Glycymeris* shell bracelets from the western Papaguería (A. Howard 1985; McGuire and Howard 1987). Many sites in the western Papaguería evidence shell production debris, though the use of shell jewelry by people there was limited (McGuire and Howard 1987). This seems to be a classic example of specialized production for food exchange (see A. Howard 1985; Mills, this volume), a common pattern in the Melanesian literature and one that characterized historic exchange relations between Papagos and Pimas (Russell 1975).

A similar case of subsistence specialization and exchange was present in the New River area, where ground-stone items were made and traded into the Phoenix Basin (Bostwick and Burton 1993; Hoffman and Doyel 1985). In exchange, the New River residents may have received buff ware and shell ornaments, which appear in New River sites, and food (Doyel 1991b). Depending on who produced these items and the distance to trading partners, exchange might have been between men, men and women, or women.

Buff ware was traded widely out of the Phoenix Basin north to the Verde Valley and south to the San Pedro (Crown 1991a). Crown

(1991a) noted an overlap in the distributions of ball courts, Hohokam shell, and buff-ware ceramics in central Arizona. Paul Fish (1989) noted the similarly widespread distribution of Hohokam ritual items such as palettes, censers, and stone bowls. Many authors have identified the development of a Hohokam "regional system" during the pre-Classic that reflects both a shared ideology and an integrated economy (Crown 1991a, 1991b; Fish 1989; Wallace, Heidke, and Doelle 1995; Wilcox and Sternberg 1983). This system involved the exchange of probably both women's and men's products: ceramics, ritual items, and socially valued goods.

Because ball courts appear to have been unrestricted in access, both women and men likely were active participants in events that periodically brought together and facilitated exchange among a variety of people.

Mortuary ceremonialism is another context in which women's and men's products accumulated, at least in part, through exchange. Plainware bowls and jars were the vessels most commonly found in cremations at Pueblo Grande (Mitchell 1994). Well-made projectile points, many of nonlocal stone, were deposited by the thousands in Hohokam cremations. David Doyel (1991b) posited that a few part-time specialists could have made the numbers of points associated with cremations. If points are considered a male item (made by men, given to men), as they appear to have been in the Classic period (see Peterson 1994), then Hohokam men might have acquired points from these specialists and deposited them as part of a mourning ceremony. Arleyn Simon and John Ravesloot (1995) have made a similar argument concerning women and deposits of pottery in mortuary contexts in the Tonto Basin. Alternatively, the mourning group might have been made up of both sexes or primarily of women (e.g., Merriam 1955) who were responsible for amassing wealth items to include in the cremation.

At Pueblo Grande, cremations were the primary loci of shell ornament deposition in the pre-Classic period (Mitchell 1994). Between 20 and 25 percent of the burials contained shell ornaments, most of which were bracelets (Stone and Foster 1994). Unfortunately, it is difficult to determine the sex of a cremated individual, and thus which sex(es) the ornaments were buried with remains unknown. The richest burials on Mound A at La Ciudad were of females (Wilcox 1987), suggesting that both women and men had access to the wealth displayed in mortuary ritual.

Classic Period (A.D. 1150 to 1450)

The Classic period in the Phoenix Basin exhibited a marked increase in the local production of items such as obsidian points and shell ornaments that had been imported during the pre-Classic. Concomitant with this increase was a marked decrease in the area over which Hohokam materials were distributed and ball courts used (Crown 1991a). This increase in production and decrease in spatial distribution suggests that men and women of the Phoenix Basin participated in more restricted yet more intense interactive networks.

David Abbott (1985, 1994; Abbott and Walsh-Anduze 1995) documented the nature of Classic-period ceramic production and exchange in the basin. Plain ware tended to be produced locally, often within individual canal systems. Pueblo Grande stands out for its greater diversity of plain-ware sources that crosscut canal systems. Abbott attributed this to its greater prominence in hosting ceremonies to which large numbers of nonresidents would have been invited. Because plain ware generally did not move great distances, Abbott assumed the vessels were exchanged as gifts among kin. Exchanges with socially close people for food or other household items could also account for the restricted distribution. In either case, the interaction was most likely among women.

Red ware presents a different picture. Much of the red ware at Pueblo Grande comes from the South Mountain area and, in the early Classic, from the Gila River as well. Abbott postulated that South Mountain villages specialized in red-ware production. He envisioned trade fairs as the context in which ceramics moved. The pattern of exchange that William Longacre (1991) and Miriam Stark (1990, 1992) documented for the Philippines, however, could have worked just as well. In the villages they studied, small groups of women potters visited other communities to exchange pots for food. Fictive kinship ties developed between potting women and their trade partners (Stark 1992), and a woman's social connections determined where she traded. Potters on occasion gave pots as gifts to their trade partners, although most vessels were exchanged for food. Potters also responded to requests from trade partners. In the Phoenix Basin, considering the preference for red-ware bowls in Classic-period inhumations and ceremonial precincts (Abbott and Walsh-Anduze 1995; Mitchell 1994), it is possible that burial preparations were the occasions on which Pueblo Grande women commissioned red-ware vessels from their trade partners in the South Mountain area.

By A.D. 1300, Gila and Tonto Polychrome vessels had become common in the Phoenix Basin (Doyel 1991b). Some were made locally (Crown and Bishop 1987), whereas others were imported from east-central Arizona (Schaller 1994). Technologically, Salado Polychrome represents a unique combination of attributes emulated by Hohokam, Ancestral Pueblo, and Mogollon populations. The unique quality of Salado Polychrome technology and the lack of regional variation in technical attributes (Crown 1994) suggest that women learned the technique directly from one another rather than by copying imports. Such direct contact would further suggest that despite the reduced nature of Hohokam interaction in the Classic period, women moved over a wider area than the exchange data document.

Although finely crafted mortuary projectile points ceased to be made in the Classic period, other kinds of lithic production increased in intensity. There were greater quantities of obsidian (cores, debitage, and finished products) (Doyel 1991b; Peterson, Mitchell, and Shackley 1997; Teague 1985) and a greater diversity of sources in the Pueblo Grande obsidian assemblage than there had been during the pre-Classic period (Peterson 1994). This greater diversity might have appeared because Pueblo Grande was more involved in regional interaction (Abbott 1994) than were other sites in the Phoenix Basin from which we have collections. At Pueblo Grande, obsidian from sources more than 200 kilometers away was represented in raw form. Peterson, Mitchell, and Shackley (1997) suggested that men might have embedded raw material procurement into long-distance trips focused on other procurement activities, such as obtaining shell.

Points remained appropriate burial accompaniments. At Pueblo Grande, most points were from burials, and 73 percent of them were with adult males (Peterson 1994). These Classic-period points are relatively uniform in shape; points from northern Arizona tend to have longer blades, which may relate to stylistic distinctions or to the availability of larger cores (Peterson 1994).

Shell ornament exchange also changed dramatically in the Classic period, with a marked reduction in the production of bracelets and other items in the western Papaguería and the appearance of shell ornament production in the Phoenix Basin (A. Howard 1985; McGuire and Howard 1987). At platform mound sites generally, according to Crown and Fish (1996), shell ornaments were differentially distributed among men and women. For Pueblo Grande specifically, presence-and-absence data on shell from inhumations show that roughly equal proportions of men and women (59 percent and 52 percent, respectively) were buried with shell of any sort (Mitchell 1994:Appendix A), and roughly equal proportions were buried with shell bracelets and pendants (Gross and Stone 1994). Male burials, however, tended to receive greater *numbers* of shell ornaments—an average of 44 per burial versus an average of 14 for female burials (Mitchell 1994). Stone disk beads, on the other hand, tended to be associated with female burials. The stone is largely slate or steatite, both of which were available more locally than shell.

Acquisition of the raw material might also have been more in the hands of men as sources of shell became increasingly distant from the Phoenix Basin. Ann Howard (1985) postulated that besides the western Papaguería, the Trincheras area of northern Mexico might have become a supplier of shell, given the appearance in the Hohokam repertoire of a new species of *Glycymeris* that lives farther south in the Gulf of California.

In general, the economic system in the Classic-period Phoenix Basin was characterized by a series of community specializations (Crown 1991b; Doyel 1991b; Gasser and Miksicek 1985) involving both women's and men's crafts and products. Although trade fairs have been postulated as the means by which materials moved around the basin (Abbott 1994; Doyel 1991b), ethnographic data from Melanesia indicate that large quantities of materials can move around regions simply on the basis of multiple individual trade partnerships (Healey 1990; Lepowsky 1993; see also Wallace and Heidke 1986). Thus, a tighter network of social relations among men, among women, and perhaps among families across the basin than is implied by the trade-fair model seems likely, given the quantities of economic goods that were made in households but traded basinwide.

Current data do not document a particularly coherent system of valuables exchange. Unlike ornamentation in the pre-Classic period, with its emphasis on shell bracelet exchange, durable ornamentation in the Classic period was less standardized. Beads became much more prominent, but not in quantities that indicate large-scale giveaways or the accumulation of corporate wealth. At some sites stone beads are emphasized, and at others, shell beads (Stone and Foster 1994). Although men averaged more ornaments than women, some women nonetheless had access to large quantities of ornaments.

In sum, the widely shared nature of both design and technological styles in ceramics suggests that women were active in exchanging the products of their labor across the entire Hohokam world. Personal trade partnerships and community-level aggregations (e.g., at ball courts or platform mounds) are envisioned as the mechanisms by which women exchanged their products. Similarly, men's trade partnerships probably moved the serrated points of the pre-Classic across the basin. Both men and women participated in the exchange for shell ornaments, but men are expected to have undertaken the very long-distance expeditions to the Gulf of California to acquire shell.

THE ANCESTRAL PUEBLO AREA

Although portions of the Ancestral Pueblo area (e.g., Black Mesa, Chaco Canyon, Mesa Verde) have witnessed research as intense as that in the Hohokam area, large expanses remain relatively unknown, and information can be spotty. The following analysis pieces together literature on Ancestral Pueblo exchange.

One hallmark of Ancestral Pueblo exchange is the early development and persistence of community specialization in ceramic production and long-distance exchange (50 to 100+ km). Reconstructing the contexts in which people moved large quantities of material over long distances on foot presents a challenge in dealing with Ancestral Pueblo exchange.

Basketmaker III (A.D. 500 to 700)

In the northern San Juan River area, households were dispersed; many made their own gray ware, but others obtained such vessels through exchange. White ware, constituting less than 10 percent of the ceramic assemblage, was nonlocal (Blinman and Wilson 1993; Wilson and Blinman 1995). The limited range of tempers and clays in imported white wares suggests some degree of specialization. Although different white-ware production areas can be distinguished on the basis of temper and paint, design style is uniform across the northern Southwest (Hegmon 1995:56).

Lithic raw material was exchanged relatively widely in the Black Mesa area (Gumerman and Dean 1989).

Ornaments included *Olivella* and *Glycymeris* shell beads, as well as turquoise. Locally available materials (including garnet, shale, and steatite in the Chaco area) were also made into beads (Mathien 1984). Many burials excavated by A. V. Kidder and Samuel Guernsey (1919) in the Marsh Pass area contained necklaces of shell and stone beads, along with stone pendants. Ornaments tended to be associated more with subadults than with adults, however.

In sum, both women's and men's products appear to have circulated widely in relatively small quantities during the Basketmaker III period, suggesting the participation of both genders in long-distance exchange networks of dispersed trade partners.

Pueblo I (A.D. 700 to 900)

This period saw some degree of aggregation, although many households remained dispersed. Virtually all households produced gray ware. White ware circulated at a regional level, indicating some degree of specialization. A few potters appear to have produced for entire communities (Hegmon, Hurst, and Allison 1995). White-ware types were characterized by abrupt stylistic boundaries and were distributed locally (Wilson and Blinman 1995; Hegmon 1995; Hegmon, Hurst, and Allison 1995; Wilson and Blinman 1991), suggesting that the immediate networks within which women interacted were fairly tightly bounded. Michelle Hegmon (1995) noted, however, that white-ware technology, including the selection of particular temper types, was widely shared, suggesting interaction among women beyond their immediate localities.

Red-ware bowls made in southeastern Utah began to be exported some distance (50–75 km; Hegmon 1995) into the Dolores River

(Blinman and Wilson 1993) and Black Mesa areas (Gumerman and Dean 1989). This red-ware production may be the first example of community specialization in the Southwest (Hegmon, Hurst, and Allison 1995). The clinal distribution of red ware (Wilson and Blinman 1995) suggests down-the-line exchange. That traded red-ware vessels were less variable than vessels found at the source suggests that a subset of southeastern Utah potters, perhaps the better ones, was involved in exchange (e.g., see DeBoer and Lathrap 1979).

Ornaments tended to be made of local materials or shell; turquoise was rare (Mathien 1984; Windes 1992). The 34 burials at Chaco Canyon that date to this period contained only ceramics, with no sex data on their distribution.

Decorated ceramics, and red-ware bowls in particular, tended to be more frequent at Pueblo I sites or roomblocks that contained kivas (Blinman 1989; Hegmon 1995). Stephen Plog (1989) argued that by Pueblo II times, ritual contexts had become appropriate settings for exchange. Ceremonial feasting might also have created a demand for the import of certain decorated pottery, particularly red ware. Presumably, it was women who did the cooking and serving, using vessels made by other women and obtained through down-the-line or direct exchange among women. On the basis of the ethnographic data discussed earlier, we can infer that the intensity of women's production of and exchange for items used in ceremonies (in this case decorated serving bowls) increased as the tempo of ceremonial activity increased.

Pueblo II (A.D. 900 to 1100)

In this period, settlements tended to be dispersed, except in Chaco Canyon, but the numbers and sizes of habitations increased. In some areas, such as the Mesa Verde region, gray ware was still produced by most households. In others, such as Black Mesa and the Virgin Anasazi, gray ware was produced for long-distance exchange from upland to lowland areas (Hays-Gilpin, personal communication 1997; Allison 1997). The distances over which gray ware moved were sizable, sometimes exceeding 100 kilometers. In both the Navajo Mountain and Moapa Valley areas, virtually all of the gray ware was imported during this period.

In the Mesa Verde area, white ware increased in frequency while red ware decreased. White ware was traded over longer distances (Wilson and Blinman 1995), and production intensity increased, as is evidenced by the appearance of multihousehold kilns (Bernardini 1997). On Black Mesa, imported San Juan Red Ware was replaced by more locally made Tsegi Orange Ware (Gumerman and Dean 1989).

The reduction in long-distance exchange connections evidenced in the decrease in San Juan Red Ware is mirrored in the increasingly circumscribed distribution of different types of white ware (Hantman and Plog 1982; Plog 1990). Toll, Blinman, and Wilson (1992), however, suggested that differences among types have to do with technical differences in paste, paint, and surface treatment rather than differences in design. They argued that there was instead a great deal of commonality in white-ware design styles, centered on the use of hatching (Toll, Blinman, and Wilson 1992). Moreover, they suggest that plain wares were similar in surface and rim treatment over much of the Ancestral Pueblo area as well. They also noted a widespread shift from mineral to carbon paint and a loss of hatching in the 1100s (see also Lang 1982; Wilson 1996). This stylistic commonality across the broad expanse of the Ancestral Pueblo area, from Black Mesa to the Rio Grande, suggests that despite greater intensity of interaction among women at the subregional level, women regularly communicated with each other outside their subregions, probably through marriage and participation in multicommunity ceremonies.

Lithic raw materials were traded over shorter distances during the Pueblo II period, and consequently there was a decrease in the diversity of lithic sources (Plog 1990).

Chaco Canyon

Community specialization during late Pueblo II–early Pueblo III is prominent in the Chaco Canyon system; communities 50 to 60 kilometers away in the Chuska Mountains supplied about half of the plain ware and much of the white ware (Mills et al. 1997; Toll 1981, 1991). The scale of importation vastly outstripped that found elsewhere during Pueblo II. H. Wolcott Toll (1991) estimated that roughly 49,000 vessels were imported into Pueblo Alto alone over a 60-year period. Although import levels approaching 1,000 vessels per year appear staggering, they are consistent with ethnographic data collected from small-scale potting communities. For example, potting villages in the Amphlettes Islands of Melanesia produced 300 to 350 vessels (6 vessels per potter) a month in exchange for food (Lauer 1970). In the Philippine village of Dalupa (Stark 1990), with a population of 400, 77 households produced 2,800 pots for exchange in a single year.

Although both towns and villages received pots from the Chuskas, these vessels were more abundant in towns. Town dwellers also imported more jar forms than the villagers did. The high frequency of sooting on these jars and their large sizes suggest greater emphasis on cooking, perhaps for feasting, at the town sites (Toll 1981, 1984).

The mechanism(s) that brought the Chuska pots into the canyon are unclear. Given the meccalike nature of Chaco Canyon, it is not unreasonable to expect that yearly pilgrimages might have been made from pueblos in the San Juan Basin, during which vessels were traded. The diversity of white-ware sources at Pueblo Alto (Toll 1984) is reminiscent of the ceramic diversity at Pueblo Grande and may reflect the diverse origins of the participants in ceremonial activities.

Although local materials dominate the lithic assemblage in the canyon, by the tenth century high frequencies of nonlocal material, especially Washington Pass chert, suggest direct procurement (Cameron 1984). Trade partners (male?) might have brought the material into the canyon, or men might have quarried it directly, perhaps during beam-harvesting expeditions.

Ornamentation was rare at Chacoan small sites, but when it occurred it was more often associated with adults than subadults (there are no data on ornament distribution by sex). White, red, and black stone beads appear to have been imported, because no production debris was found. Stone beads tended to be concentrated at the small sites, whereas turquoise was present in much greater frequencies at the large sites, especially Pueblo Bonito (Toll 1991; Windes 1992).

The emphasis on turquoise ornament production in Chaco Canyon coincided with a particularly intensive period of mining in the Cerrillos Hills of central New Mexico (Warren and Mathien 1985). Chacoan ceramics were rare in the Cerrillos Hills area, suggesting that contemporaneous populations in the Rio Grande region might have supplied the turquoise. Alternatively, Chacoans could have made short-term expeditions to the source. This kind of expedition was likely undertaken by men.

Although turquoise (Windes 1992) and shell were broadly distributed over the Ancestral Pueblo area, they were particularly concentrated at the great houses in Chaco Canyon and nowhere were more abundant than in burial chambers at Pueblo Bonito (Akins 1986; Judd 1954; Pepper 1920). Of the burials sexed and described at Pueblo Bonito in rooms 32, 33, 320, 326, and 329, adult males appear to have been directly associated with the greatest quantity of ornaments, in the form of shell and turquoise beads and pendants (e.g., room 33; Akins 1986:115). Subadults and women were also interred with substantial quantities of ornaments. Large numbers of ceramic vessels, finely woven cloth, and some baskets accompanied these elaborate graves.

Several researchers have noted that large quantities of ornaments also occurred in these elaborate burials unassociated with any particular person, as in the corner caches in room 33 (Akins 1986), as well as in kiva niches (e.g., Chetro Ketl; Akins 1986; Lekson 1983; Toll 1991).

Pueblo III (A.D. 1100–1300)

Production for long-distance exchange characterized white ware and some gray ware during the Pueblo III period. Little Colorado White Ware was exchanged over a wide area in northern Arizona from roughly A.D. 1050 to 1250 (PII–PIII). It was produced in the Hopi Buttes area and traded to people living in the San Francisco Peaks, Grand Canyon, and Chevelon areas. Amy Douglass (1987) argued that the lack of fall-off in the distribution of Little Colorado White Ware for more than 100 kilometers from its source suggests that exchange systems, at least in this area, had not shrunk during Pueblo II (contra Hantman and Plog 1982).

Imported Tusayan Gray Ware decreased to 30 percent in the Navajo Mountain area as local pottery production increased, probably due to the depopulation of Black Mesa (Hays-Gilpin, personal communication 1997).

In southwestern Colorado, most households continued to produce gray ware. White-ware exchange increased in intensity but decreased in distance (Blinman and Wilson 1993; Wilson and Blinman 1995), probably owing to increased local demand. Production by women who were part-time potters might not have been able to meet the needs of regional populations, perhaps because of increasing use of white ware in feasting (Bernardini 1997); hence the contraction in exchange distance. In addition, the use of communal kilns suggests that larger groups of women cooperated in the production of white ware (Bernardini 1997).

In the Kayenta area, with the contraction of populations, there appears to have been a decrease in the exchange of material goods. Nonetheless, uniformity in technological and design styles indicates continued interaction among women (Gumerman and Dean 1989). By A.D. 1200, however, Kayenta women were exporting their vessels to the Tusayan and Mesa Verde regions and to areas to the south. The increase in the tempo of interaction presaged southward migrations out of the Kayenta area.

White Mountain Red Ware was traded widely, particularly St. Johns Polychrome (Carlson 1982), which was distributed down the line as far east as the Rio Grande Valley and perhaps to the western Great Plains, north to the Mesa Verde area, west to Gila Bend, and south to northern Chihuahua.

Santa Fe Black-on-white, produced in the northern Rio Grande, exhibits the by now familiar pattern of variability in paste but broad stylistic uniformity that characterizes much of Southwestern decorated pottery. It was traded locally, within areas defined by the paste attributes (Habicht-Mauche 1995). The stylistic uniformity indicates interaction among women at a larger scale than that documented by the commodity exchange.

Although the intensity of ritual activities increased markedly during the Pueblo III period, durable ornaments did not play an obvious role in ritual elaboration. For example, ceramic vessels continued to dominate burial goods in the Zuni area. Ornaments appeared in small quantities with both adults and children (Howell 1994).

Pueblo IV (A.D. 1300–1600)

Migration is the hallmark of the Pueblo IV period throughout the Ancestral Pueblo area. Regions once densely occupied were abandoned; areas that had supported sparse populations for centuries were faced, in the span of a few generations, with the immigration of thousands of people. Villages larger than any seen before in the Southwest were established. Migration of this scale by definition involves the reconfiguration of interactive relations.

The process of migration generally begins with the collection of information about potential destinations. Information can be provided by kin, trade partners, or more mobile members of the community who maintain contact with their homeland (Duff 1998). These information-gathering contacts are diffuse in nature, and so it is not surprising that this kind of interaction is poorly visible in the archaeological record. The Mesa Verde area, for example, shows no evidence of long-distance trade contacts that might have presaged plans to move (Lipe 1995). Only the Kayenta-Tusayan area discussed earlier provides clear evidence that exchange relations were initiated or intensified before migration.

In the Mogollon Rim area, immigrant potters from the Kayenta-Tusayan area, in concert with local potters, developed a unique technological style known as Salado Polychrome (Crown 1994). Although Salado Polychrome is unique technically, it shares a design style, the Pinedale style, with many other red- and yellow-slipped wares, including Rio Grande Glaze I, White Mountain Red Ware, Hopi Yellow Ware, and Zuni Glaze Ware, making it a true horizon style (Crown 1994). This style is also evidenced in rock and kiva art, suggesting that men adopted it as well.

The importance of Salado Polychrome specifically (and red- and yellow-slipped Pinedale-style bowls more generally) lies in their apparent association with the spread of what Crown (1994) termed the Southwestern regional cult. She argued that this cult derived from the migration of Kayenta-Tusayan populations into the Mogollon Rim area early in the Pueblo IV period, and she believed it developed in response to the fact that Pueblo IV village populations, because of migration, included people of diverse backgrounds and heritages. If this was the case, then it is women's products that express participation in the cult most clearly in the archaeological record. If food preparation and distribution by women were important in ceremonies associated with this cult, as they are in many ceremonies held by historic Southwestern peoples (Beaglehole 1937; Bernardini 1997; Ford 1972b; Parsons 1932; Spielmann 1998; Titiev 1944), then the association between women's products and a new design style could be an expression of women's centrality to the new cult.

Recent ceramic analyses have documented the rapidity with which women on either side of the Mogollon Rim learned new technological and design styles in response to immigration, first from the Kayenta-Tusayan area and then from the Colorado Plateau to below the Mogollon Rim (Crown 1994; Mills 1998; Triadan 1998; Zedeño 1994). These ceramics were both locally made and imported (Triadan 1998; Zedeño 1994), as were the gray ware and plain red ware (Zedeño 1994).

A different kind of ceramic exchange developed in the Homol'ovi area later in the Pueblo IV period. Adams (1998) argued that although Homol'ovi populations maintained affiliations with both the Hopi Mesas and the upper Little Colorado drainage in the early Pueblo IV period (about A.D. 1280–1330), subsequently the Hopis were able to gain control over the region by setting up a colony (Homol'ovi II) whose purpose was to produce cotton. In return for cotton, Homol'ovi II residents obtained large quantities of yellow-ware ceramics (90 percent of their decorated ware) from the Hopi Mesas (largely from Awatovi; Bishop et al. 1988), and shell and obsidian perhaps through other exchange connections. The close association between Awatovi and Homol'ovi II suggests that women might have been supplying relatives, rather than distant trade partners, with pottery.

In the eastern Pueblo area, women who moved from the Four Corners continued to produce white-ware ceramics in the styles they had used in their homeland. In the Rio Grande Valley, particularly from Albuquerque northward, a number of designs from McElmo Black-on-white and Mesa Verde Black-on-white appear in Santa Fe, Vallecitos, and Galisteo Black-on-whites (Lang 1982).

In the early 1300s, the Albuquerque area was also the locus of a new ceramic technology, glaze ware, which involved a change in paint composition and in tempering materials (Herhahn 1995; Huntley and Herhahn 1996). Black-on-white production declined earliest in the Albuquerque area because of this new technology (Lang 1982). Knowledge of how to make glaze paints and the firing regime necessary to vitrify them spread across the Rio Grande area fairly rapidly in the 1300s, suggesting direct contact among women. Recipes for the paint were variable during the fourteenth century (Huntley and Herhahn 1996), but by the mid-1400s, glaze paint composition was remarkably uniform, suggesting a shared concept among women potters of what a glaze paint should be (Huntley and Herhahn 1996). The Galisteo Basin became dominant in glaze production and perhaps paint production during this century, although other parts of the Rio Grande, such as the Salinas and Cochiti areas, continued to make their own glaze wares as well as import them long distances (Capone 1995; Herhahn n.d.; Warren 1981).

Most glaze bowls were significantly larger than the indigenous white-ware bowls. In an earlier publication (Spielmann 1998), I inferred from this fact that a new context of food serving, possibly ceremonial feasting, which might have accompanied the development and dissemination of Pinedale-style Glaze A ceramics in the Rio Grande, was instrumental in the rapid adoption of glaze ware across much of the Rio Grande Valley.

Red- and yellow-slipped glaze ware was virtually the only decorated ware over much of the Pueblo IV Rio Grande from Santa Fe southward. Two white wares (Biscuit Ware and Jemez Black-on-white [not a true "ware"]), however, were far more abundant than glaze ware in the northern Rio Grande. The distributions of Biscuit Ware (a product of the northern Tewa area), Jemez Black-on-white (a product confined almost entirely to the Jemez area), and glaze ware were characterized by distinct boundaries (Futrell 1998; Graves and Eckert 1998). William Graves and Suzanne Eckert (1998) demonstrated marked differences in iconography on these three wares and proposed that they reflected ideological differences. Interestingly, glaze ware was exchanged and used over the most ethnically diverse portion of the Rio Grande, as one would expect from Crown's (1994) model of the Southwestern regional cult. Biscuit Ware and Jemez Black-on-white, in contrast, appear to have been confined to distinct ethnic groups (Futrell 1998; Graves and Eckert 1998).

The gendered aspect of this patterning has to do with the fact that, as witnessed in the development of Salado Polychrome, women's products figured prominently in the expression of ritual affiliation and in the celebration of ceremonial feasts sponsored by aggregated populations of the Pueblo IV period. Women perhaps created and certainly controlled the iconography that united large numbers of disparate people (glaze area) or expressed ethnic unity (Biscuit and Jemez). Different rock-art styles coincide with the distributions of Biscuit Ware and Rio Grande Glaze Ware, however, indicating that iconography that may have been produced by men also expressed these ideological distinctions.

Obsidian was relatively rare in Rio Grande Pueblo IV sites until the fifteenth century, when exchange for obsidian, ceramics, and possibly cotton increased in intensity (Cameron 1991; Spielmann 1996). Point styles were fairly similar at a gross level, dominated by small, triangular side-notched points.

Ornamentation presents the researcher with an interesting dilemma in the Pueblo IV Southwest. Ornaments are uncommon in the archaeological record, both in middens and in mortuary rituals, but they are prominent in the pictorial record, particularly in Rio Grande kiva murals. This dichotomy between pictorial and actual wealth warrants investigation.

With regard to the mortuary record, ornamentation is rare in all areas except below the Mogollon Rim. At Hawikku, for example, the most common ornament category was miscellaneous shell, found in only 50 of 955 burials. Ornamentation was *not* a distinguishing feature of burials defined as those of leaders (Howell 1994). Only 11 percent of the Hawikku burials were sexed, and data in Todd Howell's dissertation indicate that shell ornaments were strongly associated with men. Turquoise was rare; when it appeared with women it was invariably in the form of turquoise-inlaid combs.

In contrast, shell ornaments appeared to be particularly abundant at Grasshopper Pueblo. R. J. Bradley's (1996) pan-Southwestern study of the distribution of shell ornaments documented a concentration of *Glycymeris* shell bracelets and pendants at Grasshopper. Men and women had similar ornament frequencies (Whittlesey 1978:210, 212) but differed in some of the kinds of ornaments associated with them. *Glycymeris* shell pendants appeared exclusively with men, whereas shell and bone rings were exclusively with women. Women had more stone disk beads and turquoise mosaic pendants. Both men and women had stone pendants, shell bracelets, shell beads, and turquoise mosaic earrings (Whittlesey 1978:212). Of burials considered particularly "rich" (n = 20), 12 were men and 5 were women. Thus, as among the Hohokam, although men appear to have been buried with somewhat larger quantities of ornaments, ornaments were also acquired by women with some frequency, and some women were richly appointed. Greater differences in ornamentation existed within the sexes than between them.

In the Rio Grande, burials were relatively unadorned. If present, ornaments were usually associated with subadults (Hayes, Warren, and Young 1981; Kidder 1958; Palkovich 1980). The concentration of ornaments with subadults in Pueblo IV sites is reminiscent of the Basketmaker III burial record and of societies in which ornaments circulated in generalized rather than competitive exchange systems.

The unadorned nature of Pueblo IV burials in the Rio Grande stands in marked contrast to the remarkable ornamentation depicted in the kiva murals at Pottery Mound (Hibben 1975). Many individuals are depicted wearing multiple strands of white (shell) beads, often interspersed with red (coral) beads. Black beads occur on occasion. Shell pendants are common, and earrings are depicted as well. Where sex is identifiable, roughly equal numbers of men and women are depicted wearing or directly associated with necklaces (7 females, 6 males). In addition, large quantities of necklaces are shown hanging from a rack (kiva 2, layer 1, north wall) and in a basket between a seated man and woman.

Interestingly, the one depiction of a dead person, a woman, in the Pottery Mound murals shows her unadorned (kiva 2, layer 1). This dovetails with the archaeological mortuary record, which indicates that ornamentation of adults was rare.

Murals at the site of Kuaua (Dutton 1963), though less elaborate, nonetheless depict a fair amount of ornamentation equally distributed among males and females. As at Pottery Mound, the most common ornaments are necklaces of white shell beads interspersed with red beads. Shell pendants, bracelets, and earrings are also depicted. Despite the fact that many of the representations in the Pottery Mound and Kuaua murals are of mythical individuals, one is struck by the abundance of shell in paintings and the scarcity of actual shell in all excavated contexts in most Pueblo IV sites.

In summary, the record of exchange for the Ancestral Pueblos is largely, though not exclusively, a ceramic one. Data presented here suggest that women retained control over the products of their labor both locally and over long distances. Some products were exchanged down the line in a series of local transactions (e.g., Pueblo I red ware; San Juan Red Ware), whereas others were carried over long distances to large-scale ceremonies in which both men and women likely participated (e.g., Chuska white and plain wares at Chaco). Finally, the rapid dissemination of technological styles over fairly large regions (e.g., Salado Polychrome and Rio Grande Glaze Ware) suggests that women were in direct contact with one another over fairly long distances. Extant lithic (e.g., Washington Pass chert, Rio Grande obsidian) and ornament data indicate that men's and women's exchange networks were similar in their geographic extent.

THE MOGOLLON AREA

Late Pithouse (A.D. 550–1000)

Exchange relations in the Mogollon area during the Late Pithouse period were more widespread and of greater intensity than those of the subsequent Classic Mimbres period. Paul Minnis (1985) noted that Late Pithouse sites had more shell and turquoise items than those of later periods. Mimbres Boldface Black-on-white was distributed more widely than later black-on-whites. Palettes were more frequent (M. Nelson, personal communication 1997). Twenty-one percent of the Late Pithouse burials at Galaz Ruin contained ornaments (Anyon and LeBlanc 1984).

For sites in the Forestdale Valley, J. Jefferson Reid (1989) commented on a pattern also documented by William Beeson (1966) in which ceramics and cradle-board flattening patterns were diverse, combining both Ancestral Pueblo and Mogollon styles. Reid argued for a pattern of ethnic co-residence going back to the A.D. 600s. At the very least, women with different ways of making pots and caring for infants were present at these sites.

Classic (A.D. 1000–1150)

Minnis (1985) noted an overall contraction in the exchange sphere of Mimbres-area materials during the Classic period, although Mimbres Classic ceramics were distributed over a fairly broad zone from eastern Arizona to western Texas. Few nonlocal ceramics and little obsidian entered the Classic Mimbres sites.

Ornamentation was less pronounced, with only 12 to 18 percent of the burials from Classic-period sites containing ornaments (Gilman 1990). Nonetheless, ornamentation was considerably more elaborate in Classic Mimbres burials than elsewhere, with some burials containing one to two shell bracelets, small turquoise pendants, and a dozen or so beads (Gilman 1990). In her comprehensive analysis of the distribution of shell ornaments in the Southwest, R. J. Bradley (1996) noted that *Glycymeris* shell bracelets were particularly concentrated in the Mogollon area. Indeed, one-third of the bracelets in her sample (outside the Hohokam area) came from Swartz Ruin.

Interestingly, ornamentation is rare in the only pictorial record we have for the Mimbres: paintings on Mimbres Classic Black-on-white pots. In a sample of several hundred vessels included in the Mimbres Foundation archive of Mimbres vessels, of the 35 vessels that depict males, only 2 show individuals with ornaments (necklaces). Of the 27 vessels that depict females, only 3 show ornamentation (necklaces), and 2 of these vessels appear to have been painted by the same person.

Postclassic (A.D. 1150–1450)

The Postclassic period witnessed a remarkable change in interaction with peoples outside the Mimbres area as the Mimbres population dispersed. Locally made ceramics included a diversity of styles (Chupadero Black-on-white, Tularosa Black-on-white, Tularosa Fillet Rimmed, El Paso Polychrome; Hegmon, Hurst, and Allison 1998; Nelson 1999). Hearths and grinding facilities were similarly diverse, causing Hegmon, Nelson, and Ruth (1998) to postulate that women were marrying into the Mimbres area and continuing to make pottery and set up households in the style of their natal villages. The situation is somewhat reminiscent of the earlier occupations in the Forestdale area and of Crown's (1985b, 1991b) description of the Late Classic Phoenix Basin, where the dispersed population interacted to the north and south of the basin but did not constitute a culturally distinct entity.

Darrell Creel (1994) noted that the Mimbres Valley proper was not entirely abandoned by aggregated populations; these populations simply moved downriver and occupied fewer large sites. This move south might have been facilitated by the development of exchange relations with southern populations in the Late Classic period. Small quantities of El Paso Polychrome, Chupadero Black-on-white, and Playas Red appear at Classic-period Mimbres sites. Like the Pueblo III Kayenta women, Classic Mimbres women might have been the ones to develop trade partnerships with populations to the south that would have facilitated relatively large-scale migration down the drainage during the Black Mountain phase. This decorated pottery continued to be imported after the Black Mountain phase villages were established.

By the Late Postclassic period, two relatively uniform ceramic traditions had crystallized out of the diversity. Women in the northern part of the area made (and exchanged) ceramics in the Tularosa style, whereas women in the south made (and exchanged) ceramics in the styles of the El Paso area.

In sum, the Mogollon record of exchange is much more limited than that from other areas of the Southwest, and less is known about the gender distribution of burial accompaniments. In the Classic period, few items were exchanged beyond the local region. Interestingly, for the Postclassic, women's products define a broad but loose network of exchange relations encompassing an area from El Paso to central New Mexico. That women appear to have been marrying into the Mimbres region from these diverse areas suggests that women could have been involved in these long-distance exchanges.

DISCUSSION

Women and Exchange

The primary, archaeologically visible exchange item attributed to women in this analysis is pottery. Both plain and decorated wares were exchanged over varying distances. The changes in scale of exchange may have to do with changes in population density, which in turn affected the sizes of marriage networks, level of demand, and sizes of the areas from which participants in ceremonies were drawn. Ecological complementarity also appears to have played a role in long-distance exchange for ceramics, as in the cases of the Virgin Anasazi and the Chuska-Chaco connection. James Allison (1997) suggested that there was a mutualistic relationship between fuel-rich and food-rich populations.

Regardless of the spatial extent over which a particular ware was traded, the data suggest that women's information concerning ceramic production extended beyond their trading area. Toll, Blinman, and Wilson's argument (1992) that both white-ware design styles and gray-ware decorative styles were similar across much of the Ancestral Pueblo area during the Pueblo II period, for example, and the nearly synchronous switch from mineral to organic paint in the 1100s document a wider sphere of women's interaction than is indicated by the distribution of particular white-ware types. Circulation of women as marriage partners and interaction among women at regular regional ceremonies were likely the mechanisms by which technical and design-style commonalities in pottery production developed and pots circulated. The degree to which families or individuals were mobile between regions, however, remains unclear.

Red- and yellow-slipped wares vary in the degree to which production was specialized. Community or even regional specialization often characterized the production of these wares—for example, Pueblo I red ware, Classic-period Hohokam red ware, and Rio Grande Glaze Ware. The mechanisms by which these items were exchanged are not obvious. Down-the-line exchange, women potters to women consumers, appears to account for the movement of San Juan Red Ware into southwestern Colorado. In the Phoenix Basin, red ware could easily have moved out of the South Mountain communities to communities north of the Salt River through a combination of personal trade partnerships between women north and south of the Salt and trade at multicommunity ceremonies.

Movement of Rio Grande Glaze Ware, as between the Galisteo Basin and the Salinas area, is comparable in distance to the Chuska-Chaco connection. Although the ceremonial centrality of Chaco Canyon might have promoted periodic concentrations of people there from throughout the San Juan Basin, there is no place as obviously centralized for the Rio Grande. It may be the case, however, that people were drawn to the Galisteo Basin pueblos to witness or participate in ceremonies. Recent research by Jeannette Mobley-Tanaka (n.d.) indicates that Galisteo Basin potters redefined the iconography on glaze ware in the early 1400s, and this iconography was then adopted by other glaze producers. Research by Deborah Huntley and Cynthia Herhahn (1996) indicates that the Galisteo Basin glaze recipe was also emulated by glaze-ware potters throughout the Rio Grande. Because this is an aspect of technological style and would have required instruction, it appears likely that women from outlying regions visited the Galisteo Basin pueblos with some regularity.

The Melanesian literature discussed earlier is replete with examples of women gaining status through the distribution of wealth items in ceremonial contexts or by producing particularly attractive items with high exchange value (pots, mats, baskets). How do the pots made and exchanged by women of the Southwest fit into this picture?

Traded decorated ceramic vessels in the Southwest were often domestic items that were also used in ceremonial contexts, as either serving bowls (Pueblo I red ware, glaze ware) or mortuary vessels (Mimbres Black-on-white, Hohokam red ware), or perhaps both. Assuming that women prepared and served the food in precontact ceremonial feasts, it must have been up to the women to procure enough decorated vessels to meet the feasting needs of the community. The display of more bowls or particularly fine bowls in the context of public food distribution might have brought individual women a certain degree of prestige. Whether these bowls can be considered "wealth," however, is arguable.

Mortuary rituals, in some times and places, presented women with another context in which their products were emphasized. Mortuary rituals across the Southwest were highly varied. In some cases, individuals were interred with large numbers of pots (e.g., Chaco Canyon, Phoenix Basin). In some of these situations, as Simon and Ravesloot (1995) argued, women might have been expressing their connections with the deceased. In others, as at Pueblo Bonito, the ceramic accumulation was so large and unique (cylinder vessels) that families or relatives of the deceased might have stockpiled or commissioned vessels.

Women's wealth in the precontact Southwest remains elusive. There is little evidence in either the Southwestern or the more general ethnographic literature to support the argument that pots represented wealth.

Men and Exchange

Lithic artifacts have only been touched upon in this chapter, in part owing to the lack of attention to post-Archaic point styles across the Southwest and in part owing to the paucity of lithic literature in general. From the information discussed earlier, however, it appears that exchange for lithic raw material tended to parallel that of pots and pot styles. As stylistic zones shrank, so did the distances over which lithic raw materials moved (Pueblo I Black Mesa), and as ceramics began to circulate widely, so did obsidian (Pueblo IV Rio Grande). Washington Pass chert, like Chuska ceramics, was imported into Chaco Canyon in Pueblo II times. Thus, men's and women's durable products tended to move at the same geographic scale.

Projectile point styles, however, had a different distribution, generally being much more widespread than the distribution of particular raw materials. This broad distribution of point styles appears similar to the broad distributions of ceramic styles, again suggesting that men's and women's information networks might have been equally extensive.

Points may have been a form of wealth briefly in the Southwest. The large number and high quality of points accompanying pre-Classic Hohokam cremations suggest that their acquisition from specialists and their deliberate destruction in public mortuary contexts might have been a means by which men could gain status.

Except for the pre-Classic Hohokam points, I have identified no durable item that could be convincingly argued was men's wealth. David Wilcox (1987) proposed that textiles were men's wealth among the Classic-period Hohokam, but we have little evidence concerning the production and distribution of cloth from this area. Textiles are a light, easily transported and elaborated item and often constitute wealth in middle-range societies. Whether textiles represented only men's wealth in the Southwest, however, is arguable. Although upright looms are associated with kivas in Pueblo IV and are thus thought to have been used by men, we have no such association between looms and a gendered locality for the Hohokam. Moreover, Ruth Underhill (1979a) argued that the backstrap loom, used by women historically, had greater antiquity than the upright loom in the Southwest.

Ornaments as Wealth

Unlike exchange systems in Melanesia, those in the precontact Southwest only occasionally focused on amassing ornaments, principally of shell and turquoise. For the most part, ornaments were widely distributed in small quantities and likely moved through gift exchange among men and women, much as they do in the !Kung generalized exchange system, *hxaro*.

There are three contexts, however, in which the accumulation of ornaments appears to have been an important focus of long-distance exchange. Among the pre-Classic Hohokam, *Glycymeris* shell bracelets were widely exchanged and, like projectile points, were included in cremations. Unfortunately, their association with particular sexes is unknown, owing to the difficulty of sexing cremations.

The second area that accumulated ornaments was Chaco Canyon. As Toll (1991) noted, Pueblo Bonito so far has produced the vast majority of ornaments, principally turquoise but also some shell. In the Bonito burials, although there was much that was not associated with individual interments, adult males exhibited the greatest amount of ornamentation in comparison with subadults and women (e.g., four male burials in and under room 33). Nonetheless, some women and subadults were ornamented, indicating that wealth might have been corporate rather than associated with a particular sex.

Clearly, we are not dealing with prestige-goods exchange, because wealth did not pass out of the canyon in appreciable quantities. The unique concentration of ornaments in the Bonito burials is different from what would be expected in the kinds of ceremonial exchange systems involving ornaments in Melanesia. At Chaco Canyon, ornaments were amassed and cached rather than circulated in the payment of social debts.

The murals at Pottery Mound (Hibben 1975) provide an example of how these ornaments might have been used and, in fact, may hark back to earlier times of abundance (McGuire 1986). The lavish displays of ornaments, particularly turquoise, in ceremonial contexts and the wearing of ornaments at Pueblo Bonito probably enhanced the prestige of entire elite families. We do not know whether residents of other great houses in the canyon also amassed ornaments and competed for prestige among themselves. Excavations at Pueblo del Arroyo, Pueblo Alto, and Chetro Ketl, however, failed to uncover anything approaching the quantities of exotic ornaments found at Pueblo Bonito.

The third example of ornament concentration—that evident in the Mogollon Highlands—has received less attention than Chaco and the Hohokam. From the Late Pithouse to the Pueblo IV periods, sites in the Mogollon Highlands contained a greater quantity of shell ornaments, particularly bracelets, than anywhere else outside the Hohokam area (and the site of Casas Grandes; R. J. Bradley 1996). Given the variability in ornamentation exhibited by the Galaz and especially the Grasshopper burials, it is possible that these shell items were socially valued goods that both men and women accumulated. Men, however, appear to have been more active in their accumulation.

To conclude, ornament accumulation in general is not especially prominent in the Southwestern archaeological record. In the three cases in which we can demonstrate more intensive trade in ornaments, both men and women were associated with many of the same items. There are greater distinctions among women and among men in ornaments than between men and women. Men, however, appear to have had a greater variety and/or quantity of turquoise and shell jewelry, suggesting a certain degree of gender hierarchy in the acquisition of these socially valued goods. Nonetheless, we can envision both women and men operating in the public contexts in which such wealth was displayed.

The ceramic and the more limited lithic data suggest greater equality than difference in the extent and intensity of women's and men's interactive networks. Beginning at Zuni, with Coronado's encounter with a man from Pecos, the ethnohistoric and ethnographic records are replete with examples of men traveling among the pueblos. Although the precontact data discussed here cannot demonstrate that women traveled widely throughout the Southwest, widely shared technological styles nonetheless document that women, too, were involved in long-distance communication networks. The regional systems of interaction that archaeologists have defined across the Southwest were the products of both male and female exchange relations.

11

Gender Models in the Southwest

A Sociocultural Perspective

Louise Lamphere

The chapters in this book make a number of important contributions to both the anthropological study of gender and the study of Southwestern cultures through time. Their authors take us beyond the temptation to make the contemporary Hopis or Zunis a generalized model for gender in Pueblo society, with the corresponding assumption that a matrilineal "tribal-level" organization held sway in precontact times and that any contrasts among contemporary pueblos arose through Spanish colonial contact. Instead, they demonstrate that there was a rich and changing history of gender relations in each of three culture areas—the Hohokam, the Mogollon, and the Ancestral Pueblo—and that there were regional variations as well as temporal ones. By carefully examining the division of labor in a number of spheres—hunting, agriculture, craft production, cooking, and trade—the contributors to this volume offer us a much clearer idea of how tasks were divided in particular time periods in the past and in various culture areas, giving us a much more nuanced sense of the important variability in men's and women's work lives. These data on the gender division of labor, along with material on health status, violence, and the accumulation of wealth and goods in burials, can begin to help us build models of gender relations and show how these might be linked to relations among kin groups and communities. In other words, we can now begin to evaluate evidence for gender hierarchies versus equality and evidence for a relationship between gender and social differentiation (unequal differences among households, kin groups, and communities).

In this short commentary, I use sociocultural approaches to gender in order to build two models of gender relations that I feel will help us understand the dynamics and oscillations that occurred during Southwestern prehistory as gender relations and political-ritual relations changed.

ISSUES OF POWER, STATUS, AND HIERARCHY

Most sociocultural theories about power, status, and authority draw from two major traditions in social theory: those that stem from the work of Marx and those that rely heavily on the insights of Weber. For those working from a Marxist position, power and authority are rooted in productive relations. To use one example, Karen Sacks (now Karen Brodkin), in her book *Sisters and Wives* (1979), used a modes-of-production analysis. In revising her earlier approach, voiced in "Engels Revisited: Women, the Organization of Production and Private Property" (1974), she relied more heavily on Marx than on Engels. She argued that institutionalized power (or the recognized right to make decisions for others, commonly called authority) "rests ultimately on the possession of socially critical property, the means of production" (1979:72). In communal modes of production (usually found in foraging societies), all members are owners of productive property, whereas in class societies a small group or class owns and controls productive property. In kin corporate modes of production (the model most relevant to tribal-level societies, including those in the historical and prehistoric Southwest), productive property is held by kinspeople, and "every individual has access to at least some productive property." Power exists to the extent that these corporations control unequal amounts of productive property and members within them have unequal access to their kin group's property (Sacks 1979:73). Women have access to property as "sisters" in kin groups or as members of female associations, age groups, or secret societies. In the eighteenth century, for example, Iroquois matrons, as senior members and "sisters" in the matrilineal *gens* (the localized clan grouping), held control over agricultural production, supervised households, provisioned war parties, and could nominate and depose sachems (male chiefs who were heads of clans), village leaders, and tribal officeholders (Brown 1975). In the nineteenth century, Cheyenne and Arapaho quilling societies were a source of women's power in Plains Indian societies (see Schneider 1983).

Sacks, like other Marxists, has argued that in many societies men and women held equal control of productive resources and political power. In contrast, those who have based their gender analysis on Weberian notions of power, authority, and status have argued for both universal gender asymmetry and for the idea that some societies were egalitarian. Sherry Ortner and Harriet Whitehead (1981) provide an example of the gender asymmetry position. Their introduction to *Sexual Meanings* relies heavily on Weber's notions of status without drawing on his ideas about economic class or political power and authority. Weber differentiated classes based on "life chances" and economic interests from status groups determined by the "social estimation of honor." Although the control of wealth often led to high social honor, there was always some slippage between the two. Weber treated class and status as relatively independent variables. Power and legitimate authority, a third set of constructs, were based on notions of the ability to control others, or the probability that certain commands would be obeyed by a given group of persons (see Gerth and Mills 1946:180, 187; Giddens 1971:156)

Ortner and Whitehead focused on "prestige structures," or sets of positions that result from a particular line of social evaluation (1981:13). Gender constitutes an important prestige structure, and one of many in any individual society. Gender affects other ranking systems, however. Prestige structures, such as those based on age, wealth, charisma, ritual expertise, or physical prowess, tend to be genderized and made consistent with one another. Thus, larger prestige structures are located in a male-dominated public sphere, and categories such as warrior, statesman, and elder are essentially male roles, whereas women are often defined in terms of their relations to men (as wives, mothers, sisters, and a variety of other kin statuses) (Ortner and Whitehead 1981:8). Ortner and Whitehead assumed that prestige structures were always hierarchical and entailed a ranking of higher or lower on whatever dimension is being evaluated. They found little evidence in the ethnographic record that female prestige was consistently higher than male prestige. Thus, social honor in relation to gender was always a matter of ranking males above females.

In contrast, Alice Schlegel, in her introduction to *Sexual Stratification* (1977a), did not assume a gender ranking along the dimensions she discussed: rewards, prestige, and power. Her notion of rewards relied on Weberian ideas of "economic interests in the possession of goods or opportunities for income" or the "disposition of material property" rather than on the Marxist concept of a "means of production" or "productive control." Her concept of prestige as "deference granted an individual, role, or category" seems clearly based on Weber's ideas about "social honor," and her discussion of power and authority owes much to Weber's definitions, since she argues that authority is one form of power, or the "recognized and legitimated right to make decisions concerning others." Men and women derive their power "from their ability to control their own persons and activities and the persons and activities of others," by whatever means (1977a:8). In her analysis of Hopi society, Schlegel argued that the sexes were divided into "two domains of action," the domestic and the political-religious. The domestic organization of the lineage and house was under the control of women, while the religious and political organization of the Hopi village was under the control of male community leaders. At the level of the clan, in between the household and the community, authority was shared by a brother-and-sister pair. This system was supported by an ideology of sexual balance or equality between the principles of maleness and femaleness (Schlegel 1977b:246).

These three examples from feminist sociocultural anthropology illustrate the range of ways in which we have looked at gender relations: one based on the control of productive resources, with notions of power growing out of this control and little attention given to prestige; one based primarily on notions of prestige; and a third hinging on economic variables, power, and prestige, treated as three separate dimensions. Sacks and Schlegel would agree that there is a range of societies, including some that are egalitarian; Ortner and Whitehead would argue that all societies have some kind of gender hierarchy. Other models seem to be variations on these three. Eleanor Leacock (1981) and Christine Gailey (1987b) have argued for models based on the control of economic resources, whereas many other scholars have seen gender stratification as an issue of multiple dimensions sometimes operating in different spheres: domestic, public, religious (Errington 1990). Finally, some feminist anthropologists have emphasized issues of value (prestige) but have pushed for emic (indigenous) notions of value and argued that some systems place femaleness higher than maleness, or they see a balance (Sanday 1981).

How can we use these kinds of models to examine the archaeological record in the Southwest? How can we get from abstract concepts like power, prestige, and productive control to some of the concrete relations that can be "seen" in the archaeological record? First, we have to confront issues of how to get at productive control using data on the gender division of labor as well as evidence that some households or kin groups could accumulate wealth. Second, we need to think about how to measure notions of value. And third, we need models relating productive control, power, and value (prestige) to gender. All of these issues involve figuring out how to recognize hierarchy (or lack of it) from evidence of gender difference versus similarity and how to assess household or kin-group equality versus differentiation.

TWO MODELS

I have found Sherry Ortner's approach in "Gender Hegemonies," an essay in her book *Making Gender* (1996:138–72), an enormously helpful way to examine gender relationships in a more historical and processual light. Borrowing from Gramsci and Williams, Ortner reversed her previous position and built a new approach for understanding both egalitarian and nonegalitarian gender systems. She used the term "hegemony" to describe the set of ideas implicitly accepted by members of a culture as the way in which the world operates. For Ortner, however, the term not only encapsulated ideas about prestige and value but also included practices that were about the exercise of power. Hegemonic ideas and practices were the dominant ones, but Ortner also assumed that there were subversive, challenging, and "counterhegemonic" ideas and practices. In addition, I think it is important to reinsert into this model the notion of an economic base.

Coming as it does from Marxist theory, the notion of hegemony goes hand in hand with the idea that those who control the means of production or have accumulated economic resources also create and control the hegemonic ideas and use political power to reinforce and reproduce them.

One of the positive aspects of the Ortner model is that one can characterize a hegemony in relatively emic (rather than etic) terms. Doing this for the Southwest entails the extensive use of ethnographic analogy, drawing on what we know about Southwestern cultures in the late nineteenth and early twentieth centuries. Southwestern notions of power were tied not to the secular world but to ideas about the supernatural and about ritual power. Power derived from knowledge acquired directly through visions, dreams, or techniques of divination or through learning the proper ritual actions, the proper ways to construct ritual objects, or the songs and prayers that brought the aid of supernatural beings.

It is important here not to project a Western split between the human and the supernatural, or between the natural world and the supernatural, but to see both as imbued with the same forces. For traditional Southwestern Native Americans, humans and other beings (including those that existed in the mythological past) are composed of the same elements and are part of the same universe. For example, in Navajo cosmology, the primary elements—moisture, air, substance, and heat—make up not only the universe but also the Diyin Diné'e, or Holy People, and the Diné, or Navajos. "All persons who live now or who have ever lived in the Navajo world—hooghan, baskets, corn plants, corn beetles, humans, cradles, mountains, prayers—were and are constructed of the same fundamental elements, linked by metaphoric structures including complementarity, permeated by vibration in the form of sound or movement, and possessed of the same seven senses and anatomical components, including mind, eyes, ears, legs, and feet" (Schwarz 1997:35–36). Similarly, Alfonso Ortiz (1969) showed how Tewa cosmology incorporates a fourfold model of the universe that merges both sacred places inhabited by beings Westerners would call supernaturals and Tewa villages inhabited by the Dry Food People (or Tewa), including those who have been initiated into one of the societies and have become "Made People." There are six categories of "persons," including three who are living and three who are supernatural beings, which mirror each other. Thus, the Towa é, literally translated as "persons," are represented both by six pairs of supernaturals (brothers) and by six male human beings who are selected each year "to head those of our traditional ways" (Ortiz 1969:64). For the Zunis, both the "raw people" (who eat raw food, can change their form, and are given sacrifices by the cooked people) and the cooked, or daylight, people are "people" in the sense that they have the same bodily qualities and treat each other as kin (Tedlock 1979:499).

A second important theme present in Southwestern ethnographic material is the division between those with ritual knowledge (and power) and "ordinary people," a division found in several Pueblo social structures. There is some variability in the participation of women in the societies that confer ritual power, but most of the contemporary evidence indicates that most of those with ritual or political power are or were male, though a few women may play important counterhegemonic roles.

Three contemporary examples of these distinctions come from the Zunis, the Tewas, and the Hopis. Zunis distinguish between "daylight people" and ordinary Zunis who have not been initiated (who are poor or without religion). Males are initiated into the kachina society to become "valuable or protected," a status women already enjoy because of their connection with birth. At Zuni, women are rarely initiated into the kachina society, and then usually to cure them from being frightened by kachinas. (There was one female member of a kiva group in 1930.) Women participate as "wives of male members, preparing feasts for kachina impersonators, helping with costumes, and providing an admiring audience" (Tedlock 1979:502). Women can be initiated into the medicine societies or the rain priesthoods (but are ineligible for the bow priesthood) (Ladd 1979b:85).

Tewas express this difference in the concepts of "dry food people" and "Made People," or those who belong to one of eight different societies. One of these is the women's society. Women are also ritual assistants to four other societies, and two women are lay assistants to the winter and summer chiefs.

Hopis distinguish between the *pavansinom,* the "most powerful" or "most important" people, and the *sukavungsinom*, the "grassroots" or "common" people. Peter Whitely (1988) described the "important people" as the members of the core lineage segments with principal ceremonial offices. "Their authority rests in the religious societies and is repeatedly validated in myth and ritual. Ritual action, because of its intent to affect instrumentally the conditions of existence, is simultaneously political action." He concluded: "The power—to make significant transformations in the world—derives from various sorts of esoteric knowledge, the primary locus of which is in ritual. Initiation into a religious society confers power, but the greatest proportion adheres to the chief-priests. Their specialized knowledge is kept with strict secrecy from ordinary participants" (Whitely 1988:69). Furthermore, political decision making is deliberative; the authority of the *pavansinom* lies in the ritual capacity to plan the future course of events. At Oraibi in the late nineteenth century, the main chief-priests were all male. There were three women's societies, however: Lakon, Owaqquol, and Maraw. The rituals of the first two are usually referred to as "Basket Dances," and they stress fertility and the celebration of the harvest. Maraw, which is related to the male Wuwtsim society, is associated with fertility and the fruits of warfare (Whitely 1988; also see Levy 1993). Discussions of the Oraibi split mention only male leaders in this period.

In using these ethnographic data to interpret the prehispanic archaeological record, it is important to distinguish between periods when hierarchies of ritual power were less pronounced and periods when they were more pronounced. At some times, the differences between "important people" and "common people" (between ritual specialists and the initiated rest) might have been damped down, and women might have had their own societies or been frequent participants in societies and kiva groups that gave them the status of important people. These would have been times when most adults became initiated and both sexes had wide opportunity to acquire ritual knowledge. During these periods, the village leader (*kikmongwi*, *pekwin*, etc.) was probably a spokesman for all and a consensus articulator. These times might have contrasted with periods when people placed greater cultural emphasis on ritual—periods for which ritual activities are more evident in the grave goods of a few elaborate burials and for which there might be spatial or residential evidence for a ritual elite. Ritual structures that are village- or community-wide or that seem to have served primarily for male ritual activities would perhaps indicate that women participated in ritual in limited ways or had their own religious societies.

Finally, there is also a pervasive theme of gender dualism in most of the ethnographic accounts of Ancestral Pueblo religion, as well as in accounts of the Navajo and Piman peoples. Supernaturals are often paired—male and female, two females, or two males (sisters or brothers). The important symbolism of four and the use of four directions, four colors, four stones, animals, and so forth in ritual often lead to a pairing and balancing of genders as part of this larger framework. Certainly female supernatural figures are very important. The two sisters Iatiku (mother of the Corn clan) and Nautsiti (mother of the Sun clan) are important in the Acoma origin story (Gutierrez 1991:3–7). Blue Corn Woman and White Corn Maiden were the first mothers of each of the moieties among the Tewa (Ortiz 1969:13). And Spider Grandmother gives crucial help to male figures in Hopi stories (Clemmer 1995:15, 16).

In what follows I examine evidence concerning (1) the division of labor as it relates to the control of productive resources, (2) Southwestern notions of power as they help us to develop an emic sensibility about how to examine both power/authority and prestige (notions of social honor), and (3) gender dualism in religious ideology as it, too, relates to prestige and social honor. I propose two models, one that I call the "balance model," and the other, the "ritual power model." Each model is a way of presenting economic, political, and ideological relations that are hegemonic, but it also contains parts of the other model (or counterhegemonic tendencies) within it. In the balance model, the allocation of productive resources and mechanisms for redistribution are such that they damp down the possibility that some households or kin groups can accumulate more resources than others. Ritual-political power is similarly downplayed. Archaeologically, this model would be manifested in evidence that kin groups and households were the important ritual units and that both males and females had access to ritual spaces and ritual items. In the ritual power model, which I discuss at greater length later, it is ritual power that underpins differential social honor or prestige.

DIVISIONS OF LABOR

Ethnological work on the gender division of labor, especially work on large cross-cultural samples, has tended to classify tasks (such as cooking, hunting, and agriculture) as "male" or "female." Single-culture studies of gender have dwelt less on careful analysis of the division of labor than on topics related to conflict, power, ritual, and, more recently, the colonial encounter. One of the important contributions of the chapters in this volume is their analysis of the division of labor within the whole complex of activities and processes that come under the headings of "hunting," "pottery production," and "agriculture," for example.

In these chapters, we see two models of the division of labor: the overlapping and the complementary. What I have termed the balance model can include either of these two types. Overlap in the division of labor can occur in several ways. First, men and women can do the same tasks. Second, a complex of tasks that occurs over time in several locations, such as hunting, pottery making, or cloth production, can involve some steps completed by men and others by women. And third, production at one site and in one time period can include mixed-gender groups rather than single-gender groups.

Sue Ellen Jacobs has argued for overlapping sex roles among the Tewas, but she gives virtually no examples in which men and women actually perform the same tasks (Jacobs 1995:208–9). Among Navajos in the subsistence economy of the 1930s, however, there are a number of examples. Both men and women herded sheep, sheared them, and helped in the birthing of lambs. Both men and women participated in planting fields, weeding crops, and harvesting them. To use an archaeological example from this book, Christine Szuter suggests that women could have been involved along with men in hunting small game (e.g., rabbit hunting as depicted on Mimbres pottery).

Regarding the second type of overlap (participation of one gender within a complex of activities usually attributed to a different gender), Szuter discusses the possibilities that women produced feathers for arrowheads while tending birds and carried game from kill sites. As an example of the third type of overlap (gender-integrated production at one site), Barbara Mills argues that shell production in pre-Classic Hohokam sites was organized by household rather than by gender. "Shell working is a labor-intensive process that combines flaking, cutting, and abrading of the raw material. Reamers and a variety of ground-stone abraders were found in nearly every structure. Although shell working might have been a men's activity in situations of less intensive production, women and children's labor was probably used at these sites to increase output" (Mills, this volume). The second, or complementary, version of the division of labor is consistent with either the balance model or the ritual power model. It entails a highly differentiated but complementary gender division of labor in which (1) men and women do very different activities, (2) the steps involved in these activities tend to be done by only one gender, with minor participation by the other, and (3) production sites involve the work of only one gender. The contributors to this volume generally agree that for the early time periods in the Southwest there is more evidence for overlap, whereas gender differentiation in tasks is more clearly evident in later time periods (e.g., after A.D. 900 or 1000).

A complementary division of labor might support hierarchy rather than balance. In the former case, a complementary division of labor with more male-only or female-only task complexes would support important power differences between men and women. This might be specifically the case when women's work load is particularly heavy relative to men's. Thus the complementary division of labor can be a double-edged sword. For example, if women are pressed into hours and hours of corn grinding in communal mealing rooms, and if they also devote large amounts of energy to cooking, child care, and pottery making, then women might consequently hold fewer ritual roles, participate less in long-distance trade networks, and perform fewer other activities that would balance men's important ritual power. In contrast, in contexts where the power associated with ritual is widely dispersed among kin groups and among men and women, and where there is little in the way of control over productive resources by kin groups whose leaders are "important people," a complementary division of labor would make little difference and might even signal "high social honor." For example, women could hold prestige as excellent potters or providers of vast amounts of food for feast days.

THE RITUAL POWER MODEL

In this model, notions of ritual power are hegemonic, and the importance of ritual power undergirds the higher social honor or prestige afforded ritual practitioners (heads of sacred societies, heads of kin groups that hold society paraphernalia). Furthermore, the complementary division of labor (and much clearer differences between males and females in productive activities) becomes part of the hegemony and supports the social differences between "important people" and "commoners." Craft production (turquoise bead manufacture, pottery) could be focused on display for ritual occasions, and agricultural work, hunting, and food processing would often be harnessed for ritual feasting. Archaeologically, one would expect to see some indications (in burials, for example) that prestige was being accorded to ritual practitioners. If there were few avenues for women to become "powerful people," then one could argue for increasing male dominance and a gender hierarchy. There might also be indications that control over productive resources (agricultural products, craft items, wealth items) was more concentrated in some households than in others. This would be reflected in residential and ritual architecture.

There are four periods outlined in these chapters and in other literature on Southwestern archaeology that are good candidates for the more hierarchical hegemony in which ritual power resided with "important or powerful people," most of whom were probably male. In each of these cases there is clear evidence for inequalities between kin groups, and men and women of higher-ranking groups apparently had greater access to productive resources, ritual power, and prestige than did men and women of lower-ranking groups. In some instances, women in the kin groups of "important people" might have had some advantages over "ordinary women." But both sets of women still engaged in productive and reproductive work, particularly pottery making and corn grinding. In addition, it is not clear that women were subordinate to men in their own kin group, because aspects of a complementary division of labor (the balance model) still held sway. There is less evidence for overlapping patterns, which means that it is possible to make contradictory arguments regarding power and prestige. On one hand, women's work loads increased and women might have been more confined, yet on the other, they could have been part of women's work groups, produced socially valued goods, participated in trade networks, and contributed to ritual activities through the provision of food or the care of ritual paraphernalia. Classic Hohokam, Classic Chaco, and Postclassic Rio Grande Pueblo are examples of economic-political and social structures to which the ritual power model probably applies. The transition from Classic to Postclassic Mimbres is one in which a ritual power model could have been the guiding hegemony on a smaller scale, but counterhegemonic forces tipped the scale to a new period when a more balanced hegemony was reasserted.

Classic Hohokam: Confinement or Integration?

For the Hohokam Classic period (A.D. 1150–1400), there is ample evidence of increasing social differentiation and the emergence of an elite. Domestic architecture changed to include walled compounds made up of from 3 to 69 rooms; the larger compounds were probably occupied by a number of households. Some compounds also incorporated platform mounds, which included structures that were used for residence. Food processing, food preparation, pottery production, and fiber processing all took place in the rooms and courtyards on top of the mounds. Other households continued to occupy pit structures. Patricia Crown and Suzanne Fish (1996:807) argued that "the high incidence of exotic artifacts found in association with the mounds and the unusual architecture of the mounds and their surrounding compounds imply that ritual activities occurred in association with the mounds as well. It is likely that the elite occupying the mounds derived at least some of their power through ritual performance and possession of esoteric knowledge. Whether women were directly involved in the performance of ritual is unknown, but their presence on the mounds and in the compounds surrounding the mounds indicates that they were not segregated from ritual structures during the Classic period."

Elites living on the mounds and those living in the compounds below and nearby utilized an extensive system of canals (which were originally built in some areas during the pre-Classic). This irrigation system potentially underwrote the production of agricultural surpluses, although it is not clear that some households or kin groups controlled substantially more production than others.

Shell production in the Classic period indicates that "households in compounds associated with platform mounds seem to have made and used a greater proportion of shell items than did households farther away" (Mills, this volume). Mills concluded that elite households participated in shell production and that production of shell items used in ritual and as symbols of authority was by men.

The evidence from burials is complex. Although women were buried on some platform mounds, there were two mounds without female burials, whereas men were consistently buried on the tops of the platforms. There seem to have been few differences between female burials on the tops of mounds and those in nearby compounds. Although the grave lot values—the measure Jill Neitzel uses in her chapter—of the materials buried with females were higher during the Classic period than during the pre-Classic, there was a greater proportion of adult males and children among those who had the wealthiest graves. Women tended to be buried with utilitarian objects, including spindle whorls, pestles, manos, and higher frequencies of ceramic vessels, whereas Classic-period men were more likely to have been buried with ornamental or ritual items, axes, abraders, and smaller numbers of ceramic vessels. Men also tended to be buried in adobe boxes located on mounds and in adobe-lined pits, indicating that more effort was put into male burials. Crown and Fish concluded that "adult males were accorded greater social honor at death than females" (1996:810).

What are we to make of these data, which indicate the prominence of males in ritual roles (buried in special places with ornamental and ritual materials) and the (literally) elevated status of households engaged in ritual activities? There does seem to be ample evidence for a ritual-political system in which power and prestige were in the hands of elite males. The situation for women is much more ambiguous, and one could argue that women's activities supported the ritual system but at the same time confined them. Or one could argue that women's activities provided a counterhegemonic tendency that "put the brakes" on ritual power and integrated women's economic and reproductive roles more clearly into the structure, giving them a parallel basis for control over resources (pottery), power, and prestige. From this description, we see three groups of women, those on the platform mounds associated with "elite families," those in compounds but not on platforms, and those living in pit structures. Among all three groups there was a clearly differentiated division of labor, with shell work being done by men and pottery making by women. Within the sets of activities entailed in cloth making, there was still an important gender division of labor. Females spun agave and cotton thread, and males wove the cloth.

Crown and Fish (1996) also argued that overall, women's work loads increased during the Hohokam Classic period. They began making tortillas on the *comal,* a more labor-intensive process of preparing corn for consumption. They produced highly polished red ware and Salado Polychrome pottery, which required more steps and time in manufacture. And they contributed to the production of clothing by processing agave fibers for thread and spinning cotton. (Men were assumed to have dug up the agave and to have woven both agave-fiber garments and cotton on upright looms; Crown and Fish 1996:805.)

In some senses, there seem to have been few differences between the women in the courtyards on the mounds and those in the courtyards below. The enclosed courtyards could have promoted greater cohesion, cooperation, and loyalty among households in the same kin group. Senior women might have exercised leadership in women's activities, and a walled compound might have made it possible for fewer adults to watch the children, freeing some women for productive activities. On the other hand, women might have been more secluded from the outside world and less in contact with the entire village community, whereas men and women living in unenclosed pit structures might have had greater access to community activities, interaction, and gossip (Crown and Fish 1996:806). Crown and Fish (1996:813) tended to see women's productive activities as "keeping power in balance," or, in my terms, as providing a counterhegemonic tendency to male access to exotics, ritual items, and the spoils of warfare and hence to places in a system of ritual-political power and prestige. I think a convincing argument could be made that increased female labor means that women end up supporting a system that gives them less autonomy.

Chaco Canyon, A.D. 1050–1130: Widening Social Differences

The time when a ritually based power system seems to have been best developed was the late Pueblo II–early Pueblo III period at Chaco Canyon, particularly the years between A.D. 1075 and 1115. Evidence for social differentiation and a ritual elite is found most prominently in architecture and the division between great houses and small houses, a difference made prominent by the building boom in the late eleventh century. Although new construction on Chetro Ketl and Pueblo Alto had begun earlier, a great deal of construction took place between 1075 and 1115. Earlier, during the Bonito phase (A.D. 900–1050), clusters of small-house sites were associated with one or more great kivas. These small sites, many of them on the south side of the canyon, were occupied for a century and remodeled many times.

In contrast, the great houses, including Pueblo Bonito, Chetro Ketl, Pueblo Alto, and Pueblo del Arroyo, were multistoried buildings with stunning examples of masonry. Recent research indicates that large parts of these structures were used primarily for storage and ceremonial activities. Only a few suites exhibit evidence of having been inhabited on a permanent, year-round basis. Thomas Windes (1987) concluded that only a small percentage of the population actually lived in the great houses. In addition, there are relatively few burials at Chaco. This and the lack of enough arable land to support more than 2,000 people (Judge 1984:8) indicate that Chaco was a ritual center and that not all those who utilized it lived there permanently. The extensive network of roads connecting outliers like Salmon Ruin, Kin Ya'a, and Pueblo Pintado to sites in Chaco Canyon and to Pueblo Alto support this notion.

Status differences between those who lived in great houses and those occupying small houses are indicated by data on health and nutrition. Nancy Akins (1986) argued that "authority-holding elites" in Pueblo Bonito had greater access to nutritional resources and enjoyed better health. Pueblo Bonito males and females were taller (by 4.6 cm) than males and females in outlying pueblos. Life expectancy was greater and fertility lower at Pueblo Bonito (Nelson et al. 1994:100).

Neitzel (this volume, table 4.9) suggests that the burial data for Chaco indicate that there was a male-dominated hierarchy in the Chaco great houses between A.D. 900 and 1050. Male grave lot values in great houses were higher than female ones. (In the small houses, female grave lot values were higher.) Included in the richest burials throughout the Southwest are two burials from Pueblo Bonito, both males interred with thousands of turquoise beads, pendants, effigies, and other objects, including offerings. Akins concluded that these were individuals of the greatest authority and power in a three-tiered social ranking system (Akins 1986:115–17, 133, 162–63). There were no male burials dating between 1030 and 1150 at Chaco, but hierarchy with indications of important wealth differences continued. At Aztec Ruin, a Chacoan outlier dating between 1100 and 1300, there are also two adults buried with beads, disks, pendants, pots, and projectile points (Morris 1924:155–61), indicating the accumulation of wealth. Women's burials at Chaco tend to include ordinary goods such as mats, baskets, cotton, and pitchers, whereas men's burials have more manos, jars, and throwing sticks (Jill Neitzel, personal communication).

Data on the division of labor also suggest differences between great houses and small houses. In the small sites, grinding was done with movable metates set into adobe mealing bins that integrated spaces from a number of adjacent structures (Bustard 1996). In contrast, the great houses had grinding complexes found in room suites. There were also communal grinding rooms with 10 to 12 mealing bins. Michelle Hegmon and her colleagues (this volume) argue that these grinding rooms were used for food preparation on a suprahousehold scale.

Male and female craft production tells a different story. Recent research has indicated that much of the pottery and turquoise found at Chaco was produced outside the canyon. Between A.D. 1040 and 1200, about 30 percent of all ceramics at Chaco were made in the Chuska area, especially near Washington Pass (Mills, this volume). This amounts to about 1,000 vessels a year, most of them going to larger sites (Spielmann, this volume). Mills suggests that although men might have been involved in procuring wood, temper, and clay, women might not only have made the pottery but also have been involved in bringing vessels to Chaco Canyon during "pilgrimages" or feasts. There seem to have been extensive trade networks that connected the Chuska sites with Chaco, and women from the Chuskas might have traded their pottery for food with women in villages closer to Chaco, or they themselves might have brought the pottery to Chaco for feasts or for trading (Spielmann, this volume).

Men might at times have been absent from Chaco itself in order to procure turquoise, timbers for houses, and game to supplement what must have been a depleted faunal population (Mills, this volume). Men seem to have been involved in working turquoise for ornaments in kivas in Chaco Canyon (2 of the 11 excavated ornament production areas with dates between A.D. 920 and 1220 were in kivas; Mathien 1984, cited in Mills, this volume). There seem to have been few producers, however—perhaps just one or two individuals. Much of the shell and turquoise seems to have been concentrated in the great houses in Chaco Canyon, particularly in the elaborate burials mentioned earlier.

I suggest that between A.D. 1050 and 1130, the differentiation between kin groups in the great houses and those in the small houses indicates a significant difference in status, possibly between those who were "important people"—most likely male ritual specialists and their sisters, male kin, wives, and children (organized into some sorts of kin groups, possible matrilocal or bilateral extended families or matrilineages)—and "ordinary" people living in small houses and outlying villages. The data also point to a more differentiated division of labor in the great houses, with women spending more time grinding corn (though possibly only in relation to feasting rather than every day), and men more engaged in hunting, procuring turquoise, and carrying building materials from faraway sites. The emphasis on ritual goods in male graves and on ordinary goods in female graves might mean that male ritual activities were becoming dominant while females spent long hours in necessary but supplementary work to support the rituals (particularly corn grinding and food preparation).

The counterhegemonic tendencies here come from the small houses and from outlying villages in areas such as the Chuska Mountains. On one hand, one could argue that the production of valuable pottery by women in distant villages and the use of female trade networks to bring pots and/or food into Chaco Canyon might indicate the calling in of economic resources for ritual purposes—the way in which potlatching or feasting in "big man" systems operates. On the other hand, if such rituals served as redistribution systems rather than as systems for appropriating goods, then women involved in craft production and trade might have retained a measure of autonomy and leverage, even prestige.

The Pueblos after A.D. 1300: Women's Work in Larger Villages

Michelle Hegmon and her co-authors (this volume) argue that the Pueblo IV period brought an important change in Ancestral Pueblo organization, coincident with large-scale migration into the Rio

Grande area. Villages in the 1300s were highly formalized and carefully planned. These authors point out that the unit pueblo structure (living quarters, storage rooms, and kivas) disappeared, "in favor of integrated community architecture, the dissociation of kivas from households and their extension to larger organizations, the reduced social scale of households, and the increased visibility of food preparation." These were large villages with a dramatic increase in the amount of food prepared outdoors. There are also single mealing bins, suggesting that households were smaller and that women did not do mealing in larger groups of kin. Kivas contain anchor holes for upright looms, indicating male weavers working in ritual spaces controlled by males. Hegmon and colleagues argue that larger social units (such as moieties, religious societies, clans, or sodalities) used these kivas.

In the late thirteenth century, the *comal*, fire dogs, and rectangular fire pits were all introduced to produce tortillas and *piki* bread. There is some indication that the use of *comales*, the fine grinding of meal or flour, and the use of oil for frying were all part of an effort to cook corn quickly and might reflect an increased concern with fuel (Crown, this volume). These techniques also increased women's work loads.

In terms of craft production, a new ceramic technology, glaze ware, spread rapidly across the Albuquerque area, suggesting direct contact among women (Spielmann, this volume) and a shared concept among women potters of what a glaze paint should be. Because most glaze bowls were significantly larger than the indigenous white-ware bowls, ceremonial feasting may have been important, too.

Hegmon and her co-authors argue that women's prestige declined with the end of the unit pueblos. Women lost power as a result of a decline of household symbolism, exclusion from the kiva, and the end of special grinding rooms. They retained some autonomy through exterior grinding and ongoing contributions to ritual food (Hegmon, Ortman, and Mobley-Tanaka, this volume, table 2.3).

Mimbres Reorganization: Increased Household and Gender Autonomy

In an article on Mimbres abandonment and reorganization, Hegmon, Nelson, and Ruth (1998) compared material from pre–A.D. 1150 Mimbres Classic sites with material from Postclassic sites dating after 1150. The Classic-period sites consisted of both field houses composed of 3 or fewer rooms and larger villages of 50 to 100 rooms. In the later period, the villages were abandoned and the field houses were remodeled and expanded, usually to 5 to 15 rooms. The shift, then, was from aggregated villages to dispersed hamlets of only a few households.

The authors, utilizing data on pottery and the presence of different hearth and mealing facility forms, argued that during the Classic period, the "entire region appeared to have a strong 'Mimbres focus,' with a homogeneous material culture. At least in the Mimbres Valley, this focus may have involved the fairly strong social control necessary to organize large aggregates of people and cope with the increasingly over-exploited environment" (Hegmon, Nelson, and Ruth 1998:158). These homogeneous villages were replaced by small hamlets with a high degree of diversity, and regional networks and alliances were expanded. Since women presumably made the pottery, during the Postclassic they were learning different traditions and combining Cibola and Mimbres styles. From this evidence, Hegmon, Ortman, and Mobley-Tanaka (this volume) argue that women were maintaining their own networks independently of men. Altogether during this period there was residential mobility, with smaller kin groups moving out of villages, perhaps abandoning a more ritually centralized system. At the same time, female craft production and trade networks became reorganized and possibly stronger. Contrasted with the Chaco situation, female pottery production was not in the service of a centralized ritual-political system.

CONCLUSION

The Classic Hohokam, Chaco Canyon, and Pueblo IV examples are ones in which we see increasing differentiation between elite and nonelite households that probably represents the increasing importance of ritual power and the ability of "important or powerful people" (mostly male) to centralize and redistribute goods and resources. The Mimbres example, in contrast, is one in which a ritual system "devolved" into a balance model of small household clusters.

In all these cases, women retained their important productive and reproductive roles in both elite and nonelite households and wider kin groups. They continued to produce pottery, and there is no indication that elite women, even if confined in Hohokam compounds and the tops of ceremonial mounds, became completely dependent on male-generated economic resources. This is also true of women who lived at Pueblo Bonito and the other Chacoan great houses and in the post-1300 Rio Grande large villages. Their role in food processing was equally important, in addition to cooking, child care, and possibly other craft production. In a class-divided society, one would expect to see elite women primarily as consumers rather than producers and more differences in wealth associated with elite versus nonelite women. That utilitarian goods appear in female burials in both Classic Hohokam mounds and Chacoan great-house sites suggests elite female participation in productive and food processing activities. On the other hand, one could argue that elite women were often pressed into work for the ritual hierarchy, particularly carrying out the hard labor of corn grinding in communal grinding rooms. Counterhegemonic tendencies are indicated at both the elite and nonelite levels, in the former case in the rare instances where elaborate female burials indicate possible high ritual status, and in the latter case, where female trade networks (mostly in pottery and often in nonelite villages) suggest control of religiously oriented activities. The Mimbres case is particularly intriguing because it suggests that at times of cultural and population shifts, when communities broke up and were reorganized on a smaller scale, women profited as the system devolved into a much more balanced one.

In sum, these chapters contribute to building an approach to gender and hierarchy that is complex and nuanced. As such they have important implications for the study of gender more broadly. For those working in the Southwest, particularly in sociocultural anthropology, this volume gives time depth to the study of gender and hierarchy and lays out the range of variability among societies before European contact. Much of the contemporary anthropological work on gender in the Southwest has focused on the nineteenth- and twentieth-century Pueblos and Navajos, who are often thought of in terms of the balance model. Without a careful examination of gender and hierarchy for the Classic-period Hohokam, eleventh-century Chaco Canyon, and the Rio Grande region during Pueblo IV, we would have a very inaccurate sense of how gender relations have been constituted in the Southwest. We would fail to see how, in certain periods, hierarchy increased yet women continued to play important economic and domestic roles, many of them undergirding ritual activities that were in the hands of men. In other times and places (Postclassic Mimbres and some historical Pueblo situations), hierarchy decreased, and the balance model seems more appropriate as an account of gender relations. Certainly, this volume should affect how we teach and write about cultures of the Southwest.

In anthropology more generally, this volume can contribute to gender theory involving the study of societies that are often thought to be "middle-range"—pastoralists and sedentary horticulturalists who are not part of state-level, class-based societies. There is a lack of conceptual clarity in how to think about gender in these societies, which are often labeled "tribal." They are found in great numbers in the Americas, Africa, and Oceania and have undergone transformations during the colonial period and in the nineteenth and twentieth centuries through the policies of the larger nation-states in which they are embedded. Clearly there are regional patterns that have significant time depth, and as this volume shows, it is important to include archaeological material in the analysis of gender for any particular region.

We need, however, to get beyond thinking only in terms of how simple economic types (horticulturalists or pastoralists), kinship systems (patrilineal or matrilineal forms), or political models (tribes or chiefdoms) might define gender relations. Here, this volume is a model. By examining particular topics (agriculture, hunting, cuisine, trade, etc.) across sites and time periods, the authors unravel the complexities of gender relations. They are able to show that women contributed to a number of spheres in which female participation might not be assumed (hunting and trade come to mind). They are also able to demonstrate that hierarchy increased in the ritual and religious sphere in the prehispanic Southwest while women continued to contribute economically (through craft production and trade). Corn grinding and food producing are the most ambiguous activities. It is possible to argue that these activities brought women together, creating solidarity and anchoring women in an important role within a ritual structure that emphasized feasting. Alternatively, one can see the increased work load as subordinating women and decreasing their autonomy. It would be interesting to investigate whether these same relationships hold for other regions or whether very different patterns have emerged.

In these kinds of middle-range societies there is likely to be a wide variety of patterns, since gender hierarchy does not neatly dovetail with class hierarchy as it does in state-level societies. We will need a number of different models to encompass the variation found worldwide in different historical time periods and as these societies have been transformed under colonialism and nation-state building. This volume goes a long way toward making such a theory of gender relations in midrange societies possible.

References

Aberle, D.

1961 Matrilineal Descent in Cross-Cultural Perspective. In *Matrilineal Descent,* edited by D. Schneider and K. Gough, pp. 655–727. Berkeley: University of California Press.

Abbott, D. R.

1984 A Technological Assessment of Ceramic Variation in the Salt-Gila Aqueduct Area: Toward a Comprehensive Documentation of Hohokam Ceramics. In *Hohokam Archaeology along the Salt-Gila Aqueduct, Central Arizona Project, vol. 8: Material Culture,* edited by L. S. Teague and P. L. Crown, pp. 3–117. Arizona State Museum Archaeological Series 150. Tucson: University of Arizona.

1985 Spheres of Intra-Cultural Exchange and the Ceramics of the Salt-Gila Project. In *Proceedings of the 1983 Hohokam Symposium,* part 2, edited by A. E. Dittert and D. E. Dove, pp. 419–38. Arizona Archaeological Society Occasional Paper 2. Phoenix.

1994 Hohokam Social Structure and Irrigation Management: The Ceramic Evidence from the Central Phoenix Basin. Ph.D. diss., Arizona State University.

1996 Ceramic Exchange and a Strategy for Reconstructing Organizational Developments among the Hohokam. In *Interpreting Southwestern Diversity: Underlying Principles and Overarching Patterns,* edited by P. R. Fish and J. J. Reid, pp. 147–58. Anthropological Research Papers 48. Tempe: Arizona State University.

Abbott, D. R., and M. E. Walsh-Anduze

1995 Temporal Patterns without Temporal Variation: The Paradox of Hohokam Red Ware Ceramics. In *Ceramic Production in the American Southwest,* edited by B. J. Mills and P. L. Crown, pp. 88–114. Tucson: University of Arizona Press.

Adams, E. C.

1991 *The Origin and Development of the Pueblo Katsina Cult.* Tucson: University of Arizona Press.

1996 Understanding Aggregation in the Homol'ovi Pueblos: Scalar Stress and Social Power. In *River of Change: Prehistory of the Middle Little Colorado River Valley, Arizona,* edited by E. C. Adams, pp. 1–14. Arizona State Museum Archaeological Series 185. Tucson: University of Arizona.

1998 Late Prehistory in the Middle Little Colorado River Area: A Regional Perspective. In *Migration and Reorganization: The Pueblo IV Period in the American Southwest,* edited by K. A. Spielmann, pp. 53–63. Anthropological Research Papers 51. Tempe: Arizona State University.

Adams, E. C., and K. A. Hays

1991 *Homol'ovi II: Archaeology of an Ancestral Hopi Village, Arizona.* Anthropological Papers of the University of Arizona 55. Tucson: University of Arizona Press.

Adams, J. L.

1993 Technological Development of Manos and Metates on the Hopi Mesas. *Kiva* 58:331–44.

1999 Refocusing the Role of Food Grinding Tools as Correlates for the Subsistence Strategies of Gatherers and Early Agriculturalists in the American Southwest. *American Antiquity* 64:475–98.

Adams, K.

1994A Regional Synthesis of *Zea mays* in the Prehistoric American Southwest. In *Corn and Culture in the Prehistoric New World,* edited by S. Johannessen and C. Hastorf, pp. 273–302. Boulder, CO: Westview Press.

Adams, P.

1969 The Effect of Experimental Malnutrition on the Development of Long Bones. *Biblioteca Nutritio et Dieta* 13:69–73.

Adler, M. A.

1996 Land Tenure, Archaeology, and the Ancestral Pueblo Social Landscape. *Journal of American Archaeology* 15:337–71.

Adler, M. A., ed.

1996 *The Prehistoric Pueblo World,* A.D. *1150–1350.* Tucson: University of Arizona Press.

Adler, M. A., and A. Johnson

1996 Appendix: Mapping the Puebloan Southwest. In *The Prehistoric Pueblo World, A.D. 1150–1350*, edited by M. A. Adler, pp. 255–74. Tucson: University of Arizona Press.

Akins, N. J.

1986 *A Biocultural Approach to Human Burials from Chaco Canyon, New Mexico.* Reports of the Chaco Center 9. Santa Fe: National Park Service.

Allen, L. H.

1984 Functional Indicators of Nutritional Status of the Whole Individual or the Community. *Clinical Nutrition* 3:169–75.

Allen, W. H., C. F. Merbs, and W. H. Birkby

1985 Evidence for Prehistoric Scalping at Nuvakwewtaqa (Chavez Pass) and Grasshopper Ruin, Arizona. In *Health and Disease in the Prehistoric Southwest*, edited by C. F. Merbs and R. J. Miller, pp. 23–42. Anthropological Research Papers 34. Tempe: Arizona State University.

Allison, J.

1997 Craft Specialization and Exchange in Egalitarian Societies: A Virgin Anasazi Case Study. Ph.D. diss., Arizona State University.

Allison, M. J.

1984 Paleopathology in Peruvian and Chilean Populations. In *Paleopathology at the Origins of Agriculture*, edited by M. N. Cohen and G. J. Armelagos, pp. 515–30. New York: Academic Press.

Alloway, D.

1994 The Shaman's Ears. *The Cache: Collected Papers on Texas Archaeology* 2, pp. 1–9. Texas Archaeological Stewardship Network, Office of the State Archaeologist, Austin.

Ames, K. M.

1995 Chiefly Power and Household Production on the Northwest Coast. In *Foundations of Inequality*, edited by T. D. Price and G. M. Feinman, pp. 155–88. New York: Plenum Press.

Anderson, B.

1972 The Idea of Power in Javanese Culture. In *Culture and Politics in Indonesia*, edited by C. Holt, pp. 1–69. Ithaca: Cornell University Press.

Anderson, R. L.

1989 *Art in Small-Scale Societies.* Englewood Cliffs, NJ: Prentice-Hall.

Angel, J. L.

1978 Pelvic Inlet Form: A Neglected Index of Nutritional Status. *American Journal of Physical Anthropology* 48:378.

Anyon, R., and S. A. LeBlanc

1980 The Architectural Evolution of Mogollon-Mimbres Communal Structures. *Kiva* 45:253–77.

1984 *The Galaz Ruin: A Prehistoric Mimbres Village in Southwestern New Mexico.* Albuquerque: Maxwell Museum of Anthropology and University of New Mexico Press.

Apodaca, A.

1952 Corn and Custom: The Introduction of Hybrid Corn to Spanish American Farmers in New Mexico. In *Human Problems in Technological Change: A Casebook,* edited by E. Spicer, pp. 35–39. Troy, NY: Russell Sage Foundation.

Appadurai, A.

1981 Gastro-Politics in Hindu South Asia. *American Ethnologist* 8:494–511.

Ardener, S.

1981 Ground Rules and Social Maps for Women: An Introduction. In *Women and Space: Ground Rules and Social Maps,* edited by S. Ardener, pp. 11–34. New York: St. Martin's Press.

Arnold, D. E.

1985 *Ceramic Theory and Cultural Process.* Cambridge: Cambridge University Press.

Arnold, J. E.

1996 The Archaeology of Complex Hunter-Gatherers. *Journal of Archaeological Method and Theory* 3:77–126.

Awe, B.

1977 The Iyalode in the Traditional Yoruba Political System. In *Sexual Stratification: A Cross-Cultural View,* edited by A. Schlegel, pp. 144–60. New York: Columbia University Press.

Bahr, D. M.

1983 Pima and Papago Social Organization. In *Handbook of North American Indians, vol. 10: Southwest,* edited by A. Ortiz, pp. 178–92. Washington, D.C.: Smithsonian Institution.

Bailey, R. C., and R. Aunger, Jr.

1989 Net Hunters vs. Archers: Variation in Women's Subsistence Strategies in the Ituri Forest. *Human Ecology* 17:273–97.

Baker, B. J., and G. J. Armelagos

1988 The Origin and Antiquity of Syphilis: Paleopathological Diagnosis and Interpretation. *Current Anthropology* 29:703–20.

Balfet, H.

1965 Ethnographical Observations in North Africa and Archaeological Interpretations: The Pottery of the Maghreb. In *Ceramics and Man,* edited by F. R. Matson, pp. 161–77. Chicago: Aldine.

Ballereau, D.

1987 A Complete Survey of Petroglyphs from Cerros La Proveedora and Calera, Sonora. In *Rock Art Papers,* vol. 5, edited by K. Hedges, pp. 95–112. San Diego Museum of Man Papers 23. San Diego.

Barber, E.

1994 *Women's Work: The First 10,000 Years.* New York: W. W. Norton.

Barlow, K.

1985 The Role of Women in Intertribal Trade among the Murik of Papua New Guinea. *Research in Economic Anthropology* 7:95–122.

Bartlett, K.

1933 *Pueblo Milling Stones of the Flagstaff Region and Their Relation to Others in the Southwest.* Flagstaff: Museum of Northern Arizona.

Bar-Yosef, O., and R. H. Meadow

1995 The Origins of Agriculture in the Near East. In Last Hunters, *First Farmers: New Perspectives on the Prehistoric Transition to Agriculture,* edited by T. D. Price and B. Gebauer, pp. 39–94. Santa Fe: School of American Research Press.

Bass, P.

1994 A Gendered Search through Some West Texas Rock Art. In *New Light on Old Art: Recent Advances in Hunter-Gatherer Rock Art Research,* edited by D. S. Whitley and L. L. Loendorf, pp. 67–74. Institute of Archaeology Monograph 36. Los Angeles: University of California.

Bass, W. M.

1971 *Human Osteology.* Columbia: University of Missouri Archaeological Museum Society.

Batchelor, C.

1996a Clay Figurines: Bibliography. Draft of annotated bibliography prepared for the Elden Pueblo Project, Coconino National Forest, Flagstaff, AZ.

1996b Clay Figurines. Slide lecture for Northern Arizona Archaeology Society, Flagstaff, AZ.

Bayendor, D., and D. L. Martin

1989 Sexual Dimorphism, Stature, and Robusticity in the Prehistoric Anasazi (Abstract). *American Journal of Physical Anthropology* 78:189.

Bayham, F. E.

1976 Faunal Exploitation. In *Desert Resources and Hohokam Subsistence: The Conoco Florence Project,* pp. 110–21. Archaeological Series 103. Tempe: Arizona State University.

1982 A Diachronic Analysis of Prehistoric Animal Exploitation at Ventana Cave. Ph.D. diss., Arizona State University.

Bayman, J. M.

1996 Hohokam Craft Production and Platform Mound Community Organization in the Tucson Basin. In *Interpreting Southwestern Diversity: Underlying Principles and Overarching Patterns,* edited by P. R. Fish and J. J. Reid,. pp. 159–71. Anthropological Research Papers 48. Tempe: Arizona State University.

Beaglehole, E.

1937 *Notes on Hopi Economic Life.* Yale University Publications in Anthropology 15. New Haven.

Beaglehole, E., and P. Beaglehole

1935 *Hopi of the Second Mesa.* Menasha, WI: American Anthropological Association.

Beals, R. L., G. W. Brainerd, and W. Smith

1945 *Archaeological Studies in Northeast Arizona: A Report on the Archaeological Work of the Rainbow Bridge–Monument Valley Expedition.* Berkeley: University of California Press.

Bean, L. J., and K. S. Saubel

1972 *Temalpakh: Cahuilla Indian Knowledge and Use of Plants.* Banning, CA: Malki Museum Press.

Beeson, W. J.

1966 Archaeological Survey near St. Johns, Arizona: A Methodological Study. Ph.D. diss., University of Arizona.

Bender, B.

1978 Gatherer-Hunter to Farmer: A Social Perspective. *World Archaeology* 10:204–22.

1985 Emergent Tribal Formations in the American Midcontinent. *American Antiquity* 50:52–62.

Bender, D. R.

1967 A Refinement of the Concept of Household: Families, Co-residence, and Domestic Functions. *American Anthropologist* 69:493–504.

Bennett, W. C., and R. M. Zingg

1935 *The Tarahumara: An Indian Tribe of Northern Mexico.* Chicago: University of Chicago Press.

Benson, S. L.

1986 Activity-Induced Pathology in a Puebloan Population: Grasshopper, Arizona. M.A. thesis, Arizona State University.

Bernardini, W.

1997 Women's Labor and Inter-Household Economic Collaboration: Pueblo II and III Kiln Firing Groups in the American Southwest. M.A. thesis, Arizona State University.

1999 Reassessing the Scale of Social Action at Pueblo Bonito, Chaco Canyon, New Mexico. *Kiva* 64:447–70.

Bernard-Shaw, M.

1984 The Stone Tool Assemblage of the Salt-Gila Aqueduct Project Sites. In *Hohokam Archaeology along the Salt-Gila Aqueduct, Central Arizona Project, vol. 8: Material Culture,* edited by L. Teague and P. Crown, pp. 373–444. Arizona State Museum Archaeological Series 150. Tucson: University of Arizona.

Berreman, G. D.

1981 Social Inequality: A Cross-Cultural Analysis. In *Social Inequality: Comparative and Developmental Approaches,* edited by G. D. Berreman, pp. 3–40. New York: Academic Press.

Bertelsen, R., A. Lillehammer, and J. Naess

1987 *Were They All Men? An Examination of Sex Roles in Prehistoric Society.* Stavanger, Norway: Arkeologist Museum i Stavanger.

Binford, L. R.

1971 Mortuary Practices: Their Study and Their Potential. In *Approaches to the Social Dimensions of Mortuary Practices,* edited by J. A. Brown, pp. 6–29. Memoirs of the Society for American Archaeology 25. Washington, D.C.

1980 Willow Smoke and Dogs' Tails: Hunter-Gatherer Settlement Systems and Archaeological Site Formation. *American Antiquity* 45:4–20.

Birket-Smith, K.

1965 *The Paths of Culture.* Madison: University of Wisconsin Press.

Bishop, R., V. Canouts, S. De Atley, A. Qoyawayma, and C. W. Aikens

1988 The Formation of Ceramic Analytical Groups: Hopi Pottery Production and Exchange, A.D. 1300–1600. *Journal of Field Archaeology* 15:317–37.

Black, M.

1984 Maidens and Mothers: An Analysis of Hopi Corn Metaphors. *Ethnology* 23:279–88.

Blakely, R. L.

1977 Sociocultural Implications of Demographic Data from Etowah, Georgia. In *Biocultural Adaptation in Prehistoric America,* edited by R. L. Blakely, pp. 45–66. Athens: University of Georgia Press.

Blakeslee, D. J.

1975 The Plains Interband Trade System: An Ethnohistoric and Archaeological Investigation. Ph.D. diss., University of Wisconsin.

Blanton, R. E., G. M. Feinman, S. A. Kowalewski, and P. N. Peregrine

1996 A Dual-Processual Theory for the Evolution of Mesoamerican Civilization. *Current Anthropology* 37:1–14.

Bledsoe, C.

1990 School Fees and the Marriage Process for Mende Girls in Sierra Leone. In *Beyond the Second Sex: New Directions in the Anthropology of Gender,* edited by P. Sanday and R. Goodenough, pp. 281–309. Philadelphia: University of Pennsylvania Press.

Bleed, Peter

1986 The Optimal Design of Hunting Weapons: Maintainability or Reliability. *American Antiquity* 51:737–47.

Blinman, E.

1989 Potluck in the Protokiva: Ceramics and Ceremonialism in Pueblo I Villages. In *The Architecture of Social Integration in Prehistoric Pueblos,* edited by W. D. Lipe and M. Hegmon, pp. 113–24. Cortez, CO: Crow Canyon Archaeological Center.

1993 Anasazi Pottery: Evolution of a Technology. *Expedition* 35:14–23.

Blinman, E., and C. D. Wilson

1993 Ceramic Perspectives on Northern Anasazi Exchange. In *The American Southwest and Mesoamerica: Systems of Prehistoric Exchange,* edited by J. E. Ericson and T. G. Baugh, pp. 65–94. New York: Plenum.

Blitz, J.

1993 Big Pots for Big Shots: Feasting and Storage in a Mississippian Community. *American Antiquity* 58:80–93.

Bloomer, W. W.

1989 Moon House: A Pueblo III Period Cliff Dwelling Complex in Southeastern Utah. M.A. thesis, Washington State University.

Bodine, J. J.

1979 Taos Pueblo. In *Handbook of North American Indians, vol. 9: Southwest,* edited by A. Ortiz, pp. 255–67. Washington, D.C.: Smithsonian Institution.

Bohrer, V. L.

1960 Zuni Agriculture. *El Palacio* 67:181–202.

1991 Recently Recognized Cultivated and Encouraged Plants among the Hohokam. *Kiva* 56:227–36.

Boserup, E.

1965 *The Conditions of Agricultural Growth: The Economics of Agrarian Change under Population Pressure.* Chicago: Aldine.

1970 *Woman's Role in Economic Development.* London: Earthscan.

Bostwick, T.

1988 *An Investigation of Archaic Subsistence and Settlement in the Harquahala Valley, Maricopa County, Arizona.* Flagstaff, AZ: Northland Research.

1996 Scenes of Power: Rock Art of the South Mountains, Arizona. Paper presented at the 61st annual meeting of the Society for American Archaeology, New Orleans.

Bostwick, T. W., and J. H. Burton

1993 A Study in Sourcing Hohokam Basalt Ground Stone Implements. *Kiva* 58:357–72.

Bourdieu, P.

1973 The Berber House. In *Rules and Meaning*, edited by M. Douglas, pp. 98–110. London: Penguin.

Bradley, B. A.

1992 Excavations at Sand Canyon Pueblo. In *The Sand Canyon Archaeological Project: A Progress Report*, edited by W. D. Lipe, pp. 79–98. Crow Canyon Archaeological Center Occasional Paper 2. Cortez, CO.

1993 Planning, Growth, and Functional Differentiation at a Prehistoric Pueblo: A Case Study from SW Colorado. *Journal of Field Archaeology* 20:23–42.

1996 Pitchers to Mugs: Chacoan Revival at Sand Canyon Pueblo. *Kiva* 61:241–57.

Bradley, C.

1989 Reliability and Inference in the Cross-Cultural Coding Process. *Journal of Quantitative Anthropology* 1:353–71.

1993 Women's Power, Children's Labor. *Cross-Cultural Research* 27:70–96.

Bradley, R. J. E.

1996 The Role of Casas Grandes in Prehistoric Shell Exchange Networks within the Southwest. Ph.D. diss., Arizona State University.

Brady, J.

1996a Ground Stone and Grinding Technology in the Postclassic Period, Eastern Mimbres Region. Seminar paper on file, Arizona State University.

1996b Mobility and Ceramic Assemblages in the Mogollon Region. M.A. thesis, University of Oklahoma.

Braithwaite, M.

1982 Decoration as Ritual Symbol: A Theoretical Proposal and an Ethnographic Study in Southern Sudan. In *Symbolic and Structural Archaeology*, edited by I. Hodder, pp. 80–88. Cambridge: Cambridge University Press.

Brandt, E. A.

1977 The Role of Secrecy in a Pueblo Society. In *Flowers of the Wind: Papers on Ritual, Myth, and Symbolism in California and the Southwest*, edited by T. C. Blackburn, pp. 11–28. Socorro, NM: Ballena Press.

1980 On Secrecy and the Control of Knowledge: Taos Pueblo. In *Secrecy: A Cross-Cultural Perspective*, edited by S. Tefft. New York: Human Sciences Press.

1994 Egalitarianism, Hierarchy, and Centralization in the Pueblos. In *The Ancient Southwestern Community*, edited by W. H. Wills and R. Leonard, pp. 9–24. Albuquerque: University of New Mexico Press.

Braun, D. P.

1983 Pots as Tools. In *Archaeological Hammers and Theories*, edited by A. Keene and J. Moore, pp. 108–34. New York: Academic Press.

1987 Coevolution of Sedentism, Pottery Technology, and Horticulture in the Central Midwest, 200 B.C.–A.D. 600. In *Emergent Horticultural Economies of the Eastern Woodlands*, edited by W. F. Keegan, pp. 153–82. Center for Archaeological Investigations Occasional Paper 7. Carbondale: Southern Illinois University.

Breitburg, E.

1993 The Evolution of Turkey Domestication in the Greater Southwest and Mesoamerica. In *Culture and Contact: Charles C. Di Peso's Gran Chichimeca*, edited by A. Woosley and J. Ravesloot, pp. 153–72. Albuquerque: University of New Mexico Press.

Breternitz, C. D., D. E. Doyel, and M. P. Marshall

1982 *Bis Sa' ani: A Late Bonito Phase Community on Escavada Wash, Northwest New Mexico.* Navajo Nation Papers in Anthropology 14. Window Rock, AZ: Navajo Nation Cultural Resource Management Program.

Breternitz, D. A., C. K. Robinson, and G. T. Gross, compilers

1986 *Dolores Archaeological Program: Final Synthetic Report.* Denver: Bureau of Reclamation Engineering and Research Center.

Brew, J. O.

1946 *Archaeology of Alkali Ridge, Southeastern Utah.* Papers of the Peabody Museum of American Archaeology and Ethnology, vol. 21. Cambridge, MA: Harvard University.

1979 Hopi Prehistory and History to 1850. In *Handbook of North American Indians, vol. 9: Southwest*, edited by A. Ortiz, pp. 514–23. Washington, D.C.: Smithsonian Institution.

Bridges, P. S.

1989 Changes in Activities with the Shift to Agriculture in the Southeastern United States. *Current Anthropology* 30:385–94.

1990 Osteological Correlates of Weapon Use. In *A Life In Science: Papers in Honor of Lawrence Angel*, edited by J. Buikstra, pp. 87–98. Center for American Archaeology Scientific Papers 6.

Brightman, R.

1996 The Sexual Division of Foraging Labor: Biology, Taboo, and Gender Politics. *Comparative Studies in Society and History* 38:687–729.

Brody, J. J.

1977 *Mimbres Painted Pottery.* Albuquerque: University of New Mexico Press.

Brooks, J.

1944 Journal of Thales H. Haskell. *Utah Historical Quarterly* 12:69–95.

Brown, C. H.

1985 Mode of Subsistence and Folk Biological Taxonomy. *Current Anthropology* 26:43–64.

Brown, G. M.

1990 Nuvakwewtaqa and the Chavez Pass Region: An Overview. In *Technological Change in the Chavez Pass Region, North Central Arizona,* edited by G. M. Brown, pp. 5–20. Anthropological Research Papers 41. Tempe: Arizona State University.

Brown, J. A.

1989 The Beginnings of Pottery as an Economic Process. In *What's New? A Closer Look at the Process of Innovation,* edited by S. E. van der Leeuw and R. Torrence, pp. 203–24. London: Unwin Hyman.

Brown, J. K.

1970 A Note on Sexual Division of Labor. *American Anthropologist* 72:1073–78.

1975 Iroquois Women: An Ethnohistoric Note. In *Towards an Anthropology of Women,* edited by R. Reiter. New York: Monthly Review Press.

1979 Economic Organization and the Position of Women among the Iroquois. In *Women and Society: An Anthropological Reader,* edited by S. W. Tiffany, pp. 48–74. St. Alban's, VT: Eden Press.

1992 Lives of Middle-Aged Women. In *In Her Prime: New Views of Middle-Aged Women,* edited by V. Kerns and J. Brown, pp. 17–30. Urbana: University of Illinois Press.

Browner, C. H., and S. Perdue

1988 Women's Secrets: Bases for Reproductive and Social Autonomy in a Mexican Community. *American Ethnologist* 15:85–97.

Brumfiel, E. M.

1991 Weaving and Cooking: Women's Production in Aztec Mexico. In *Engendering Archaeology: Women and Prehistory,* edited by J. M. Gero and M. W. Conkey, pp. 224–51. Oxford: Basil Blackwell.

1992 Breaking and Entering the Ecosystem—Gender, Class, and Faction Steal the Show. *American Anthropologist* 94:551–67.

1996a Figurines and the Aztec State: Testing the Effectiveness of Ideological Domination. In *Gender and Archaeology,* edited by R. P. Wright, pp. 143–66. Philadelphia: University of Pennsylvania Press.

1996b The Quality of Tribute Cloth: The Place of Evidence in Archaeological Argument. *American Antiquity* 61:453–62.

Brumfiel, E. M., and T. K. Earle

1987 Specialization, Exchange, and Complex Societies: An Introduction. In *Specialization, Exchange, and Complex Societies*, edited by E. M. Brumfiel and T. K. Earle, pp. 1–9. Cambridge: Cambridge University Press.

Brunson, J. L.

1989 The Social Organization of the Los Muertos Hohokam: A Reanalysis of Cushing's Hemenway Expedition Data. Ph.D. diss., Arizona State University.

Buckley, T., and A. Gottlieb

1988 A Critical Appraisal of Theories of Menstrual Symbolism. In *Blood Magic: The Anthropology of Menstruation*. Berkeley: University of California Press.

Buikstra, J. E., J. Bullington, D. Charles, D. Cook, S. Frankenberg, L. Konigsberg, J. Lambert, and L. Xue

1987 Diet, Demography, and the Development of Horticulture. In *Emergent Horticultural Economies of the Eastern Woodlands*, edited by W. F. Keegan, pp. 67–86. Center for Archaeological Investigations Occasional Paper 7. Carbondale: Southern Illinois University.

Buikstra, J. E., and D. C. Cook

1980 Paleopathology: An American Account. *Annual Reviews in Anthropology* 9:433–70.

Bunzel, R.

1932 *Zuni Ceremonialism*. Forty-seventh Annual Report of the Bureau of American Ethnology, pp. 1929–1930. Washington, D.C.: Smithsonian Institution.

1972 [1929] *The Pueblo Potter: A Study of Creative Imagination in Primitive Art*. New York: Dover.

Burton, J. F.

1991 *The Archeology of Sivu'ovi: The Archaic to Basketmaker Transition at Petrified Forest National Park*. Publications in Anthropology 55. Western Archeological and Conservation Center. Tucson: National Park Service.

Burton, M. L., L. A. Brudner, and D. R. White

1977 A Model of the Sexual Division of Labor. *American Ethnologist* 4:227–51.

Burton, M. L., and D. R. White

1984 Sexual Division of Labor in Agriculture. *American Anthropologist* 86:568–83.

Burton, M. L., D. R. White, and M. Dow

1982 *Sexual Division of Labor in Old World Agriculture*. Michigan State University Working Paper 5. Lansing: Michigan State University.

Bustard, W. J.

1996 Space as Place: Small and Great House Spatial Organization in Chaco Canyon, New Mexico, A.D. 1000–1150. Ph.D. diss., University of New Mexico.

Byrne, B.

1994 Access to Subsistence Resources and the Sexual Division of Labor among Potters. *Cross-Cultural Research* 28:225–50.

Cameron, C.

1984 A Regional View of Chipped Stone Raw Material Use in Chaco Canyon. In *Recent Research on Chaco Prehistory*, edited by W. J. Judge and J. D. Schelberg, pp. 137–52. Reports of the Chaco Center 8. Albuquerque: U.S. Department of the Interior.

1990 The Effect of Varying Estimates of Pit Structure Use-Life on Prehistoric Population Estimates in the American Southwest. *Kiva* 55:155–65.

Cameron, J.

1991 Lithics. In *Subsistence and Exchange at Gran Quivira Pueblo, New Mexico*, edited by K. A. Spielmann, pp. 89–115. Report submitted to the National Park Service Southwestern Regional Office. Santa Fe.

Capone, P.

1995 Mission Pueblo Ceramic Analyses: Implications for Protohistoric Interaction Networks and Cultural Dynamics. Ph.D. diss., Harvard University.

Carlson, R. L.

1965 *Basketmaker III Sites near Durango, Colorado.* University of Colorado Studies, Series in Anthropology 8. Boulder.

1982 The Polychrome Complexes. In *Southwestern Ceramics: A Comparative Review*, edited by A. H. Schroeder, pp. 201–34. Arizona Archaeologist 15. Phoenix: Arizona Archaeological Society.

Carr, C.

1994 A Cross-Cultural Survey of the Determinants of Mortuary Practices. In *The Pueblo Grande Project, vol. 7: An Analysis of Classic Period Mortuary Patterns*, edited by D. R. Mitchell, pp. 7–69. Soil Systems Publications in Archaeology 20. Phoenix.

Castetter, E. F., and W. H. Bell

1942 *Pima and Papago Indian Agriculture.* Albuquerque: University of New Mexico Press.

1951 *Yuman Indian Agriculture.* Albuquerque: University of New Mexico Press.

Castetter, E. F., W. H. Bell, and A. Grove

1938 *The Early Utilization and Distribution of Agave in the American Southwest.* Albuquerque: University of New Mexico Press.

Castetter, E. F., and R. M. Underhill

1935 *Ethnobiological Studies in the American Southwest, 2: The Ethnobiology of the Papago Indians.* Albuquerque: University of New Mexico Press.

Cater, J. D., and M. L. Chenault

1988 Kiva Use Reinterpreted. *Southwestern Lore* 54:19–32.

Cattanach, G. S., Jr.

1980 *Long House, Mesa Verde National Park, Colorado.* Archaeological Research Series 7-H. Washington, D.C.: National Park Service.

Chan, E.

1989 Compact Femoral Tissue: An Indicator of Nutritional Deficiencies in Black Mesa Anasazi Infants. Senior honor's thesis, Hampshire College.

Childs, T. S.

1991 Style, Technology, and Iron Smelting Furnaces in Bantu-Speaking Africa. *Journal of Anthropological Archaeology* 10:332–59.

Childs, T. S., and D. Killick

1993 Indigenous African Metallurgy: Nature and Culture. *Annual Review of Anthropology* 22:317–37.

Christensen, D. D.

1994 *Rock Art, Ceramics, and Textiles: The Validity of Unifying Art Motifs.* Rock Art Papers 11, pp. 107–16. San Diego Museum Papers 31. San Diego.

Christenson, A. L.

1991 The Microenvironment of Cliffdwellings in Tsegi Canyon, Arizona. *Kiva* 57:39–54.

Ciolek-Torrello, R. S.

1985 A Typology of Room Function at Grasshopper Pueblo. *Journal of Field Archaeology* 12:41–63.

1989 Room Function and Households at Grasshopper Pueblo. In *Mogollon Variability,* edited by C. Benson and S. Upham, pp. 107–19. The University Museum Occasional Papers 15. Las Cruces: New Mexico State University.

Ciolek-Torrello, R. S., and J. J. Reid

1974 Change in Household Size at Grasshopper. *Kiva* 40:39–48.

Claassen, C.

1992 Questioning Gender: An Introduction. In *Exploring Gender through Archaeology: Selected Papers from the 1991 Boone Conference,* edited by C. Claassen, pp. 1–9. Monographs in World Archaeology 11. Madison, WI: Prehistory Press.

1997 Women's Lives in Prehistoric North America. In *Women in Prehistory: North America and Mesoamerica,* edited by C. Claassen and R. Joyce, pp. 65–87. Philadelphia: University of Pennsylvania Press.

Claassen, C., ed.

1992 *Exploring Gender through Archaeology: Selected Papers from the 1991 Boone Conference.* Monographs in World Archaeology 11. Madison, WI: Prehistory Press.

1994 *Women in Archaeology.* Philadelphia: University of Pennsylvania Press.

Claassen, C., and R. Joyce, eds.

1997 *Women in Prehistory: North America and Mesoamerica.* Philadelphia: University of Pennsylvania Press.

Clark, G. A.

1967 A Preliminary Analysis of Burial Clusters at the Grasshopper Site, East-Central Arizona. M.A. thesis, University of Arizona.

Clemmer, R.

1995 *Roads in the Sky: The Hopi Indians in a Century of Change.* Boulder, CO: Westview Press.

Cohen, M., and S. Bennett

1993 Skeletal Evidence for Sex Roles and Gender Hierarchies in Prehistory. In *Sex and Gender Hierarchies,* edited by B. D. Miller, pp. 273–96. Cambridge: Cambridge University Press.

Cole, S.

1989 Iconography and Symbolism in Basketmaker Rock Art. In *Rock Art of the Western Canyons,* pp. 59–85. Colorado Archaeological Society Memoir 3. Denver: Denver Museum of Natural History.

Collier, J. F.

1988 *Marriage and Inequality in Classless Societies.* Stanford, CA: Stanford University Press.

Collier, J. F., and M. Z. Rosaldo

1981 Politics and Gender in Simple Societies. In *Sexual Meanings: The Cultural Construction of Gender and Sexuality,* edited by S. B. Ortner and H. Whitehead, pp. 275–329. Cambridge: Cambridge University Press.

Conkey, M. W., and J. M. Gero

1991 Tensions, Pluralities, and Engendering Archaeology: An Introduction to Women and Prehistory. In *Engendering Archaeology: Women and Prehistory,* edited by J. M. Gero and M. W. Conkey, pp. 3–30. Oxford: Basil Blackwell.

Conkey, M. W., and J. Spector

1984 Archaeology and the Study of Gender. In *Advances in Archaeological Method and Theory,* vol. 7, edited by M. B. Schiffer, pp. 1–38. New York: Academic Press.

Connell, R. W.

1987 *Gender and Power: Society, the Person, and Sexual Politics.* Cambridge: Polity Press.

Cordell, L.

1984 *Prehistory of the Southwest.* New York: Academic Press.

1997 *Archaeology of the Southwest.* New York: Academic Press.

Cordell, L., and G. Gumerman, eds.

1989 *Dynamics of Southwest Prehistory.* Washington, D.C.: Smithsonian Institution Press.

Cosgrove, H. S., and C. B. Cosgrove

1932 *The Swarts Ruin: A Typical Mimbres Site in Southwestern New Mexico.* Papers of the Peabody Museum of American Archaeology and Ethnology 15. Cambridge, MA: Harvard University.

Costin, C.

1991 Craft Specialization: Issues in Defining, Documenting, and Explaining the Organization of Production. In *Archaeological Method and Theory,* vol. 3, edited by M. B. Schiffer, pp. 1–56. Tucson: University of Arizona Press.

1993 Textiles, Women, and Political Economy in Late Prehispanic Peru. *Research in Economic Anthropology* 14:3–28.

1996 Exploring the Relationship between Gender and Craft in Complex Societies: Methodological and Theoretical Issues of Gender Attribution. In *Gender and Archaeology,* edited by R. P. Wright, pp. 111–40. Philadelphia: University of Pennsylvania Press.

Coulam, N. J., and A. R. Schroedl

1996 Early Archaic Clay Figurines from Cowboy and Walters Caves in Southeastern Utah. *Kiva* 61:401–12.

Coward, R.

1985 *Female Desires.* New York: Grove Press.

Crabtree, P. J.

1991 Gender Hierarchies and the Sexual Division of Labor in the Natufian Culture of the Southern Levant. In *The Archaeology of Gender,* edited by D. Walde and N. D. Willows, pp. 384–91. Calgary, Alberta: Archaeological Association of the University of Calgary.

Cravioto, R. O., R. K. Anderson, E. E. Lockhart, F. P. Miranda, and R. S. Harris

1945 The Nutritive Value of the Mexican Tortilla. *Science* 102:91–93.

Creamer, W.

1993 *The Architecture of Arroyo Hondo Pueblo, New Mexico.* Santa Fe: School of American Research Press.

Creel, D. G.

1994 Interpreting the End of the Mimbres Classic. Paper presented at the spring meeting of the Arizona Archaeological Council, Tucson.

1999 The Black Mountain Phase in the Mimbres Area. In *The Casas Grandes*

World, edited by C. Schaafsma and C. Riley, pp. 107–20. Salt Lake City: University of Utah Press.

Crockett, S. J., and D. J. Stuber

1992 Prestige Value of Foods: Change over Time. *Ecology of Food and Nutrition* 27:51–64.

Crossette, B.

1996 New Tally of World Tragedy: Women Who Die Giving Life. *New York Times*, June 11: A12.

Crotty, H. K.

1983 *Honoring the Dead: Anasazi Ceramics from the Rainbow Bridge–Monument Valley Expedition.* UCLA Museum of Cultural History Monograph Series 22. Los Angeles.

1994 East Meets West at Pottery Mound: Ceramics, Kiva Architecture, and Murals with a Western Flavor in a Rio Grande Pueblo. Paper presented at the 59th annual meeting of the Society for American Archaeology, Anaheim.

Crown, P. L.

1984a Design Variability in Salt-Gila Aqueduct Red-on-Buff Ceramics. In *Hohokam Archaeology along the Salt-Gila Aqueduct, Central Arizona Project, vol. 8: Material Culture*, edited by L. S. Teague and P. L. Crown, pp. 205–48. Arizona State Museum Archaeological Series 150. Tucson: University of Arizona.

1984b An X-Ray Fluorescence Analysis of Hohokam Ceramics. In *Hohokam Archaeology along the Salt-Gila Aqueduct, Central Arizona Project, vol. 8: Material Culture*, edited by L. S. Teague and P. L. Crown, pp. 277–310. Arizona State Museum Archaeological Series 150. Tucson: University of Arizona.

1985a Morphology and Function of Hohokam Small Structures. *Kiva* 50:75–94.

1985b Intrusive Ceramics and the Identification of Hohokam Exchange Networks. In *Proceedings of the 1983 Hohokam Symposium*, part 2, edited by A. E. Dittert and D. E. Dove, pp. 439–57. Arizona Archaeological Society Occasional Paper 2. Phoenix.

1987 Classic Period Hohokam Settlement and Land Use in the Casa Grande Ruins Area, Arizona. *Journal of Field Archaeology* 14:147–62.

1991a The Hohokam: Current Views of Prehistory and the Regional System. In *Chaco and Hohokam*, edited by P. L. Crown, and W. J. Judge, pp. 135–57. Santa Fe: School of American Research Press.

1991b The Role of Exchange and Interaction in Salt-Gila Basin Hohokam Prehistory. In *Exploring the Hohokam*, edited by G. J. Gumerman, pp. 383–415. Albuquerque: University of New Mexico Press.

1994 *Ceramics and Ideology: Salado Polychrome Pottery.* Albuquerque: University of New Mexico Press.

Crown, P. L., and R. L. Bishop

1987 The Manufacture of Salado Polychromes. *Pottery Southwest* 14:1–4.

Crown, P. L., and S. K. Fish

1996 Gender and Status in the Hohokam Pre-Classic to Classic Transition. *American Anthropologist* 98:803–17.

Crown, P. L., and W. H. Wills

1995a The Origins of Southwestern Containers: Women's Time Allocation and Economic Intensification. *Journal of Anthropological Research* 51:173–86.

1995b Economic Intensification and the Origins of Ceramics in the Greater American Southwest. In *The Emergence of Pottery*, edited by W. Barnett and J. Hoopes, pp. 241–56. Washington, D.C.: Smithsonian Institution Press.

Cushing, F. H.

1920 Zuni Breadstuff. *Indian Notes and Monographs*, vol. 8, pp. 7–642.

Cutler, H., and L. Blake

1976 Corn from Snaketown, Appendix 4. In *The Hohokam: Desert Farmers and Craftsmen*, by E. Haury, pp. 365–66. Tucson: University of Arizona Press.

Danforth, M. E., D. C. Cook, and S. G. Knick III

1994 The Human Remains from Carter Ranch Pueblo, Arizona. *American Antiquity* 59:88–101.

Darling, J. A.

1993 Mass Inhumation and the Execution of Witches in the North American Southwest. Unpublished paper. Office of Archaeological Studies. Santa Fe: Museum of New Mexico.

Dean, J. S.

1969 *Chronological Analysis of Tsegi Phase Sites in Northeastern Arizona.* Papers of the Laboratory of Tree-Ring Research 3. Tucson: University of Arizona Press.

1970 Aspects of Tsegi Phase Social Organization: A Trial Reconstruction. In *Reconstructing Prehistoric Pueblo Societies*, edited by W. Longacre, pp. 140–74. Albuquerque: University of New Mexico Press.

1991 Thoughts on Hohokam Chronology. In *Exploring the Hohokam: Prehistoric Desert Peoples of the American Southwest*, edited by G. J. Gumerman, pp. 61–149. Albuquerque: University of New Mexico Press.

1996 Kayenta Anasazi Settlement Transformations in Northeastern Arizona: A.D. 1150–1350. In *The Prehistoric Pueblo World, A.D. 1150–1350*, edited by M. A. Adler, pp. 29–47. Tucson: University of Arizona Press.

DeBoer, W.

1991 The Decorative Burden. In *Ceramic Ethnoarchaeology*, edited by W. Longacre, pp. 144–61. Tucson: University of Arizona Press.

DeBoer, W., and D. Lathrap

1979 The Making and Breaking of Shipibo-Conibo Ceramics. In *Ethnoarchaeology: Implications of Ethnography for Archaeology,* edited by C. Kramer, pp. 102–38. New York: Columbia University Press.

Dennis, W.

1940 *The Hopi Child.* New York: D. Appleton-Century Co.

Densmore, F.

1929 *Papago Music.* Washington, D.C.: Government Printing Office.

Devereux, G.

1937 Institutionalized Homosexuality of the Mohave Indians. *Human Biology* 9:498–527.

Diehl, M. W.

1996 The Intensity of Maize Processing and Production in Upland Mogollon Pithouse Villages A.D. 200–1000. *American Antiquity* 61:102–15.

di Leonardo, M.

1991 Gender, Culture, and Political Economy: Feminist Anthropology in Historical Perspective. In *Gender at the Crossroads of Knowledge,* edited by M. di Leonardo, pp. 1–48. Berkeley: University of California Press.

Di Peso, C. C.

1956 *The Upper Pima of San Cayetano del Tumacacori: An Archaeohistorical Reconstruction of the Ootam of Pimeria Alta.* Amerind Foundation Publications 7. Dragoon, AZ.

1974a *Casas Grandes: A Fallen Trading Center of the Gran Chichimeca, vol. 1: Preceramic-Viejo Periods.* Flagstaff: Northland Press.

1974b *Casas Grandes: A Fallen Trading Center of the Gran Chichimeca, vol. 2: The Medio Period.* Dragoon, AZ: Amerind Foundation.

Di Peso, C. C., J. B. Rinaldo, and G. J. Fenner

1974a *Casas Grandes: A Fallen Trading Center of the Gran Chichimeca, vols. 6 (Ceramics and Shell)* and *7 (Stone and Metal).* Amerind Foundation Publications 9. Dragoon, AZ.

1974b *Casas Grandes: A Fallen Tradition Center of the Gran Chichimeca, vol. 8: Bones, Perishables, Commerce, Subsistence, and Burials.* Flagstaff: Northland Press.

Divale, W., and M. Harris

1976 Population, Warfare, and the Male Supremacist Complex. *American Anthropologist* 78:521–38.

Dobres, M. A.

1992 Reconsidering Prehistoric "Venus" Figurines: A Feminist Inspired Re-analysis. In *Ancient Images, Ancient Thought: The Archaeology of Ideology,* edited by A. Goldsmith et al., pp. 245–61. Calgary, Alberta: University of Calgary Press.

1995 Gender and Prehistoric Technology: On the Social Agency of Technical Strategies. *World Archaeology* 27:25–49.

Doebley, J., and V. Bohrer

1983 Maize Variability and Cultural Selection at Salmon Ruin, New Mexico. *Kiva* 49:19–37.

Doelle, W. H., F. W. Huntington, and H. D. Wallace

1987 Rincon Phase Reorganization in the Tucson Basin. In *The Hohokam Village: Site Structure and Organization*, edited by D. Doyel, pp. 71–96. Glenwood Springs, CO: Southwestern and Rocky Mountain Division of the American Association for the Advancement of Science.

Dohm, K.

1994 The Search for Anasazi Village Origins: Basketmaker II Dwelling Aggregations on Cedar Mesa. *Kiva* 60:257–76.

Donley-Reid, L.

1990 The Power of Swahili Porcelain, Beads, and Pottery. In *Powers of Observation*, edited by S. Nelson and A. Kehoe, pp. 47–60. Archaeological Papers of the American Anthropological Association 2.

Doolittle, W.

1992 House-lot Gardens in the Gran Chichimeca: Ethnographic Cause for Archaeological Concern. In *Gardens of Prehistory: The Archaeology of Settlement Agriculture in Greater Mesoamerica*, edited by T. W. Killion, pp. 69–91. Tuscaloosa: University of Alabama Press.

Dorsey, G. A.

1899 The Hopi Indians of Arizona. *Popular Science Monthly* 55:732–50.

Douglass, A. A.

1987 Prehistoric Exchange and Sociopolitical Development: The Little Colorado White Ware Production-Distribution System. Ph.D. diss., Arizona State University.

Downs, J. F.

1966 The Significance of Environmental Manipulation in Great Basin Cultural Development. In *The Current Status of Anthropological Research in the Great Basin, 1964*, edited by W. d'Azevedo, pp. 138–52. University of Nevada Social Sciences and Humanities Publication 1. Desert Research Institute. Reno: University of Nevada.

Doyal, L.

1995 *What Makes Women Sick? Gender and the Political Economy of Health.* New Brunswick, NJ: Rutgers University Press.

Doyel, D. E.

1974 *Excavations in the Escalante Ruin Group, Southern Arizona.* Tucson: Arizona State Museum, University of Arizona.

1991a Hohokam Cultural Evolution in the Phoenix Basin. In *Exploring the Hohokam*, edited by G. Gumerman, pp. 231–78. Albuquerque: University of New Mexico Press.

1991b Hohokam Exchange and Interaction. In *Chaco and Hohokam*, edited by P. L. Crown and W. J. Judge, pp. 225–52. Santa Fe: School of American Research Press.

Dozier, E. P.

1970 *The Pueblo Indians of North America*. New York: Holt.

Draper, P.

1975 !Kung Women: Contrasts in Sexual Egalitarianism in Foraging and Sedentary Contexts. In *Toward an Anthropology of Women*, edited by R. R. Reiter, pp. 252–82. New York: Monthly Review Press.

1997 Institutional, Evolutionary, and Demographic Contexts of Gender Roles: A Case Study of !Kung Bushmen. In *The Evolving Female*, edited by M. E. Morbeck, A. Galloway, and A. Zihlman, pp. 220–32. Princeton: Princeton University Press.

Driver, J. C.

1990 Meat in Due Season: The Timing of Communal Hunts. In *Hunters of the Recent Past*, edited by L. B. Davis and B. O. K. Reeves, pp. 11–33. London: Unwin Hyman.

DuCros, H., and L. Smith

1992 *Women in Archaeology: A Feminist Critique*. Canberra: Australian National University.

Duff, A. I.

1998 The Process of Migration in the Late Prehistoric Southwest. In *Migration and Reorganization: The Pueblo IV Period in the American Southwest*, edited by K. A. Spielmann, pp. 31–52. Anthropological Research Papers 51. Tempe: Arizona State University.

Duffy, A.

1986 Reformulating Power for Women. *Canadian Review of Sociology and Anthropology* 23:22–46.

Duke, P.

1965 *Fort Lewis College Archaeological Investigations in Ridges Basin, Colorado:* 1965–1982. Occasional Papers of the Center for Southwest Studies 4.

Dunnigan, T.

1983 Lower Pima. In *Handbook of North American Indians, vol. 10: Southwest*, edited by A. Ortiz, pp. 217–29. Washington, D.C.: Smithsonian Institution.

Dutton, B.

1963 *Sun Father's Way*. Albuquerque: University of New Mexico Press.

Eaton, L.

1991 The Heart of the Region: The Anthropology Collections of the Museum of Northern Arizona. *American Indian Art* 16:46–53.

Eddy, F. W.

1966 *Prehistory of the Navajo Reservoir District, Northwestern New Mexico.* Museum of New Mexico Press Papers in Anthropology 15. Santa Fe

Effland, R. W., Jr.

1988 An Examination of Hohokam Mortuary Practices from Casa Buena. In *Excavations at Casa Buena: Changing Hohokam Land Use along the Squaw Peak Parkway,* vol. 2, edited by J. B. Howard, pp. 693–794. Soil Systems Publications in Archaeology 11. Phoenix.

Eggan, F.

1950 *Social Organization of the Western Pueblos.* Chicago: University of Chicago Press.

Ehrenberg, M.

1989 *Women in Prehistory.* Norman: University of Oklahoma Press.

Ekejiuba, F.

1995 Down to Fundamentals: Women-Centered Heartholds in Rural West Africa. *Development* 1:72–76.

Ellis, C. J.

1997 Factors Influencing the Use of Stone Projectile Tips: An Ethnographic Perspective. In *Perspectives on Projectile Technology,* edited by H. Knecht. New York: Plenum Publishing.

Ellis, F. H.

1964 Archaeological History of Nambe Pueblo, Fourteenth Century to the Present. *American Antiquity* 30:34–42.

1979a Isleta Pueblo. In *Handbook of North American Indians, vol. 9: Southwest,* edited by A. Ortiz, pp. 351–65. Washington, D.C.: Smithsonian Institution.

1979b Laguna Pueblo. In *Handbook of North American Indians, vol. 9: Southwest,* edited by A. Ortiz, pp. 438–49. Washington, D.C.: Smithsonian Institution.

El-Najjar, M. Y., D. J. Ryan, C. G. Turner, and B. Lozoff

1976 The Etiology of Porotic Hyperostosis among the Prehistoric and Historic Anasazi Indians of the Southwestern United States. *American Journal of Physical Anthropology* 44:477–88.

Elson, M. D., and D. R. Abbott

2000 Organizational Variability in Platform Mound-Building Groups of the American Southwest. In *Alternative Leadership Strategies in the Prehispanic Southwest,* edited by B. J. Mills. Tucson: University of Arizona Press.

Elson, M. D., M. T. Stark, and D. A. Gregory, eds.

1995 *The Roosevelt Community Development Study: New Perspectives on Tonto Basin Prehistory*. Anthropological Papers 15. Tucson: Center for Desert Archaeology.

Ember, C.

1983 The Relative Decline in Women's Contribution to Agriculture with Intensification. *American Anthropologist* 85:285–305.

Errington, S.

1990 Recasting Sex, Gender, and Power: A Theoretical and Regional Overview. In *Power and Difference: Gender in Island Southeast Asia,* edited by J. Atkinson and S. Errington, pp. 1–58. Palo Alto, CA: Stanford University Press.

Espenshade, C. T.

1997 Mimbres Pottery, Births, and Gender: A Reconsideration. *American Antiquity* 62:733–36.

Estioko-Griffin, A., and P. Bion Griffin

1981 Woman the Hunter: The Agta. In *Woman the Gatherer,* edited by F. Dahlbe, pp. 121–51. New Haven: Yale University Press.

Etienne, M.

1980 Women and Men, Cloth and Colonization: The Transformation of Production-Distribution Relations among the Baule (Ivory Coast). In *Women and Colonization,* edited by M. Etienne and E. Leacock, pp. 214–38. New York: J. F. Bergin.

Euler, R. C.

1966 A Large Clay Figurine from Prescott, Arizona. *Kiva* 22:4–7.

Ezell, P. H.

1961 *The Hispanic Acculturation of the Gila River Pimas.* Memoirs of the American Anthropological Association, vol. 63, no. 5, part 2. Washington, D.C.

Ezzo, J. A.

1992 Dietary Change and Variability at Grasshopper Pueblo, Arizona. *Journal of Anthropological Archaeology* 11:219–89.

Ezzo, J. A., and W. Deaver

1996 *Data Recovery at the Costello-King Site: A Late Archaic Site in the Northern Tucson Basin.* Tucson: Statistical Research, Inc.

Fane, D.

1991 The Southwest. In *Objects of Myth and Memory: American Indian Art at the Brooklyn Museum,* edited by D. Fane, I. Jacknis, and L. M. Breen, pp. 45–159. Brooklyn: The Brooklyn Museum in association with the University of Washington Press.

Farb, P., and G. Armelagos

1980 *Consuming Passions.* New York: Houghton Mifflin.

Feil, D. K.

1978 Women and Men in the Enga Tee. *American Ethnologist* 5:263–79.

1984 *Ways of Exchange: The Enga Tee of Papua New Guinea.* Queensland: University of Queensland Press.

Feinman, G. M.

1995 The Emergence of Inequality: A Focus on Strategies and Processes. In *Foundations of Social Inequality,* edited by T. D. Price and G. M. Feinman, pp. 255–79. New York: Plenum Press.

1999 Rethinking Our Assumptions: Economic Specialization at the Household Scale in Ancient Ejutla, Oaxaca, Mexico. In *Pottery and People: A Dynamic Interaction,* edited by J. M. Skibo and G. M. Feinman, pp. 81–98. Salt Lake City: University of Utah Press.

Feinman, G. M., and J. Neitzel

1984 Too Many Types: An Overview of Sedentary Prestate Societies in the Americas. In *Advances in Archaeological Method and Theory,* vol. 7, edited by M. B. Schiffer, pp. 39–102. New York: Academic Press.

Ferguson, T. J.

1995 *Historic Zuni Architecture and Society: An Archaeological Application of Space Syntax.* Anthropological Papers of the University of Arizona 60. Tucson: University of Arizona Press.

Fewkes, J. W.

1904 *Two Summer's Work in Pueblo Ruins.* Twenty-second Annual Report of the Bureau of American Ethnology. Washington, D.C.: Smithsonian Institution.

1919 *Prehistoric Villages, Castles, and Towers of Southwestern Colorado.* Bureau of American Ethnology Bulletin 70. Washington, D.C.: Smithsonian Institution.

Fewkes, J. W., and A. M. Stephen

1892 The Mam-srau'-ti: A Tusayan Ceremony. *American Anthropologist* 5:217–45.

Fink, T. M., and C. F. Merbs

1991 Paleonutrition and Paleopathology of the Salt River Hohokam: A Search for Correlates. *Kiva* 56:293–317.

Finkler, K.

1994 *Women in Pain: Gender and Morbidity in Mexico.* Philadelphia: University of Pennsylvania Press.

Fish, P. R.

1989 The Hohokam. In *Dynamics of Southwest Prehistory,* edited by L. S. Cordell and G. J. Gumerman, pp. 19–63. Washington, D.C.: Smithsonian Institution Press.

Fish, P. R., and S. K. Fish

1984 Agricultural Maximization in the Sacred Mountain Basin. In *Prehistoric Agricultural Societies in the Southwest,* edited by S. Fish and P. Fish, pp. 147–60. Anthropological Research Papers 33. Tempe: Arizona State University.

1991 Hohokam Political and Social Organization. In *Exploring the Hohokam: Prehistoric Desert Peoples of the American Southwest,* edited by G. J. Gumerman, pp. 151–75. Albuquerque: University of New Mexico Press.

Fish, P. R., S. K. Fish, C. Brennan, D. Gann, and J. Bayman

1993 Marana: Configuration of a Hohokam Platform Mound Site. In *Proceedings of the Second Salado Conference, Globe Arizona, 1992,* edited by R. Lange and S. Germick, pp. 62–68. Arizona Archaeological Society Occasional Paper. Phoenix.

Fish, S. K., and P. R. Fish

1991 Comparative Aspects of Paradigms for the Neolithic Transition in the Levant and the American Southwest. In *Perspectives on the Past: Theoretical Biases in Mediterranean Hunter-Gatherer Research,* edited by G. A. Clark, pp. 396–410. Philadelphia: University of Pennsylvania Press.

1994 Prehistoric Farmers of the Southwest. *Annual Review of Anthropology* 23:83–108.

Fish, S. K., and P. R. Fish, eds.

1984 *Prehistoric Agricultural Strategies in the Southwest.* Anthropological Research Papers 33. Tempe: Arizona State University.

Fish, S. K., P. R. Fish, and J. Madsen

1990 Sedentism and Settlement Mobility in the Tucson Basin Prior to A.D. 1000. In *Perspectives on Southwestern Prehistory,* edited by P. Minnis and C. Redman, pp. 76–91. Boulder, CO: Westview Press.

1992 Evolution and Structure of the Classic Period Marana Community. In *The Marana Community in the Hohokam World,* edited by S. K. Fish, P. R. Fish, and J. H. Madsen, pp. 20–40. Anthropological Papers of the University of Arizona 56. Tucson: University of Arizona Press.

Fish, S. K., P. R. Fish, and J. Madsen, eds.

1992 *The Marana Community in the Hohokam World.* Anthropological Papers of the University of Arizona no 56. Tucson: University of Arizona Press.

Fish, S. K., and G. P. Nabhan

1991 Desert as Context: The Hohokam Environment. In *Exploring the Hohokam: Prehistoric Desert Peoples in the American Southwest,* edited by G. Gumerman, pp. 29–60. Albuquerque: University of New Mexico Press.

Flanagan, J. G.

1989 Hierarchy in Simple "Egalitarian" Societies. *Annual Review of Anthropology* 18:245–66.

Fontana, B. L., W. J. Robinson, C. W. Cormack, and E. E. Leavitt, Jr.

1966 *Papago Indian Pottery.* Seattle: University of Washington Press.

FoodPro

1996 Software for Dietary and RDA Assessment.

Ford, R. I.

1972a An Ecological Perspective on the Eastern Pueblos. In *New Perspectives on the Pueblos,* edited by A. Ortiz, pp. 1–17. Albuquerque: University of New Mexico Press.

1972b Barter, Gift, or Violence: An Analysis of Tewa Intertribal Exchange. In *Social Exchange and Interaction,* edited by E. N. Wilmsen, pp. 21–45. Museum of Anthropology Anthropological Paper 46. Ann Arbor: University of Michigan.

1981 Gardening and Farming before A.D. 1000: Patterns of Prehistoric Cultivation North of Mexico. *Journal of Ethnobiology* 1:6–27.

1984 Ecological Consequences of Early Agriculture in the Southwest. In *Papers on the Archaeology of Black Mesa,* vol. 2, edited by S. Plog and S. Powell, pp. 127–38. Carbondale: Southern Illinois University Press.

1994 Corn Is Our Mother. In *Corn and Culture in the Prehistoric New World,* edited by S. Johannesson and C. A. Hastorf, pp. 513–25. Boulder, CO: Westview Press.

Foucault, M.

1980 *Power/Knowledge.* New York: Pantheon Books.

1994 Two Lectures. In *Culture/Power/History,* edited by N. Dirks, G. Eley, and S. Ortner, pp. 200–221. Princeton: Princeton University Press.

Fowler, C. S.

1986 Subsistence. In *Handbook of North American Indians, vol. 11: Great Basin,* edited by W. d'Azevedo, pp. 64–97. Washington, D.C.: Smithsonian Institution Press.

Fratt, L., and M. Biancaniello

1993 Homol'ovi III Ground Stone in the Raw: A Study of the Local Sandstone Used to Make Ground Stone Artifacts. *Kiva* 58:373–92.

French, M.

1985 *Beyond Power: On Women, Men and Morals.* New York: Ballantine.

1977 *The Women's Room.* New York: Jove.

Friedl, E.

1975 *Women and Men: An Anthropologist's View.* New York: Holt, Rinehart, and Winston.

Futrell, M.

1998 Interaction among the Biscuit, Glaze, and Jemez Black-on-white Ceramic Zones in the Protohistoric Period of New Mexico. In *Migration and Reorganization: The Pueblo IV Period in the American Southwest,* edited by

K. A. Spielmann, pp. 285–92. Anthropological Research Papers 51. Tempe: Arizona State University.

Gailey, C. W.

1987a Evolutionary Perspectives on Gender Hierarchy. In *Analyzing Gender: A Handbook of Social Science Research,* edited by B. B. Hess and M. M. Ferree, pp. 32–67. Newbury Park, CA: Sage Publications.

1987b *Kinship to Kingship: Gender Hierarchy and State Formation in the Tongan Islands.* Austin: University of Texas Press.

Galinat, W. C.

1988 The Origin of Maiz de Ocho. *American Anthropologist* 90:682–83.

Garn, S. M.

1970 *The Earlier Gain and Late Loss of Bone in Nutritional Perspective.* Springfield, IL: C. C. Thomas.

Gasser, R. E., and S. Kwiatkowski

1991 Food for Thought: Recognizing Patterns in Hohokam Subsistence. In *Exploring the Hohokam: Prehistoric Desert Peoples in the American Southwest,* edited by G. Gumerman, pp. 417–60. Albuquerque: University of New Mexico Press.

Gasser, R., and C. Miksicek

1985 The Specialists: A Reappraisal of Hohokam Exchange and the Archaeobotanical Record. In *Proceedings of the 1983 Hohokam Symposium,* part 2, edited by A. E. Dittert, Jr., and D. E. Dove, pp. 483–98. Arizona Archaeological Society Occasional Paper 2. Phoenix.

Gebbie, D. A. M.

1981 *Reproductive Anthropology: Descent through Woman.* New York: Wiley and Sons.

Genoves, S.

1967 Proportionality of the Long Bones and Their Relation to Stature among Mesoamericans. *American Journal of Physical Anthropology* 26:67–78.

Gero, J. M.

1991 Genderlithics: Women's Roles in Stone Tool Production. In *Engendering Archaeology: Women and Prehistory,* edited by J. M. Gero and M. W. Conkey, pp. 163–93. Oxford: Basil Blackwell.

Gero, J. M., and M. W. Conkey, eds.

1991 *Engendering Archaeology: Women and Prehistory.* Oxford: Basil Blackwell.

Gerth, H. H., and C. W. Mills

1946 *From Max Weber: Essays in Sociology.* New York: Oxford University Press.

Gewertz, D. B.

1983 *Sepik River Societies.* New Haven, CT: Yale University Press.

Gibbs, L.

1987 Identifying Gender Representations in the Archaeological Record: A Contextual Study. In *The Archaeology of Contextual Meaning*, edited by I. Hodder, pp. 79–89. Cambridge: Cambridge University Press.

Giddens, A.

1971 *Capitalism and Modern Social Theory*. Cambridge: Cambridge University Press.

Gifford, E. W.

1931 *The Cocopa*. University of California Publications in American Archaeology and Ethnology 31, pp. 257–334. Berkeley: University of California.

Gill, S.

1987 *Mother Earth: An American Story*. Chicago: University of Chicago Press.

Gillespie, W.

1976 Culture Change at the Ute Canyon Site: A Study of the Pithouse-Kiva Transition in the Mesa Verde Region. M.A. thesis, University of Colorado.

1988 Vertebrate Faunal Remains. In *Hohokam Archaeology along Phase B of the Tucson Aqueduct, Central Arizona Project, vol. 2: Excavations at Fastimes AZ (AA:12:384), A Rillito Phase Site in the Avra Valley*, edited by J. Czaplicki and J. Ravesloot, pp. 234–68. Arizona State Museum Archaeological Series 178. Tucson: University of Arizona.

Gilman, A.

1981 The Development of Social Stratification in Bronze Age Europe. *Current Anthropology* 22:1–8.

Gilman, P. A.

1987 Architecture as Artifact: Pitstructures and Pueblos in the American Southwest. *American Antiquity* 52:538–64.

1990 Social Organization and Classic Mimbres Period Burials in the SW United States. *Journal of Field Archaeology* 17:457–69.

Gilman, P. A., V. Canouts, and R. L. Bishop

1994 The Production and Distribution of Classic Mimbres Black-on-white Pottery. *American Antiquity* 59:695–709.

Glass, M.

1984 Faunal Remains from Hohokam Sites in the Rosemont Area, Northern Santa Rita Mountains. In *Hohokam Habitation Sites in the Northern Santa Rita Mountains*, edited by A. Ferg et al. Arizona State Museum Archaeological Series no. 147, vol. 2, part 2. Tucson: University of Arizona.

Goffman, E.
1976 *Gender Advertisements.* London: Macmillan.

Goldstein, L. G.
1976 Spatial Structure and Social Organization: Regional Manifestations of Mississippian Society. Ph.D. diss., Northwestern University.
1981 One-Dimensional Archaeology and Multi-Dimensional People: Spatial Organization and Mortuary Analysis. In *The Archaeology of Death,* edited by R. Chapman, I. Kinnes, and K. Randsborg, pp. 53–70. Cambridge: Cambridge University Press.

Goodman, A. H., and T. L. Leatherman
1995 Political Economic Perspectives in Biological Anthropology. Paper presented at the annual meeting of the American Association of Anthropology, Washington D.C.

Goodman, A. H., D. L. Martin, and G. J. Armelagos
1995 The Biological Consequences of Inequality in Prehistory. *Rivista di Antropologia* 73:1–9.

Goodman A. H., D. L. Martin, C. P. Klein, M. S. Peele, N. A. Cruse, L. R. McEwen, A. Saeed, and B. M. Robinson
1993 Cluster Bands, Wilson Bands, and Pit Patches: Histological and Enamel Surface Indicators of Stress in Black Mesa Anasazi Population. *Journal of Paleopathology* 2:115–27.

Goodman, A. H., R. B. Thomas, A. C. Swedlund, and G. J. Armelagos
1988 Biocultural Perspectives on Stress in Prehistoric, Historical, and Contemporary Population Research. *Yearbook of Physical Anthropology* 31:169–202.

Goodman, M. J., P. B. Griffin, A. A. Estioko-Griffin, and J. S. Grove
1985 The Compatibility of Hunting and Mothering among the Agta Hunter-Gatherers of the Philippines. *Sex Roles* 12:1199–1209.

Goody, J.
1973 Bridewealth and Dowry in Africa and Eurasia. In *Bridewealth and Dowry,* edited by J. Goody and S. J. Tambiah, pp. 1–58. Cambridge: Cambridge University Press.
1982 *Cooking, Cuisine, and Class.* Cambridge: Cambridge University Press.

Gordon, J. E., I. Chitkara, and J. Wyon
1963 Weanling Diarrhea. *American Journal of Medical Sciences* 245:345–77.

Gordon, J. E., J. B. Wyon, and W. Ascoli
1967 The Second Year Death Rate in Less Developed Countries. *American Journal of the Medical Sciences* (Sept.):121–44.

Gough, G. R.
1987 The Indian Hill Ceremonial Fertility Site Complex. In *Rock Art Papers,* vol. 5, edited by K. Hedges, pp. 55–60. San Diego Museum Papers 23. San Diego.

Graham, M.

1994 *Mobile Farmers: An Ethnoarchaeological Approach to Settlement Organization among the Rarámuri of Northwestern Mexico.* International Monographs in Prehistory, Ethnoarchaeological Series 3. Ann Arbor, MI.

Grant, C.

1978 *Canyon de Chelly: Its People and Rock Art.* Tucson: University of Arizona Press.

Graves, W. M. II

1996 Social Power and Prestige Enhancement among the Protohistoric Salinas Pueblos, Rio Grande Valley, New Mexico. M.A. thesis, Arizona State University.

Graves, W., and S. Eckert

1998 Decorated Ceramic Distributions and Ideological Developments in the Northern and Central Rio Grande Valley, New Mexico. In *Migration and Reorganization: The Pueblo IV Period in the American Southwest,* edited by K. A. Spielmann, pp. 263–83. Anthropological Research Papers 51. Tempe: Arizona State University.

Grayson, D. K.

1988 *Danger Cave, Last Supper Cave, and Hanging Rock Shelter.* Anthropological Papers of the American Museum of Natural History 66. New York.

Green, T.

1996 Ground Stone Assemblage Variation across the Pajarito Plateau: Subsistence and Society. Paper presented at the 61st annual meeting of the Society for American Archaeology, New Orleans.

Gregory, D. A.

1991 Hohokam Exchange and Interaction. In *Chaco and Hohokam: Prehistoric Regional Systems in the American Southwest,* edited by P. L. Crown and W. J. Judge, pp. 159–93. Santa Fe: School of American Research Press.

Grenard, J. E., and J. Grenard

1992 Ballcourts in Ritual: Another Look-See. *The Petroglyph* 28(6):6–7.

Griffin, P. B.

1967A High-Status Burial from Grasshopper Ruin, Arizona. *Kiva* 33:37–53.

Griswold, G.

1970 *Aboriginal Patterns of Trade between the Columbia Basin and the Northern Plains.* Archaeology in Montana 11 (2–3). Missoula: Montana Archaeological Society.

Gross, G. T., and T. Stone

1994 Marine Shell. In *The Pueblo Grande Project, vol. 4: Material Culture,* edited by M. S. Foster, pp. 167–202. Soil Systems Publications in Archaeology 20. Phoenix.

Guernsey, S. J.
1931 *Explorations in Northeastern Arizona.* Papers of the Peabody Museum, vol. 12, no. 1. Cambridge, MA: Harvard University.

Gumerman, G. J.
1984 *A View From Black Mesa: The Changing Face of Archaeology.* Tucson: University of Arizona Press.
1988 A Historical Perspective on Environment and Culture in Anasazi Country. In *The Anasazi in a Changing Environment,* edited by G. J. Gumerman, pp. 1–24. Cambridge: Cambridge University Press.
1994 Patterns and Perturbations in Southwest Prehistory. In *Themes in Southwest Prehistory,* edited by G. J. Gumerman, pp. 3–10. Santa Fe: School of American Research.

Gumerman, G. J., ed.
1994 *Themes in Southwest Prehistory.* Santa Fe: School of American Research Press.

Gumerman, G. J., and J. S. Dean
1989 Prehistoric Cooperation and Competition in the Western Anasazi Area. In *Dynamics of Southwest Prehistory,* edited by L. S. Cordell and G. J. Gumerman, pp. 99–148. Washington, D.C.: Smithsonian Institution Press.

Gumerman, G., IV
1996 Southwestern Foodways: Beyond Nutrition. Draft ms. on file with C. Szuter.

Gutierrez, R. A.
1991 *When Jesus Came, the Corn Mothers Went Away: Marriage, Sexuality, and Power in New Mexico, 1500–1846.* Stanford, CA: Stanford University Press.

Guyer, J. I.
1988 The Multiplication of Labor: Historical Methods in the Study of Gender and Agricultural Change in Modern Africa. *Current Anthropology* 29:247–72.

Haas, J., and W. Creamer
1993 *Stress and Warfare among the Kayenta Anasazi of the Thirteenth Century A.D.* Fieldiana: Anthropology n.s. 21. Chicago: Field Museum of Natural History.

Haas, J. D., and G. G. Harrison
1977 Nutritional Anthropology and Biological Adaptation. *Annual Review of Anthropology* 6:69–101.

Habicht-Mauche, J. A.
1995 Changing Patterns of Pottery Manufacture and Trade in the Northern Rio Grande Region. In *Ceramic Production in the American Southwest,* edited by B. J. Mills and P. L. Crown, pp. 167–199. Tucson: University of Arizona Press.

1998 Pottery, Food, Hides, and Women: Labor, Production, and Exchange across the Protohistoric Plains-Pueblo Frontier. In *The Archaeology of Regional Interaction in the Prehistoric Southwest*, edited by M. Hegmon, pp. 209–31. Boulder: University Press of Colorado.

Hackbarth, M.

1987 A Descriptive Summary of the Excavation Results at Locus E, AZ AA:12:2, Muchas Casas. In *Field Investigations at the Marana Community Complex,* pp. 121–50. Anthropological Field Studies 14. Office of Cultural Resource Management. Tempe: Arizona State University.

Hagopian, J.

1995 Ceramic Vessels and Status Differentiation: A Case Study from Black Mesa, Arizona. M.A. thesis, Northern Arizona University.

Hantman, J. L., and S. Plog

1982 The Relationship of Stylistic Similarity to Patterns of Material Exchange. In *Contexts for Prehistoric Exchange,* edited by J. E. Ericson and T. K. Earle, pp. 237–63. New York: Academic Press.

Hard, R. J.

1990 Agricultural Dependence in the Mountain Mogollon. In *Perspectives on Southwestern Prehistory,* edited by P. E. Minnis and C. L. Redman, pp. 135–49. Boulder, CO: Westview Press.

Hard, R. J., R. P. Mauldin, and G. R. Raymond

1996 Mano Size, Stable Carbon Isotope Ratios, and Macrobotanical Remains as Multiple Lines of Evidence of Maize Dependence in the American Southwest. *Journal of Archaeological Method and Theory* 3:253–318.

Hard, R. J., and W. Merrill

1992 Mobile Agriculturalists and the Emergence of Sedentism: A Perspective from Northern Mexico. *American Anthropologist* 94:601–20.

Harding, T. G.

1967 *Voyagers of the Vitiaz Strait.* Seattle: University of Washington Press.

Hargrave, L. L.

1970 *Mexican Macaws: Comparative Osteology and Survey of Remains from the Southwest.* Anthropological Papers of the University of Arizona 20. Tucson: University of Arizona Press.

Harris, D. R., and G. C. Hillman

1989 *Foraging and Farming: The Evolution of Plant Exploitation.* London: Unwin-Hyman.

Harris, M.

1993 The Evolution of Human Gender Hierarchies: A Trial Formulation. In *Sex and Gender Hierarchies,* edited by B. D Miller, pp. 57–79. Cambridge: Cambridge University Press.

Harris, M., and E. B. Ross

1987 *Death, Sex, and Fertility: Population Regulation in Preindustrial and Developing Societies.* New York: Columbia University Press.

Harry, K.

1997 Ceramic Production, Distribution, and Consumption in Classic Period Communities. Ph.D. diss., University of Arizona.

Hart, G.

1992 Imagined Unities: Constructions of "The Household" in Economic Theory. In *Understanding Economic Processes,* edited by S. Ortiz and S. Lees, pp. 111–29. Monographs in Economic Anthropology 10. Lanham, MD: University Press of America.

Hartman, B.

1996 The Global Politics of Health and Healthcare for Women. *Reproductive Rights* 86:10–15.

Hastorf, C. A.

1991 Gender, Space and Food in Prehistory. In *Engendering Archaeology: Women and Prehistory,* edited by J. M. Gero and M. W. Conkey, pp. 132–62. Oxford: Basil Blackwell.

Haury, E. W.

1934 *The Canyon Creek Ruin and the Cliff Dwellings of the Sierra Ancha.* Medallion Papers 14. Globe, AZ: Gila Pueblo.

1936 *The Mogollon Culture of Southwestern New Mexico.* Medallion Papers 20. Globe, AZ: Gila Pueblo.

1938 Pottery. In *Excavations at Snaketown, Material Culture,* edited by H. Gladwin, E. Haury, E. Sayles, and N. Gladwin, pp. 168–220. Medallion Papers 25. Globe, AZ: Gila Pueblo.

1940 *Excavations in the Forestdale Valley, East-Central Arizona.* University of Arizona Bulletin 11. Tucson: University of Arizona.

1945 *The Excavation of Los Muertos and Neighboring Ruins in the Salt River Valley, Southern Arizona.* Papers of the Peabody Museum of American Archaeology and Ethnology 24. Cambridge, MA: Harvard University.

1950 *The Stratigraphy and Archaeology of Ventana Cave.* Tucson: University of Arizona Press.

1976 *The Hohokam: Desert Farmers and Craftsmen.* Tucson: University of Arizona Press.

Haury, E. W., and L. L. Hargrave

1931 *Recently Dated Pueblo Ruins in Arizona.* Smithsonian Miscellaneous Collections 82. Washington, D.C.

Haury, E. W. and E. B. Sayles

1947 *An Early Pit House Village of the Mogollon Culture, Forestdale Valley, Arizona.* University of Arizona Bulletin 18, no. 4. Social Sciences Bulletin 16.

Hawkes, K.

1991 Showing Off: Tests of an Hypothesis about Men's Foraging Goals. *Ethnology and Sociobiology* 12:29–54.

Hawkey, D. E.

1988 Use of Upper Extremity Enthesopathies to Indicate Habitual Activity Patterns. M.A. thesis, Arizona State University.

Hayden, B.

1981 Research and Development in the Stone Age: Technological Transitions among Hunter-Gatherers. *Current Anthropology* 22:519–48.

1990 Nimrods, Piscators, Pluckers, and Planters: The Emergence of Food Production. *Journal of Anthropological Archaeology* 9:31–69.

Hayden, B., M. Deal, A. Cannon, and J. Casey

1986 Ecological Determinants of Woman's Status among Hunter-Gatherers. *Human Evolution* 1:449–74.

Hayden, J. D.

1957 *Excavations 1940 at University Indian Ruin, Tucson, Arizona.* Technical Series 5. Globe, AZ: Southwestern Parks and Monuments.

Hayes, A. C., and J. A. Lancaster

1975 *Badger House Community, Mesa Verde National Park.* National Park Service Reports in Archaeology 7E. Washington, D.C.

Hayes, A. C., J. Young, and H. Warren

1981 *Excavation of Mound 7, Gran Quivira National Monument, New Mexico.* Publications in Archaeology 16. Washington, D.C.: National Park Service.

Hays, K. A.

1984 Rock Art of Northern Black Mesa. In *Excavations on Black Mesa, 1982: A Descriptive Report,* edited by D. L. Nichols and F. E. Smiley, pp. 517–40. Southern Illinois University at Carbondale Center for Archaeological Investigations, Research Paper 39. Carbondale.

1990 Chiefs without Chiefdoms, Tribes without Big Men: Priesthood and Power in Pueblo Society. Paper presented at the annual meeting of the American Anthropological Association, Washington, D.C.

1992 Anasazi Ceramics as Text and Tool: Toward a Theory of Ceramic Design "Messaging." Ph.D. diss., University of Arizona.

1993 When Is a Symbol Archaeologically Meaningful? Meaning, Function, and Prehistoric Visual Arts. In *Archaeological Theory: Who Sets the Agenda?* edited by N. Yoffee and A. Sherratt, pp. 81–92. Cambridge: Cambridge University Press.

Hays-Gilpin, K. A.

1993 *Symbolic Archaeology, Science, and Other False Dichotomies.* Paper presented at the New Mexico Archaeological Council Symposium on Archaeological Method and Theory, Albuquerque, NM.

1994 Gender Constructs in the Material Culture of Seventh-Century Anasazi Farmers in Northeastern Arizona. Paper presented at the Gender and Material Culture Conference, University of Exeter, United Kingdom.

1995 Conception and Birth in Basketmaker and Puebloan Rock Art, Landscape, and Architecture. Paper presented at a meeting of the Native American Art Studies Association, Tulsa, Oklahoma.

1996 Anasazi Iconography: Medium and Motif. In *Interpreting Southwestern Diversity: Underlying Principles and Overarching Patterns*, edited by P. R. Fish and J. J. Reid, pp. 55–67. Anthropological Research Papers 48. Tempe: Arizona State University.

Healey, C.

1990 *Maring Hunters and Traders: Production and Exchange in the Papua New Guinea Highlands.* Berkeley: University of California Press.

Hedges, K.

1983 A Re-examination of Pomo Baby Rocks. In *American Indian Rock Art*, vol. 9, edited by F. G. Bock, pp. 10–21. El Toro, CA: American Rock Art Research Association.

Hegmon, M.

1989 Social Integration and Architecture. In *The Architecture of Social Evolution in Prehistoric Pueblos*, edited by W. D. Lipe and M. Hegmon, pp. 5–14. Crow Canyon Archaeological Center Occasional Paper 1. Cortez, CO.

1994 Boundary-Making Strategies in Early Pueblo Societies: Style and Architecture in the Kayenta and Mesa Verde Regions. In *The Ancient Southwestern Community: Models and Methods for the Study of Prehistoric Social Organization*, edited by W. H. Wills and R. D. Leonard, pp. 171–90. Albuquerque: University of New Mexico Press.

1995 *The Social Dynamics of Pottery Style in the Early Puebloan Southwest.* Crow Canyon Archaeological Center Occasional Paper 5. Cortez, CO.

1996 Variability in Food Production, Strategies of Storage and Sharing, and the Pithouse-to-Pueblo Transition in the Northern Southwest. In *Evolving Complexity and Environmental Risk in the Prehistoric Southwest*, edited by J. A. Tainter and B. B. Tainter, pp. 223–50. Proceedings, vol. 24, Santa Fe Institute, Studies in the Sciences of Complexity. Reading, MA: Addison-Wesley.

Hegmon, M., W. Hurst, and J. R. Allison

1995 Production for Local Consumption and Exchange: Comparisons of Early Red and White Ware Ceramics in the San Juan Region. In *Ceramic Production in the American Southwest*, edited by B. J. Mills and P. L. Crown, pp. 30–62. Tucson: University of Arizona Press.

Hegmon, M., M. C. Nelson, and S. Ruth

1998 Abandonment and Reorganization in the Mimbres Region of the American Southwest. *American Anthropologist* 100:148–62.

Hegmon, M., and W. R. Trevathan

1996 Gender, Anatomical Knowledge, and Pottery Production: Implications of an Anatomically Unusual Birth Depicted on Mimbres Pottery from Southwestern New Mexico. *American Antiquity* 61:747–54.

Heidke, J., E. Miksa, and M. Wiley

1996 Ceramic Artifacts. In *Archaeological Investigations of Early Village Sites in the Middle Santa Cruz Valley: Analyses and Synthesis,* edited by J. Mabry, pp. 13-1–13-54. Anthropological Papers 19. Tucson: Center for Desert Archaeology.

Henderson, T. K.

1987a The Growth of a Hohokam Village. In *The Hohokam Village: Site Structure and Organization,* edited by D. Doyel, pp. 97–126. Glenwood Springs, CO: Southwestern and Rocky Mountain Division of the American Association for the Advancement of Science.

1987b *Structure and Organization at La Ciudad.* Anthropological Field Studies 18. Tempe: Arizona State University.

Hendon, J. A.

1996 Archaeological Approaches to the Organization of Domestic Labor: Household Practice and Domestic Relations. *Annual Review of Anthropology* 25:45–61.

1999 Multiple Sources of Prestige and the Social Evaluation of Women in Prehispanic Mesoamerica. In *Material Symbols: Culture and Economy in Prehistory,* edited by J. Robb. Center for Archaeological Investigations Occasional Paper 26. Carbondale: Southern Illinois University.

Herhahn, C.

1995 An Exploration of Technology Transfer in the Fourteenth-Century Rio Grande Valley, New Mexico: A Compositional Analysis of Glaze Paints. M.S. thesis, Arizona State University.

n.d. Glazeware Petrographic Analysis Descriptive Report for Gran Quivira (LA 120), Quarai (LA 95), Pueblo Colorado (LA 476), and Pueblo Blanco (LA 51). Manuscript in the possession of K. Spielmann.

Hermann, N. P.

1993 Burial Interpretations. In *Across the Colorado Plateau: Anthropological Studies for the Transwestern Pipeline Expansion Project,* vol. 18, edited by C. Cohen, D. Bunds, and N. Cella, pp. 77–95. Albuquerque, NM: Maxwell Museum of Anthropology.

Herrington, L.

1982 Water Control Systems of the Mimbres Classic Phase. In *Mogollon Archaeology: Proceeding of the 1980 Mogollon Conference,* edited by P. H. Beckett, pp. 75–90. Ramona, CA: Acoma Books.

Hewett, E. L.

1904 Archaeology of Pajarito Park. *American Anthropologist* n.s. 6:629–59.

1937 *Indians of the Rio Grande Valley.* Santa Fe: School of American Research.

1953 *The Pajarito Plateau and its Ancient People.* Santa Fe: School of American Research.

Hibben, F.

1975 *Kiva Art of the Anasazi at Pottery Mound.* Las Vegas: K. C. Publications.

Hill, J. N.

1970 *Broken K Pueblo: Prehistoric Social Organization in the American Southwest.* Anthropological Papers of the University of Arizona 18. Tucson.

Hill, K., H. Kaplan, K. Hawkes, and A. M. Hurtado

1985 Men's Time Allocation to Subsistence Work among the Ache of Eastern Paraguay. *Human Ecology* 13:29–54.

Hill, W. W.

1982 *An Ethnography of Santa Clara Pueblo, New Mexico.* Edited and annotated by C. H. Lange. Albuquerque: University of New Mexico Press.

Hillier, B., and J. Hanson

1984 *The Social Logic of Space.* Cambridge: Cambridge University Press.

Hillman, G. C., and M. S. Davies

1990 Measured Domestication Rates in Wild Wheats and Barley under Primitive Cultivation, and Their Archaeological Implications. *Journal of World Prehistory* 4:157–222.

Hodder, I.

1992 Gender Representation and Social Reality. In *Theory and Practice in Archaeology,* edited by I. Hodder, pp. 254–61. Oxford: Basil Blackwell.

Hodge, F. W.

1939 A Square Kiva at Hawikuh. In *So Live the Works of Men,* edited by D. D. Brand and F. E. Harvey, pp. 195–214. Albuquerque: University of New Mexico Press.

Hoffer, C. P.

1972 Mende and Sherbro Women in High Office. *Canadian Journal of African Studies* 6:151–64.

Hoffman, J. M.

1993 Human Skeletal Remains. In *The Duckfoot Site,* edited by R. R. Lightfoot and M. C. Etzkorn, pp. 253–96. Occasional Paper 3, Crow Canyon Archaeological Center.

Hoffman, T. L., and D. E. Doyel

1985 Ground Stone Tool Production in the New River Basin. In *Hohokam Settlement and Economic Systems in the New River Drainage, Arizona,* edited by D. E. Doyel and M. D. Elson, pp. 521–64. Soil System Publications in Archaeology 4. Phoenix.

Hoffman, T. L., D. E. Doyel, and M. D. Elson

1985 Ground Stone Tool Production in the New River Basin. In *Proceedings of the 1983 Hohokam Symposium,* part 2, edited by A. E. Dittert, Jr., and D. E. Dove, pp. 655–86. Arizona Archaeological Society Occasional Paper 2. Phoenix.

Howard, A. V.

1985 A Reconstruction of Hohokam Interregional Shell Production and Exchange within Southwestern Arizona. In *Proceedings of the 1983 Hohokam Symposium,* part 2, edited by A. E. Dittert, Jr., and D. E. Dove, pp. 459–72. Arizona Archaeological Society Occasional Paper 2. Phoenix.

1993 Marine Shell Artifacts and Production Processes at Shelltown and the Hind Site. In *Shelltown and the Hind Site: A Study of Two Hohokam Craftsman Communities in Southwestern Arizona,* edited by W. S. Marmaduke and R. J. Martynec, pp. 321–423. Flagstaff: Northland Research.

Howard, J. B.

1985 Courtyard Groups and Domestic Cycling: A Hypothetical Model of Growth. In *Proceedings of the 1983 Hohokam Symposium,* part 1, edited by A. E. Dittert, Jr., and D. E. Dove, pp. 311–26. Arizona Archaeological Society Occasional Paper 2. Phoenix.

Howell, T. L.

1994 Leadership at the Ancestral Zuni Village of Hawikku. Ph.D. diss., Arizona State University.

1995 Tracking Zuni Gender and Leadership Roles across the Contact Period in the Zuni Region. *Journal of Anthropological Research* 51:125–47.

Huckell, B. B.

1984 *The Archaic Occupation of the Rosemont Area, Northern Santa Rita Mountains, Southeastern Arizona.* Arizona State Museum Archaeological Series 147. Tucson: University of Arizona.

1990 Late Preceramic Farmer-Foragers in Southeastern Arizona: A Cultural and Ecological Consideration of the Spread of Agriculture into the Arid Southwestern United States. Ph.D. diss., University of Arizona.

Huckell, L. W.

1998 Macrobotanical Remains. In *Archaeological Investigations of Early Village Sites in the Middle Santa Cruz Valley,* edited by J. Mabry, pp. 57–148. Anthropological Papers 19. Tucson: Center for Desert Archaeology.

Hughes, I.

1977 *New Guinea Stone Age Trade.* Terra Australis 3, Research School of Pacific Studies. Canberra: Australian National University.

Hunter-Anderson, R. L.

1986 *Prehistoric Adaptation in the American Southwest.* Cambridge: Cambridge University Press.

Huntington, F. W.

1986 *Archaeological Investigations at the West Branch Site: Early and Middle Rincon Occupation in the Southern Tucson Basin.* Institute for American Research Anthropological Paper 5. Tucson.

Huntley, D., and C. Herhahn

1996 Technological Change and the Development of Rio Grande Valley Craft Specialization. Paper presented at the 1996 Chacmool Conference, University of Calgary, Calgary, Alberta.

Hurtado, A. M., K. Hawkes, K. Hill, and H. Kaplan

1985 Female Subsistence Strategies among Ache Hunter-Gatherers of Eastern Paraguay. *Human Ecology* 13:1–26.

Hyder, W. D.

1997 Basketmaker Social Identity: Rock Art as Culture and Praxis. In *Rock Art as Visual Ecology: International Rock Art Congress Proceedings,* vol. 1, edited by P. Faulstich, pp. 31–42. Tucson: American Rock Art Research Association.

Iliff, F. G.

1954 *People of the Blue Waters: My Adventures among the Walapai and Havasupai Indians.* New York: Harper Brothers.

Irwin-Williams, C.

1973 The Oshara Tradition: Origins of Anasazi Culture. *Eastern New Mexico Contributions in Anthropology* 5:1–21. Portales: Eastern New Mexico University.

Ivanhoe, F.

1985 Elevated Orthograde Skeletal Plasticity of Some Archaeological Populations from Mexico and the American Southwest: Direct Relation to Maize Phytate Nutritional Load. In *Health and Disease in the American Southwest,* edited by C. Merbs and R. Miller, pp. 165–76. Anthropological Papers 34. Tempe: Arizona State University.

Jackson, T. L.

1991 Pounding Acorn: Women's Production as Social and Economic Focus. In *Engendering Archaeology: Women in Prehistory,* edited by J. M. Gero and M. W. Conkey, pp. 301–28. Oxford: Basil Blackwell.

Jacobs, D.

1992 Increasing Ceremonial Secrecy at a Salado Platform Mound. In *Developing Perspectives on Tonto Basin Prehistory,* edited by C. L. Redman, G. E. Rice, and K. E. Pedrick, pp. 45–60. Roosevelt Monograph Series 2, Anthropological Field Studies 26, Office of Cultural Resource Management. Tempe: Arizona State University.

1994 *Archaeology of the Salado in the Livingston Area of Tonto Basin. Roosevelt Platform Mound Study: Report on the Livingston Management Group, Pinto Creek Complex,* part 1. Roosevelt Monograph Series 3, Anthropological Field Studies 32, Office of Cultural Resource Management. Tempe: Arizona State University.

Jacobs, S. E.

1995 Continuity and Change in Gender Roles at San Juan Pueblo. In *Women and Power in Native North America,* edited by L. F. Klein and L. A. Ackerman, pp. 177–213. Norman: University of Oklahoma Press.

James, S.

1987 Hohokam Patterns of Faunal Exploitation at Muchas Casas. In *Studies in the Hohokam Community of Marana,* edited by G. Rice, pp. 171–286. Anthropological Field Studies 15, Office of Cultural Resource Management. Tempe: Arizona State University.

James, S. R.

1994 Regional Variation in Prehistoric Pueblo Households and Social Organization: A Quantitative Approach. Ph.D. diss., Arizona State University.

Jeançon, J. A

1923 *Excavations in the Chama Valley, New Mexico.* Bureau of American Ethnology Bulletin 81. Washington, D.C.: Smithsonian Institution.

Jett, S. C., and P. B. Moyle

1986 The Exotic Origins of Fishes Depicted on Prehistoric Mimbres Pottery from New Mexico. *American Antiquity* 51:688–720.

Johns, T.

1990 *With Bitter Herbs They Shall Eat It: Chemical Ecology and the Origins of Human Diet and Medicine.* Tucson: University of Arizona Press.

Johnson, P.

n.d. Faunal Remains from the Big Ditch Site. Unpublished ms. in the possession of C. Szuter.

Jones, T. L.

1996 Mortars, Pestles, and Division of Labor in Prehistoric California: A View from Big Sur. *American Antiquity* 61:243–64.

Jorgensen, J. G.

1980 *Western Indians: Comparative Environments, Languages, and Cultures of 172 Western American Indian Tribes.* San Francisco: W. H. Freeman and Company.

1983 Comparative Traditional Economics and Ecological Adaptations. In *Handbook of North American Indians, vol. 10: Southwest,* edited by A. Ortiz, pp. 684–710. Washington, D.C.: Smithsonian Institution.

Josephides, L.

1985 *The Production of Inequality.* London: Tavistock.

Joyce, R.

1992 Images of Gender and Labor in Classic Maya Society. In *Exploring Gender through Archaeology: Selected Papers from the 1991 Boone Conference,* edited by C. Claasen, pp. 63–70. Monographs in World Archaeology 11. Madison, WI: Prehistory Press.

1996 The Construction of Gender in Classic Maya Monuments. In *Gender and Archaeology,* edited by R. P. Wright, pp. 167–95. Philadelphia: University of Pennsylvania Press.

Judd, N. M.

1954 *The Material Culture of Pueblo Bonito.* Smithsonian Institution Miscellaneous Collections, vol. 124. Washington, D.C.

Judge, W. J.

1984 New Light on Chaco Canyon. In *New Light on Chaco Canyon,* edited by D. G. Noble. Santa Fe: School of American Research Press.

1989 Chaco Canyon–San Juan Basin. In *Dynamics of Southwest Prehistory,* edited by L. S. Cordell and G. J. Gumerman, pp. 209–61. Washington, D.C.: Smithsonian Institution Press.

Jung, C. G.

1968 *Psychology and Alchemy.* 2d ed. Bollingen Series 20. Princeton, NJ: Princeton University Press.

Kaemlein, W.

1955 Yuma Dolls and Yuma Flutes in the Arizona State Museum. *Kiva* 20:1–10.

Kaldahl, E. J.

1997 Where the Knapper Works: Intra-Site Spatial and Gender-Related Manufacturing Variation among Pueblo Flintknappers (A.D. 1200s–1325). Paper presented at the annual meeting of the Society for American Archaeology, Nashville.

1999 Late Prehistoric Technological and Social Reorganization along the Mogollon Rim, Arizona. Ph.D. diss., University of Arizona.

Kane, A. E., and C. K. Robinson, compilers

1988 *Dolores Archaeology Program. Anasazi Communities at Dolores: McPhee Village.* Denver: Bureau of Reclamation Engineering and Research Center.

Kantner, J., and N. Mahoney, eds.

2000 *Great House Communities across the Chacoan Landscape.* Anthropological Papers of the University of Arizona. Tucson: University of Arizona Press. In press.

Katz, S. H., M. L. Hediger, and L. A. Valleroy

1974 Traditional Maize Processing Techniques in the New World. *Science* 184:765–73.

Katzenberg, M. A., and P. A. Walker

1992 Perimortem Cranial Trauma in Prehistoric Native Americans in Southwest Colorado [Abstract]. In *Papers on Paleopathology Presented at the Nineteenth Annual Meeting of the Paleopathology Association, Las Vegas, Nevada, 31 March–1 April, 1992,* edited by Eve Cockburn, p. 15.

Keeley, L. H.

1995 Protoagricultural Practices among Hunter-Gatherers: A Cross-Cultural Survey. In *Last Hunters, First Farmers: New Perspectives on the Prehistoric Transition to Agriculture,* edited by T. D. Price and A. B. Gebauer, pp. 243–72. Santa Fe: School of American Research Press.

Kelly, R. L.

1991 Sedentism, Sociopolitical Inequality, and Resource Fluctuations. In *Between Bands and States,* edited by S. A. Gregg, pp. 135–58. Center for Archaeological Investigations Occasional Paper 9. Carbondale: Southern Illinois University.

Kennard, E. A.

1979 Hopi Economy and Subsistence. In *Handbook of North American Indians, vol. 9: Southwest,* edited by A. Ortiz, pp. 552–58. Washington, D.C.: Smithsonian Institution Press.

Kennedy, J. G.

1963 Tesguino Complex: The Role of Beer in Tarahumara Culture. *American Anthropologist* 65:620–40.

Kennedy, K. A. R.

1983 Morphological Variations in Ulnar Supinator Crests and Fossae as Identifying Markers of Occupational Stress. *Journal of Forensic Science* 28:871–76.

1989 Skeletal Markers of Occupational Stress. In *Reconstruction of Life from the Skeleton,* edited by M. Y. Iscan and K. A. R. Kennedy, pp. 129–60. New York: Alan R. Liss.

Kent, K. P.

1957 *The Cultivation and Weaving of Cotton in the Prehistoric Southwestern United States.* Transactions of the American Philosophical Society, n.s. 47(3). Philadelphia.

1983 *Prehistoric Textiles of the Southwest.* Albuquerque: University of New Mexico Press.

Kent, S.

1990a Activity Areas and Architecture: An Interdisciplinary View of the Relationship between Use of Space and Domestic Built Environments.

In *Domestic Architecture and the Use of Space: An Interdisciplinary Cross-Cultural Study*, edited by S. Kent, pp. 1–8. Cambridge: Cambridge University Press.

1990b A Cross-Cultural Study of Segmentation, Architecture, and the Use of Space. In *Domestic Architecture and the Use of Space: An Interdisciplinary Cross-Cultural Study*, edited by S. Kent, pp. 127–52. Cambridge: Cambridge University Press.

Kenzle, S.

1993 Enclosing Walls: A Study of Architectural Function in the American Southwest. M.A. thesis, University of Calgary.

Kessler, E.

1976 *Women: An Anthropological View.* New York: Holt, Rinehart, and Winston.

Kidder, A. V.

1958 *Pecos, New Mexico: Archaeological Notes.* Papers of the R. S. Peabody Foundation for Archaeology 5. Andover, MA: Phillips Academy.

Kidder, A. V., and S. J. Guernsey

1919 *Archaeological Explorations in Northeastern Arizona.* Bureau of American Ethnology Bulletin 65. Washington, D.C.

Kintigh, K. W.

1985 *Settlement, Subsistence, and Society in Late Zuni Prehistory.* Anthropological Papers of the University of Arizona 44. Tucson: University of Arizona Press.

Kisselburg, J. A.

1987 Specialization and Differentiation: Non-Subsistence Economic Pursuits in Courtyard Systems at La Ciudad. In *The Hohokam Village: Site Structure and Organization*, edited by D. E. Doyel, pp. 159–70. Glenwood Springs, CO: American Association for the Advancement of Science.

Klein, L. F., and L. Ackerman

1995 *Women and Power in Native North America.* Norman: University of Oklahoma Press.

Kliks, M. M.

1985 Studies on the Traditional Herbal Anthelmintic *Chenopodium ambrosioides L.*: Ethnopharmacological Evaluation and Clinical Field Trials. *Social Science and Medicine* 21:879–86.

Klima, B.

1953 Paleolithic Huts of Dolni Vestonice. *Antiquity* 27:4–14.

Kohler, T.

1992a Field Houses, Villages, and the Tragedy of the Commons in the Early Northern Anasazi Southwest. *American Antiquity* 57:617–35.

1992b Prehistoric Human Impact on the Environment in the Upland North American Southwest. *Population and Environment* 13:255–68.

1996 Prehistoric Villages as Complex Adaptive Systems. *Bulletin of the Santa Fe Institute* 7:30–32.

Kornfeld, M., and J. Francis

1991 A Preliminary Historical Outline of Northwestern High Plains Gender Systems. In *The Archaeology of Gender*, edited by D. Walde and N. D. Willows, pp. 444–51. Calgary, Alberta: Archaeological Association of the University of Calgary.

Kosse, K.

1996 Middle-Range Societies from a Scalar Perspective. In *Interpreting Southwestern Diversity: Underlying Principles and Overarching Patterns*, edited by P. Fish and J. Reid, pp. 87–96. Anthropological Research Papers 48. Tempe: Arizona State University.

Kottak, C.

1975 *Cultural Anthropology*. New York: Random House.

Kramer, C.

1985 Ceramic Ethnoarchaeology. *Annual Review of Anthropology* 14:77–102.

Kristiansen, K.

1984 Ideology and Material Culture: An Archaeological Perspective. In *Marxist Perspectives in Archaeology*, edited by M. Spriggs, pp. 72–100. Cambridge: Cambridge University Press.

Kuhnlein, J., and D. H. Calloway

1979 Adventitious Mineral Elements in Hopi Diets. *Journal of Food Science* 44:282–85.

Kunitz, S. J., and R. C. Euler

1972 *Aspects of Southwestern Paleoepidemiology*. Prescott College Anthropological Reports 2. Prescott, AZ.

Kurz, R. B.

1987 Contributions of Women to Subsistence in Tribal Societies. *Research in Economic Anthropology* 8:31–59.

Kuzawa, C.

1996 Patterns of Age-Related Bone Loss in a Classic Hohokam Population from Pueblo Grande. *Ascent* 4:9–18.

Ladd, E. J.

1979a Zuni Economy. In *Handbook of North American Indians, vol. 9: Southwest*, edited by A. Ortiz, pp. 534–39. Washington, D.C.: Smithsonian Institution.

1979b Zuni Social and Political Organization. In *Handbook of North American Indians, vol. 9: Southwest*, edited by A. Ortiz, pp. 482–91. Washington, D.C.: Smithsonian Institution.

Lallo, J., G. J. Armelagos, and J. C. Rose

1978 Paleoepidemiology of Infectious Disease in the Dickson Mounds Population. *Medical College of Virginia Quarterly* 14:17–23.

Lamphere, L.

1974 Strategies, Cooperation, and Conflict among Women in Domestic Groups. In *Women, Culture, and Society*, edited by M. Z. Rosaldo and L. Lamphere, pp. 97–112. Stanford, CA: Stanford University Press.

1987 Feminism and Anthropology: The Struggle to Reshape Our Thinking about Gender. In *The Impact of Feminist Research in the Academy*, edited by C. Faarnham, pp. 11–33. Bloomington: Indiana University Press.

1993 The Domestic Sphere of Women and the Public World of Men: The Strengths and Limitations of an Anthropological Dichotomy. In *Gender in Cross-Cultural Perspective*, edited by C. B. Brettell and C. F. Sargent, pp. 67–77. Englewood Cliffs, NJ: Prentice Hall.

Lancaster, J.

1986 Ground Stone. In *Short-term Sedentism in the American Southwest*, edited by B. Nelson and S. LeBlanc, pp. 177–90. Albuquerque: University of New Mexico Press.

Lang, R. W.

1982 Transformation in White Ware Pottery of the Northern Rio Grande. In *Southwestern Ceramics: A Comparative Review*, edited by A. H. Schroeder, pp. 153–200. Arizona Archaeologist 15. Phoenix: Arizona Archaeological Society.

Lang, R. W., and A. H. Harris

1984 *The Faunal Remains from Arroyo Hondo Pueblo, New Mexico: A Study in Short-Term Subsistence Change.* Santa Fe: School of American Research Press.

Lange, C.

1959 *Cochiti: A New Mexico Pueblo, Past and Present.* Austin: University of Texas Press.

Langford, B. L.

1986 The Southwest Museum. *American Indian Art* 12:30–37.

Larsen, C. S.

1987 Bioarchaeological Interpretations of Subsistence Economy and Behavior from Human Skeletal Remains. *Advances in Archaeological Method and Theory* 10:339–445.

Laski, V.

1958 *Seeking Life.* Philadelphia: American Folklore Society.

Lauer, P. K.

1970 Amphlett's Islands' Pottery Trade and the Kula. *Mankind* 7:165–83.

Lawton, H. W., P. J. Wilke, M. DeDecker, and W. M. Mason

1976 Agriculture among the Paiute of Owens Valley. *Journal of California Archaeology* 3:13–50.

Leacock, E.

1975 Class, Commodity, and the Status of Women. In *Women Cross-Culturally: Change and Challenge*, edited by R. R. Rohrlich-Leavitt, pp. 601–16. The Hague: Mouton.

1978 Women's Status in Egalitarian Society: Implications for Social Evolution. *Current Anthropology* 19:247–75.

1981 *Myths of Male Dominance: Collected Articles on Women Cross-Culturally.* New York: Monthly Review Press.

1993 Women in Samoan History: A Further Critique of Derek Freeman. In *Sex and Gender Hierarchies,* edited by B. D. Miller, pp. 351–65. Cambridge: Cambridge University Press.

Leatherman, T. L., J. S. Luerssen, L. B. Markowitz, and R. B. Thomas

1986 Illness and Political Economy: The Andean Dialectic. *Cultural Survival Quarterly* 10:19–21.

Lebeuf, A. M. D.

1963 The Role of Women in the Political Organization of African Societies. In *Women of Tropical Africa,* edited by R. Paulme, pp. 93–119. London: Routledge.

LeBlanc, S. A.

1982 Temporal Change in Mogollon Ceramics. *In Southwestern Ceramics: A Comparative Review,* edited by A. H. Schroeder, pp. 107–28. Arizona Archaeologist 15. Phoenix: Arizona Archaeological Society.

1983 *The Mimbres People: Ancient Pueblo Painters of the American Southwest.* London: Thames and Hudson.

1997 A Comment on Hegmon and Trevathan's "Gender, Anatomical Knowledge, and Pottery Production." *American Antiquity* 62:723–26.

1999 *Prehistoric Warfare in the American Southwest.* Salt Lake City: University of Utah Press.

Lechtman, H.

1977 Style in Technology: Some Early Thoughts. In *Material Culture: Styles, Organization, and Dynamics of Technology,* edited by H. Lechtman and R. Merrill, pp. 3–20. New York: West.

Lederman, R.

1986 *What Gifts Engender.* Cambridge: Cambridge University Press.

1990a Big Men, Large and Small? Towards a Comparative Perspective. *Ethnology* 29:3–15.

1990b Contested Order: Gender and Society in the Southern New Guinea Highlands. In *Beyond the Second Sex: New Directions in the Anthropology of Gender,* edited by P. Sanday and R. Goodenough, pp. 43–73. Philadelphia: University of Pennsylvania Press.

Lee, R. B.

1992 Work, Sexuality, and Aging among !Kung Women. In *In Her Prime: New Views of Middle-Aged Women*, edited by V. Kerns and J. Brown, pp. 35–48. Urbana: University of Illinois Press.

Leh, L. L.

1942 *A Preliminary Report on the Monument Ruins in San Juan County, Utah.* University of Colorado Studies, Series C, vol. 1, no. 3.

Lekson, S. H.

1983 *The Architecture and Dendrochronology of Chetro Ketl.* National Park Service, Reports of the Chaco Center 6. Albuquerque, NM.

1986 *Great Pueblo Architecture of Chaco Canyon, New Mexico.* Albuquerque: University of New Mexico Press.

Lepowsky, M.

1990 Gender in an Egalitarian Society: A Case Study from the Coral Sea. In *Beyond the Second Sex: New Directions in the Anthropology of Gender*, edited by P. Sanday and R. Goodenough, pp. 169–223. Philadelphia: University of Pennsylvania Press.

1993 *Fruit of the Motherland.* New York: Columbia University Press.

Levy, J.

1982 *Social and Religious Organization in Bronze Age Denmark: An Analysis of Ritual Hoard Finds.* British Archaeological Reports, International Series 124. Oxford.

Levy, J. E.

1993 *Orayvi Revisited: Social Stratification in an "Egalitarian" Society.* Santa Fe: School of American Research Press.

Lewis, O.

1942 *The Effects of White Contact upon Blackfoot Culture, with Special Reference to the Role of the Fur Trade.* Philadelphia: American Ethnological Society Monographs.

Lightfoot, K. G., and S. Upham

1989 Complex Societies in the Prehistoric American Southwest: A Consideration of the Controversy. In *The Sociopolitical Structure of Prehistoric Southwestern Societies*, edited by S. Upham, K. G. Lightfoot, and R. A. Jewett, pp. 3–30. Boulder, CO: Westview Press.

Lightfoot, R. R.

1994 *The Duckfoot Site, vol. 2: Archaeology of the House and Household.* Occasional Paper no 4. Cortez, CO: Crow Canyon Archaeological Center.

Lightfoot, R. R., and K. A. Kuckelman

1994 Warfare and the Pueblo Abandonment of the Mesa Verde Region. Paper presented at the 59th annual meeting of the Society for American Archaeology, Anaheim, CA.

1995 Ancestral Pueblo Violence in the Northern Southwest. Paper presented at the 60th annual meeting of the Society for American Archaeology, Minneapolis.

Lilley, I.

1985 Chiefs without Chiefdoms? Comments on Prehistoric Sociopolitical Organization in Western Melanesia. *Archaeology of Oceania* 20:60–65.

Lindauer, O., and B. Zaslow

1994 Homologous Style Structures in Hohokam and Trincheras. *Kiva* 59:319–44.

Lindsay, A. J., Jr., J. R. Ambler, M. A. Stein, and P. M. Hobler

1968 *Survey and Excavations North and East of Navajo Mountain, Utah, 1959–1962.* Museum of Northern Arizona Bulletin 45, Glen Canyon Series 8. Flagstaff: Northern Arizona Society of Science and Art.

Linton, R.

1941 Primitive Art. *Kenyon Review* 3:34–51.

Lipe, W.

1989 Social Scale of Mesa Verde Anasazi Kivas. In *The Architecture of Social Integration in Prehistoric Pueblos,* edited by W. D. Lipe and M. Hegmon, pp. 53–72. Crow Canyon Archaeological Center Occasional Paper 1. Cortez, CO.

1992 Summary and Concluding Comments. In *The Sand Canyon Archaeological Project: A Progress Report,* edited by W. D. Lipe, pp. 121–34. Crow Canyon Archaeological Center Occasional Paper 2. Cortez, CO.

1995 The Depopulation of the Northern San Juan: Conditions in the Turbulent 1200s. *Journal of Anthropological Archaeology* 14:143–69.

Lister, R. H., and F. C. Lister

1978 *Anasazi Pottery.* Albuquerque: University of New Mexico Press.

Loftin, J. D.

1991 *Religion and Hopi Life in the Twentieth Century.* Bloomington: Indiana University Press.

Longacre, W. A.

1970 *Archaeology as Anthropology: A Case Study.* Anthropological Papers of the University of Arizona 17. Tucson.

1991 Sources of Ceramic Variability among the Kalinga of Northern Luzon. In *Ceramic Ethnoarchaeology,* edited by W. A. Longacre, pp. 95–111. Tucson: University of Arizona Press.

1996 Modes of Ceramic Production and Distribution: Some Observations from Philippine Ethnoarchaeology. Paper presented at the annual meeting of the Society for American Archaeology, New Orleans.

Lovejoy, C. O., R. S. Meindl, T. R. Pryzbeck, T. S. Barton, K. Heiple, and D. Kotting

1977 Paleodemography of the Libben Site, Ottowa County, Ohio. *Science* 198:291–93.

Lovejoy, C. O., and E. Trinkaus

1980 Strength and Robusticity of the Neanderthal Tibia. *American Journal of Physical Anthropology* 53:465–70.

Lowell, J.

1991a *Prehistoric Households at Turkey Creek Pueblo, Arizona.* Anthropological Papers of the University of Arizona 54. Tucson: University of Arizona Press.

1991b Reflections of Sex Roles in the Archaeological Record: Insights from Hopi and Zuni Ethnographic Data. In *The Archaeology of Gender,* edited by D. Wade and N. D. Willows, pp. 452–61. Calgary, Alberta: Archaeological Association of the University of Calgary.

Luebben, R. A.

1985 Excavation of Four Small Pueblo III Period Sites Situated near Yucca House, Colorado. *Journal of Intermountain Archeology* 4:1–24.

Mabry, J. B.

1998 Conclusions. In *Archaeological Investigations of Early Village Sites in the Middle Santa Cruz Valley,* edited by J. Mabry, pp. 757–92. Anthropological Papers 19. Tucson: Center for Desert Archaeology.

Macintyre, M.

1983 Kune on Tubetube and in the Bwanabwana Region of the Southern Massim. In *The Kula: New Perspectives on Massim Exchange,* edited by J. W. Leach and E. Leach, pp. 369–79. Cambridge: Cambridge University Press.

Magers, P. C.

1986 Weaving at Antelope House. In *Archaeological Investigations at Antelope House,* edited by D. P. Morris, pp. 224–76. Washington, D.C.: National Park Service.

Mann, M.

1986 *The Sources of Social Power.* Cambridge: Cambridge University Press.

Manning, S. J.

1992 The Lobed-Circle Image in the Basketmaker Petroglyphs of Southwestern Utah. *Utah Archaeology* 1992:1–37.

Marmaduke, W. S., and R. J. Martynec, eds.

1993 *Shelltown and the Hind Site: A Study of Two Hohokam Craftsman Communities in Southwestern Arizona.* Flagstaff: Northland Research.

Marshall, M. P., J. R. Stein, R. W. Loose, and J. E. Novotny

1979 *Anasazi Communities of the San Juan Basin.* Public Service Company of New Mexico and New Mexico State Planning Division, Albuquerque and Santa Fe.

Marshall, Y., ed.

1998 Intimate Relations issue. *World Archaeology 29*, no. 3.

Martin, D. L.

1990 Women and Children: Subgroups at Risk in the Transition to Agriculture. Paper presented at the 6th Conference on Hunting and Gathering Societies, University of Alaska, Fairbanks.

1992 Political Economic Perspectives on Skeletal Biology and the American Southwest. Paper presented at the Wenner-Gren Conference on Political Economic Perspectives in Biological Anthropology, A. H. Goodman and T. L. Leatherman, organizers. Cabo San Lucas, Baja California, Mexico.

1997 Violence against Women in the La Plata River Valley (A.D. 1000–1300). In *Troubled Times: Violence and Warfare in the Past*, edited by D. Martin and D. W. Frayer, pp. 45–76. Amsterdam: Gordon and Breach.

1998 Owning the Sins of the Past: Historical Trends, Missed Opportunities, and New Directions in the Study of Human Remains. In *Building a New Biocultural Synthesis*, edited by A. H. Goodman and T. L. Leatherman, pp. 171–90. Ann Arbor: University of Michigan Press.

Martin, D. L., N. J. Akins, A. H. Goodman, and A. C. Swedlund

n.d. *Harmony and Discord: Bioarchaeology of the La Plata Valley.* Santa Fe: Museum of New Mexico Press. In press.

Martin, D. L., and A. H. Goodman

1995 Demography, Diet, and Disease in the Transitional Basketmaker III–Pueblo Period. In *Studies in Ridges Basin Archaeology*, edited by F. E. Smiley and S. A. Gregg, pp. 1–48. Animas–La Plata Monograph Series, Research Paper 4. Flagstaff: Northern Arizona University.

Martin, D. L., A. H. Goodman, G. J. Armelagos, and A. L. Magennis

1991 *Black Mesa Anasazi Health: Reconstructing Life from Patterns of Death and Disease.* Southern Illinois University at Carbondale, Center for Archaeological Investigations, Occasional Paper 14.

Martin, D. L., A. L. Magennis, and J. C. Rose

1987 Cortical Bone Maintenance in an Historic Afro-American Cemetery from Cedar Grove, Arkansas. *American Journal of Physical Anthropology* 74:255–64.

Martin, D. L., and W. D. Seefeldt

1991 Prehistoric Obstetrics: Why Anasazi Women Died Young on Black Mesa, Arizona (A.D. 800–1150). Poster presented at the 60th annual meeting of the American Association of Physical Anthropology, Milwaukee.

Martin, M. K., and B. Voorhies

1975 *Female of the Species.* New York: Columbia University Press.

Martin, P. S.

1961 A Human Effigy of Stone from a Great Kiva near Springerville, Arizona. *Kiva* 26:1–5.

Martin, P. S., W. A. Longacre, and J. N. Hill

1967 *Chapters in the Prehistory of Eastern Arizona, 3.* Fieldiana: Anthropology 57. Chicago: Field Museum of Natural History.

Martin, P. S., and J. B. Rinaldo

1950 *Sites of the Reserve Phase, Pine Lawn Valley, Western New Mexico.* Fieldiana: Anthropology 38(3). Chicago: Field Museum of Natural History.

1960 *Table Rock Pueblo, Arizona.* Fieldiana: Anthropology 51(2). Chicago: Field Museum of Natural History.

Masse, W. B.

1980 *Excavations at Gu Achi: A Reappraisal of Hohokam Settlement and Subsistence in the Arizona Papaguería.* Publications in Anthropology 12. USDI Western Archaeological and Conservation Center. Tucson: National Park Service.

Mathien, F. J.

1984 Social and Economic Implications of Jewelry Items of the Chaco Anasazi. In *Recent Research on Chaco Prehistory,* edited by W. J. Judge and J. D. Schelberg, pp. 173–86. Reports of the Chaco Center 8, Division of Cultural Research, U.S. Department of the Interior. Albuquerque: National Park Service.

Matson, R. G.

1991a *The Origins of Southwestern Agriculture.* Tucson: University of Arizona Press.

1991b Basketmaker II Subsistence: Carbon Isotopes and Other Dietary Indicators from Cedar Mesa, Utah. *American Antiquity* 56:444–59.

Mauldin, R.

1993 The Relationship between Ground Stone and Agricultural Intensification in Western New Mexico. *Kiva* 58:317–30.

Maxwell, T. D., and K. F. Anschuetz

1992 The Southwestern Ethnographic Record and Prehistoric Agricultural Diversity. In *Gardens in Prehistory,* edited by T. Killion, pp. 35–69. Tuscaloosa: University of Alabama Press.

McAnany, P. A.

1992 A Theoretical Perspective on Elites and the Economic Transformation of Classic Period Maya Households. In *Understanding Economic Process: Monographs in Economic Anthropology* 10, edited by S. Ortiz and S. Lees, pp. 85–103. Lanham, MD: University Press of America.

McBrearty, S., and M. Moniz

1991 Prostitutes or Providers? Hunting, Tool Use, and Sex Roles in Earliest Homo. In *The Archaeology of Gender*, edited by D. Walde and N. D. Willows, pp. 71–82. Calgary, Alberta: Archaeological Association of the University of Calgary.

McCafferty, K. E., and D. M. Mittler

1996 Vertebral Osteophytosis in a Hohokam Population. *Ascent* 4:19–30.

McCafferty, S. D., and G. G. McCafferty

1991 Spinning and Weaving as Female Gender Identity in Post-Classic Mexico. In *Textile Traditions of Mesoamerica and the Andes: An Anthology*, edited by M. B. Schevill, J. C. Berlo, and E. B. Dwyer. New York: Garland.

McCreery, P., and E. Malotki

1994 *Tapamveni: The Rock Art Galleries of Petrified Forest and Beyond.* Petrified Forest, AZ: Petrified Forest Museum Association.

McCreery, P., and J. McCreery

1986 A Petroglyph Site with Possible Hopi Ceremonial Association. In *American Indian Rock Art*, vol. 2, edited by E. Snyder, pp. 1–7. El Toro, CA: American Rock Art Research Association.

McElmurry, B. J., K. F. Norr, and R. S. Parker

1993 *Women's Health and Development.* Boston: Jones and Bartlett.

McGaw, J.

1996 Reconceiving Technology: Why Feminine Technologies Matter. In *Gender and Archaeology*, edited by R. Wright, pp. 79–110. Philadelphia: University of Pennsylvania Press.

McGee, W. J.

1898 *The Seri Indians.* U.S. Bureau of American Ethnology, Annual Report 17 (part 1), pp. 1–344. Washington, D.C.

McGowan, C.

1978 Female Fertility and Rock Art. In *American Indian Rock Art*, vol. 4, edited by E. Snyder, A. J. Bock, and F. Bock, pp. 26–40. El Toro, CA: American Rock Art Research Association.

McGregor, J. C.

1943 Burial of an Early American Magician. *Proceedings of the American Philosophical Society* 86: 270–89.

McGuire, R. H.

1986 Economies and Modes of Production in the Prehistoric Southwestern Periphery. In *Ripples in the Chichimec Sea*, edited by F. J. Mathien and R. H. McGuire, pp. 243–69. Carbondale: Southern Illinois University Press.

1992 *Death, Society, and Ideology in a Hohokam Community.* Boulder, CO: Westview Press.

McGuire, R. H., and A. V. Howard

1987 The Structure and Organization of Hohokam Shell Exchange. *Kiva* 52:113–46.

McGuire, R. H., and D. J. Saitta

1996 Although They Have Pretty Captains, They Obey Them Badly: The Dialectics of Prehispanic Western Pueblo Social Organization. *American Antiquity* 61:197–216.

McNeish, A. S.

1986 The Interrelationship between Chronic Diarrhoea and Malnutrition. In *Diarrhoea and Malnutrition in Childhood,* edited by A. Smith-Walker and A. S. McNeish, pp. 1–6. London: Buttersworth.

Meigs, A.

1990 Multiple Gender Ideologies and Statuses. In *Beyond the Second Sex: New Directions in the Anthropology of Gender,* edited by P. Sanday and R. Goodenough, pp. 101–12. Philadelphia: University of Pennsylvania Press.

Mellaart, J.

1975 *The Neolithic of the New East.* New York: Charles Scribner.

Merbs, C. F.

1983 *Patterns of Activity-Induced Pathology in a Canadian Inuit Population.* Mercury Series Paper 119. Ottowa, Canada: National Museum of Man.

1989 Trauma. In *Reconstruction of Life from the Skeleton,* edited by M. Y. Iscan and K. A. R. Kennedy, pp. 161–99. New York: Alan R. Liss.

Merbs, C. F., and E. Vestergaard

1985 The Paleopathology of Sundown, a Prehistoric Site near Prescott, Arizona. In *Health and Disease in the Prehistoric Southwest,* edited by C. Merbs and R. Miller, pp. 85–103. Anthropological Research Papers 34. Tempe: Arizona State University.

Merriam, C. H.

1955 *Studies of California Indians.* Edited by the staff of the Department of Anthropology, University of California. Berkeley: University of California Press.

Merrill, W. L.

1978 Thinking and Drinking: A Rarámuri Interpretation. In *The Nature and Status of Ethnobotany,* edited by R. Ford, pp. 101–17. Museum of Anthropology Anthropological Paper 67. Ann Arbor: University of Michigan.

Meskell, L.

1998 Running the Gamut: Gender, Girls, and Goddesses. *American Journal of Archaeology* 102:181–85.

Messer, E.

1978 *Zapotec Plant Knowledge: Classification, Uses, and Communication about Plants in Mitla, Oaxaca, Mexico.* Memoirs of the Museum of Anthropology, University of Michigan 10 (2). Ann Arbor.

Mick-O'Hara, L.

1994 Nutritional Stability and Changing Faunal Resource Use in La Plata Valley Prehistory. Ph.D. diss., University of New Mexico.

Miksicek, C.

1984 Historic Desertification, Prehistoric Vegetation Change, and Hohokam Subsistence in the Salt-Gila Basin. In *Hohokam Archaeology along the Salt-Gila Aqueduct, Central Arizona Project, vol. 7: Environment and Subsistence,* edited by L. Teague and P. Crown, pp. 53–80. Arizona State Museum Archaeological Series 150. Tucson: University of Arizona.

Miles, J. S.

1966 Diseases Encountered at Mesa Verde, Colorado: Evidences of Disease. In *Human Palaeopathology,* edited by S. Jarcho, pp. 91–97. New Haven, CT: Yale University Press.

Miller, B. D., ed.

1993 *Sex and Gender Hierarchies.* Cambridge: Cambridge University Press.

Miller, B. D.

1993 The Anthropology of Sex and Gender Hierarchies. In *Sex and Gender Hierarchies,* edited by B. D. Miller, pp. 3–31. Cambridge: Cambridge University Press.

Mills, B. J., ed.

2000 *Alternative Leadership Strategies in the Prehispanic Southwest.* Tucson: University of Arizona Press.

Mills, B. J.

1989 Ceramics and Settlement in the Cedar Mesa Area, Southeastern Utah: A Methological Approach. Ph.D. diss., University of New Mexico.

1993 Functional Variation in the Ceramic Assemblages. In *Across the Colorado Plateau: Anthropological Studies for the Transwestern Pipeline Expansion Project, vol. 16: Interpretation of Ceramic Artifacts,* by B. Mills, C. Goetze, and N. Zedeño, pp. 301–46. Albuquerque: Office of Contract Archeology and Maxwell Museum of Anthropology, University of New Mexico.

1995a The Organization of Protohistoric Zuni Ceramic Production. *In Ceramic Production in the American Southwest,* edited by B. Mills and P. Crown, pp. 200–230. Tucson: University of Arizona Press.

1995b Gender and the Reorganization of Historic Zuni Craft Production: Implications for Archaeological Interpretation. *Journal of Anthropological Research* 51:149–72.

1998 Migration and Pueblo IV Community Reorganization in the Silver Creek Area, East-Central Arizona. In *Migration and Reorganization: The Pueblo IV Period in the American Southwest,* edited by K. A. Spielmann, pp. 65–80. Anthropological Research Papers 51. Tempe: Arizona State University.

1999 Ceramics and the Social Contexts of Consumption in the Northern Southwest. In *Pottery and People: A Dynamic Interaction,* edited by J. M. Skibo and G. M. Feinman, pp. 99–114. Salt Lake City: University of Utah Press.

2000 Alternative Models, Alternative Strategies: Leadership in the Prehispanic Southwest. In *Alternative Leadership Strategies in the Prehispanic Southwest,* edited by B. J. Mills. Tucson: University of Arizona Press.

Mills, B. J., A. Carpenter, and W. Grimm

1997 Sourcing Chuskan Ceramics: Petrographic and Experimental Analyses. *Kiva* 62:261–82.

Mills, B. J., and P. L. Crown

1995 Ceramic Production in the American Southwest: An Introduction. In *Ceramic Production in the American Southwest,* edited by B. Mills and P. Crown, pp. 1–29. Tucson: University of Arizona Press.

Mills, B. J., and P. L. Crown, eds.

1995 *Ceramic Production in the American Southwest.* Tucson: University of Arizona Press.

Mills, B. J., S. A. Herr, and S. Van Keuren, eds.

1999 *Living on the Edge of the Rim: Excavations and Analysis of the Silver Creek Archaeological Research Project, 1993–1998.* Arizona State Museum Archaeological Series 192. Tucson: University of Arizona.

Minnis, P. E.

1985 *Social Adaptation to Food Stress: A Prehistoric Southwestern Example.* Chicago: University of Chicago Press.

1988 Four Examples of Specialized Production at Casas Grandes, Northwestern Chihuahua. *Kiva* 53:181–93.

1989 Prehistoric Diet in the Northern Southwest: Macroplant Remains from Four Corners Feces. *American Antiquity* 54:543–63.

Mintz, S.

1971 Men, Women, and Trade. *Comparative Studies in Society and History* 13:247–69.

1985 *Sweetness and Power: The Place of Sugar in Modern History.* New York: Viking Press.

Mitchell, D. R.

1991 An Investigation of Two Classic Period Hohokam Cemeteries. *North American Archaeologist* 12:109–27.

1994 The Pueblo Grande Burial Artifact Analysis: A Search for Wealth, Ranking, and Prestige. In *The Pueblo Grande Project, vol. 7: An Analysis of Classic Period Hohokam Mortuary Practices*, edited by D. R. Mitchell, pp. 129–80. Soil Systems Publications in Archaeology 20. Phoenix.

Mitchell, D. R., ed.

1994a *The Pueblo Grande Project, vol. 2: Feature Descriptions, Chronology, and Site Structure.* Soil Systems Publications in Archaeology 20. Phoenix.

1994b *The Pueblo Grande Project, vol. 7: An Analysis of Classic Period Mortuary Patterns.* Soil Systems Publications in Archaeology 20. Phoenix.

Mobley-Tanaka, J. L.

1990 Community and Community Interaction at Chimney Rock, Colorado. M.A. thesis, University of Colorado.

1997a Gender and Ritual Space in the Pithouse to Pueblo Transitions: Subterranean Mealing Rooms in the North American Southwest. *American Antiquity* 62:437–48.

1997b The History and Prehistory of Yellow Jacket. *Southwestern Lore* 63.

n.d. A Preliminary Analysis of Designs on Sourced Glaze Wares at Gran Quivira (LA120), New Mexico. Report in the possession of K. Spielmann.

Mohr Chavez, K. L.

1992 The Organization of Production and Distribution of Traditional Pottery in South Highland Peru. In *Production and Distribution: An Integrated Approach*, edited by G. J. Bey and C. A. Pool, pp. 49–92. Boulder, CO: Westview Press.

Molleson, T.

1994 The Eloquent Bones of Abu Hureyra. *Scientific American*:70–75.

Moore, H. L.

1986 *Space, Text, and Gender: An Anthropological Study of the Marakwet of Kenya.* New York: Guilford Press.

1992 Households and Gender Relations: The Modeling of the Economy. In *Understanding Economic Process: Monographs in Economic Anthropology* 10, edited by S. Ortiz and S. Lees, pp 131–48. Lanham, MD: University Press of America.

Moore, J., and E. Scott

1997 *Invisible People and Processes: Writing Gender and Childhood into European Archaeology.* London: Leicester University Press.

Morelli, G.

1997 Growing Up Female in a Farmer Community and a Forager Community. In *The Evolving Female*, edited by M. E. Morbeck, A. Galloway, and A. Zihlman, pp. 209–19. Princeton, NJ: Princeton University Press.

Morley, S. G.

1914 The Excavation of the Cannonball Ruins in Southwestern Colorado. *American Anthropologist* n.s. 10:596–610.

Morris, D. H.

1990 Changes in Groundstone following the Introduction of Maize into the American Southwest. *Journal of Anthropological Research* 46:177–94.

Morris, E. A.

1980 *Basketmaker Caves in the Prayer Rock District, Northeastern Arizona.* Anthropological Papers of the University of Arizona 35. Tucson: University of Arizona Press.

Morris, E. H.

1924 *Burials in the Aztec Ruin.* Anthropological Papers of the American Museum of Natural History 31 (part 3). New York.

1925 Exploring the Canyon of Death. *National Geographic* 48:262–300.

1939 *Archaeological Studies in the La Plata District, Southwestern Colorado and Northwestern New Mexico.* Carnegie Institution of Washington, Publication 519. Washington, D.C.

1951 Basketmaker III Human Figurines from Northeastern Arizona. *American Antiquity* 7:33–40.

Morris, E. H., and R. F. Burgh

1954 *Basket Maker II Sites near Durango, Colorado.* Carnegie Institution Publication 604. Washington, D.C.

Morris, J. N.

1991 *Archaeological Investigations of the Hovenweep Laterals.* Four Corners Archaeological Project Report 14. Cortez, CO: Complete Archaeological Service Associates.

Morss, N.

1954 *Clay Figurines of the American Southwest.* Papers of the Peabody Museum of American Archaeology and Ethnology 44. Cambridge, MA.

Moulard, B.

1984 *Within the Underworld Sky.* Pasadena: Twelvetrees Press.

Mukhopadhyay, C. C., and P. J. Higgins

1988 Anthropological Studies of Women's Status Revisited: 1977–1987. *Annual Review of Anthropology* 17:461–95.

Munson, M.

2000 Sex, Gender, and Status: Human Images from the Classic Mimbres. *American Antiquity* 65:127–44.

Munson, N.

1996 An Investigation of Spanish Influence at Pecos Pueblo Utilizing Musculoskeletal Stress Markers. M.A. thesis, Arizona State University.

Murdock, G. P., and C. Provost

1973 Factors in the Division of Labor by Sex: A Cross-Cultural Analysis. *Ethnology* 12:203–25.

Murphy, R. F., and Y. Murphy

1980 Women, Work and Property in a South American Tribe. In *Theory and Practice: Essays Presented to Gene Weltfish,* edited by S. Diamond, pp. 179–94. New York: Mouton.

Nagy, B. L., and D. E. Hawkey

1993 Correspondence of Osteoarthritis and Muscle Use in Reconstructing Prehistoric Activity Patterns. Paper presented at the 20th annual meeting of the Paleopathology Association, Toronto.

Nash, J.

1978 The Aztecs and the Ideology of Male Dominance. *Signs* 4:349–62.

1993 *Crafts in Global Markets: Changes in Artisan Production in Middle America.* Albany: State University of New York Press.

Nash, M.

1961 The Social Context of Economic Choice in a Small Society. *Man* 61:186–91.

Neff, L. S.

1996 Ancient Pueblo Spinning Traditions in the Northern Southwest. M.A. thesis, Northern Arizona University.

Neitzel, J.

1991 Hohokam Material Culture and Behavior: The Dimensions of Organizational Change. In *Exploring the Hohokam: Prehistoric Desert Peoples of the American Southwest,* edited by G. J. Gumerman, pp. 177–230. Albuquerque: University of New Mexico Press.

Nelson, B.

1986 Ceramics. In *Short-Term Sedentism in the American Southwest: The Mimbres Valley Salado,* edited by B. Nelson and S. LeBlanc, pp. 121–40. Albuquerque: University of New Mexico Press.

1991 Ceramic Frequency and Use-Life: A Highland Mayan Case in Cross-Cultural Perspective. In *Ceramic Ethnoarchaeology,* edited by W. Longacre, pp. 162–81. Tucson: University of Arizona Press.

Nelson, B. A., and R. Anyon

1996 Fallow Valleys: Asynchronous Occupations in Southwestern New Mexico. *Kiva* 61:241–56.

Nelson, B. A., D. L. Martin, A. C. Swedlund, P. R. Fish, and G. J. Armelagos

1994 Studies in Disruption: Demography and Health in the Prehistoric American Southwest. In *Understanding Complexity in the Prehistoric Southwest,* edited by G. Gumerman and M. Gell-Mann, pp. 59–112. New York: Addison, Wesley.

Nelson, M. C.

1991 The Study of Technological Organization. In *Archaeological Method and Theory,* vol. 3, edited by M. B. Schiffer, pp. 57–100. Tucson: University of Arizona Press.

1993 Changing Occupational Patterns among Prehistoric Horticulturalists in Southwest New Mexico. *Journal of Field Archaeology* 20:43–57.

1999 *Mimbres during the Twelfth Century: Abandonment, Continuity, and Reorganization.* Tucson: University of Arizona Press.

Nelson, M. C., and M. Hegmon

1995 Eastern Mimbres Archaeological Project: Archaeological Research on the Ladder Ranch, 1995. Report submitted to Turner Foundation.

Nelson, S. M.

1993 Gender Hierarchy and the Queens of Silla. In *Sex and Gender Hierarchies,* edited by B. D. Miller, pp. 297–315. Cambridge: Cambridge University Press.

1997 *Gender in Archaeology: Analyzing Power and Prestige.* London: Altamira Press.

Nerlove, S. B.

1974 Women's Workload and Infant Feeding Practices: A Relationship with Demographic Implications. *Ethnology* 13:207–14.

Nesbitt, P. H.

1938 *Starkweather Ruin: A Mogollon-Pueblo Style Site in the Upper Gila Area of New Mexico, and Affiliative Aspects of the Mogollon Culture.* Logan Museum Publications in Anthropology, Bulletin 6. Beloit, WI.

Netting, R. M.

1990 Population, Permanent Agriculture, and Polities: Unpacking the Evolutionary Portmanteau. In *The Evolution of Political Systems: Sociopolitics in Small-Scale Sedentary Societies,* edited by S. Upham, pp. 21–61. Cambridge: Cambridge University Press.

1993 *Smallholders, Householders: Farm Families and the Ecology of Intensive, Sustainable Agriculture.* Palo Alto, CA: Stanford University Press.

Nicholas, L. M., and G. M. Feinman

1989 A Regional Perspective on Hohokam Irrigation in the Lower Salt River Valley, Arizona. In *The Sociopolitical Structure of Prehistoric Southwestern Societies,* edited by S. Upham, K. G. Lightfoot, and R. A. Jewett, pp. 199–236. Boulder, CO: Westview Press.

Nicholas, L. M., and J. Neitzel

1984 Canal Irrigation and Sociopolitical Organization in the Lower Salt River Valley: A Diachronic Analysis. In *Prehistoric Agricultural Strategies in the Southwest,* edited by S. K. Fish and P. R. Fish, pp. 161–78. Anthropological Research Papers 33. Tempe: Arizona State University.

Nichols, D. L., and F. E. Smiley

1985 An Overview of Black Mesa Archaeology. In *Excavations on Black Mesa, 1983: A Descriptive Report,* edited by A. L. Christenson and W. J. Parry, pp. 47–82. Center for Archaeological Investigations, Research Paper 46. Carbondale: Southern Illinois University.

Ninez, V. K.

1984 *Household Gardens: Theoretical Considerations on an Old Survival Strategy.* Potatoes in Food Systems Research Report 1. Lima, Peru: International Potato Center.

Ogilvie, M.

1993 Sexual Division of Labor as Reflected in Skeletal Morphology at Pottery Mound, New Mexico. Class paper, Anthropology 570, University of New Mexico.

1996 Imaging: A Non-invasive Approach to Behavioral Reconstruction in Preceramic Populations. Paper presented at the Archaic Conference, New Mexico Archaeological Council Meeting, Albuquerque.

O'Kane, W. C.

1950 *Sun in the Sky.* Norman: University of Oklahoma Press.

O'Laughlin, T. C.

1980 *The Keystone Dam Site and Other Archaic and Formative Sites in Northwest El Paso, Texas.* Publications in Anthropology 8. El Paso Centennial Museum.

Ortiz, A.

1969 *The Tewa World: Space, Time, Being, and Becoming in a Pueblo Society.* Chicago: University of Chicago Press.

1979 San Juan Pueblo. In *Handbook of North American Indians, vol. 9: Southwest,* edited by A. Ortiz, pp. 278–95. Washington, D.C.: Smithsonian Institution.

Ortman, S. G.

1998 Corn Grinding and Community Organization in the Pueblo Southwest, A.D. 1150–1550. In *Migration and Reorganization: The Pueblo IV Period in the American Southwest,* edited by K. A. Spielmann, pp. 165–92. Anthropological Research Papers 51. Tempe: Arizona State University.

Ortner, D. J., and W. G. J. Putschar

1981 *Identification of Pathological Condition in Human Skeletal Remains.* Washington, D.C.: Smithsonian Institution Press.

Ortner, S. B.

1974 Is Female to Male as Nature Is to Culture? In *Women, Culture, and Society,* edited by M. Z. Rosaldo and L. Lamphere, pp. 67–87. Stanford, CA: Stanford University Press.

1981 Gender and Sexuality in Hierarchical Societes: The Case of Polynesia and Some Comparative Implications. In *Sexual Meanings: The Cultural Construction of Gender and Sexuality,* edited by S. B. Ortner and H. Whitehead, pp. 359–409. Cambridge: Cambridge University Press.

1996 *Making Gender: The Politics and Erotics of Culture.* Boston: Beacon Press.

Ortner, S. B., and H. Whitehead

1981 Introduction: Accounting for Sexual Meanings. In *Sexual Meanings: The Cultural Construction of Gender and Sexuality,* edited by S. Ortner and H. Whitehead, pp. 1–27. Cambridge: Cambridge University Press.

Ortner, S. B., and H. Whitehead, eds.

1981 *Sexual Meanings: The Cultural Construction of Gender and Sexuality.* Cambridge: Cambridge University Press.

O'Shea, J. M.

1981 Social Configurations and the Archaeological Study of Mortuary Practices: A Case Study. In *The Archaeology of Death,* edited by R. Chapman, I. Kinnes, and K. Randsborg, pp. 39–52. Cambridge: Cambridge University Press.

1984 *Mortuary Variability: An Archaeological Investigation.* New York: Academic Press.

1995 Mortuary Custom in the Bronze Age of Southeastern Hungary: Diachronic and Synchronic Perspectives. In *Regional Approaches to Mortuary Practices,* edited by L. A. Beck, pp. 125–45. New York: Plenum.

Page, R. G.

1940 Hopi Land Patterns. *Plateau* 13:29–36.

Paige, K. E., and J. M. Paige

1981 *The Politics of Reproductive Ritual.* Berkeley: University of California Press.

Palkovich, A. M.

1980 *Pueblo Population and Society: The Arroyo Hondo Skeletal and Mortuary Remains.* Santa Fe: School of American Research Press.

1984 Agriculture, Marginal Environments, and Nutritional Stress in the Prehistoric Southwest. In *Paleopathology at the Origins of Agriculture,* edited by M. N. Cohen and G. J. Armelagos, pp. 425–61. New York: Academic Press.

1985 Disease and Mortality Patterns in the Burial Rooms of Pueblo Bonito: Preliminary Considerations. In *Recent Research on Chaco Prehistory,* edited by W. J. Judge and J. D. Schelberg, pp. 103–13. Albuquerque, NM: Division of Cultural Research, National Park Service.

1987 Endemic Disease Patterns in Paleopathology: Porotic Hyperostosis. *American Journal of Physical Anthropology* 74:527–37.

Paoletti, J. B.

1997 The Gendering of Infants' and Toddlers' Clothing in America. In *The Material Culture of Gender the Gender of Material Culture,* edited by K. Martinez and K. Ames, pp. 27–36. Henry Francis du Pont Winterthur Museum, Delaware.

Parsons, E. C.

1919 Waiyautitsa of Zuni, New Mexico. *Scientific Monthly* 9:443–57.

1932 Isleta, New Mexico. *Forty-seventh Annual Report of the Bureau of American Ethnology for the Years 1929–1930*, pp. 193–466. Washington, D.C.

1939 *Pueblo Indian Religion.* Chicago: University of Chicago Press.

Patterson, A., and M. Patterson

1993 The Rock Art of Bluff, Utah, and the Pendant Circle Complex. In *Utah Rock Art*, vol. 12, edited by F. Harris, pp. 187–211. Green River, UT: Utah Rock Art Research Association, John Wesley Powell Museum.

Patterson-Rudolph, C.

1990 *Petroglyphs and Pueblo Myths of the Rio Grande.* Santa Fe: Ancient City Press.

1997 *On the Trail of Spider Woman: Petroglyphs, Pictographs, and Myths of the Southwest.* Santa Fe, NM: Ancient City Press.

Paul, L., and B. Paul

1978 The Maya Midwife as Sacred Specialist: A Guatemalan Case. *American Ethnologist* 2:707–26.

Peacock, N. R.

1991 Rethinking the Sexual Division of Labor: Reproduction and Women's Work among the Efe. In *Gender at the Crossroads of Knowledge: Feminist Anthropology in the Postmodern Era*, edited by M. di Leonardo, pp. 339–60. Berkeley: University of California Press.

Peckham, S.

1979 When Is a Rio Grande Kiva? In *Collected Papers in Honor of Bertha Pauline Dutton*, edited by A. H. Schroeder, pp. 55–79. Papers of the Archaeological Society of New Mexico 4. Albuquerque.

Pennington, C. W.

1963 *The Tarahumar of Mexico: Their Environment and Material Culture.* Salt Lake City: University of Utah Press.

1969 *The Tepehuan of Chihuahua: Their Material Culture.* Salt Lake City: University of Utah Press.

1980 *The Pima Bajo of Central Sonora, Mexico, vol. 1: Their Material Culture.* Salt Lake City: University of Utah Press.

Pepper, G. H.

1906 Human Effigy Vases from Chaco Canyon, New Mexico. In *Boas Anniversary Volume*, pp. 320–34. New York: American Museum of Natural History.

1909 The Exploration of a Burial Room in Pueblo Bonito, New Mexico. In *Putnam Anniversary Volume*, by his friends and associates, pp. 196–252. New York: G. E. Stechert.

1920 *Pueblo Bonito.* Anthropological Papers of the American Museum of Natural History 27. New York.

Peterson, J.

1994 Chipped Stone. In *Pueblo Grande Project: Material Culture*, edited by M. S. Foster, pp. 49–118. Soil Systems Publications in Archaeology 20, vol. 4. Phoenix.

Peterson, J., D. Mitchell, and M. S. Shackley

1997 The Social and Economic Contexts of Lithic Procurement: Obsidian from Classic-Period Hohokam Sites. *American Antiquity*:231–59.

Peterson, J. T.

1978 *The Ecology of Social Boundaries: Agta Foragers of the Philippines.* Illinois Studies in Anthropology 11. Urbana: University of Illinois Press.

Phagan, C. J.

1988 Nonflaked Lithic Tool Use: Food Preparation. In *Dolores Archaeological Program: Supporting Studies: Additive and Reductive Technologies*, compiled by E. Blinman, C. J. Phagan, and R. H. Wilshusen, pp. 179–204. Denver: USDI Bureau of Reclamation Engineering and Research Center.

Pierce, C.

1996 Why Corrugated? A Functional and Historical Analysis of the Change from Smooth to Corrugated Cooking Pots in the American Southwest. Paper presented at the 61st annual Meeting of the Society for American Archaeology, New Orleans.

Plog, S.

1989 Ritual, Exchange, and the Development of Regional Systems. In *The Architecture of Social Integration in Prehistoric Pueblos*, edited by W. D. Lipe and M. Hegmon, pp. 143–54. Cortez, CO: Crow Canyon Archaeological Center.

1990 Sociopolitical Implications of Stylistic Variation in the American Southwest. In *The Uses of Style in Archaeology*, edited by M. Conkey and C. Hastorf, pp. 61–73. Cambridge: Cambridge University Press.

1995 Equality and Hierarchy: Holistic Approaches to Understanding Social Dynamics in the Pueblo Southwest. In *Foundations of Social Inequality*, edited by T. D. Price and G. M. Feinman, pp. 189–206. New York: Plenum Press.

1997 *Ancient Peoples of the American Southwest.* London: Thames and Hudson.

Plog, S., and S. Powell

1984 Patterns of Culture Change: Alternative Interpretations. In *Papers on the Archaeology of Black Mesa, Arizona*, vol. 2, edited by S. Plog and S. Powell, pp. 209–16. Carbondale: Southern Illinois University Press.

Population Reports

1988 *Mother's Lives Matter: Maternal Health in the Community.* Population Reports. Series L, Issues in World Health, no. 7. Baltimore, MD: Johns Hopkins University.

Potter, J.

1995 The Effects of Sedentism on the Processing of Hunted Carcasses in the Southwest: A Comparison of Two Pueblo IV Sites in Central New Mexico. *Kiva* 60:411–28.

1997 Communal Ritual and Faunal Remains: An Example from the Dolores Anasazi. *Journal of Field Archaeology* 24:353–64.

1998 The Open Space Structure of Pueblo IV Period Settlements in the Southwest. In *Migration and Reorganization: The Pueblo IV Period in the American Southwest,* edited by K. A. Spielmann, pp. 137–63. Anthropological Research Papers 51. Tempe: Arizona State University.

Powell, M. L.

1988 *Status and Health in Prehistory: A Case Study of the Moundville Chiefdom.* Washington, D.C.: Smithsonian Institution Press.

Powell, S.

1983 *Mobility and Adaptation: The Anasazi of Black Mesa, Arizona.* Carbondale: Southern Illinois University Press.

Prentice, G.

1986 Origins of Plant Domestication in the Eastern United States: Promoting the Individual in Archaeological Theory. *Southeastern Archaeology* 5:103–19.

Preucell, R.

1988 Seasonal Agricultural Circulation and Residential Mobility: A Prehistoric Example from the Pajarito Plateau, New Mexico. Ph.D. diss., University of California, Los Angeles.

Progress of Nations

1996 *Vital Statistics on Maternal Morbidity and Mortality.* New York: World Health Organization.

Prudden, T. M.

1903 The Prehistoric Ruins of the San Juan Watershed in Utah, Arizona, Colorado, and New Mexico. *American Anthropologist* 5:224–88.

Quinn, N.

1977 Anthropological Studies on Women's Status. *Annual Review of Anthropology* 6:181–225.

Raisz, L. G.

1982 Osteoporosis. *Journal of the American Geriatric Society* 30:127–38.

Raisz, L. G., and B. E. Kream

1983 Regulation of Bone Formation. *New England Journal of Medicine* 309:29–35.

Randsborg, Klaus

1974 Social Stratification in Early Bronze Age Denmark: A Study in the Regulation of Cultural Systems. *Praehistorische Zeitschrift* 49:38–61.

1986 Women in Prehistory: The Danish Example. *Acta Archaeologica* 55:143–54.

Rautman, A. E.

1997 Changes in Regional Exchange Relationships during the Pithouse to Pueblo Transition in the American Southwest: Implications for Gender Roles. In *Women in Prehistory*, edited by C. Claassen and R. Joyce, pp. 100–118. Philadelphia: University of Pennsylvania Press.

Ravesloot, J. C.

1987 *The Archaeology of the San Xavier Bridge Site (AZ BB:13:14), Tucson Basin, Southern Arizona.* Cultural Research Management Division, Arizona State Museum, University of Arizona, Tucson.

1988 *Mortuary Practices and Social Differentiation at Casas Grandes, Chihuahua, Mexico.* Anthropological Papers of the University of Arizona 49. Tucson.

1992 Anglo-American Acculturation of the Gila River Pima: The Mortuary Evidence. Paper presented at the 25th Annual Conference on Historical and Underwater Archaeology, Kingston, Jamaica.

Ravesloot, J. C., J. S. Dean, and M. Foster

1995 New Perspectives on the Casas Grandes Tree-Ring Dates. In *The Gran Chichimeca: Essays on the Archaeology and History of Northern Mesoamerica*, edited by J. E. Reyman, pp. 240–51. Brookfield, VT: Ashgate.

Rea, A.

1997 *At the Desert's Green Edge: Ethnobotany of the Pima Indians.* Tucson: University of Arizona Press.

Reid, J. J.

1989 A Grasshopper Perspective on the Mogollon of the Arizona Mountains. In *Dynamics of Southwest Prehistory*, edited by L. S. Cordell and G. J. Gumerman, pp. 65–97. Washington, D.C.: Smithsonian Institution Press.

Reid, K. C.

1989 A Materials Science Perspective on Hunter-Gatherer Pottery. In *Pottery Technology: Ideas and Approaches*, edited by G. Bronitsky, pp. 167–80. Boulder, CO: Westview.

Reinhard, K. J.

1988 Cultural Ecology of Prehistoric Parasitism on the Colorado Plateau as evidenced by Coprology. *American Journal of Physical Anthropology* 77:355–66.

1990 Archaeoparasitology in North America. *American Journal of Physical Anthropology* 82:145–63.

Renaud, E. B.

1929 Prehistoric Female Figurines from America and the Old World. *The Scientific Monthly* 28:507–12.

1938 *Petroglyphs of North Central New Mexico.* Archaeological Survey Series, Eleventh Report, Department of Anthropology. Denver: University of Denver.

Reverby, S. M., and D. O. Helly

1992 Introduction: Converging on History. In *Gendered Domains: Rethinking Public and Private in Women's History,* edited by D. Helly and S. Reverby, pp. 1–24. Ithaca: Cornell University Press.

Rice, G. E., ed.

1987 *The Hohokam Community of La Ciudad.* Office of Cultural Resource Management Report 69. Tempe: Arizona State University.

1998 *A Synthesis of Tonto Basin Prehistory: The Roosevelt Archaeology Studies, 1989 to 1998.* Roosevelt Monograph Series 12, Anthropological Field Studies 41, Office of Cultural Resource Management. Tempe: Arizona State University.

Rice, P. M.

1991 Women and Prehistoric Pottery Production. In *The Archaeology of Gender,* edited by D. Wade and N. D. Willows, pp. 436–43. Calgary, Alberta: Archaeological Association of the University of Calgary.

Rinaldo, J., and E. Bluhm

1956 Late Mogollon Pottery types of the Reserve Area. *Fieldiana: Anthropology* 36:149–87.

Robb, J.

1999 Secret Agents: Culture, Economy, and Social Reproduction. In *Material Symbols: Culture and Economy in Prehistory,* edited by J. E. Robb, pp. 3–15. Center for Archaeological Investigations Occasional Paper 26. Carbondale: Southern Illinois University Press.

Roberts, F. H. H.

1929 *Shabik'eschee Village: A Late Basketmaker Site in the Chaco Canyon, New Mexico.* Bureau of American Ethnology Bulletin 92. Washington, D.C.: Smithsonian Institution.

Robins, M. R.

1998 Modeling San Juan Basketmaker Socio-economic Organization: A Preliminary Study in Rock Art and Social Dynamics. M.A. thesis, Northern Arizona University.

Robins, M. R., and K. Hays-Gilpin

n.d. The Bird in the Basket: Basketmaker III Iconography. In *Adaptation, Community, Integration, and Ritual: Recent Research into the Basketmaker III Period in the Northern Southwest,* edited by P. F. Reed. Salt Lake City: University of Utah Press. In press.

Robinson, W. J.

1959 Burial Customs at the Point of Pines Ruin. Master's thesis, Department of Anthropology, University of Arizona, Tucson.

Rogers, R.

1980 The Chemistry of Pottery Smudging. *Pottery Southwest* 7:2–4.

Rogers, S.

1975 Female Forms of Power and the Myth of Male Dominance: Models of Female/Male Interaction in Peasant Society. *American Ethnologist* 2:727–56.

Rohn, A. H.

1971 *Mug House, Mesa Verde National Park, Colorado.* Archaeological Research Series 7D. Washington, D.C.: National Park Service.

1989 Northern San Juan Prehistory. In *Dynamics of Southwestern Prehistory,* edited by L. S. Cordell and G. J. Gumerman, pp. 149–78. Washington, D.C.: Smithsonian Institution Press.

Roosevelt, A. C.

1988 Interpreting Certain Female Images in Prehistoric Art. In *The Role of Gender in Precolumbian Art and Architecture,* edited by V. Miller, pp. 1–34. Washington, D.C.: University Press of America.

Rosaldo, M. Z.

1974 Women, Culture, and Society: A Theoretical Overview. In *Women, Culture, and Society,* edited by M. Rosaldo and L. Lamphere, pp. 17–42. Stanford, CA: Stanford University Press.

1980 The Use and Abuse of Anthropology: Reflections on Cross-Cultural Understandings. *Signs* 5:389–417.

Roscoe, W.

1989 The Semiotics of Gender on Zuni Kachinas. *Kiva* 55:1:49–70.

1991 *The Zuni Man-Woman.* Albuquerque: University of New Mexico Press.

Rosenberg, E. M.

1980 Demographic Effects of Sex-Differential Nutrition. In *Nutritional Anthropology,* edited by N. Jerome, R. Kandel, and G. Pelto, pp. 183–203. New York: Redgrave.

Roth, B. J., and B. B. Huckell

1992 Cortaro Points and the Archaic of Southern Arizona. *Kiva* 57:353–70.

Russell, F.

1975 *The Pima Indians.* Twenty-sixth Annual Report of the Bureau of American Ethnology for the Years 1904–1905. Reprint. Tucson: University of Arizona Press.

Russo, P., and C. Cramoy

1984 Nutrition and Pregnancy. In *Nutrition in the Twentieth Century,* edited by M. Winick, pp. 47–90. New York: John Wiley.

Sacks, K.

1974 Engels Revisited: Women, the Organization of Production, and Private Property. In *Women, Culture and Society,* edited by M. Rosaldo and L. Lamphere, pp. 207–22. Stanford, CA: Stanford University Press.

1976 State Bias and Women's Status. *American Anthropologist* 78:565–69.

1979 *Sisters and Wives: The Past and Future of Sexual Equality*. Westport, CT: Greenwood.

Sanday, P. R.

1973 Toward a Theory of the Status of Women. *American Anthropologist* 75:1682–1700.

1974 Women's Status in the Public Domain. In *Women, Culture, and Society,* edited by M. Z. Rosaldo and L. Lamphere, pp. 189–206. Stanford, CA: Stanford University Press.

1981 *Female Power and Male Dominance: On the Origins of Sexual Inequality.* Cambridge: Cambridge University Press.

1990 Introduction. In *Beyond the Second Sex: New Directions in the Anthropology of Gender,* edited by P. Sanday and R. Goodenough, pp. 1–19. Philadelphia: University of Pennsylvania Press.

Sando, J.

1979 Jemez Pueblo. In *Handbook of North American Indians, vol. 9: Southwest,* edited by A. Ortiz, pp. 418–29. Washington, D.C.: Smithsonian Institution.

Sassaman, K. E.

1992a Lithic Technology and the Hunter-Gatherer Sexual Division of Labor. *North American Archaeologist* 13:249–62.

1992b Gender and Technology at the Archaic-Woodland "Transition." In *Exploring Gender through Archaeology: Selected Papers from the 1991 Boone Conference,* edited by C. Claasen, pp. 71–79. Monographs in World Archaeology 11. Madison,WI: Prehistory Press.

1995 The Social Contradictions of Traditional and Innovative Cooking Technologies in the Prehistoric American Southeast. In *The Emergence of Pottery,* edited by B. Barnett and J. Hoopes, pp. 223–40. Washington, D.C.: Smithsonian Institution Press.

Saul, M. B.

1981 Appendix B: Disposal of the Dead at Las Colinas. In *The 1968 Excavations at Mound 8, Las Colinas Group, Phoenix, Arizona,* edited by L. C. Hammack and A. P. Sullivan, pp. 257–68. Arizona State Museum Archaeological Series 154. Tucson.

1988 Mortuary Deposits. In *The 1982–1984 Excavations at Las Colinas: Material Culture,* edited by D. A. Gregory and C. Heathington, pp. 413–59. Arizona State Museum Archaeological Series no. 162, vol. 4. Tucson: University of Arizona.

Saxe, A. A.

1970 Social Dimensions of Mortuary Practices in a Mesolithic Population from Wadi Halfa, Sudan. Ph.D. diss., University of Michigan.

Sayles, E. B.

1983 *The Cochise Cultural Sequence in Southeastern Arizona.* Anthropological Papers of the University of Arizona 42. Tucson: University of Arizona Press.

Schaafsma, P.

1975 *Rock Art in the Cochiti Reservoir District.* Papers in Anthropology 16. Santa Fe: Museum of New Mexico.

1992 *Rock Art in New Mexico.* Rev. ed. Santa Fe: Museum of New Mexico Press.

Schachner, G.

1999 Pueblo I Period Ritual Control and Transformation in the Northern San Juan Region. M.A. thesis, Arizona State University.

Schaller, D. M.

1994 Geographic Sources of Phoenix Basin Plainware Based on Petrographic Analysis. In *Pueblo Grande Project: Ceramics and the Production and Exchange of Pottery in the Central Phoenix Basin,* part 1, edited by D. R. Abbott, pp. 17–90. Soil Systems Publications in Archaeology 20, vol. 3. Phoenix.

Schiffer, M. B.

1975 Behavioral Chain Analysis: Activities, Organization, and the Use of Space. In *Chapters in the Prehistory of Eastern Arizona, 4. Fieldiana: Anthropology* 65:103–19.

1987 *Formation Processes of the Archaeological Record.* Albuquerque: University of New Mexico Press.

1990 Technological Change in Water-Storage and Cooking Pots: Some Predictions from Experiment. In *The Changing Roles of Ceramics in Society: 26,000 b.p. to the Present,* edited by W. D. Kingery, pp. 119–36. Westerville, OH: American Ceramic Society.

Schiffer, M. B., and J. Skibo

1987 Theory and Experiment in the Study of Technological Change. *Current Anthropology* 28:595–622.

Schlanger, S. H.

1988 Patterns of Population Movement and Long-Term Population Growth in Southwestern Colorado. *American Antiquity* 53:773–93.

1994 Food Processing, Mealing Rooms, and the Organization of Prehistoric Society in the American Southwest. Paper presented at the 59th annual meeting of the Society for American Archaeology, Anaheim, CA.

1995 Men's Houses and Women's Places: Gender and Power Relations during the Pithouse to Pueblo Transition. Paper presented at the 60th annual meeting of the Society for American Archaeology, Minneapolis.

1996a Corn, Control, and Complementary Relations in Pueblo Society. Paper presented at the annual meeting of the American Anthropological Association, San Francisco.

1996b Corn Grinding, Mealing Rooms, and Prehistoric Society in the American Southwest. Unpublished ms. Museum of Indian Arts and Culture, Laboratory of Anthropology, Museum of New Mexico. Santa Fe.

Schlanger, S. H., and R. H. Wilshusen

1993 Local Abandonments and Regional Conditions in the North American Southwest. In *Abandonments of Settlements and Regions: Ethnoarchaeological and Archaeological Approaches*, edited by C. M. Cameron and S. A. Tomka, pp. 85–98. Cambridge: Cambridge University Press.

Schlegel, A.

1977a Toward a Theory of Sexual Stratification. In *Sexual Stratification: A Cross-Cultural View*, edited by A. Schlegel, pp. 1–40. New York: Columbia University Press.

1977b Male and Female in Hopi Thought and Action. In *Sexual Stratification: A Cross-Cultural View*, edited by A. Schlegel, pp. 245–69. New York: Columbia University Press.

1977c An Overview. In *Sexual Stratification: A Cross-Cultural View*, edited by A. Schlegel, pp. 344–57. New York: Columbia University Press.

Schlegel, A., ed.

1977 *Sexual Stratification: A Cross-Cultural View.* New York: Columbia University Press.

Schlegel, A., and H. B. Barry III

1986 The Cultural Consequences of Female Contribution to Subsistence. *American Anthropologist* 88:142–50.

1991 *Adolescence: An Anthropological Inquiry.* New York: Free Press.

Schneider, J. S.

1996 Quarrying and Production of Milling Implements at Antelope Hill, Arizona. *Journal of Field Archaeology* 23:299–311.

Schneider, M. J.

1983 Women's Work: An Examination of Women's Roles in Plains Indians Arts and Crafts. In *The Hidden Half: Studies of Plains Indian Women*, edited by P. Albers and B. Medicine. New York: University Press of America.

Schulting, R. J.

1995 *Mortuary Variability and Status Differentiation on the Columbia-Fraser Plateau.* Burnaby, B.C.: Archaeology Press.

Schwarz, M. T.

1997 *Molded in the Image of Changing Woman: Navajo Views on the Human Body and Personhood.* Tucson: University of Arizona Press.

Scott, C. J.

1983 The Evolution of Mimbres Pottery. In *Mimbres Pottery: Ancient Art of the American Southwest*, pp. 39–68. New York: Hudson Hills.

Scudder, T.

1962 *Ecology of the Gwembe Tonga.* Manchester: Manchester University Press.

Sedlin, E. D., H. M. Frost, and A. R. Villanueva

1963 Variations in Cross-Section Area of Rib Cortex with Age. *Journal of Gerontology* 18:9–13.

Semé, M.

1984 The Effects of Agricultural Fields on Faunal Assemblage Variation. In *Papers on the Archaeology of Black Mesa, Arizona,* vol. 2, edited by S. Plog and S. Powell, pp. 139–57. Carbondale: Southern Illinois University Press.

Seymour, D. J.

1988 An Alternative View of Sedentary Period Hohokam Shell-Ornament Production. *American Antiquity* 53:812–29.

Seymour, D. J., and M. B. Schiffer

1987 A Preliminary Analysis of Pithouse Assemblages from Snaketown, Arizona. In *Method and Theory for Activity Area Research: An Ethnoarchaeological Approach,* edited by S. Kent, pp. 549–603.

Shackley, M. S.

1990 Early Hunter-Gatherer Procurement Ranges in the Southwest: Evidence from Obsidian Geochemistry and Lithic Technology. Ph.D. diss., Arizona State University.

1996 Elko or San Pedro? A Quantitative Analysis of Late Archaic Projectile Points from White Tanks, Yuma County, Arizona. *Kiva* 61:413–32.

Shafer, H. J.

1982 Classic Mimbres Phase Households and Room Use Patterns. *Kiva* 48:17–27.

1985 A Mimbres Potter's Grave: An Example of Mimbres Craft Specialization? *Bulletin of the Texas Archaeological Society* 56:185–200.

1991 Archaeology at the NAN Ruin: The 1987 Season. *The Artifact* 29:1–43.

1995 Architecture and Symbolism in Transitional Pueblo Development in the Mimbres Valley, SW New Mexico. *Journal of Field Archaeology* 22:23–47.

1996 The Classic Mimbres Phenomenon and Some New Interpretations. Lecture presented at the ninth Mogollon Conference, Silver City, NM.

1999 The Mimbres Classic and Postclassic. In *The Casas Grandes World,* edited by C. F. Schaafsma and C. L. Riley, pp. 121–33. Salt Lake City: University of Utah Press.

Shaffer, B. S., and K. M. Gardner

1995 The Rabbit Drive through Time: Analysis of the North American Ethnographic and Prehistoric Evidence. *Utah Archaeology* 8:13–25.

Shaffer, B. S., K. M. Gardner, and J. F. Powell

1996 Prehistoric and Ethnographic Pueblo Gender Roles: Continuity of Lifeways from the Eleventh Century to the Early Twentieth Century. Paper presented at the fourth Gender and Archaeology Conference, East Lansing, MI.

1997 Who's Who in Mimbres Pottery Motifs: Identifying the Sex of Portrayed Human Figures. Poster presented at the annual meeting of the Society for American Archaeology, Nashville, TN.

1999 Sexual Division of Labor in the Prehistoric Puebloan Southwest as Portrayed by Mimbres Potters. In *Sixty Years of Mogollon Archaeology: Papers from the Ninth Mogollon Conference,* edited by S. M. Whittlesey, pp. 112–17. Tucson: SRI Press.

Shaffer, B. S., H. A. Nicholson, and K. M. Gardner

1995 Possible Mimbres Documentation of Pueblo Snake Ceremonies in the Eleventh Century. *North American Archaeologist* 16:17–32.

Shaffer, B. S., and C. P. Schick

1995 Environment and Animal Procurement by the Mogollon of the Southwest. *North American Archaeologist* 16:117–32.

Shanks, M., and C. Tilley

1982 Ideology, Symbolic Power, and Ritual Communication: A Reinterpretation of Neolithic Burial Practices. In *Symbolic and Structural Archaeology,* edited by I. Hodder, pp. 129–54. Cambridge: Cambridge University Press.

Shelley, P., and C. Irwin-Williams, eds.

1980 *Investigations at the Salmon Site: The Structure of Chacoan Society in the Northern Southwest.* Portales: Eastern New Mexico University.

Shennan, S.

1993 After Social Evolution: A New Archaeological Agenda? In *Archaeological Theory: Who Sets the Agenda?,* edited by N. Yoffee and A. Sherratt, pp. 53–59. Cambridge: Cambridge University Press.

Shennan, S. E.

1975 The Social Organization of Branc. *Antiquity* 49:279–88.

1985 From Minimal to Moderate Ranking. In *Ranking, Resource, and Exchange,* edited by C. Renfrew and S. Shennan, pp. 27–32. Cambridge: Cambridge University Press.

Shepard, A. O.

1939 Technology of La Plata Pottery. In *Archaeological Studies in the La Plata District,* by E. H. Morris, pp. 249–87. Carnegie Institution of Washington Publication 528. Washington, D.C.

Shepard, H. W.

1938 Report on the Project for the Technical Improvement of Pueblo Pottery. Ms. on file, Laboratory of Anthropology, Museum of New Mexico. Santa Fe.

Shipek, F. C.

1989 An Example of Intensive Plant Husbandry: The Kumeyaay of Southern California. In *Foraging and Farming: The Evolution of Plant Exploitation*, edited by D. R. Harris and G. C. Hillman, pp. 159–70. London: Unwin-Hyman.

Short, S. A.

1999 A Method for Systematic Comparison of Representational Images Based on Generative Grammars. Paper presented at the 1999 International Rock Art Congress, Ripon, WI.

Sillitoe, P.

1985 Divide and No One Rules: The Implications of Sexual Divisions of Labor in the Papua New Guinea. *Man* 20:494–522.

Simon, A. W., and J. C. Ravesloot

1995 Salado Ceramic Burial Offerings: A Consideration of Gender and Social Organization. *Journal of Anthropological Research* 51:103–24.

Sires, E. W.

1984 Hohokam Architecture and Site Structure. In *Hohokam Archaeology along the Salt-Gila Aqueduct, Central Arizona Project, vol. 9: Synthesis and Conclusions*, edited by L. S. Teague and P. L. Crown, pp. 115–40. Arizona State Museum Archaeological Series 150. Tucson: University of Arizona.

1987 Hohokam Architectural Variability and Site Structure during the Sedentary-Classic Transition. In *The Hohokam Village: Site Structure and Organization*, edited by D. Doyel, pp. 171–82. Glenwood Springs, CO: Southwestern and Rocky Mountain Division of the American Association for the Advancement of Science.

Skibo, J., and E. Blinman

1999 Exploring the Origins of Pottery on the Colorado Plateau. In *Pottery and People*, edited by J. Skibo and G. Feinman, pp. 171–83. Salt Lake City: University of Utah Press.

Skibo, J. M., and M. B. Schiffer

1995 The Clay Cooking Pot: An Exploration in Women's Technology. In *Expanding Archaeology*, edited by J. M. Skibo, W. H. Walker, and A. E. Nielsen, pp. 80–91. Salt Lake City: University of Utah Press.

Smiley, F. E.

1985 Chronometric and Early Agricultural Adaptations in Northeastern Arizona: Approaches to the Interpretation of Radiocarbon Dates. Ph.D. diss., University of Michigan.

Smith, B. D.

1992 *Rivers of Change: Essays on Early Agriculture in Eastern North America.* Washington, D.C.: Smithsonian Institution Press.

Smith, M. F.

1988 Function from Whole Vessel Shape: A Method and an Application to Anasazi Black Mesa, Arizona. *American Anthropologist* 90:912–22.

Smith, W.

1952a *Excavations in Big Hawk Valley, Wupatki National Monument, Arizona.* Bulletin 24. Flagstaff: Museum of Northern Arizona.

1952b *Kiva Mural Decorations at Awatovi and Kawaika-a, with a Survey of Other Wall Paintings in the Pueblo Southwest.* Papers of the Peabody Museum of American Archaeology and Ethnology, vol. 37. Cambridge, MA: Harvard University.

1972 *Prehistoric Kivas of Antelope Mesa.* Papers of the Peabody Museum of Archaeology and Ethnology 39(1). Cambridge, MA: Harvard University.

1990 [1952] When Is a Kiva? In *When Is a Kiva and Other Questions about Southwestern Archaeology*, edited by R. H. Thompson, pp. 59–75. Tucson: University of Arizona Press. [Originally published in *Excavations in Big Hawk Valley*, pp. 154–65.]

Smith, W., and J. M. Roberts

1954 *Zuni Law: A Field of Values.* Peabody Museum of American Archaeology and Ethnology Paper 44 (1). Cambridge, MA: Harvard University.

Smith, W., R. B. Woodbury, and N. F. S. Woodbury

1966 *The Excavation of Hawiku by Frederick Webb Hodge: Report of the Hendricks-Hodge Expedition*, 1917–1923. Contributions from the Museum of the American Indian, Heye Foundation, vol. 20. New York.

Snodgrass, O. T.

1975 *Realistic Art and Times of the Mimbres Indians.* El Paso: privately published by O. T. Snograss.

Snow, D. H.

1982 The Rio Grande Glaze, Matte-Paint, and Plainware Tradition. In *Southwestern Ceramics: A Comparative Review*, edited by A. Schroeder, pp. 235–78. Arizona Archaeologist 15. Phoenix: Arizona Archaeological Society.

1990 Tener Comal y Metate: Protohistoric Rio Grande maize Use and Diet. In *Perspectives on Southwestern Prehistory*, edited by P. Minnis and C. Redman, pp. 289–300. Boulder, CO: Westview Press.

Sobolik, K. D., L. S. Zimmerman, and B. M. Guilfoyl

1997 Indoor versus Outdoor Firepit Usage: A Case Study from the Mimbres. *Kiva* 62:283–300.

Solway, J. S.

1992 Middle-Aged Women in Bakgalagadi Society (Botswana). In *In Her Prime: New Views of Middle-Aged Women*, edited by V. Kerns and J. K. Brown, pp. 49–58. Urbana: University of Illinois Press.

Spain, D.

1992 *Gendered Spaces.* Chapel Hill: University of North Carolina Press.

Sparling, J.

1974 Analysis of Faunal Remains from the Escalante Ruin Group. In *Excavations in the Escalante Ruin Group, Southern Arizona,* edited by D. E. Doyel, pp. 215–53. Arizona State Museum Archaeological Series 37. Tucson: University of Arizona.

Spencer, R. F., and J. D. Jennings

1965 *The Native Americans: Prehistory and Ethnology.* New York: Harper and Row.

Sperling, S., and Y. Beyene

1997 A Pound of Biology and a Pinch of Culture or a Pinch of Biology and a Pound of Culture? The Necessity of Integrating Biology and Culture in Reproductive Studies. In *Women in Human Evolution,* edited by L. Hager, pp. 137–52. New York: Routledge.

Speth, J. D.

1990 Seasonality, Resource Stress, and Food Sharing in So-Called "Egalitarian" Foraging Societies. *Journal of Anthropological Archaeology* 9:148–88.

Speth, J. D., and S. L. Scott

1989 Horticulture and Large-Mammal Hunting: The Role of Resource Depletion and the Constraints of Time and Labor. In *Farmers as Hunters: The Implications of Sedentism,* edited by S. Kent, pp. 71–77. Cambridge: Cambridge University Press.

Speth, J. D., and K. A. Spielmann

1983 Energy Source, Protein Metabolism, and Hunter-Gatherer Subsistence Strategies. *Journal of Anthropological Archaeology* 2:1–31.

Spielmann, K. A.

1995 Glimpses of Gender in the Prehistoric Southwest. *Journal of Anthropological Research* 51:91–102.

1996 The Evolution of a Frontier: Plains-Pueblo Relations in the Fifteenth Century. In *Interpreting Southwestern Diversity: Underlying Principles and Overarching Patterns,* edited by P. Fish and J. J. Reid, pp. 35–40. Anthropological Research Papers 48. Tempe: Arizona State University.

1998 Ritual Influences on the Development of Rio Grande Glaze A Ceramics. In *Migration and Reorganization: The Pueblo IV Period in the American Southwest,* edited by K. A. Spielmann, pp. 253–61. Anthropological Research Papers 51. Tempe: Arizona State University.

Spier, L.

1928 *Havasupai Ethnography.* New York: American Museum of Natural History.

1933 *Yuman Tribes of the Gila River.* Chicago: University of Chicago Press.

Spiro, M. E.

1993 Gender Hierarchy in Burma: Cultural, Social, and Psychological Dimensions. In *Sex and Gender Hierarchies*, edited by B. D. Miller, pp. 316–33. Cambridge: Cambridge University Press.

Spray, J.

1996 La Plata Valley. *El Palacio* (June):16–22.

Stahl, A. B.

1989 Plant-Food Processing: Implications for Dietary Quality. In *Foraging and Farming: The Evolution of Plant Exploitation*, edited by D. R. Harris and G. C. Hillman, pp. 171–94. London: Unwin Hyman.

Stark, M.

1990 Pottery Exchange from an Ethnoarchaeological Perspective. Ms. in the possession of K. Spielmann.

1992 From Sibling to Suki: Social Relations and Spatial Proximity in Kalinga Pottery Exchange. *Journal of Anthropological Archaeology* 11:137–51.

Steinbock, R. T.

1976 *Paleopathological Diagnosis and Interpretation.* Springfield, IL: Charles C. Thomas.

Stephen, A. M

1936 *Hopi Journal of Alexander M. Stephen*, vols. 1 and 2, edited by E. C. Parsons. New York: Columbia University Press.

Stevenson, M. C.

1887 The Religious Life of the Zuni Child. *Fifth Annual Report of the Bureau of American Ethnology for the Years 1883–1884*, pp. 533–55. Washington, D.C.: Smithsonian Institution.

1904 The Zuni Indians: Their Mythology, Esoteric Fraternities, and Ceremonies. *Twenty-third Annual Report of the Bureau of American Ethnology*, pp. 3–634. Washington, D.C.: Smithsonian Institution.

Steward, J. H.

1938 *Basin-Plateau Aboriginal Sociopolitical Groups.* Bureau of American Ethnology Bulletin 120. Washington, D.C.: U.S. Government Printing Office.

Stickel, E. G.

1968 Status Differentiation at the Rincon Site. *University of California at Los Angeles Archaeological Survey Annual Report* 10, pp. 209–61.

Stiger, M. A.

1977 Anasazi Diet: The Coprolite Evidence. M.A. thesis, University of Colorado.

1979 Mesa Verde Subsistence Patterns from Basketmaker to Pueblo III. *Kiva* 44:133–44.

Stinson, S. L.

1996 Roosevelt Red Ware and the Organization of Ceramic Production in the Silver Creek Drainage. M.A. thesis, University of Arizona.

Stirling, M.

1942 *Origin Myth of Acoma and Other Records.* Bureau of American Ethnology Bulletin 135. Washington, D.C.: Smithsonian Institution.

Stodder, A. W.

1984 Paleoepidemiology of the Mesa Verde Region Anasazi: Demography, Stress, Migration. M.A. thesis, University of Colorado.

1987 The Physical Anthropology and Mortuary Practice of the Dolores Anasazi: An Early Pueblo Population in Local and Regional Perspective. In *Dolores Archaeological Program Supporting Studies: Settlement and Environment,* edited by K. L. Peterson an J. D. Orcutt, pp. 339–504. U.S. Bureau of Reclamation Engineering and Research Center, Colorado.

1990 Paleoepidemiology of Eastern and Western Pueblo Communities in Protohistoric New Mexico. Ph.D. diss., University of Colorado.

Stoltman, J. B.

1999 The Chaco-Chuska Connection: In Defense of Anna O. Shepard. In *Pottery and People: A Dynamic Interaction,* edited by J. M. Skibo and G. M. Feinman, pp. 9–24. Salt Lake City: University of Utah Press.

Stone, T., and M. S. Foster

1994 Miscellaneous Artifacts. In *The Pueblo Grande Project, vol. 4: Material Culture,* edited by M. S. Foster, pp. 203–62. Soil Systems Publications in Archaeology 20. Phoenix.

Storey, R.

1988 Preindustrial Urban Lifestyle and Child Health. Paper presented at the 87th annual meeting of the American Anthropological Association, Phoenix.

Strathern, M.

1972 *Women in Between.* London: Seminar Press.

1984 Domesticity and the Denigration of Women. In *Rethinking Women's Roles: Perspectives from the Pacific,* edited by D. O'Brien and S. Tiffany, pp. 13–31. Berkeley: University of California Press.

Stubbs, S. A., and W. S. Stallings, Jr.

1953 *The Excavation of Pindi Pueblo, New Mexico.* Monographs of the School of American Research 18. Santa Fe.

Swentzell, R.

1990 Remembering Tewa Pueblo Houses and Spaces. *Native Peoples* (Winter):6–12.

Szuter, C. R.

1991a *Hunting by Prehistoric Horticulturalists in the American Southwest.* New York: Garland.

1991b Hunting by Hohokam Desert Farmers. *Kiva* 56:277–92.

Szuter, C. R., and F. Bayham

1989 Sedentism and Animal Procurement among Desert Horticulturalists of the North American Southwest. In *Farmers as Hunters: The Implication of Sedentism,* edited by S. Kent, pp. 80–95. Cambridge: Cambridge University Press.

Tainter, J. A.

1975 The Archaeological Study of Social Change: Woodland Systems in West-Central Illinois. Ph.D. diss., Northwestern University.

1978 Mortuary Practices and the Study of Prehistoric Social Systems. In *Advances in Archaeological Method and Theory,* vol. 1, edited by M. B. Schiffer, pp. 105–41. New York: Academic Press.

Tani, M.

1994 Why Should More Pots Break in Larger Households? Mechanisms Underlying Population Estimates from Ceramics. In *Kalinga Ethnoarchaeology,* edited by W. Longacre, pp. 51–70. Washington, D.C.: Smithsonian Institution Press.

Teague, L.

1984 Role and Ritual in Hohokam Society. In *Hohokam Archaeology along the Salt-Gila Aqueduct, Central Arizona Project, vol. 9: Synthesis and Conclusions,* edited by L. S. Teague and P. L. Crown, pp. 155–85. Arizona State Museum Archaeological Series 150. Tucson: University of Arizona.

1985 The Organization of Hohokam Exchange. In *Proceedings of the 1983 Hohokam Symposium,* part 2, edited by A. E. Dittert, Jr., and D. E. Dove, pp. 397–418. Arizona Archaeological Society Occasional Paper 2. Phoenix.

1998 *Textiles in Southwestern Prehistory.* Albuquerque: University of New Mexico Press.

Tedlock, D.

1979 Zuni Religion and World View. In *Handbook of North American Indians, vol. 9: Southwest,* edited by A. Ortiz, pp. 499–508. Washington, D.C.: Smithsonian Institution.

Thomas, C. M., and J. H. King

1985 Hohokam Figurine Assemblages: A Suggested Ritual Context. In *Proceedings of the 1983 Hohokam Conference,* part 2, edited by A. E. Dittert, Jr., and D. E. Dove, pp. 687–732. Arizona Archaeological Society Occasional Paper 2. Phoenix.

Thoms, H.

1947 The Role of Nutrition in Pelvic Variation. *American Journal of Obstetrics and Gynecology* 54:62–73.

Tice, K. E.

1995 *Kuna Crafts, Gender, and the Global Economy.* Austin: University of Texas Press.

Tiffany, S.

1979a Women, Power, and the Anthropology of Politics: A Review. *International Journal of Women's Studies* 2:430–42.

1979b Introduction: Theoretical Issues in the Anthropological Study of Women. In *Women and Society: An Anthropological Reader,* edited by S. W. Tiffany, pp. 1–35. Montreal: Eden Press Women's Publications.

Titiev, M.

1944 *Old Oraibi: A Study of the Hopi Indians of Third Mesa.* Papers of the Peabody Museum of American Archaeology and Ethnology 22 (1). Cambridge, MA: Harvard University.

1972 *The Hopi Indians of Old Oraibi.* Ann Arbor: University of Michigan Press.

Toll, H. W.

1981 Ceramic Comparisons concerning Redistribution in Chaco Canyon, New Mexico. In *Production and Distribution: A Ceramic Viewpoint,* edited by H. Howard and E. L. Morris, pp. 83–121. British Archaeological Reports, International Series 120. Oxford.

1984 Trends in Ceramic Import and Distribution in Chaco Canyon. In *Recent Research on Chaco Prehistory,* edited by W. J. Judge and J. D. Schelberg, pp. 115–35. U.S. Department of the Interior, Reports of the Chaco Center 8. Albuquerque, NM: National Park Service.

1985 Pottery, Production, Public Architecture, and the Chaco Anasazi System. Ph.D. diss., University of Colorado.

1991 Material Distributions and Exchange in the Chaco System. In *Chaco and Hohokam: Prehistoric Regional Systems in the American Southwest,* edited by P. L. Crown and W. J. Judge, pp. 77–107. Santa Fe: School of American Research Press.

1992 Patterns of Basketmaker III Occupation in the La Plata Valley, New Mexico. Paper presented at the 56th annual meeting of the Society for American Archaeology, New Orleans.

1993 The Role of the Totah in Regions and Regional Definition. Paper presented at the 5th Occasional Anasazi Symposium, San Juan College, Farmington, NM.

1995 *An Analysis of Variability and Condition of Cavate Structures in Bandelier National Monument.* Intermountain Cultural Resources Center Professional Paper 53. Anthropology Program, National Park Service, U.S. Department of the Interior.

Toll, H. W., ed.

1995 *Soil, Water, Biology, and Belief in Prehistoric and Traditional Southwestern Agriculture.* New Mexico Archaeological Council Special Publication 2. Albuquerque.

Toll, H. W., E. Blinman, and C. D. Wilson

1992 Chaco in the Context of Ceramic Regional Systems. In *Anasazi Regional Organization and the Chaco System*, edited by D. E. Doyel, pp. 147–57. Maxwell Museum of Anthropology Anthropological Paper 5. Albuquerque: University of New Mexico.

Toll, H. W., and P. J. McKenna

1987 The Ceramography of Pueblo Alto. In *Artifactual and Biological Analyses: Investigations at the Pueblo Alto Complex, Chaco Canyon, New Mexico, 1975–1979*, vol. 3, no. 1, edited by J. Mathien and T. Windes, pp. 19–230. Publications in Archeology 18F. Santa Fe: National Park Service.

Toll, M. S.

1993 The Archaeobotany of the La Plata Valley in Totah Perspective. Paper presented at the 5th Occasional Anasazi Symposium, San Juan College, Farmington, NM.

Torrence, R.

1983 Time Budgeting and Hunter-Gatherer Technology. In *Hunter-Gatherer Economy in Prehistory*, edited by G. Bailey, pp. 11–22. Cambridge: Cambridge University Press.

Triadan, D.

1989 Defining Local Ceramic Production at Grasshopper Pueblo, Arizona. M.A. thesis, Lateinamerikainstitut, Freie Universität Berlin, Germany. (On file in the Arizona State Museum Library, University of Arizona, Tucson.)

1997 *Ceramic Commodities and Common Containers: Production and Distribution of White Mountain Red Ware in the Grasshopper Region, Arizona.* Anthropological Papers of the University of Arizona 61. Tucson: University of Arizona Press.

1998 Socio-Demographic Implications of Pueblo IV Ceramic Production and Circulation: Sourcing White Mountain Redware from the Grasshopper Region, Arizona. In *Migration and Reorganization: The Pueblo IV Period in the American Southwest*, edited by K. A. Spielmann, pp. 233–52. Anthropological Research Papers 51. Tempe: Arizona State University.

Trinkaus, E., S. E. Churchill, and C. B. Ruff

1994 Postcranial Robusticity in Homo II: Humeral Bilateral Asymmetry and Bone Plasticity. *American Journal of Physical Anthropology* 93:1–34.

Trippell, E. J.

1889 The Yuma Indians. *The Overland Monthly* (2d series) 13:561–84; 14:1–11. San Francisco: Overland Publishing Company.

Truell, M. L.

1992 *Excavations at 29SJ627, Chaco Canyon, New Mexico, vol. 1: The Architecture and Stratigraphy.* Reports of the Chaco Center 11. Branch of Cultural Research, U.S. Department of the Interior. Santa Fe: National Park Service.

Tschopik, H., Jr.
1941 *Navajo Pottery Making: An Inquiry into the Affinities of Navajo Painted Pottery.* Papers of the Peabody Museum of American Archaeology and Ethnology, vol. 17, no. 1. Cambridge, MA: Harvard University.

Tsing, A. L.
1993 *In the Realm of the Diamond Queen.* Princeton, NJ: Princeton University Press.

Turner, C. G. III, and L. Lofgren
1966 Household Size of Prehistoric Western Pueblo Indians. *Southwestern Journal of Anthropology* 22:117–32.

Udall, L.
1969 *Me and Mine.* Tucson: University of Arizona Press.

Ulijaszek, S. J., and S. S. Strickland
1993 *Nutritional Anthropology: Prospects and Perspective.* London: Smith-Gordon.

Underhill, R. M.
1936 *The Autobiography of a Papago Woman.* Menasha, WI: American Anthropological Association.
1939 *Social Organization of the Papago Indians.* Columbia University Contributions to Anthropology 20. New York: Columbia University Press.
1946 *Papago Indian Religion.* New York: Columbia University Press.
1979a *Pueblo Crafts.* New York: AMS Press.
1979b *Papago Woman.* Prospect Heights, IL: Waveland Press.

United Nations
1995 *The World's Women 1995.* New York: United Nations.

Van Blerkom, L. M.
1985 The Evolution of Human Infectious Disease in the Eastern and Western Hemispheres. Ph.D. diss., University of Colorado.

Vandiver, P., O. Soffer, B. Klima, and J. Svoboda
1989 The Origins of Ceramic Technology at Dolni Vestonice, Czechoslovakia. *Science* 246:1002–8.

Van Keuren, S., S. L. Stinson, and D. R. Abbott
1997 Specialized Production of Hohokam Plainware Ceramics in the Lower Salt River Valley. *Kiva* 63:155–75.

Varien, M. D., ed.
1999 *The Sand Canyon Archaeological Project: Site Testing, Version 1.0.* Cortez, CO: Crow Canyon Archaeological Center.

Varien, M. D.

1990 *Excavations at Three Prehistoric Sites along Pia Mesa Road, Zuni Indian Reservation, McKinley County, New Mexico.* Revised Zuni Archaeology Program Report 233. Zuni, NM.

1999 *Sedentism and Mobility in a Social Landscape: Mesa Verde and Beyond.* Tucson: University of Arizona Press.

Varien, M. D., W. D. Lipe, M. A. Adler, I. M. Thompson, and B. A. Bradley

1996 Southwest Colorado and Southeast Utah Settlement Patterns, A.D. 1100 to 1300. In *The Prehistoric Pueblo World, A.D. 1150–1350,* edited by M. A. Adler, pp. 86–113. Tucson: University of Arizona Press.

Vehik, S. C.

1975 Sociocultural Implications of Central European Early Bronze Age Mortuary Practices. Ph.D. diss., University of Missouri.

Verdon, M.

1980 Shaking Off the Domestic Yoke, or the Sociological Significance of Residence. *Comparative Studies in Society and History* 22:109–32.

Vivian, P.

1994 Anthropomorphic Figures in the Pottery Mound Murals. In *Kachinas in the Pueblo World,* edited by P. Schaafsma, pp. 81–91. Albuquerque: University of New Mexico Press.

Vivian, R. G., D. N. Dodgen, and G. H. Hartmann

1978 *Wooden Ritual Artifacts from Chaco Canyon New Mexico: The Chetro Ketl Collection.* Anthropological Papers of the University of Arizona 32. Tucson: University of Arizona Press.

Voth, H. R.

1905 *Traditions of the Hopi.* Anthropological Series vol. 8, Field Columbian Museum Publication 96. Chicago.

1912 *The Oraibi Marau Ceremony.* Field Museum of Natural History Publication 156, Anthropological Series vol. 11, no. 1. Chicago.

Walde, D., and N. D. Willows, eds.

1991 *The Archaeology of Gender.* Calgary, Alberta: Archaeological Association of the University of Calgary.

Walker, P. L.

1985 Anemia among Prehistoric Indians of the American Southwest. In *Health and Disease in the Prehistoric Southwest,* edited by C. F. Merbs and R. J. Miller, pp. 139–63. Anthropological Research Papers 34. Tempe: Arizona State University.

1989 Cranial Injuries as Evidence of Violence in Prehistoric Southern California. *American Journal of Physical Anthropology* 80:313–23.

Walker, W. H.

1996 Ritual Deposits: Another Perspective. In *River of Change: Prehistory of the Middle Little Colorado River Valley, Arizona,* edited by E. C. Adams, pp. 75–91. Arizona State Museum Archaeological Series 185. Tucson: University of Arizona.

Wall, D.

1994 *The Archaeology of Gender: Separating the Spheres in Urban America.* New York: Plenum.

Wallace, H. D., and J. M. Heidke

1986 Ceramic Production and Exchange. In *Archaeological Investigations at the Tanque Verde Wash Site: A Middle Rincon Settlement in the Eastern Tucson Basin,* edited by M. D. Elson, pp. 233–70. Institute for American Research Anthropological Paper 7. Tucson.

Wallace, H. D., J. M. Heidke, and W. H. Doelle

1995 Hohokam Origins. *Kiva* 60:575–618.

Ward, A., ed.

1978 *Limited Activity and Occupation Sites.* Center for Anthropological Studies Contribution 1. Albuquerque: Center for Anthropological Studies.

Ward, M. C.

1999 *A World Full of Women.* 2d ed. Boston: Allyn and Bacon.

Warren, A. H.

1981 A Petrographic Study of the Pottery of Gran Quivira. In *Contributions to Gran Quivira Archaeology,* edited by A. Hayes, pp. 67–73. National Park Service Publications in Archaeology 17. Washington, D.C.

Warren, A. H., and F. J. Mathien

1985 Prehistoric and Historic Turquoise Mining in the Cerrillos District: Time and Place. Ms. on file, Chaco Center, National Park Service, University of New Mexico, Albuquerque.

Wason, P. K.

1994 *The Archaeology of Rank.* Cambridge: Cambridge University Press.

Watson, P. J., and M. C. Kennedy

1991 The Development of Horticulture in the Eastern Woodlands of North America: Women's Role. In *Engendering Archaeology: Women and Prehistory,* edited by J. M. Gero and M. W. Conkey, pp. 255–75. Oxford: Basil Blackwell.

Watson, P. J., S. A. LeBlanc, and C. L. Redman

1980 Aspects of Zuni Prehistory: Preliminary Report on Excavations and Survey in the El Morro Valley of New Mexico. *Journal of Field Archaeology* 7:201–18.

Weber, S. A., and P. D. Seaman, eds.

1985 *Havasupai Habitat: A. F. Whiting's Ethnography of a Traditional Indian Culture.* Tucson: University of Arizona Press.

Webster, L.

1997 Effects of European Contact on Textile Production and Exchange in the North American Southwest: A Pueblo Case Study. Ph.D. diss., University of Arizona.

Weigle, M.

1989 *Creation and Procreation: Feminist Reflections on Mythologies of Cosmogony and Parturition.* Philadelphia: University of Pennsylvania Press.

Weiner, A. B.

1976 *Women of Value, Men of Renown.* Austin: University of Texas Press.

1986 Forgotten Wealth: Cloth and Women's Production in the Pacific. In *Women's Work,* edited by E. Leacock and H. I. Safa, pp. 96–110. South Hadley, MA: Bergin and Garvey.

1992 *Inalienable Possessions: The Paradox of Keeping while Giving Away.* Berkeley: University of California Press.

Weismantel, M. J.

1988 *Food, Gender, and Poverty in the Ecuadorian Andes.* Philadelphia: University of Pennsylvania Press.

Welch, P. D., and C. M. Scarry

1995 Status-Related Variation in Foodways in the Moundville Chiefdom. *American Antiquity* 60:397–419.

Wesson, A. L., and D. L. Martin

1995 Women Carried Heavy Loads while Men Were Weaving: Precontact Sexual Division of Labor at Black Mesa, Arizona. Paper presented at the 64th annual meeting of the American Association of Physical Anthropology, Oakland, CA.

West, C., and D. H. Zimmerman

1987 Doing Gender. *Gender and Society* 1:125–51.

Wetherington, R.

1968 *Excavations at Pot Creek Pueblo.* Fort Burgwin Research Center Publication 6. Taos, NM.

Wetterstrom, W.

1986 *Food, Diet, and Population at Prehistoric Arroyo Hondo Pueblo, New Mexico.* Santa Fe: School of American Research Press.

Wheat, J. B.

1955 *Mogollon Culture prior to A.D. 1000.* American Anthropological Association Memoir 82. Menasha, WI.

1984 Yellow Jacket Canyon Archaeology. In *Insights into the Ancient Ones,* 2d ed., edited by J. H. Berger and E. F. Berger, pp. 60–66. Cortez, CO: Mesa Verde Press.

White, D. R., M. L. Burton, and L. A. Brudner

1977 Entailment Theory and Method: A Cross-Cultural Analysis of the Sexual Division of Labor. *Behavior Science Research* 12:1–24.

Whiteley, D. S.

1994 By the Hunter, For the Gatherer: Art, Social Relations, and Subsistence Change in the Prehistoric Great Basin. *World Archaeology* 25:356–73.

Whitely, P.

1988 *Deliberate Acts: Changing Hopi Culture through the Oraibi Split.* Tucson: University of Arizona Press.

Whitman, W.

1940 The San Ildefonso of New Mexico. In *Acculturation in Seven American Indian Tribes,* edited by R. Linton. New York: D. Appleton-Century.

Whittaker, J. C.

1987 Individual Variation as an Approach to Economic Organization: Projectile Points at Grasshopper Pueblo, Arizona. *Journal of Field Archaeology* 14:465–79.

Whittlesey, S. M.

1978 Status and Death at Grasshopper Pueblo: Experiments Toward an Archaeological Theory of Social Correlates. Ph.D. diss., University of Arizona.

1984 Uses and Abuses of Mogollon Mortuary Data. In *Recent Research in Mogollon Archaeology,* edited by S. Upham, F. Plog, D. G. Batcho, and B. E. Kauffman, pp. 276–84. University Museum, New Mexico State University, Occasional Papers 10. Las Cruces.

Whittlesey, S. M., and J. J. Reid

1997 Mortuary Ritual and Organizational Inferences at Grasshopper Pueblo, Arizona. In *Ancient Burial Practices of the American Southwest,* edited by D. R. Mitchell and J. L. Brunson-Hadley. Albuquerque: University of New Mexico Press.

Whyte, Martin

1978 *The Status of Women in Preindustrial Societies.* Princeton, NJ: Princeton University Press.

Wiessner, P.

1977 *Hxaro*: A Regional System of Reciprocity for Reducing Risk among the !Kung San. Ph.D. diss., University of Michigan.

Wilcox, D. R.

1987 *Frank Midvale's Investigation of the Site of La Ciudad.* Anthropological Field Studies 19. Tempe: Arizona State University.

1991a Hohokam Religion: An Archaeologist's Perspective. In *The Hohokam: Ancient People of the Desert,* edited by D. G. Noble, pp. 47–61. Santa Fe: School of American Research Press.

1991b Hohokam Social Complexity. In *Chaco and Hohokam: Prehistoric Regional Systems in the American Southwest,* edited by P. L. Crown and W. J. Judge, pp. 252–75. Santa Fe: School of American Research Press.

1996 Organizational Parameters of Southwest/Mesoamerican Connectivity. Paper presented at 1996 Southwest Symposium, Arizona State University, Tempe.

Wilcox, D. R., and J. Haas

1994 The Scream of the Butterfly: Competition and Conflict in the Prehistoric Southwest. In *Themes in Southwest Prehistory*, edited by G. J. Gummerman, pp. 211–38. Santa Fe: School of American Press.

Wilcox, D. R., T. R. McGuire, and C. Sternberg

1981 *Snaketown Revisited.* Arizona State Museum Archaeological Series 155. Tucson: University of Arizona.

Wilcox, D. R., and C. Sternberg

1983 *Hohokam Ballcourts and Their Interpretation.* Arizona State Museum Archaeological Series 160. Tucson: University of Arizona.

Wilk, R. R.

1984 Households in Process: Agricultural Change and Domestic Transformation among the Kekchi Maya of Belize. In *Households: Comparative and Historical Studies of the Domestic Group*, edited by R. M. Netting, R. R. Wilk, and E. J. Arnould, pp. 217–44. Berkeley: University of California Press.

1991 The Household in Anthropology: Panacea or Problem? *Reviews in Anthropology* 20:1–12.

Wilk, R. R., ed.

1989 *The Household Economy: Reconsidering the Domestic Mode of Production.* Boulder, CO: Westview Press.

Wilk, R. R., and R. M. Netting

1984 Introduction. In *Households: Comparative and Historical Studies of the Domestic Group*, edited by R. M. Netting, R. R. Wilk, and E. J. Arnould, pp. xiii–xxxviii. Berkeley: University of California Press.

Williams, R.

1977 *Marxism and Literature.* Oxford: Oxford University Press.

Wills, W. H.

1988a *Early Prehistoric Agriculture in the American Southwest.* Santa Fe: School of American Research Press.

1988b Early Agriculture and Sedentism in the American Southwest. *Journal of World Prehistory* 2:445–88.

1991 Organization Strategies and the Emergence of Prehistoric Villages in the American Southwest. In *Between Bands and States*, edited by S. A. Gregg, pp. 161–89. Occasional Paper 9. Carbondale: Center for Archaeological Investigations.

1992 Plant Cultivation and the Evolution of Risk-Prone Economies in the Prehistoric American Southwest. In *Transitions to Agriculture in Prehistory*, edited by A. B. Gebauer and T. D. Price, pp. 153–76. Monographs in World Prehistory 4. Madison, WI: Prehistory Press.

1995 Archaic Foraging and the Beginning of Food Production in the American Southwest. In *Last Hunters, First Farmers: New Perspectives on the Prehistoric Transition to Agriculture*, edited by T. D. Price and A. B. Gebauer, pp. 215–42. Santa Fe: School of American Research Press.

1996 The Transition from the Preceramic to the Ceramic Period in the Mogollon Highlands of Western New Mexico. *Journal of Field Archaeology* 23:335–59.

Wills, W. H., and B. B. Huckell

1994 Economic Implications of Changing Land-Use Patterns in the Late Archaic. In *Themes in Southwest Prehistory*, edited by G. J. Gumerman, pp. 33–52. Santa Fe: School of American Research Press.

Wills, W. H., and T. C. Windes

1989 Evidence for Population Aggregation and Dispersal during the Basketmaker III Period in Chaco Canyon, New Mexico. *American Antiquity* 54:347–69.

Wilshusen, R. H., ed.

1995 *The Cedar Hill Special Treatment Project: Late Pueblo I, Early Navajo, and Historic Occupations in Northwestern New Mexico.* Research Paper 1, La Plata Archaeological Consultants. Dolores, CO.

Wilshusen, R. H.

1986 The Relationship between Abandonment Mode and Ritual Use in Pueblo I Anasazi Protokivas. *Journal of Field Archaeology* 13:245–54.

1991 Early Villages in the American Southwest: Cross-Cultural and Archaeological Perspectives. Ph.D. diss., University of Colorado.

Wilshusen, R. H., and E. Blinman

1992 Pueblo I Village Formation: A Reevaluation of Sites Recorded by Earl Morris on Ute Mountain Ute Tribal Lands. *Kiva* 57:251–69.

Wilshusen, R. H., and C. D. Wilson

1995 Reformatting the Social Landscape in the Late Pueblo I–Early Pueblo II Period: The Cedar Hill Data in Regional Context. In *The Cedar Hill Special Treatment Project: Late Pueblo I, Early Navajo, and Historic Occupations in Northwestern New Mexico*, edited by R. H. Wilshusen, pp. 43–80. Research Paper 1, La Plata Archaeological Consultants. Dolores, CO.

Wilson, C. D.

1996 Ceramic Pigment Distributions and Regional Interaction: A Re-examination of Interpretations in Shepard's "Technology of La Plata Pottery." *Kiva* 62:83–102.

Wilson, C. D., and E. Blinman

1991 Early Anasazi Ceramics and the Basketmaker Transition. Paper presented at the Anasazi Symposium, Mesa Verde National Park, CO.

1995 Changing Specialization of White Ware Manufacture in the Northern San Juan Region. In *Ceramic Production in the American Southwest,* edited by B. J. Mills and P. L. Crown, pp. 68–87. Tucson: University of Arizona Press.

Windes, T. C.

1984 A New Look at Population in Chaco Canyon. In *Recent Research on Chaco Prehistory,* edited by W. J. Judge and J. D. Schelberg, pp. 75–87. Reports of the Chaco Center 8. Albuquerque, NM: National Park Service.

1987 *Investigations in the Pueblo Alto Complex, Chaco Canyon, New Mexico, vol. 1: Summary of Tests and Excavations at the Pueblo Alto Community.* Publications in Anthropology 18F, Chaco Canyon Studies. Santa Fe: National Park Service.

1992 Blue Notes: The Chacoan Turquoise Industry in the San Juan Basin. In *Anasazi Regional Organization and the Chaco System,* edited by D. E. Doyel, pp. 159–68. Maxwell Museum of Anthropology Anthropological Paper 5. Albuquerque: University of New Mexico.

1993 *The Spadefoot Toad Site: Investigations at 29SJ629, Chaco Canyon, New Mexico,* vol. 1. Reports of the Chaco Center 12, Branch of Cultural Research, Division of Anthropology. Santa Fe: National Park Service.

Windes, T. C., and D. Ford

1992 The Nature of the Early Bonito Phase. In *Anasazi Regional Organization and the Chaco System,* edited by D. E. Doyel, pp. 75–86. Anthropological Papers 5, Maxwell Museum of Anthropology, University of New Mexico. Albuquerque.

1996 The Chaco Wood Project: The Chronometric Reappraisal of Pueblo Bonito. *American Antiquity* 61:295–310.

Wing, E., and A. Brown

1979 *Paleonutrition: Method and Theory in Prehistoric Foodways.* New York: Academic Press.

Winter, J. C.

1977 *Hovenweep 1976.* San Jose State University, Anthropology Department, Archeological Report 3.

Wolf, D. L.

1991 Does Father Know Best? A Feminist Critique of Household Strategy Research. *Research in Rural Sociology and Development* 5:29–44.

Wolf, E.

1990 Facing Power: Old Insights, New Questions. *American Anthropologist* 92:586–96.

Woodbury, R. B.

1965 *Prehistoric Agriculture at Point of Pines, Arizona.* Memoirs of the Society of American Archaeology 17. Salt Lake City.

Woosley, A.

1980 Agricultural Diversity in the Prehistoric Southwest. *Kiva* 45:315–35.

Worthington, B. S., J. Vermeersch, and R. Williams

1990 *Nutrition in Pregnancy and Lactation.* St. Louis, MO: Mosby.

Wright, K. I.

1994 Ground-Stone Tools and Hunter-Gatherer Subsistence in Southwest Asia: Implications for the Transition to Farming. *American Antiquity* 59:238–63.

Wright, R. P.

1991 Women's Labor and Pottery Production in Prehistory. In *Engendering Archaeology: Women and Prehistory*, edited by J. M. Gero and M. W. Conkey, pp. 194–223. Oxford: Basil Blackwell.

1996 Technology, Gender, and Class: Worlds of Difference in Ur III Mesopotamia. In *Gender and Archaeology*, edited by R. P. Wright, pp. 79–110. Philadelphia: University of Pennsylvania Press.

Wright, R. P., ed.

1996 *Gender and Archaeology.* Philadelphia: University of Pennsylvania Press.

Wyckoff, L. L.

1985 *Designs and Factions: Politics, Religion, and Ceramics on the Hopi Third Mesa.* Albuquerque: University of New Mexico Press.

Wylie, A.

1985 The Reaction against Analogy. In *Advances in Archaeological Method and Theory 8*, edited by M. B. Schiffer, pp. 63–111. London: Academic Press.

1992 Feminist Theories of Social Power: Some Implications for a Processual Archaeology. *Norwegian Archaeological Review* 25:51–68.

Yanagisako, S. J.

1979 Family and Household: The Analysis of Domestic Groups. *Annual Review of Anthropology* 8:161–205.

Yohe, R. M. II, M. E. Newman, and J. S. Schneider

1991 Immunological Identification of Small-Mammal Proteins on Aboriginal Milling Equipment. *American Antiquity* 56:659–66.

Young, K., C. Wolkowitz, and R. McCullagh, eds.

1981 *Of Marriage and the Market: Women's Subordination in International Perspective.* London: CSE Books.

Young, L. C., and T. Stone

1990 The Thermal Properties of Textured Ceramics: An Experimental Study. *Journal of Field Archaeology* 17:195–203.

Young, M. J.

1987 Women, Reproduction, and Religion in Western Puebloan Society. *Journal of American Folklore* 100:436–45.

Zack-Horner, J.

1996 Aggregation and the Faunal Record: A Comparative Analysis in the Silver Creek Area of the Mogollon Plateau. M.A. thesis, University of Arizona.

Zaslow, B.

1981 *Pattern Dissemination in the Prehistoric Southwest and Mesoamerica: A Comparison of Hohokam Decorative Patterns with Patterns from the Upper Gila Area and from the Valley of Oaxaca.* Anthropological Research Papers 25. Tempe: Arizona State University.

Zaslow, B., and A. E. Dittert, Jr.

1977 *Pattern Technology of the Hohokam.* Anthropological Research Papers 2. Tempe: Arizona State University.

Zedeño, M. N.

1994 *Sourcing Prehistoric Ceramics at Chodistaas Pueblo, Arizona: The Circulation of People and Pots in the Grasshopper Region.* Anthropological Papers of the University of Arizona 58. Tucson: University of Arizona Press.

Index

Note: *f* indicates a figure, and *t*, a table

School of American Research
Advanced Seminar Series

Published by SAR Press

Chaco & Hohokam: Prehistoric Regional Systems in the American Southwest
Patricia L. Crown & W. James Judge, eds.

Recapturing Anthropology: Working in the Present
Richard G. Fox, ed.

War in the Tribal Zone: Expanding States and Indigenous Warfare
R. Brian Ferguson & Neil L. Whitehead, eds.

Ideology and Pre-Columbian Civilizations
Arthur A. Demarest & Geoffrey W. Conrad, eds.

Dreaming: Anthropological and Psychological Interpretations
Barbara Tedlock, ed.

Historical Ecology: Cultural Knowledge and Changing Landscapes
Carole L. Crumley, ed.

Themes in Southwest Prehistory
George J. Gumerman, ed.

Memory, History, and Opposition under State Socialism
Rubie S. Watson, ed.

Other Intentions: Cultural Contexts and the Attribution of Inner States
Lawrence Rosen, ed.

Last Hunters–First Farmers: New Perspectives on the Prehistoric Transition to Agriculture
T. Douglas Price & Anne Birgitte Gebauer, eds.

Making Alternative Histories: The Practice of Archaeology and History in Non-Western Settings
Peter R. Schmidt & Thomas C. Patterson, eds.

Senses of Place
Steven Feld & Keith H. Basso, eds.

Cyborgs & Citadels: Anthropological Interventions in Emerging Sciences and Technologies
Gary Lee Downey & Joseph Dumit, eds.

Archaic States
Gary M. Feinman & Joyce Marcus, eds.

Critical Anthropology Now: Unexpected Contexts, Shifting Constituencies, Changing Agendas
George E. Marcus, ed.

The Origins of Language: What Nonhuman Primates Can Tell Us
Barbara J. King, ed.

Regimes of Language: Ideologies, Polities, and Identities
Paul V. Kroskrity, ed.

Biology, Brains, and Behavior: The Evolution of Human Development
Sue Taylor Parker, Jonas Langer, & Michael L. McKinney, eds.

Published by Cambridge University Press

Dreaming: Anthropological and Psychological Interpretations
Barbara Tedlock, ed.

The Anasazi in a Changing Environment
George J. Gumerman, ed.

Regional Perspectives on the Olmec
Robert J. Sharer & David C. Grove, eds.

The Chemistry of Prehistoric Human Bone
T. Douglas Price, ed.

The Emergence of Modern Humans: Biocultural Adaptations in the Later Pleistocene
Erik Trinkaus, ed.

The Anthropology of War
Jonathan Haas, ed.

The Evolution of Political Systems
Steadman Upham, ed.

Classic Maya Political History: Hieroglyphic and Archaeological Evidence
T. Patrick Culbert, ed.

Turko-Persia in Historical Perspective
Robert L. Canfield, ed.

Chiefdoms: Power, Economy, and Ideology
Timothy Earle, ed.

Published by University of California Press

Writing Culture: The Poetics and Politics of Ethnography
James Clifford & George E. Marcus, eds.

PUBLISHED BY UNIVERSITY OF NEW MEXICO PRESS

RECONSTRUCTING PREHISTORIC PUEBLO SOCIETIES
William A. Longacre, ed.

NEW PERSPECTIVES ON THE PUEBLOS
Alfonso Ortiz, ed.

STRUCTURE AND PROCESS IN LATIN AMERICA
Arnold Strickon & Sidney M. Greenfield, eds.

THE CLASSIC MAYA COLLAPSE
T. Patrick Culbert, ed.

METHODS AND THEORIES OF ANTHROPOLOGICAL GENETICS
M. H. Crawford & P. L. Workman, eds.

SIXTEENTH-CENTURY MEXICO: THE WORK OF SAHAGUN
Munro S. Edmonson, ed.

ANCIENT CIVILIZATION AND TRADE
Jeremy A. Sabloff & C. C. Lamberg-Karlovsky, eds.

PHOTOGRAPHY IN ARCHAEOLOGICAL RESEARCH
Elmer Harp, Jr. ed.

MEANING IN ANTHROPOLOGY
Keith H. Basso & Henry A. Selby, eds.

THE VALLEY OF MEXICO: STUDIES IN PRE-HISPANIC ECOLOGY AND SOCIETY
Eric R. Wolf, ed.

DEMOGRAPHIC ANTHROPOLOGY: QUANTITATIVE APPROACHES
Ezra B. W. Zubrow, ed.

THE ORIGINS OF MAYA CIVILIZATION
Richard E. W. Adams, ed.

EXPLANATION OF PREHISTORIC CHANGE
James N. Hill, ed.

EXPLORATIONS IN ETHNOARCHAEOLOGY
Richard A. Gould, ed.

ENTREPRENEURS IN CULTURAL CONTEXT
Sidney M. Greenfield, Arnold Strickon, & Robert T. Aubey, eds.

THE DYING COMMUNITY
Art Gallaher, Jr., & Harlan Padfield, eds.

SOUTHWESTERN INDIAN RITUAL DRAMA
Charlotte J. Frisbie, ed.

LOWLAND MAYA SETTLEMENT PATTERNS
Wendy Ashmore, ed.

SIMULATIONS IN ARCHAEOLOGY
Jeremy A. Sabloff, ed.

CHAN CHAN: ANDEAN DESERT CITY
Michael E. Moseley & Kent C. Day, eds.

SHIPWRECK ANTHROPOLOGY
Richard A. Gould, ed.

ELITES: ETHNOGRAPHIC ISSUES
George E. Marcus, ed.

THE ARCHAEOLOGY OF LOWER CENTRAL AMERICA
Frederick W. Lange & Doris Z. Stone, eds.

LATE LOWLAND MAYA CIVILIZATION: CLASSIC TO POSTCLASSIC
Jeremy A. Sabloff & E. Wyllys Andrews V, eds.

Photo by Katrina Lasko

Participants in the School of American Research advanced seminar "Sex Roles and Gender Hierarchies in Middle-Range Societies: Engendering Southwestern Prehistory," Santa Fe, New Mexico, March 1997. Left to right: Michelle Hegmon, Debra L. Martin, Christine R. Szuter, Louise Lamphere, Barbara J. Mills, Patricia L. Crown, Kelley Hays-Gilpin, Katherine A. Spielmann, Suzanne K. Fish, Jill Neitzel.

www.ingramcontent.com/pod-product-compliance
Lightning Source LLC
Chambersburg PA
CBHW020813270326
41928CB00006B/361

* 9 7 8 0 9 3 3 4 5 2 1 7 6 *